A GUIDE TO PL/I AND STRUCTURED PROGRAMMING, 3RD EDITION

SEYMOUR V. POLLACK

Washington University

THEODOR D. STERLING

Simon Fraser University

HOLT, RINEHART AND WINSTON
NEW YORK   CHICAGO   SAN FRANCISCO   ATLANTA   DALLAS
MONTREAL   TORONTO   LONDON   SYDNEY

Library of Congress Catalog Card Number: 80-12448
Pollack, Seymour V
  A guide to PL/1 and structured programming.
  Includes bibliographies.
  1. PL/1 (Computer program language) I. Sterling,
Theodor D., joint author. II. Title.
QA76.73.P25P65   1980   001.6'424   75-20466
ISBN 0-03-55821-5

Printed in the United States of America
0   1   2   3   144   9   8   7   6   5   4   3   2   1

PREFACE TO THE THIRD EDITION

When the computer age completed its second decade, even the grizzled veterans had to admit their amazement over the fact that the tremendous growth of computer technology and usage had persisted that long. Yet, with the approach of a fourth decade, there still seems to be no shortage of revolutions to fuel continuing acceleration. Nor is this ongoing supply of revolutions confined to those oriented exclusively around breakthroughs in memory technology, integrated circuits, or other hardware advances. In fact, it is one such revolution that prompts the appearance of this edition so soon (relatively) after its predecessor.

This revolution (and it is not really less than that) focuses on the processes of defining, developing, and maintaining effective computer applications. Its essence lies in a fundamental change in the way these processes are perceived. For a long time, conventional wisdom assigned to these processes an artistic, almost transcendental characteristic. Conception of a computer application, and its subsequent implementation as a successful computer program, were crafts whose nature evaded precise definition. Thus, there were no exact rules (and, many contended, there could not be any) that one might follow to "guarantee" a successful result, i.e., an accurate and reliable program that consistently does what it is supposed to do. Instead, one acquired the requisite skills and insights by sitting at the feet (or at the terminal, as it were) of a master and scrutinizing his or her works. Although this attitude predominated, it was by no means universal. Almost from the beginning, the population of computing researchers and practitioners included those who felt that their attempts at systematizing the computerization process eventually would succeed. Meanwhile, however, the programming art was, by and large, an ad hoc process supported here and there by useful rules of thumb and household hints.

The current view of the computerization process is very different from the one outlined above, and this difference is at the heart of the revolution. While certainly not a science equipped with precise, reproducible cause-effect relationships, the sequence of events leading to an effective computer application now is seen to be a relatively well-disciplined and orderly one, far from the willy-nilly aspect of earlier perceptions.

There are no natural laws or brilliant formulas whose discovery catalyzed this turnaround. In fact, the revolutionary nature of this revised view did not become clear for some time, and for a very simple reason: the ad hoc approach worked. The acuity of hindsight makes it easy to take pot shots at the undisciplined formulation of algorithms and their disorderly reduction to computer programs, but the fact is that the incredible growth of computing could not have been sustained without a mounting horde of successful implementations. That same hindsight reveals that the severe limitations of the ad hoc approach did not become apparent until the size and complexity of new computer applications exceeded some vaguely defined level. Then, the lack of order began to take its toll, resulting in a rapidly increasing incidence of logical errors. Moreover, because the newer applications were more ambitious and convoluted, their very complexity made these errors increasingly difficult to track down. Eventually, the overall effect was that a growing proportion of an installation's computing costs were incurred in repairing faults that kept appearing in programs released for routine use as "error-free". Initial suspicions became convictions as study after study produced figures of program maintenance costs exceeding 60 percent, 70 percent, and even 80% of overall computing costs in a wide variety of industrial, commercial, scientific, and governmental environments. These revelations provided additional motivation for an already ongoing range of inquiries into the nature of the computerization process. This effort was intensified, and the revolution was on.

In our view, the central idea behind the revised perception of computerization is the recognition that the end result of the process is an *operating, reliable computer program* that can and should be treated as an engineered product. This means that the successful production of a program can be effected by the application of the same design and engineering methodologies that have served for many decades in the development of other types of products. It is no coincidence that the systematic design and development of computer programs and program systems has come to be known as software engineering, nor is it an idle apellation.

The aspect of computerization that concerns us directly in this book is a most crucial one, i.e., the design and implementation of the program itself. Consistent with its larger framework, this process is characterized by the imposition of a sense of orderliness, a systematic way of doing things. This consists of a set of rules, guidelines, concepts, and practices which, when taken together, have been given the name *structured programming*.

There is nothing mysterious or exotic about structured programming. On the contrary, its basic purpose is to simplify the programming process, thereby heightening the likelihood of producing a program that is easier to formulate and develop. Emphasis is placed on devising the clearest and simplest way to express a particular processing intent. To support this emphasis, structured programming defines a number of standardized programming components called *constructs*. These are set forth as the building blocks from which all well-structured programs are to be synthesized, regardless of the programming language in which the program ultimately is written.

PL/I is particularly well suited for writing structured programs because most of the standard constructs have direct counterparts in PL/I statement types. This is no mere coincidence. It is important to understand that the ideas relating to structured programming did not spring full-blown from a single source. Instead, they have been fed by multiple streams including formal studies of programming practices, some very creative thinking, the useful household hints mentioned before, and a healthy dose of common sense. Consequently, many of these ideas were recognized and incorporated in PL/I prior to their augmentation and institutionalization as structured programming, and prior editions of this book reflected their presence.

In the current edition, these principles are emphasized more fully, within a larger perspective that views the programming process as a systematic activity. There is no need to defend structured programming; that part of the revolution is over. While it is no panacea, structured programming has demonstrated repeatedly its substantial advantages in reducing the proportion of errors in the initial version of a program, simplifying the process of tracking down and eliminating those errors, and decreasing (often dramatically) the amount of maintenance required once a program is in routine use. Accordingly, there is no need to compare structured programming techniques with the less disciplined ones being replaced. It is much more effective to inculcate good practices from the start than to study less useful ones, only to have to unlearn them. By the same token, material dealing with structured programming per se is integrated fully with the discussion of PL/I's features and their use by taking advantage of the "naturally" structured aspects of the language. Avoidance of such artificial separation makes every PL/I program example a structured programming example as well. Incidentally, these examples continue to provide valuable insights with regard to the behavior and use of PL/I's features in a structured programming context. Infusion of discipline and orderliness into the programming process does not lessen the importance (or the effectiveness) of learning by example.

Our thanks go to Howard Bomze and Phil Samuels in Saint Louis, and to Doreen Godwin and Carol Rourke in Vancouver for their invaluable help in preparing this edition. We wish them all the best.

S. V. P., St. Louis
T. D. S., Vancouver

CONTENTS

I   STRUCTURING A PL/I PROGRAM   1

I.1   ACTION OF THE PL/I COMPILER   2

I.2   BASIC INSTRUCTION TYPES   4

I.2.1   Definition of Program Limits   4

I.2.2   Definition of Variables   5

I.2.3   Internal Manipulation of Numbers   7

I.2.3.1   numerical constants   8
I.2.3.2   arithmetic operations   8
I.2.3.3   PL/I default actions   11
I.2.3.4   shifting data in storage   11

I.2.4   ⌄ Input-Output (I/O) Statements   **12**
         ⌄ I.2.4.1   the **GET DATA** and **PUT DATA** statements   **12**
         ⌄ I.2.4.2   format control with the **PUT DATA** statement   **14**
I.2.5   √ Illustrative Programs   **15**
I.2.6   Control and Decision Statements   **18**
         I.2.6.1   program loops   **19**
         I.2.6.2   the **DO** loop   **20**
         I.2.6.3   the **DO-WHILE** construct   **21**
I.2.7   Relational Operations   **22**
I.2.8   The **IF-THEN-ELSE** Construct   **23**

I.3   PROGRAM EXECUTION   **24**

PROBLEMS   **27**

SUMMARY OF IMPORTANT TERMS   **32**

SUPPLEMENTARY READING   **35**

II   PROGRAM DEVELOPMENT AND IMPLEMENTATION   **37**

II.1   PROGRAM DEVELOPMENT   **38**

II.2   AIDS IN PROGRAM DEVELOPMENT   **50**
         II.2.1   The Source Listing   **50**
         II.2.2   The Cross-Reference Guide   **52**
         II.2.3   Diagnostic Messages   **52**

II.3   A SUMMARY OF SOURCE PROGRAM FORMAT RULES   **56**

PROBLEMS   **57**

SUMMARY OF IMPORTANT TERMS   **61**

SUPPLEMENTARY READING   **62**

III   NUMERICAL DATA FORMS   **63**

III.1   BASIC TYPES OF NUMBERS   **63**
         III.1.1   Base   **64**

III.1.2   Scale   **65**

III.1.3   Mode   **66**

III.1.4   Precision   **66**
 III.1.4.1   precision of floating point numbers   **66**
 III.1.4.2   precision of fixed point numbers   **66**
 III.1.4.3   scaling of fixed point numbers   **67**

III.2   EXPRESSION OF NUMERICAL VALUES   **68**

III.2.1   Appearance of Decimal Constants   **69**
 III.2.1.1   fixed point decimal numbers   **69**
 III.2.1.2   floating point decimal numbers   **69**

III.2.2   Binary Numbers   **71**
 III.2.2.1   fixed point binary constants   **71**
 III.2.2.2   binary floating point constants   **72**

III.3   SELECTION OF BASE AND SCALE   **72**

PROBLEMS   **77**

SUMMARY OF IMPORTANT TERMS   **78**

SUPPLEMENTARY READING   **79**

IV   DECLARATION AND USE OF NUMERICAL VARIABLES   **81**

IV.1   DECLARATION   **81**
 IV.1.1   Combinations of Attributes   **82**
 IV.1.2   Defaults   **82**
 IV.1.3   Shorthand Forms for Declarations   **83**
 IV.1.4   The **INITIAL** Attribute   **84**
 IV.1.5   Implied Declarations   **85**
 IV.1.6   Changing the Defaults   **85**
  IV.1.6.1   the **RANGE** specifications   **86**
  IV.1.6.2   the **VALUE** specifications   **87**
  IV.1.6.3   exceptions to programmer-defined defaults   **88**

IV.2   USE OF NUMERICAL VARIABLES   **88**
 IV.2.1   Decimal Fixed Variables   **89**
 IV.2.2   Binary Fixed Variables   **89**
 IV.2.3   Floating Point Variables   **89**
 IV.2.4   Input and Output of Numerical Variables   **89**

IV.2.5   Complex Numbers   **91**
           IV.2.5.1   complex notation in PL/I   **91**
           IV.2.5.2   internal operations with complex numbers   **95**
IV.2.6   Accuracy and Rounding   **97**

PROBLEMS   **98**

SUMMARY OF IMPORTANT TERMS   **103**

SUPPLEMENTARY READING   **104**

V   **NON-NUMERIC DATA**   **105**

V.1   CHARACTER STRINGS   **105**
          V.1.1   Representation of Character Strings   **106**
          V.1.2   Declaration of Character Variables   **107**
                    V.1.2.1   assignment of character strings to variables   **107**
                    V.1.2.2   shorthand forms for character constants   **108**
                    V.1.2.3 initialization of character strings   **108**
                    V.1.2.4   the **VARYING** attribute   **109**
          V.1.3   Input-Output of Character Strings   **110**
                    V.1.3.1   input forms   **110**
                    V.1.3.2   output forms   **111**
          V.1.4   Assignment Statements   **112**
          V.1.5   Concatenation   **113**
          V.1.6   Use of Character Strings in Decision Structures   **114**
                    V.1.6.1   construction of character string tests   **114**
                    V.1.6.2   alphabetization   **115**

V.2   ALTERNATE DESCRIPTION OF STRINGS: The **PICTURE**
          Attribute   **118**
          V.2.1   Declaration of **PICTURE** Variables   **118**
                    V.2.1.1   picture description of numerical data   **118**
                    V.2.1.2   shorthand forms for numerical picture
                                   declarations   **120**

          V.2.2   Input/Output of Numerical **PICTURE** Variables   **121**
          V.2.3   **PICTURE** Descriptions of Non-numeric Strings   **123**
          V.2.4   Other Descriptive Facilities   **126**
                    V.2.4.1   specification of scale factors   **126**
                    V.2.4.2   suppression of high order zeros   **126**
                    V.2.4.3   pictures for complex data   **127**

PROBLEMS   127

SUMMARY OF IMPORTANT TERMS   130

SUPPLEMENTARY READING   131

VI   ARRAYS   133

VI.1   BASIC ORGANIZATIONAL PROPERTIES   134
   VI.1.1   Dimensionality of Arrays   134
   VI.1.2   One-Dimensional Arrays   135
   VI.1.3   Two-Dimensional Arrays   135
   VI.1.4   Higher-Dimensional Arrays   137

VI.2   DECLARATION OF ARRAYS   138
   VI.2.1   Assignment of Attributes to Arrays   139
   VI.2.2   Internal Organization of Arrays   140
   VI.2.3   Initialization of Arrays   141
   VI.2.4   Special Subscripts   143

VI.3   INTERNAL HANDLING OF ARRAYS   144
   VI.3.1   Operations on an Entire Array   144
   VI.3.2   Operations Involving More than One Array   145
   VI.3.3   Subscripts as Variables   146
   VI.3.4   Manipulation of Parts of Arrays   150
      VI.3.4.1   manipulation of cross sections   150
      VI.3.4.2   DO loops and arrays   154

VI.4   INPUT/OUTPUT OF ARRAYS   156
   VI.4.1   Transmission of Entire Arrays   157
   VI.4.2   Input/Output of Parts of Arrays   158
      VI.4.2.1   input/output of array cross sections   158
      VI.4.2.2   input/output of sequences of elements   159

VI.5   ADDITIONAL PROPERTIES OF ARRAYS   161
   VI.5.1   Multiple Names for Arrays   161
      VI.5.1.1   the DEFINED attribute   162
      VI.5.1.2   duplicate names for parts of arrays   162
      VI.5.1.3   more complex array definition: the iSUB specification   163

VI.5.1.4   the **POSITION** specification   **167**

VI.5.2   Arrays with Variable Sizes   **168**

PROBLEMS   **170**

SUMMARY OF IMPORTANT TERMS   **175**

SUPPLEMENTARY READING   **176**

√VII   STRUCTURES **177**

VII.1   DECLARATION OF STRUCTURES   **178**

VII.1.1   Assignment of Levels in Structures   **181**
VII.1.2   Naming Elements in Structures   **184**
VII.1.3   Naming Minor Structures   **185**
VII.1.4   The **LIKE** Attribute   **186**

VII.2   INPUT/OUTPUT OF STRUCTURES   **187**

VII.3   INTERNAL MANIPULATION OF STRUCTURES   **188**

VII.4   THE **BY NAME** OPTION   **190**

VII.5   INTERACTION OF ARRAYS AND STRUCTURES   **192**
VII.5.1   Inclusion of arrays in Structures   **193**
VII.5.2   Arrays of Structures   **195**

PROBLEMS   **197**

SUMMARY OF IMPORTANT TERMS   **201**

√VIII   TRANSMISSION OF DATA STREAMS   **203**

VIII.1   LIST-DIRECTED STREAM TRANSMISSION: **GET/PUT LIST**   **204**

VIII.1.1   The **GET LIST** Statement   **205**
    VIII.1.1.1   list-directed input of arrays   **206**
    VIII.1.1.2   the **DO** loop in a **GET LIST** statement   **206**

VIII.1.2   The **PUT LIST** Statement   **208**
    VIII.1.2.1   the **PAGE** option   **208**
    VIII.1.2.2   the **LINE** option   **208**
    VIII.1.2.3   the **SKIP** option   **209**
    VIII.1.2.4   expressions in **PUT LIST** statements   **210**

VIII.2   DATA-DIRECTED TRANSMISSION: **GET/PUT DATA**   **210**

VIII.2.1   The **GET DATA** Statement   **211**
    VIII.2.1.1   data-directed input of arrays   **212**
    VIII.2.1.2   data-directed input of structures   **212**

VIII.2.2   The **PUT DATA** Statement   **213**

VIII.3   EDIT-DIRECTED DATA TRANSMISSION: **GET/PUT EDIT**   **214**

VIII.3.1   Edit-Directed Input: The **GET EDIT** Statement   **215**
    VIII.3.1.1   basic form of the **GET EDIT** statement   **216**
    VIII.3.1.2   the **COLUMN** specification   **216**
    VIII.3.1.3   the **F** specification   **217**
    VIII.3.1.4   the **E** specification   **218**
    VIII.3.1.5   the **C** specification   **219**
    VIII.3.1.6   the **A** specification   **219**
    VIII.3.1.7   the **P** specification   **220**
    VIII.3.1.8   the **X** specification   **220**
    VIII.3.1.9   the **SKIP** specification   **221**

VIII.3.2   Iterative Specifications   **222**

VIII.3.3   Blank Data   **223**

VIII.3.4   Operation of the **GET DATA**; Statement   **223**

VIII.3.5   Edit-Directed Input of Data Aggregates   **223**
    VIII.3.5.1   edit-directed input of entire arrays   **225**
    VIII.3.5.2   **GET EDIT** statements with built-in **DO** loops   **225**

VIII.3.6   Extension of Format Capabilities   **226**
    VIII.3.6.1   the remote format specification   **227**
    VIII.3.6.2   variable format specification   **229**

VIII.3.7   Edit-Directed Output: The **PUT EDIT** Statement   **232**
    VIII.3.7.1   allocation of spaces on the print line   **233**
    VIII.3.7.2   fixed-point output format   **233**
    VIII.3.7.3   floating-point output format   **234**
    VIII.3.7.4   other format specifications   **234**
    VIII.3.7.5   control of line and column positions   **235**
    VIII.3.7.6   overprinting   **236**

VIII.3.8 The **P** Specification **238**
       VIII.3.8.1 picture codes for character strings **238**
       VIII.3.8.2 picture codes for fixed point numbers **239**
       VIII.3.8.3 picture codes for floating point numbers **239**

VIII.4 INTERNAL EDITING: THE **STRING** OPTION **244**
   VIII.4.1 The **GET STRING** Statement **244**
   VIII.4.2 The **PUT STRING** Statement **245**

PROBLEMS **245**

SUMMARY OF IMPORTANT TERMS **253**

IX INTERNAL ARITHMETIC MANIPULATIONS 255

IX.1 EVALUATION OF ARITHMETIC EXPRESSIONS **256**
   IX.1.1 Priority of Arithmetic Operations **256**
   IX.1.2 Conversion in Mixed Arithmetic Expressions **258**
   IX.1.3 Precision of Converted Results **259**
       IX.1.3.1 precision rules for converting binary numbers **260**
       IX.1.3.2 precision rules for converting decimal numbers **261**
   IX.1.4 precision rules for arithmetic operations **262**
       IX.1.4.1 addition and subtraction **263**
       IX.1.4.2 multiplication **263**
       IX.1.4.3 precision rules for division **263**
       IX.1.4.4 precision of exponentiation **264**
       IX.1.4.5 precision of final results **264**

IX.2 BUILT-IN FUNCTIONS FOR ARITHMETIC OPERATIONS **264**
   IX.2.1 Functions for Use with Single-Valued Variables **265**
       IX.2.1.1 the **ABS** function **265**
       IX.2.1.2 the **SIGN** function **266**
       IX.2.1.3 the **PRECISION** function **266**
       IX.2.1.4 base-changing functions **266**
       IX.2.1.5 scale-changing functions **267**
       IX.2.1.6 functions for manipulating complex numbers **267**
       IX.2.1.7 basic arithmetic functions **268**
       IX.2.1.8 the modulus function **269**
       IX.2.1.9 numerical adjustment functions **270**
       IX.2.1.10 selection function **271**
       IX.2.1.11 common algebraic funntions **271**
       IX.2.1.12 trigonometric functions **272**

IX.2.1.13   hyperbolic functions   **273**
IX.2.1.14   inverse functions   **273**
IX.2.1.15   error functions   **273**
IX.2.2   Built-In Functions for Data Aggregates   **274**
IX.2.2.1   the summation function   **274**
IX.2.2.2   the product function   **275**
IX.2.2.3   the polynomial function   **275**

IX.3   SOME COMPUTATIONAL DIFFICULTIES   **276**

PROBLEMS   **278**

SUMMARY OF IMPORTANT TERMS   **285**

SUPPLEMENTARY READING   **285**

X   **MANIPULATION OF CHARACTER STRINGS**   **287**

X.1   DEVELOPMENT OF CHARACTER STRING EXPRESSIONS   **287**
X.1.1   Concatenation of Strings   **288**
X.1.1.1   expansion of strings   **288**
X.1.1.2   the **LENGTH** function   **288**
X.1.1.3   the **REPEAT** function   **290**
X.1.2   Extraction and Decomposition of Character Strings   **290**
X.1.2.1   basic properties of the substring function   **290**
X.1.2.2   substrings as pseudovariables   **291**
X.1.2.3   the **STRING** pseudovariable   **292**
X.1.2.4   automatic replacement: the **TRANSLATE** function   **294**

X.2   EXAMINATION OF CHARACTER STRINGS   **295**
X.2.1   The **INDEX** Function   **295**
X.2.2   The **VERIFY** Function   **296**

X.3   RELATIONS WITH OTHER DATA FORMS   **297**
X.3.1   Character Strings in Arithmetic Expressions   **297**
X.3.2   Arithmetic in Character String Expressions   **298**
X.3.2.1   conversion of numbers to character strings   **298**
X.3.2.2   the **CHAR** function   **300**

PROBLEMS   **301**

SUMMARY OF IMPORTANT TERMS   303

SUPPLEMENTARY READING   304

XI   BIT STRINGS   305

XI.1   REPRESENTATION OF BIT STRING DATA   306

XI.2   INPUT/OUTPUT OF BIT STRING DATA   306
XI.2.1   List-Directed and Data-Directed Transmission   306
XI.2.2   Edit-Directed Transmission   309

XI.3   INTERNAL MANIPULATIONS   309
XI.3.1   Logical Operations   310
XI.3.2   Expressions Involving Bit Strings of Length 1   314
XI.3.3   General Expressions with Logical and Comparative Operators   316
XI.3.4   Bit Strings and the IF Statement   317
XI.3.5   Built-In Functions for Bit Strings   318
XI.3.5.1   the BOOL function   318
XI.3.5.2   the UNSPEC function   321
XI.3.5.3   the HIGH and LOW functions   321
XI.3.5.4   the ANY and ALL functions   322
XI.3.5.5   the BIT function   322

PROBLEMS   323

SUMMARY OF IMPORTANT TERM   325

SUPPLEMENTARY READING   326

XII   CONTROL OF SEQUENCE IN A PROCEDURE   327

XII.1   THE GO TO STATEMENT   328
XII.1.1   Statement Label Variables   329
XII.1.2   Declaration of Label Variables for Efficient Processing   330
XII.1.3   Arrays of Label Variables   330

XII.2   THE CASE CONSTRUCT   331

XII.3   EXPANDED USES OF THE **IF** STATEMENT   **334**
    XII.3.1   The **THEN IF** Clause   **336**
    XII.3.2   The **ELSE IF** Clause   **340**

XII.4   THE **DO** STATEMENT   **342**
    XII.4.1   Nesting of **DO** Groups   **342**
    XII.4.2   Extensions to the **DO** Loop   **344**
        XII.4.2.1   the **WHILE** clause   **344**
        XII.4.2.2   multiple iterative specifications   **345**
        XII.4.2.3   re-use of the **DO** loop index   **346**
        XII.4.2.4   changing the repetition increment: the **BY** phrase   **347**
        XII.4.2.5   negative increments   **348**
        XII.4.2.6   nonintegers as increments in a **DO** loop   **349**
        XII.4.2.7   the full-blown **DO** statement   **351**
    XII.4.3   **DO** Loops with multidimensional Arrays   **351**
    XII.4.4   Transmission of Multidimensional Arrays   **354**

PROBLEMS   **358**

SUMMARY OF IMPORTANT TERMS   **361**

SUPPLEMENTARY READING   **362**

XIII   **CONTROL OF PL/I PROGRAM ORGANIZATION**   **363**

XIII.1   TYPES OF BLOCKS   **364**
    XIII.1.1   Procedures   **364**
        XIII.1.1.1   external procedures   **366**
        XIII.1.1.2   internal procedures   **367**
    XIII.1.2   The **BEGIN** Block   **367**
    XIII.1.3   Relationships Between Blocks in a Program   **369**
    XIII.1.4   The **PROCESS** Statement   **371**

XIII.2   TRANSFER OF CONTROL BETWEEN PROCEDURES   **372**
    XIII.2.1   Function Procedures   **372**
        XIII.2.1.1   invocation of function procedures   **374**
        XIII.2.1.2   arguments versus parameters   **374**
        XIII.2.1.3   attributes of returned values — the **RETURNS** option   **375**

XIII.2.1.4   alternate entries for function procedures   **376**
XIII.2.1.5   multiple returns in a function   **378**
XIII.2.2   Subroutines   **379**
XIII.2.2.1   invocation of subroutine procedures   **379**
XIII.2.2.2   formal parameters in a subroutine   **379**
XIII.2.2.3   processing of data aggregates in subroutines   **380**
XIII.2.2.4   alternate returns from subroutines   **381**
XIII.2.3   Activation of Internal Procedures   **382**

XIII.3   TRANSFER OF INFORMATION BETWEEN PROCEDURES   **385**
XIII.3.1   Transfer of Numerical Information   **385**
XIII.3.2   Arithmetic Expressions as Arguments   **386**
XIII.3.3   The **GENERIC** Attribute   **387**
XIII.3.4   Non-Numeric Arguments   **388**
XIII.3.4.1   character and bit-string arguments   **388**
XIII.3.4.2   use of statement labels as arguments   **389**
XIII.3.4.3   use of entry points as arguments   **390**
XIII.3.4.4   dummy arguments   **392**

XIII.4   RECOGNITION OF NAMES IN A PROGRAM   **393**
XIII.4.1   The **STATIC** and **AUTOMATIC** Attributes   **394**
XIII.4.1.1   scope of variables   **395**
XIII.4.1.2   scope of entry names   **396**
XIII.4.1.3   alteration of scope   **396**
XIII.4.1.4   the **BUILTIN** Attribute   **397**
XIII.4.2   Extension of Scope: **EXTERNAL** and **INTERNAL** Attributes   **398**
XIII.4.3   The **BEGIN** Block   **400**

XIII.5   RECURSIVE PROCEDURES   **401**

PROBLEMS   **403**

SUMMARY OF IMPORTANT TERMS   **407**

SUPPLEMENTARY READING   **409**

XIV   DATA RECORDS, DATA SETS, AND FILES   **411**

XIV.1   ORGANIZATION OF DATA SETS   **413**
XIV.1.1   Internal Construction of Records   **413**

XIV.1.2   Basic Declaration of Files   **414**

XIV.1.3   Direction of Transmission   **416**
    XIV.1.3.1   the **INPUT** attribute   **416**
    XIV.1.3.2   the **OUTPUT** attribute   **416**
    XIV.1.3.3   the **UPDATE** attribute   **417**
    XIV.1.3.4   the **PRINT** attribute   **417**

XIV.1.4   Data Transmission Attributes   **418**

XIV.2   ACCESS METHODS FOR DATA RECORDS   **419**

XIV.2.1   The **SEQUENTIAL** Attribute   **419**
    XIV.2.1.1   the **BACKWARDS** attribute   **420**
    XIV.2.1.2   the **KEYED** attribute   **420**
    XIV.2.1.3   buffered input/output operations   **421**

XIV.2.2   The **DIRECT** Attribute   **423**

XIV.2.3   File Declaration Defaults   **423**

XIV.3   THE **ENVIRONMENT** SPECIFICATIONS   **425**

XIV.3.1   Files and Data Sets   **425**

XIV.3.2   Records and Blocks   **425**
    XIV.3.2.1   fixed length records   **427**
    XIV.3.2.2   variable length records   **427**
    XIV.3.2.3   spanned records   **428**
    XIV.3.2.4   undefined length records   **430**

XIV.3.3   Specification of Buffers   **430**

XIV.3.4   Data Set Organization   **430**
    XIV.3.4.1   the **CONSECUTIVE** attribute   **431**
    XIV.3.4.2   the **INDEXED** attribute   **431**
    XIV.3.4.3   the **REGIONAL** attribute   **435**

XIV.4   RELATIONSHIP BETWEEN FILES AND EXTERNAL STORAGE DEVICES   **439**

XIV.5   ACTIVATION OF FILES   **440**

XIV.5.1   The **TITLE** Option   **441**

XIV.5.2   File Variables   **442**

XIV.5.3   Additional Options for **PRINT** Files   **443**
    XIV.5.3.1   the **PAGESIZE** option   **443**
    XIV.5.3.2   the **LINESIZE** option   **444**

XIV.5.4   Additional Remarks About **OPEN** and **CLOSE** Statements   **444**

PROBLEMS   **445**

SUMMARY OF IMPORTANT TERMS   **445**

SUPPLEMENTARY READING   **447**

XV   **MANIPULATION OF FILES AND DATA SETS**   **449**

XV.1   The **READ** Statement   **451**
XV.1.1   The **KEYTO** Option   **454**
XV.1.2   The **KEY** Option   **454**
XV.1.3   The **IGNORE** Option   **456**
XV.1.4   Buffered Files   **458**
XV.1.4.1   locate mode input   **459**
XV.1.4.2   pointers and pointer variables   **459**
XV.1.4.3   based variables and pointers   **459**
XV.1.4.4   the **SET** option   **460**
XV.1.4.5   handling variable format record files   **460**

XV.2   THE **WRITE** STATEMENT   **462**
XV.2.1   The **KEYFROM** Option   **463**
XV.2.2   The **LOCATE** Statement   **464**
XV.2.3   Punched Card Output   **466**

XV.3   UPDATE FILE HANDLING   **467**
XV.3.1   The **REWRITE** Statement   **467**
XV.3.2   Deletion and Addition of Records   **468**

XV.4   USE OF FILE NAMES AS ARGUMENTS   **470**

PROBLEMS   **470**

SUMMARY OF IMPORTANT TERMS   **472**

SUPPLEMENTARY READING   **473**

XVI   **CONTROL OF EXECUTION**   **475**

XVI.1   SERVICE OPERATIONS   **476**
XVI.1.1   General Aids   **477**
XVI.1.1.1   the **TIME** function   **477**

XVI.1.1.2   the **DATE** function   **477**

XVI.1.2   Communications with the Operator   **477**
XVI.1.2.1   the **DISPLAY** instruction   **478**
XVI.1.2.2   the **REPLY** instruction   **478**

XVI.1.3   Input/Output Services   **478**
XVI.1.3.1   the **COUNT** function   **478**
XVI.1.3.2   the **LINENO** function   **478**

XVI.2   THE HANDLING OF INTERRUPTIONS   **480**

XVI.2.1   Computational Conditions   **482**
XVI.2.1.1   the **CONVERSION** condition   **482**
XVI.2.1.2   the **ONCHAR** function   **482**
XVI.2.1.3   the **ONSOURCE** function   **483**
XVI.2.1.4   the **SIZE** condition   **484**
XVI.2.1.5   the **FIXEDOVERFLOW** condition   **485**
XVI.2.1.6   the **OVERFLOW** condition   **485**
XVI.2.1.7   the **UNDERFLOW** condition   **485**
XVI.2.1.8   the **ZERODIVIDE** condition   **486**
XVI.2.1.9   the **SUBSCRIPTRANGE** condition   **486**
XVI.2.1.10   the **STRINGRANGE** condition   **486**

XVI.2.2   Input/Output Interrupt Conditions   **487**
XVI.2.2.1   the **NAME condition**   **487**
XVI.2.2.2   the **UNDEFFINEDFILE** condition   **487**
XVI.2.2.3   the **TRANSMIT** condition   **488**
XVI.2.2.4   the **RECORD** condition   **488**
XVI.2.2.5   the **KEY** condition   **488**
XVI.2.2.6   the **ENDPAGE** condition   **489**

XVI.2.3   Interruptions as Debugging Aids   **490**
XVI.2.3.1   the **SNAP** option   **490**
XVI.2.3.2   the **ONLOC** option   **491**
XVI.2.3.3   the **ONCODE** function   **492**
XVI.2.3.4   the **ERROR** and **FINISH** conditions   **493**
XVI.2.3.5   the **CHECK** condition   **493**

XVI.2.4   Do-It-Yourself Interruptions   **498**
XVI.2.4.1   the **ON CONDITION** statement   **498**
XVI.2.4.2   simulation of standard interruptions   **499**

XVI.2.5   Enabling and Disabling Interrupt Conditions   **499**

XVI.2.6   Scope of an Interrupt Condition   **501**

XVI.2.7   Scope of Condition Prefixes   **504**

PROBLEMS   **507**

SUMMARY OF IMPORTANT TERMS   **507**

SUPPLEMENTARY READING   **508**

XVII CONTROL OF STORAGE   509

XVII.1 BASED VARIABLES   **510**
    XVII.1.1 Declaration of Based Variables   **510**
    XVII.1.2 Allocation of Based Variables   **511**
        XVII.1.2.1   multiple allocations of based variables   **511**
        XVII.1.2.2   allocation of based arrays   **512**
        XVII.1.2.3   allocating based structures   **513**
        XVII.1.2.4   the **REFER** option   **513**
    XVII.1.3 Pointer Qualifiers   **515**
    XVII.1.4 Basic Properties of Pointer Variables   **516**
        XVII.1.4.1   declaration of pointers   **517**
        XVII.1.4.2   assignment of values of pointer variables   **517**
        XVII.1.4.3   the **ADDR** function   **518**
        XVII.1.4.4   the **NULL** built-in function   **518**
        XVII.1.4.5   use of based variables to describe other variables   **519**
    XVII.1.5 The **AREA** Attribute   **521**
        XVII.1.5.1   allocation of areas   **521**
        XVII.1.5.2   allocation of storage in areas   **522**
        XVII.1.5.3   the **AREA** condition   **522**
        XVII.1.5.4   offset variables   **522**
        XVII.1.5.5   the **NULLO** built-in function   **524**
        XVII.1.5.6   other properties of areas   **525**
    XVII.1.6 Freeing Based Variables   **525**
        XVII.1.6.1   freeing amidst multiple allocations   **526**
        XVII.1.6.2   freeing parts of areas   **527**
        XVII.1.6.3   the **EMPTY** built-in function   **527**

XVII.2 LIST PROCESSING   **528**
    XVII.2.1 Organization of Lists   **531**
    XVII.2.2 Manipulation of Lists   **533**
        XVII.2.2.1   chaining through a list   **533**
        XVII.2.2.2   searching a list   **533**
        XVII.2.2.3   insertion in a list   **534**
        XVII.2.2.4   deletion from a list   **536**

XVII.2.3 Lists and Areas   **537**

XVII.3   CONTROLLED STORAGE   **539**

XVII.3.1 Special Properties of Controlled Variables   **540**
XVII.3.1.1   the "pushdown" and "pop-up" concept   **540**
XVII.3.1.2   the **ALLOCATION** function   **541**
XVII.3.1.3   controlled variables as parameters   **541**
XVII.3.2 Asterisk Notation for Controlled Variables   **543**

PROBLEMS   **545**

SUMMARY OF IMPORTANT TERMS   **549**

SUPPLEMENTARY READING   **551**

XVIII CONTROL OF COMPILATION   **553**

XVIII.1 COMPILE-TIME STATEMENTS   **555**
XVIII.1.1 Activation and Reactivation of Compile-Time Variables   **556**
XVIII.1.1.1 the %**DEACTIVATE** statement   **557**
XVIII.1.1.2 the %**ACTIVATE** statement   **557**
XVIII.1.2 Sequential Replacement Rescanning   **557**
XVIII.1.3 Compile-Time Declaration   **560**
XVIII.1.4 The Compile-Time Assignment Statement   **560**
XVIII.1.5 Compile-Time Decision Statements   **560**
XVIII.1.5.1 the %**IF** statement   **561**
XVIII.1.5.2 the %**DO** group   **562**
XVIII.1.5.3 the compile-time null statement   **562**
XVIII.1.5.4 the %**GO TO** statement   **563**
XVIII.1.6 SUBSTR as a Compile-Time Built-In Function   **564**
XVIII.1.7 The %**INCLUDE** Statement   **565**

XVIII.2 COMPILE-TIME PROCEDURES   **568**

PROBLEMS   **571**

SUMMARY OF IMPORTANT TERMS   **571**

SUPPLEMENTARY READING   **572**

XIX **ASYNCHRONOUS PROCESSING**   **573**

    XIX.1   THE TASK CONCEPT   **574**
        XIX.1.1   The TASK Option and TASK Attribute   **574**
        XIX.1.2   Creation and Termination of a Task   **575**
            XIX.1.2.1   task creation   **575**
            XIX.1.2.2   termination of tasks   **576**

    XIX.2   EVENTS AND EVENT VARIABLES   **576**
        XIX.2.1   Declaration of Events   **576**
        XIX.2.2   Setting of Event Variables   **577**

    XIX.3   SYNCHRONIZATION OF TASKS   **578**
        XIX.3.1   The **WAIT** Statement   **578**
        XIX.3.2   The **DELAY** Statement   **581**

    XIX.4   Priority in Asynchronous Processing   **581**
        XIX.4.1   Setting Priorities of Tasks   **581**
        XIX.4.2   The **PRIORITY** Function   **582**
        XIX.4.3   Use of Priorities During Task Creation   **583**

    XIX.5   HANDLING OF FILES IN ASYNCHRONOUS PROCESSING   **583**
        XIX.5.1   Locking and Unlocking of Records   **583**
        XIX.5.2   Use of the **EVENT** Option in File Manipulation   **584**

    SUMMARY OF IMPORTANT TERMS   **585**

    SUPPLEMENTARY READING   **586**

APPENDIX A. FLOWCHARTING   **587**

APPENDIX B. DATA CONVERSION   601

B.1   CONVERSION SITUATIONS   603
         B.1.1   Assignment   604
         B.1.2   Arguments   604
         B.1.3   Subscripts, Formats, and Options   604
         B.1.4   Expressions   604

B.2   DETERMINATION OF SOURCE AND TARGET
         ATTRIBUTES   605
         B.2.1   Conversion to Arithmetic Operations   605
         B.2.2   Conversion Rules for Relational Operands   606
         B.2.3   Conversion for Logical Operators   607
         B.2.4   Conversion for Concatenation   608

B.3   MECHANISMS FOR CONVERSION   608
         B.3.1   Arithmetic Conversion   608
                    B.3.1.1   mode conversion   608
                    B.3.1.2   precision conversion   608
                    B.3.1.3   base conversion   609
                    B.3.1.4   scale conversion   609
         B.3.2   Conversion Between Numeric Character and Arithmetic   610
         B.3.3   Conversion Between Bit String and Arithmetic   611
         B.3.4   Conversion Between Character Strings and Arithmetic
                    Types   611
         B.3.5   Conversion Between Numeric Character and Bit Strings   611
         B.3.6   Conversion Between Numeric Character and Character
                    Strings   612
         B.3.7   Conversion Between Character and Bit Strings   612
B.4   COMMON PROBLEMS AND THEIR AVOIDANCE   613
         B.4.1   Fixed Point Overflow   613
         B.4.2   Inaccurate Results   613
         B.4.3   Difficulties in Converting Arithmetic Values to Character
                    strings   614

APPENDIX C. COLLATING SEQUENCES FOR CHARACTER SETS   615

APPENDIX D. PL/I COMPILERS 619

D.1   BACKGROUND 619
      D.1.1   The IBM PL/I-F Compiler 620
      D.1.2   The PL/C Compiler 620
      D.1.3   The **PLUTO** Compiler 620
      D.1.4   The IBM Optimizing and Checkout Compilers 621
      D.1.5   The IBM Subset Compiler 621
      D.1.6   **PLAGO** (PL/I Load and Go) 622
      D.1.7   Other Compilers 622

D.2   TREATMENT OF LANGUAGE DIFFERENCES 622
      D.2.1   Statement Types 623
      D.2.2   Attributes 628
      D.2.3   Built-In Functions 630
      D.2.4   Pseudovariables 632
      D.2.5   **ON** Conditions 634

APPENDIX E. ABBREVIATIONS FOR PL/I KEYWORDS 635

INDEX 637

I STRUCTURING A PL/I PROGRAM

Learning to program is very much like learning a language. Just as fluency of speech depends on how soon the student starts to converse, so will he become facile in PL/I more quickly if he begins to write programs from the start. A PL/I compiler has the happy facility of enabling us to write workable programs with only a cursory knowledge of it. We shall exploit this ability immediately. The student will find that, by working the exercise problems in this chapter and inventing others, he will be able to examine the basic features of PL/I and, by using them, become acquainted with the anatomy of programs.

In presenting these introductory concepts, we have used a notation that differentiates *Bold* between literal and generic information. Terms written in bold capitals (such as **PROCEDURE** *type* or **END**) are members of PL/I's permanent vocabulary (often referred to as *keywords*) and always appear in programs exactly as shown. Words in lowercase type are to be interpreted as generic words, referring to an item in general. Thus, the word "label" indicates that some kind of word or symbol, chosen by the programmer, is to appear in a particular place. In illustrative

Keywords
Generic words

1

statements in the text, the specific word selected to replace a generic word is written in large capitals and treated literally.

This notation also uses a vertical series of dots to indicate the presence of a portion of a program whose contents are not germane to the issue under discussion. Other aspects of this notation, which prevails throughout the text, include spacing between terms and use of parentheses. These will usually be self-explanatory.

I.1   ACTION OF THE PL/I COMPILER

Any program, regardless of its organization or the language in which it is written, consists of a sequence of instructions, which are carried out in a certain order. This order may be permanently fixed during the design so that the program operates exactly the same way each time it is used, or it may contain logical mechanisms that will alter the sequence depending on prevailing conditions during a particular run. When a program is written in a high-level language, its instructions, in their original form, bear no relation to those the computer is designed to accept. In order to build fast, reliable computers, it is necessary at present to design their circuits around a repertoire of commands that are specific for each type of machine and look nothing like instructions in a natural language.

Each individual instruction in a *machine language* is so trivial by human standards that it would require several (sometimes dozens) to produce the equivalent of a single human command. For example, suppose we have two values, X and Y, and we want to calculate a value Z representing their sum. In ordinary mathematical notation, we would say

$$Z = X + Y$$

with the implication that X and Y were values made available to us either from some external source or stored in our memory. Once the result is calculated and written down, it is immediately available for inspection. To do the same thing in a computer, we must provide the machine with an entire series of instructions in which the actual addition plays a relatively small part. If we were to represent the individual machine instructions in narrative form, a program to perform the simple addition $Z = X + Y$ would appear somewhat as follows, assuming that the values X and Y are available to the machine in some acceptable form:

1. Start of program.
2. Reserve a particular location in the computer's memory for the value that we have called X. (We shall refer to this particular location from now on as the *address* of X.)
3. Reserve a second memory location for the value that we have called Y. (We will refer to this particular location from now on as the *address* of Y.)
4. Reserve another location in memory for the value that we shall call Z. (We shall refer to this particular location from now on as the *address* of Z.)
5. Here is the designation for the peripheral device from which the values for X and Y will be coming.

6. Bring in the next two available values from the device specified in Step 5.

7. Store the two values just received in address X and Y, respectively.

8. Take the value currently in address X and reproduce that value in address Z.

9. Take the current value in address Y and add it to the current value in address Z.

10. Here is a description of the device on which the results will be displayed.

11. Transmit the current values in addresses X, Y, and Z to the display device specified previously.

12. End of program; there are no further instructions.

If this is what is required to add two numbers together, you can readily imagine what kind of a production it would take to get something useful done with such a language. To make matters even less convenient, these instructions, in order to be intelligible to the computer, would each have to be represented in a special binary code consisting of long strings of ones and zeros.

PL/I's goal (as is the case with any other high-level language) is to simplify the process of instruction and relieve the user from the arduous, complex, and time-consuming task of having to produce a program directly in machine language. The vehicle for such relief is the PL/I compiler, a very extensive, closely knit structure of procedures and routines designed to scan each high-level instruction, analyze it to determine what sequence of machine language would be required to produce the equivalent actions, and actually produce those instructions in machine language. Thus, in a very real sense, the compiler represents an automatic programmer. Because of this interpretive and analytical ability, the programmer working with PL/I can instruct the compiler to produce a machine language program equivalent to the one listed above, with a set of instructions that can be as simple as the following:

PL/I Instruction	*Compiler Action*
PROCEDURE;	Step 1 above.
DECLARE X,Y,Z;	Steps 2-4. With no further specifications PL/I assumes that X, Y, and Z will contain numbers rather than letters or other symbols.
GET DATA (X,Y);	Steps 5-7. The assignment of a particular device for all input is built into the supervisory system by which programs and jobs are assembled and executed at each installation. Unless otherwise instructed, PL/I refers to the assigned input device.
Z = X + Y;	Steps 8-9.
PUT DATA (X,Y,Z);	Steps 10-11. Again, a standard output device is assumed.
END;	Step 12.

If our particular procedure had called for Z to be calculated as

$$Z = \frac{2.7X^3 + 12Y^2}{31 - 3XY}$$

instead of the sum of X and Y, the calculation of Z would have required something like 21 machine language instructions. However, the equivalent PL/I program would still contain the same number of statements as before. The Z = X + Y; step would simply be replaced by

$$Z = (2.7*X**3 + 12*Y**2)/(31 - 3*X*Y);$$

which is still a single "instruction" as far as the PL/I programmer is concerned.

I.2 BASIC INSTRUCTION TYPES

The full list of commands available to the PL/I programmer is an imposing one and may even seem formidable to some. However, one of the most interesting features of the language's structure is its modularity. More than any of its predecessors, PL/I's apparent size can shrink to match the requirements and background of the user without losing its integrity as a language. It is quite possible for entire programs, and fairly complex ones at that, to be written with a small subset of the full vocabulary, as if that constituted the extent of the language. In fact, such PL/I extracts have been implemented and are used routinely for an extensive variety of applications. (References to these PL/I subsets are given at the end of this chapter.) The PL/I subset we shall explore in this chapter is quite simple; yet it allows us to deal with a wide range of situations.

Regardless of their degree of complexity, the instructions in PL/I, as with most other programming languages, can be conveniently categorized into a small number of functional groups. In terms of our basic vocabulary, some of these groups may be represented only by a single type of command. However, if we become familiar with these groupings at this early stage, it will facilitate the process of systematically building up our PL/I vocabulary by introducing new instructions as additional members of particular categories.

I.2.1 Definition of Program Limits

A PL/I program consists of one or more unified modules called *procedures*. As with any other programming language, it is necessary to provide the compiler with signals for defining the beginning and end of a procedure. The form these signals take will depend on whether the procedure is one of several used by the program or whether it operates in a supervisory capacity, pulling other procedures together. For our present purposes, it will suffice to consider a program as consisting of a single procedure.

The start of such a procedure is signaled by the statement

label: **PROCEDURE OPTIONS(MAIN);**

where "label" is a name assigned to the program by the programmer. As such, it must start with a letter consisting entirely of letters and digits, and contain no blanks. (The **OPTIONS (MAIN)**" part tells PL/I that this is the procedure that will receive initial control.)

All procedures must end with the statement

END label; *optional*

"label" in this case may be omitted. If it is used, it must be the same as the one used in the **PROCEDURE** statement. For example, the sequence

START: **PROCEDURE OPTIONS(MAIN);**

.
.
.

other statements

.
.
.

END START;

shows how these statements are used to bracket a program. Note also that each statement terminates with a semicolon (;). This symbol signals PL/I that it has reached the end of a statement. If this signal is missing, PL/I will proceed until it is stopped by another semicolon, or will even try to insert one at a likely spot. Failure to end a statement with a semicolon will thus cause needless errors.

I.2.2   Definition of Variables

In dissecting the simple process of adding two numbers, we saw that the sequence of machinelike instructions did not concern themselves with the values to be added. Instead, X and Y were names assigned to the addresses of locations in the processor where the values were stored, and the instructions dealt with the current contents of those locations.

One of the basic duties of the PL/I compiler, therefore, is to make it easy for the programmer to reserve locations in storage and assign convenient names to them. Since the internal circuitry permanently assigns a number to each unit of storage (a unit corresponds to a portion of storage capable of holding a single character of information), the compiler must assign a numerical designation (address) to each name specified by the programmer. It must keep track of these assignments so that it can always determine which locations are still available and refer to the proper address when the corresponding name is used.

The easiest and surest way to reserve storage is with a statement having the general form

DECLARE name;

where "name" is an identifier assigned by the programmer. Such names can be one or several characters long and, for our present purposes, must start with A-H or O-Z. (Names starting

A-H, O-Z
I - N SPECIAL PROPERTIES

with I-N automatically are assigned special properties, which will be discussed later.) A number of names may be declared in this fashion with a single statement. Thus

   DECLARE X, X1, X2, X3;

will reserve four areas in storage, which, for the duration of the program, will be known as X, X1, X2, and X3. Similarly,

   DECLARE TIME, RATE, FORTISSIMO;

will reserve three areas in storage, which will be referred to from then on as TIME, RATE, and FORTISSIMO.

PL/I will recognize and handle many different types of information as long as they are explicitly defined by the user. When such specifications are lacking, the compiler makes certain assumptions and then proceeds. For the first declaration shown above, the compiler operates on the basis that X, X1, X2, and X3 will always contain numbers having the form

$$\pm n.dE \pm pp \qquad \textit{No specifies in declare}$$

where n.d represents a number, written in ordinary notation, which may have digits on either side of the decimal point, and pp is a one- or two-digit number indicating the power of ten by which the number n.d is to be multiplied to obtain its proper magnitude. Either the n or the d part may be ommitted if not needed; if d is omitted, so may the decimal point. Positive signs may be omitted as well. This form of numerical representation is known as *floating-point*. Several typical floating-point numbers and their actual magnitudes are shown below.

Floating-point Form	Magnitude
2E0	2.0
3.12E+01	31.2
3.12E+04	31200.
3.12E−06	0.00000312
−6.4E−00	−6.4
−6.42E−01	−0.642
−0.27E−03	−0.00027
0.683E+03	683.
−21.04E−01	−2.104

Internally, such numbers are stored using a total number of digits automatically set by PL/I at some fixed value, depending on the particular implementation. A typical length is six digits, so that the number −3.71 could be represented in floating-point form as −3.71000E+00.

I.2.3 Internal Manipulation of Numbers

Manipulative commands available in PL/I allow the programmer to generate new data internally (as opposed to bringing it in from some external source), perform mathematical operations on these data (as well as those introduced as input), and shift such information around in the processor. The basic command used for these operations is the <u>assignment statement</u> having the general form

  name = expression;

where <u>"name" refers to some variable name designated by the programmer, and "expression" consists of one or more terms connected by mathematical operators.</u> The use of the symbol "=" in PL/I deserves some special attention. In all of our previous mathematical dealings we have been accustomed to treating that sign as a symbol of equality. If we encountered a statement such as

$$distance = velocity \times time$$

we would interpret this to mean that the product of velocity and time produces a result that is numerically equal to the distance. This is not quite the case in PL/I. Since we are dealing with the contents of locations rather than with actual values, it will be more fruitful if we consider the equals sign as representing an abbreviation for the words <u>"is replaced by."</u> Thus, if the distance equation were to appear as a PL/I assignment, it would look like this:

  DISTANCE = VELOCITY * TIME;

and would represent a command to "take the current contents of the storage location designated by the name VELOCITY, multiply those contents by the value presently stored in the location TIME and place the result in location DISTANCE." Although for all practical purposes the eventual outcome is the same, the conceptual difference is an important one in several respects. For example, the rules of ordinary algebra make the writing of a statement such as

$$X = X + 3;$$

inconsistent, for how can a value be three more than itself? In PL/I, however, this type of statement $(X = X + 3;)$ becomes perfectly plausible since it represents an instruction to "take the current contents of location X, increase that value by 3, and place the result back in location X, wiping out what was there before." With this fundamental concept in mind, we can proceed to the operations.

I.2.3.1 Numerical Constants

Sometimes we wish to refer to a value that does not change. In such a case we write the value itself, in ordinary notation, rather than a symbolic name for a location containing the value. We have already used this capability several times: The statement $X = X + 3$; considered above is an example. A very useful application is one in which we wish to assign a specific value to a variable. For instance, the assignment of the value -12.4 to X is handled merely by writing

$$X = -12.4;$$

I.2.3.2 Arithmetic Operations

PL/I provides five basic numerical operations, which can be combined in a wide variety of ways to synthesize more complex processes. Each of these operations is represented by a specific symbol, as shown in Table 1.1.

TABLE 1.1. Symbols for Arithmetic Operators

Symbol	Operation
+	Addition
−	Subtraction
*	Multiplication
/	Division
**	Exponentiation

These operators are used to connect constants and variables to form expressions in assignment statements. As such, they must always appear explicitly and can never be implied. The use of a statement such as

$$Z = XY;$$

will not be interpreted as a statement representing the equality of Z with the product of X and Y, as it is in ordinary algebraic notation. Instead, PL/I will begin searching its tables of names to determine whether a location has been assigned to the name XY. Consequently, that statement must appear unambiguously as

$$Z = X * Y;$$

Note that it is not necessary to use blanks to set off an operator from an adjacent constant or variable. Their usage, therefore, is strictly a matter of individual convenience. As a result, the forms

$$Z=X+2*Y-3;$$
$$Z = X + 2 * Y - 3;$$

and

$$Z = X + 2 * Y - 3;$$

are equivalent as far as the PL/I compiler is concerned. Table 1.2 shows some typical numerical expressions constructed with these operators.

TABLE 1.2. Use of Operators to Synthesize Arithmetic Expressions in PL/I

Algebraic Expression	PL/I Equivalent
$2X - 3Y$	$2*X - 3*Y$
$X^2 + 4Y^4$	$X**2 + 4*Y**4$
$3X - \dfrac{7.6Y}{Z}$	$3*X - 7.6*Y/Z$
$\dfrac{X}{Y^2} + \dfrac{18.9Y^{.6}}{4}$	$X/Y**2 + 18.9*Y**.6/4$
$.58XY^2 - 1.74X^3Y^{.7}$	$.58*X*Y**2 - 1.74*X**3*Y**.7$
$\dfrac{X}{Y} + 2.7X + \dfrac{3XY^2}{5}$	$X/Y + 2.7*X + 3*X*Y**2/5$

Assume that all variables are named by single letters.

Since computers do not share our ability to scan several lines of information at the same time, we cannot expect them to react to an algebraic expression the same way we do. For example, the rules of algebra leave no doubt as to what operations are implied by the expression

$$Y = \frac{2X + 7}{3X - 4}$$

However, since this expression must be rewritten as a continuous string of numbers and symbols before it can be read at all, it becomes necessary to apply a somewhat different set of rules. Based on the examples shown in Table 1.2, if we were to transform the above expression into

$$Y = 2*X + 7/3*X - 4;$$

it would be interpreted as if it were

$$Y = 2X + \frac{7X}{3} - 4$$

To overcome these difficulties and to provide the necessary flexibility for arithmetic operations, the programmer can make these expressions more explicit by including parentheses. Thus, the inclusion of parentheses will allow PL/I to make the proper distinction in our example if we write it as

$$Y = (2*X + 7)/(3*X - 4);$$

Once parentheses are introduced, they are treated as in ordinary algebraic notation. Table 1.3 shows some examples.

TABLE 1.3. Use of Parentheses in PL/I Expressions

Algebraic Expressions	PL/I Equivalent
$\dfrac{X-2}{3Y}$	$(X-2)/(3*Y)$
$\dfrac{X-2}{3Y} + 7X$	$(X-2)/(3*Y) + 7*X$
$\dfrac{X-2}{3Y+7X}$	$(X-2)/(3*Y+7*X)$
$(X+Y)(2X-Y)$	$(X+Y)*(2*X-Y)$
$\dfrac{(3X-7Y)^2}{2X}$	$(3*X-7*Y)**2/(2*X)$
$\dfrac{X-4}{2+\dfrac{Y}{3}}$	$(X-4)/(2+Y/3)$
$7Z\left(\dfrac{X-4}{2+\dfrac{Y}{3}}\right)^2$	$7*Z*((X-4)/(2+Y/3))**2$

At this stage we need not concern ourselves with the exact nature of the rules by which PL/I analyzes and operates on an arithmetic expression. Since there is no practical limit to the number of parentheses that may be introduced in an arithmetic expression (as long as they are used in properly nested pairs), we shall be fairly liberal with them.

There is no significant limit to the complexity or length of arithmetic expressions the language can handle. Rather, the restrictions lie with the individual programmer and are dictated by the amount of bookkeeping he is willing to do. Assuming, for instance, that variables X, Y, W, T, G, and B have been declared and do in fact contain specific numerical values, a statement such as

$$Z = 2*X*Y/17*G + W*(X*W*G**3/(B-7*T) + 21/(T-X));$$

is perfectly legitimate. However, keeping track of all the operators and parentheses may be too cumbersome. In that case, it may be more convenient to break the command into several chunks, namely,

$$Z1 = 2*X*Y/17*G;$$
$$Z2 = X*W*G**3/(B-7*T);$$
$$Z3 = 21/(T-X);$$
$$Z = Z1 + W*(Z2+Z3);$$

where Z1, Z2, and Z3 are temporarily used variables.

I.2.3.3 PL/I Default Actions

We have already encountered some instances in which PL/I gives unusual freedom to the programmer. For example, we declared X, Y, and Z without specifying what X, Y, and Z stood for or what their properties were. In the absence of precise designations, the PL/I compiler assumes X, Y, and Z to be numbers of a specific format. This predefined action, one of many such automatic responses built into the compiler, is known as a *default*. Since the system is permeated with such features, the student should keep in mind that, for many circumstances, PL/I will make specific assumptions and pursue some course when the programmer has failed to make clear exactly what he means. When the programmer is aware of the default actions that the compiler will take, and if this is in line with the program as intended, he has a powerful device for saving time and space. However, where the programmer simply forgets to specify a particular action or procedure, he may cause himself needless grief and errors because the compiler will assume that he has meant to specify a particular action or property and go ahead and include it in its final sequence of instructions. In the beginning at least, the student should be very careful to specify the intended actions explicitly and in detail. ✳

I.2.3.4 Shifting Data in Storage

A transfer of information from one location to another is merely a special case of the assignment statement in which no arithmetic is done and no new numbers are generated. The statement

$$Y = Z;$$

for example, will reproduce the current contents of location Z in location Y, so that both addresses contain identical information. Note that although the contents of Z will remain unchanged, the previous contents of Y are wiped out by this command, necessitating specific action if it is desired to preserve that value. If we want to exchange the contents of two locations, say X and Y, we must set up a sequence of instructions including a temporary variable (call it HOLD):

DECLARE X, Y, HOLD;

HOLD = X;

X = Y;

Y = HOLD;

I.2.4 Input-Output (I/O) Statements

PL/I provides the programmer with an extensive repertoire of commands for sending information to and from the processor. Yet, for all their versatility, these commands are surprisingly easy to construct. This simplicity is maintained in part by dividing various transmission modes into distinct categories, thus allowing the user to select the type of input/output instruction that, with only simple specifications, will suit the data input or display requirements, rather than having to work with a heavily qualified all-inclusive statement.

One basic mode of data transmission is known as *stream I/O*, in which PL/I treats both input and output as continuous streams of data. To the compiler, such streams have no physical beginning or end. Instead, the flow of the stream to or from the processor is turned on or off by the program wherever and whenever the programmer desires. Under this concept, the command following the last I/O statement in a procedure merely constitutes the final interruption in flow, leaving the input and output streams waiting for further use. This idea of data streams is completely general, having nothing to do with the physical form of the data. There is no required connection between the amount of data on a punched card, for example, and the length of, or the stopping point in, a stream. If an input instruction should direct a number of values to be read so that the processor stops in the middle of a card, the next input instruction will cause the transmission process to pick up exactly where it left off (unless the programmer takes steps to the contrary) regardless of the number of intervening commands before this next instruction is reached.

I.2.4.1 The **GET DATA** and **PUT DATA** Statements

One of the forms of stream I/O allows the user to submit input data as a stream of miniature assignment-like statements separated by commas and punctuated by semicolons. A basic form for this command is

GET DATA (name1, name2, etc.);

where (name1, name2, etc.) is a list of variable names stipulating the locations in which the data items are to be stored. The input transmitted by this type of statement is prepared in the form

   name1 = value, name2 = value, etc.;

For example, a card punched as shown below, can be

$$A=76, B=-29, C=0, D=321.4;$$

read by means of the statement

   GET DATA (A,B,C,D);

with the result that floating-point numbers representing values of 76, -29, 0, and 321.4 are stored in locations A, B, C, and D, respectively. Because the data card contains both names and values it is not necessary to maintain any particular order. For example, the card

B=−29,   D=321.4,   A=76,   C=0;

would produce the same result.

   When output data are to be transmitted from the processor, exactly the same structure applies, except that the basic command is now the **PUT** statement, namely,

   PUT DATA (name1, name2, etc.);

When encountering such a statement, PL/I will produce instructions that direct the computer to copy the information stored in the specified addresses and place it in the output stream. Each value is accompanied by the name associated with its location, thus forming a series of assignmentlike statements. Assume that the values A, B, C, and D are those read in by the **GET DATA** statement shown before. If we assume further that the values are stored as six-digit floating-point numbers, then the statement

   PUT DATA   (D,C,A,B);

will produce the following output:

$$D=3.21400E+02   C=0.00000E+00   A=7.60000E+01   B=-2.90000E+01;$$

Note that the order in which the data items appear is determined strictly by the order in which the **PUT** statement specifies them. This has nothing to do with the order in which they were read or computed.

   Upon closer examination of these **GET** and **PUT** statements, it may occur to the student that these may be a bit *too* simple. Nowhere in these statements has any reference been made to the input or output device involved. It is true that the rules for constructing **GET DATA** and **PUT DATA** statements allow for the inclusion of such specifications. The lack of such definitions, however, points out the importance of PL/I default capabilities with regard to input/output. When PL/I runs across a **GET** or **PUT** statement in which no input source or output destination is specified, the compiler assumes by default that **SYSIN** or **SYSPRINT** is to be used, respectively. For program execution, the programmer can designate the devices to be used for the **SYSIN** and **SYSPRINT** files, or he can allow still another default to operate by which the supervisory routines will cause **SYSIN** to refer to the same input source from which the program was read and **SYSPRINT** to refer to the same printer on which the program listing is printed. For our purposes, it will be convenient to assume that **SYSIN** is a card reader and **SYSPRINT** is a line printer unless specified otherwise. It should be understood, however, that such definitions are relatively easy to change and may vary, even from one job to the next.

I.2.4.2   Format Control with the **PUT DATA** Statement

When the **PUT DATA** statement is used in its basic form, control of the physical positioning of the output on the page is left to PL/I. The appearance of such output is not a fixed characteristic of the language, but varies with the particular version of the compiler being used. A particular compiler may be set to print three values per line regardless of the length of the list in the **PUT** statement. Thus, if A, B, C, D, E, and F currently contain values of 1, 3, 5, 7, 9, and 11, respectively, the statement

PUT DATA (A,B,C,D,E,F);

will produce

$$A = 1.00000E + 00 \quad B = 3.00000E + 00 \quad C = 5.00000E + 00$$
$$D = 7.00000E + 00 \quad E = 9.00000E + 00 \quad F = 1.10000E + 01;$$

and the statements

PUT DATA (A,B);   **PUT DATA** (C,D,E,F);

will result in the same thing (except for an extra semicolon); namely,

$$A = 1.00000E + 00 \quad B = 3.00000E + 00; \quad C = 5.00000E + 00$$
$$D = 7.00000E + 00 \quad E = 9.00000E + 00 \quad F = 1.10000E + 01;$$

The **PUT DATA** statement can be augmented with embellishments that provide some limited control of the output format. For the present, we shall introduce one such refinement that allows the user to specify the start of a new line. This is done with the statement

PUT SKIP DATA (name1, name2, etc.);

Thus, using the six values in the previous example, the statements

PUT DATA (A,B); **PUT SKIP DATA** (C,D,E,F);

now will produce

$$A = 1.00000E + 00 \quad B = 3.00000E + 00;$$
$$C = 5.00000E + 00 \quad D = 7.00000E + 00 \quad E = 9.00000E + 00$$
$$F = 1.10000E + 01;$$

I.2.5 Illustrative Programs

In tackling any programming job, the student should be clear about the nature of the problem to be solved, the general method he will use in solving the problem, and the specific flow of instructions he will employ to implement that solution on the computer. Proper documentation of the precise requirements will save him from serious errors such as the development of a correct solution to a problem that differs from the one he intended to solve.

The general methods and rules by which problems are solved are usually referred to as _algorithms._ Very often the same problem may be solved by more than one algorithm. The algorithm chosen for a particular problem will depend very much on the inventiveness of the programmer, his need to preserve time (either for programming or for the machine), and the flexibility of the programming language being used. The student should adopt the habit of making a _flowchart_ for himself. There are many rules for flowcharting, and no hard and fast procedures need to be adopted. (For some useful methods of flowcharting, the student is referred to Appendix A.)

Although we still lack some fundamental instructions, it is now possible for us to construct a variety of PL/I procedures that are complete in themselves and will work. A look at a few examples will be fruitful.

Illustration 1

Let us begin with a simple problem: finding the hypotenuse (HYP) of a right triangle, given the lengths of the two sides (SIDE1 and SIDE2) punched on a card as shown below. The output is to show values for all three sides.

```
SIDE1 = 174.7,SIDE2 = 215.3;
```

Our solution will make use of the relationships

$$HYP = \sqrt{SIDE1^2 + SIDE2^2} = (SIDE1^2 + SIDE2^2)^{.5}$$

The resulting PL/I program would read

```
TRNGL: PROCEDURE OPTICNS (MAIN);
       DECLARE SIDE1, SIDE2, HYP;
       GET DATA (SIDE1,SIDE2);
       HYP = (SIDE1 ** 2 + SIDE2 ** 2)**.5;
       PUT DATA (SIDE1,SIDE2,HYP);
       END TRNGL;
```

Illustration 2

We are interested in determining the present value (call it WORTH) of a piece of capital goods which cost a certain amount originally (PRICE) and which has depreciated over a particular length of time (AGE). The rate of depreciation is such that the item will have been completely written off at the end of some period of years (AMORT).

Our method of solution (algorithm) will be to employ the relationship

$$\text{WORTH} = \text{PRICE} - \frac{\text{PRICE}}{\text{AMORT}} \times \text{AGE}$$

To build a PL/I program around this algorithm, let us assume that the values for the input variables are punched on a data card in the order of PRICE, AMORT, and AGE. The output is to include a display of these values as well as the calculated value of WORTH. Our program would then be

```
DEPREC: PROCEDURE OPTIONS (MAIN);
        DECLARE PRICE, AMORT, AGE, WORTH;
        GET DATA (PRICE,AMORT,AGE);
        WORTH = PRICE - (PRICE/AMORT)*AGE;
        PUT DATA (PRICE,AMORT,AGE);
        PUT SKIP DATA (WORTH);
        END DEPREC;
```

and, with input presented as shown below,

```
PRICE=10000,  AMORT=25,  AGE=11;
```

the resulting output will be as follows:

```
PRICE= 2.00000E+04      AMORT= 2.50000E+01      AGE= 1.10000E+01;
WORTH= 1.12000E+04;
```

Note that, by printing the value of WORTH with a separate **PUT SKIP DATA** statement, we forced the program to begin a new output line.

Illustration 3

Let us try something a bit more complex this time. We have a set of two linear equations in the form

$$a_1x + b_1y = c_1$$

$$a_2x + b_2y = c_2$$

where a_1, a_2, b_1, b_2, c_1, and c_2 are numerical values to be brought in as input for use in determining the values of x and y.

A number of possible algorithms can be designed, all of which will provide correct solutions to these equations. The one used here has been selected arbitrarily. It should be pointed out, however, that in more complex situations the choice of an algorithm is often a problem requiring serious deliberation of such factors as accuracy, memory size, machine speed, and programming time. We shall be meeting such situations in subsequent problems.

The algorithm to be used here is a straightforward substitution. That is, we shall transform the first of the two equations to obtain an expression for x. This expression will then be used to replace x in the second equation, resulting in a single equation in which the only unknown quantity is y expressed in terms of a, b, and c.

$$y = \frac{a_1c_2 - a_2c_1}{a_1b_2 - a_2b_1}$$

Having obtained y, we can solve for x by

$$x = \frac{c_1 - b_1y}{a_1} \text{ or } x = \frac{c_2 - b_2y}{a_2}$$

Our program would be designed to read in values of a_1, a_2, b_1, b_2, c_1, c_2 in that order, perform the calculations indicated above, and print out the original input values with the derived values of x and y. With these requirements in mind, we can write

```
SOLVE: PROCEDURE OPTIONS (MAIN);
       DECLARE A1,A2,B1,B2,C1,C2,X,Y;
       GET DATA (A1,A2,B1,B2,C1,C2);
       Y = (A1*C2 - A2*C1)/(A1*B2 - A2*B1);
       X = (C1 - B1*Y)/A1;
       PUT DATA(A1,A2);
       PUT SKIP DATA(B1,B2);
       PUT SKIP DATA(C1,C2);
       PUT SKIP DATA(X,Y);
       END SOLVE;
```

Given the input values shown below,

$$\text{A1=8 , A2=6 , B1=11 , B2=9 , C1=2 , C2=3 ;}$$

the program produces the following results:

```
A1=  8.00000E+00        A2=  6.00000E+00;
B1=  1.10000E+01        B2=  9.00000E+00;
C1=  2.00000E+00        C2=  3.00000E+00;
X=-2.50000E+00          Y=  2.00000E+00;
```

Now that we have examined some complete procedures we can make note of some of the
guidelines underlying the physical preparation of PL/I statements. Although the compiler does
not necessarily restrict the program to punched cards, we shall use that medium throughout:

1. There is no set starting or ending point for a PL/I statement; however, because of
    operating system conventions, use of column 1 is usually disallowed. Local rules may
    limit the right-hand extremity (some installations require stopping at column 72, for
    example) but these variations depend on the installation.

2. More than one statement may appear on a card (see the procedure in Illustration 3).

3. Aside from their obvious necessity in separating words, blanks may be used to
    improve legibility between any statement components. For example, the blanks
    around the = sign in Illustration 1 are optional (as evidenced by their removal in
    Illustration 2 without effect). The student should note that the apparently haphazard
    use of blanks in these illustrative procedures is intended to emphasize PL/I's flexibil-
    ity in this regard. Incidentally, any number of blanks may appear in succession.

I.2.6 Control and Decision Statements

Although we are able to write complete PL/I programs with the basic statements covered so
far, we still suffer from some fundamental restrictions. The severity of these limitations can
easily be seen by examining any one of the three illustrative programs developed in the
previous section. Let us look at the second of these.

As it stands, the program is designed to read in those values required for calculation of the
depreciation, which can then be subtracted from the original cost, also read in, to obtain the
present value. Once the results have been printed, however, it is over. Should we want to
repeat the process for a different set of input values representing a different piece of capital
goods or a different depreciation time, there is no mechanism available for going back to the
beginning of the program, reading in a new set of values, and performing the calculations once
again. Instead, with the program in its present state, it is necessary to reenter the entire set of
instructions as if we were starting a completely new job. This type of operation is highly
inefficient. In fact, with shorter programs, it is often true that it takes considerably more time

to bring the instructions in and prepare the program for operation than it does to do the actual processing. One way of averting this situation would have been to extend the program by repeating the set of instructions so that two cases would have been handled during a particular run:

```
DEPREC: PROCEDURE OPTIONS (MAIN);
        DECLARE PRICE, AMORT, AGE, WORTH;

        GET DATA (PRICE,AMORT,AGE);
        WORTH = PRICE - (PRICE/AMORT)*AGE;
        PUT SKIP DATA(PRICE,AMORT,AGE,WORTH);

        GET DATA (PRICE,AMORT,AGE);
        WORTH = PRICE - (PRICE/AMORT)*AGE;
        PUT SKIP DATA(PRICE,AMORT,AGE,WORTH);
        END DEPREC;
```

Such an algorithm will work if we always expect each run to consist of exactly two cases, a very unreal situation. It would be more likely for a typical run to be called upon to handle dozens, perhaps hundreds, of cases. Under these circumstances it would be ludicrous to write a program in this manner, even assuming that sufficient storage were available for all of these instructions.

I.2.6.1 Program Loops

Repetitive calculation and processing can be handled effectively by providing a mechanism that will allow a single sequence of instructions to be repeated rather than necessitating the duplication of the instructions. The technique for effecting such repetitions is called *looping*, and a particular sequence to be repeated is a *loop*.

When a loop is part of a program, we usually construct the loop to repeat itself in a controlled way. Regardless of the number of repetitions, sooner or later something happens (because we designed for it to happen) that will cause a break in this pattern, and the program will go on to do something else. This may or may not be another loop. Regardless of its nature, it is distinct from the previous activity. Thus, we need to think of a loop as a structural unit consisting of two components:

1. The process itself — the required action(s) performed by the loop each time it goes through a cycle.

2. A controlling mechanism that regulates the repetitive process by determining whether it should stop or continue.

There are various ways to express such control, the choice depending largely on the nature of the algorithm and the requirements imposed by the application. By way of introduction, we shall examine some of PL/I's powerful facilities for constructing loops by specifying automatic control mechanisms.

1.2.6.2   The **DO** Loop

One way of controlling a loop is to decide ahead of time that the loop will be repeated a certain number of times. Thus, such a process is easily regulated by setting up a counter that keeps track of how many times the loop has gone through its cycle. Before each cycle is started, the counter's value specifies that cycle's number. (This means that before the program starts through the loop, the counter will be set *(initialized)* to 1, thereby indicating that the first cycle is about to be started). When a cycle is completed, the counter is increased by 1 and tested against a *limiting value*, i.e., the required number of cycles. If the requirement already has been met (i.e., the counter exceeds the limit), the program breaks the pattern, skips by the loop, and goes on to the next part of the program.

This type of loop is specified very easily in PL/I. It begins with a **DO** statement containing the necessary control information and concludes with an **END** statement, so that PL/I "knows" the exact extent of the loop. Between these two boundaries are placed whatever statements it takes to describe the processing to be repeated. This construction is called a **DO** *loop*.

Illustration 4

We shall acquaint ourselves with the **DO** loop by revising the algorithm in Illustration 2 so that it computes the present value for each of 36 sets of input data:

```
DPRC36: PROCEDURE OPTIONS (MAIN);
        DECLARE PRICE, AMORT, AGE, WORTH;

        DO K = 1 TO 36;
           GET DATA (PRICE,AMORT,AGE);
           WORTH = PRICE - (PRICE/AMORT)*AGE;
           PUT DATA (PRICE,AMORT,AGE);
           PUT SKIP DATA (WORTH);
        END;

        END DPRC36;
```

The **DO** statement provides the necessary elements of control in the form of

1.   an *index variable* (K in this example) that counts the number of cycles;

2.   a *starting value* (1 in this case);

3.   a *limiting value* (36 for this program) against which the index variable can be tested before each cycle.

Note that the index variable is not declared, since its entire existence is tied to the loop. (K could be used quite properly as the index variable for another loop elsewhere in the same program). Also of interest is the fact that the loop's boundaries (the **DO** and **END** statements) are equipped with the same label (as was shown for the **PROCEDURE** and **END** statements that bracket a program). This is not required for a **DO** loop, but it is a very convenient feature, especially in more intricate programs using many loops.

label: Do   ;

:

END label;

This control structure is such a fundamental component in many well-designed programs that it is considered as a single conceptual activity. The control thus implemented is simple and powerful, but rather restrictive. It means that every time we run our trusty depreciator, we must supply exactly 36 sets of input data for it to process. For most situations, this is an unreasonable requirement. An alternative approach is to allow the number of sets to vary from run to run and supply that number as part of the input. For this purpose we define an additional variable NSETS into which this value will be read. Once it is available, it can be used as a limiting value for the **DO** loop, so that the **DO** statement now would say

LOOP: DO K = 1 TO NSETS;

The revised program is shown below.

```
DPRC: PROCEDURE OPTIONS (MAIN);
      DECLARE PRICE, AMORT, AGE, WORTH, NSETS;
      GET DATA (NSETS);

      DO K = 1 TO NSETS;
        GET DATA (PRICE,AMORT,AGE);
        WORTH = PRICE - (PRICE/AMORT)*AGE;
        PUT DATA (PRICE,AMORT,AGE);
        PUT SKIP DATA (WORTH);
      END;

      END DPRC;
```

I.2.6.3   The **DO-WHILE** Construct

Another, more general type of **DO** loop can be constructed by using a different control mechanism. Instead of counting the cycles and breaking the pattern when the loop has been repeated a certain number of times, this type of control allows the repetitions to continue as long as a specified condition exists. As soon as that condition changes, the loop is bypassed and the program continues with the next activity.

This type of loop, called a **DO-WHILE** construct, is controlled by a **DO** statement formed as follows:

label: **DO WHILE** (condition);

The condition inside the parentheses is some kind of test whose outcome is either true or false. Prior to the start of each cycle, this condition is tested and, if found to be true, the repetition is performed. If not, the processing in the loop is bypassed and the program continues beyond it.

Illustration 5

We shall illustrate a **DO-WHILE** construct by generalizing the procedure in Illustration 4. Instead of requiring the user to specify how many input sets there will be in a given run, we shall use a special signal to stop the run. That is, the procedure will be designed to look for a particular input value. As long as that value does not appear, the loop continues to repeat, irrespective of the number of input sets. In this example, a price of zero will serve as the signal to end the run. This is a reasonable choice in this context, since an actual price of zero will not occur. (Such signals are known in the computing jargon as *sentinels* or *dummy values*).

The modified procedure, then, reads the first set of input values before the loop starts. This "primes" the system so that the loop control has something to test prior to its first cycle. As long as the condition turns out to be true (i.e., PRICE is greater than zero), the program performs the computations, reads the next input set, and is ready to test again:

```
DPRCR: PROCEDURE OPTIONS (MAIN);
       DECLARE PRICE, AMORT, AGE, WORTH;
       GET DATA (PRICE,AMORT,AGE);

       DO WHILE (PRICE ¬= 0);
         WORTH = PRICE - (PRICE/AMORT)*PAGE;
         PUT DATA (PRICE,AMORT,AGE);
         PUT SKIP DATA (WORTH);
         GET DATA (PRICE,AMORT,AGE);
       END;

       END DPRCR;
```

The **DO-WHILE** construct, like the **DO** loop, is a fundamental component of structured programs. Note that the **DO-WHILE** construct has a peculiar but very useful property: Since the loop starts with a test, it is possible to have a situation in which the loop does not even go through one cycle. In Illustration 5, for example, this would happen if our first input set had a PRICE of zero. The test (PRICE > 0) would fail, the loop would be bypassed and that would be that, regardless of whether or not there are additional input sets. In this context, such behavior may not seem particularly useful, but it can be of considerable value in other processes.

I.2.7   Relational Operations

The test used to control the loop in Illustration 5 is an example of a *relational operation* — an elementary rule for comparison that can be used as a basis for a "true" or "false" decision. PL/I provides six *relational operators* for the construction of such tests:

```
=  :   — equal to
¬ = :  — not equal to
<  :   — less than
< = :  — less than or equal to
> = :  — greater than or equal to
>  :   — greater than
```

A basic comparison is formed by combining two expressions with one of these operators (as we did with PRICE > 0). Of course, the expressions used in these comparisons can become as complicated as the application dictates. For instance, assuming variables S, T, and U have been defined and given values, we can specify a test such as

$$3.8 * (S+T)/(2.6/S) < = 16 * (U-7.2*T)/(T+2*U)$$

without changing the basic structure: This still is a comparison between two numerical values, with the outcome being either "true" or "false".

I.2.8 The **IF-THEN-ELSE** Construct

Besides providing a powerful basis for controlling loops, the ability to describe comparisons serves as a more general vehicle for setting up a limitless range of decision rules. The structured programming component for specifying these rules is called an **IF-THEN-ELSE** *construct*. This is nothing more than a comparison followed by a choice of two actions:

```
IF comparison
THEN
   action1;
ELSE
   action2;
```

These actions are mutually exclusive: action1 is taken when the outcome of the comparison is "true", in which case action2 is ignored. The exact opposite occurs when the outcome is "false". Typically, this construct is used in well-designed programs as follows:

```
IF comparison
THEN
   action1;
ELSE action2;
action3;
```

Based on the outcome of the comparison, *either* action1 or action2 is taken. Then, *regardless of which of the two alternatives was followed*, action3 is performed.

This is a very simple and innocent-looking construct, even though the comparison could be quite involved. However, do not yawn. There is much more here than a first glance would indicate. The versatility of this construct, and its embodiment by PL/I's corresponding **IF-THEN-ELSE** statement combination, lies in the fact that the alternative actions (action1 and action2 in the general form shown earlier) may be arbitrarily simple or complex. There is no minimum or maximum limit on the number of statements in which such an action must be described. Moreover, there are very few restrictions on the *kinds* of actions that may be specified. Thus, one of the actions well might be another **IF-THEN-ELSE** construct. We shall not deal with the consequences of this power until later in the text. It is sufficient here to point out that this structural component is a crucial building block in almost all programs.

Illustration 6

Using the control facilities already described, we shall develop a program that reads in pairs of numbers X and Y. For each pair, the program prints a value Z, computed as follows:

Z = 2X + Y when X is less than Y
Z = 1.72X - Y when X is not less than Y

After the last input set has been processed, the program is to print the number of sets handled by that run. X can be zero, but never below zero.

We shall use -1 as an end-of-data signal, thereby allowing us to build a **DO-WHILE** loop around the condition (X > -1). Inside the loop, an **IF-THEN-ELSE** construct will be set up to compute each value of Z after determining how it will be done. The statements are shown below:

```
ILL6: PROCEDURE OPTIONS (MAIN);
       DECLARE X,Y,Z,NPAIR;
       NPAIR = 0;
       GET DATA (X,Y);

       DO WHILE (X >= 0);
         NPAIR = NPAIR+1;
         IF X < Y
         THEN
             Z=2*X+Y;
         ELSE
             Z=1.72*X-Y;
         PUT SKIP DATA (X,Y,Z);
         GET DATA (X,Y);
       END;

       PUT SKIP DATA (NPAIR);
       END ILL6;
```

Let us recapitulate what happens here:

1. A counter NPAIR is set (initialized) to zero.

2. A set of X and Y values is brought in to give the loop control something to test at the start.

3. Once the test passes (X is 0 or more), NPAIR is increased by 1, X and Y are compared (by the **IF** statement), and Z is computed in accordance with the comparison's outcome.

4. X, Y, and Z are printed.

5. The next set of input is read and the loop is ready to repeat, starting with the test for X.

6. As soon as there is a negative value for X, the test in the **WHILE** statement will prevent the loop from being executed again. Instead, it will be bypassed.

7. Once the loop is bypassed, the program concludes after printing NPAIR's value.

I.3   PROGRAM EXECUTION

A program written in PL/I cannot be interpreted directly by the machine and, therefore, cannot be executed in its initial form. The actual processing is instigated by the machine language instructions generated from the original program by the PL/I compiler and introduced into the processor by the system under which it operates. Although the specific details surrounding the process by which such a machine language program is introduced and executed may vary widely with the hardware and software used, we can present a general picture of the sequence of operations involved, so that the student will have an idea how this occurs and gain insight into some basic duties and capabilities of an operating system. For convenience, we shall assume that the universal form of input to our operating system is the punched card and that its output is a printer. It should be realized, however, that the general concepts apply irrespective of the type of peripheral device used or the number of different devices involved.

We shall consider the initial input to consist of the user's PL/I program and his data; the final output will be considered a display of the results produced by processing the data according to the instructions in the program. The operations involved in producing this final output usually occur automatically, without the participation or cognizance of the user, although they include a number of steps in which information is transferred to and from the central processor.

This process is basically the same regardless of the physical medium used to prepare the program. Thus, the nature of the information being transferred, and the activities performed in response, have little to do with whether the programmer is using punched cards or lines typed on a terminal.

In order to initiate this processing, the user must supply some directions in addition to his or her actual program and data. (Part of this information, of course, specifies the fact that the program is being submitted on cards, through a terminal, etc.). The general nature of this *information* and the sequence in which it is usually submitted are shown schematically in Figure 1.1 (which assumes punched cards to be the mode of input), and can be outlined as follows:

1. The input package must be introduced by a set of instructions to the operating system. These instructions serve to identify the job, the user, and the type of operation being requested. In our case, the specifications indicate to the system that we are submitting a PL/I program to be transformed into an executable set of machine language instructions. This tells the system that the PL/I compiler is required, and the system will go about the business of making PL/I available and ready for use. The system can use these signals to prepare additional internal instructions that will check on the success of the compilation. If the compilation proves successful, that is, if there are no errors detected in the PL/I instructions, preparations can be made for the actual processing of the data.

2. These system instructions are followed by the set of PL/I statements that are read in and listed as part of the output. This is called the *source program*. On encountering the signal that indicates the conclusion of the user's program, the system triggers the compiler to begin the process of producing a machine language program called the *object program*. The resulting set of instructions is stored temporarily on some convenient device for subsequent use. If the compilation was successful, the user is notified by a message to that effect. If not, a record of the types of errors encountered and their locations in the

user's program are displayed so that he can examine the listing of this program and make the appropriate corrections.

3. The PL/I instructions are followed by additional commands to the system indicating that the machine language program produced by the compiler is to be brought into memory and readied for use on the data. These directions cause the system to check the status of the program. If compilation was successful, processing will go ahead by assignment of specific locations to these machine language instructions (object program), and they will be placed in those locations. If procedural errors in the source program were sufficiently serious to prevent compilation, the commands to continue processing would be ignored and the job terminated.

4. The group of system instructions described above is followed by a specific instruction indicating that the information following in the input package represents data for the program. At this point, the system turns control of the processor over to the object

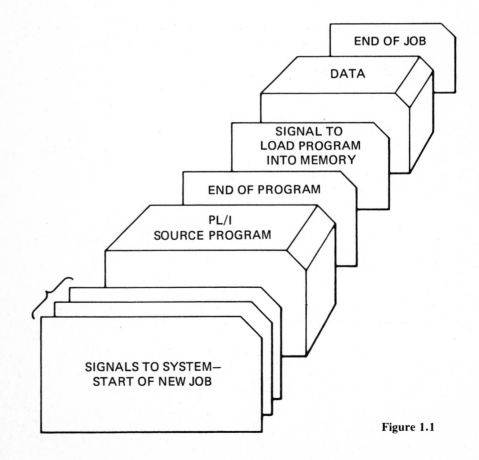

Figure 1.1

program, which then proceeds to process those data. If the data are in the form expected by the program, processing proceeds routinely; otherwise, the user is notified of an error condition and control is turned back to the system, causing the remaining cards to be read in without any subsequent processing until a card is spotted signalling the beginning of the next job. Of course, if the incoming information is being prepared, a line at a time, on a terminal, there is no need for the system to look for (and bypass) additional information; it simply curtails that job and asks for the next one.

5. The last data item is followed by a signal to the system indicating that there are no more items pertaining to this job. Once the program has finished processing, and whatever output called for by the actual program has been produced, the system generates additional output informing the user that the job is finished (as far as it is concerned), and it goes on to begin the next job.

Once a PL/I program has been successfully compiled and tested to the point where the user is convinced that the program is operating properly, there is no need to resubmit the original source deck for compilation each time a run is to be made. Instead, one of two things may be done. If the program is to be used only occasionally, the user may include as part of the instructions to the system (Step 1 above) a request that the object program be produced in permanent form—say, on punched cards. After this is done, these cards can be submitted for subsequent runs, in lieu of the PL/I program, with appropriate instructions to the system, thereby saving the time required to compile the program, store it, and bring it back into the processor for execution. Should the program be intended for constant use, it may be made part of the permanent system library. It is then added to other library programs and executive routines so that it is no longer necessary to submit the program as part of the user's package. Instead, these can be replaced by a reference to the program that has been given a unique name. Upon encountering this reference, the system will consult its catalog of programs, find the proper one, and bring it into storage.

PROBLEMS

Assume that each variable consists of a single letter.

1. Express in ordinary form the values of the following numbers:

a.	3.2E0	f.	$-.083E+2$
b.	7E+02	g.	1E4
c.	.7E+3	h.	$-2.7244E00$
d.	174E−4	i.	0E+03
e.	6.2743E−03	j.	0.000359E−2

2. Express the following numbers in floating-point form using one digit to the left of the decimal point and five to the right: (Example: $372 = 3.72000E+2$)

a. 42

b. -17.76

c. 3960

d. 249000

e. -0.00000000063

f. 0.0167458

g. 3.14159

h. 314.1590

i. 602568000

j. $-13\frac{1}{2}$

3. Express in conventional form the results of the following calculations:

a. $3.62E0+414.1E+0$

b. $17E1+.2E3$

c. $-3.25E-1+161E-1$

d. $3240E-3-.002E+4$

e. $8.5E-3+391520E-3$

f. $2E1*1.4E-3$

g. $-3E-1*477E-4$

h. $150E-2/6E-3$

i. $2.20E0+33E-1+4E5$

j. $99E-3-1.4E2/7E-1$

4. Express the results of the following calculations in floating-point form using the specifications given for Problem 2:

a. $41E-1*200E+01-1.5E2$

b. $62.4E-3*100E-2/40E-1$

c. $33.3E-2/4E-3+1.623E+01$

d. $.007E2*.0002E7/.00004E3$

e. $325000E-5+3.25E03-32.5E-5$

f. $70000E-04+.00000007E6+77000E-3/.11E3$

5. Write the following expressions in acceptable PL/I form:

a. $3X + 2Y$

b. $3X - 2XY$

c. $4.2X^2 + 2.4Y^2$

d. $137X^2Y^3 - \dfrac{.029X^{1.5}}{2.7Y^{2.7}}$

e. $\dfrac{58.2X^{5.82}}{17Y} + \dfrac{3X^2Y^{.5}}{2XY^2Z}$

f. $3(X+2Y)^{3.2}$

g. $\dfrac{X^2Y}{7X+Y}$

h. $\dfrac{2Y^2X}{7X^2+3} - \dfrac{(41.7)^2}{3(X+Y^2Z)}$

i. $2(X+Y)(X^2-2Y-Z)^2$

j. $\dfrac{3ZY^8 - 2X^{2.1}}{14Z^2 + \left(\dfrac{2X}{Y+1}\right)^{7.7}}$

6. Evaluate Z in the following statements. Express your results in conventional form.

   a.   Z = 2*X**2+3**Y;
        X = 15, Y = 4

   b.   Z = X+4*Y**3/3*Y+7*X;
        X = 3.4, Y = 6

   c.   Z = 3*X*Y/2*X**2+3*X*Y;
        X = 2, Y = 5

   d.   Z = 3*X*Y/(2*X**2+3*X*Y);
        X = 2, Y = 5

   e.   Z = X**3+3+X/4*Y**2*X−3/6*X*Y;
        X = 2, Y = 3

   f.   Z =2*((X+Y)*(X−3*Y))**3)*(3*Y)/2;
        X = 3, Y = 4

7. Write a program to read in a set of four values (A, B, C, and D) and print out values of their sum (call it E), their product (call it F), and the difference between the former and the latter (call it G).

8. Modify the program in Problem 7 to repeat the process 27 times.

9. Write PL/I statements for each of the following computations:

   (a) Calculate the sum (call it N20) of the first 20 integers and print the result.

   (b) Calculate 7! (call it N7FACT) and print the result.

   (c) Read eleven sets of three numbers X1, X2, and X3. For each set, calculate Y, obtained from the formula

$$Y = \frac{X1\,(X2\text{-}X3)}{X1+X2}$$

   print X1, X2, X3 and Y for each set. After all eleven sets have been processed, print SUMY, the sum of all the Y values.

   (d) Input consists of a value called BREAK, followed by 14 values for X. After reading and printing BREAK, compute and print B1, the sum of all the X values less than BREAK, and B2, the sum of all the X values not less than BREAK.

   (e) Input consists of nine sets of three values V1, V2, and V3. In addition to printing each set as it is read, the program is to:

      (1) Compute and print SUMV12, the sum of the nine products V1 X V2.

      (1) Compute and print SUMV13, the sum of all the products V1 x V3 in which V1 is less than V.

      (3) Compute and print SUMV23, the sum of the products V2 x V3 in which V2 is equal to or greater than V1.

10. Write PL/1 statements for each of the following computations:

   (a) Read (and print) an integer value N and compute the sum of the squared values of the first N integers. Call that sum SUMSQR and print the result.

(b) Read in two integers N1 and N2. After these two values are printed, compute and print a value HSUM12, obtained by taking half of the sum of the integers from N1 through N2. (Note: to keep things simple, assume for this problem that both the input values are positive and that N1 always is less than N2. Later on, as our fluency grows, we shall no longer allow ourselves such simplifications).

(c) Input consists of a single value for a variable Y followed by a succession of values for a second variable X. After reading and printing Y, compute a value SUMX consisting of the sum of incoming X values. This summation process is to continue as long as SUMX does not exceed Y. When the point is reached where this process can continue no longer (that is, the next value of X would place SUMX beyond Y), print SUMX, along with the last value of X used in the sum. Assume that there always will be enough values of X available to make this processing possible.

(d) Modify the procedure in Problem 10 (c) by printing an additional value NUMX, an integer representing the number of X values used to prepare SUMX. Input consists of an arbitrary succession of positive integer values for a variable K. (K can never be 0 or less). Compute and print:

   (1)   SUMK, the sum of all the input values.

   (2)   NUMBIG, the number of times a particular value of K is larger than the previous value.

   (3)   NUMSML, the number of times a particular value of K is less than or equal to the previous value.

Define any additional variables you need for this procedure.

11.   Read in some integer B and calculate the sum of the first B even numbers (call it TOTAL) and print it.

12.   Read in a list of 21 numbers (call them A1, A2, and so on) and square every other one. Print the squared values and their sum (call it TOTAL).

13.   Write a program that reads an integer X and produces the following output: Starting with a variable D set at 1, it uses D as the diameter of a circle and prints the diameter, circumference, area, and the volume of a cylinder with a height equal to its diameter. The program repeats for D of 2,3,4, and so on, through a diameter of X.

14.   If we characterize an arithmetic series by its first term F, the constant difference between terms D, and the number of terms T, then the value of its last term V is given by

$$V = F + D(T - 1)$$

and the sum of the first T terms (call it S) can be found by

$$S = \frac{T}{2} (F + V)$$

Write a program that reads values of F, D, and T, and prints F, D, T, V, and S. The program produces this output for each of a succession of input values until it finds a D value of zero.

15. If a certain amount of principal P is invested at an interest rate R compounded C times a year, the total amount T after Y years will be

$$T = P \left(1 + \frac{R}{C}\right) YC$$

Write a program that reads a single set of values for P,R,C and Y. Using these values, it prints P,R and C, followed by a table in which T is given for YRS = 1,2,3, and so on, through Y.

16. Generalize the program in Problem 15 so that it will produce tables for a succession of input values. Each new table is to start on a new page. (*Note:* The PL/I statement **PUT PAGE;** causes the paper in the line printer to be advanced to the next page.) Use a P value of zero to indicate the end of the run.

17. Produce a table showing values of X, X^2, X^3, and $\sqrt{X}$ for X values of 1, 2, 3, ..., 40.

18. Write a program that reads an integer TOP and produces a table showing values of X, X^2, X^3 and $\sqrt{X}$ for X values of 1, 2, 3, ..., TOP.

19. Write a program that reads an integer TOP and a fraction F and produces a table showing values of X, X^{**F}, X^{**F+1} and X^{**2F} for X values of 1, 2, 3, ..., TOP.

20. Write a program that reads two integers TOP and R and produces a table showing values of X, TOP $-$ X, X(TOP $-$ X) and $R\sqrt{X}$ for X values of 1, 1.5, 2, 2.5, ..., TOP.

21. Produce a table of squares and cubes of the first 50 numbers divisible by 7 and print them out in rows of three.

22. Write a program to solve for the unknowns of sets of three simultaneous equations with up to three unknowns each (that is, some equations in the set may have only one or two unknowns). Print each result on a new line and set up a counter that will keep track of the number of equations solved.

23. A firm pays its salesmen 4 percent commission on all items selling for less than $100 and 3 percent on all items selling for more. If the salesman is related to the boss or the boss's wife, he gets 6 percent commission on all items. Such salesmen are recognizable by their employee numbers, all of which are multiples of 23. No employee number is larger than 5000. Each employee has a monthly summary card containing the following information in the order given: employee number, total sales on items that sell for less than $100, and total sales on items that sell for more than $100. Write a program that will print the number of employees related to the boss or his wife and the extra cost to the firm incurred by rampant nepotism.

24. A number (called ANUMBER) is to be read into the machine. If the number is even, the program reads the next number; if it is odd, the number is squared and printed out. No input number will exceed 470 or go below zero.

25. A series of the age (in whole years) and identification number of each subject in an experiment is read into the machine in that order. A program is to be written that should print the identification number of each subject over ten years of age. It also should keep track of all subjects under ten and over ten and print out these counts after all subjects have been run through the machine.

SUMMARY OF IMPORTANT TERMS

Address
: A (numerical) designator permanently assigned to a physical storage location that distinguishes it from all other elements of storage in the processor.

Algorithm
: A finite set of procedural rules, stated in a given sequence, which describes some type of process or problem solution.

Assignment statement
: A statement of the form *variable = expression*; whose execution causes the indicated expression to be evaluated and its result placed in the location associated with the designated variable.

Comment
: Remarks and other information interspersed in (but not an intrinsic part of) a source program. Comments in PL/I are denoted by the form /*...*comment...*/*.

Compiler
: A set of processing procedures that analyze a high-level language source program and produce an operationally equivalent object program in a machine-oriented language.

Construct
: A basic component used in building a structured program (such as **IF-THEN-ELSE**). Conversely, a program is structured if it is composed entirely of constructs.

DECLARE statement

The primary vehicle for providing PL/I with information defining a variable and describing its attributes.

Default

A set of attributes for prescribed actions built into a system and automatically assumed or followed in the absence of explicit specifications pertaining to those attributes or actions. For example, PL/I uses a default input source when one is specified in a particular **GET** statement.

DO Loop

A construct in which some processing activity is repeated a controlled number of times, the number of repetitions being regulated by a mechanism specified in a **DO** statement.

DO-WHILE

A construct that specifies a loop in which some processing activity is preceded by a test whose outcome determines whether that activity will be performed another time. (Since the test is performed prior to the activity, it is possible to enter and leave a **DO-WHILE** construct without performing the activity at all).

Dummy data

Values that are chosen to be patently and intentionally spurious so that they can be used as special indicators; for example, to signal the end of data.

END statement

The statement used to indicate the conclusion of a major structural component in a PL/I program. Components so ended include procedures, **DO** groups, and **BEGIN** blocks.

Floating point

A form for representing numerical values in which a particular magnitude is expressed as a fraction times an implied base raise to a particular power. For example, in PL/I, the magnitude 2431.6 can be expressed as 0.24316×10^4, in which case the floating-point designation would be $0.24316E+04$.

Flowchart

A schematic diagram that provides a graphical representation of the sequence of events and the flow of logic in a particular procedure.

GET DATA

A type of input statement in which the data items to be transmitted to the processor are expected to be in the form $name = value, name = value, \ldots;$.

GO TO statement

A statement type that explicitly directs the flow of processing to some designated (labeled) statement at some arbitrary point in the procedure.

High Level Language

A programming language whose statements can specify activities that are arbitrarily more complex than those performed by a single machine instruction.

IF statement

A primary vehicle for constructing and specifying explicit tests and comparisons that form the basis for subsequent action. For example, in the statement **IF** $X=3*B$ **THEN** $Z=Y+X$; Z will not be computed unless the outcome of the indicated test is successful.

IF-THEN-ELSE

A construct which describes a true-false test, along with the two mutually exclusive activities stemming from the outcome of the test.

Infinite loop	A repetitive sequence of statements in which the faulty operation (or absence) of a logical control mechanism forces the procedure to cycle through that sequence indefinitely.
Keyword	A term or phrase (such as **DECLARE** or **GO TO** in PL/I) that is a permanent member of a programming language's vocabulary.
Label	A name that may be optionally attached to a PL/I statement so that it can be referred to in some other part of a procedure. Thus, the statement HERE: $X=B+Y$; is identified by the label HERE, thereby providing a reference point for some other statement such as **GO TO** HERE;.
Loop	A sequence of statements constructed with the intent of executing them repeatedly, under the control of a suitable logical mechanism that regulates the number of cycles in accordance with the dictates of the particular situation.
Machine language	A collection of instruction types recognized by the circuitry of a particular processor.
Object program	A set of machine-oriented instructions produced by a compiler from a source program written in a higher-level language.
Operating system	An extensive network of procedures, designed for and implemented on a particular type of processing system, that supervise, monitor, schedule and control all activities on that processing system.
PAGE	An output option, which can be specified as part of a **PUT** statement. Its presence forces the program to start a new page before printing.
Procedure	The major structural component of a PL/I program. In this context the smallest possible PL/I program consists of a single procedure.
PROCEDURE statement	The type of statement that signals the beginning of any PL/I procedure.
PUT DATA statement	A convenient statement type for producing labeled output. The basic form **PUT DATA** (V1,V1,...etc.); produces the output v1=value v2=value ... ;.
SKIP	An option in the **PUT** statement (for example, **PUT SKIP DATA** (list);) that forces the program to start a new line before printing any output.
Source program	A sequence of statements written in a high-level language such that they cannot be executed directly by a processor. Instead, they must be converted by a compiler or other language processing program to an equivalent executable object program.
Stream input/output	A method of data transmission to and from a processor in which the input or output is treated as a continuous stream of characters punctuated by directions in the program.

Structured Program	Representation of an algorithm in a particular programming language such that its entire extent consists only of recognized constructs. Unconditional sequences, **DO-WHILE**, and **IF-THEN-ELSE** are considered to be the simplest set of constructs needed to synthesize a structured program.
SYSIN	In IBM implementations of PL/I, **SYSIN** is the default input source.
SYSPRINT	In IBM implementations of PL/I, **SYSPRINT** is the default output destination.
Variable	A designated storage location whose contents are expected to vary from time to time during the execution of a program.

SUPPLEMENTARY READING

General

Baer, R., *The Digital Villain*. Reading, Mass.: Addison-Wesley, 1972.

Rothman, S., and Mosmann, C., *Computers and Society*. Chicago: Science Research, 1972.

Sterling, T. D., and Pollack, S. V., *Computing and Computer Science: A First Course with PL/I*. New York: Macmillan, 1970.

PL/I Subsets

Conway, R., and others, *PL/C, the Cornell Compiler for PL/I*. Ithaca: Cornell University Press, 1971.

Pollack, S. V., and Sterling, T. D. *Essentials of PL/I*. New York: Holt, Rinehart and Winston, 1973.

PL/I Subset Language Specifications, IBM Form No. c28-6809. White Plains, N.Y.: IBM Corporation.

II PROGRAM DEVELOPMENT AND IMPLEMENTATION

In examining the programs in the previous chapter, we concentrated on the basic form and properties of individual statements, seeking to gain some insight into their general behavior. To facilitate the development of this background, we operated under two assumptions:

1. Once a method of solution (that is, an algorithm) has been established for a given problem, its implementation as a program is well defined.

2. Once a particular procedure is seen to solve a certain set of problems, it will continue to do so.

Although these assumptions may appear reasonable for some very trivial problems, their applicability degrades rather quickly. In fact, much of the effort associated with the program development process often concerns itself with identifying and accommodating the complications surrounding an apparently "straightforward" algorithm. Moreover, every computer installation can relate numerous episodes in which unforeseen circumstances have thwarted processing by a program that had been operating routinely for years, thereby demonstrating the futility of persistent belief in the second assumption.

Accordingly, it usually is not enough to implement an algorithm that provides the "correct" answers. An important aspect of program development deals with the recognition and anticipation of procedural circumstances that could cause a program to malfunction. When appropriate safeguards are introduced to avert such situations, they often represent more programming steps than the basic algorithm itself.

We shall examine some of the basic techniques used to support the process of algorithm development, along with some of the services that are made available to facilitate the identification and correction of programming errors.

II.1   PROGRAM DEVELOPMENT

Illustration 7

To provide a focus around which some of these developmental concepts may be examined, we shall consider a relatively ordinary problem: given a set of starting dates (month, day, and year) and elapsed times (expressed as years, months, and days), we should like to devise a procedure that computes the corresponding final dates (month, day, and year) for any number of cases. We shall simplify the requirements somewhat by ignoring the occurrence of leap years.

The definition of a suitable algorithm requires immediate recognition of the fact that we must perform three separate additions: days to days, months to months, and years to years. Accordingly, these operations will be specified as individual steps. Furthermore, since we want the computations to be performed over and over for any number of input cases, there will need to be some kind of **DO** loop in which each cycle represents the processing for a single case. Consequently, there must be some way of stopping this loop. To do this we shall take advantage of the fact that the numerical value of the starting month must be between 1 and 12; accordingly, we shall decide that a starting month of zero will signal the end of the run.

With these conditions in mind, we can begin defining the general flow of our algorithm. This process is aided greatly by the ability to depict such flow graphically. For this reason, it is a very good idea to express the algorithm's steps in terms of a *flow diagram* or *flowchart*. Various systems are used for this purpose, their common goal being to provide a convenient, easily legible "picture" of an algorithm in which each general type of activity is represented by a standardized symbol. We shall use two such systems here:

1.   The ANSI (American National Standards Institute) system. This method shows each step in a separate box (whose shape depends on the type of activity), with the boxes connected by arrows that show the sequence of events.

2.   The N-S system (named for Nassi and Schneiderman, its originators). This method, designed to emphasize a program's structure, depicts a program as a single enclosed box, with the sequence of events (implied rather than explicitly stated) proceeding from top to bottom. Each type of program construct has its own symbol, and that symbol appears within the overall enclosure.

The various symbols are defined and summarized in Appendix A. Meanwhile, we shall introduce the use of such diagrams and charts as a natural part of program development, defining symbols and boxes as we need them.

Illustration 7 is a good place to start. Without working through the design in any more detail, we know that we shall read a set of input data and test the starting month for zero to determine whether or not the run is completed. Once the decision is made to continue, the input values are printed (the practice of displaying the input "as received" is known as an *echo check*), following which the new date is computed and printed. The procedure then reads the next input and is directed to the test for zero, at which point the process repeats. This flow is represented in the diagrams of Figure 2.1(a) and 2.1(b).

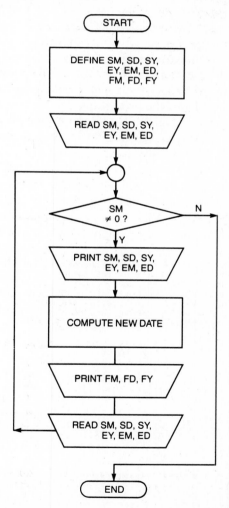

Figure 2.1a

Figure 2.1(a) gives us an opportunity to become acquainted with some of the ANSI flowcharting symbols. Note that the program begins and ends with oblong *terminators*, so that the chart's extent is very clear. A rectangular box, used for internal activities not involving decisions, defines the program's variables, followed by a trapezoid (input/output) showing the first input set being read. The **DO-WHILE** *construct* begins with a diamond-shaped box (which expresses a true-or-false decision) with two alternatives: one of them takes the program through the processing, which consists of the computation of new dates (a rectangular box), input of a new set (the trapezoid), and doubling back to the test at the beginning of the **DO** loop; the second alternative takes the program around the loop, thereby bringing it (in this case) to its conclusion.

In Figure 2.1(b) processing starts at the top of the N-S chart with a rectangular box (used for all activities except decisions) defining the variables and the next one reading the first input set. The **DO-WHILE** construct is shown in the next box, in which the inverted L-shaped symbol contains the test with which the construct begins. The activity inside the **DO-WHILE** box is repeated as long as the preceding test allows. When that is no longer the case (i.e., the starting month is zero in this example), the loop is bypassed and the program continues with the next box which, in this instance, concludes the processing.

Once we are satisfied with the general flow, we can expand our pictorial representation to include more details. Specifically, we can replace the "compute new date" specification with the three actual calculations. This is shown in the revised flowchart of Figure 2.1(c) (the N-S diagram would be changed correspondingly) and the procedure itself is shown below. The lines beginning and ending with /*............*/ are known as comment lines. These are not part of the PL/I program; rather, they are notes to the reader designed (by the programmer) to help clarify the PL/I statements. Note that the statements are a direct reflection of the flowchart. As a matter of fact, it turns out that, even for surprisingly complicated algorithms, a clear represen-

```
ILL7: PROCEDURE OPTIONS (MAIN);
     /***********************************************************/
     /* SM,SD AND SY ARE THE STARTING MONTH, DAY AND YEAR    */
     /* EY,EM AND ED ARE THE ELAPSED YEARS, MONTHS AND DAYS */
     /* FM,FD AND FY ARE THE FINAL MONTH, DAY AND YEAR       */
     /* THE BLANK LINES IN THIS LISTING ARE MADE BY PLACING */
     /* BLANK CARDS AT THE APPROPRIATE POINTS.               */
     /***********************************************************/

         DECLARE SM,SD,SY,EY,EM,ED,FM,FD,FY;
         GET DATA (SM,SD,SY,EY,EM,ED);

         DO WHILE (SM ¬ = 0);
           PUT SKIP DATA (SM,SD,SY);
           PUT SKIP DATA (EY,EM,ED);
           FY = SY+EY;
           FM = SM+EM;
           FD = SD+ED;
           PUT SKIP DATA (FM,FD,FY);
           PUT SKIP;
           GET DATA (SM,SD,SY,EY,EM,ED);
         END;

     /***********************************************************/
     /* NOTE THAT THE STATEMENT  PUT SKIP;   CAUSES THE      */
     /* PROGRAM TO SKIP A LINE IN THE OUTPUT. THIS WILL LEAVE*/
     /* A BLANK LINE BETWEEN SUCCESSIVE CASES.               */
     /***********************************************************/

         END ILL7;
```

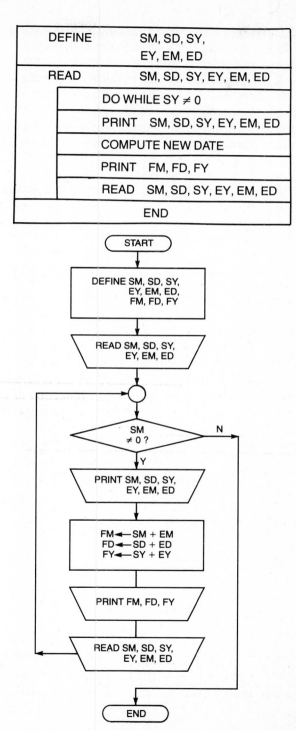

DEFINE	SM, SD, SY, EY, EM, ED

READ	SM, SD, SY, EY, EM, ED

DO WHILE SY ≠ 0

PRINT SM, SD, SY, EY, EM, ED

COMPUTE NEW DATE

PRINT FM, FD, FY

READ SM, SD, SY, EY, EM, ED

END

Figure 2.1b

START

DEFINE SM, SD, SY,
EY, EM, ED,
FM, FD, FY

READ SM, SD, SY,
EY, EM, ED

SM ≠ 0 ?   N

Y

PRINT SM, SD, SY,
EY, EM, ED

FM ← SM + EM
FD ← SD + ED
FY ← SY + EY

PRINT FM, FD, FY

READ SM, SD, SY,
EY, EM, ED

END

Figure 2.1c

tation of an algorithm's flow and structure often reduces the actual preparation of the program statements to a relatively straightforward, almost simplistic task.

Results for some sample cases (Figure 2.2) are as expected, but their appearance is awkward. Floating-point form and its supporting arithmetic are very useful for handling extensive computations, expecially those in which the expected magnitudes of the results are not easy to predict. However, the situation here requires only simple arithmetic, and the data are restricted to integers. Consequently, it is appropriate to use a form called *fixed point*, which is less powerful computationally but more convenient for display.

SM= 4.00000E+00	SD= 7.00000E+00	SY= 1.90900E+03;
EY= 1.20000E+01	EM= 7.00000E+00	ED= 1.20000E+01;
FM= 1.10000E+01	FD= 1.90000E+01	FY= 1.92100E+03;
SM= 8.00000E+00	SD= 2.10000E+01	SY= 1.87600E+03;
EY= 4.10000E+01	EM= 3.00000E+00	ED= 6.00000E+00;
FM= 1.10000E+01	FD= 2.70000E+01	FY= 1.91700E+03;
SM= 7.00000E+00	SD= 3.00000E+00	SY= 1.95700E+03;
EY= 2.40000E+01	EM= 0.00000E+00	ED= 2.50000E+01;
FM= 7.00000E+00	FD= 2.80000E+01	FY= 1.98100E+03;

Figure 2.2

Illustration 7A

We shall change to fixed point form by renaming the variables in Illustration 7, thereby taking advantage of another default feature: *PL/I variable names beginning with I, J, K, L, M, or N automatically are treated as fixed-point integers unless otherwise specified.* Accordingly, the statements now will appear as shown below (sample output is given in Figure 2.3):

NM1=	4	ND1=	7	NY1=	1909;
NY=	12	NM=	7	ND=	12;
NM2=	11	ND2=	19	NY2=	1921;
NM1=	8	ND1=	21	NY1=	1876;
NY=	41	NM=	3	ND=	6;
NM2=	11	ND2=	27	NY2=	1917;
NM1=	7	ND1=	3	NY1=	1957;
NY=	24	NM=	0	ND=	25;
NM2=	7	ND2=	28	NY2=	1981;
NM1=	3	ND1=	27	NY1=	1958;
NY=	2	NM=	4	ND=	24;
NM2=	7	ND2=	51	NY2=	1960;

Figure 2.3

The convenience of fixed-point display is immediately seen. Apparent also is the fact that there is a serious flaw in the procedure, as evidenced by the last case in Figure 2.3. Although mathematically "correct" (4 + 28 indeed equals 32), we run afoul of the calendar, in which context the result is inconsistent. Obviously, the procedure will work only part of the time unless further processing is incorporated to detect and handle such incongruities.

```
ILL7A: PROCEDURE OPTIONS (MAIN);

/*********************************************************/
/* NOW, WE SHALL CHANGE OUR VARIABLE NAMES TO MAKE USE   */
/* OF PL/I'S AUTOMATIC FEATURE (CALLED A DEFAULT) IN     */
/* WHICH VARIABLES NAMES STARTING WITH I-N ARE TREATED   */
/* AUTOMATICALLY AS FIXED POINT INTEGERS. NM1,ND1 AND    */
/* NY1 ARE STARTING MONTH, DAY AND YEAR, NY, NM AND ND   */
/* ARE ELAPSED YEARS, MONTHS AND DAYS, AND NM2, ND2 AND  */
/* NY2 ARE THE FINAL MONTH, DAY AND YEAR.                */
/*********************************************************/

        DECLARE NM1,ND1,NY1,NM,ND,NY,NM2,ND2,NY2;
        GET DATA (NM1,ND1,NY1,NY,NM,ND);

        DO WHILE (NM1¬ = 0);
          PUT SKIP DATA (NM1,ND1,NY1);
          PUT SKIP DATA (NY,NM,ND);
          NM2 = NM1+NM;
          ND2 = ND1+ND;
          NY2 = NY1+NY;
          GET DATA (NM1,ND1,NY1,NY,NM,ND);
        END;

        END ILL7A;
```

Let us examine the nature of these additional requirements. The general difficulty stems from the fact that a legitimate starting date, when processed against an equally legitimate elapsed time, may produce an "impossible" day in an "impossible" month. For example, an elapsed time of 3 years, 5 months, and 17 days applied to a starting date of October 26, 1968 (10/26/68), would produce a final date of 15/43/71:

		M	D	Y
start:		10	26	1968
elapsed:	+	5	17	3
final:		15	43	1971

Since the years do not cycle, the use of simple addition is adequate for that part of it. Consequently, our adjustment process can start with the final month. Recognizing that the numbering cycle repeats beyond 12, we can test for a value that exceeds this limit and reduce the value of the final month by 12. Compensation is effected by adding one to the value of the final year. Thus, 15/43/71 is expressed as (15 -12)/43/(71 + 1), or 3/43/72:

	M	D	Y
Initial result:	15	43	1971
month adjustment:	− 12	+	1
adjusted result:	3	43	1972
day adjustment:	+1	−31	
final result:	4	12	1972

In more general terms, we can say that the procedure needs the following type of decision rule: if the final month turns out to exceed a value of 12, the procedure must subtract 12 from the value and add 1 to the value of the final year.

Adjustment of the day number will not be so easy. By inspecting the partially corrected date developed above, we "know" that 3/43 can be corrected by subtracting 31 (since there are 31 days in March) and compensating for the subtraction by adding 1 to the month, so that our final date comes out 4/12/72. This final adjustment seems simple enough: if the day value exceeds the number of days in the month designated by N M2, subtract that number of days from N D2 and add 1 to N M2. However, in transferring that decision rule from its description in English to a proper sequence of PL/I statements, we must take into account the fact that the number of days in each month is not constant, nor do the differences vary from month to month in a nice orderly cycle. Consequently, we must implement this final decision rule as a series of tests, each of which takes care of one of the three possible lengths (28, 30 or 31 days).

Illustration 7B

In order to implement the adjustment described above, we shall exploit PL/I's ability to specify complex actions resulting from tests. Recall that the basic **IF-THEN-ELSE** construct (discussed in Section I.2.8) provides for the specification of two alternative actions, each one of arbitrary complexity. In order to preserve this structural concept, it should be possible to view each action as a single entity, regardless of the number of program statements required to express it.

PL/I enables the programmer to define such actions by writing "compound statements". The mechanism that makes it possible for the compiler to distinguish these actions from other sequences of statements is the **DO** *group*, indicated by bracketing each action with a simple **DO** statement at the beginning and an **END** statement at its conclusion. This reflects the **IF-THEN-ELSE** construct exactly as seen below:

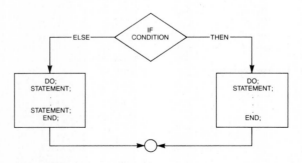

Using these facilities, we can modify our new date computations to include the additional tests:

1. Compute NM2 and N D2 by direct addition (NM1+NM and N D1+N D, respectively) and initialize adjustment factors (N MADJ and N DADJ) to zero.

2. IF NM2 exceeds 12, adjust N M2 downward, compensating by incrementing N Y2.

3. Check N D2 to see whether it needs further evaluation. (If it is less than 29, it does not, and processing can continue from Step 8).

4. Check for February. Recompute the adjustment factors (NMA DJ and N DA DJ) if it is, and continue with Step 8. If it is not, continue with Step 5.

5. Check whether N D2 exceeds 30. If it does not, continue with Step 8. If it does, set the day adjustment (N DA DJ) to 31, NMA DJ to 1, and continue with Step 6.

6. IF NM2 is not a 30-day month (i.e., 4, 6, 9 or 11), continue with Step 8. Otherwise, adjust N DA DJ to 30 and continue with Step 8.

7. If N D2 is exactly 31, and N M2 is a 31-day month, readjust N DA DJ and NMA DJ to zero and continue with Step 8. Otherwise, avoid the adjustment and continue with Step 8.

8. Use NMA DJ and N DA DJ for final adjustments to N D2 and N M2.

9. Print the output results (N M2, N D2 and N Y2) and read the next set of input values.

10. End of the date computation process.

Flowcharts for the revised program are given in Figure 2.4 and then corresponding statements are given below:

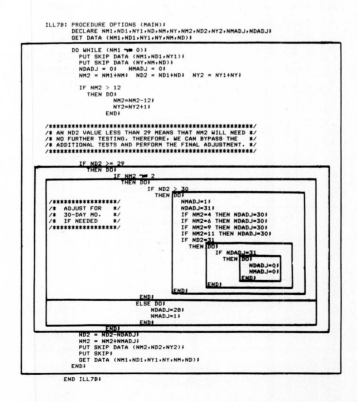

```
ILL7B: PROCEDURE OPTIONS (MAIN);
       DECLARE NM1,ND1,NY1,ND,NM,NY,NM2,ND2,NY2,NMADJ,NDADJ;
       GET DATA (NM1,ND1,NY1,NY,NM,ND);

       DO WHILE (NM1 ¬= 0);
       PUT SKIP DATA (NM1,ND1,NY1);
       PUT SKIP DATA (NY,NM,ND);
       NDADJ = 0;   NMADJ = 0;
       NM2 = NM1+NM;  ND2 = ND1+ND;  NY2 = NY1+NY;

       IF NM2 > 12
          THEN DO;
                  NM2=NM2-12;
                  NY2=NY2+1;
               END;

/************************************************************/
/* AN ND2 VALUE LESS THAN 29 MEANS THAT NM2 WILL NEED */
/* NO FURTHER TESTING. THEREFORE, WE CAN BYPASS THE */
/* ADDITIONAL TESTS AND PERFORM THE FINAL ADJUSTMENT. */
/************************************************************/

       IF ND2 >= 29
          THEN DO;
                  IF NM2 ¬= 2
                     THEN DO;
                            IF ND2 > 30
                               THEN DO;
                                      NMADJ=1;
/*****************/             NDADJ=31;
/* ADJUST FOR  */             IF NM2=4 THEN NDADJ=30;
/* 30-DAY MO.  */             IF NM2=6 THEN NDADJ=30;
/* IF NEEDED   */             IF NM2=9 THEN NDADJ=30;
/*****************/             IF NM2=11 THEN NDADJ=30;
                                      IF ND2=31
                                         THEN DO;
                                                IF NDADJ=31
                                                   THEN DO;
                                                          NDADJ=0;
                                                          NMADJ=0;
                                                        END;
                                              END;
                                    END;
                          END;
                     ELSE DO;
                            NDADJ=28;
                            NMADJ=1;
                          END;
                END;
       ND2 = ND2-NDADJ;
       NM2 = NM2+NMADJ;
       PUT SKIP DATA (NM2,ND2,NY2);
       PUT SKIP;
       GET DATA (NM1,ND1,NY1,NY,NM,ND);
       END;

    END ILL7B;
```

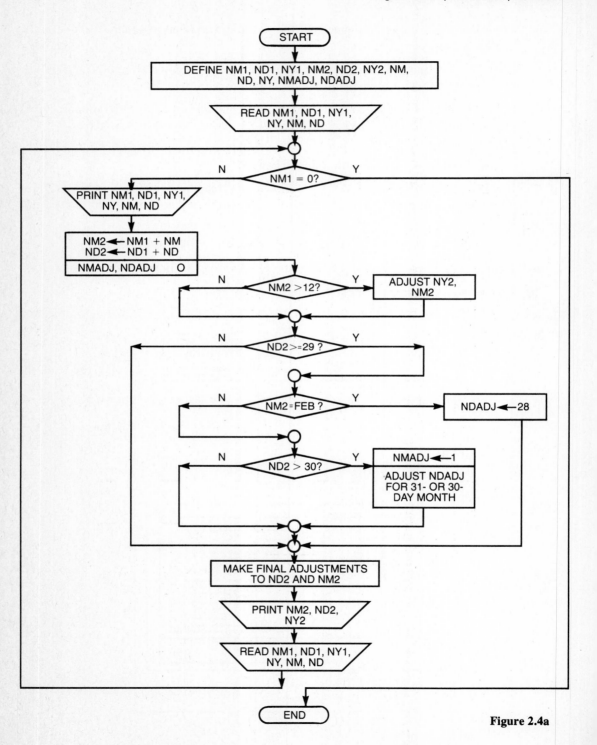

Figure 2.4a

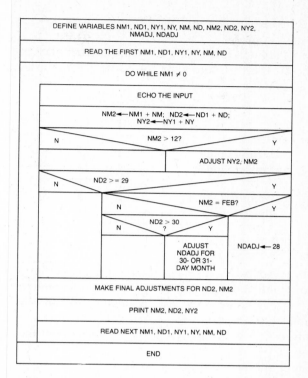

Figure 2.4b

As can be seen in Figure 2.5, the modified procedure now operates properly on the cases

NM1=	4	ND1=	7	NY1=	1909;
NY=	12	NM=	7	ND=	12;
NM2=	11	ND2=	19	NY2=	1921;
NM1=	3	ND1=	27	NY1=	1958;
NY=	2	NM=	4	ND=	24;
NM2=	8	ND2=	20	NY2=	1960;
NM1=	6	ND1=	24	NY1=	1967;
NY=	12	NM=	5	ND=	16;
NM2=	12	ND2=	10	NY2=	1979;

Figure 2.5

that had caused trouble previously. However, a proclamation that the procedure "works" still would be premature. Evidence to the contrary is provided by the two cases shown in Figure 2.6. In order to determine what type of remedial action has to be taken with regard to the

NM1=	8	ND1=	27	NY1=	1959;
NY=	4	NM=	4	ND=	18;
NM2=	13	ND2=	14	NY2=	1963;
NM1=	7	ND1=	31	NY1=	1947;
NY=	26	NM=	6	ND=	30;
NM2=	2	ND2=	30	NY2=	1974;

Figure 2.6

procedure, it will be useful to follow the course of processing for these examples so that we can discern what went wrong.

Consider the first set of input in Figure 2.6: when the number of elapsed months (4) is added to the starting month (8), the resulting value of 12 represents a legitimate month, so no adjustment is applied to NM2 or NY2.

	M	D	Y
starting value:	8	27	1959
elapsed value:	4	18	4
computed value:	12	45	1963
adjustment:	+ 1	− 31	
final value:	13	14	1963

Since the computed value of ND2 (45) does require adjustment, the procedure works its way through the various tests until it determines (by process of elimination) that NM2 is a 31-day month. Accordingly, ND2 is reduced by 31 to a value of 14 and NM2 is increased by 1 to compensate. This brings it to a value of 13, clearly requiring further adjustment. However, there is no mechanism to deal with this type of contingency and the results are printed as shown.

The second set of input in Figure 2.6 is processed with similar lack of success. In this case the initially computed value NM2 (13) was found to need adjustment and the necessary arithmetic ensued: NM2 was increased by 1 to 1974. Then, the computed ND2 value of 61 (31 + 30) is adjusted to 30, and NM2 is incremented correspondingly, to a "final" value of 2. Again, there is no provision for assessing the need to adjust further.

	M	D	Y
starting value:	7	31	1947
elapsed value:	6	30	26
computed value:	13	61	1973
month adjustment:	− 12		+ 1
adjusted value:	1	61	1974
day adjustment:	+ 1	− 31	
final value:	2	30	1974

Illustration 7C

These difficulties are handled in this version of the procedure by including an additional test for NM2 after ND2's initial adjustment. This is implemented merely by introducing an additional iteration around the processing (steps 5-8 in Illustration 7B) that adjusts N Y2, N M2 and N D2. If further adjustment is required, the appropriate action will be taken the second time around; if not, the processing will be bypassed, and the final "adjustment" (with zeros) will have no effect. This change is seen in the revised listing shown below and output is repeated in Figure 2.7.

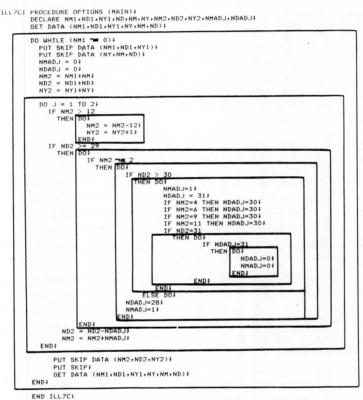

```
ILL7C: PROCEDURE OPTIONS (MAIN);
       DECLARE NM1,ND1,NY1,ND,NM,NY,NM2,ND2,NY2,NMADJ,NDADJ;
       GET DATA (NM1,ND1,NY1,NY,NM,ND);
DO WHILE (NM1 ¬= 0);
   PUT SKIP DATA (NM1,ND1,NY1);
   PUT SKIP DATA (NY,NM,ND);
   NMADJ = 0;
   NDADJ = 0;
   NM2 = NM1+NM;
   ND2 = ND1+ND;
   NY2 = NY1+NY;
   DO J = 1 TO 2;
      IF NM2 > 12
         THEN DO;
              NM2 = NM2-12;
              NY2 = NY2+1;
              END;
      IF ND2 >= 29
         THEN DO;
              IF NM2 ¬= 2
                 THEN DO;
                      IF ND2 > 30
                         THEN DO;
                              NMADJ=1;
                              NDADJ = 31;
                              IF NM2=4 THEN NDADJ=30;
                              IF NM2=6 THEN NDADJ=30;
                              IF NM2=9 THEN NDADJ=30;
                              IF NM2=11 THEN NDADJ=30;
                              IF ND2=31
                                 THEN DO;
                                      IF NDADJ=31
                                         THEN DO;
                                              NDADJ=0;
                                              NMADJ=0;
                                              END;
                                      END;
                              END;
                      ELSE DO;
                           NDADJ=28;
                           NMADJ=1;
                           END;
                      END;
              END;
      ND2 = ND2-NDADJ;
      NM2 = NM2+NMADJ;
   END;
   PUT SKIP DATA (NM2,ND2,NY2);
   PUT SKIP;
   GET DATA (NM1,ND1,NY1,NY,NM,ND);
END;
END ILL7C;
```

By now it is clear that the implementation of an effective procedure often depends on a thorough analysis of the circumstances that might prevail during the operation of that procedure. Even after such careful consideration, it is imprudent to release a program for routine use without an accompanying set of detailed qualifications. The procedure we have been modifying throughout this chapter exemplifies this necessity: hidden beneath our concern for uneven cycles and impossible dates is the persistent assumption that the elapsed time (in years, months, and days) always will be submitted to the program in reduced form. That is, NM is expected to be less than 12. (For instance, an elapsed time expressed as 17 months, 21 days would be "incorrect" in that form; as a matter of fact, these input values might produce erroneous results when submitted to any version of the program discussed. The "proper" input values for this time period must be 1 year, 5 months, 26 days). Accordingly, the program must be accompanied by operating instructions that specifically restrict the input to that form consistent with the procedural design.

NM1=	4	NC1=	7	NY1=	1909;
NY=	12	NM=	7	ND=	12;
NM2=	11	ND2=	19	NY2=	1921;
NM1=	3	ND1=	27	NY1=	1958;
NY=	2	NM=	4	ND=	24;
NM2=	8	ND2=	20	NY2=	1960;
NM1=	6	ND1=	24	NY1=	1967;
NY=	12	NM=	5	ND=	16;
NM2=	12	ND2=	1C	NY2=	1979;
NM1=	8	ND1=	27	NY1=	1959;
NY=	4	NM=	4	ND=	18;
NM2=	1	ND2=	14	NY2=	1964;
NM1=	7	ND1=	31	NY1=	1947;
NY=	26	NM=	6	ND=	30;
NM2=	3	ND2=	2	NY2=	1974;

Figure 2.7

II.2   AIDS IN PROGRAM DEVELOPMENT

Conversion of a suitable algorithm into an effective program is beset by further difficulties. A major set of obstacles stems from failure to comply with some part of the interlocking network of syntactic rules governing the action of the compiler. Depending on its type and context, such a violation may precipitate a variety of effects, ranging from the compiler's interception and automatic correction of the fault to its complete bafflement and paralysis. Because of PL/I's unprecedented default mechanisms, its range of responses to syntactic violations includes extensive attempts to apply remedial actions in preference to a forced halt in its compilation. Expectedly, this approach often produces results that are at odds with the programmer's intent. However, it should be borne in mind that these actions are taken not to make the statement "correct," but rather to override these recognizable errors. Thus, instead of requiring a separate run to find each error (by having the run stop at the point of detection), it is possible to identify a number of them during a single compilation. In support of this general facility, the mechanisms for interception and consequent default action are complemented by an extensive array of messages that provide the programmer with information regarding the location of the error, its possible cause, and the nature of the "remedy" applied. Thus, even if the "correction" was not suitable in the programmer's context, it is accompanied by sufficient information to allow the programmer to implement appropriate corrections.

The number and variety of these diagnostic services that PL/I provides is far too great for us to consider in detail. Moreover, their nature and content vary with the particular version of the compiler at a given facility. Consequently, we shall restrict our examination to an overview of these capabilities so that there is a basis for further study. References to sources giving complete descriptions of such facilities are included at the end of the chapter.

II.2.1   The Source Listing

As part of the compilation process, PL/I produces a source program listing that appears to be little more than a literal reproduction of the stream of characters submitted by the programmer. Actually, a considerable amount of analysis has already been performed by the time this list is printed. The listing of the example program in Figure 2.9 shows the results of some of this work. (The original punched cards are shown for reference in Figure 2.8). Along the left side of the listing, PL/I adds a column of numbers that refer to program statements. These correspond to entries in an internal table where PL/I keeps track of the machine instructions generated from the source language. (The additional columns will be of interest later). Every statement receives such a numerical designation, whether it has a label or not, and this number is referred

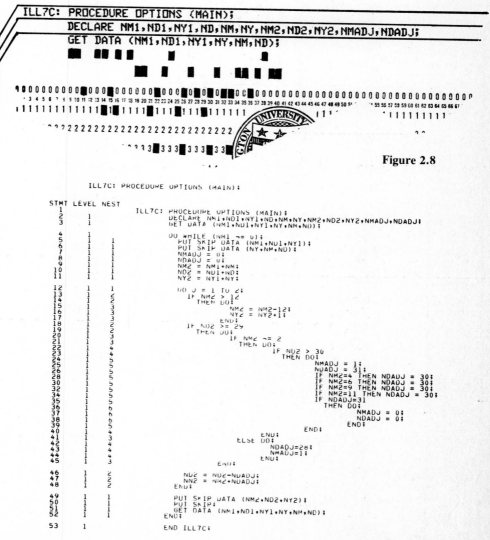

Figure 2.8

```
                    ILL7C: PROCEDURE OPTIONS (MAIN);

STMT LEVEL NEST
   1                        ILL7C: PROCEDURE OPTIONS (MAIN);
   2        1                      DECLARE NM1,ND1,NY1,ND,NM,NY,NM2,ND2,NY2,NMADJ,NDADJ;
   3        1                      GET DATA (NM1,ND1,NY1,NY,NM,ND);

   4        1                      DO WHILE (NM1 ¬= 0);
   5        1    1                    PUT SKIP DATA (NM1,ND1,NY1);
   6        1    1                    PUT SKIP DATA (NY,NM,ND);
   7        1    1                    NMADJ = 0;
   8        1    1                    NDADJ = 0;
   9        1    1                    NM2 = NM1+NM;
  10        1    1                    ND2 = ND1+ND;
  11        1    1                    NY2 = NY1+NY;

  12        1    1                    DO J = 1 TO 2;
  13        1    2                      IF NM2 > 12
  14        1    3                        THEN DO;
  15        1    3                           NM2 = NM2-12;
  16        1    3                           NY2 = NY2+1;
  17        1    3                        END;
  18        1    2                      IF ND2 >= 29
  19        1    3                        THEN DO;
  20        1    3                           IF NM2 ¬= 2
  21        1    4                             THEN DO;
  22        1    4                               IF ND2 > 30
  23        1    4                                 THEN DO;
  24        1    5                                    NMADJ = 1;
  25        1    5                                    NDADJ = 31;
  28        1    5                                    IF NM2=4 THEN NDADJ = 30;
  30        1    5                                    IF NM2=6 THEN NDADJ = 30;
  32        1    5                                    IF NM2=9 THEN NDADJ = 30;
  34        1    5                                    IF NM2=11 THEN NDADJ = 30;
  35        1    5                                    IF NDADJ=31
  36        1    6                                      THEN DO;
  37        1    6                                         NMADJ = 0;
  38        1    6                                         NDADJ = 0;
  39        1    5                                      END;
  40        1    4                                 END;
  41        1    3                             ELSE DO;
  42        1    4                                 NDADJ=28;
  43        1    4                                 NMADJ=1;
  44        1    4                             END;
  45        1    3                           END;

  46        1    2                      ND2 = ND2-NDADJ;
  47        1    2                      NN2 = NM2+NMADJ;
  48        1    2                    END;

  49        1    1                    PUT SKIP DATA (NM2,ND2,NY2);
  50        1    1                    PUT SKIP;
  51        1    1                    GET DATA (NM1,ND1,NY1,NY,NM,ND);
  52        1    1                  END;

  53        1              END ILL7C;
```

Figure 2.9

to in subsequently produced input, such as diagnostic messages. Note that each line of printout corresponds to a single punched card regardless of the number of statements that may appear on the card. However, the statement numbering is consistent with the physical appearance of the statements themselves, so that statement number 26 is followed in that column by statement number 28, indicating the presence of the additional statement on the first of the two consecutive lines. Note that the test portion of an **IF** statement and its associated action are treated as two statements (for example, statements 13-14).

II.2.2   The Cross-Reference Guide   *Fig 2.10*

As part of its analysis, the compiler also produces a summary of the occurrences of various names throughout the program. To illustrate its construction, this guide (termed a *cross-reference table*) is shown in Figure 2.10 for Illustration 7C. Each name (positioned in alphabetical order) is associated with source listing's statement number, (DCL NO.) in which it is defined. For example, ILL7C's usage is established in statement 1, since ILL7C is the label identifying the procedure. Similarly, NY2 is related to statement 2, where it is defined by declaration. The right-most column enumerates the attributes assigned to each name (either through explicit statements in the program or by default) and gives the statement numbers in which that name appears. Thus, the attachment of ND1 to a statement (number 2, as indicated by DCL NO.) establishes it as a FIXED BINARY integer; consultation of the referenced statements in the source listing (3, 5, 10 and 51) reveals them to be the ones in which ND1 is specified for use or change in a statement. The compiler is very meticulous about correct reporting of a name's occurrences. Note that NY2's cross-references include two citations for statement 16, since there are two appearances in the statement.

   SYSIN and **SYSPRINT** warrant special attention: since there is no explicit reference to either name in the program, there are no designations in the DCL NO. column. However the absence of such specifications in the input and output statements (3, 5, 6, 49-51) forced PL/I to include the default names, whereupon the newly defined associations were included in the table.

   The table's completeness makes it a useful aid in tracking down a variety of errors. For example, it would not be implausible to depress the wrong key while keypunching, so that statement 47 referred to NN2 instead of NM2 (Figure 2.11a). As a result, NN2 will show up in the cross-reference table (Figure 2.11b), together with the appropriate statement number. The attribute listing also provides valuable tutorial information about some of the compiler's default activities. (Unexplained attributes will be discussed later; their default values are satisfactory in most instances.)

II.2.3   Diagnostic Messages

Illustration 8

   Although we have not yet covered enough material to take advantage of the extensive

```
ILL7C: PROCEDURE OPTIONS (MAIN);

          ATTRIBUTE AND CROSS-REFERENCE TABLE

DCL NO.   IDENTIFIER        ATTRIBUTES AND REFERENCES

1  ******** ILL7C    ENTRY,BINARY,FIXED(15,0)

2  ******** J        AUTOMATIC,ALIGNED,BINARY,FIXED(15,0)
                     12

2  ******** ND       AUTOMATIC,ALIGNED,BINARY,FIXED(15,0)
                     3,6,10,51

2  ******** ND1      AUTOMATIC,ALIGNED,BINARY,FIXED(15,0)
                     3,5,10,51

2  ******** ND2      AUTOMATIC,ALIGNED,BINARY,FIXED(15,0)
                     10,18,22,46,46,49

2  ******** NDADJ    AUTOMATIC,ALIGNED,BINARY,FIXED(15,0)
                     8,25,27,29,31,33,34,37,42,46,47

2  ****** NM         AUTOMATIC,ALIGNED,BINARY,FIXED(15,0)
                     3,6,9,51

2  ****** NM1        AUTOMATIC,ALIGNED,BINARY,FIXED(15,0)
                     3,4,5,9,51

2  ****** NM2        AUTOMATIC,ALIGNED,BINARY,FIXED(15,0)
                     9,13,15,20,26,28,30,32,47,47,49

2  ******** NMADJ    AUTOMATIC,ALIGNED,BINARY,FIXED(15,0)
                     7,24,36,43

2  ****** NY         AUTOMATIC,ALIGNED,BINARY,FIXED(15,0)
                     3,6,11,51

2  ****** NY1        AUTOMATIC,ALIGNED,BINARY,FIXED(15,0)
                     3,5,11,51

2  ****** NY2        AUTOMATIC,ALIGNED,BINARY,FIXED(15,0)
                     11,16,16,49

   SYSIN             FILE,EXTERNAL
                     3,51

   SYSPRINT          FILE,EXTERNAL
                     5,6,49,50
```

Figure 2.10

diagnostic services the compiler makes available, it is important even at this stage to become acquainted with their basic form. To provide this introduction, we shall write a simple

```
46    1    2              ND2 = ND2-NDADJ;
47    1    2              NN2 = NM2+NDADJ;
48    1    2            END;

49    1    1            PUT SKIP DATA (NM2,ND2,NY2);
50    1    1            PUT SKIP;
51    1    1            GET DATA (NM1,ND1,NY1,NY,NM,ND);
52    1    1          END;

53    1            END ILL7C;
```

(a)

```
2    ********* NDADJ            AUTOMATIC,ALIGNED,BINARY,FIXED(15,0)
                                8,25,27,29,31,33,34,37,42,46,47

2    ********* NM               AUTOMATIC,ALIGNED,BINARY,FIXED(15,0)
                                3,6,9,51

2    ********* NM1              AUTOMATIC,ALIGNED,BINARY,FIXED(15,0)
                                3,4,5,9,51

2    ********* NM2              AUTOMATIC,ALIGNED,BINARY,FIXED(15,0)
                                9,13,15,15,20,26,28,30,32,47,49

2    ********* NMADJ            AUTOMATIC,ALIGNED,BINARY,FIXED(15,0)
                                7,24,36,43

     ********* NN2              AUTOMATIC,ALIGNED,BINARY,FIXED(15,0)
                                47
```

(b)

Figure 2.11

procedure that reads successive sets of values A and B and, for each set, computes a value D from the formula

$$D =(A + B) (A - B) + 2B$$

and prints that value, along with A and B. A counter (which we shall call N) keeps track of the number of sets processed, and prints that number at the end of the run. For purposes of this illustration, we shall define a restriction that the values for A and B in a given set will never be the same, thereby allowing us to use that as a criterion to define the end of the run.

In preparing this procedure, whose listing appears in Figure 2.12a, we have "forgotten" momentarily that multiplication cannot be implied, but must be explicitly indicated. Hence, statement 8, which reads

$$D = (A+B) (A-B)+2*B;$$

should have read

$$D = (A+B)*(A-B)+2*B;$$

```
STMT LEVEL NEST BLOCK MLVL   SOURCE TEXT

   1   1                1        ILLB: PROCEDURE OPTIONS (MAIN);
   2   1                         DECLARE A,B,D,N;
   3   1                1        N = 0;        GET DATA (A,B);

   5   1                1        DO WHILE (A ¬= B);
   6   1     1          1          N = N+1;
   7   1     1          1          D = (A+B) (A-B) + 2*B;
   ERROR IN STMT     7  INCOMPLETE EXPRESSION (SY10)
         FOR STMT     7  PL/C USES  D=(A+B)*(A-B)+2*B;
   8   1     1          1          IF A > B THEN PUT SKIP DATA (A,B,D); ELSE PUT SKIP DATA (B,A,D);
  11   1     1          1        END;
  12   1                1        PUT SKIP (2) DATA (N);
  13   1                1        END ILLB;
```

Figure 2.12a

A look at this figure, produced by the PL/C implementation of PL/I, indicates that the PL/C compiler has spotted an error and produced some diagnostic information as part of its output. In this particular instance it was able to do something about the error, and it reported what it did: it inserted an asterisk and used the resulting statement. As it turns out, this modification coincides with the original intent, so that this time the compiler can be said to have acted "reasonably." Another implementation, the IBM PL/I-F compiler, threw up its hands when confronted with the identical situation, choosing to delete the entire statement before continuing with the compilation. However, PL/I's reference to that statement in its diagnostic messages (Figure 2.12b), has pinpointed the problem, even though nothing "constructive" was done about it.

```
COMPILER DIAGNOSTICS.


SEVERE ERRORS.

   IEM0126I      7   IMPLEMENTATION RESTRICTION. STATEMENT NUMBER 7 HAS TOO MANY ERRORS TO BE INTERPRETED. THE

                     STATEMENT HAS BEEN DELETED.

   IEM0109I      7   TEXT BEGINNING '' IN OR FOLLOWING STATEMENT NUMBER 7 HAS BEEN DELETED.


ERRORS.

   IEM0096I      7   SEMI-COLON NOT FOUND WHEN EXPECTED IN STATEMENT NUMBER 7 .   ONE HAS BEEN INSERTED.


WARNINGS.

   IEM0227I          NO FILE/STRING OPTION SPECIFIED IN ONE OR MORE GET/PUT STATEMENTS. SYSIN/SYSPRINT HAS BEEN

                     ASSUMED IN EACH CASE.

   IEM0764I          ONE OR MORE FIXED BINARY ITEMS OF PRECISION 15 OR LESS HAVE BEEN GIVEN HALFWORD STORAGE. THEY

                     ARE FLAGGED '**********' IN THE XREF/ATR LIST.
```

Figure 2.12b

Illustration 8A

Sometimes when the error is sufficiently unambiguous that it can be analyzed directly, the compiler can be relied on to take helpful corrective action. Such an instance is seen in this version of illustration 8 in which the word **THEN** was ommitted from the **IF** statement (Figure

2.13a). The resulting diagnostic message, shown in Figure 2.13b, indicates that the compiler obligingly put the **THEN** in and went ahead.

```
IL8A: PROCEDURE OPTIONS (MAIN);
      DECLARE A,B,D,N;
      N = 0;       GET DATA (A,B);

      DO WHILE (A ¬= B);
         N = N+1;
         D = (A+B)*(A-B) + 2*B;
         IF A > B       PUT SKIP DATA (A,B,D);  ELSE PUT SKIP DATA (B,A,D);
      END;

      PUT SKIP (2) DATA (N);
      END IL8A;
```

(a)

```
COMPILER DIAGNOSTICS.


8    THEN INSERTED IN IF STATEMENT NUMBER 8
```

(b)

Figure 2.13

II.3 A SUMMARY OF SOURCE PROGRAM FORMAT RULES

In writing the PL/I programs examined thus far, we have used certain rules of construction, some of which were stated explicitly, whereas others were implied. For purposes of convenience, these are enumerated below, together with additional formatting information.

1. Column 1 of a punched card (or a line on a terminal) should not be used in a PL/I program. Permissible columns vary from one implementation to another but the most typical ranges are 2-80 and 2-72. PL/I statements may begin or end in any column within the permissible range.

2. Several statements may appear on the same line or card; however, it is a good practice to limit statements to one per line. (In special cases, groups of analogous statements may appear together in the same card/line without affecting simplicity or clarity).

3. Statements may be continued from one card/line to another, within the permissible range of columns.

4. Comments in PL/I source programs begin with /* and end with */. Anything at all (except, of course, */) may appear in a comment and comments may appear anywhere in a program.

5. While statements may begin and end anywhere within the permissible range (see (1) above), it is very helpful to emphasize a program's structure by indenting various components. The following formats have been found to be particularly useful:

    (a) **IF-THEN-ELSE:**

> **IF** test condition
>   **THEN**
>   action;
>   **ELSE**
>   action;

    (b) Loops:

> **DO** specification;
>   action;
> **END**;

In addition, insertion of a blank card/line between program components (such as loops or initializing sections) enhances clarity.

6. Names of variables must begin with one of the following 29 characters: A through Z,$,#, or @. Subsequent characters may include any of the ten digits 0 through 9 and the break character ____. Maximum allowable length is 31 characters. It is a good idea to invent names that carry some meaning with regard to the things they represent.

7. Statement labels are constructed in accordance with the same rules defined for variable names. Any statement may be labeled, with the exception of declarations; however, emphasis on structured program design will minimize the need for such labels. **PROCEDURE** statements must be labelled.

PROBLEMS

1. Select the illegal statement labels and indicate why they cannot be used:

a.	B*2*C	f.	AX+Y/2Z
b.	$23	g.	START HERE
c.	NET PAY	h.	#HRS.__OVER
d.	¢__LOST	i.	#HRS.__LESS__BREAK
e.	@PRICE__LESS	j.	2WX__P.8

2. Modify the procedure in Illustration 7c to take leap years into account.

3. Write a program that reads in sets of X, Y, and Z values and prints those values of Y for which X^2 is no more than eight less that the product of Y and Z. No value of Z will ever fall below -17.

4. Write a program that reads in pairs of A and B values and maintains running totals of the A's and B's read in at any time. Whenever the sum of A values exceeds twice that of the B values, both sums are to be printed, together with the number of values used to compute each sum, and new sums are to be calculated, starting with the next pair of values. No individual value of B will ever be larger than 4.5 times the values of the corresponding A.

5. The Consolidated Schmichik Company awards its top salesman of the year with a bonus and an expense-paid, 3-day holiday fiesta in New Diana, Texas. To determine who the lucky winner is, total sales figures are accumulated for each of the five men on consolidated's crack sales team. Each sales transaction is recorded on a separate punched card that contains the following information in the order given:

a. Salesmen's identification number (1, 2, 3, 4, or 5).

b. Month of sale (January is denoted by 1, February, 2, and so on).

c. Year of sale.

d. Type of schmichik sold (types are 10, 14, or 23).

e. Number of schmichiks sold.

f. Unit price, given as dollars per schmichik.

Write a program that prints the number of the winning salesman, together with his total sales.

6. Write a program that reads in sets of three values, D, E, and F, and assigns a sequence number to each set as it is read in. The program is to print the sequence number and the values for each set in which F is midway between E and D, at the end of the run, the program is to print the total number of sets for which this condition exists. D is never the smallest value in a given set.

7. A bank's program compares monthly loan payments against amounts owed. Input is submitted to the program in the following order:

LOAN (borrower's identification, expressed as a five-digit integer)

PR (the amount still owed)

DUE (the amount of the monthly installment)

PAID (the amount of this payment).

The program is to print a line of output for each transaction in accordance with the following rules:

a. If the amount still outstanding is the same as that covered by a monthly payment and the size of the current payment is equal to that amount, print only the identification number.

b. If the amount of the current payment is the same as the amount required for a monthly installment, credit the payment and print the identification and the new amount still outstanding.

c. If the amount paid is less than the total amount due, print the identification number, amount due, amount paid, the difference between the two amounts, and the new amount still outstanding.

d. If no payment is recorded for a particular account (that is, PAID is zero) print only the identification and the amount still owed.

Use an identification number of 0 to signal the end of the data.

e. Assuming this was an actual process, list the kinds of input errors you think would be likely to occur, and indicate what remedial steps you would incorporate in your procedure.

8. Write a program that reads sets of four values D, E, F and G. Print the input on a separate line. Then process the values such that they end up with the lowest one in D, next lowest in E, and so on. Print another line of output, showing the sorted values. Repeat for additional input sets, stopping only when both D and F are zero.

9. The arithmetic mean XM of a collection of N values of X is given by

$$XM = \frac{\Sigma X}{N}$$

and the standard deviation D can be computed as

$$D = \sqrt{\frac{\Sigma x^2 - (\Sigma x)^2}{N-1}}$$

Write a program that reads a value of N, followed by N values of X. The program is to print N, XM, and D.

10. Modify the program specified in the previous problem so that it computes XM and D without reading an input value for N. Instead, the program is to operate on the basis that X cannot be zero.

11. Write a program that reads a value N, followed by a value X, followed in turn by coefficients a_0, a_1, ... a_N of the Nth degree polynomial

$$Y = a_0 + a_1 X + a_2 X^2 + ... + a_N X^N$$

The program is to print N and each of the coefficients on a separate line, followed by a final line displaying X and Y.

12. Modify the program in the previous problem so that it computes and prints X and Y for each of a succession of X's. Use X = 0 to signal the end of the input.

13. Modify the program in Problem 12 so that it processes any number of X's for any number of polynomials. Use X = 0 to signal the last value for a particular polynomial and N = 0 to signal the end of a run.

14. Let S represent the sum of the series

$$\frac{1}{2^2} - \frac{1}{4^2} + \frac{1}{6^2} - \frac{1}{8^2} + \cdots$$

Write a program that reads a number N and prints a line showing N, followed by the first N terms of the series given above. Repeat this process for any number of input values of N. Use a value of 0 to stop the run.

15. Write sequences of statements to express each of the following decision processes.

(a)

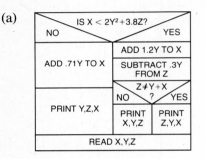

(b)

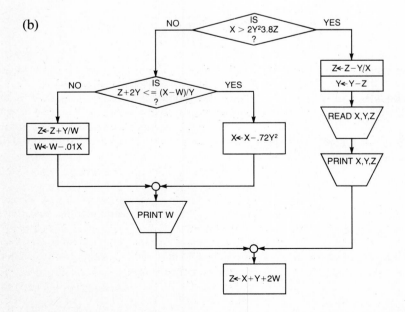

16. Explore the types of error messages generated by your PL/I compiler by submitting a source program with intentionally introduced errors. A number of suggestions follow:

    a. Misspell one or more of the keywords (for example, **PROCEDURE** or **DECLARE**).

    b. Keypunch an unlabeled statement starting in column 1.

    c. Include a blank in a variable name.

    d. Use the same label name for two different statements.

    e. Omit the **END** statement.

    f. Omit an arithmetic operator in an assignment statement.

    g. Run two keywords together (for example **GETDATA**).

    h. Use two consecutive arithmetic operators in an assignment statement.

    i. Punch a semicolon instead of a colon after a label.

    j. Open a comment and forget to close it.

SUMMARY OF IMPORTANT TERMS

Compound statement	A sequence of statements always executed together, as if the entire collection were a single statement.
Cross-reference table	A compiler-produced summary, listing the occurrences of all the names used in a program.
DO group	A sequence of statements enclosed by **DO** and **END** that can be used as a compound statement to describe a single conceptual activity. A **DO** group may appear only as an alternative activity after **THEN** and/or **ELSE** in an **IF-THEN-ELSE** construct.
Echo check	A practice, in program implementation, in which steps are included to print (or transmit to some other output device) a copy of the input data "as received." This information is then available for process check out and other types of verification.
Fixed point	A representational form in which numerical values are expressed as $\pm nnn...n.nn...n$. (The sign is optional for positive values.)

Naming conventions

In the absence of explicit specifications, PL/I variable names beginning with I-N are automatically assumed to represent fixed-point numbers. All others are assumed to represent floating-point numbers.

Relational operation

A specification that defines a rule for performing a comparison. The eight relational operators available in PL/I are $=$, $\neg =$, $<$, $<=$, $>$, $>=$, $\neg <$, and $\neg >$.

Source listing

A compiler-produced display (printout) showing the program as submitted, each line corresponding to a punched card. Sequential statement numbers (assigned by the compiler) are included, along with some organizational information about the program components.

SUPPLEMENTARY READING

Conway, R., and others, *PL/C, the Cornell Compiler for PL/I*. Ithaca: Cornell University Press, 1971. See, especially, pp. 40-57.

PL/I (F) Programmer's Guide, IBM document No. GC28-6594. White Plains, N.Y.: IBM Corporation.

III NUMERICAL DATA FORMS

In setting up our programs thus far, we have been able to use two different types of numbers by exploiting PL/I's default mechanisms relating to variable names. These facilities, while providing a certain measure of convenience, represent no more than the surface layer of an extensive array of features that allow the programmer to endow the numbers he uses with many different combinations of attributes. Some of these, when explicitly declared, will bring additional attributes along by default. Others require explicit definition in order to get at the more specialized properties.

III.1 BASIC TYPES OF NUMBERS

PL/I must be informed of the properties of the numbers it is to manipulate by explicit declaration; otherwise, it will assume them by default. These properties can be described in terms of four primary attributes: *base, scale, mode,* and *precision*. By assigning various combinations of these attributes, it is possible for the programmer to control the form in which the data are stored, manipulated, and displayed.

III.1.1 Base

The *base* attribute determines the number system that will be used to store a particular value. This may be either **DECIMAL**, in which case the number will be represented internally as a series of digits to the base 10, or it may be **BINARY**, causing it to be represented as a series of 1's and 0's, that is, a number to the base 2. We can illustrate the conceptual difference by selecting a decimal quantity, say 108, and writing it in the form

$$108 = 100 + 8 = 1 \times 10^2 + 0 \times 10^1 + 8 \times 10^0$$

Binary numbers must have exactly the same construction except that their expression as a sum involves only 1s and 0s, each multiplied by a different power of two, rather than ten. Since

$$2^0 = 1$$
$$2^1 = 2$$
$$2^2 = 4$$
$$2^3 = 8$$
$$2^4 = 16$$
$$2^5 = 32$$
$$2^6 = 64$$

We can express the magnitude 108 as a binary number by combining $64 + 32 + 8 + 4$, or

$$1 \times 2^6 + 1 \times 2^5 + 0 \times 2^4 + 1 \times 2^3 + 1 \times 2^2 + 0 \times 2^1 + 0 \times 2^0$$

or 1101100_2.

III.1.2 Scale

Numerical values may have a *scale* of either **FIXED** or **FLOAT**. We have already encountered both basic forms as delivered by PL/I's defaults. In addition to their obvious difference in appearance, there are important distinctions between fixed- and floating-point numbers with regard to the way they are represented in storage.

When a floating-point number is stored, its exponent and fractional portions are kept in separate subareas of the assigned storage location. With numbers having the **FIXED** attribute, an exponent is, of course, not used. Instead, the entire storage location is devoted to the actual value. Use of the floating-point form allows the programmer to store a wider range of magnitudes than is usually possible with fixed-point format. This can be illustrated as follows: suppose our storage was able to accommodate up to six decimal digits in a single location. In fixed-point format, all six digits would be available for the value, so that the largest number that could be represented in the location would be 999999 or

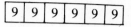

represented pictorially. By the same token, the number closest to zero that could be stored there would be .000001. (An actual decimal point is not stored; instead, PL/I sets up the bookkeeping required to keep track of the magnitude). Now let us suppose that when the circuits are directed to store numbers in floating-point form, one of the six digits is allocated for the exponent. Under these circumstances, the location can still contain a maximum of six nines, but their implied meaning can be pictured as

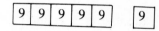

or $.99999 \times 10^9$ or 999,990,000. Similarly, the smallest number that could be accommodated (except for zero) would be $.00001 \times 10^{-9}$ or .00000000000001. This extended range is necessary in a very wide variety of applications, so that the use of floating-point form often is preferred in spite of the lower speed of floating-point operations when compared to fixed-point arithmetic.

III.1.3   Mode

Many engineering problems are handled by means of number concepts involving square roots of negative numbers. Since the existence of such quantities is inconsistent with conventional algebraic rules, such quantities are termed *imaginary numbers*. The unit of imaginary numbers is called i and is equal to $\sqrt{-1}$. All other imaginary numbers can then be expressed as multiples of i. For example,

$$\sqrt{-64} = \sqrt{64}\sqrt{-1} = 8\sqrt{-1} = 8i$$

To distinguish them from imaginary numbers, ordinary numbers are called *real* numbers. Furthermore, quantities containing both a real and imaginary component are called *complex numbers*.

To make such concepts and facilities available to the PL/I programmer, the language provides two alternative *modes* for numbers, namely, **REAL** or **COMPLEX**. Since the use of complex numbers is germane in a relatively limited number of contexts, the **COMPLEX** attribute is never assigned by default. Accordingly, this has not been of concern to us thus far, and we shall continue to omit explicit references to the mode except when dealing specifically with complex numbers.

These three basic attributes are summarized in Table 3.1.

TABLE 3.1 Descriptive Attributes of
Numbers Recognized by PL/I

Attributes	Alternatives
Base	**DECIMAL** or **BINARY**
Scale	**FIXED** or **FLOAT**
Mode	**REAL** or **COMPLEX**

III.1.4   Precision

This attribute concerns itself with the internal size and arrangement of numbers. When we perform arithmetic operations manually, we use a visual decimal point to make sure that proper magnitudes are maintained. Furthermore, we keep track of the number of digits used to represent each value so that the final results will be consistent with the values used to obtain them. For the same reason, the program must set up and maintain a set of indicators that provide similar information about each numerical value being stored. Since the actual decimal point is not carried along with the number, each value must be accompanied by some type of specifications that tell the program how the digits are allocated. For example, if the digits

were stored in adjacent positions without additional specifications, there would be no way of knowing whether they represented the single value 7329.463 or 7.329463, two separate values (such as .732 and 9463 or 7.32 and 946.3), part of a value (such as 1.46 ⟨7329463⟩ 88), or any one of a tremendous variety of possible combinations. The information that PL/I uses for this purpose is supplied to it by defining the precision as part of the declaration for a variable.

III.1.4.1   Precision of Floating-Point Numbers

For floating-point numbers, precision is specified by giving the effective number of digits (which we shall call p) that are to be stored. Thus, for example, a value of $.12747 \times 10^2$ is said to have a precision of (5). The same value expressed as $.1274700 \times 10^2$ has a precision of (7).

III.1.4.2   Precision of Fixed-Point Numbers

For fixed-point numbers (regardless of base), physical size is given as the number of digits and magnitude is defined by the location of the decimal or binary point. If we call the <u>total</u>

number of digits w and we let d represent the number of digits to the right of the decimal or binary point, the precision of any fixed-point number can be specified in the form (w,d). Table 3.2 shows some examples of fixed-point numbers and their respective precisions expressed in (w,d) format.

TABLE 3.2 Various Precision Specifications for
Fixed-Point Numbers

Base	Digits	Intended Value	Precision
Decimal	125	12.5	(3,1)
		1.25	(3,2)
		.125	(3,3)
		125	(3,0)
		125	(3)
Binary	1101101	110110.1	(7,1)
		11.01101	(7,5)
		.1101101	(7,7)
		110.1101	(7,4)
		1101101.	(7,0)

III.1.4.3 Scaling of Fixed-Point Numbers

If we look a little more closely at the second part of the precision specification for fixed-point numbers (the d in w,d), we can discover that this specification carries the same type of information given by the exponent portion of a floating-point number. This similarity is seen by referring to Table 3.2. In the first entry, application of the precision (3,1) to the three digits 125 produces a result equivalent to multiplication by 10^{-1}. (That is, a d of 1 corresponds to an exponent of -1). By the same token, d values of 2 and 3 (as shown in the next two entries of the table) correspond to exponent values of -2 and -3, respectively. Thus, in a very real sense, d specifies the amount of *scaling* that is to be done to represent the proper magnitude of a fixed point number. In fact, d is technically referred to as the *scale factor*. The difference between the scaling of fixed- and floating-point numbers is that the scaling of the former is *fixed* at the time the number is declared, whereas that of floating-point numbers may vary dynamically — that is, *float* around.

PL/I's automatic scaling facilities allow a degree of flexibility beyond that shown in Table 3.2. Use of the scale factor may be generalized to include situations where a value's required fractional digits (d) exceed the total number of digits (w) associated with that value. For example, it is possible for a fixed decimal number to be stored as 6749 while representing an actual value of .006749. This situation is described by applying the same method of expression used before: we have a four-digit number which we wish to be treated as if there were six digits to the right of an assumed decimal point. Accordingly, the appropriate precision specification is (4,6). Similarily, a value stored as 28074 and described as having precision (5,8) will be used in computations as the value .00028074.

The same type of extension can be applied to very large fixed-point integers whose low-order digits are zeros. To illustrate, suppose that the value associated with a particular variable X takes the form of a five-digit decimal integer in which the last two digits are zeros. (That is, sample values for X would be 14700, 90600, 56800, and so on). Accordingly, it is possible to restrict storage to the first three digits without "losing" anything, so long as the mechanism is available to apply the proper scaling when the variable participates in some type of computation. A precision of (3,−2) describes this situation: w is 3 because only three digits are being stored; d is −2 because the assumed decimal point must be positioned two places to the right of the rightmost digit of the stored value. Thus, a number stored as 158 and described by precision (3,−2) would be treated as 15800. Looking at it another way, the −2 indicates that the stored value must be divided by 10^{-2} to obtain the proper magnitude. Table 3.3 gives some additional examples of fixed-point precision specifications in which d is negative or exceeds w.

These same precision rules (including their extensions) apply to binary fixed-point numbers as well as those whose base is decimal. Some examples are shown in Table 3.3.

TABLE 3.3 Precision Specifications for Fixed-Point Numbers
Illustrating Extended Scaling

Base	Digits	Intended Value	Precision
Decimal	125	.0125	(3,4)
		.000125	(3,6)
		1250.	(3,−1)
		12500.	(3,−2)
Binary	1101101	.001101101	(7,9)
		.0001101101	(7,10)
		11011010.	(7,−1)
		1101101000.	(7,−3)

III.2 EXPRESSION OF NUMERICAL VALUES

We have been using fixed-point and floating-point decimal numbers without specific concern about the form in which they are expressed. The ability to do this represents an additional reflection of PL/I's default mechanisms, which permit the compiler to accept a wide variety of forms without restrictive imposition on the user. This tolerance, which applies to input data as well as numerical constants used in PL/I statements, will be examined further in this section.

III.2.1   Appearance of Decimal Constants

Extensive conversion mechanisms, all of which operate automatically, allow the programmer to dissociate the form in which a number is expressed from that ultimately used to store the number. Accordingly, we have exploited that flexibility by expressing numerical values "naturally." However, along with these versatile arrangements there are certain operating limits that should be known.

III.2.1.1   Fixed-Point Decimal Numbers

We have already seen that the expression of fixed-point decimal constants follows conventional notation exactly. Numbers such as 7, −18.45, 322.0, .507200 and 0.507200 are perfectly legitimate fixed-point constants. Whether or not these values are preserved when stored in final form will depend on the attributes of the variables in which these values are placed.

The length of a fixed-point constant (the number of digits used to store it) can be controlled by the programmer via the **DECLARE** statement or by the compiler's defaults. For most implementations, fixed-point decimal constants may be as long as 15 digits, irrespective of the position of the decimal point. Since there is no exponent to adjust as with floating-point variables, the number of digits used for a particular variable immediately defines the maximum value. Hence, with a limit of 15 digits, the largest acceptable value would be 999999999999999, unless a negative scale factor were used.

III.2.1.2   Floating-Point Decimal Numbers

The largest floating-point decimal value accepted by PL/I varies with the particular version of the compiler being used. A typical maximum is 7.2×10^{75} (7.2E+75 in PL/I notation.) By the same token, there is a minumum recognizable magnitude aside from zero itself. A typical value for this limit is 2.4×10^{-78} (2.4E−78 in PL/I notation). When a number (either read in *or* computed during a program) exceeds the allowable maximum, the resulting situation is known as *overflow*. An *underflow* occurs when a value is encountered that falls between the acceptable minimum and zero. An overflow is automatically treated by the program as an error that may terminate the job; an underflow causes a result of zero to be assumed. However, PL/I has provisions that allow the programmer to control the action resulting from such circumstances. These facilities are discussed in the chapter dealing with control of execution.

The maximum number of digits that may be used to express a floating-point decimal value is usually 16. Thus, a number such as

$$4.231556018772963E+04$$

will be accepted, whereas

$$4.2315560187729638E+04$$

will not. In most PL/I implementations, the assignment or input of a number with too many digits will result in an error condition that may either terminate the proceedings or cause the guilty number to be truncated on the right. For example, if our compiler had a 16-digit limit, a statement in a program such as

$$A = 31.7682405991342688E+00;$$

might produce a message such as "floating-point constant beginning '31.7682405' in statement number XX is too long and has been truncated on the right." The XX refers to the source listing. If the compiler is preset to continue with the job despite this error, it will store the constant as a 16-digit number and the statement **PUT DATA** (A); will produce A=3.176824059913426E+01;. Note that there is no rounding. If a number containing more than 16 digits should be generated during some calculation, the necessary truncations will occur automatically.

```
ILIN: PROCEDURE OPTIONS (MAIN);
      DECLARE A,B,C,D;
      GET DATA (A,B,C);

      DO WHILE (A  = 0);
        D = A+B+C;
        PUT SKIP DATA (A,B,C);
        PUT SKIP DATA (D);
        GET DATA (A,B,C);
      END;

      END ILIN;
```

(a)

A=27000E-3 B=32.8 C = 1.074E+03;   (b)

A=11011B   B = 3280E-02 C=1074;   (c)

A=2.7E1   B=32.8   C=.1074E4;   (d)

A = 27,B=3.28E1,C=1074;   (e)

A= 2.70000E+01   B= 3.28099E+01   C= 1.07401E+03;
D= 1.13382E+03;

(f)

Figure 3.1

While not always practical, PL/I's floating-point notation is an acceptable form for input. For instance, the sequence of statements shown in Figure 3.1a will operate properly on any of the forms shown in Figures 3.1b, 3.1c, 3.1d, and 3.1e (as well as many others) to produce the results shown in Figure 3.1f).

III.2.2   Binary Numbers

Because of PL/I's extensive automatic conversion facilities, values to be stored as binary numbers need not be expressed that way when specified as constants in the program or as part of the input. However, there are numerous occasions when the context of a given procedure makes it appropriate for the programmer to specify a binary value as a string of ones and zeros. Capabilities for such specifications parallel those described for decimal constants.

III.2.2.1   Fixed-Point Binary Constants

The representation of fixed-point binary numbers is identical to that used for decimal values, with the exceptions that only the digits 0 and 1 may be used and a **B** is added at the end of a value. This serves as a signal to PL/I that the quantity immediately preceding the **B** is to be treated as a binary number. Otherwise, there would be no direct way of telling whether numbers such as 101 meant decimal 101 or binary 101, the latter being equivalent to a value of 5 in the decimal system. Hence, the binary constant is written as 101**B**. As with decimal values, a period is used to separate integers from fractions. A number of examples are given in Table 3.4, and additional material about the conversion between binary and decimal numbers is cited at the end of the chapter.

TABLE 3.4   Examples of Binary Fixed-Point Constants

Decimal Equivalent	Precision (w,d)	Written As
37.125	(12,5)	0100101.00100B
8.0625	(8,4)	1000.0001B
8.0625	(10,5)	01000.00010B
3.375	(7,3)	0011.011B
.09375	(9,6)	000.000110B
89.	(9,2)	1011001.00B
−7.75	(7,4)	−111.1100B
115.5625	(11,4)	1110011.1001B

The maximum number of digits that may be assigned to a binary fixed-point value is related to the internal organization of the processor on which PL/I is implemented. A typical value for this maximum (used in the IBM System 360 and 370 computers) is 31 binary digits, thus enabling a fixed-point binary value to be as large as $2^{31} - 1$.

III.2.2.2   Binary Floating-Point Constants

The general format for representing floating-point binary numbers is the same as for decimal numbers, with two important exceptions: As in the fixed-point binary case, a **B** must be included immediately after the last digit of the number (the rightmost digit of the exponent) so that the compiler can recognize it as a binary value. The second difference has to do with the use of the exponents. To maintain consistency of floating-point notation, the exponent in a binary floating-point number indicates the power of two by which that number is to be multiplied to obtain its proper magnitude. However, in the interest of brevity and convenience, a small inconsistency has been introduced. Although the exponent refers to a power of two and is part of a binary representation, it is written as a *decimal* number. We shall examine an example to see exactly how this format works.

Suppose we wanted to express the number 27.5 in binary floating-point form using eight binary digits. If we were to write it as a fixed-point binary number, its form would be 11011.100B. An equivalent floating-point form would be 11011.100E+00B. Since binary arithmetic is completely analogous to decimal manipulations, multiplication of a binary number by two causes the binary point to shift one place to the right in exactly the same way that multiplication of a decimal number by ten causes the decimal point to shift one place to the right. Conversely, division by two causes the binary point to shift one place to the left. Hence, if we wish to shift the binary point in any direction without changing the actual value of the number, we must compensate by increasing or decreasing the exponent accordingly. The following shows how this manipulation works for the binary value 11011.100B (27.5) using a length of eight bits:

$$11011.100E+00B$$
$$1101.1100E+01B$$
$$110.11100E+02B$$
$$11.011100E+03B$$
$$1.1011100E+04B$$
$$110111.00E-01B$$
$$11011100.E-02B$$
$$.11011100E+05B$$

It is easy to see that expression of the exponent as a binary number can very quickly become awkward. For example, 1101110.E−09B would otherwise have to appear as 1101110.E−1001B.

III.3   SELECTION OF BASE AND SCALE

The versatility of PL/I, which allows the programmer to devise numerous workable ways of handling a given situation, also may present him with complications regarding the choice of methodology and techniques. One such area is the selection of an appropriate combination of base, scale, and precision for numerical items to be used in a particular procedure. It is impossible to define a set of strict rules regarding the preferability of one combination of attributes over another. However, there are guidelines that can be helpful in enhancing computational efficiency and possibly avoiding difficulties that may arise in the development of very large or very small numbers.

In general, it is a good idea to restrict the use of fixed-point numbers to those types of variables that will not be involved in extensive computations. Items that usually are eligible for treatment as fixed-point quantities include counters and dollar amounts whose computational involvement will be limited to addition and subtraction. More extensive arithmetic, particularly those procedural steps involving chained multiplications and divisions, may produce loss of digits when performed on fixed-point numbers. The difficulty stems from the fact that the precision specification controls the number of positions that are allocated for value and the number of digits to be carried during computations. Consequently, the programmer must provide sufficient storage to accommodate the entire range of expected values, as well as for the appropriate number of digits. Although such a specification can be provided for initial values, it may turn out to be insufficient if a variable is to be subjected to computations that extend the value beyond the range originally reserved for it. Consequently, such variables are best treated as floating-point numbers, in which case the range problems and the consequent risk of precision loss are greatly alleviated. We shall see later on that, once the computations have been completed, the programmer is not restricted to displaying the output in floating-point form.

Computers generally perform arithmetic on binary numbers faster than they handle corresponding operations on decimal values. Consequently, the former base is preferred, with the implication that the programmer is assured of the variable's adequacy to represent the anticipated range of values. When it is difficult to predict this range, it is possible to play it safe by using maximum binary floating-poing precision (which is 53 on most IBM implementations). Bear in mind that the use of a binary floating-point variable does not mean that values to be assigned or read into that variable need be expressed explicitly in that form. The programmer still can use whatever form is convenient for the occasion, letting PL/I's mechanisms take care of any conversion.

Illustration 9

To review some of the facilities discussed earlier, we shall combine them in the context of a complete procedure. At the same time this example will serve as a vehicle for the introduction of a few additional features. These will be treated as conveniences, with a more detailed scrutiny of their properties appearing later.

Kopf Drayage Corporation uses three types of vehicles to haul goods for customers. Based on accumulated data, the company has developed the following equations for fuel consumption:

$$\text{Type 1: FLCON} = 4.4 - 0.00022 \times \text{PYLD}$$

$$\text{Type 2: FLCON} = 4.14 - 0.00000189 \times \text{PYLD}^{1.2}$$

$$\text{Type 3: FLCON} = 3.96 - (0.000207 \times \text{PYLD} - 0.00000061 \times \text{PYLD}^2)$$

where PYLD represents the weight of the payload in pounds and FLCON is the fuel consumption in miles per gallon. Each time a vehicle completes its point-to-point delivery, an input card is prepared containing the vehicle type, number of miles traveled (to the nearest mile), and the weight of the payload (to the nearest pound). At the end of the week, the cards are to be processed by a program that produces the output listed below.

For each delivery: vehicle type, distance, payload weight, fuel consumption and amount of fuel used

For each vehicle type: number of deliveries, total distance, total payload weight and total amount of fuel consumed

For all types: total number of deliveries, total distance traveled, total payload weight and total amount of fuel consumed

Before getting into the details of the procedure, we can establish that its overall structure consists of two basic components: There is a set of calculations that must be performed for each input card, this process repeating until all of the input has been read. At that point, the required summary information can be produced and displayed. Up to now our technique for defining the end of the data has been built on the use of an "impossible" value as a test criterion. (For example, a type number of zero could be used in this problem.) A more versatile mechanism is available for detecting the last input card regardless of its contents, thereby eliminating the necessity for devising a special test for each particular situation. When the collection of input is associated with the default name **SYSIN** (as it usually is in this text) a test for the end of the data can be specified as follows:

ON ENDFILE (SYSIN) action;

This type of statement sets up an automatic mechanism which is in force during any statements executed after the execution of the **ON** statement. There is no effect on the course of events until there is no more input, at which time the indicated action is taken. Thus, by inserting a statement that says

ON ENDFILE (SYSIN) NDFILE = 0;

ahead of the input statement (or statements) in a program, that program becomes equipped with a test that will automatically cause the **DO-WHILE** loop to be bypassed when there is no more input.

It should be noted that this is one specific use of a more general facility that allows the construction of tests for a wide variety of circumstances. These will be developed in subsequent discussions dealing with the control of execution.

Further examination of the processing for each input card indicates that the course of the

```
ILL9: PROCEDURE OPTIONS (MAIN);

/****************************************************/
/* FLCON IS THE FUEL CONSUMPTION                    */
/* PYLD IS THE PAYLOAD                              */
/* NTYPE IS THE VEHICLE TYPE                        */
/* MILES IS THE NO. OF MILES FOR A DELIVERY         */
/* GLNS IS THE AMOUNT OF FUEL USED FOR A DELIVERY   */
/* NDEL1, NDEL2, NDEL3 AND NDELT ARE THE NOS. OF    */
/*     DELIVERIES FOR TYPES 1,2,3 AND THE TOTAL,    */
/*        RESPECTIVELY                              */
/* PYLD1, PYLD2, PYLD3 AND PYLDT ARE THE PAYLOAD    */
/*           TOTALS                                 */
/* MILES1, MILES2, MILES3 AND MILEST ARE THE MILEAGE*/
/*        TOTALS                                    */
/* GLNS1, GLNS2, GLNS3 AND GLNST ARE THE FUEL       */
/*         USAGE TOTALS                             */
/* NDFILE IS A SWITCH INITIALIZED TO 1 AND SET TO 0 */
/*     WHEN THERE ARE NO MORE INPUT VALUES.         */
/****************************************************/
        DECLARE FLCON,PYLD,NTYPE,MILES,GLNS,NDEL1,NDEL2,NDEL3,NDELT,
                PYLD1,PYLD2,PYLD3,PYLDT,MILES1,MILES2,MILES3,MILEST,
                GLNS1,GLNS2,GLNS3,GLNST,NDFILE;

     NDEL1 = 0;   NDEL2 = 0;   NDEL3 = 0;
     PYLD1 = 0;   PYLD2 = 0;   PYLD3 = 0;
     GLNS1 = 0;   GLNS2 = 0;   GLNS3 = 0;
     NDFILE = 1;
     ON ENDFILE (SYSIN) NDFILE = 0;
     GET DATA (NTYPE,MILES,PYLD);
     DO WHILE (NDFILE  = 0);
       IF NTYPE = 1
         THEN DO;
                 FLCON = 4.4-2.2E-4*PYLD;
                 GLNS = MILES/FLCON;
                 NDEL1 = NDEL1+1;
                 PYLD1 = PYLD1+PYLD;
                 MILES1 = MILES1+MILES;
                 GLNS1 = GLNS1+GLNS;
              END;
       IF NTYPE = 2
         THEN DO;
                 FLCON = 4.14-1.89E-6*PYLD**1.2;
                 GLNS = MILES/FLCON;
                 NDEL2 = NDEL2+1;
                 PYLD2 = PYLD2+PYLD;
                 MILES2 = MILES2+MILES;
                 GLNS2 = GLNS2+GLNS;
              END;
       IF NTYPE = 3
         THEN DO;
                 FLCON = 3.96-(2.07E-4*PYLD+6.1E-7*PYLD**1.4);
                 GLNS = MILES/FLCON;
                 NDEL3 = NDEL3+1;
                 PYLD3 = PYLD3+PYLD;
                 MILES3 = MILES3+MILES;
                 GLNS3 = GLNS3+GLNS;
              END;
       PUT SKIP DATA (NTYPE,MILES,PYLD,FLCON,GLNS);
       GET DATA (NTYPE,MILES,PYLD);
     END;
```

```
/***********************************************************/
/* ONCE ALL THE INPUT DATA HAVE BEEN READ AND PRO-     */
/* CESSED, THE END OF FILE SIGNAL WILL SET NDFILE TO   */
/* ZERO, AND THE LOOP WILL BE BYPASSED.                */
/***********************************************************/

          NTYPE = 1;
          PUT SKIP (2) DATA (NTYPE);
          PUT SKIP DATA (NDEL1, MILES1);
          PUT SKIP DATA (PYLD1, GLNS1);
          NTYPE = 2;
          PUT SKIP (2) DATA (NTYPE);
          PUT SKIP DATA (NDEL2, MILES2);
          PUT SKIP DATA (PYLD2, GLNS2);
          NTYPE = 3;
          PUT SKIP (2) DATA (NTYPE);
          PUT SKIP DATA (NDEL3, MILES3);
          PUT SKIP DATA (PYLD3, GLNS3);

/***********************************************************/
/* NOW FOR THE FINAL SUMMARY FIGURES.                  */
/***********************************************************/

          NDELT = NDEL1 + NDEL2 + NDEL3 +
          MILEST = MILES1 + MILES2 + MILES3;
          PYLDT = PYLD1 + PYLD2 + PYLD3;
          GLNST = GLNS1 + GLNS2 + GLNS3;
          PUT SKIP (3) DATA (NDELT,MILEST);
          PUT SKIP DATA (PYLDT,GLNST);

          END ILL9;
```

computations will depend on the type of vehicle: fuel consumption is calculated differently for each type. Furthermore, separate totals must be maintained for each type in accordance with the requirements of the problem. Once the computations are complete and the appropriate totals have been updated, the information printed for each delivery is the same for all types. Consequently, it will be convenient to specify three mutually exclusive sets of actions followed by a common output statement.

PL/I provides a very effective way to implement such constructions. The basic mechanism is a "compound statement" that can be attached to an **IF** statement and treated as a single activity. Such a structure needs boundaries, and they are supplied by the statements **DO**; and **END**; at the start and conclusion of the sequence, respectively. Accordingly, the resulting form is

IF condition **THEN DO**;

       statements

       END;

This type of construction, called a **DO** group, will be used as a framework for the three actions required in this procedure.

Now, some additional details can be set down. Groups of four variables (one for each type and one for the total) will be established for fuel usage and payload (both of which will be handled as floating-point numbers), as well as number of deliveries and total miles (both of which will be handled as fixed-point integers). The resulting programming is shown below and sample output is given in Figure 3.2.

```
NTYPE=        2      MILES=       817   PYLD= 8.14000E+03  FLCON= 4.04684E+00  GALNS= 2.01885E+02;
NTYPE=        1      MILES=       644   PYLD= 9.21800E+03  FLCON= 2.37203E+00  GALNS= 2.71496E+02;
NTYPE=        2      MILES=       707   PYLD= 6.88600E+03  FLCON= 4.06378E+00  GALNS= 1.73975E+02;
NTYPE=        2      MILES=       983   PYLD= 8.81700E+03  FLCON= 4.03746E+00  GALNS= 2.43469E+02;
NTYPE=        3      MILES=       429   PYLD= 1.24060E+04  FLCON= 1.06355E+00  GALNS= 4.03365E+02;
NTYPE=        3      MILES=      1107   PYLD= 1.14850E+04  FLCON= 1.28781E+00  GALNS= 8.59595E+02;
NTYPE=        1      MILES=       356   PYLD= 5.28000E+03  FLCON= 3.23840E+00  GALNS= 1.09930E+02;

NTYPE=        1;
NDEL1=        2      MILES1=     1000;
PYLD1= 1.44980E+04   GLNS1= 3.81426E+02;

NTYPE=        2;
NDEL2=        3      MILES2=     2507;
PYLD2= 2.38430E+04   GLNS2= 6.19330E+02;

NTYPE=        3;
NDEL3=        2      MILES3=     1536;
PYLD3= 2.38910E+04   GLNS3= 1.26296E+03;

NDELT=        7      MILEST=     5043;
PYLDT= 6.22320E+04   GLNST= 2.26371E+03;
```

Figure 3.2

PROBLEMS

1. Express the following quantities as fixed-point binary numbers:

   a. 102

   b. .3125

   c. 2¾

   d. −26.5

   e. 15.125

   f. 3675E02

   g. 3×10^2

   h. −562.5E−02

   i. $11^{-5}/_{32}$

   j. 10025×10^{-2}

2. Convert the following to fixed-point decimal numbers:

   a. 11011B

   b. 10001110.01B

   c. 001100.11B

   d. 110000011.1B

   e. 1001.1001B

   f. 1110111.101B

3. Express the following as fixed-point decimal numbers:

   a. 1100E01B

   b. 10011.001E−2B

   c. 0.1011E04B

   d. 100.101E3B

4. Give the base, scale and precision for the following:

    a. 12.568

    b. 10101.1111

    c. 0.1E4

    d. .11011B

    e. −12.568E2

    f. 10101.1111E+9B

    g. −11.10E1

    h. −16478.000902

5. The digits 217486 have been placed in a particular area of storage. Show what the implied magnitude would be for each of the following precisions:

    a. (6,2)

    b. (6,0)

    c. (6,4)

    d. (6,6)

    e. (6,9)

    f. (6,−3)

6. Make the necessary conversions in the following expressions and show each result (X) as a fixed-point decimal number with precision (6,3):

    a. X = 7.2+.607E+01;

    b. X = −101.11+101.11B;

    c. X = 2*1101E1B−3E−2;

    d. X = 101.10B*3E0;

7. Assuming that Z is stored as a floating-point decimal number in the form $\pm d.dddddE\pm dd$, give the value in Z after each of the following statements:

    a. Z = 3.4+2.70E−06;

    b. Z = −61.7+61.7E−01;

    c. Z = 12.5*1011B;

    d. Z = 6.2*(3E1−11000B);

    e. Z = 101.11+4.8E−2;

    f. Z = 10.1B*(11100B−2.0E+3);

    g. Z = (101E+03B+2.2E+01)*400E−02;

    h. Z = (1011B*(1101101B−101))/5.2E1

8. Rewrite the program in Illustration 9 so that it handles (accidental) occurrences of unexpected values of NTYPE. An erroneous NTYPE should not stop the run.

SUMMARY OF IMPORTANT TERMS

Base	The number system in which a particular value is expressed. In PL/I the base may be **DECIMAL** or **BINARY**.
Compound statement	A sequence of statements that are treated organizationally as a single activity. For example, the construction **IF...THEN DO;...END;** is an instance of a compound statement.
DO group	An organizational component in a PL/I procedure attached to an **IF** statement and consisting of the sequence **DO;**...statements...**END;**.

Initialization	The process of placing a known starting value in a variable so that it can be used properly for subsequent computations. For example, a variable in which a running sum is to be accumulated would be initialized to zero prior to the start of the accumulation process.
Mode	An attribute of PL/I numerical variables that indicates whether a given variable may have an imaginary component (**COMPLEX**) or not (**REAL**). The default always is **REAL**.
ON ENDFILE	A PL/I statement type that sets up a mechanism that detects the end of data from a given input source and forces the program to perform a specified action. This situation is detected even in the absence of such a statement, but the default action is to terminate processing.
Overflow	A situation resulting from the appearance of a number (by computation or other means) that exceeds the largest expressible value for the processor being used.
Precision	An attribute of PL/I numerical variables that indicates their extent in terms of the number of fractional digits and (for fixed-point numbers) the total number of digits.
Scale	An attribute of PL/I numerical variables that indicates their internal representational form. The scale may be **FIXED** or **FLOAT** regardless of base or mode.
Scale factor	The number of places a radix point has to be shifted (+ for left, − for right) in order to adjust the apparent magnitude of a scaled number to its actual value.
Scaling	The process of adjusting a numerical value by shifting its decimal (or binary, or any other radix) point so that the apparent magnitude is arbitrarily different from the actual magnitude.
Underflow	A situation resulting from the appearance in a processor of a nonzero numerical value that is smaller than the smallest number expressible in that processor.

SUPPLEMENTARY READING

Sterling, T.D., and Pollack, S.V., *Computing and Computer Science: A First Course with PL/I*. New York: Macmillan, 1970, Chapter 3.

IBM System/360 PL/I Reference Manual, IBM Publication C28-8201. White Plains, N.Y.: IBM Corporation, 1968, Chapter 3.

IV DECLARATION AND USE OF NUMERICAL VARIABLES

PL/I's facility for assigning attributes to variables based on the first letter of the variable name is simple and convenient; however, it limits us to the use of variables which are either **DECIMAL FLOAT** or **BINARY FIXED**. If the programmer wishes to take advantage of the extensive numerical capabilities that PL/I provides, he must explicitly make his intentions known to PL/I using additional features of the **DECLARE** statement. Even in this situation, PL/I still provides a system of default actions that can reduce the amount of information that the programmer must specify. The wide variety of numerical capabilities offered by PL/I presents the programmer with an additional problem: that of deciding which of the many possible choices of numerical capabilities is most suited to his present purpose. In this chapter we shall examine these problems and shall also consider some additional facilities for the input and output of numerical variables.

IV.1   DECLARATION

If the programmer wishes to use a variable, X, he can declare his intention by writing

DECLARE X; *✓ Float decimal*

and PL/I's default action will associate with X a location which can contain a **FLOAT DECIMAL** (6) number. If for some reason the programmer wishes X to be a **FIXED DECIMAL** (7,2) number, he can override PL/I's default action by simply appending these attributes to the declaration of X. The declaration thus becomes

DECLARE X **FIXED DECIMAL** (7,2);

IV.1.1   Combinations of Attributes

The example above is just one illustration of a general capability in PL/I. It is possible to declare any consistent combination of base, scale, mode, and precision. The two base attributes are **BINARY** and **DECIMAL**; the two scale attributes are **FLOAT** and **FIXED**; the two mode attributes are **COMPLEX** and **REAL**; and the precision attribute is written as either one or two numbers contained in parentheses. The attributes may be written in any order *except* that the precision attribute must follow one of the others. This is to avoid confusing it with the dimension attribute, which must appear first and which we shall study in a later chapter. A combination of these attributes is consistent, provided that it does not specify more than one base, scale, or mode, and provided that the precision attribute of a **FLOAT** variable consists of a single number enclosed in parentheses. Thus, for example, the declaration

DECLARE Z **FLOAT FIXED DECIMAL** (7);

is inconsistent because it contains two scale attributes **FLOAT** and **FIXED**. Similarly, the declaration

DECLARE T **DECIMAL FLOAT** (7,3);

is inconsistent because the variable has been declared to have the attribute **FLOAT** and the precision specification contains a scale factor. If the scale factor is omitted in the precision attribute of a **FIXED** variable it is assumed to be zero by default.

IV.1.2   Defaults

When the programmer explicitly includes attributes in the declaration of a variable, PL/I continues to apply defaults. In our above examples we did not ever specify a mode attribute. Because complex variables are only used in certain specialized situations, PL/I's default in the absence of a mode specification is to assume that it should be **REAL**. Thus, all of our examples above are equivalent to declarations in which the attribute **REAL** is included in addition to the ones shown.

To understand how PL/I applies default attributes to a variable let us consider the following three cases:

1. The programmer declares the variable without mentioning any base, scale, mode, or precision attributes. In this case, PL/I assigns the attributes **DECIMAL FLOAT REAL** (6) if the first letter of the variable name is either A-H or O-Z. On the other hand, if the first letter of the variable name is I-N, then PL/I assigns the attributes **BINARY FIXED REAL** (15,0). This is the case we have been using so far in our example programs.

2. The programmer declares the variable with a partial set of attributes; that is, he uses at least one base, scale, or mode attribute and also leaves at least one of the base, scale, mode, and precision attributes unspecified. In this case, PL/I fills in the missing attributes, as indicated in Table 4.1.

3. The programmer declares the variable with a complete set of attributes. In this case, of course, nothing is left to default.

IV.1.3 Shorthand Forms for Declarations

To reduce the number of statements that the programmer must prepare, PL/I allows several variables to be declared in a single **DECLARE** statement. Further contraction of declarations may be achieved if several of the variables share a common set of attributes. It is possible to group variables within parentheses and state the common attribute or attributes once for the entire group. This technique is known as *factoring of attributes* and may be applied to any number of variables. For example, we can replace the statement

DECLARE B **FIXED** (5,3), C **FIXED** (5,3), D **FIXED** (5,3);

with the shortened form

DECLARE (B,C,D) **FIXED** (5,3);

It is possible to shorten declarations even if all of the attributes are not shared among the variables. Thus, the statement

DECLARE E **FLOAT BINARY** (24), F **FIXED BINARY** (31,4), G **FIXED BINARY** (31,8);

can be written as

DECLARE (E **FLOAT** (24), F **FIXED** (31,4), G **FIXED** (31,8)) **BINARY**;

Variables with factored attributes may be included as part of a more extensive declaration. Accordingly, a construction such as

DECLARE (A,A1,A2) **FIXED** (7,2), B, B1, B2, N, (C,C1) **BINARY FLOAT**;

is quite valid.

TABLE 4.1 Default Attributes for Numeric Variables

Missing Attribute	Default		
Base Scale Mode	**DECIMAL** **FLOAT** **REAL**		
	If the Other Attributes are	Then the Default Precision is	Maximum Precision
Precision	**DECIMAL FIXED** **DECIMAL FLOAT** **BINARY FIXED** **BINARY FLOAT**	(5,0) (6) (15,0) (21)	15 16(33)* 31 53(109)*

*Optimizing and checkout compilers.

IV.1.4 The INITIAL Attribute

There are a number of reasons for assigning a particular value to a variable immediately after storage has been reserved for it. (Initialization of a counter or a sum, as in Illustration 9, is one such usage.) It is possible to perform such initialization as part of the **DECLARE** statement by using the form

DECLARE name base scale mode (precision) **INITIAL** (m);

where (m) represents the actual value to be placed in the assigned location at that time. For example, the statement

DECLARE X FIXED (5,2); **INITIAL** (0);

is equivalent to the sequence

DECLARE X **FIXED** (5,2); X = 0;

The **INITIAL** attribute can also be used in a factored declaration:

DECLARE (X,Y,Z) **FIXED** (6,3) **INITIAL** (4.2);

will place a value of 4.2 in each of the locations named. Since the assignment of a numerical attribute instructs PL/I to make any necessary base or scale conversion, it is possible to write statements such as

DECLARE (A **FIXED** (5,2), B, **FLOAT** (7), C **BINARY FIXED** (18)) **INITIAL** (8);

and have the values 008.00, 8.000000E+00 and 000000000000001000 **B** placed in A, B, and C, respectively.

IV.1.5 Implied Declarations

PL/I's default facilities, which assign certain attributes to numerical variables based on nothing more than their declared names, also can operate without the declaration. If a variable name appears in an assignment statement without having been declared, PL/I will automatically reserve storage for that variable in accordance with the default attributes associated with the first letter of that variable's name. Thus, in the statement

G = 27.2+8*X;

if G does not appear in any **DECLARE** statement, then PL/I will assume that the programmer will be satisfied to have G declared with default attributes (**DECIMAL FLOAT** (6)) and act accordingly. This is also true if the variable appears in an input-output statement; for example,

GET LIST (G);

would also cause G to be given default attributes if it is not otherwise declared. This is a good time to stress the fact that it is necessary either to initialize, assign a value to, or read a value into a variable before using it in some situation where it must have a value. Thus, if X in the above statement has never been assigned a value, inconsistent results will be obtained. However, some versions of PL/I accept such usage by exercising an additional default that sets all variables without **INITIAL** attributes to zero at the beginning of the program.

IV.1.6 Changing the Defaults

The Optimizing and Checkout Compilers make it possible for the programmer to extend the properties and attributes that may be assigned by default. Although this may be of considerable convenience in a particular setting, it specifically does not allow the programmer to override those attributes that are assigned explicitly or contextually. Consequently, the main purpose of this facility is to help simplify program organization by permitting the programmer to establish associations between certain types of variables and certain sets of attributes. Once established, these relationships are used automatically in the same way as other default mechanisms.

The basic vehicle for implementing such extensions is the **DEFAULT** statement. We shall confine our examination to the more commonly used form, with an appropriate reference at the end of the chapter to a more comprehensive discussion.

IV.1.6.1   The **RANGE** Specification

Earlier in the chapter we referred to a convention (built into the compiler) that automatically assigns a particular set of attributes to a variable based solely on the initial letter of its name. For the Optimizing and Checkout Compilers, this relationship need not be permanent. By means of the **RANGE** specification in a **DEFAULT** statement, it is possible to redefine this convention in almost any desirable manner. By using a statement having the general form

   DEFAULT RANGE (letters) attributes;

the programmer can set up a rule that will be used by the compiler to assign a specified set of attributes to variables whose names begin with a particular letter or a particular combination of letters. For example, the statement

   DEFAULT RANGE (X) **FIXED DECIMAL**;

causes the compiler to assign the attributes **FIXED DECIMAL** to any declared variable whose name begins with X, regardless of the letters or digits used for subsequent characters in that name. Note that no precision was given in the **DEFAULT** statement, so the precision defined in the built-in default rules would be used automatically.

This type of specification could be restricted further by indicating a combination of letters. For example, the statement

   DEFAULT RANGE (XV) **FIXED DECIMAL**;

would set up a relationship whereby the attributes **FIXED DECIMAL** (and default precision) would be assigned to all explicitly or implicitly declared variables whose names started with the sequence XV.

Another version of the **RANGE** specification can be used to define a series of defaults for a sequence of initial letters. This is done by specifying the form

   DEFAULT RANGE (letter:letter) attributes;

The two letters within the parentheses represent the beginning and end of an alphabetical sequence, so all variables with names whose initial letters are in that range will be assigned the accompanying attributes. For example,

   DEFAULT RANGE (W:Z) **FLOAT BINARY**;

sets up a default such that all declared variables whose names begin with W, X, Y, or Z will have the attributes **FLOAT BINARY** with default precision. Note that in all of these examples there was no mode specified in the **DEFAULT** statement. Accordingly, the attribute **REAL** would be assigned by the built-in default mechanisms.

The **RANGE** specification may be used to define a convention that encompasses all variables. For this type of specification the form is

DEFAULT RANGE (*) attributes;

Thus, the statement

DEFAULT RANGE (*) **FIXED DECIMAL**;

makes arrangements for all declared variables, regardless of their initial letter (this includes all 29 "letters" of the extended alphabet). These will have an assigned scale of **FIXED** and a base of **DECIMAL**. (The other attributes, of course, will come from the original defaults.) This facility is much more useful when applied in conjunction with the **VALUE** specification, as described in the next section.

IV.1.6.2   The **VALUE** Specification

Since the precision is specified as a numerical value, special facilities are required to change such defaults. This need is fulfilled in the **DEFAULT** statement by an additional specification having the general form

VALUE (attributes (precision));

Note that the **VALUE** feature will not work properly with only a precision specification; other attributes also must be included, even though there appears to be a redundancy. For example, the statement

DEFAULT RANGE (X) **FIXED DECIMAL VALUE** (**FIXED DECIMAL** (6,3));

defines a default mechanism in which all variables whose names begin with X (and are declared with no explicit base or scale attributes) will be assigned the attributes **FIXED DECIMAL** (6,3). Had we written

DEFAULT RANGE (X) **VALUE** (**FIXED DECIMAL** (6,3));

the resulting default would be quite different: this time, the scale and base of an appropriately named variable will *not* automatically be set to **FIXED DECIMAL**. What happens instead is that when a variable whose name begins with X is declared with the **FIXED DECIMAL** explicitly specified, but with the prism defined by the **DEFAULT** statement will supply a precision of (6,3). If base and/or scale are unspecified, the ordinary defaults take over. Thus, assuming the previous **DEFAULT** statement, the sequence

DECLARE X **FIXED DECIMAL INITIAL** (7); X2 = X;

will produce a fixed decimal variable named X with precision (6,3), as expected; however, even though X2 begins with the "right" letter, the absence of explicit specifications will force the assignment of **FLOAT DECIMAL** (6).

Several precision specifications may be associated with a single **VALUE** specification, thereby defining different default precisions for different combinations of base/scale/mode. To illustrate, consider the following statement:

DEFAULT RANGE (W:Z) **VALUE** (**FIXED BINARY** (31), **FLOAT BINARY** (53),
FIXED   DECIMAL (8,4));

As indicated by the **RANGE** part of the specification, this provides new defaults for variables whose names begin with W, X, Y, or Z. Specifically, when such a variable is declared with the explicit attributes **FIXED BINARY**, its precision will be (31); on the other hand, if such a variable is declared explicitly as **FLOAT BINARY**, its associated precision automatically will be (53); furthermore, such variables declared as **FIXED DECIMAL** automatically will receive a precision of (8,4). Declaration without these explicit attributes causes the regular defaults to operate, W or no W.

Several **RANGE** specifications may be factored into a single **DEFAULT** statement. Thus, a form such as

DEFAULT (RANGE (X:Y) **FLOAT, RANGE** (A) **FIXED) BINARY**;

is perfectly valid: variable names beginning with X or Y will be associated with the attributes **FLOAT BINARY**, whereas those beginning with A will be associated with the attributes **FIXED BINARY**.

IV.1.6.3   Exceptions to Programmer-Defined Defaults

Despite a **DEFAULT** statement to the contrary, it is possible to single out particular variable names for exemption from these new defaults. This is done by adding the keyword **SYSTEM** to that variable's declaration. For instance, the sequence

DEFAULT RANGE (X) **FIXED DECIMAL**;

DECLARE X4 SYSTEM;

will result in the attributes **REAL FLOAT DECIMAL** (6) being assigned to X4. Had we omitted the word **SYSTEM** from the declaration, X4 would have been given the attributes **REAL FIXED DECIMAL** (5).

IV.2   USE OF NUMERICAL VARIABLES

PL/I's default rules do not in any way attempt to assign attributes to a variable on the basis of the purpose for which the variable is used. Thus it is up to the programmer to know the situations in which one type of numeric variable is more appropriate than another, and act accordingly. In the following paragraphs we shall outline a few of the more common situations in which it is appropriate to use the various types of PL/I variables.

IV.2.1 Decimal Fixed Variables

Decimal fixed variables are especially appropriate in dealing with numbers that represent amounts of money. They are also useful for simple counters or to read in or write out values representing the number of times something has occurred, the number of objects in a certain category, and so on. Because of their decimal format, they are efficiently used in input and output. If numerous additions and subtractions must be performed, so that the computation outweighs the need to do input and output, then binary numbers should be considered. If the computations involve numerous multiplications, divisions, or exponentiations, then floating-point should probably be used.

IV.2.2 Binary Fixed Variables

Binary fixed variables are also useful as simple counters and are an excellent choice for calculations involving integers. Because computers can do binary arithmetic more efficiently than they can do decimal arithmetic, binary fixed variables are preferable to decimal fixed variables if extensive computations are to be done. On the other hand, if it is necessary to read the number in or write it out frequently, then decimal fixed may be a better choice. It is almost always preferable to use binary fixed numbers in the case of variables that are used in association with arrays (which we shall study in a later chapter). PL/I requires that the subscripts of an array be in binary. Thus if decimal variables are used instead, conversion to binary is necessary.

IV.2.3 Floating-Point Variables

Floating-point variables are ideal for situations in which extensive computations must be done, especially if multiplications, divisions, or exponentiations are involved, because the number of integral and fractional places is quite difficult to predict even after just a few multiplications or divisions. Variables used in mathematical formulas, or to represent quantities such as distance, time, speed, and so on, should almost always be in floating point. In fact, almost any variable that is used in a situation other than those mentioned under decimal and binary fixed-point numbers should probably be floating-point.

The observant student may have noticed that although we discussed decimal and binary fixed-point numbers separately, we have treated floating-point numbers under a single heading. There is a good reason for this: Internally, PL/I uses only one form of floating-point number. Thus, whether the programmer calls it **DECIMAL FLOAT** or **BINARY FLOAT**, it's all the same to PL/I. This is just one example of a situation in which PL/I makes it appear to the programmer that one thing is happening when, for its own convenience, PL/I is actually doing something quite different. As long as the programmer cannot tell the difference, everyone winds up happy.

IV.2.4 Input and Output of Numerical Variables

In preparing data for input to a procedure, we have allowed its form to be dictated by convenience. By doing so we have exploited PL/I's automatic conversion mechanisms that mediate between the two sets of attributes. This is but one aspect of more general facility, which focuses around the idea that *the declaration determines the internal representation of a variable*. For example, if we write the sequence of statements

DECLARE A FLOAT DECIMAL (5);

GET DATA (A);

and the particular value of A were punched as 11.75, it would be stored as 1.17500E+01. This is true independently of the way it is punched on the input card. It could appear as 11.75, 11.75E+0, 1175E−2, 11.750, or even 1011.11B. On the other hand, if a statement such as **PUT DATA** (A); is executed, the form in which the output is displayed depends on the form in which it is stored (as defined by the declaration).

These same conversion mechanisms also operate in assignment statements. For example, if variable B is declared as **FIXED DECIMAL** (6,2) and B receives a value through the assignment statement

B = 643;

the internal representation of B would correspond to a value of 0643.00. Subsequent display of this variable would produce a value of 643.00, the leftmost 0 having been supressed automatically.

Although these conversion mechanisms prevail for all numerical variables, there is one exception in the way they operate with binary variables. As long as values being assigned to binary variables are represented as legitimate numerical forms (any allowable combination of base, scale, mode, and precision), proper conversion will take place. However, when it comes to the display of binary values, PL/I takes matters into its own hands. The assumption is that the user is not interested in a string of 1's and 0's, and would rather see an equivalent representation as a decimal quantity. Consequently, appropriate conversion to decimal form is made before the value is printed, even though the programmer did not explicitly request this. If we wrote the following as part of a procedure:

DECLARE I FLOAT BINARY (21), **J FIXED BINARY** (7,2);

I = 1.01111E+3B; J = 1101.11B;

PUT DATA (I,J);

the output would read

I = 1.17500E+01 J=13.7;

In order to obtain the display as a string of binary digits, special measures must be taken by the programmer. (These techniques are discussed with other operations on bit strings).

This automatic conversion mechanism generalizes to include values produced by any computations in PL/I, regardless of their complexity. Consequently, we can specify a computational expression that will generate a result in, say, floating point form and force its conversion to fixed-point by assigning it to a variable whose declared scale is **FIXED**. For example, the sequence

DECLARE A,B,C,D **FIXED** (7,2);

GET DATA (A,B,C);

D = A+(B*C)**2.1−C/(B-A);

will place a fixed point number in D even though A,B, and C were used as floating point numbers. Subsequent output of D (via a statement like **PUT DATA** (D);) will display it in fixed point form.

Illustration 9A

We shall modify Illustration 9 to take advantage of this conversion facility by allowing some of our computed results to be converted (and ultimately displayed) in the more natural fixed-point format. Towards this end, we shall declare FLCON, GALNS, GLNS1, GLNS2, GLNS3 and GLNST as fixed-point variables.

In addition to these changes in attributes, we shall use this illustration to introduce a second, more compact input form. The use of **GET LIST** instead of **GET DATA** relieves the programmer of the necessity for expressing each of his input values as a miniature assignment statement. Thus, the input shown in Figure 4.1a, which would be read with the statement

GET DATA (NTYPE,MILES,PYLD);

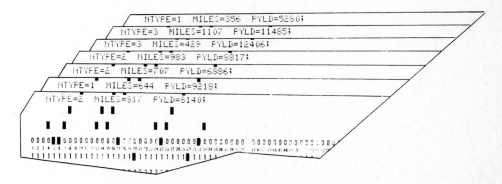

Figure 4.1a

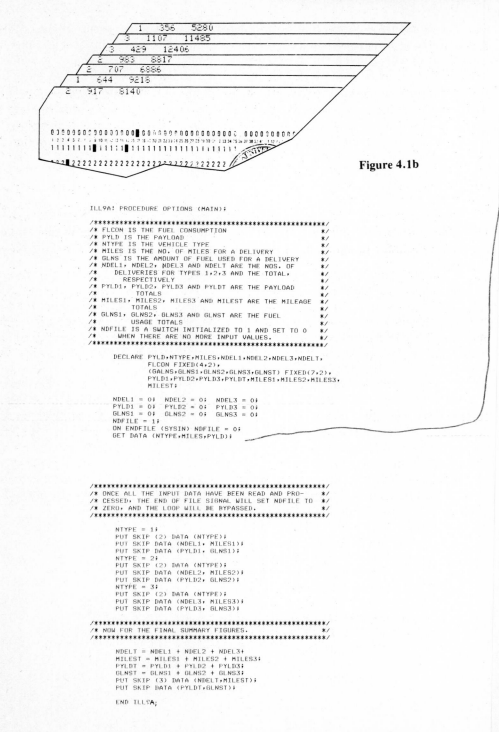

Figure 4.1b

```
ILL9A: PROCEDURE OPTIONS (MAIN);

/**********************************************************/
/* FLCON IS THE FUEL CONSUMPTION                        */
/* PYLD IS THE PAYLOAD                                  */
/* NTYPE IS THE VEHICLE TYPE                            */
/* MILES IS THE NO. OF MILES FOR A DELIVERY             */
/* GLNS IS THE AMOUNT OF FUEL USED FOR A DELIVERY       */
/* NDEL1, NDEL2, NDEL3 AND NDELT ARE THE NOS. OF        */
/*    DELIVERIES FOR TYPES 1,2,3 AND THE TOTAL,         */
/*    RESPECTIVELY                                      */
/* PYLD1, PYLD2, PYLD3 AND PYLDT ARE THE PAYLOAD        */
/*        TOTALS                                        */
/* MILES1, MILES2, MILES3 AND MILEST ARE THE MILEAGE    */
/*        TOTALS                                        */
/* GLNS1, GLNS2, GLNS3 AND GLNST ARE THE FUEL           */
/*        USAGE TOTALS                                  */
/* NDFILE IS A SWITCH INITIALIZED TO 1 AND SET TO 0     */
/*    WHEN THERE ARE NO MORE INPUT VALUES.              */
/**********************************************************/

      DECLARE PYLD,NTYPE,MILES,NDEL1,NDEL2,NDEL3,NDELT,
            FLCON FIXED(4,2),
            (GALNS,GLNS1,GLNS2,GLNS3,GLNST) FIXED(7,2),
            PYLD1,PYLD2,PYLD3,PYLDT,MILES1,MILES2,MILES3,
            MILEST;

      NDEL1 = 0;   NDEL2 = 0;   NDEL3 = 0;
      PYLD1 = 0;   PYLD2 = 0;   PYLD3 = 0;
      GLNS1 = 0;   GLNS2 = 0;   GLNS3 = 0;
      NDFILE = 1;
      ON ENDFILE (SYSIN) NDFILE = 0;
      GET DATA (NTYPE,MILES,PYLD);




/**********************************************************/
/* ONCE ALL THE INPUT DATA HAVE BEEN READ AND PRO-      */
/* CESSED, THE END OF FILE SIGNAL WILL SET NDFILE TO    */
/* ZERO, AND THE LOOP WILL BE BYPASSED.                 */
/**********************************************************/

      NTYPE = 1;
      PUT SKIP (2) DATA (NTYPE);
      PUT SKIP DATA (NDEL1, MILES1);
      PUT SKIP DATA (PYLD1, GLNS1);
      NTYPE = 2;
      PUT SKIP (2) DATA (NTYPE);
      PUT SKIP DATA (NDEL2, MILES2);
      PUT SKIP DATA (PYLD2, GLNS2);
      NTYPE = 3;
      PUT SKIP (2) DATA (NTYPE);
      PUT SKIP DATA (NDEL3, MILES3);
      PUT SKIP DATA (PYLD3, GLNS3);

/**********************************************************/
/* NOW FOR THE FINAL SUMMARY FIGURES.                   */
/**********************************************************/

      NDELT = NDEL1 + NDEL2 + NDEL3;
      MILEST = MILES1 + MILES2 + MILES3;
      PYLDT = PYLD1 + PYLD2 + PYLD3;
      GLNST = GLNS1 + GLNS2 + GLNS3;
      PUT SKIP (3) DATA (NDELT,MILEST);
      PUT SKIP DATA (PYLDT,GLNST);

      END ILL9A;
```

Previous example pg 75

can be simplified to the form shown in Figure 4.1b when the procedure is designed to read the data with the statement

GET LIST (NTYPE,MILES,PYLD);

We shall use this input facility for the data in this procedure, noting that in choosing between these two input forms the programmer must weigh the conciseness of the unlabeled format against the accompanying loss of convenient identification. The sample output shown in Figure 4.2 indicates the effect on the display forms; the program is shown on the preceeding page.

List used on pg. 97

appears incorrect Doesn't show GET LIST Uses GET DATA

IV.2.5   Complex Numbers

In the previous chapter we introduced complex numbers as a basic data type in PL/I. Now we shall examine this capability further and see its use in an example program.

IV.2.5.1   Complex Notation in PL/I

The basic distinction between imaginary constants and real ones in PL/I is the presence or absence of the letter I at the end of the constant. Thus, the imaginary fixed decimal constant 14i appears in PL/I as 14I. PL/I does not actually have complex constants, but the same effect can be achieved by combining a real and an imaginary constant with an addition or subtraction operator. Thus the complex value 17.2 - 24.9i would be written in fixed decimal as 17.2 - 24.9I. Note that no multiplication sign is used between the I and the constant by which it is multiplied. The same rules apply for floating-point and binary complex numbers. Table 4.2 summarizes these rules for a typical complex value. In order to maintain consistency during arithmetic manipulations, PL/I finds it convenient to treat all quantities involving imaginary components as complex numbers. Thus, if we have a purely imaginary number (one containing no real component), it is represented and carried internally as a complex number having a real part equal to zero. Nevertheless, real and imaginary constants and real and complex variables may all be freely intermixed in a single expression. PL/I's ever-present conversion mechanisms will sort it all out. Although each complex quantity consists of two separate numbers, PL/I treats them as a single logical entity. Both components of a complex variable have the same base, scale, and precision.

TABLE 4.2 Complex Number Notations
for the Value 34 + 12i

Base and Scale	Form
FIXED DECIMAL	00034 + 00012I
FLOAT DECIMAL	3.40000E+01 + 1.20000E+01I
FIXED BINARY	000000000100010B + 000000000001100BI
FLOAT BINARY	1.00010 ... 0E+05B + 1.10000 ... 0E+03BI

```
NTYPE=  2    MILES=   917    PYLD= 9.14000E+03    FLCON= 4.03    GALNS= 227.91;
NTYPE=  1    MILES=   644    PYLD= 9.21900E+03    FLCON= 2.37    GALNS= 212.05;
NTYPE=  2    MILES=   707    PYLD= 6.88600E+03    FLCON= 4.06    GALNS= 174.36;
NTYPE=  2    MILES=   983    PYLD= 8.81700E+03    FLCON= 4.03    GALNS= 244.31;
NTYPE=  3    MILES=   429    PYLD= 1.24060E+04    FLCON= 1.06    GALNS= 406.75;
NTYPE=  3    MILES=  1107    PYLD= 1.14850E+04    FLCON= 1.28    GALNS= 869.29;
NTYPE=  1    MILES=   356    PYLD= 5.28000E+03    FLCON= 3.23    GALNS= 110.33;


NTYPE=  1;
NDEL1=  2    MILES1= 1000;
PYLD1= 1.44990E+04    GLNS1= 382.38;

NTYPE=  2;
NDEL2=  3    MILES2= 2607;
PYLD2= 2.48430E+04    GLNS2= 646.58;

NTYPE=  3;
NDEL3=  2    MILES3= 1536;
PYLD3= 2.38910E+04    GLNS3= 1276.04;

NDELT=  7    MILEST= 5143;
PYLDT= 6.32330E+04    GLNST= 2305.00;
```

Figure 4.2

IV.2.5.2   Internal Operations with Complex Numbers

Manipulations of complex quantities in PL/I proceed according to the set of rules governing their use in algebra. If $a + bi$ and $c + di$ are two complex numbers,

$$a+bi + c+di = (a+c) + (b+d)i$$
$$a+bi - (c+di) = (a-c) + (b-d)i$$
$$(a+bi)(c+di) = (ac-bd) + (bc+ad)i$$
$$\frac{a+bi}{c+di} = \frac{(ac+bd)}{(c^2+d^2)} + \frac{(bc-ad)}{(c^2+d^2)} i$$

The procedures for performing these calculations are built into PL/I so that the program need only indicate the operations. For example, the statements

DECLARE (A,B,C) **FIXED COMPLEX** (5,2);

A = 3+7I; B = 2+4I; C = A/B;

will produce a value of 1.7+0.1I in C.

Illustration 10

To exemplify the design of a program involving complex numbers, we shall call upon a perennial favorite: a procedure for the solution of quadratic equations. The problem is to design a procedure so that for the general quadratic equation

$$ax^2 + bx + c = 0;$$

it will read in sets of values for the three constants a, b, and c, and print the roots x_1 and x_2 for each set.

The algorithm we shall use is based on the general solution for quadratic equations:

$$x_1 = \frac{-b + \sqrt{b^2 - 4ac}}{2a}$$
$$x_2 = \frac{-b - \sqrt{b^2 - 4ac}}{2a}$$

These formulas are always valid; however, when the quantity $(b^2 - 4ac)$ is less than 0, x_1 and x_2 will be complex numbers having the respective values

$$x_1 = \frac{-b}{2a} + \left(\frac{\sqrt{4ac-b^2}}{2a}\right)i$$
$$x_2 = \frac{-b}{2a} - \left(\frac{\sqrt{4ac-b^2}}{2a}\right)i$$

As we do not know in advance how many sets of constants we shall be processing in a given run, we shall use the end of file test to stop the run. In addition, we shall use unlabeled input data in conjunction with a **GET LIST** statement. The input and output are shown in Figure 4.3 and the program appears below:

A	B	C
3	-24	45
5	-11	-75
2.5	16	48
5	8	3.2

Figure 4.3a

$x_1 = 5.0+0i$ $x_2 = 3.0+0i$

$x_1 = 5.0+0i$ $x_2 = -3.0+0i$

$x_1 = -3.2+3i$ $x_2 = -3.2-3i$

$x_1 = -0.8+0i$ $x_2 = -0.8+0i$

Figure 4.3b

```
A= 3.00000E+00        B=-2.40000E+01        C= 4.50000E+01;
X1= 5.00000E+00+0.00000E+00I              X2= 3.00000E+00+0.00000E+00I;

A= 5.00000E+00        B=-1.00000E+01        C=-7.50000E+01;
X1= 4.99999E+00+0.00000E+00I              X2=-2.99999E+00+0.00000E+00I;

A= 2.50000E+00        B= 1.60000E+01        C= 4.80999E+01;
X1=-3.19999E+00+2.99999E+00I              X2=-3.19999E+00-2.99999E+00I;

A= 5.00000E+00        B= 8.00000E+00        C= 3.19999E+00;
X1=-7.99609E-01+0.00000E+00I              X2=-8.00390E-01+0.00000E+00I;
```

Figure 4.3c

```
A= 3.00000E+00        B=-2.40000E+01        C= 4.50000E+01;
X1=      5.0000+0.0000I                   X2=      3.0000+0.0000I      ;

A= 5.00000E+00        B=-1.00000E+01        C=-7.50000E+01;
X1=      5.0000+0.0000I                   X2=     -3.0000+0.0000I      ;

A= 2.50000E+00        B= 1.60000E+01        C= 4.80999E+01;
X1=     -3.2000+3.0000I                   X2=     -3.2000-3.0000I      ;

A= 5.00000E+00        B= 8.00000E+00        C= 3.19999E+00;
X1=     -0.8000+0.0000I                   X2=     -0.8000+0.0000I      ;
```

Figure 4.3d

```
ILL10: PROCEDURE OPTIONS (MAIN);
       DECLARE A,B,C,T,N, (D,TC,X1,X2) COMPLEX;

/********************************************************/
/*  D IS THE TEST VALUE B**2 - 4*A*C            */
/*  T AND TC ARE VARIABLES USED TO STORE        */
/*    INTERMEDIATE VALUES TO AVOID REDUNDANT    */
/*    CALCULATIONS.                             */
/*  X1 AND X2, THE ROOTS, ARE DECLARED AS COM-  */
/*    PLEX SO THAT THEY CAN BE USED FOR ALL     */
/*    INPUT. IF THE ROOTS ARE REAL THE IMAGINARY */
/*    COMPONENTS WILL PRINT AS ZEROS.           */
/*  N IS A VARIABLE USED TO SET UP A LOOP THAT  */
/*    WOULD GO ON FOREVER IF IT WERE NOT FOR THE */
/*    ENDFILE CONDITION.                        */
/********************************************************/

       ON ENDFILE (SYSIN) STOP;  /* STOP IS A PL/I */
                                 /* STATEMENT THAT */
                                 /* MEANS STOP.    */
       N = 1;
       GET LIST (A,B,C);

       DO WHILE (N=1);
          PUT SKIP (2) DATA (A,B,C);
          T = -B/(2*A);
          D = B**2 - 4*A*C;
          TC = D**.5/(2*A);
          X1 = T+TC;    X2 = T-TC;
          PUT SKIP DATA (X1,X2);
          GET LIST (A,B,C);
       END;

       END ILL10;
```

IV.2.6   Accuracy and Rounding

When we do arithmetic by hand, we usually calculate "accurate" results, using as many digits as the problem requires. If some intermediate operation reveals the need for additional decimal places, we simply provide them. This is not always possible on a computer, since its computational abilities may be restricted by the way it does arithmetic, its storage characteristics, and other organizational features. Consequently, a processor actually can "run out of places" when it performs certain types of arithmetic.

One effect of these limitations occurs in the process of conversion between number types. For example, if we solve the quadratic equations by hand, using sets of input values as shown in Figure 4.3a, we obtain the results given in Figure 4.3b. Since the program embodies the conventional equations, we would expect the same results when it is used on the same input. However, as seen in Figure 4.3c, most of the results differ from the (expected) exact values. Furthermore, the echo check of the input values reveals a slight discrepancy in the third and fourth sets as a result of the conversion process.

When the desired number of places can be defined, based on the problem's requirements, it is possible to counteract this behavior by forcing PL/I to perform some rounding. This is requested by means of a *built-in function* named **ROUND**. The programmer simply specifies the fixed-point expression to be rounded, accompanied by the number of places to which the rounding should occur. For example, assuming that X, A, and W are **DECIMAL FIXED** (10,5), the statement

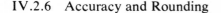

$$Y = ROUND\ ((2*X+A)W,3);$$

will perform the indicated computations, round the result to three decimal places (that is, to the nearest thousandth), and place the rounded result in Y. Of course, the final appearance of the result will be governed by the attributes of the destination variable Y. Although the process of rounding involves a number of operations, its inclusion as a built-in function means that the sequence of operations has been already defined and made a part of PL/I's procedural library and is accessible to the programmer by means of its name, **ROUND**. Accordingly, the programmer can treat it as a single conceptual operation. A variety of additional built-in functions are available and we shall introduce them in subsequent discussions.

Illustration 10A

PL/I's rounding capability is exploited in this illustration. In this version of the program, the roots X1 and X2 are rounded to two places after they are computed. It is necessary to apply the **ROUND** function to fixed-point values to round to a specific number of places. On floating-point data, the **ROUND** function rounds in the last internal binary place regardless of the number of places requested. The revised output is shown in Figure 4.3d and the listing appears below:

```
ILL10A: PROCEDURE OPTIONS (MAIN);
        DECLARE A,B,C,T, (D,TC) COMPLEX,
                (X1,X2) FIXED COMPLEX (8,4),
                N INITIAL (1);

        ON ENDFILE (SYSIN) STOP;
        GET LIST (A,B,C);

        DO WHILE (N = 1);
          PUT SKIP(2) DATA (A,B,C);
          T = -B/(2*A);
          D = B**2 - 4*A*C;
          TC = D**.5/(2*A);
          X1 = T+TC;           X2 = T-TC;
          X1 = ROUND(X1,2);    X2 = ROUND(X2,2);
          PUT SKIP DATA (X1,X2);
          GET LIST (A,B,C);
        END;

        END ILL10A;
```

PROBLEMS

1. Show what the stored value would be when an input value of 84.1875 is read into each of the variables declared as shown below. Use IBM System 360/370 default precision or those values in effect at your installation if they differ.

    a. **DECLARE** IA3;

    b. **DECLARE** A3I;

    c. **DECLARE** J41 **FIXED** (4);

    d. **DECLARE** A20 **FIXED** (8,1);

    e. **DECLARE** GH4I **FLOAT**;

    f. **DECLARE** K822 **FIXED**;

    g. **DECLARE** K822 **FIXED** (10);

    h. **DECLARE** L12A **BINARY**;

    i. **DECLARE** IC4 **FLOAT** (10);

    j. **DECLARE** W **COMPLEX**;

    k. **DECLARE** J7 **FLOAT COMPLEX** (6);

    l. **DECLARE** N8 **COMPLEX FLOAT** (9);

2. Write a program that reads sets of two numerical values (let us call them A and B) and stores them as fixed-point decimal numbers, each having five digits, two of which are to the right of the decimal point. For each set, a line is to be printed showing the larger value, the smaller one and then their sum. If that sum exceeds 141.99, no further processing is required for that set; otherwise, A and B are to be replaced by twice their respective values and a new sum generated. Furthermore, a line is to be printed showing these new values, larger one first, followed by the new sum. At the end of the run the program is to print the total number of sets processed, the number of sets for which new values had to be assigned and the number of sets that were printed in reverse order (that is, B followed by A).

3. Write a program that reads sets of numerical values (let us call them A, B, C, and D) and stores them as four-digit fixed-point decimal integers. For each set, the program computes A + D and B + C. When it finds that A + D exceeds B + C, it is to print a line showing A, D, and A + D, followed by a line showing B, C, and B + C. Otherwise, it is to print these two lines in reverse order. In addition, the procedure is to test A + B against C + D. If A + B is greater, print A, B, and A + B, followed by a line showing C, D, and C + D. If A + B is not greater than C + D, print the same two lines in reverse order. At the end of the run, print the number of sets processed, the number in which A + D exceeds B + C but A + B does not exceed C + D, the number in which the reverse is true, and the number in which both are true (that is A + B is greater than C + D and A + D is greater than B + C).

4. A land tax office wishes to produce a summary of assessments on property within its jurisdiction. Each parcel of property is a rectangular area whose characteristics are punched on a card as follows: parcel number (call it PARCEL), which can range from 1 to 46900; land type (call it TYPE), which is 1, 2, 3, 4, or 5; length (call it LENGTH) in feet to the nearest foot. (This value many range from 25 to 1130 feet.) Width (call it WIDTH) in feet to the nearest foot, ranging from 18 to 950 feet. Assessment schedule is as follows:

Type	Assessment Rate
1	$0.89/acre
2	$0.96/acre
3	$1.09/acre
4	$1.57/acre
5	$1.91/acre

Write a program that prints a line for each parcel showing to the nearest penny, its number, type, area in square feet, and total assessment. At the end of the parcel listing, print a line for each land type showing to the nearest hundredth of a percent, the type number, number of parcels in that type, total area in square feet, total assessment to the nearest cent, and percent of the total assessment for all the land. Finally, print an additional line for all grand totals, excluding percent. An acre is the area equivalent to that of 208- × 208-foot square. All values should appear as fixed-point numbers with appropriate precision.

5. The Lustreless Bath Oil Company must adjust the viscosity of its product to some particular level, depending on the altitude of the locale to which a particular batch of bath oil is being shipped. The equation defining the altitude effect is

$$VF = 4.47 - 0.0152 \times \text{altitude} + 0.00038 \times \text{altitude}^2$$

where VF is the desired final viscosity in bath oil viscosity units and the altitude is in feet.

To make the adjustment, it is necessary to add viscosity correction fluid (VCF) in an amount that depends on the type (fragrance) of bath oil being made and the initial viscosity (VI) as it leaves the reactor. The equations as determined for the five Lustreless fragrances are given below:

$$\text{Lilac} \qquad \frac{VI-VF}{WT} = .027 + .0076VI^{.72}$$

$$\text{Gardenia} \qquad \frac{VI-VF}{WT} = .029 + .0081VI^{.72}$$

$$\text{Spice} \qquad \frac{VI-VF}{WT} = .031 + .0081VI^{.74}$$

$$\text{Money} \qquad \frac{VI-VF}{WT} = .034 + .0085VI^{.77}$$

$$\text{Garlic} \qquad \frac{VI-VF}{WT} = .039 + .0097VI^{.78}$$

where WT is the number of grams to be added. The following information is available as input: (a) month (1 through 12); (b) day (1 through 31); (c) vat number (1 through 737); (d) type of oil (one of the above-mentioned fragrances); (e) VI; and (f) altitude of destination in feet (−512 to 14,770).

Write a program to collect these data for each vat. (You must select your own designations for type of oil.) For each vat, print a line containing the month, day, vat number, type, and WT. Once the last vat's data have been processed (you must determine how to recognize this), print five additional lines showing the total amount of VCF required for each type of oil in this set of data. The assumption is that VCF will lower the viscosity. There may, however, be cases in which a particular vat has an initial viscosity (VI) equal to or below the required VF. For these cases, no correction is made, and WT should be printed as zero. Use fixed-point variables where appropriate.

6. A bank summarizes payments on all its loans at the end of each year. Each debtor has 13 data cards. The first card shows his identification number (from 00001 to 99999), the total amount owed at the beginning of the year (from 000000.01 to 999999.99), and monthly interest rate (from .002 to .015). The next 12 cards contain his identification number, the number of the month (01 to 12), and the amount paid (from 00000000.00 to 99999999.99).

Write a program to print one line for each debtor, giving his identification number, the amount owed at the beginning of the year, and the amount still in debt at the end of the year. (The second amount may be larger than the first, the same, smaller, or zero.) At the end of the output, there should be a line giving the total number of debtors, the total number of payments handled, the total amount owed to the bank at the beginning of the year, and the total amount owed at the end of the year. All printouts should be in fixed-decimal format.

7. A series of digits (each having a value from 0 to 9) is available as input. There is no indication regarding how many such digits there are, and the number of digits may vary from run to run. Write a program that categorizes these digits into three groups: 0-2, 3-6, and 7-9. Output is to consist of the following: number of input values examined, number of values in each group, and, for each group, the number of consecutive pairs of values belonging to the same group. For example, the sequence 0 3 5 4 7 2 1 6 6 9 8 2 consists of 12 digits. Four of them belong to the first group, five to the second group and the remaining three to the third group. There are three consecutive pairs in the first group (3 5, 5 4, and 6 6), as well as one pair each for the first and third groups (2 1 and 9 8, respectively).

8. The English Channel Tunnel Project is going badly. Morale is low, the turnover is intolerable, and the next shipment of wine is not due for weeks. To keep things going, the Tunnel Authority decided to implement a bold payment plan: On a given day, all employees' pay will be set at 0.1 Franc per day, and it will double on each successive day from that day on. New employees will start at the 0.1 Franc rate, with the same rules applying to them. Très bien!

　　When an employee has had enough of the Channel and resigns, a card is prepared showing his employee number (1-9999) and the number of days he has worked under the bold new plan. Write a program that prints a line of output for each employee read in, showing his number, number of days worked, and total pay.

9. A number of workers have approached the Tunnel Authority with the following proposition: Each of them has in mind a particular amount of money he wishes to make and is willing to be hired for the number of days required to reach or exceed that amount. Each employee is given a number (as in Problem 8), and a card is prepared containing that number as well as the desired earnings. Write a program that reads these data, and for each card prints a line containing the employee number, desired earnings, minimum number of whole days required to reach or exceed those earnings, and the actual earnings for that period.

10. The Knishville Savings and Loan Association wants to introduce a service that will allow a borrower to specify the amount of his monthly payment, and KSLA will give him a schedule based on the amount of his loan. Write a program that produces such a schedule in accordance with the following specifications: The interest on the loan is to be charged at a rate of ½ percent per month on the unpaid balance. Input for a given loan consists of the borrower's account number (six digits), the amount of his loan, and the size of the desired payment. Print this information on the first output line, followed by a line for each payment giving the payment number, the amount credited against the principal, the amount going for interest, and the new amount owed. The final payment probably will be different from the others. After the last payment print the total amount of interest.

11. Modify the program in the previous problem so that it handles any number of successive loan schedules.

12. Revise the program in Problem 11 to reject a schedule request when the specified monthly amount does not exceed the interest due on the first payment. For example, a borrower wishing to pay off a $10,000 loan at $50 per month is never going to do it with the interest rate of ½ percent per month.

13. Generalize the program in Problem 12 so that the interest rate may be specified separately for each case.

14. Write a program that finds a root for the general equation

$$f(x) = a_n x^n + a_{n-1} x^{n-1} + a_{n-2} x^{n-2} + \ldots + a_1 x + a_0 = 0$$

where n will never exceed a value of 5, using the following method:

a.   Find values x_0 and x_1 such that $f(x_0) < 0$ and $f(x_1) > 0$.

b.   Compute $x_2 = \dfrac{x_0 + x_1}{2}$ and evaluate $f(x_2)$.

c.   If $f(x_2) < 0$, then use x_2 as the new value for x_0.

If $f(x_2) > 0$, then use x_2 as the new value for x_1.

(Of course, if $f(x_2) = 0$, we have a solution).

d.   Once the new assignment is made either to x_0 or x_1, compute the positive difference between x_0 and x_1. (Note: This may involve a test to see which value is greater in order to determine which is subtracted from which.)

e.   If the difference obtained in d is $< .001$, consider x_2 a satisfactory solution. Otherwise, go back to b and repeat.

Input consists of n, the degree of the equation, followed by n + 1 coefficients, starting with a_n, a_{n-1}, ..., all the way down to a_0. Print the coefficients in the same order, followed by the final value for x.

15.   Write the program for Problem 14 so that it can used repeatedly for different sets of input values.

16.   Write the program for Problem 14 or 15 so that the output consists of the coefficients, as before, followed by a line for each try showing x_0, x_1, x_2, and the difference computed in d. The last line contains the final value for x and a value TRIES, indicating the number of tries.

17.   The value of π can be computed using Leibnitz's formula:

$$\pi = 4(1 - 1/3 + 1/5 - 1/7 + \ldots)$$

Reliable sources give the value as 3.14159265. Write a program that computes π to 2, 3, 4, 5, 6, 7, and 8 decimal places and prints a line showing each value, along with the smallest number of terms it required to obtain that accuracy.

18.   Caries' Clinging Candies manufactures confections to be sold under local brand names. The basic mixture, to which desired flavoring is added, consists of two ingredients whose relative proportions are determined strictly by price. Ingredient A costs 29 cents a pound and B (the good stuff) costs 81 cents a pound. Write a program that computes mixtures for a succession of requirements. Each input set consists of a batch number (five-digit integer), total number of pounds in the mixture, and the final price per pound. The final price is the amount charged. To cover costs of flavoring, packaging and other overhead and profit, C^3 sets its price at double its cost for A and B in a given blend.

Output is to show the batch number, weight of the order, its price per pound, and the weights of A and B used to fill the order. If a set of specifications present an impossible situation (required price is too low) print a line with that batch number and zeros for A and B. If a price is too high, honest C^3 wants the program to print the same information as before, with an additional line showing the batch number and the total amount of excess (required total price − actual total price).

19.   Prices change. To reflect this, write the program for Problem 18 so that each set of input consists of a batch number, total pounds, final price per pound, and the current costs for A and B (in dollars and cents per pound).

SUMMARY OF IMPORTANT TERMS

Built-in function	An arbitrarily complicated procedure that may be treated as if it were a single (conceptual) operation. It is "built-in" in the sense that it is available as an intrinsic part of the language, with its name being one of the permanent keywords. Consequently, a reference to that name (in proper context) is all that is necessary to incorporate the procedure into a program.
Character string	An item of information consisting of an arbitrary succession of any characters (letters, digits or other symbols) recognized by the system. (The complete list of such characters is given in Appendix C.)
Complex number	A constant or variable consisting of a real value and an imaginary value.
COMPLEX	The attribute associated with complex numbers. This must always be declared explicitly; it is never assigned by default.
DEFAULT statement	A vehicle (in the IBM Optimizing and Checkout Compilers) for extending the default attributes that may be implied in a declaration.
ELSE clause	An alternative action that may be specified as part of an **IF** statement. This action will be performed when the condition tested by the **IF** statement is found to be false.
Factoring of attributes	A concise way of declaring a number of variables with a common set of attributes.
GET LIST statement	A mode of data transmission to the processor in which the input consists of the actual values to be transmitted, separated by blanks or commas.
Implied declaration	Use of a variable name in such a way that its context forces the PL/I compiler to assign appropriate default attributes to that variable and reserve storage for it. For example, the statement **GET LIST** (X); without prior reference to X implies a declaration for X.
INITIAL attribute	An optional attachment to a **DECLARE** statement that allows the programmer to assign values to variables as part of the declaration process.

RANGE specification	Part of a **DEFAULT** statement, which defines starting letters of variable names to which the new defaults apply. (Available only in the Optimizing and Checkout Compilers.)
REAL	The attribute describing real numbers (alternative to **COMPLEX**). Numerical variables always are **REAL** unless explicitly declared with the attribute **COMPLEX**.
Real numbers	Numerical values that have no imaginary components.
ROUND	A built-in function that allows the programmer to specify the rounding of a value to a specified number of places.
STOP	A statement that terminates all activity for that program.
SYSTEM specification	An option used in a **DECLARE** statement to override the attributes set up by the programmer via a **DEFAULT** statement and use the standard ones. (Available only in the Optimizing and Checkout Compilers.)
THEN clause	An alternative activity, specified as part of an **IF** statement. This activity will be performed if the test in the **IF** statement is found to be true. Thus, the entire complex, consisting of the test and its two alternative consequences, can be thought of structurally as **IF ...THEN...ELSE...**;
VALUE specification	An option in a **DEFAULT** statement that allows definition of new defaults for those attributes expressed as numbers (such as precision). (Available only in the Optimizing and Checkout Compilers.)

SUPPLEMENTARY READING

IBM OS PL/I Checkout and Optimizing Compilers: Language Reference Manual, IBM Publication SC33-0009. White Plains, N.Y., IBM Corporation, 1971, pp. 23-28, 83-87.

IBM System/360 PL/I Reference Manual, IBM Publication C28-8201. White Plains, N.Y.: IBM Corporation, 1968, pp. 28-32.

V NON-NUMERIC DATA

One of the primary aspects that significantly distinguishes PL/I from many of its predecessors is the amount of attention devoted to the handling of nonnumeric data. The facilities available for recognizing and processing characters constitute a major facet of the language, which parallels that constructed for the manipulation of numbers. To a certain extent, some of these operations represent direct counterparts of those performed on numerical values; others, of course, are necessarily unique to the nature of character data. In this chapter we shall take a first look at the basic operations in order to develop some proficiency and become used to the idea of handling words, sentences, strings of any kind, and even complete text materials.

V.1 CHARACTER STRINGS

PL/I considers nonnumeric data as consisting of sequences of characters called *strings*. These may consist of any legitimate characters in any combination and, for all practical purposes, in any number. A character string has all the properties associated with an item of data: it can be given a name, read in or printed, moved around in storage, and combined with or isolated from other strings; and decisions can be made based on its contents.

V.1.1   Representation of Character Strings

As is true with numbers, it is possible to express character strings as constants or place them in reserved storage associated with variable names. The compiler recognizes the appearance of a character string constant by the presence of a single quotation mark ' at the beginning and end of the string. Everything between those marks is interpreted and handled literally, so that all the characters, including each blank, will be transmitted, stored, and moved exactly as they are. Table 5.1 shows some examples of character string constants. Notice that a string consisting entirely of numbers is not treated as a numerical value. Because of the quotation marks, this is just another string of characters as far as the compiler is concerned. The same is true with a string of 1's and 0's. There is, however, another type of string, called a *bit string*, whose composition is restricted to 1's and 0's. This is a separate type of data, having special properties, which we shall explore in a separate chapter.

Because PL/I uses single quotation marks to indicate the beginning and end of the character string constant, it is obvious that we shall run into some trouble when we try to handle a character string that itself contains one or more quotation marks. PL/I accommodates this contingency by requiring the inclusion of an extra quotation mark for every quotation mark we want to use in a character string. Thus, if we wanted to create a character string consisting of the five characters DON'T, it would have to be written as 'DON'' T'.

TABLE 5.1 Examples of Character Strings in PL/I

Strings Represented as	Will Be Stored as
'237.4W'	237.4W
'/*THIS STRING HERE*/'	/*THIS STRING HERE*/
'2X(5Y−23Z)**5'	2X(5Y−23Z)**5
'2*X*(5*Y−23*Z)**5'	2*X*(5*Y−23*Z)**5
'2(X−Y'	2(X−Y

Table 5.2 sheds some additional light on the representation of character strings containing quotation marks.

TABLE 5.2 Examples of Character Strings with Quotations Marks

If We Want to Store	We Must Write
IT'S A GIFT!	'IT''S A GIFT!'
"DON'T GO." SHE SAID	'''''DON''T GO,''''' SHE SAID.'
"WHO?" I ASKED, "ME?"	'''''WHO?''''' I ASKED, '''''ME?'''''
IT'S JOE'S	'IT''S JOE''S'
"IT'S JOE'S," THEY CRIED	'''''IT''S JOE''S,''''' THEY CRIED.'

V.1.2   Declaration of Character Variables

The method of assigning names to character string variables does not differ in any way from that used for numerical variables. For such allocations, the declaration has the general form

DECLARE name **CHARACTER** (n);

where n is a decimal integer representing the number of characters to be accommodated. The **CHARACTER** attribute is never assigned by default; thus, the programmer must always declare every **CHARACTER** variable explicitly. There is a limit of 32767 on the string length given in such a declaration. When determining the number of positions to assign, it is not necessary to count the quotation marks at the beginning and end of a character string or the extra ones used to designate internal quotation marks. These are not actually part of the character string; rather, they serve as indicators to the compiler. Once a length has been specified for a string in this fashion, that many positions are always available and that number will always be accessed when a reference is made to the variable name. Let us say we want to store the eight-character constant 'PAY RATE' for subsequent use. The statements

DECLARE PR **CHARACTER** (8);

PR = 'PAY RATE';

would assign the necessary storage and place the eight characters, PAY RATE, in that location. Subsequent reference to PR will always produce that character string until the programmer changes it. Thus, the statement

PUT DATA (PR);

will produce the following display:

PR = 'PAY RATE';

V.1.2.1   Assignment of Character Strings to Variables

Reference to a character string variable name implies a reference to all of the storage associated with that name irrespective of the length of the string assigned to that variable. Should the situation arise in which a character string is to be stored under a particular name and the number of positions associated with that name exceeds the length of the string supplied, the variable will be filled with the available characters starting at the left, and the remainder will automatically be filled in with blanks. Thus, if variable PR is declared as shown before and we say

PR = 'PAID';

the resulting contents of PR will be the eight characters PAIDƀƀƀƀ (where each ƀ represents a single blank). If the reverse should occur (that is, an attempt is made to assign a character string constant to a variable having insufficient length) PL/I will accommodate as much as the length will allow, starting with the leftmost character, and truncate the rest. Accordingly, the statement

  PR = 'PAID UNTIL MAY';

will fill PR with the eight characters PAIDbUNT, the rest disappearing forever into the Great Character Bucket.

V.1.2.2   Shorthand Forms for Character String Constants

When one or more characters are repeated in a string, a shorthand method can be used to represent this. The string MICROMICRO for example, can be represented by writing (2) 'MICRO'. By the same token, the statement

  B = (3)'12.4';

will place the 12 characters 12.412.412.4 in location B (assuming B had been declared with sufficient length). Another shorthand form is available, but its use is associated predominantly with the construction of character string expressions. Accordingly, discussion of its properties and usage is included as part of the examination of character string manipulation.

Factoring of character declarations is possible. For instance, the statement

  DECLARE U CHARACTER(9), **V CHARACTER**(9), **W CHARACTER**(9);

can be rewritten as

  DECLARE (U,V,W) **CHARACTER**(9);

Consistent with the overall declaration process, it is perfectly legitimate to include character string variables as part of a more comprehensive declaration statement.

V.1.2.3   Initialization of Character Strings

Use of the **INITIAL** attribute with character string variables is routine. Accordingly, the statements

  DECLARE B CHARACTER(4); B = 'EVEN';

and

  DECLARE B CHARACTER(4) **INITIAL** ('EVEN');

produce identical results. Initialization with a character constant that is longer or shorter than a string's declared length proceeds in accordance with the rules governing ordinary string assignments (V.1.2.1).

V.1.2.4   The **VARYING** Attribute

Increased convenience in the assignment and handling of character strings is provided by a PL/I feature that allows the programmer to treat suitably declared variables as if their length expanded and contracted to match their current contents. This capability operates through the **VARYING** attribute, whose use in the declaration is as follows:

DECLARE name **CHARACTER** (n) **VARYING**;

or

DECLARE name **VARYING CHARACTER** (n);

where n now represents the maximum expected length to be accommodated by that variable during the course of the procedure. If n is declared to be 41, for example, this means that 41 positions always will be available for that variable even if they are not all in use. Should the length of a string to be stored in that variable fall below the maximum, the procedure (through appropriate bookkeeping) will "adjust" the current length; when a different string is substituted, a new adjustment is made. The effect of using this attribute can be seen by examining the following sequence of statements:

DECLARE (B, C **VARYING**) **CHARACTER** (9);

B = 'FEFFEL';   C = 'FEFFEL';

PUT DATA (B,C);

Since B is declared with a fixed length of nine, assignment of the six characters FEFFEL fills the first six positions of B, forcing PL/I to provide the necessary three blanks to fill out the rest of the string. However, when the same string is assigned to C, its apparent length "shrinks" to six, and thus the result of the output statement is as follows:

B = 'FEFFEL ';   C = 'FEFFEL';

Some maximum value greater than 0 must, of course, be stipulated in the declaration in order for the **VARYING** attribute to be effective. However, once that maximum has been defined, it is possible for the apparent length to "contract" to zero, signifying that the variable is completely empty at that time. (Note that, in this context, a string containing nothing is quite different from one containing blanks). A variable length string can be evacuated by assigning nothing to it, viz.

C = '';

In support of this facility, PL/I keeps track of the current apparent length of each variable length character string. This information is made conveniently available to the programmer by means of a built-in function named **LENGTH**. If C is declared as a **CHARACTER** string, the statement

$$N = \textbf{LENGTH} \ (C);$$

will place in N an integer indicating the number of characters currently stored in C. If C is not **VARYING**, this merely will be the declared length of C. This value is like any other number in that it can be printed and/or used in any computational process.

Table 5.3 summarizes the properties associated with **VARYING** strings.

TABLE 5.3 Properties of the **VARYING** Attribute

Statements	Contents of C	LENGTH(C)
DECLARE C CHARACTER (8); C=D;	PLATES␢␢	8
DECLARE C CHARACTER (8) **INITIAL** ('PLAT');	PLAT␢␢␢␢	8
DECLARE C CHARACTER (8) **VARYING**; C=D;	PLATES	6
DECLARE C CHARACTER (6) **VARYING**; C='PLAT';	PLAT	4
DECLARE C CHARACTER (6) **VARYING**; C=D;	PLATES	6
DECLARE C CHARACTER (6) **VARYING INITIAL** ('PLATE');	PLATE	5
DECLARE C CHARACTER (6) **VARYING**; C=E;	PLATER	6

*Assume the following: **DECLARE D CHARACTER** (6), E **CHARACTER** (7); D='PLATES'; E='PLATERS';

V.1.3   Input/Output of Character Strings

Input/output of character data can be handled by the same statements used for numerical values. It is not necessary to change the form or to add anything to it. Instead, the necessary provisions consist of an appropriate declaration and the presentation of the data in proper form. The latter requirement is fulfilled by placing single quotation marks at the beginning and end of each character string.

V.1.3.1   Input Forms

Character data to be read with a **GET LIST** statement are submitted as character string constants separated by blanks or commas. When the **GET DATA** statement is to be used for input, each value is presented to the program as a miniature assignment statement. Figure 5.1 illustrates the two forms, together with appropriate input statements. Note that even though the variable names are included in the input of Figure 5.1b, it is still necessary to declare all character string variables explicitly.

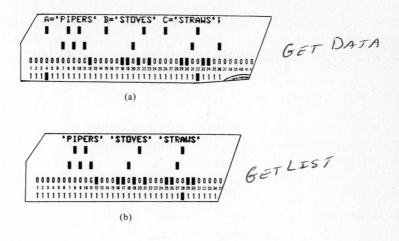

(a)

(b)

Figure 5.1

V.1.3.2   Output Forms

Display of character string values with the **PUT DATA** statement is as expected: each value is enclosed in single quotation marks and presented as an assignment statement. Though not discussed till now, it comes as no surprise that there is a **PUT LIST** statement that produces unlabeled values. Moreover, when **CHARACTER** values are printed using **PUT LIST**, PL/I obligingly removes the quotes in the same spirit as its change of binary variables to decimal before printing. Accordingly, assuming that the values shown in Figure 5.1 were read into variables defined by the statement

DECLARE B CHARACTER (6), (A,C) **CHARACTER** (8);

then the statement

PUT LIST (A,C,B);

will produce the following display:

PIPERS STRAWS STOVES

Of course, numerical variables also may be printed in this fashion, and any arbitrary mixture of variables may be specified in a single statement. The **SKIP** option is applicable here as well.

The **PUT LIST** statement allows the transmission of expressions and constants as well as variables. This is especially useful when the programmer desires to use a character value to label output.

An additional capability is provided when character output is to be produced; the programmer can generate character strings as part of the **PUT LIST** statement itself. Such strings are called *literals*. This is done simply by specifying the constant within the parenthetical list. For instance, the statement

   PUT LIST ('TOP OF THE PAGE');

will cause the string TOP OF THE PAGE to be printed.

Constants, variables and expressions can be printed with the same statement in any desired order. It is perfectly valid to do the following:

   DECLARE (PAY,TAX) **FIXED** (5,2); **GET LIST** (PAY,TAX);

   PUT SKIP LIST ('SAM''S NET PAY = ',PAY-TAX);

If the values read in for PAY and TAX are 325.42 and 21.38, respectively, then the output line would read

   SAM'S NET PAY = 304.04

The procedure may be given more flexibility. Let us say we want to list the names and heights of a number of people while letting the recipients know exactly what we are about. This can be done by writing

   DECLARE A CHARACTER (6), X **FIXED** (2); **GET LIST** (X,A);

   PUT SKIP LIST ('NAME IS',A,' AND HEIGHT IS ',X,'IN.');

If A were read in as 'DUNKLE' and X's value is 70, the output would read

   NAME IS DUNKLE AND HEIGHT IS 70 IN.

V.1.4   Assignment Statements

If a character string is to be assigned to a particular variable, that variable must be declared. We cannot write a statement such as

   D = 'LOOK MA';

without having declared D as a character variable. If we omit the declaration, PL/I will try to do what it always does when it runs across an undeclared variable; that is, it will assign default attributes to it as specified in Chapter IV. In this case, D would be considered a location for a floating-point decimal variable, and trouble would be encountered in converting the character string to that form. Of course, a statement like D='−125.83'; would be valid.

It is also possible (as we have seen) to write direct replacement statements of the form A = B; where both A and B should be explicitly declared as character string variables. If A were declared with a length of four, B's length were six, and their respective contents were 'TWIG' and 'BRANCH', the statement A = B; would change the contents of A to 'BRAN', whereas the statement B = A; would change B's contents to 'TWIGᵇᵇ' and not to 'TWIGCH'.

V.1.5   Concatenation

Since character strings do not generally contain numerical values, it would usually be meaningless to use the ordinary arithmetic operations for the construction of character string expressions. Instead, PL/I provides an appropriate operator for string manipulation. The process triggered by this operator is known as *concatenation*, and the symbol used to represent it is II. As a result of concatenation, the strings on either side of the operator are combined to produce a single string. For example, the following sequence

DECLARE Y CHARACTER (3), **Z CHARACTER** (6);

Y = 'ZUM';

Z = Y II Y;

Z will contain the string ZUMZUM. The ability to concatenate is by no means limited to two strings, nor are there any restrictions with regard to mixing constants and variables. Hence, the sequence

DECLARE B CHARACTER (5),**C CHARACTER** (6),**D CHARACTER** (17);

B = 'YOUNG'; C = 'MALONE';

D = B II 'DOCTOR' II C;

will place the string YOUNGDOCTORMALONE in location D. If we want to separate the words in the string by blanks, these must be specified as part of the constant. Thus,

D = B II ' DOCTOR ' II C;

Table 5.4 gives additional examples showing the results of concatenation.

TABLE 5.4 Use of the Concatenation Operator*

Expression	Resulting String
AIICIIA	2314 AND 2314
'FIND'IIAII'NOT'IIB	FIND2314NOTBJ44*
BIICIICII'C'	BJ44*ᵇANDᵇᵇANDᵇC
AII','IIBIICII'MORE'	2314,BJ44* AND MORE

Assume: A = '2314';   B = 'BJ44';   C = 'ᵇANDᵇ';

V.1.6   Use of Character Strings in Decision Structures

The incorporation of a decision mechanism based on the contents of the character string is very easily done in PL/I by using character strings as the testing ingredients in the ordinary **IF** statement. Although all of the relational operators are available for use in such comparisons, the most common type of decision structure involving character strings centers around the test for equality or inequality.

V.1.6.1   Construction of Character String Tests

The character strings being compared in an **IF** statement may be constants, variables, or combinations of these concatenated together. A sequence of statements such as

DECLARE A **CHARACTER** (7),B **CHARACTER** (4),C **CHARACTER** (17);

A = 'INCOME '; B = 'TAX ';

C = 'INCOME TAX RETURN';

IF C = A‖B‖'RETURN' **THEN GO TO** CHECK;

would produce an equal comparison in the **IF** statement and the **GO TO** statement following the word **THEN** would be executed. When such a comparison is made between two character strings of unequal length, an appropriate number of blanks is automatically added to the right of the shortest string so that the resulting lengths are equalized for the comparison. This addition, it should be understood, is temporary and is not reflected in the subsequent contents of either string. Consider the following sequence:

```
          .
          .
          .
```

DECLARE B **CHARACTER** (4), C **CHARACTER** (6);

GET LIST (B,C); **PUT SKIP LIST** (B,C);

IF B=C **THEN PUT SKIP LIST** ('B AND C ARE EQUAL');

        ELSE PUT SKIP LIST ('B AND C ARE DIFFERENT');

```
          .
          .
          .
```

If this sequence were used to read strings B and C having respective values of 'SHOP' and 'SHOPƀƀ', the two strings would be considered equal and the appropriate message would be printed. This will occur only when the extra characters in the longer string are blanks. If B and C are 'SHOP' and 'SHOPPE', or 'SHOP' and 'ƀƀSHOP', the comparison for equality would have failed. As the various facets of the language are explored, we shall find that this restriction is a temporary one and can be circumvented by built-in functions for dealing with parts of strings.

V.1.6.2   Alphabetization

Availability of the other relational operators for character string comparisons offers additional conveniences. Perhaps the most frequently used facility in this regard is based on the fact that each unique character is represented in storage by its own numerical code (see Appendix B). These codes are assigned in such a way that the code for 'A' is less than that for 'B', and so on. Consequently, a test to determine whether one letter is "greater than" some other letter is tantamount to a test for alphabetical order. This same property extends to strings of characters, so that a string containing the five characters *CATCH* will test as being "greater than" a string containing the seven characters *BROUGHT*, indicating that it follows the longer string in an alphabetically ordered sequence. The different string lengths do not impede the comparison since PL/I pads the shorter string with blanks at the right end and the blank is alphabetically "earlier" than any of the letters or digits.

Illustration 11

A genealogist, having stumbled across some ancient Druid records punched on cards, is interested in obtaining certain information from them. Each card contains the following observations for an individual Druid in the order listed:

last name;

height in inches, to the nearest inch;

weight in pounds, to the nearest pound;

annual income in Rieglochs, to the nearest Riegloch.

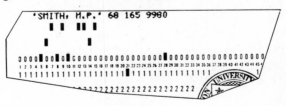

Figure 5.2

A typical card is shown in Figure 5.2. Our genealogist wants to find the records for all Druids named Smith or whose names begin with Smith and, for each such individual, to print the name, height, weight, and obesity index, the latter calculated as the number of pounds per inch of height. He is also interested in knowing how many such people there were, together with their average height, weight, and obesity index. For all others, he wants to print the name, height and weight.

Our strategy will be to read in each card and check to see whether the name is Smith. To do

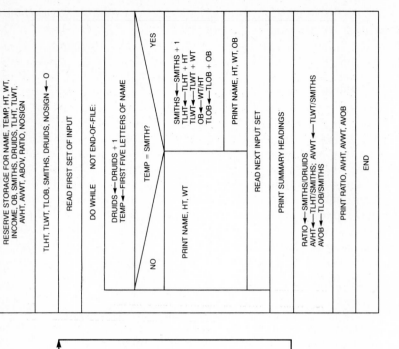

Figure 5.3b

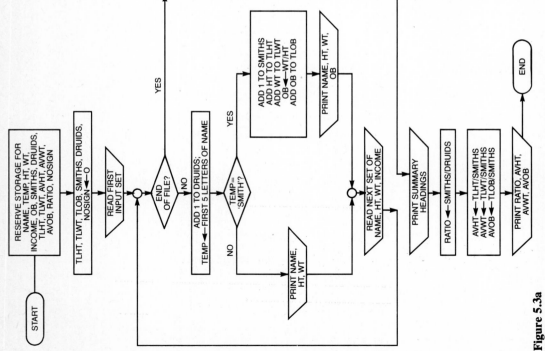

Figure 5.3a

this, we shall exploit PL/I's habit of truncating character string constants that are too long to fit in their assigned variables. Each incoming name will be reproduced in a variable name TEMP with length five, thereby providing us with the first five characters of the name. Consequently, if those characters are SMITH, we can conclude either that the entire name is Smith or that it is some longer name beginning with SMITH. If it is, obesity index will be calculated, and that value, with the height and weight, will be added to their respective totals. This information can then be printed. Notice that all the information on the card must be read in, even though some of it is not required for this procedure. Since there is no direct way to skip information with a **GET LIST** statement, we shall merely store the unwanted information without referring to it subsequently. As an additional feature, we shall accumulate and print the total number of records processed and the percentage of people named Smith. The flowchart is shown in Figure 5.3, a sample output appears in Figure 5.4, and the source statements follow:

```
ILL11: PROCEDURE OPTIONS (MAIN);

/************************************************************/
/*   NAME:    THE VARIABLE CONTAINING THE NAME.            */
/*   TEMP:    STORES THE FIRST 5 CHARACTERS OF THE NAME    */
/*            SO THAT IT CAN BE COMPARED WITH 'SMITH'      */
/*   HT:      HEIGHT;   WT:      WEIGHT                     */
/*   OB:      OBESITY INDEX                                */
/*   INCOME:  THE VARIABLE FOR STORING INCOME              */
/*   TLHT:    TOTAL HEIGHT;    TLWT:    TOTAL WEIGHT        */
/*   TLOB:    TOTAL OF OBESITY INDEX VALUES                */
/*   SMITHS:  TOTAL SMITHS;    DRUIDS:   TOTAL DRUIDS       */
/*   AVHT:    AVERAGE HEIGHT;   AVWT:    AVERAGE WEIGHT     */
/*   AVOB:    AVERAGE OBESITY INDEX                         */
/*   RATIO:   RELATIVE NUMBER OF SMITHS                    */
/************************************************************/
          DECLARE  (NAME,TEMP) CHARACTER(5),
                   HT FIXED(2), WT FIXED(3), INCOME FIXED(5),
                   (TLHT,TLWT,SMITHS,DRUIDS) FIXED(7) INITIAL (0),
                   (OB,TLOB,RATIO,AVHT,AVWT,AVOB) FIXED(8,4),
                   NDSIGN FIXED BINARY INITIAL (0);

          TLOB = 0;
          PUT LIST ('SMITHS AMONG THE DRUIDS');
          PUT SKIP(2) LIST ('NAME','HEIGHT','WEIGHT','OBINDEX');
          PUT SKIP;       ON ENDFILE (SYSIN) NDSIGN = 1;
          GET LIST (NAME,HT,WT,INCOME);

          DO WHILE (NDSIGN = 0);
            TEMP = NAME;
            DRUIDS = DRUIDS+1;
            IF TEMP = 'SMITH'
              THEN DO;
                     TLHT = TLHT+HT;    TLWT = TLWT+WT;    OB = WT/HT;
                     TLOB = TLOB+OB;    SMITHS = SMITHS+1;
                     PUT SKIP LIST (NAME,HT,WT,OB);
                   END;
              ELSE PUT SKIP LIST (NAME,HT,WT);
            GET LIST (NAME,HT,WT,INCOME);
          END;

/*   WE ARE READY TO PRODUCE THE SUMMARY. ALL COMPUTED     */
/*   RESULTS WILL BE ROUNDED TO TWO SECIMAL PLACES.        */

          PUT SKIP (2) LIST ('NO. OF DRUIDS:  ',DRUIDS);
          PUT SKIP LIST ('NO. OF SMITHS:  ',SMITHS);
          RATIO = ROUND(SMITHS/DRUIDS,2);
          PUT SKIP LIST ('RATIO OF SMITHS TO DRUIDS:  ',RATIO);
          AVHT = ROUND(TLHT/SMITHS,2);
          AVWT = ROUND(TLWT/SMITHS,2);
          AVOB = ROUND(TLOB/SMITHS,2);
          PUT SKIP LIST ('AVERAGE HEIGHT FOR SMITHS:  ',AVHT);
          PUT SKIP LIST ('AVERAGE WEIGHT FOR SMITHS:  ',AVWT);
          PUT SKIP LIST ('AVERAGE OBINDEX FOR SMITHS:  ',AVOB);
          STOP;
          END ILL11;
```

```
SMITHS AMONG THE DRUIDS

NAME                        HEIGHT              WEIGHT              OB.INDEX

FEFFEL, J.W.                66                  123
SMITH, K.L.                 71                  187                 2.6338
SMITHFIELD, U.U             70                  197                 2.8142
SMITH, H.P.                 68                  165                 2.4264
FUPNIK, F.D.                63                  108
SMITHSON, J.J.              73                  175                 2.3972
SMITH, F.X.                 70                  165                 2.3571

NO. OF DRUIDS:                     7
NO. OF SMITHS:                     5
RATIO OF SMITHS TO DRUIDS:                     0.7100
AVERAGE HEIGHT FOR SMITHS:                    70.4000
AVERAGE WEIGHT FOR SMITHS:                   177.8000
AVERAGE OB. INDEX FOR SMITHS:                  2.5300
```

Figure 5.4

V.2   ALTERNATE DESCRIPTION OF STRINGS: THE **PICTURE** ATTRIBUTE

If it is known in advance that the content of certain variables will be restricted to particular types of characters, such as numbers only or letters and numbers (*alphameric* characters) only, these variables may be conveniently described by means of the **PICTURE** attribute. This feature provides a set of special codes for representing different types of characters in a string. When a variable is described by this attribute, PL/I expects the contents of that variable at any time to conform to that description and will treat any discrepancies as errors.

V.2.1   Declaration of **PICTURE** Variables

Declaration for the **PICTURE** attribute follows the general form

   DECLARE name **PICTURE** 'codes';

where "name" has its usual meaning and "codes" refers to a series of character codes used to describe the variable. The length of the variable is not explicitly defined, as it is in an ordinary character string declaration. Instead, it is deduced by the compiler from the codes appearing in the **PICTURE** specification. All declared **PICTURE** designations must be enclosed by single quotation marks.

V.2.1.1   Picture Description of Numerical Data

When it is known that a particular variable will always contain numbers, it can be described in a **PICTURE** specification by a series of special codes designating the length of the variable and its order of magnitude. Although a declaration of this type results in the storage of a numerical value that can ultimately be used like any other number (arithmetic can be performed on it), the method of storage is somewhat different than for conventional arithmetic variables, so some type of conversion is necessary prior to its participation in computational expressions. This conversion is automatic, and the programmer need not be directly concerned with it; however, it should be understood that this process takes time and, therefore, should be used only when necessary. Numerical variables declared in this manner also differ from ordinary arithmetic variables with respect to the techniques available for displaying them. In addition to a straightforward printout by means of an ordinary **PUT LIST** or **PUT DATA** statement, a wide variety of editing functions are available to control the appearance of such a variable. Many of these features are unique to **PICTURE** variables; the resulting appearance of the numerical output cannot conveniently be duplicated by combinations of other statements.

The presence of a 9 in a **PICTURE** declaration indicates that a particular position in the variable will always be occupied by a numerical digit. Consequently, the specification for fixed-point decimal variable consists of a string of 9's equal in length to the number of digits to be allocated for this variable. Thus, if we write

DECLARE D **PICTURE** '99999';

PL/I will reserve sufficient storage to accommodate five decimal digits. If decimal places are to be specified, the code letter V is included in the description at that position in the string where a decimal point is *assumed* to be. If we rewrote the above declaration as

DECLARE D **PICTURE** '99V999';

the implication would be that D is a five-digit number, with its three rightmost digits to the right of an imaginary decimal point. Enough information is provided that, when the programmer desires it, conversion to a conventional numerical value can be performed and the proper magnitude will be preserved. For example, if we were to write

DECLARE C **FIXED**(5,3), D **PICTURE** '99V9' **INITIAL**(23.7);

C = D; **PUT LIST** (C,D);

the output generated by the last statement would appear as

23.700   237 → see Table pg. 122 appears OK

If the values of a numeric variable described by a **PICTURE** are expected to be negative, the sign must be explicitly indicated in the specification. This is done by using the letter S either to the left of the first 9 in the declaration or to the right of the last. A description such as

DECLARE C **PICTURE** '999V9';

would store the number −149 as '149' and subsequent conversion to a numeric variable (with attributes, say, **FIXED**(4,1)) would produce 149. To pick up the sign, we would have to say

DECLARE C **PICTURE** 'S999V9';

When it is desired to specify a variable in floating-point form, the **PICTURE** attribute can be used to designate the parts of the numerical string referring to the exponent and the actual number. As in the fixed-point case, a 9 is used to denote the presence of each numeric character and V indicates the location of the *implied* decimal point. In addition, a K is placed at the point in the specification where the letter E would normally go when an ordinary floating-point number is specified. Immediately after the K, the programmer can include an S to indicate that the sign of the exponent is to be explicitly shown. If this S is omitted (which it may be), the program assumes that all exponents will be positive. Following these specifications, of course, are one or more 9's to indicate the portion of the variable that will contain the value of the exponent. Suppose we had the statement

   DECLARE C **PICTURE** '9V99KS99';

and we had placed the value 2.63E+04 in location C. This should appear internally as '263+04'. Conversion to a floating-point number would then produce 2.63E+04.

V.2.1.2   Shorthand Forms for Numerical Picture Declarations

When a **PICTURE** declaration is used to reserve space for numerical variables containing a large number of digits, it is possible to shorten the written specification by using the form

   PICTURE '(m)9';

where (m) is a repetition factor showing how many 9's are meant to be specified. This feature can be used to replace a statement such as

   DECLARE D **PICTURE** '99999999';

with the statement

   DECLARE D **PICTURE** '(8)9';

The same thing can be done to both sides of the implied decimal point, so we can replace

   DECLARE C **PICTURE** '9999999V999999';

with

   DECLARE C **PICTURE** '(7)9V(6)9';

This feature may be used for shortening floating-point picture specifications. There are no provisions for handling binary numbers with pictures. Table 5.5 shows additional examples.

TABLE 5.5 Description of Numerical Strings with the **PICTURE** Attribute*

Description of C	Assigned/Input Value	Value in C†	Description of D	Value in D† After D=C;
'999'	C=193;	193	**FIXED(3)**	193
'999V9'	C=43.8	043(·)8	**FIXED(5,2)**	043(·)80
'999V9'	C=438;	438(·)0	**FIXED(5,2)**	438(·)00
'(7)9'	C=6120	0006120	**FIXED(5,0)**	06120
'(3)9V(4)9'	C=18569	569(·)0000	**FIXED(7,4)**	569(·)0000
'(3)9V(4)9'	C=18.569;	018(·)5690	**FIXED(7,4)**	018(·)5690
'99V9'	C=−26.4;	26(·)4	**FIXED(3,1)**	26(·)4
'S99V9'	C=−26.4;	−26(·)4	**FIXED(3,1)**	−26(·)4
'S99V9'	C=−7.4;	−07(·)4	**FIXED(3,1)**	−07(·)4
'999'	C='72'.	072	**FIXED(3,1)**	72(·)0
'V99K9'	C=.16E2	(·)16+2	**FLOAT(5)**	.16000E+02
'99V99K99'	C=−20.18E+03;	20(·)18+03	**FLOAT(6)**	.201800E+05
'S99V99KS99'	C=−20.18E−03;	−20(·)18−03	**FLOAT(6)**	−0.201800E−01
'99V99'	C='12.7';	12(·)70	**FIXED(4,2)**	12(·)70
'9V999KS99'	C=.3728	3(·)728−01	**FLOAT(5)**	.37280E+00
'9V999KS99'	C='3728'	3(·)728+03	**FLOAT(5)**	.37280E+04

*C is a numerical string; D is a numerical variable.

† (·) denotes the position of the implied decimal point.

V.2.2 Input/Output of Numerical **PICTURE** Variables

Input flexibility for these variables is the same as that obtainable for the other numerical forms. The information provided by the **PICTURE** specification is sufficient to allow PL/I to perform whatever conversions are necessary between the input form of a numerical value and that which conforms to the specifications in the picture. The flexibility includes conversion from character strings to numeric form as long as the input characters are limited to numerical digits, signs, and decimal points. The examples shown in Table 5.5 apply to input values as well as those set by assignment. For instance, a value punched as 43.8, when read into a variable C declared as **PICTURE** '999V9', will be stored as 043.8 and will imply a numerical value of 43.8.

Note, however, that if a value is punched a 6438, the program would assume (reasonably) that we are trying to read 6438 into a variable that will accommodate nothing larger than 999.9. As a result it will take what it can (438) and store it as 438.0. Similarly, as seen by the sixth entry in Table 5.6, an input value of 174 presented to a variable declared as **PICTURE** '9V99' is truncated to 4 and stored as 4.00.

The display of numerical string variables is consistent with their specifications; an instruction to print such a variable produces a literal duplication of the form specified by the declaration. Since the description, as we have seen it so far, designates the location of an implied decimal point, a request to print such a variable will not produce an actual period at the designated spot in the number, even though the value is handled internally with its proper magnitude. Table 5.6 shows how such output would look for various **PICTURE** specifications.

To make such output more readable, additional specifications must be included in the **PICTURE** description. Many codes are available for such editing purposes, some of which will be introduced here to aid in legibility. The inclusion of a period in a numerical **PICTURE** description will cause that point to appear when the value is printed. If we write

> **DECLARE** B **PICTURE** '99V.99';
>   ↑

and location B contains the four digits 2371, a **PUT LIST** statement will produce 23.71. The form '99.V99' is also acceptable. Table 5.6 shows some additional examples.

The use of decimal points in a **PICTURE** declaration is not as straightforward as it would appear. Their presence influences the treatment of input as well as the appearance of output. The eighth entry in Table 5.6 illustrates this. Specification of the period without the V forces the program to stop reading when a decimal point is encountered in an input value. Thus, a value of 1.74 intended for a variable declared as **PICTURE** '9.99' will not be read as 1.74. Instead, it will be stopped at the period, treated as the single character 1 and stored as 001. Then, when it is printed, the program obligingly inserts the period in accordance with the declaration, and the value appears as 0.01. The addition of the V corrects this (as seen in the seventh entry of Table 5.6).

TABLE 5.6 Appearance of Printed Numerical Strings

Description of Numerical String	Appearance of Input Value	Appearance of Output Value
'9999'	2746	2746
'9999'	'815'	0815
'9999'	−32	0032
'S999'	−32	−032
'9V99'	1.74	174
'9V99'	174	400
'9.V99'	1.74	1.74
'9.99'	1.74	0.01
'V9999KS99'	241.5	2415+03
'V9999KS99'	2.415E+2	2415+03
'.V9999KS99'	241.5	.2415+03
'.9999ES99'	241.5	.2415E−01
'S9.9999ES99'	−71628	−7.1628E+04
'S9.(4)9ES99'	−0.00479	−4.7900E−07

When displaying numbers stored as floating-point pictures, no E appears in the printout unless the programmer provides for it. This is done by replacing the K in the **PICTURE** specification with an E. Some examples of this form are seen in Table 5.6.

Here again, however, the programmer must understand the underlying operations in order to use these features effectively. Note the difference between the eleventh and twelfth entries in Table 5.6: With the V included, the 241.5 is converted as expected. Once the V is omitted, the same input value (241.5) is stored as the four numeric characters 2415, and the exponent is set at -01 to compensate for the implied shift in the decimal point. Then, when the value is printed, the program merely inserts a period in the specified position *without any associated adjustment in the exponent.* Accordingly, it appears as .2415E-01. (The presence of the E does not affect this process). This is seen again in the last two entries. The -71628 is stored as -71628E$+00$; its subsequent display includes a period in its specified position. Similarly, the -0.00479 is stripped of high-order zeros and stored as -47900E-07. (Note that at this instant the value is proper: -47900E-07 is indeed equivalent to -0.00479.) Then, the period is inserted as specified and the result appears as -4.7900E-07.

V.2.3 **PICTURE** Descriptions of Nonnumeric Strings

Three symbols are available for specifying strings whose contents are not necessarily limited to numerical digits. The most tolerant of these is X, whose presence in a picture specification indicates that the particular position in the string may contain any character at all. Hence, the two statements

DECLARE D CHARACTER(5);

DECLARE D PICTURE 'XXXXX';

produce the same results: storage is reserved for a character string named D, having length of five positions, any of which could contain any of the characters acceptable by the computer.

A somewhat more restrictive specification can be prescribed for nonnumeric character strings. If it is known that the contents of a string will be restricted to letters of the alphabet or blanks, this may be specified in a PICTURE by means of an A, as in the statement

DECLARE C PICTURE 'AAAAA';

which specifies a string having a length of five characters, none of which could be anything except A-Z or blank.

The third picture character, 9, we have already used for denoting a digit in a numeric string; in this context, however, it denotes either a digit or a blank. It is perfectly acceptable to mix these specifications in a single **PICTURE** description if that level of detail is desired. Of course, it is necessary to use at least one A or X; otherwise we would have a numeric picture. Thus, if we were to write

DECLARE D PICTURE 'AXX99';

we would be describing a character string with a length of five in which the first position will always be one of the 26 letters or blank, the next two positions can be anything at all and the final two will always be numerical digits or blank. The use of symbolic specifications such as V, K, or S is not allowed in such nonnumeric strings. When a string is described in this way, the implied restrictions are checked every time an attempt is made to change the value of that string. Whenever there is an inconsistency (such as trying to read a digit into the first position of the string declared in the preceding statement), the transaction will not be allowed and the processing will be interrupted. Additional examples of this usage are shown in Table 5.7.

TABLE 5.7 Properties of Nonnumeric Picture Specifications

Description of String	Specified Value	Stored/Printed Value
'99X99'	'12.16'	12.16
'99X99'	'24W68'	24W68
'99XX9'	'24W873'	24W87
'99A99'	'12.16'	-illegal-
'XXXX'	'1.8J'	1.8J
'AAAA'	'W.WW'	-illegal-
'AAA9'	'BAW32'	BAW3
'999'	'80732'	732
'XXX'	'80732'	807

Illustration 11A

To summarize the properties of picture variables, we shall use them in the processing described in Illustration 11. The affected part of the listing, which produces the output shown in Figure 5.5a, operates on the same type of input as before, and is as follows:

```
SMITHS AMONG THE DRUIDS

NAME                    HEIGHT              WEIGHT              OB.INDEX

FEFFEL, J.W.            66                  123
SMITH, K.L.            71                  187                 +0002.6338
SMITHFIELD, U.U        70                  197                 +0002.8142
SMITH, H.P.            68                  165                 +0002.4264
FUPNIK, F.D.           63                  108
SMITHSON, J.J.         73                  175                 +0002.3972
SMITH, F.X.            70                  165                 +0002.3571

NO. OF DRUIDS:          0C00007
NC. OF SMITHS:          0000005
RATIO OF SMITHS TO DRUIDS:                 +0000.7100
AVERAGE HEIGHT FOR SMITHS:                 +0070.4000
AVERAGE WEIGHT FOR SMITHS:                 +0177.8000
AVERAGE OB. INDEX FOR SMITHS:              +0002.5300
```

Figure 5.5a

```
ILL11A: PROCEDURE OPTIONS (MAIN);

       DECLARE NAME PICTURE '(15)X',  TEMP PICTURE '(5)X',
               HT PICTURE '99', WT PICTURE '999',
               INCOME PICTURE '(5)9',
               (TLHT,TLWT,SMITHS,DRUIDS) PICTURE '(7)9' INITIAL (0),
               (OB,TLOB,RATIO,AVHT,AVWT,AVOB) PICTURE 'S(4)9.V(4)9',
               NDSIGN PICTURE '9' INITIAL (0);

       TLOB = 0;
       PUT SKIP LIST ('SMITHS AMONG THE DRUIDS');
       PUT SKIP(2) LIST ('NAME','HEIGHT','WEIGHT','OBINDEX');
       PUT SKIP;     ON ENDFILE (SYSIN) NDSIGN = 1;
       GET LIST (NAME,HT,WT,INCOME);

       DO WHILE (NDSIGN = 0);
         TEMP = NAME;      DRUIDS = DRUIDS+1;
         IF TEMP = 'SMITH'
           THEN DO;
                   TLHT = TLHT+HT;    TLWT = TLWT+WT;
                   OB = WT/HT;   TLOB = TLOB+OB;   SMITHS = SMITHS+1;
                   PUT SKIP LIST (NAME,HT,WT,OB);
                 END;
           ELSE PUT SKIP LIST (NAME,HT,WT);
       END;

       PUT SKIP(2) LIST ('NO. OF DRUIDS:  ',DRUIDS);
       PUT SKIP LIST ('NO. OF SMITHS:  ',SMITHS);
       RATIO = ROUND(SMITHS/DRUIDS,2);
       PUT SKIP LIST ('RATIO OF SMITHS TO DRUIDS:  ',RATIO);
       AVHT = ROUND(TLHT/SMITHS,2);   AVWT = ROUND(TLWT/SMITHS,2);
       AVOB = ROUND(TLOB/SMITHS,2);
       PUT SKIP LIST ('AVERAGE HEIGHT FOR SMITHS:',AVHT);
       PUT SKIP LIST ('AVERAGE WEIGHT FOR SMITHS:',AVWT);
       PUT SKIP LIST ('AVERAGE OB. INDEX FOR SMITHS:',AVOB);
       STOP;
       END ILL11A;
```

Note that the picture declarations for OB, TLOB, RATIO, and so on must include the V as well as the physical decimal point. If we had omitted the V (using the specification 'S(4)9. (4)9'), PL/I would not have sufficient information to scale properly, and thus the output would appear as in Figure 5.5b.

```
SMITHS AMONG THE DRUIDS

NAME                   HEIGHT               WEIGHT              OB.INDEX

FEFFEL, J.W.           66                   123
SMITH, K.L.            71                   187                 +0000.0002
SMITHFIELD, U.U        70                   197                 +0000.0002
SMITH, H.P.            68                   165                 +0000.0002
FUPNIK, F.D.           63                   108
SMITHSON, J.J.         73                   175                 +0000.0002
SMITH, F.X.            70                   165                 +0000.0002

NO. OF DRUIDS:         0000007
NO. OF SMITHS:         0000005
RATIO OF SMITHS TO DRUIDS:               +0000.0000
AVERAGE HEIGHT FOR SMITHS:               +0000.0070
AVERAGE WEIGHT FOR SMITHS:               +0000.0177
AVERAGE OB. INDEX FOR SMITHS:            +0000.0002
```

Figure 5.5b

V.2.4   Other Descriptive Facilities

Additional conveniences are available through the **PICTURE** specification. Since they are not used as commonly as the other features, they are included primarily for completeness, and are discussed separately in this section.

V.2.4.1   Specification of Scale Factors

When declaring fixed-point variables by means of the **PICTURE** specification, it is possible to include a scale factor. The general form is

PICTURE 'codesF(n)';

where (n) is a signed or unsigned decimal constant.

This scale factor indicates that the number described by the picture has an assumed decimal point whose position is n digits to the right of where it would be otherwise. If we had a five-digit string of numbers (say, 21468), which we were to place in some location B described by

DECLARE B PICTURE '999V99';

it would be treated as if its value were 214.68. If our description were to be changed to read

DECLARE B PICTURE '999V99F(2)';

the same five digits would have an implied value of 21468. The primary use of picture scale factors is to avoid storing high- or low-order zeros. Thus, an intended value of 765000, when assigned to a numeric string declared as '999F (3)', will be stored as 765, but its use in computations will be with its proper magnitude. Table 5.8 shows some additional examples.

TABLE 5.8   Use of Scale Factor in
Picture Specifications

Description	Specified Value	Stored Form
'S99F(2)'	−6100	−61
'9999V9F(4)'	27198000	27198
'(5)9V(3)9F(3)'	675820000	00675820
'99V999F(7)'	675820000	67582
'999F(−6)'	.000791	791
'9V99F(−4)'	.000791	791

V.2.4.2   Suppression of High Order Zeros

The character Z can be used in place of 9 to indicate a position that can contain a digit, with the additional provision that, if the digit is a leading (nonsignificant) zero, it will be stored as a blank. For instance, the sequence

DECLARE T PICTURE 'ZZZ9V.99';

T = 12.87; **PUT LIST** (T);

will cause ƀƀ12.87 to be printed and will also be stored internally in the same form.

V.2.4.3   Pictures for Complex Data

The description of complex variables requires no additional codes in the **PICTURE** specification. Instead, the declaration is augmented by including the **COMPLEX** attribute. The statement

DECLARE E COMPLEX PICTURE '999V9';

will allocate storage for both the real and imaginary components of the complex variable E. Since there is no change required in the **PICTURE** attribute itself, all of the codes described for real numerical variables are available for complex variables as well. For example,

DECLARE Z COMPLEX PICTURE 'S9V999KS99';

describes a complex variable Z. If we say

Z = −6.3 + 24.88I;

the internal form would be '−6300+00+2488+01'.

PROBLEMS

1.   Write the following as PL/I character string constants:

   a.   #24J47

   b.   NO, I'M NOT ARMSTRONG-JONES!

   c.   'TWAS BRILLIG

   d.   IT'S TOO LATE; I WON'T GO.

e.   "I HEARD HER CRY 'HELP'," HE EXCLAIMED.
(note that " is a single character that is different from '.)

2.   Three character strings are punched as shown below:

            'IMPORTANCE' 'TIME' 'MUSIC'

Indicate what the output would look like in the following sequences:

  a.   **DECLARE A CHARACTER**(8), **B CHARACTER**(4), **C CHARACTER**(5);
      GET LIST(A,C,B); **PUT LIST**(A,B,C);

  b.   **DECLARE** (A,B) **CHARACTER**(8), **C CHARACTER**(4);
      GET LIST(A,C,B); **PUT LIST**(C,B,A);

  c.   **DECLARE** (A,B,C) **CHARACTER**(10);
      GET LIST(C,A,B); **PUT LIST**(A,B,C);

  d.   **DECLARE** (A,B,C) **CHARACTER**(8);
      GET LIST(C,B,A); C = A; B = A; **PUT LIST**(A,C,B);

  e.   **DECLARE** (A,B,C) **CHARACTER**(6)**VARYING**;
      GET LIST(A,B,C); B = C; A = B; **PUT LIST**(A,B,C);

  f.   **DECLARE** (A,B,C) **CHARACTER**(10)**VARYING**;
      GET LIST(A,C,B); C = A; **PUT LIST**(A,B,C);

3.   Show the contents of location D as a result of the statements given below. Use the following values: A = 'IS'; B = 'NEVER'; C = '32.2';

  a.   **DECLARE D CHARACTER**(22); D = 'W'||A||C||.'||B||'44!';

  b.   **DECLARE D CHARACTER**(20); D = C||A||''||B||'33. '||B;

  c.   **DECLARE D CHARACTER**(14); D = C||'C'||(2)B||'B'||(2)'A';

  d.   **DECLARE D CHARACTER**(30)**VARYING**; D = B||'WRITE'||(3)C;

  e.   **DECLARE D CHARACTER**(15)**VARYING**; D = (3)'B'||B||...'||C||'C';

4.   Show the results of each output statement given below, using the following values:

      DECLARE ACHARACTER(4), **B CHARACTER**(5), **C CHARACTER**(6),
              D CHARACTER (8) **VARYING**;
              A = 'FLAG'; B = 'STAGE'; C = 'POWDER';

    a.   **DECLARE E CHARACTER**(10)**VARYING**; **D** = 'OFFER';
        E=D||A||'A'; N=**LENGTH**(E); **PUT LIST**(E,N);

    b.   **DECLARE E CHARACTER**(22)**VARYING**; D='TREBLE';
        E=A||B||D; N=2*(**LENGTH**(B)+1); **PUT LIST**(E,N);

   c. **DECLARE E CHARACTER(25)VARYING; D='SET';**
       E=B||C||(2)D; D=E;
       M=LENGTH(D); N=40−LENGTH(E); PUT LIST(N,M,D,E);

   d. (A little tricky, but you can do it!)
       DECLARE E CHARACTER(30)VARYING; D='AFAR';
       E=D||A||B; D=E; E=E||D; N=3*(LENGTH(D)+LENGTH(E));
       PUT LIST(D,E,N);

5. A punched card contains three pieces of data, A, B, and C:

$$1237 \quad 31.48 \quad \text{'TRIUMPH'}$$

Show the results of the statement **PUT LIST(A,B,C);** for the following declarations

   a. **DECLARE A PICTURE'(4)9', B PICTURE '999V9', C PICTURE '(8)A';**

   b. **DECLARE A PICTURE '(5)X', B PICTURE '9999V.ES99';**
       C PICTURE '(9)X';

   c. **DECLARE (A,B) PICTURE '9999.999', C PICTURE '(4)X(3)A';**

6. An insurance firm has instituted an incentive program in which the person with the highest sales of the month is singled out for special commendation and a cash award. The computer is used to select the monthly winner by going through the monthly sales summary cards. These cards contain the following information in this order: (a) salesman's name (25 characters); (b) month (2 digits); (c) year (2 digits); (d) total sales in dollars (6 digits); and (e) number of previous monthly awards (2 digits). Because of the processing requirements, all of the cards for all months must be kept together. The size of the award is $100 if it is the saleman's first award (big sports), $250 if it is his second, $400 if he has had two previous awards, and so on. Write a program that will identify the deserving salesman for a given month (specified as input). Determine the size of his award and print a message illustrated by the following:

     Salesman of the month for 3/67 is A. V. Jenkins, with sales of 362,471 dollars.

     His award is 550 dollars.

7. Write a program that reads an unknown number of input cards, with each card containing four words. No word is longer than ten letters. The program is to print each set of words in alphabetical order (rearranged if necessary) on a separate line. After the last card has been processed, the program is to print the number of cards processed and the number of cards on which the words already were in alphabetical order and needed no rearranging.

8. Using the same input as in the previous problem, write a program that prints each set of words on a line in order by length (longest word first), followed by the average length for each set of words. For example, a card containing the strings

     'ANY' 'THROUGH' 'BELTS' 'BE'

would produce the following line:

THROUGH BELTS ANY BE 4.25

After all the cards have been processed, the program is to print the number of cards processed and the average word length. (Compute the overall average by averaging the individual word lengths rather than by averaging the card averages.)

9. Using the same input as described in Problem 7, write a program that performs the following processing: For each card, a line is printed showing those words beginning with S or W, followed by a string in which the eligible words are concatenated. No rearranging is necessary. That is, the words may be printed and concatenated in the order in which they appear. After all cards have been processed, the program is to print the number of cards processed and the number of cards eligible for concatenation.

10. A set of input cards are available with each card containing three words ranging in length from three to ten letters. Write a program that processes each card by interchanging the first two letters of the longest and shortest words on that card. When such an interchange is made, the program is to print a line containing the original three words in order of increasing length, followed by the two new "words," longer one first. If at least two of the words on a card are of equal length, no processing is to be performed and the three words are merely printed "as received." After the final card has been processed, the program is to print the number of cards processed and the number of interchanges.

SUMMARY OF IMPORTANT TERMS

Alphabetic characters	(In PL/I) A set of characters consisting of the letters A-Z and the additional three characters #. $, and @.
Alphameric characters	(In PL/I) A set of characters consisting of the alphabetic characters and the decimal digits 0-9.
CHARACTER attribute	The attribute assigned explicitly to all declared character string variables. This cannot be implied.
Character constant	A string of characters used directly as an expression or a term in an expression. To distinguish this value from a string of characters that represent the name of a variable in which a character string is stored, the constant is indicated by placing a single quote mark at its beginning and end.
Concatenation	A character string operator, denoted by ‖, that is used to join two character strings to form a larger one.
Length	A built-in function that provides the current length of a character string declared with the **VARYING** attribute.
Literal	In this context, synonymous with a constant: a term that represents its own value and not a symbolic reference to a value.
Numerical characters	In PL/I, the set of characters consisting of the decimal digits 0-9.

PICTURE attribute

An alternate method for describing the composition of declared character string variables. Use of this specification allows the restriction of selected characters in such variables to members of the alphabetic or numerical sets.

POSITION option

A specification that allows the declaration of a character string variable derived by overlaying a specified part of another character string.

PUT LIST

An output statement that produces a display of specified values (with no accompanying identification) whose format is controlled by default.

VARYING attribute

A specification that may be added to a character string declaration to indicate that the apparent length of that string may change from time to time, up to designated maximum.

SUPPLEMENTARY READING

IBM OS PL/I Checkout and Optimizing Compilers: Language Reference Manual, IBM Publication SC33-0009. White Plains, N.Y.: IBM Corporation, 1971, pp. 29-30, 47, 296-304.

IBM System/360 PL/I Reference Manual, IBM Publication C28-8201. White Plains, N.Y.: IBM Corporation, 1968, pp. 32-34, 205-214.

VI ARRAYS

Our consideration of variables and their names has included a wide variety of attributes, but has been limited by the restriction that the designation of a variable name resulted in its association with a unique location in storage that would always contain either a single numerical value or a particular string of characters.

In many instances it would be a great convenience to be able to assign one name to a group of locations, each of which contains a separate variable whose value can change at any time. There are frequent occasions when a variable can consist of many subclasses, so it is advantageous to be able to refer to any one of these as a member of some larger collection. For instance, we may want to base certain calculations on the ages, weights, and heights of the members of the population. It would be almost impossible to give a name to each subject's age and declare it separately. Instead, we would want to refer to a variable called AGE and assign different locations to the ages of different people, with any of these ages always being available. Similarly, we may want to treat pay rates, temperatures, prices, or any other collection of measurements in a like manner.

The ability to handle data in this fashion often facilitates the development of algorithms, since it may allow them to be organized in a manner more consistent with the nature of the problem to be solved. The resulting programs are usually easier to write and produce more efficient processing.

VI.1 BASIC ORGANIZATIONAL PROPERTIES

When a group of values represents similar measurements, readings, or observations, such values can be organized into a collection called an *array*. Arrays are a very versatile method of organization. The programmer can refer to the array by a single name, thereby allowing the entire collection to be treated as an entity. This gives him a capability of using single statements to specify operations that will be performed on all of the array's members. If the programmer is working with a set of temperature readings for which he has chosen the collective name TEMP, he can write simple statements involving that name and the operations implied by such commands will be performed in sequence on each member of the array. Yet the programmer still retains the ability to manipulate each temperature independently. PL/I includes provisions for identifying subgroups of an array and specifying operations to be performed on them.

VI.1.1 Dimensionality of Arrays

Complete independence of each member of an array is assured by establishing organizational indicators that endow each element with a unique identity. Since the value for each element can vary independently, it cannot serve as a primary criterion for identification. Instead, uniqueness is achieved by categorizing an array into organizational subgroups and locating each element with regard to its placement in these groups. The simplest level of organization breaks an array down into one set of subgroups, with each division containing a single element; more intricate constructions use several such categorizations, with each element belonging to a unique combination of subgroups.

The number of different categorizations thus constitutes an index to the array's degree of complexity. This indicator is known as the *dimensionality* of the array. From the programmer's point of view, the dimensionality represents the number of criteria that must be specified in order to identify a member of the array uniquely.

The naming of array elements reflects this approach. Each member's name is constructed by supplementing the array's collective name with a *subscript* in which each of the appropriate criteria is denoted. For example, if C is the name of an array of 12 elements, in which only one criterion is used to differentiate among them, C is said to be a *one-dimensional* array, in which the first element is known as C(1) and the seventh element is uniquely referred to as C(7). Similarly, if an array E is organized into two types of subgroups, these types are called *rows* and *columns*, and the array is said to be *two-dimensional*. Accordingly, each element's subscript consists of two parts: a row number and column number, so that element E(4,2) designates that element belonging to row 4 and column 2. We shall explore these organizational properties in the sections that follow.

VI.1.2   One-Dimensional Arrays

The simplest type of array is a collection of data in which a single indicator immediately pinpoints any particular member. As an example, consider the array PRICES shown in Table 6.1, which represents prices per square yard for various hypothetical construction materials. It is readily apparent that if we know the type of material we can immediately identify its price by where it is placed in the list and distinguish it from all other prices in the array. Thus, the third member of PRICES is simply identified as PRICES(3).

TABLE 6.1   Organization of a
One-Dimensional Array
Named PRICES

Type	Name	Value
1	PRICES(1)	1.25
2	PRICES(2)	1.15
3	PRICES(3)	1.62
4	PRICES(4)	1.25
5	PRICES(5)	1.50

VI.1.3   Two-Dimensional Arrays

A two-dimensional array requires the specification of two properties or characteristics to pinpoint one of its members uniquely. Such an aggregate is shown in Table 6.2. Each member of this array still represents a price per square yard for some hypothetical building material. To find a particular price this time, two things must be known: the type of material and the quantity to be purchased. Consequently, the array is organized to reflect these dimensions. All prices referring to materials of the same type are listed together horizontally in the same *row*. At the same time, all prices referring to a particular quantity of purchase are listed vertically in the same *column*. It is then possible to refer to any particular price by identifying the row and column to which it belongs. Thus, the price located in the second row, third column, is $1.11.

Since the array COSTS consists of 5 rows and 4 columns, its 20 elements are said to be organized as a 5 × 4 array. The subscript assigned to members of two-dimensional arrays consists of the row and column number, in that order, enclosed by parentheses. Referring to Table 6.2, the value of $1.11, which we saw was located in the second row and third column, can be identified by the reference COSTS(2,3). Similarly, the value in COSTS(3,2) is $1.56.

TABLE 6.2 Organization of a Two-Dimensional
Array Named COSTS 5 rows(types)
× 4 columns (purchased quantities)

Type	Number of Square Yards Purchased			
	1-50	51-100	101-500	Over 500
1	1.25	1.21	1.16	1.12
2	1.15	1.13	1.11	1.09
3	1.62	1.56	1.51	1.47
4	1.25	1.24	1.23	1.22
5	1.47	1.44	1.40	1.35

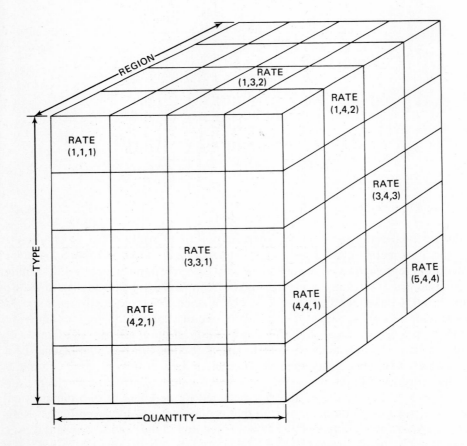

Figure 6.1

VI.1.4 Higher-Dimensional Arrays

There are many situations in which more than two criteria are required to provide unique identification for an element in an array. For example, the price schedule for the building materials may depend not only on the type and the amount purchased but also on the geographic region where delivery is to be made. Accordingly, we can construct an array called RATE, having three dimensions, each of which we must specify to locate a particular member. Its organization must now arrange prices not only according to type and quantity but also region. This is shown diagrammatically in Figure 6.1.

With the addition of a third dimension, *each type must now be represented as a table of purchase quantities and regions* (rows and columns). One convenient method for arranging the data of a three-dimensional array is depicted in Table 6.3. Reference to a particular member

TABLE 6.3 Organization of a 5 × 4 × 4 Array Named
RATE by Type (rows), Amount of
Purchase (columns), and region (blocks)

Type	Quantity	Region 1	2	3	4
	1-50	1.25	1.27	1.28	1.31
	51-100	1.21	1.23	1.25	1.26
1	101-500	1.16	1.16	1.17	1.17
	500	1.12	1.14	1.15	1.16
	1-50	1.15	1.18	1.20	1.21
	51-100	1.13	1.17	1.19	1.20
2	101-500	1.11	1.13	1.14	1.16
	500	1.09	1.12	1.13	1.14
	1-50	1.62	1.64	1.65	1.67
	51-100	1.56	1.58	1.62	1.65
3	101-500	1.51	1.55	1.58	1.62
	500	1.47	1.51	1.53	1.55
	1-50	1.25	1.27	1.29	1.30
	51-100	1.24	1.25	1.27	1.29
4	101-500	1.23	1.24	1.25	1.26
	500	1.22	1.23	1.24	1.25
	1-50	1.50	1.51	1.53	1.54
	51-100	1.47	1.48	1.50	1.51
5	101-500	1.44	1.45	1.47	1.49
	500	1.40	1.42	1.44	1.46

of a three-dimensional array is completely consistent with the general rules for subscripting: each subscript now consists of the type, quantity, and region numbers, in that order. Hence, the value in RATE(2,3,4) is $1.16.

The dimensionality of arrays can certainly extend well beyond three. Treatment of higher-dimension arrays is exactly analogous to that described for the simpler organizations. The limits on dimensionality prescribed by PL/I are well beyond those imposed by our ability to keep track of them. The amount of data required to fill multidimensional arrays and the capacity of even the largest processors to accommodate them constitute a practical restriction on the number of useful dimensions; for example, a three-dimensional array with dimensions 10 x 10 x 5 (not at all unusual in a real situation) contains 500 individual elements. The addition of a fourth dimension with six categories immediately jumps the number of elements to 3000. A ten-dimensional array of six subcategories per dimension would require 3,477,846 items of data to fill it.

Note that the organization of data into such arrays does not necessarily imply that each member of an array must contain a meaningful value. For example, it may very well be that a particular type of material in the array called RATE cannot be made available to one of the regions regardless of price (there may be a local law preventing its distribution). An entire row of values from that region would thus be eliminated. If such vacancies represent a relatively small number of elements in the total array, it is still convenient to organize the data as a full array. Nonexistent values can be handled in a variety of ways, depending on the individual situation. For most cases it is appropriate to use zeros or blanks for them.

VI.2   DECLARATION OF ARRAYS

Reservation of storage for arrays is handled as part of PL/I's general declaration mechanism. To indicate that a single name is to refer to an entire collection of values, its declaration must be accompanied by sufficient information for PL/I to determine the size and dimensionality of the array. These specifications are given in the form of a parenthesized list placed immediately after the array name:

DECLARE array (m,n,etc.) atttributes;

Each of the values (m, n, etc.) within the parentheses gives the size for that particular dimension of the array. The statement

DECLARE X(10,20) **FIXED DECIMAL**(5,2);

will cause PL/I to reserve 200 positions in storage for the accommodation of an array X consisting of 10 rows and 20 columns. Each element of this array will be stored as a fixed decimal value having five digits, two of which will be to the right of the assumed decimal point. The same number of locations would be reserved by the statement

DECLARE Y(200) **FIXED DECIMAL**(5,2);

but the collection would be treated as a simple list of 200 values, rather than ten subgroups containing 20 values each. Once an array has been declared in this manner, consistency must be maintained whenever referring to an element in that array. The specification Y(2,5) would be meaningless in terms of the declaration made above and would produce an error message.

VI.2.1   Assignment of Attributes to Arrays

When storage is allocated for an array, any legitimate combination of attributes may be assigned to it by exactly the same mechanism used for single-valued variables. Arrays may be mixed with such variables in the same declaration, and such statements may include factoring. The form

Factoring

DECLARE(A,X(10),B,Y(3,8)) **FIXED DECIMAL** (6,3);

is perfectly legitimate and will result in the allocation of a storage position for each of the single-valued variables A and B, reservation of ten locations for the one-dimensional array X, and 24 locations for the two-dimensional array Y. Values to be stored in any of these locations will be handled as fixed decimal numbers with precision (6,3).

If two or more arrays have the same dimension, the dimension attribute may be factored; however, it must always precede all other attributes. For example,

DECLARE ((A,B)(10),C) **FIXED DECIMAL** (8,2);

is legal, whereas

DECLARE ((A,B) **FLOAT**(7), C **FIXED**(5,2))(5,4,3) **BINARY**;

is not, because, when expanded, the factored dimension attribute does not appear first.

The declaration of such arrays is by no means limited to numerical values. We may declare arrays of character strings, values with the **PICTURE** attribute, or any other type of variable that PL/I recognizes. The only limitation is that all of the members of a particular array must have identical attributes. Thus, the single statement

DECLARE (A,J(11)**BINARY**) **FIXED**(6,2),Y,X(4,6) **FIXED**(6,3),

  B(8) **CHARACTER**(10),D(6,5,2);

will produce the following allocations:

- A single-valued fixed-point decimal variable A with precision (6,2).

- An 11-element fixed binary array J, with each member having a precision of (6,2).

- A single-valued floating-point decimal variable Y with default precision.

- A two-dimensional fixed decimal array X consisting of four rows and six columns, with each element being stored with precision (6,3).

- A one-dimensional array, B, consisting of eight character strings, each ten characters long.

- A three-dimensional array, D, with dimensionality 6 x 5 x 2, giving 60 elements in all. Each value is to be stored as a floating-point decimal number with default precision.

VI.2.2   Internal Organization of Arrays

The fact that we can "find" any element in an array by citing the proper subscripts implies the use of a consistent organizational scheme that governs the internal sequencing of array elements. Familiarity with this arrangement will allow the programmer to exploit a number of the facilities for handling arrays and parts of arrays.

PL/I assigns consecutive locations in storage to elements of an array such that the last (rightmost) subscript varies most rapidly. This sequence is referred to as *row major order*. When dealing with a two-dimensional array, this means that the sequence starts with the first row, element by element, followed by the second row, and so on. Thus, if X is a 3 x 2 array, its six elements will be stored in the following sequence:

$$X(1,1) \; X(1,2) \; X(2,1) \; X(2,2) \; X(3,1) \; X(3,2)$$

Accordingly, element X(3,1) is the fifth sequential element in a 3 x 2 array. Based on this organizational rule, we can state a more general formula for locating the position of an element in any two-dimensional array: if v is a two-dimensional array having m rows and n columns, and v(i,j) is an element in that array belonging to row i and column j, the p_{ij}, the position of that element, can be computed as follows:

$$p_{ij} = n(i\text{-}1) + j$$

Thus, if W is an 8 x 12 array, then the position of the element W(7,5) is 12(7 − 1) + 5 or 77 in the array.

Three-dimensional arrays follow an extension of the same rule. For example, a 2 x 3 x 2 array, W, is shown below:

$$W(1,1,1), \; W(1,1,2), \; W(1,2,1), \; W(1,2,2), \; W(1,3,1), \; W(1,3,2),$$

$$W(2,1,1), \; W(2,1,2), \; W(2,2,1), \; W(2,2,2), \; W(2,3,1), \; W(2,3,2)$$

We see that $W(1,3,2)$ is the sixth element in the sequence and $W(2,3,1)$ is the eleventh. The positional formula for three-dimensional arrays can be stated as an extension of the previous one. If n is dimensioned as c x d x e and $v(i,j,k)$ indicates an element in the array, then

$$p_{ijk} = de(i-1) + e(j-1) + k$$

For example, if array R is 5 x 4 x 6, then element $R(3,3,4)$ would occupy a position 4 x 6(3 − 1) + 6(3 − 1) + 4, or 64th in the sequence of 120 elements.

VI.2.3   Initialization of Arrays

The **INITIAL** attribute can be used to assign starting values to some or all members of an array by including it in the **DECLARE** statement. In its simplest form, it will cause the same value to be assigned to each member of an array. To do this, the **INITIAL** specification must be accompanied by a *repetition factor* that indicates the number of elements to receive the designated initial value. That is, the statement

DECLARE X(12) **FIXED**(6,3) **INITIAL**((12)6);

will reserve 12 positions of storage for an array called X and a value of 006.000 will be placed in each of these 12 positions. Note that the repetition factor must appear. If we were to say simply

DECLARE X(12) **FIXED**(6,3) **INITIAL**(6);

PL/I would not find anything wrong with such a declaration. However, only the first of X's 12 elements would receive the indicated value; the others would have undetermined values, leading to possible trouble later on.

It is possible to initialize arrays so that all of the members do not necessarily contain the same value. This is done by listing the desired value for each element in the array as part of the **INITIAL** specification. Referring again to the one-dimensional array X, suppose that we wished to initialize the first five of its elements to 8.4 and the remaining seven to −6. The appropriate declaration would read

DECLARE X(12) **FIXED**(6,3) **INITIAL**((5) 8.4,(7) −6);

Repetition factors can be combined with individual specifications to produce any desired type of initialization. For example, the statement

DECLARE Y(2,4) **FIXED DECIMAL**(6) **INITIAL**(3,(3)5,(2)18,−9,24);

will fill Y with the values shown below:

	1	*2*	*3*	*4*
1	000003	000005	000005	000005
2	000018	000018	−000009	000024

The repetition factor can be extended for use in repeated sequences of initial values. Writing the statement

DECLARE Z(8) **FIXED**(5,2) **INITIAL**((2)(0,(2)3,1));

will fill array Z with the values as shown below:

000.00	003.00	003.00	001.00
000.00	003.00	003.00	001.00

Similarly, the statement

DECLARE IDENT (5,5) **FIXED** (5,2) **INITIAL** ((5)(1,(5)0));

would produce the following 5 x 5 "identity" matrix:

	1	*2*	*3*	*4*	*5*
1	1	0	0	0	0
2	0	1	0	0	0
3	0	0	1	0	0
4	0	0	0	1	0
5	0	0	0	0	1

If more constants are specified in the **INITIAL** designation than there are elements in the array, PL/I will use as many as it needs, starting from the leftmost value. If the opposite is true, PL/I will use all the values it is given, leaving the rest of the array uninitialized.

Initialization works just as well for nonnumeric arrays. If we were to write

DECLARE GAGGLE(76) **CHARACTER**(6) **INITIAL** ((76)(1)'EXPERT');

we would create as formidable an array of experts as anyone could want. The (1) is necessary to prevent PL/I from erroneously interpreting the (76) as a string repetition factor. If we were to write simply (76) 'EXPERT', this would indicate to PL/I that GAGGLE(1) was to be initialized to the value 'EXPERTEXPERT...EXPERT' (repeated 76 times) and GAG-GLE(2) through GAGGLE(76) were to be left uninitialized. Since GAGGLE(1) is only six characters long 75 of the experts would simply disappear.

VI.2.4   Special Subscripts

When we make a declaration such as

DECLARE X(2,5) **FIXED**(5,2);

the combination of explicit and default attributes will cause ten positions in storage to be allocated to the name X. These will be handled in two groups (rows) of five elements each. The contents of each element will be treated as a real fixed decimal quantity having precision (5,2). There is an additional implication: the specification of the number of rows and columns immediately limits the range of subscripts. In this particular case, the row number must be either 1 or 2. Similarly, the column subscript cannot be anything but 1, 2, 3, 4, or 5. Although this is usually adequate, there are occasions when it is more convenient to shift the range of assigned subscripts in an array. PL/I permits great flexibility in such assignments by means of the following declarative form:

DECLARE array (m1:m2,n1:n2, etc.) attributes;

The designations m1:m2 represent the respective bounds for the first subscript, n1:n2 provides similar information for the second dimension, and so on. If we were to state

DECLARE Y(12:20) **FIXED DECIMAL**(7,1);

the result would be the allocation of nine locations for elements of the fixed decimal array X. A reference to X(12) would cause the first of these locations to be accessed, X(14) would refer to the third of these locations, and so on. Under these circumstances, a designation such as X(1) would be outside the stipulated range of subscripts, resulting in an operational error. Note that PL/I calculates the total number of required positions from the specified bounds.

The subscript range can be shifted in any direction to suit the programmer's convenience. This includes the use of negative numbers and zero. For example, the statement

DECLARE W (6, −12:12);

sets up storage for an array of 150 floating-point decimal numbers with default precision. That is, there are six rows (numbered 1 through 6) and 25 columns numbered −12, −11, −10, ..., −1, 0, 1, 2, ..., 11, 12.

VI.3   INTERNAL HANDLING OF ARRAYS

One of PL/I's most powerful facilities allows the programmer to specify internal operations for entire arrays by means of single statements. Extension of these basic capabilities provides total control over the selection of portions of arrays.

VI.3.1   Operations on an Entire Array

If X is an appropriately declared array, we can specify the performance of arithmetic operations on the entire array by including X, without subscripts, in an assignment statement. As a very simple example, we can write

   $X = 2*X**2 + 1;$

thereby replacing each member of array X with one more than twice the square of its previous value. Single-valued variables may also be involved. For instance, if X is declared as 5 x 4 array and A and B are single-valued numerical variables, then the statement

   $X = 2*A*X + 3*B;$

is exactly equivalent to a series of 20 statements for the individual elements:

   $X(1) = 2*A*X(1) + 3*B;$
   $X(2) = 2*A*X(2) + 3*B;$

.
.
.

.

   $X(20) = 2*A*X(20) + 3*B;$

(This assumes, of course, that X, A, and B had values placed in them prior to their use here).

   Assignment statements such as the one above can also include individual members of arrays, but the programmer must be fully aware of the sequence of events. Suppose that Y(1) is the first member of an array of eight values and its current value is 7. A programmer writing the statement

   $Y = Y + Y(1);$

and expecting each member of Y to be increased by 7 is in for a surprise. We can reconstruct what happens by assigning hypothetical values to each member of Y and going through the operations.

| 7 | 6 | 11 | 22 | 17 | 7 | 4 | 18 |

The program will perform the indicated operations starting with the first element. Accordingly, the value of Y(1) will be increased by 7, yielding a value of 14. The addition now will be repeated for each subsequent element in the array. Note, however, that the *current* value of Y(1) will be used as the cycle of operations is repeated so that elements Y(2) through Y(8) will each be increased by 14 rather than 7. Consequently, the results of the statement are as shown below:

| 14 | 20 | 25 | 36 | 31 | 21 | 18 | 32 |

By the same token, the statement

    Y = Y/Y(1);

will replace the value of Y(1) with a 1. As a result, all the other elements will be divided by 1, thereby causing no change in their values. In order to get around this, the programmer must provide an extra statement so that the sequence could read something like this:

    Z = Y(1);   Y = Y/Z;

VI.3.2.   Operations Involving More Than One Array

PL/I allows the programmer to write the statements such as

    A = 2*B;

where A and B are both arrays that have been declared with the same number of dimensions and identical bounds in each corresponding dimension. (Note that they need not have identical attributes; as long as PL/I can make the conversion, the usage is legal.) As a result of the statement shown above, each element in A will contain a value twice as large as the one in the corresponding element of B. Taking this a step further, we can write

    DECLARE (A(3,5),B(3,5),C(3,5)) **FIXED** (6,3);

                    .

                    .

                    .

    C = A/(2*B)+B(2,3);

As a result, B(2,3) will be treated just as if it were a single-valued variable and, in turn, will be added to the quotient of each set of corresponding elements from arrays A and B. The order in which such operations are repeated corresponds to that in which the elements of the arrays are stored. Hence, in the situation cited above, the first cycle will divide the contents of A(1,1) by twice the value in B(1,1) and add the value in B(2,3) to that quotient, storing the result in C(1,1). The second cycle will do the same thing using A(1,2), B(1,2), and B(2,3), the latter value remaining unchanged for all cycles. This process continues until the last element in array C is computed by evaluating

$$A(3,5)/(2*B(3,5)) + B(2,3)$$

and placed in its proper location of C(3,5). Thus, we can use one simple statement to represent a series of operations that otherwise would require a sequence of loops.

Specification of array manipulations by simple assignment statements of the type illustrated above will not work unless all of the arrays involved in a particular statement have the same number of dimensions, even though they may have the same total number of elements. If we said

DECLARE (X(10),Y(2,5)); ..... Y = X+2;

the compiler would generate an error message indicating that the number of dimensions in the arrays did not match. By the same token, it is necessary for corresponding dimensions in each array to be the same size. PL/I will allow statements such as

DECLARE(X(2,4),Y(2,4),Z(2,4)); ..... Z = X*Y;

the result being that Z(1,1) will contain a value equal to the product of X(1,1) and Y(1,1); Z(1,2) will contain the product of X(1,2) and Y(1,2); and so on. However, PL/I will *not* accept statements such as

DECLARE(X(2,4),Y(4,2),Z(2,4)); ..... Z = X*Y;

because the number of rows and columns in array Y differ from those specified for arrays X and Z, even though the number of dimensions and the total number of elements are the same.

VI.3.3 Subscripts as Variables

The ability to treat an array element like any other single-valued variable is extended considerably by the fact that the element's subscripts themselves may be variables or expressions. That is, a designation such as X(I,J) for an element of array X is perfectly legitimate. I or J differs in no way from any other variable in that its value may be received as input or assigned as the result of some computation.

Illustration 12

Kopf Drayage Company (from Illustration 9) has expanded its operations so that now it uses six types of vehicles, each with its own characteristic equation for fuel consumption:

Type 1: $FLCON = 4.4 - 0.00022PYLD$

Type 2: $FLCON = 4.14 - 0.00000189PYLD^{1.2}$

Type 3: $FLCON = 3.96 - 0.000207PYLD - 0.00000061PYLD^{1.4}$

Type 4: $FLCON = 4.9 - 0.000161PYLD + 0.0000025PYLD^{1.1}$

Type 5: $FLCON = 5.11 - 0.000372PYLD^{0.8}$

Type 6: $FLCON = 6.86 - 0.000293PYLD + 0.00174PYLD^{0.6}$

However, the requirements have not changed. Using the same kind of input, we are to generate output for individual deliveries as well as a summary of overall activity.

This time, we shall handle these requirements more conveniently by setting up a number of arrays in which to accumulate the various total figures. Thus, six-element arrays would be used for GALNS(the number of gallons consumed by each type of vehicle), PAYLOAD (the number of pounds carried by each type), NMILES (the distance traveled by each type).

In addition, we shall take advantage of the array handling facilities to simplify the construction of the actual computations. Note that although each type of vehicle has its own characteristic equation for fuel consumption, all six equations can be characterized as being specific instances of the following general type:

$$FLCON = a + b(PYLD) + c(PYLD) d$$

Accordingly, we can set up an additional array for each constant across the six types of vehicles. Then, the computation of fuel consumption can be expressed as a single assignment statement in which the appropriate equation is "built" as needed by selecting the appropriate constants from their respective arrays. Hence, if NTYPE represents the type of vehicle (as read from the current set of input vaules), the single statement could be constructed as follows:

FLCON = A(NTYPE) + B(NTYPE)*PYLD + C*PYLD**D(NTYPE);

Based on the equation given before, we can summarize the values to be used for the additional arrays as shown in Table 6.4. The procedure, shown below, is used to produce the sample output shown in Figure 6.2.

```
KOPF DRAYAGE - INDIVIDUAL DELIVERIES
TYPE            MILES              PAYLOAD                  MI./GAL.              GALLONS
       2            989          1.22030E+04                  3.98                 248.75
       1           1007          6.52000E+03                  2.96                 341.00
       1            755          1.00000E+04                  2.19                 345.25
       2           1120          3.55000E+03                  4.10                 273.50
       3            460          1.45000E+04                  0.54                 853.25
       5            755          1.25000E+04                  4.40                 171.75
       4            995          1.32750E+04                  4.37                 227.75
       5            875          7.50000E+03                  5.03                 174.25
       1           1455          8.95000E+03                  2.43                 598.75
       3            270          8.70000E+03                  1.95                 138.75
       5            650          1.55000E+04                  4.27                 152.50
       4            880          3.75000E+03                  4.31                 204.50
       1            775          1.15000E+04                  1.86                 416.75
       6           1450          1.75000E+04                  2.34                 620.75
       4           1250          1.95630E+04                  1.88                 666.75
       3            555          7.50000E+03                  2.24                 248.50
       4            785          1.67000E+04                  2.32                 339.50
       6            440          4.77500E+03                  5.74                  76.75
       3            883          5.55000E+03                  2.70                 327.50

SUMMARY FIGURES
TYPE            NO.DEL.            MILES                    PAYLOAD               GALLONS
       1            4               3992                    36970                1701.75
       2            2               2109                    15753                 522.25
       3            4               2168                    36250                1568.00
       4            3               2915                    40013                1210.75
       5            3               2400                    41275                 552.00
       6            3               2765                    29775                 871.75

     ALL           19              16349                   200036                6426.50
```

Figure 6.2

TABLE 6.4 Values of Constants for Illustration 12

Type	A	B	C	D
1	4.4	-2.2×10^{-4}	0	1
2	4.14	0	-1.89×10^{-6}	1.2
3	3.96	-2.07×10^{-4}	-6.1×10^{-7}	1.4
4	4.9	-1.61×10^{-4}	2.5×10^{-6}	1.1
5	5.11	0	-3.72×10^{-4}	0.8
6	6.86	-2.93×10^{-4}	1.74×10^{-3}	0.6

The designation of a variable subscript is by no means restricted to a simple variable name. Any expression may be used in this context. For example, if X is a one-dimensional array and Y and Z are single-valued numerical variables, a construction such as X92.5*(Y+Z) represents a legitimate reference to an element of array X provided that the resulting value is within the subscript bounds. PL/I will evaluate the expression and convert the result as necessary, truncating any fractional portion. Of course, the programmer must know enough about the range of such calculations to make sure that they will never produce unrealistic subscripts in terms of the array to which they refer. Typical situations of this type occur when a calculated subscript value exceeds that associated with the last element of an array or falls below the value of the first element's subscript. When this occurs, PL/I normally ignores the error and

```
ILL12: PROCEDURE OPTIONS (MAIN);
/**********************************************************************/
/*  NTYPE = TYPE OF VEHICLE;        MILES = DISTANCE TRAVELED;    */
/*  PYLD = PAYLOAD;                 FLCON = MILES PER GALLON;     */
/*  GALLONS = FUEL USED FOR A DELIVERY.                          */
/*  FOR EACH OF THE SIX TYPES, VALUES FOR GALLONS, PAYLOAD,      */
/*  DISTANCE, AND NO. OF DELIVERIES ARE ACCUMULATED IN ARRAYS    */
/*  NAMED GALNS, PAYLOAD, NMILES, AND NDEL, RESPECTIVELY.        */
/*  TOTALS ARE COMPUTED IN GALNST, PAYLDT, MILEST, AND NDELT.    */
/*  A, B, C, AND D ARE ARRAYS CONTAINING THE CONSTANTS FOR       */
/*  THE EQUATIONS USED TO COMPUTE FLCON FOR THE SIX TYPES.       */
/**********************************************************************/
        DECLARE (PYLD,NTYPE,MILES,PAYLOAD(6),NMILES(6),NDEL(6),
                PAYLDT,MILEST,NDELT)          FIXED(6),
                FLCON                         FIXED(4,2),
                (GALLONS,GALNS(6),GALNST)     FIXED(7,2),
                A(6) INITIAL (4.4,4.14,3.96,4.9,5.11,6.86),
                B(6) INITIAL (-2.2E-4,0,-2.07E-4,-1.61E-4,
                             0,-2.93E-4),
                C(6) INITIAL (0,-1.89E-6,-6.1E-7,2.5E-6,-3.72E-4,
                             1.74E-3),
                D(6) INITIAL (1,1.2,1.4,1.1,0.8,0.6),
                E  FIXED (2,1),  NDFILE FIXED(1) INITIAL (0);

        PAYLOAD = 0;  NMILES = 0;  NDEL = 0;  GALNS = 0;
        ON ENDFILE (SYSIN) NDFILE = 1;
        PUT SKIP LIST ('KOPF DRAYAGE - INDIVIDUAL DELIVERIES');
        PUT SKIP LIST ('TYPE','MILES','PAYLOAD','MI./GAL.','GALLONS');
        GET LIST (NTYPE,MILES,PYLD);

        DO WHILE (NDFILE = 0);
          E = D(NTYPE);
/********************************************************************/
/*  E AVOIDS USING A SUBSCRIPTED VARIABLE AS AN EXPONENT */
/********************************************************************/
          NDEL(NTYPE) = NDEL(NTYPE)+1;
          NMILES(NTYPE) = NMILES(NTYPE)+MILES;
          PAYLOAD(NTYPE) = PAYLOAD(NTYPE)+PYLD;
          FLCON = ROUND(A(NTYPE) + B(NTYPE)*PYLD
                  + C(NTYPE)*PYLD**E,2);
          GALLONS = ROUND(MILES/FLCON,2);
          GALNS(NTYPE) = GALNS(NTYPE)+GALLONS;
          PUT SKIP LIST (NTYPE,MILES,PYLD,FLCON,GALLONS);
          GET LIST (NTYPE,MILES,PYLD);
        END;

        PUT SKIP(2) LIST ('SUMMARY FIGURES');
        PUT SKIP LIST ('TYPE','NO.DEL.','MILES','PAYLOAD','GALLONS');
        PUT SKIP;
        DO I = 1 TO 6;
          PUT SKIP LIST (I,NDEL(I),NMILES(I),PAYLOAD(I),GALNS(I);
        END;
        NDELT = SUM(NDEL);      /*--RECALL THAT SUM IS A----------*/
        MILEST = SUM(NMILES);   /*--BUILT-IN FUNCTION THAT--------*/
        PAYLDT = SUM(PAYLOAD);  /*--ADDS THE ELEMENTS IN AN ARRAY.*/
        PUT SKIP(2) LIST ('   ALL',NDELT,MILEST,PAYLDT,GALNST);

        END ILL12;
```

refers instead to the location where the nonexistent element would be located if it existed. This, of course, leads to unpredictable results. When it occurs, however, the programmer may intercede by anticipating such possiblities, testing for them, and preempting PL/I's action with one of his own. Automatic techniques for doing this are available as part of the ON statement and are discussed in a subsequent chapter dealing with control of execution. (PL/C, PLUTO, and the Checkout compiler treat this situation more carefully.)

VI.3.4   Manipulation of Parts of Arrays

Aside from the obvious necessity for manipulating single elements, there are numerous occasions calling for the application of a particular treatment to several (but not all) of an array's elements. In this section we shall examine two basic techniques that facilitate such processing.

VI.3.4.1   Manipulation of Cross Sections

When a given set of operations must be performed on a row or column (or other structural component) of a multidimensional array, we can use PL/I's cross-section notation for the description of the relevant portion of the array. Once a cross section has been defined, the resulting "reduced" array can be treated as being equivalent to a full array declared with the same organization. For example, based on the following declaration,

DECLARE X(6,5) **FIXED**(5), Y(6);

the assignment statement

Y = X(*,3);

is quite legitimate and will produce results equivalent to the sequence of statements

Y(1)=X(1,3); Y(2)=X(2,3);.....Y(6)=X(6,3);

We shall look at cross sections a little further in the following example.

Illustration 13

The A. T. Chu Company manufactures a line of nine Transcendental Essences. Each of these consists of a prescribed mixture of four basic ingredients (B.I.1 through B.I.4). The standard formulations are shown in Table 6.5, with the proportion of each ingredient expressed in parts by volume (see next page).

Although most batches are mixed using these proportions, there are frequent deviations, prompted by geographic preferences. Such a departure may have one of two effects: a customer may request a change in formulation for a given type, in which case the proportions are changed by adding an adjustment constant (specified by the user) to each of the four basic figures for that type. Alternatively, the customer may request a change in the proportion of a particular ingredient for all nine types. When this is required, each of the basic proportions for that ingredient is multiplied by a constant (specified by the customer) to produce the desired modification. Accordingly, each order consists of an order number (expressed as a six-digit integer) followed by the specified adjustment for that order. The procedure is to print the order number and the input specifications, followed by a copy of the adjusted table. Only one kind of adjustment can be specified in an order. (That is, either a specified type is to be adjusted across all four ingredients or the proportions of one of the ingredients is to be adjusted for all nine types.) If neither type of adjustment is specified for a particular order number, the table is to be printed as is. The procedure is to process any number of orders in a continuous run.

We shall make use of cross sections to help set up the basic table and to implement the adjustments specified for each order. Since the procedure must process an unknown number of arbitrarily different orders, including some that require no modification at all, there must be

TABLE 6.5 Basic Formulations for
A. T. Chu Essences

Type	Parts of B.I.1	Parts of B.I.2	Parts of B.I.3	Parts of B.I.4
1	2.0	3.7	3.5	100
2	1.8	3.6	3.5	100
3	1.6	3.4	3.5	100
4	1.5	3.2	4.0	100
5	1.4	3.1	4.0	100
6	1.3	2.8	4.0	100
7	1.2	2.8	4.3	100
8	1.1	2.7	4.3	100
9	1.0	2.5	4.3	100

some way of making sure that the table of standard proportions always is available, in unblemished form, for each order. There are numerous ways to do this, each with its own set of advantages and drawbacks. For instance, we could adjust the appropriate values right in the table itself, in which case it would be necessary to undo the adjustment before the next order is processed. Another way would be to maintain a "reference" copy of the table in which the proportions always would stay at their standard values. Adjustments would be computed in a separate copy and output would be printed from there. This is relatively simple to arrange, but it would be undesirable, especially if the situation called for a large table and storage were at a premium.

PROP
4 INGREDIENTS X 9 TYPES

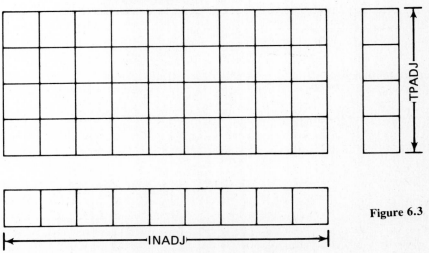

Figure 6.3

The approach in this solution will be to organize the table as a two-dimensional array in which each of the nine types is a column and each of the four ingredients a row. When an order requires a change in proportions for one of the types, the resulting changes affect one of the four columns of the array; alternatively, a change in one of the ingredients affects one of the nine rows. Consequently, we shall set up a four-element one-dimensional array (which we shall call TPADJ) to handle the first type of requirements and the nine-element one-dimensional array (which we shall call INADJ) to handle the other kind. The adjusted values will be carried in the appropriate array, whence they will be interspersed with values from the standard table during the output process. This data organization is shown in Figure 6.3 on the preceding page.

Input for each order will consist of four values: an order number (ORDER), and adjustment factor (ADJ), the type number to be adjusted (TYPE), and the ingredient number to be adjusted (INGR). A sample output is shown in Figure 6.4 and the listing is given below:

```
A.T. CHU TRANSCENDENTAL ESSENCES
ORDER NO.              100255
TYPE=   0          INGR=   0          ADJ=    1.00;

TYPE               INGR.1              INGR.2              INGR.3              INGR.4
  1                  2.00                3.70                3.50              100.00
  2                  1.80                3.60                3.50              100.00
  3                  1.60                3.40                3.50              100.00
  4                  1.50                3.20                4.00              100.00
  5                  1.40                3.10                4.00              100.00
  6                  1.30                2.80                4.00              100.30
  7                  1.20                2.80                4.30              100.00
  8                  1.10                2.70                4.30              100.00
  9                  1.00                2.50                4.30              100.00


A.T. CHU TRANSCENDENTAL ESSENCES
ORDER NO.              211211
TYPE=   0          INGR=   3          ADJ=    0.95;

TYPE               INGR.1              INGR.2              INGR.3              INGR.4
  1                  2.00                3.70                3.32              100.00
  2                  1.80                3.60                3.32              100.00
  3                  1.60                3.40                3.32              100.00
  4                  1.50                3.20                3.80              100.00
  5                  1.40                3.10                3.80              100.00
  6                  1.30                2.80                3.80              100.00
  7                  1.20                2.80                4.08              100.00
  8                  1.10                2.70                4.08              100.00
  9                  1.00                2.50                4.08              100.00


A.T. CHU TRANSCENDENTAL ESSENCES
ORDER NO.              301301
TYPE=   7          INGR=   0          ADJ=    1.10;

TYPE               INGR.1              INGR.2              INGR.3              INGR.4
  1                  2.00                3.70                3.50              100.00
  2                  1.80                3.60                3.50              100.00
  3                  1.60                3.40                3.50              100.30
  4                  1.50                3.20                4.00              100.00
  5                  1.40                3.10                4.00              100.00
  6                  1.30                2.80                4.00              100.00
  7                  2.30                3.90                5.40              101.10
  8                  1.10                2.70                4.30              100.00
  9                  1.00                2.50                4.30              100.00
```

Figure 6.4

```
ILL13: PROCEDURE OPTIONS (MAIN);
   /*************************************************************/
   /*   PROP:       TABLE OF PROPORTIONS FOR THE ESSENCES      */
   /*   TPADJ:      CUSTOMER'S ADJUSTMENTS FOR INGREDIENTS     */
   /*   INADJ:      CUSTOMER'S ADJUSTMENTS FOR ESSENCES        */
   /*************************************************************/
         DECLARE PROP (4,9) FIXED (5,2) INITIAL
                     (2,1.8,1.6,1.5,,1.4,1.3,1.2,1.1,1,3.7,3.6,3.4,
                      3.2,3.1,(2)2.8,2.7,2.5,(3)3.5,(3)4,(3)4.3,
                      (9)100),
                 (TPADJ(4),ADJ,TEMP,INADJ(9)) FIXED (5,2),
                 ORDER FIXED (6),
                 (TYPE,INGR,I,ND) FIXED (1);

      ND = 0;   ON ENDFILE (SYSIN) ND=1;
      GET LIST (ORDER,TYPE,INGR,ADJ);

      DO WHILE (ND = 0);
        PUT PAGE;
        PUT SKIP(2) LIST ('A.T. CHU TRANSCENDANTAL ESSENCES');
        PUT SKIP LIST ('ORDER NO.', ORDER);
        PUT SKIP DATA (TYPE, INGR, ADJ);
        IF TYPE = 0
          THEN DO;
                  IF INGR > 0
                    THEN INADJ = ADJ*PROP(INGR,*);
                    ELSE;             /* NO ADJUSTMENTS AT ALL. */
               END;
            ELSE DO;
                  IF INGR = 0
                    THEN TPADJ = ADJ*PROP(*,TYPE);
                    ELSE PUT SKIP (2) LIST ('IMPROPER INPUT');
               END;
        PUT SKIP (2) LIST ('TYPE','INGR.1','INGR.2',
                           'INGR.3','INGR.4');
        DO I = 1 TO 9;
          IF INGR = 0
            THEN DO;
                  IF TYPE=I THEN PUT SKIP LIST (I,TPADJ);
                            ELSE PUT SKIP LIST (I,PROP(*,I));
               END;
            ELSE DO;
                  TEMP = PROP (INGR,I);
                  PROP (INGR,I) = INADJ (I);
                  PUT SKIP LIST (I,PROP(*,I));
                  PROP (INGR,I) = TEMP;
               END;
        END;
        GET LIST (ORDER,TYPE,INGR,ADJ);
      END;

      STOP;
      END ILL13;
```

VI.3.4.2 **DO** loops and arrays

As we have seen earlier, the **DO** loop provides a convenient mechanism for setting up groups of operations to be applied to a succession of array elements. In this section we emphasize the **DO** loop's flexibility by using it for more involved array processing. One aspect of this versatility is seen in the use of variables for a loop's starting and limiting values.

Illustration 14

The Anguilla Company produces a variety of natural and synthetic lubricants for industrial purposes. Two important measures of an Anguilla lubricant's properties are the globularity (GL) and the Anguilla Number (AN), both of which vary with temperature and with the types and amounts of ingredients used to prepare the lubricant. For a given basic mixture, GL is computed in accordance with one of three formulas depending on temperature range:

$$
\begin{aligned}
&\text{From } -65°\text{F to } t_1: & &\text{GL} = a_1 + b_1 t \\
&\text{From } t_1 + 1 \text{ to } t_2: & &\text{GL} = a_2 + b_2 t + c_2 t^2 \\
&\text{From } t_2 + 1 \text{ to } 150°\text{F}: & &\text{GL} = a_3 + b_3 t + c_3 t^2 + d_3/t
\end{aligned}
$$

The various constants in the formulas (the a's, b's, c's, and d) are supplied for each basic mixture. The same is true for the cutoff temperatures, t_1 and t_2, at which points the applicable formulas change.

Once a basic mixture is prepared, it is possible to change certain of its properties by introducing two critical additives in certain proportions. The resulting AN at some temperature t can then be computed from the formula

$$
\text{AN}_t = \sqrt{g\text{GL}_t} \times \left(\frac{w_1}{w_2}\right)^{1.1}
$$

where g is the gravitational constant (32.164) and w_1 and w_2 are the respective weights of the two critical additives.

A program is required to prepare and print certain output for these lubricant orders: for each order, input is prepared consisting of an order number (six digits) and the cutoff temperatures T1 and T2. These are followed by an unknown number of input sets, with each set consisting of values for W1 and W2 accompanied by values of TS and TF. For each set of W1 and W2 values, the program is to prepare a printed table on a separate page showing values of GL and AN for each temperature starting with TS and concluding with TF. For instance, if one of the sets specifies a W1 of 70, and W2 of 80 and respective values of -20 and 35 for TS and TF, the program is to use the ratio of 70/80 in calculating AN and this should produce a table of AN values for $-20, -19, -18, ..., 33, 34, 35$.

```
ILL14:  PROCEDURE OPTIONS (MAIN);
    /************************************************************/
    /*   GL IS THE TABLE OF GLOBULARITIES FROM -65 TO 150 DEGREES; */
    /*      IT IS COMPUTED FOR EACH SET OF INPUT.                */
    /*   A1,A2,A3,B1,B2,B3,C2,C3,D3 ARE THE COEFFICIENTS FOR GL   */
    /*   AN IS THE ANGUILLA NUMBER;   ORDER IS THE ORDER NUMBER   */
    /*   T1,T2,TS, AND TF ARE TEMPERATURES USED IN COMPUTING GL,AN */
    /*   J AND GRAV ARE CONSTANTS SET AT 0 AND 32.164 RESPECTIVELY. */
    /*   W1 AND W2 ARE THE ADDITIVE WEIGHTS.                     */
    /************************************************************/
        DECLARE   (GL(-65:150),W1,W2,R,A1,A2,A3,B1,B2,B3,C2,C3,D3,GRAV)
                  FLOAT(6),
                  ORDER FIXED(6),      AN FIXED(6,3),
                  (T1,T2,TS,TF,I,J)        FIXED BINARY;

        J = 0;   GRAV = 32.164;   ON ENDFILE (SYSIN)  STOP;
        GET LIST (ORDER,T1,T2,A1,B1,A2,B2,C2,A3,B3,C3,D3);

        DO I = -65 TO 150;
          IF I <= T1
            THEN  GL(I) = A1+B1*I;
            ELSE IF I <= T2
                    THEN  GL(I) = A2+B2*I+C2*I*I;
                    ELSE  GL(I) = A3+B3*I+C3*I*I+D3/I;
        END;

    /*--THE LOOP FOR EACH SET OF INPUT DATA IS SET UP AS A--*/
    /*--"DO FOREVER" LOOP WHOSE REPEATED PROCESSING IS-------*/
    /*--BROKEN BY THE END-OF-FILE SIGNAL.------------------*/

        DO WHILE (J = 0);
          GET LIST (W1,W2,TS,TF);
          R = W1/W2;                 /*THIS AVOIDS COMPUTING W1/W2*/
          PUT PAGE;                  /*FOR EACH TEMPERATURE CHANGE*/
          PUT SKIP(2) LIST('ANGUILLA LUBRICANTS');
          PUT SKIP LIST ('ORDER NO.',ORDER);
          PUT SKIP DATA(A1,B1);  PUT SKIP DATA(A2,B2,C2);
          PUT SKIP DATA(A3,B3,C3,D3);
          PUT SKIP(2) LIST('TEMP','GL','AN');   PUT SKIP;

          DO I=TS TO TF;
            AN = ROUND(R**1.1 * (GRAV * GL(I))**.5,3);
            PUT SKIP LIST (I,GL(I),AN);
          END;

        END;

        END ILL14;
```

Our solution will make use of **DO** loops in a number of contexts. First of all, we must use the input values of T1, T2 and the various A's, B's, C's, and D to compute a set of GL values. Since we do not know what the values of TS and TF will be for this run (in fact, we do not know how many sets of them there will be), the easiest and best thing to do is to compute a full set of GL values over the entire temperature range (-65 to 150) and have them available for the run. In doing this we shall take advantage of PL/I's facility for defining arbitrary ranges of subscripts by having the subscripts coincide with the temperatures. Thus, the GL value for -17°F will be stoed in GL(-17), and so on. This organization also will facilitate subsequent reference to GL values as they are needed in computing AN at various temperatures.

Once the full set of GL values are available, the program will enter a loop in which sets of W1, W2, TS, and TF are read. For each set, TS and TF become the limits of a **DO** loop which computes and prints successive values of AN along with corresponding temperature and GL. The listing appears below and sample input and output are shown in Figure 6.5.

```
ANGUILLA LUBRICANTS
ORDER NO.              102201
A1= 7.39999E-01    B1=-4.79999E-04;
A2= 6.29999E-01    B2=-5.29999E-05      C2= 1.19999E-06;
A3= 1.21999E-01    B3=-7.69999E-05      C3= 3.09999E-07       D3= 4.20999E-01;
W1= 7.40000E+01    W2= 9.00000E+01      R= 8.22222E-01;

TEMP                   GL                     AN

        -12            7.45759E-01            3.948
        -11            7.45279E-01            3.947
        -10            7.44799E-01            3.946
         -9            7.44319E-01            3.945
         -8            7.43839E-01            3.943
         -7            7.43359E-01            3.942
         -6            7.42879E-01            3.941
         -5            7.42399E-01            3.939
         -4            7.41919E-01            3.938
         -3            6.30169E-01            3.629
         -2            6.30110E-01            3.629
         -1            6.30054E-01            3.629
          0            6.29999E-01            3.629
          1            6.29948E-01            3.629
          2            6.29898E-01            3.629
          3            6.29851E-01            3.629
```

Figure 6.5

VI.4   INPUT/OUTPUT OF ARRAYS

It is possible to transmit entire arrays or parts of arrays to and from the processor by means of the same basic input/output statements used thus far. Since the underlying idea of an input or output stream carries over directly from single-valued variables, the extension of these facilities to arrays is quite straightforward.

VI.4.1   Transmission of Entire Arrays

If an array has been appropriately declared, all of its elements can be brought in with a single statement. The sequence

DECLARE X(10) **FIXED** (6,2); **GET LIST** (X);

will cause the next ten values in the data stream to be read in and placed in location X(1) through X(10), respectively. Any necessary conversions to match the attributes specified in the declaration will be performed automatically as part of the process. This applies as well to the **GET DATA** statement, with its usage implying the presentation of input values in assignment statement form. Thus, assuming the declaration given above, the statement

GET DATA(X);

implies the expectation that each element's value will be accompanied by the appropriate subscript:

X(1) = value X(2) = value ...... X(10) = value;

In the case of **GET DATA**, the miniature assignment statements may be in any convenient order; in fact, some elements may be omitted entirely, in which case their values are unaffected. In other cases, the order in which array elements are read in or printed out is the same as that used for initialization. Of course, this corresponds to the order in which the elements are stored. For example, if we said

DECLARE X(3,4) **FIXED**(2); **GET LIST**(X);

and the values of X were punched in the following order

17 21 14 11 6 16 −29 19 44 10 −43

the resulting contents of the array would be as follows:

17 21 14 11
06 16 −29 19
44 10 (07) −43

Since an array prepared for input with a **GET DATA** statement has each of its elements identified explicitly, there is no need to follow any specific rule for sequencing and the elements may be submitted in any order.

Use of a single statement to print an entire array places the programmer at the mercy of the default for line formats. Accordingly, the statement

PUT SKIP DATA(X);

applied to the 12 values shown before and operating under a default of five values per line will produce the following output:

X(1,1) = 17   X(1,2) = 21   X(1,3) = 14   X(1,4) = 11   X(2,1) = 6

X(2,2) = 16   X(2,3) = −29   X(2,4) = 19   X(3,1) = 44   X(3,2) = 10

X(3,3) = 7   X(3,4) = −43;

Alternatively, specification of a **PUT LIST** statement would produce the same sequence of values in the same positions but, of course, without the accompanying identifiers.

VI.4.2   Input/Output of Parts of Arrays

Since an individual element, when described properly by its subscript, is treated like any other single-valued variable, its transmission via regular **GET/PUT** statements is perfectly consistent. In fact, we have printed array elements in this manner (Illustration 13) without making any particular fuss over it. In this section we shall discuss some additional conveniences for such transmission.

VI.4.2.1   Input/Output of Array Cross Sections

The definition and manipulation of array cross sections extend to input/output, so that any subset of an array that can be described as a cross section can be transmitted to or from the processor as well. To illustrate, the following sequence of statements

DECLARE B(3,5) **CHARACTER**(5) **INITIAL** ((15)'ZOOMM');

GET LIST B(2,*); **PUT LIST**(B);

when confronted with the input shown below

'SHTUK'   'GOLLY'   'WOLLY'   'GOLLY'   'SHTUK'

will produce the following output:

```
          ZOOMM   ZOOMM   ZOOMM   ZOOMM   ZOOMM
          SHTUK   GOLLY   WOLLY   GOLLY   SHTUK
          ZOOMM   ZOOMM   ZOOMM   ZOOMM   ZOOMM
```

VI.4.2.2   Input/Output of Sequences of Elements

It is possible to construct a **GET LIST** or **PUT LIST** statement that will transmit a related group of array elements by appending a **DO** loop to the basic form. The construction is

GET LIST((name(index) **DO** index = sv **TO** lv));

where sv and lv are the starting and limiting values, respectively. For example, if Y is a 30-element array, the statement

GET LIST ((Y(J) **DO** J = 1 **TO** 9));

will cause the next nine values from the input stream to be placed in Y(1), Y(2), Y(3), ..., Y(9), in that order. *The additional parentheses are required*. The results produced by this single statement are exactly equivalent to those obtained with the following sequence:

DO J = 1 **TO** 9; **GET LIST**(Y(J)); **END**;

However, the former method is preferred in that it usually is more efficient. As is the case with a regular **DO** loop, the starting value and/or limiting value may be variables. Thus, if K has a legitimate value and Y is a 30-element array, it would be valid to write

GET LIST((Y(J) **DO** J = 1 **TO** K));

in which case the next K input values will be placed in Y(1), Y(2), ..., Y(K). This facility finds frequent use in a situation where the variable's value is itself brought in as input, after which the indicated number of array elements can be read. This is exemplified by the construction

GET LIST(K,(Y(J) **DO** J = 1 **TO** K));

Here again, the additional parentheses are required.

Illustration 15

Joule-Thomson Ice Cream, which comes in 32 inviting flavors, is sold through a national chain of the company's outlets. Each of these flavors has a standard (base) price of X.XX dollars per gallon. As part of a marketing campaign, J-T is implementing a procedure whereby certain sequences of flavors are selected for discounting at certain individual outlets. For example, flavors 5 through 12 may be discounted at outlet 10077, flavors 21 through 29 may be discounted at outlet 00565, and so on. Thus, for a selected outlet, the price of each flavor in a designated sequence is discounted by a percentage also specified as part of the input. To illustrate, the input card represented on the next page

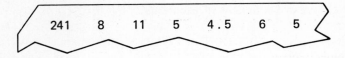

specifies that outlet 241 will have flavors 8-11 discounted as follows:

Flavor 8: 5 percent
Flavor 9: 4.5 percent
Flavor 10: 6 percent
Flavor 11: 5 percent

A procedure is required to read an unspecified number of such cards (one for each selected outlet). For each card processed, the procedure is to print a page of output showing the 32 prices, one per line. Of course, prices for the selected flavors will reflect the specified adjustments, and the corresponding discounts are to appear on the appropriate lines. No more than ten flavors are to be discounted for any one outlet, and the standard prices are to be read in ahead of the individual outlet cards.

```
ILL15: PROCEDURE OPTIONS (MAIN);
    /***********************************************************************/
    /*  THE DISCOUNTS WILL BE READ IN AS PERCENTAGES FOR CONVENIENCE*/
    /*  AFTER WHICH EACH WILL BE MULTIPLIED BY 0.01 FOR COMPUTING   */
    /*  NEW PRICES.                                                 */
    /*  F1 AND F2 ARE THE FIRST AND LAST FLAVORS IN THE DISCOUNT    */
    /*  SEQUENCE. THUS, THE NO. OF DISCOUNTED FLAVORS IS F2-F1+1.   */
    /***********************************************************************/
    DECLARE   (PRICE(32),TEMP)          FIXED(3,2),
              OUTLET                    FIXED(5),
              (F1,F2,C,I,K)             FIXED BINARY,
              DISCNT(10)                FIXED(4,2);

    C = 0;   ON ENDFILE (SYSIN) STOP;    PUT PAGE;
    GET LIST (PRICE);
    PUT SKIP(2) LIST
       ('JOULE-THOMPSON ICE CREAM - BASIC PRICE LIST');
    PUT SKIP LIST('FLAVOR','PRICE');
    DO I=1 TO 32;   PUT SKIP LIST(I,PRICE(I));   END;

    DO WHILE (C=0);
       GET LIST(OUTLET,F1,F2,(DISCNT(I) DO I=1 TO F2-F1+1));
       PUT PAGE;
       PUT SKIP(2) LIST
          ('JOULE-THOMPSON ICE CREAM CO. - DISCOUNT LIST');
       PUT SKIP LIST('OUTLET NO.',OUTLET);
       PUT SKIP(2) LIST('   FLAVOR','PRICE');
       IF F1 > 1
         THEN   DO I=1 TO F1-1;
                   PUT SKIP LIST(I,PRICE(I));
                END;
         ELSE;
         /*--K IS THE INDEX IN THE DISCOUNT LIST */
         /*--FOR A GIVEN FLAVOR                  */
       DO I = F1 TO F2;
         K = I-F1+1;
         TEMP = ROUND( PRICE(I)*(1-.01*DISCNT(K)), 2);
         PUT SKIP LIST(I,TEMP);
       END;
       IF F2 < 32
         THEN   DO I = F2+1 TO 32;   PUT SKIP LIST(I,PRICE(I));   END;
         ELSE;
    END;

    END ILL15;
```

Our solution will use a 32-element array (PRICE) for the basic prices and a 10-element array (DISCNT) for the set of discounts currently being processed. F1 and F2 will indicate the range of flavors being discounted, so that the percentage for flavor F1 will be read into DISCNT(1), flavor F2 will be read into DISCNT(2), and so on. F1 and F2 then can be used as the lower and upper limits, respectively, of a loop that will develop the discounted prices. In examining the listing for this program (shown below), it is important to note two implied properties underlying the **DO** loop mechanism:

- The loop that prepares the discounted prices contains no statement to take care of the situation in which only one flavor is to be discounted (that is, F1 = F2). Such an explicit safeguard is not needed since the looping mechanism will (properly) perform one cycle.

- The other two loops that print the remainder of the revised price list also seem "unprotected" in that there is no explicit provision for an "empty loop." Such a situation could develop if F1 were 1 or if F2 were 32. Here again the language rules governing the setup of starting and limiting values for the index variable will prevent any erroneous cycling.

VI.5   ADDITIONAL PROPERTIES OF ARRAYS

Having explored PL/I's capabilities with regard to the organization, transmission, and manipulation of arrays and their individual elements, we can turn our attention to a number of additional facilities that provide the programmer with further control.

VI.5.1   Multiple Names for Arrays

In many programming situations it may be desirable to be able to refer to a particular piece of data by more than one name. For example, it may be desirable to treat part of an array (other than a cross section) as a "separate" collection, with its own name. PL/I provides relatively convenient facilities for establishing and maintaining such relationships.

VI.5.1.1   The **DEFINED** Attribute

This feature, which makes it possible to assign more than one name to an entire array, is implemented as part of the declaration that reserves storage for the array. To illustrate, consider the following statement:

DECLARE X(7,8) **FIXED**(6,2), Y(7,8) **FIXED**(6,2) **DEFINED** X;

As expected, this causes sufficient storage to be assigned for a two-dimensional array X containing seven rows and eight columns. In addition, because of the second part of the declaration, this array will also be known as Y, and there will be complete correspondence between elements. The names X(1,1) and Y(1,1) will refer to exactly the same location and to the same value contained therein. This holds true for X(1,2) and Y(1,2), X(3,6) and Y(3,6), and so on. In this particular relationship, X is known as the *base* or *defining* variable, and Y is known as the *defined* variable.

There are several basic rules attendant to the use of defined arrays in this fashion:

1. The number of dimensions and all of the attributes must be the same for the defined and base arrays. The extent of each dimension of the defined array must be less than that of the corresponding dimension of the base array.

2. The base array must be an entire array. It cannot be a cross section of some larger array. (The Optimizing and Checkout Compilers allow the base to be a cross section.)

3. The defined array may not have the **INITIAL** attribute.

4. The use of the **DEFINED** attribute is limited to only one level. An array cannot be defined and then used as a base variable for another array.

5. Any number of defined arrays may be specified for the same defining (base) array.

6. All elements of defined arrays must refer to corresponding elements in the defining array.

VI.5.1.2   Duplicate Names for Parts of Arrays

The Optimizing and Checkout Compilers support an extended version of the **DEFINED** attribute that allows greater flexibility. For example, if we said

DECLARE X(10) **FIXED**(3), Y(6) **FIXED**(3) **DEFINED** X(4);

PL/I would duly allocate sufficient storage for the ten members of array X. Then it would set up appropriate indicators to show that X(4) also has the name Y(1), X(5) has the alias Y(2), and so on, so that the final element of the defined array (Y(6)) refers to the same location containing X(9). This is shown diagrammatically below.

X(1)	X(2)	X(3)	X(4)	X(5)	X(6)	X(7)	X(8)	X(9)	X(10)
			Y(1)	Y(2)	Y(3)	Y(4)	Y(5)	Y(6)	

If a starting subscript is not given for the base array, PL/I assumes it to be the first element of that array. Hence, if we had written

DECLARE X(10) **FIXED**(3), Y(6) **FIXED**(3) **DEFINED** X;

the assignments would have been made as follows:

X(1)	X(2)	X(3)	X(4)	X(5)	X(6)	X(7)	X(8)	X(9)	X(10)
Y(1)	Y(2)	Y(3)	Y(4)	Y(5)	Y(6)				

When specifying such defined arrays, the programmer must be careful to make sure that the defined array does not extend beyond the bounds of the base variable. A declaration such as

DECLARE V(10) **FIXED**(2), W(5) **FIXED**(3) **DEFINED** V(8);

would result in an error condition, because array V would run out of elements before the available members of W were completely assigned.

In this usage, the defined variable can also be a single-valued variable rather than an array. In the statement

DECLARE X(10) **FIXED**(2), Z **FIXED**(2), A **FIXED**(2) **DEFINED** X(7);

storage would be allocated for the ten elements of array X and the single-valued variable Z. In addition, the element X(7) would also carry the name A. (The student should keep in mind that the feature discussed in this foregoing section are supported only by the Optimizing and Checkout Compilers.)

VI.5.1.3 More Complicated Use of Defining: The iSUB Specification

It is possible to set up more complicated relationships between the elements in defined and base arrays by specifying some mathematical relationship between the subscript of each element in the defined array and the corresponding one in the base array. The specific feature used for this purpose is the iSUB specification, where i is an integer decimal constant representing a particular dimension number in the defined array. If we were to write

DECLARE X(20), Y(10) **DEFINED** X(2*1SUB);

X would be the base array and Y would be the defined array as before. In addition, Y's subscript would be represented by the name 1SUB. Since Y has only one dimension, there can be no 2SUB, 3SUB, and so on for it, and their use would result in an error condition. The result is that we have defined an array Y whose elements consist of X's even-numbered elements. Let us see how this works:

The particular element in X (the base array) corresponding to some given element in Y is determined by substituting Y's element number in the 1SUB expression as follows:

Y's Subscript	Element of X Referring to Same Location
1	X(2*1) = X(2)
2	X(2*2) = X(4)
3	X(2*3) = X(6)
.	.
.	.
9	X(2*9) = X(18)
10	X(2*10) = X(20)

Following this scheme, let us set up a declaration in which a base array X is associated with two defined arrays; that is, Y for the even-numbered elements and Z for the odd-numbered elements:

DECLARE X(20) **FIXED**(3),

           Y(10) **FIXED**(3) **DEFINED** X(2*1SUB);

           Z(10) **FIXED**(3) **DEFINED** X(2*1SUB−1);

When specifying the iSUB feature, it is not necessary for the base and defined arrays to have the same number of dimensions. Thus, if we write

DECLARE X(5,5) **FIXED**(2), Y(5) **FIXED**(2) **DEFINED** X(1SUB,1SUB);

we have defined an array Y whose elements correspond to those elements of X having the same row and column number. These elements form the *diagonal* of X, as shown in Figure 6.6.

X(1,1) Y(1)	X(1,2)	X(1,3)	X(1,4)	X(1,5)
X(2,1)	X(2,2) Y(2)	X(2,3)	X(2,4)	X(2,5)
X(3,1)	X(3,2)	X(3,3) Y(3)	X(3,4)	X(3,5)
X(4,1)	X(4,2)	X(4,3)	X(4,4) Y(4)	X(4,5)
X(5,1)	X(5,2)	X(5,3)	X(5,4)	X(5,5) Y(5)

Figure 6.6

Illustration 16

We have a two-dimensional array A consisting of 16 3-digit decimal integers arranged in four rows and four columns. It is desired to define additional arrays B, C, D and E with the following properties:

- B is to be a one-dimensional array that coincides with the second row of A.

- C is to be a one-dimensional array that coincides with the third column of A.

- D is to be a one-dimensional array whose elements coincide with those running diagonally in A from lower left to upper right.

- E is to be a two-dimensional array containing two rows and three columns that are to coincide with the lower right-hand corner of array A.

These requirements are shown diagrammatically in Figure 6.7. Array A is shown as dotted lines.

We shall describe separately the processes to determine the subscript specifications for each array:

Array B: Since this array is to correspond to elements of A whose row numbers do not change, the row specification will be a constant (2 in this case). Because the column number of each element used in the base array will be numerically the same as the element number for the corresponding member of array B, the column subscript can be specified merely by 1**SUB**.

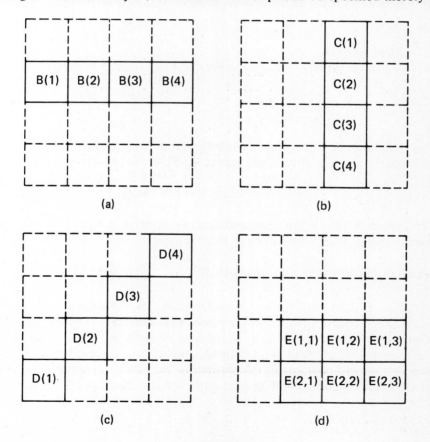

(a)　　　　　　　　　(b)

(c)　　　　　　　　　(d)

Figure 6.7

Hence, the part of our overall declaration concerned with B will read

B(4) **FIXED** (5,2) **DEFINED** A(2,1SUB);

Array C: This time it is the column number that remains constant in the base array A. There is numerical equality between the element number of the defined array and the row subscript of the base array. Accordingly, the fragment of the declaration concerned with C can read

C(4) **FIXED** (5,2) **DEFINED** A(1SUB,3);

Array D: For this array, it is necessary to vary both the row and column subscripts in the base array. If we examine Figure 6.7c, we can tabulate two relationships: one between an element in D (represented by 1SUB) and the row number of the corresponding element in A; and the other between 1SUB and the column number of the corresponding element in A.

Element in D (Value of 1SUB)	Row Numbers in A	Column Numbers in A
1	4	1
2	3	2
3	2	3
4	1	4

The column number in A is the same as 1SUB, so that part is taken care of. Since the row number in A goes in reverse order with respect to 1SUB, we can express this by saying that

$$\text{row number in A} = 5 - 1SUB$$

(for example, when 1SUB is 3, the corresponding row number in A is $5 - 3 = 2$, which agrees with our table). Accordingly, we can write the fragment

D(4) **FIXED** (5,2) **DEFINED** A(5−1SUB,1SUB);

Array E: Since E is to be a two-dimensional array, its subscript is represented by two quantities (1SUB and 2SUB). In the row dimension, we are concerned with the final two rows of array A. Consequently, the row number of the base element will always be two greater than that of the corresponding element in the defined array. Similarly, because we are dealing with the last three (rightmost) columns of the base array, A's column number will always be one greater than that for the corresponding element in array E. Thus, we can write

E(2,3) **FIXED** (5,2) **DEFINED** A(1SUB+2, 2SUB+1);

Combining these specifications and adding the declaration for the base array, we obtain the final declaration:

DECLARE A(4,4) **FIXED** (5,2), B(4) **FIXED** (5,2) **DEFINED** A(2,1SUB),

C(4) **FIXED** (5,2) **DEFINED** A(1SUB,3),

D(4) **FIXED** (5,2) **DEFINED** A(5−1SUB,1SUB),

E(2,3) **FIXED** (5,2) **DEFINED** A(1SUB+2, 2SUB+1);

VI.5.1.4   The **POSITION** Specification

The general facilities for assigning different names to the same location(s) extend to character strings as well as arrays. That is, PL/I makes it possible to treat a contiguous part of a string as a distinct entity, with its own name. This is done by means of the **DEFINED** attribute augmented with a **POSITION** specification:

DECLARE vb **CHARACTER**(1b), vd **CHARACTER**(1d) **DEFINED** vb **POSITION**(n);

In this generalization vb and vd are the base and defined variables respectively, and n specifies the position in vb corresponding to the first character of vd. Neither vd nor vb may be **VARYING**. If lb and ld are the respective lengths of the base and defined strings, n cannot exceed nb − nd + 1 (and, of course, n may not go below 1). For most PL/I implementations, n must be a decimal integer constant; however, the Optimizing and Checkout Compilers allow the use of an arithmetic expression as well.

To illustrate the use of the **POSITION** feature, consider the following declaration:

DECLARE A **CHARACTER**(12), B **CHARACTER**(6) **DEFINED** A **POSITION**(6),

C **CHARACTER**(8) **DEFINED** A **POSITION**(3);

In response, PL/I allocates storage and assigns names as represented below:

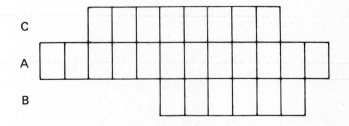

Additional flexibility is provided by the Optimizing and Checkout Compilers, both of which

allow single-valued character strings to be defined on character string arrays using arbitrary position specifications. For example, the statement

DECLARE X(10) **CHARACTER**(2), Y **CHARACTER**(7) **DEFINED** X **POSITION**(5);

defines the following relationship:

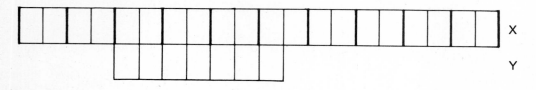

Note that the base array (X in this case) is specified without any subscript.

VI.5.2   Arrays with Variable Sizes

There are many situations in which the number of elements in an array can vary from one occasion to the next, all within the context of a particular problem. A typical example is seen in Illustration 15, where the number of flavors to be discounted may vary from one outlet to the next, with the limitation that this number would not exceed ten for any outlet. We accommodated this situation by setting up an array (which we called DISCNT) that is, sized to contain the maximum number of discount specifications. Then all or part of that array was used, depending on the particular circumstances. This is not a serious matter when the array is so small. However, when the range of variation is very wide, a situation could easily arise in which a procedure is carrying a 10,000-element array whose predominant usage is for 100 elements or less. The resulting unavailability of the unused storage can mean the difference between successful or unsuccessful implementation of a procedure.

Instead of reserving storage in advance to take care of the maximum possible needs, it is possible to delay such reservation until just before that storage actually is needed. Then, procedural arrangements can be made to define the extent of required storage, making that storage available once the extent is known. This general technique is called *dynamic storage allocation*. PL/I provides a number of ways to apply this powerful approach, and we shall introduce one of them in the context of array declaration.

It would be very nice if we could write the following sequence of statements

GET LIST (N); **DECLARE** X(N) **FIXED**(3);

thereby setting up a procedural segment in which a value N is read and used to determine the extent of an array X, which is then declared. However, it is impractical to implement such a facility without further language features. In PL/I, the ability to make such dynamic declarations is implemented by means of a special structural component called a **BEGIN** block. The basic construction is as follows:

label: **BEGIN**;

    .

    statements

    .

   END label;

If the **BEGIN** statement has a label attached to it, that same label may be appended to the **END** statement indicating the conclusion of the block. This is an organizational unit within a PL/I procedure in much the same way as a **DO** group is. However, a **BEGIN** block, in addition to grouping statements, also governs storage allocation. When such a block is set up, storage for any variables declared within its boundaries will be allocated dynamically each time it is executed rather than once and for all at the start of the program. Then, once the sequence of events takes the program out of the block's boundaries, that storage is no longer available. Should the block be entered again (as would be the case if the block were contained within some larger procedural loop), storage will be allocated anew and the amount provided this time need not bear any relation to any previous allocation.

Illustration 15a

```
ILL15A: PROCEDURE OPTIONS (MAIN);
   /*****************************************************************/
   /*   THE DISCOUNTS WILL BE READ IN AS PERCENTAGES FOR CONVENIENCE*/
   /*   WITHIN A BEGIN BLOCK WHERE THE PROPERLY SIZED ARRAY WILL BE */
   /*   ALLOCATED. ONCE INSIDE, EACH DISCOUNT WILL BE MULTIPLIED BY */
   /*   0.01 FOR COMPUTING THE NEW PRICES.                          */
   /*   F1 AND F2 ARE THE FIRST AND LAST FLAVORS IN THE DISCOUNT    */
   /*   SEQUENCE. THUS, THE NO. OF DISCOUNTED FLAVORS IS F2-F1+1.   */
   /*****************************************************************/
   DECLARE   (PRICE(32), TEMP)              FIXED(3,2),
             OUTLET                         FIXED(5),
             (F1,F2,C,I,K)                  FIXED BINARY;

   C = 0;   ON ENDFILE (SYSIN) STOP;    PUT PAGE;
   GET LIST(PRICE);
   PUT SKIP(2) LIST
      ('JOULE-THOMPSON ICE CREAM - BASIC PRICE LIST');
   PUT SKIP LIST('FLAVOR','PRICE');
   DO I=1 TO 32;   PUT SKIP LIST(I,PRICE(I));   END;

   DO WHILE (C=0);
     GET LIST (OUTLET,F1,F2);
     BEGIN;
       DECLARE DISCNT(K) FIXED(4,2);
       GET LIST(DISCNT);   PUT PAGE;
       PUT SKIP(2) LIST
          ('JOULE-THOMPSON ICE CREAM CO. - DISCOUNT LIST');
       PUT SKIP LIST('OUTLET NO.',OUTLET);
       PUT SKIP(2) LIST('   FLAVOR','PRICE');
       IF F1 > 1
          THEN DO I=1 TO F1-1;  PUT SKIP LIST(I,PRICE(I));  END;
          ELSE;
       DO I = F1 TO F2;
          K = I-F1+1;
          TEMP = ROUND( PRICE(I)*(1-.01*DISCNT(K)), 2);
          PUT SKIP LIST(I,TEMP);
       END;
       IF F2 < 32
          THEN DO I=F2+1 TO 32;  PUT SKIP LIST(I,PRICE(I));  END;
          ELSE;
     END;
   END;

   END ILL15A;
```

To see how this basic facility is used, we shall rewrite the Joule-Thompson Ice Cream procedure, making the size of DISCNT dependent on the specifications for each individual outlet. The revised listing, shown above, will still produce the same output; however, DISCNT will now vary in size with each set of input values.

PROBLEMS

1. For the array X, given below,

Row 1		Row 2		Row 3	
Column 1	*Column 2*	*Column 1*	*Column 2*	*Column 1*	*Column 2*
26.2	13.4	37.9	7.2	40.7	18.1
17.7	5.7	47.2	21.7	38.7	9.5
4.3	24.4	59.9	63.4	55.8	44.7
61.1	46.8	27.4	54.1	49.8	78.4
11.5	57.0	14.1	36.8	17.2	23.9
30.9	74.3	61.9	96.0	70.7	8.1
44.2	25.0	56.3	16.3	23.8	31.9
50.0	66.3	41.4	87.1	77.1	51.1
28.3	31.3	6.3	49.3	32.2	4.7

a. Give the values of X(2,2,4), X(3,1,5), X(1,1,6).

b. Give the subscript for the largest element.

c. Give the block number containing the smallest element.

d. Give the sum of X(3,2,2) and X(2,2,3).

e. Show the collective name for all elements in row 2.

f. Show the collective name for all elements in block 6.

g. Give the sum of all elements in X(*,2,*).

h. Give the sum of all elements in X(2,*,2).

i. Evaluate Y if $Y = 2*X(3,2,1) + 3$.

j. Evaluate Y if Y is the sum of all the values in the expression $3*X(*,*,3) - 4*X(1,2,3)$.

2. Find the positions of the designated elements in each of the arrays described below:

    a.   X(6,4) in a 12 × 7 array named X.

    b.   A(3,3) in a 6 × 6 array named A.

    c.   Y(2,7) in a 4 × 18 array named Y.

    d.   Z(6,6,6) in an 8 × 10 × 8 array named Z.

    e.   T(3,5,3) in a 5 × 5 × 5 array named T.

    f.   S(11,10,9) and S(9,10,11) in a 22 × 11 × 17 array named S.

    g.   The elements in column 3 of a 7 × 6 array named W.

    h.   R(3,*,*) of a 5 × 6 × 5 array named R.

3.   Give the subscripts for each of the following elements:

    a.   The 12th element of a 4 × 8 array.

    b.   The 9th element of a 5 × 11 array.

    c.   The 127th element of a 7 × 21 array.

    d.   The 19th element of a 4 × 11 × 17 array.

    e.   Element 71 of a 9 × 9 × 13 array.

    f.   Element 101 of a 2 × 19 × 22 array.

    g.   The 2nth element in an m x n array.

    h.   The element in position m + n in an m x n x m array.

    i.   The 23rd element in an array declared as (0:17,4:9).

    j.   The 37th element in an array declared as (4,12:22).

    k.   Element 41 in an array declared as $(-12:-8,4,-6:7)$.

4.   Indicate a general formula for computing the position p of an element in an array whose size is d1 × d2 × d3 × ... × dn.

5.   Develop a general formula for computing the position p of an element in an array whose dimensions are described as (a1:b1,a2:b2,...,an:bn).

6.   Show the contents of each array resulting from the initializations shown below:

    a.   **DECLARE** B(12) **INITIAL** (0);

    b.   **DECLARE** X(14) **INITIAL** ((3)2,6,4(5)0,0,5,5,0);

    c.   **DECLARE** D(3,6) **INITIAL** ((4)(3,−3,2,0),6,3);

    d.   **DECLARE** Y(2,4,4) **INITIAL** ((5)(0,(2)(4,7),−2),(2)2);

    e.   **DECLARE** C(6,5) **CHARACTER** (7) **INITIAL** ('FRIENDS');

f.   DECLARE E(3,8) **CHARACTER** (5) **INITIAL** ((5)'STAND');

g.   DECLARE D1(4,4) **CHARACTER** (3) **INITIAL** ((5)'STAND');

h.   DECLARE D1(4,4) **CHARACTER** (3) **INITIAL** ((16)(1)'S');

7.   Write a program in which elements of a 21 × 30 array of fixed decimal numbers with precision (4,1) are set to the following values:

- Elements having even row numbers are to be set to zero.

- Elements having odd column numbers above 18 and odd row numbers are to be set to 4.3.

- Each of the remaining elements is to be set to a value equal to the product of its row number and column number.

After printing the two headings ROW NO. and ROW SUM, the program is to print a line of output for each row in which is shown the row number and the sum of all the elements in that row.

8.   Write a program in which elements are read into a 5 × 5 array of floating-point numbers in row major order. When all of the values are in, perform the following processing:

- All elements in a given row whose values are the diagonal element in that row are to be doubled. For example, if an element in row 2 is less than the element with subscript (2,2), the value in the element is doubled.

- After these adjustments are made, a second array is to be prepared in which the rows are formed from the columns of the original array.

The program is to print the original array, followed by the adjusted array and the new array (the transpose). Each array is to be printed one row per line, with a blank line separating the arrays.

9.   Write a program that reads two-digit decimal integers into a 4 × 6 array. The values are punched in column order (that is, all the values in column 1 followed by all the values in column 2, and so on). Each element is to be processed as follows:

- If the value of the element is less than its column number, it is to be increased by the value of the column number.

- If the value of the element is equal to its column number, it is to be decreased by the product of its row and column numbers.

- Each remaining element is to be divided by an element whose row number is the same as the first element's column number, and vice versa. (For example element (2,4) would be divided by element (4,2).) Those elements for which such a match is impossible are to be left unchanged. Accordingly, an element like (3,5) would not be adjusted since there is no element (5,3) in this array).

The program is to print the original array by column (each of the six columns on a separate line). After skipping a line, this is to be followed by a partial printout of the adjusted array consisting of four lines. Each line is to show the elements of a given row having odd column numbers.

10. Rewrite the A. T. Chu procedure (Illustration 13) so that each order may specify one or more types, accompanied by individual adjustment factors for selected ingredients within each type. This time, each adjustment factor is to be used as a multiplier. Thus, an order may indicate that, for type 3, ingredients 2 and 4 are to be multiplied by 0.95 and 1.02, respectively whereas for type 7, ingredients 1 and 4 are to be multiplied by 0.88.

11. Rewrite the procedure in Illustration 15 so that the printout for each outlet includes a third column showing the discounts (as percentages) opposite the appropriate flavor numbers.

12. Rewrite the procedure in Illustration 15 so that the processing specified by the three separate loops (L1, L2, and L3) is handled in a single **DO** loop. (Do this either for the original version or for the modified procedure specified in Problem 11).

13. X is a five-element array of two-digit decimal integers. Write a procedure that reads successive sets of values for X. Each set is to be processed to produce a 5×5 array Y in which the elements of the first row are identical to those in X and those in each succeeding row contain values representing the accumulated sums of the corresponding elements in all of the preceding rows. (For example, the value in Y(4,2) would be equivalent to the sum of Y(1,2), Y(2,2), and Y(3,2).)

14. For each of the following sequences, show what will be in array Y:

    a. **DECLARE** X(10) **FIXED**(2) **INITIAL**((3)(2,4,9),0), Y **FIXED**(2) **DEFINED** X(5);

    b. **DECLARE** A(24) **FIXED**(2) **INITIAL**((4)(2(0),(2)(6,−5))),Y(7) **FIXED**(2) **DEFINED** A;

    c. **DECLARE** B(85) **FIXED**(4), Y(12) **FIXED**(4) **DEFINED** B(18); B =0; **DO** I = 1 **TO** 85; B(I) = B(I) + 85−2*I; **END**;

    d. **DECLARE** A(4,8) **CHARACTER**(5), Y(4,8) **CHARACTER**(5) **DEFINED** A; A = 'SEVEN'; A(*,7) = 'OCTAL'; A(3,*) = 'TOTAL';

    e. **DECLARE** B(30) **FIXED**(3) **INITIAL**((30)100), Y(14) **FIXED**(3) **DEFINED** B(11); **DO** I = 4 **TO** 24; B(I) = 2*B(I) − Y(6)*I; **END**;

    f. **DECLARE** X(4,5) **PICTURE** '99V.9', Y(8) **PICTURE** '99V.9' **DEFINED** X(1SUB+1,2*1SUB−1); X=−7.7; X(2,*)=12.4+ X(*,2)=6.1;

15. This season, the Craterville Music Festival will have 28 events, including symphony performances, concerts of international hog calls and responses, and rhythmic sheep shearing to the accompaniment of a synthesizer. People may subscribe by selecting any number of events and one of four ticket price categories: A category 1 ticket costs $1.75, with each successive category costing $0.75 more than its predecessor. The Festival Board requires a program that produces summary information for each subscriber. For each subscription, input is prepared consisting of the subscriber's name, the number of events to which he wishes to subscribe, the number of subscriptions, the price category, and the event numbers. Thus, the following card

'SMILOFF'   5   4   2   8   19   20   21   7

indicates that Smiloff wants four subscriptions in price category 2 to the following five events: 8, 19, 20, 21 and 7.

The program is to produce a line of output for each set of subscriptions showing the name, number of events, number of subscriptions, price category, and total cost. After the last subscriber has been processed, the program is to print a separate page showing the number of tickets sold in each category for each event. A final page is to show the revenue for each event (across all categories) and the grand total.

16. A two-dimensional array A having r rows and c columns can be multiplied by a vector VC having c elements to produce an r- element vector VR. Each element (VR_i) in the result is computed as follows:

$$VR_i = \sum_{j=1}^{c} A_{ij} VC_j$$

For example, if VR is the 2 x 3 array

$$\begin{array}{ccc} 3 & 2 & 1 \\ 4 & 5 & 6 \end{array}$$

and VC consists of the elements

$$\begin{array}{c} 7 \\ 8 \\ -1 \end{array}$$

the product VR is obtained as

$$\begin{array}{ccc} 3*7 + 2*8 + 1*\text{-}1 & = & 36 \\ 4*7 + 5*8 + 6*\text{-}1 & = & 62 \end{array}$$

Write a program that (for each input case) reads r and c, followed by the $r \times c$ elements of array A in row major order. These values are followed by the c values for the vector (one-dimensional array) VC. The program is to print A (one row per line) followed by VC (one value per line). In addition, compute and print VR (one value per line). Each set of output is to appear on a separate page, appropriately headed. r never exceeds 20 and c never exceeds 5.

17. A two-dimensional array A having r rows and c columns can be multiplied by a second array B having c rows and s columns to produce a two-dimensional array P having r rows and s columns. Each element in P (P_{ij}) is computed as follows:

$$P_{ij} = \sum_{k=1}^{c} A_{ik} B_{kj}$$

For example, A is the 3 x 4 array

$$\begin{array}{cccc} 4 & 2 & 1 & 6 \\ 5 & 3 & -1 & -2 \\ 7 & -4 & 8 & -3 \end{array}$$

and B is the 4 x 5 array

$$
\begin{array}{rrrrr}
1 & -1 & 2 & -2 & 3 \\
3 & -4 & 4 & -3 & -3 \\
6 & -5 & -6 & 5 & -2 \\
7 & 8 & -8 & -7 & 2
\end{array}
$$

the product will be a 3 x 5 array in which the first three elements of row 1 are computed as follows:

$$
\begin{aligned}
P(1,1) &= 4*1 + 2*3 + 1*6 + 6*7 = 58 \\
P(1,2) &= 4*-1 + 2*-4 + 1*-5 + 6*8 = 31 \\
P(1,3) &= 4*2 + 2*4 + 1*-6 + 6*-8 = -38
\end{aligned}
$$

The entire result is

$$
\begin{array}{rrrrr}
58 & 31 & -38 & -51 & 16 \\
-6 & -28 & 44 & -10 & 4 \\
22 & -55 & -26 & 59 & 11
\end{array}
$$

Write a program that reads a succession of input sets where each set consists of values for r, c, and s, followed by A, then B, each array in row major order. c and s each have maximum values of 5, and the maximum for r is 20. Print A and B, one row per line, then compute P and print it, one row per line. Each set of A, B and P is to appear on a separate page.

SUMMARY OF IMPORTANT TERMS

Array	An organized collection of data items stored contiguously under a collective name and sharing a common set of attributes. While reference to the collective name provides access to the entire array, it is still possible to refer to any single *element* of that array by specification of an appropriate *subscript*.
Base variable	A declared variable whose corresponding storage subsequently will be associated with one or more other (*defined*) variables. The reference (base) variable also is known as a *defining* variable.
BEGIN statement	Used specifically as the initial statement in a **BEGIN** block.
BEGIN block	A PL/I program component consisting of an arbitrary sequence of statements, starting with a **BEGIN** statement and concluding with an **END** statement. This component has the very basic advantage that variables declared within its confines are allocated *dynamically* so that they do not exist outside of the block.

Column	The term used to describe the second dimension of a multidimension array.
Cross section	An organizationally consistent subset of an array. Thus, a row or column would constitute a cross section of a multidimensional array.
DEFINED attribute	An explicitly declared attribute that designates its associated variable name as being an alternative reference to an area of storage previously associated with another name (that is, a based variable).
DEFINED variable	A variable that is declared with the **DEFINED** attribute.
Dimensionality	The number of criteria (subscripts) required to distinguish a single element from all others in an array.
DO loop	A structural component in a PL/I program (beginning with a **DO** statement and concluding with an **END** statement) that sets up a mechanism for automatic control of a cyclic sequence of operations.
Dynamic storage allocation	A technique whereby a programmer can make a designated amount of storage available at the moment it is needed, dispensing with it immediately after it has served its purpose. One mechanism for specifying dynamic storage allocation in PL/I is the **BEGIN** block.
i**SUB** specification	A PL/I option that allows the programmer to specify an arbitrarily constructed defined array on a previously declared based array.
POSITION specification	Part of a **DEFINED** description that indicates the starting point of a defined character string relative to that of its base string.
Row	The term used to refer to the first dimension of an array.
Row major order	The sequence in which array elements are stored in PL/I. The term derives from the fact that the elements are arranged so that the row number does not change until all of the succeeding dimensions have completely cycled.
Subscript	A designation that uniquely identifies an element in an array. Such identification requires one subscript for each dimension of the array.

SUPPLEMENTARY READING

IBM OS PL/I Checkout and Optimizing Compilers: Language Reference Manual. IBM Publication SC33-0009. White Plains, N.Y.: IBM Corporation, 1971, pp. 386-390.

IBM System/360 PL/I Reference Manual. IBM Publications C28-8201. White Plains, N.Y.: IBM Corporation, 1968, pp. 275-277.

VII STRUCTURES

Although arrays represent a convenient and flexible vehicle for organizing and handling collections of data, there is a basic restriction connected with their use; that is, all elements of an array must possess a common set of attributes. If an array is declared as being composed of ten strings of characters, none of its ten elements can be anything else. Similarly, the fact that an array is declared as being floating-point decimal with a particular precision means that each element will always have that combination of attributes.

It is often desirable to assign a collective name to a group of data items that may not necessarily share a set of common attributes but are nonetheless related to each other. For example, a procedure for processing medical records may be organized and implemented more conveniently if it can refer to one person's set of readings by a single name, even though that set could contain character data such as the person's name, as well as arithmetic data with various attributes such as height, weight, and blood pressure. Similarly, a listing of inventory data will usually contain names of items and other nonnumerical identifiers, as well as numerical values, such as prices or quantities on hand. In fact, such collections (usually termed *records*) represent fundamental entities of information in the widest spectrum of data processing applications irrespective of the involvement of computers.

The universality of this type of data organization is recognized in PL/I and is accomodated by aggregates called *structures*. In this chapter we shall explore the basic properties and uses of this language feature. Later on this will serve as background for the manipulation of externally stored data records.

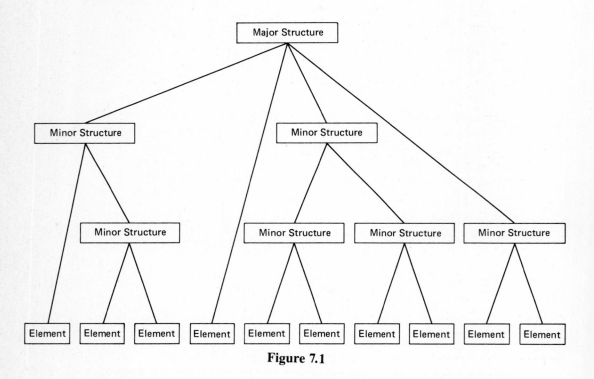

Figure 7.1

VII.1   DECLARATION OF STRUCTURES

A structure is a diverse collection of data referred to by a common name called a *major structure name*. This identifier, together with those associated with the members within the structure, are defined via the general facilities of PL/I's **DECLARE** statement. The member names contained in a structure may refer to single items or they may be collective names for smaller aggregations within the structure. When the latter is the case, the name is known as a minor structure name. A minor structure may in turn contain other minor structures, and so on. The individual items (those names to which specific numerical or character string variables can be assigned) are called *structural elements*. This hierarchical nature of a structure may be visualized by treating the structure as a tree with the major structure name as the trunk, the minor structures as the limbs, branches, or twigs, and the elements as leaves. This is shown schematically in Figure 7.1. An inverted tree is used for convenience.

A structure is declared by specifying the major structure name, followed by a list of names to be subservient to that structure. The relationship between parts of a structure is indicated by positive integer decimal constants called *levels* placed before each name and separated from it by one or more blanks. A major name always must have a level of 1. The level numbers given to minor structures and elements depend on their placement and status in the structural tree.

Suppose we were processing medical data for a group of employees and we wanted to create a structure called MED, consisting of the following data:

Description of Variable	Variable Name	Attributes
Employee's name	NAME	**CHARACTER** (20)
Employee's date of birth (month, day, year)	BIRTH	**CHARACTER** (6)
Employee's height in inches	HT	**FIXED** (2)
Employee's weight in pounds	WT	**FIXED** (3)
Age in years at examination	AGE	**FIXED** (2)

This structure is set up in PL/I by writing the statement

DECLARE 1 MED, 2 NAME **CHARACTER**(20), 2 BIRTH
  CHARACTER(6), 2 HT **FIXED**(2), 2 WT **FIXED**(3),
  2 AGE **FIXED**(2);

As seen from this declaration, the rule in PL/I is that the level number assigned to the more comprehensive name is numerically lower than that of the members contained in it. NAME, BIRTH, HT, WT, and AGE each have been given the same level number because they are all subservient to the overall structure MED, but none of these is subservient to any of the others. They can all be considered at the same level.

When an array name is declared, data attributes are specified in the declaration or assigned by PL/I's default mechanisms. With structures, however, data attributes are only assigned to or assumed for the names of elements. A structure (major or minor) refers to a group of other names and not a specific location where a value is stored. Consequently, *no data attributes are assigned to structure names*. (Structure names sometimes can have other attributes, such as **ALIGNED** or **EXTERNAL**, which we shall study later.) With regard to the structure shown before, the names NAME, BIRTH, HT, WT, and AGE each have attributes, while MED, a structure name, does not.

The hierarchy of variables employed in generating a structure is certainly not limited to two levels. Suppose that it is useful to consider the date of birth (BIRTH) as consisting of three separate entities called MONTH, DAY, and YR, each of which could be independently manipulated. Under such circumstances, the name BIRTH no longer has any data attributes attached to it directly. Instead, it is in itself a structure encompassing three elements. When we combined these three under one name, the implication was that we did not intend to do any arithmetic on them and therefore assigned the **CHARACTER** attribute to them. Now that we are considering BIRTH as three separate variables, it will be more helpful to treat each of them as a numerical quantity rather than a character string, and we shall indicate this in our new declaration. Of course, data accessed via this new declaration will have a different internal appearance than under the former declaration. By extending the PL/I convention stated above, the level number attached to each of these three variables must be greater than that attached to the minor structure name BIRTH. Thus, if we consider MONTH, DAY, and YR as fixed-point decimal variables with precision (2,0), a new declaration for the entire structure would appear as follows:

> **DECLARE** 1 MED, 2 NAME **CHARACTER**(20), 2 BIRTH,
>
> 3 MONTH **FIXED**(2), 3 DAY **FIXED**(2), 3 YR **FIXED**(2),
>
> 2 HT **FIXED**(2), 2 WT **FIXED**(3), 2 AGE **FIXED**(2);

Attribute factoring can be used to shorten this declaration producing

> **DECLARE** 1 MED, 2 NAME **CHARACTER**(20), 2 BIRTH,
>
> 3 (MONTH, DAY, YR) **FIXED**(2), 2 HT
>
> **FIXED**(2), 2 WT **FIXED**(3), 2 AGE **FIXED**(2);

Note that the level number also may be factored. We can rewrite this declaration by taking advantage of PL/I's free format for source statements to present a visual representation of the hierarchical relationship among the variables in the structure:

> **DECLARE** 1 MED,
>
> 2 NAME **CHARACTER**(20),
>
> 2 BIRTH,
>
> 3 MONTH **FIXED**(2),
>
> 3 DAY **FIXED**(2),
>
> 3 YR **FIXED**(2),
>
> 2 HT **FIXED**(2),
>
> 2 WT **FIXED**(3),
>
> 2 AGE **FIXED**(2);

This method allows much greater clarity and should be adopted. The possibilities for combining and arranging variables in a structure are virtually unrestricted; there are no practical limitations imposed by the compiler in terms of the number of variables that may be included, the combination of attributes they may possess, or the number of levels they may be assigned.

VII.1.1   Assignment of Levels in Structures

The most comprehensive name in a declared structure (the collective name under which all other members are contained) is a *major structure* name. As such, it must be assigned a level of 1 and must be the only name in that structure receiving that level. The actual elements in the structure (those variable names to which specific data attributes are assigned) are called *structural elements*, and as such must be given level numbers numerically higher than those assigned to the structure name of the structure that contains them. When some of the elements in the structure are additionally grouped under some other name, that grouping is referred to as a *minor structure*. Thus, as we have seen, BIRTH is a minor structure contained in the major structure MED.

In addition to the necessity of using a level of 1 for a major structure, there are a number of procedural rules governing the general assignments of levels.

1.   When the declaration of a structure is set up, the name of the structure, whether it be major or minor, must precede the names of the variables contained in it. Thus, as we have seen, MED is the first name in the declaration and BIRTH immediately precedes the three variables contained in it.

2.   Variables contained in a structure must be assigned level numbers numerically greater than that assigned to the structure containing them.

3.   The various level numbers assigned to portions of the structure need not be consecutive, as long as the lower-to-higher relationship is maintained between structures and elements. Thus, NAME, BIRTH, HT, WT, and AGE could have been assigned a level of 5, and MONTH, DAY, and YR could have been levels of 27.

4.   When a structure contains a minor structure and an element not contained in that minor structure, errors can be avoided by assigning the minor structure and the element the same level number. This is seen in the structure MED, where BIRTH and HT have the same level numbers, even though the former is a minor structure, itself containing several elements.

5.   A major structure is terminated by the declaration of another major structure name at level 1, by the declaration of a name without a level number, or by the end of the declaration. A minor structure is terminated by the declaration of another minor structure or structural element at the same or a lower level.

It should be understood that these rules are not inviolable and can be relaxed somewhat if the programmer has a clear and detailed idea of how the compiler processes the declaration of a structure. However, the programmer is usually much better off when he defines his structures in as straightforward a manner as possible. By using consecutive level numbers and writing out his declaration in an indented form as shown in the previous example, he will minimize the difficulties in organizing the structure without sacrificing flexibility.

Illustration 17

TABLE 7.1 Organization of Inventory
Data for the Operatic Soap
Company

SOAP
  NAME
    Trade Name (TRADE)
    Technical Name (TECHNICAL)
DATE
  Month (MONTH)
  Day (DAY)
  YEAR
    Decade (DEC)
    Unit (UNIT)
NVNTRY
  LARGE
    BOXWT
      Pounds (LBS)
      Ounces (OZ)
    Number of Boxes (NBOX)
  GIANT
    BOXWT
      Pounds (LBS)
      Ounces (OZ)
    Number of Boxes (NBOX)
  KING
    BOXWT
      Pounds (LBS)
      Ounces (OZ)
    Number of Boxes (NBOX)

The Operatic Soap Company produces a monthly summary inventory card for each of its manufactured soap products. Each card contains the following information in the order listed:

1. Trade name under which the soap is sold, expressed as a name not exceeding 15 characters.
2. Technical name of the soap, expressed as an eight-character string.

3. Month and year for which this inventory is current (for example, 0572 represents May 1972).

4. Weight of large box size, in pounds and ounces.

5. Number of large size boxes on hand (can be as high as 400,000).

6. Weight of giant size box, in pounds and ounces.

7. Number of giant size boxes available (can be as high 500,000).

8. Weight of king size box, in pounds and ounces.

9. Number of king size boxes on hand (can be as high as 250,000).

We shall develop a structure representing the contents of this inventory card. This can be done most easily by showing the hierarchical relationships among the variables on the inventory card organized in much the same way as the table of contents of a book. This is shown in Table 7.1. As in all conventional tables, we have used indentation to show that a variable is contained under a particular heading. The names shown in capital letters without parentheses represent

TABLE 7.2 Structure Declaration for
Operatic Soap Company's
Inventory Card

```
DECLARE 1 SOAP,
          2 NAME,
            3 TRADE CHARACTER(15),
            3 TECH CHARACTER(8),
          2 DATE,
            3 (MONTH, DAY) FIXED(2),
            3 YR,
              4 (DEC, UNIT) FIXED(1),
          2 NVNTRY
            3 LARGE,
              4 BOXWT,
                5 (LBS, OZ) FIXED(2),
              4 NBOX FIXED(6),
            3 GIANT,
              4 BOXWT,
                5 (LBS, OZ) FIXED(2),
              4 NBOX FIXED(6),
            3 KING,
              4 BOXWT,
                5 (LBS, OZ) FIXED(2),
              4 NBOX FIXED(6);
```

major and minor headings that will become major and minor structures in our declaration. The names in lowercase letters represent the actual structural elements, and the parenthesized names next to them are the ones to which the attributes will be assigned. We can briefly summarize the composition of our major structure SOAP by saying that it will contain three minor structures NAME, DATE, and NVNTRY. NAME will contain two elements; DATE will contain two elements and a minor structure, YEAR, which in turn will contain two elements. NVNTRY will contain three minor structures, LARGE, GIANT, and KING, each of which will contain an element and a minor structure, the latter itself containing two elements. Once this organizational setup has been defined, the assignment of level numbers then becomes a straightforward proposition, and the resulting declaration can be written as shown in Table 7.2. Examination of this table indicates that we need five levels to express the structural organization of this inventory card. Equally apparent is the fact that a number of variables have been given the same name. When this is done properly, there is no internal confusion, as we shall see in the next section.

VII.1.2   Naming Elements in Structures

The identification of a particular variable as a member of a collection is nothing new to us. We have seen that it is possible to distinguish one element from another in an array with a single name by attaching a unique subscript to the array name; in other words, we *qualify* that array name by attaching a subscript to it. Exactly the same thing can occur when we want to identify an element in a structure. In addition to specifying the name of the element, PL/I allows the programmer to extend its name by attaching to it the name of the structure in which that element is contained. When an element is identified in this manner, it is said to have a *qualified name.* The rules for constructing such names are very flexible in that they allow the programmer to specify any structure names necessary to distinguish the element uniquely from all other elements in the structure. The general form for writing such a name consists of combining the element's name with that of the structure containing it, placing them in hierarchical order from high to low, and separating them by a period, with no intervening blanks. Thus, referring to Table 7.2, the qualified name or soap's technical identifier would be SOAP.NAME.TECH.

It is obvious that there is no need to write the full qualified name for TECH in order to distinguish it from all other elements in the major structure. TECH is a unique name not used by any other element in the structure and therefore needs no additional qualifier. The real utility of qualified names lies in the fact that they allow the programmer to assign the same name to several structural elements and still maintain a mechanism for telling them apart. This is often a great convenience in keeping track of data aggregates. Thus, we have no trouble in distinguishing the three elements named NBOX, since we can refer to them as SOAP.NVNTRY.LARGE.NBOX, SOAP.NVNTRY.GIANT.NBOX, and SOAP.NVNTRY.KING.NBOX.

PL/I allows additional flexibility in the naming of structural elements by making it unnecessary to include the entire hierarchy in a qualified name. The programmer may limit the major and minor structures used in a name to those that are necessary to distinguish that element from all others. Accordingly, the three elements in SOAP named NBOX can be distinguished merely by using LARGE.NBOX, GIANT.NBOX, and KING.NBOX. The compiler can determine to which major structure a particular element belongs as long as sufficient information is given to distinguish that element from all others in that structure. Consequently, there is a variety of combinations that can be legitimately used to identify an element. To illustrate, Table 7.3 shows various ways of identifying the element SOAP.NVNTRY.GIANT.NBOX:

TABLE 7.3 Alternative Qualified Names For A Structural
Element*

FORM	REMARKS
SOAP.NVNTRY.GIANT.NBOX	OK
NVNTRY.GIANT.NBOX	OK
GIANT.NBOX	OK
NVNTRY.NBOX	ambiguous name
SOAP.GIANT.NBOX	OK
SOAP.NBOX	ambiguous name
NBOX	ambiguous name
NBOX.GIANT	improper hierarchy

*Refer to the structure in Table 7.2.

We can take further advantage of PL/I's organizational facilities by using the same name for several elements contained in different structures. For example, it might be plausible to define a major structure called CAKEMIX containing exactly the same minor structures and elements with exactly the same names as shown in Table 7.2. Then, all that would be necessary to distinguish the technical name of a soap and the technical name of a cake mix would be to refer to the former as in SOAP.TECH and to the latter as CAKEMIX.TECH.

Once the programmer is sure that the qualified name he has constructed provides the required uniqueness, he can go ahead and use it just as he would any other single-valued variable or array element, as it now refers to a particular location. Accordingly, it can appear in an input or output list, assignment statement, manipulative instruction, or comparison operation.

VII.1.3 Naming Minor Structures

Qualified names may be formed for minor structures in exactly the same way as for elements. By specifying in hierarchical order a string of names that uniquely distinguish a minor structure name from all other names in the procedure, it is possible to refer to all of the elements contained in that structure by a single collective name. Once that name has been constructed, PL/I treats it in the manner analogous to the treatment of any array cross section. Looking at Table 7.2 once again, use of the name GIANT, for example, would automatically refer collectively to the elements GIANT.LBS, GIANT.OZ, and GIANT.NBOX. In this particular case, the name GIANT would have been enough, because there is nothing else named GIANT. Turning this around, it is clear that if there is another variable named GIANT (whether it be a single-valued variable, array, or a major or minor structure), PL/I will have no trouble distinguishing between the two as long as each name is adequately qualified.

VII.1.4   The **LIKE** Attribute

When a structure or part of a structure contains elements in the same sequence and with the same attributes found in a previously declared structure, it is possible to specify this similarity in a very convenient shorthand. All that is required is to amend the declaration of the second structure by adding the attribute **LIKE** followed by the name of the major structure or the name (qualified if necessary) of the minor structure whose form and attributes are to be duplicated. The part of the structure duplicated consists of the name specified after the **LIKE** attribute, followed by every structural element encompassed by that name.

To illustrate, let us suppose that the Operatic Soap Company (from Illustration 17) has diversified into the cake mix business and stores similar inventory information on cards for each of its mixes. If we were to write an overall inventory procedure to handle cards for both types of products, we could make use of the **LIKE** attribute to avoid the necessity for specifying both parallel structures in detail. Once we have defined the major structure SOAP (as shown in Table 7.2), the simple statement

DECLARE 1 CAKE **LIKE** SOAP;

would be sufficient to specify an entire structure organized exactly like SOAP, down to the names of the elements. That is, use of the **LIKE** attribute supplies sufficient information to allow the construction of a table for CAKE so that it would recognize a qualified name such as CAKE.GIANT.NBOX.

If there are to be some differences between the two structures, the **LIKE** attribute can still be used to define those areas that are the same. For example, if Operatic's cake mixes came in only the giant size, our declaration would read

DECLARE 1 CAKE,
    2 NAME **LIKE** SOAP.NAME,
    2 DATE **LIKE** SOAP.DATE,
    2 NVNTRY **LIKE** SOAP.GIANT;

This is the same as writing

```
DECLARE 1 CAKE,
    2 NAME,
        3 TRADE CHARACTER(15), 3 TECH CHARACTER(8),
    2 DATE,
        (3 MONTH, 3 DAY) FIXED(2),
        3 YR, (4 DEC, 4 UNIT) FIXED(1),
    2 NVNTRY,
        3 BOXWT, (4 LBS, 4 OZ) FIXED(2),
        3 NBOX FIXED(6);
```

Although the structure BOXWT and the elements LBS, OZ, and NBOX have different levels in CAKE than they do in SOAP, the internal relationship between their levels has been maintained. BOXWT and NBOX still have equal level numbers, with their value being one below that of LBS and OZ.

One thing more should be noted with respect to the **LIKE** attribute. A *reference structure* (the structure named on the right side of the **LIKE** specification) cannot be one that itself was declared as being like some other structure.   *Restriction*

VII.2   INPUT/OUTPUT OF STRUCTURES

The conveniences available for transmitting structures to and from the processor are exact parallels to those discussed previously for arrays. If the unqualified name of a major structure appears in a **GET** or **PUT** statement, the elements of the entire structure will be transmitted in exactly the same order as they were declared. Thus, the statement

GET LIST (SOAP);

will cause the program to read the next 15 items in the data stream and store them in their respective locations named by the structure's declaration (see Table 7.2). In this example the first two pieces of data should be character strings, and the remaining 13 should be numbers. In any case, PL/I will attempt to perform any necessary conversions.

If a qualified name for a structural element or a minor structure is properly specified, its value can be read in by itself. Similarly, if such a name is given in an output statement, the program will independently access the particular element or minor structure and print it. For instance, referring to our now historic soap inventory card in Table 7.2, the statement

PUT LIST (LARGE.BOXWT);

will cause the program to print two fixed-point decimal values representing the number of pounds and ounces, respectively, contained in a large size box of the particular soap whose record happens to be in storage at that time. Had we written

PUT LIST(BOXWT); or **PUT LIST**(NVNTRY.BOXWT);

processing would be terminated and an error message would be produced, indicating that an ambiguous name had been used, since insufficient information has been supplied to enable the program to identify one minor structure uniquely among the three possibilities present.

When data-directed input is used, the miniature assignment statements in the input stream must contain fully qualified names. The flexibility of using only the amount of qualification needed to ensure uniqueness does not extend to variable names in the input stream. This tends to detract from the desirability of using **GET DATA** for structures.

VII.3   INTERNAL MANIPULATION OF STRUCTURES

When appropriately named, entire structures or parts of structures may appear in assignment statements, with the result that the indicated operations will be performed on all of the elements contained within the qualified name. Suppose we had a card punched as shown below

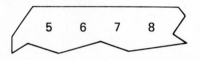

and we wrote the following sequence of instructions:

DECLARE 1 A, 2 B, (3 C, 3 D) **FIXED**(2),
                    2 E, (3 F, 3 G) **FIXED**(2);
GET LIST(A); B = 2*B + 4 − E; **PUT SKIP LIST** (B,E.F);

The processing produced by the last three statements would be exactly equivalent to the following:

GET LIST(C,D,F,G); C = 2*C + 4 − F; D = 2*D + 4− G;

PUT SKIP LIST (C,D,F);

The resulting printout would show the three values 7 8 7. In certain instances, the results obtained from assignment statements involving structures are not clear directly from the construction of the statement. We saw such a case with arrays in the statement

Y = Y + Y(1);

(as described in the previous chapter), wherein the value of Y(1) was initially added to itself and the resulting new value was used with all succeeding elements of the array. In the case of structures, the same problem comes up. Using the data in the previous example, if we were to say

B = B**2 + C;

PL/I would square the value of C, add the *original* value of C to that product, and store the result in location C. Then it would perform similar operations on D, using the new value of C. This would give C the new value $5 \times 5 + 5$, or 30, and D would be $6 \times 6 + 30$, or 66.

Assignment statements can also be written involving several structures, as long as they are identically structured. If we said

DECLARE 1 A, 2 B **FLOAT**(6), 2 C, (3 D, 3 E) **FLOAT**(6),
　　　　　　1 A1, 4 C **FIXED**(2), 4 E, (7 D, 7 F) **FIXED** (2),
　　　　　　1 A2 **LIKE** A;
GET LIST (A,A1); A2 = A + 2*A1;

the assignment would be equivalent to the following:

A2.B = A.B + 2*A1.C;

A2.C.D = A.C.D + 2*A1.E.D;

A2.C.E = A.C.E + 2*A1.E.F;

Note that although the level numbers are not the same in all the structures, the relationship between the elements is identical. Also, the difference in attributes between the corresponding elements of A and A1 is handled in the usual way by PL/I's automatic conversions.

Illustration 18

The Operatic Soap Company maintains inventory records on cards organized as shown in Table 7.2. A printout of these records has revealed that the soap with the tradename of AIDA had been erroneously punched as TOSCA. Furthermore, it was found that the new clerk who counted the boxes for the current month's inventory report was not completely familiar with the warehouse and neglected to include the contents of an entire little room. Luckily, this room contained large, giant, and king size boxes of only one type of soap, so that only one inventory record needs to be changed. We do not know the location of the card for the particular soap in the overall stack of inventory cards. Write a program to change the trade name as indicated above, correcting inventory figures for the soap in question, and print out a new inventory table, skipping a line between individual types of soap.

The procedure will be designed to expect the inventory changes to be punched on a card organized exactly as an ordinary inventory card, and a special duplicate structure will be defined to contain this information. Once this card is read in, a loop will be constructed whereby each inventory card is read and compared with the changed information. As long as no match is found, the cards will merely be printed as they were read. As soon as the proper card is identified, changes will be made and the new information printed:

```
ILL18: PROCEDURE OPTIONS (MAIN);
       DECLARE 1 SOAP, 2 NAME,
                     3 TRADE CHARACTER(15),
                     3 TECH  CHARACTER(8),
                   2 DATE,
                     (3 MONTH, 3 DAY) FIXED(2),
                     3 YEAR,
                        (4 DECADE, 4 UNIT) FIXED(1),
                   2 NVNTRY,
                     3 LARGE,
                        4 BOXWT,
                           (5 LBS, 5 OZ) FIXED(2),
                        4 NBOX FIXED(6),
                     3 GIANT,
                        4 BOXWT,
                           (5 LBS, 5 OZ) FIXED(2),
                        4 NBOX FIXED(6),
                     3 KING,
                        4 BOXWT,
                           (5 LBS, 5 OZ) FIXED(2),
                        4 NBOX FIXED(6),
                1 HOAP LIKE SOAP,
                NDFILE FIXED(1) INITIAL (0);

       ON ENDFILE (SYSIN) NDFILE=1;
       GET LIST (HOAP);
       GET LIST (SOAP);

/*---NOW WE SHALL COMPARE EACH SET OF INVENTORY DATA   ---*/
/*---AGAINST THE NAME IN HOAP TO SEE WHETHER:          ---*/
/*---  (A) THE TRADE NAME NEEDS CHANGING, AND/OR       ---*/
/*---  (B) THE INVENTORY FIGURES NEED CHANGING.        ---*/

       DO WHILE (NDFILE=0);
        IF SOAP.TRADE = 'TOSCA' THEN SOAP.TRADE = 'AIDA';
        IF SOAP.TRADE = HOAP.TRADE
          THEN DO;
               SOAP.LARGE.NBOX=SOAP.LARGE.NBOX+HOAP.LARGE.NBOX;
               SOAP.GIANT.NBOX=SOAP.GIANT.NBOX+HOAP.GIANT.NBOX;
               SOAP.KING.NBOX=SOAP.KING.NBOX+HOAP.KING.NBOX;
          END;
        PUT SKIP(2) LIST (SOAP);
        GET LIST (SOAP);
       END;

       STOP;
       END ILL18;
```

Incidentally, the thoroughness of PL/I's attribute table can be especially helpful in dealing with complex structures. Although a structure may be declared in concise form (with the **LIKE** attribute), the compiler produces a complete list of all elements, each accompanied by information about its hierarchical relations to its containing structure. This is seen in Figure 7.2, which shows part of the attribute table for Illustration 18.

VII.4 THE **BY NAME** OPTION

When properly constructed, it is possible to write a single statement to produce a series of internal manipulations for a number of elements from several structures, even though those

DCL NO.	IDENTIFIER	ATTRIBUTES AND REFERENCES
2	LBS	IN BOXWT IN KING IN NVNTRY IN SOAP,AUTOMATIC,ALIGNED,DECIMAL,FIXED (2,0)
2	LBS	IN BOXWT IN GIANT IN NVNTRY IN SOAP,AUTOMATIC,ALIGNED,DECIMAL,FIXED (2,0)
2	LBS	IN BOXWT IN LARGE IN NVNTRY IN SOAP,AUTOMATIC,ALIGNED,DECIMAL,FIXED (2,0)
2	LBS	IN BOXWT IN KING IN NVNTRY IN HOAP,AUTOMATIC,ALIGNED,DECIMAL,FIXED (2,0)
2	LBS	IN BOXWT IN GIANT IN NVNTRY IN HOAP,AUTOMATIC,ALIGNED,DECIMAL,FIXED (2,0)
2	LBS	IN BOXWT IN LARGE IN NVNTRY IN HOAP,AUTOMATIC,ALIGNED,DECIMAL,FIXED (2,0)
2	MONTH	IN DATE IN SOAP,AUTOMATIC,ALIGNED,DECIMAL,FIXED(2,0)
2	MONTH	IN DATE IN HOAP,AUTOMATIC,ALIGNED,DECIMAL,FIXED(2,0)
2	NAME	IN SOAP,AUTOMATIC,STRUCTURE
2	NAME	IN HOAP,AUTOMATIC,STRUCTURE
2	NBOX	IN KING IN NVNTRY IN SOAP,AUTOMATIC,ALIGNED,DECIMAL,FIXED(6,0) 13,13
2	NBOX	IN GIANT IN NVNTRY IN SOAP,AUTOMATIC,ALIGNED,DECIMAL,FIXED (6,0) 12,12
2	NBOX	IN LARGE IN NVNTRY IN SOAP,AUTOMATIC,ALIGNED,DECIMAL,FIXED (6,0) 11,11
2	NBOX	IN KING IN NVNTRY IN HOAP,AUTOMATIC,ALIGNED,DECIMAL,FIXED(6,0) 13
2	NBOX	IN GIANT IN NVNTRY IN HOAP,AUTOMATIC,ALIGNED,DECIMAL,FIXED (6,0) 12
2	NBOX	IN LARGE IN NVNTRY IN HOAP,AUTOMATIC,ALIGNED,DECIMAL,FIXED (6,0) 11

Figure 7.2

structures are not identically specified. The mechanism permitting this type of manipulation is the **BY NAME** option, a feature that can be included in assignment statements involving structures. When this option is specified, PL/I seeks out and operates on only those elements whose names (up to major structure level) are found to be common to all of the structures in the statement. For instance, if we had the structures

DECLARE 1 A,	DECLARE 1 A1,	DECLARE 1 A2,
2 B,	2 B,	2 B,
3 C **FIXED**(2),	3 C **FIXED**(2),	4 C **FIXED**(2),
3 D **FIXED**(2),	3 D **FIXED**(2),	4 C **FIXED**(2),
3 E **FIXED**(2),	3 E **FIXED**(2),	
2 F **FIXED**(2),	2 F **FIXED**(2),	2 G **FIXED**(2),
2 H **FIXED**(2),	2 H **FIXED**(2),	2 H **FIXED**(2),
2 W,	2 S,	2 T **FIXED**(2).
3 X **FIXED**(2),	3 X **FIXED**(2),	2 F **FIXED**(2),
3 Y **FIXED**(2);	3 Y **FIXED**(2);	

and we wrote

   A2 = A + A1 − 3, **BY NAME**;

the process would be handled as follows:

1. All members at the next level having the same name are found and compared. For our
    example these are as follows:
       A2.B, A.B, A1.B
       A2.H, A.H, A1.H
       A2.F, A.F, A1.F

2. If all similar names in a group refer to structures, PL/I generates further **BY NAME**
    assignments. If these names refer to elements, ordinary assignment statements are
    generated. When inconsistencies are found in a group (for example, one name refers
    to a structure while another is assigned to a single element), that group is abandoned.
    In our example, all the B's refer to structures and all the H's are elements, as are the
    F's. Consequently, the compiler produces the following sequence:
       A2.B = A.B + A1.B − 3, **BY NAME**;
       A2.H = A.H + A1.H −3;
       A2.F = A.F + A1.F − 3;
    Note that the order is determined by the organization of the structure to the left of the
    equals sign.

3. All **BY NAME** statements generated in Step 2 are analyzed further, producing addi-
    tional **BY NAME** statements, and so on, until all of the generated statements involve
    only elements. In our example, PL/I would have to work down one more level. The
    common names contained in the three B's are:
       A2.B.C, A.B.C, A1.B.C
       A2.B.D, A.B.D, A1.B.D
    Consequently, the dissection of the original **BY NAME** statement finally yields the
    following sequence of operations:
       A2.B.C = A.B.C + A1.B.C − 3;
       A2.B.D = A.B.D + A1.B.D − 3;
       A2.H = A.H + A1.H;   A2.F = A.F + A1.F;
    All other elements in A2 will retain their current values.

VII.5   INTERACTION OF ARRAYS AND STRUCTURES

As long as he is willing and able to do the necessary bookkeeping, the PL/I programmer can
define and work with complex collections of data involving various combinations of arrays and
structures. There are no specific restrictions imposed by the compiler in this respect: it allows
the inclusion of arrays as multivalued structural members and permits the synthesis of larger
arrays of values in which each division of an array is in itself an entire structure. As it is

impossible to explore the variety of combinations obtained by applying these capabilities, we shall present them as extensions of the basic techniques for organizing arrays and structures.

VII.5.1   Inclusion of Arrays In Structures

It is not necessary to restrict structural elements to single-valued variables. Such elements may consist of collections of values grouped into arrays with exactly the mechanisms used as for ordinary array declarations.

Illustration 19

Let us suppose that a manufacturer of industrial immersion heaters maintains a file of punched cards, each containing definitive information about a particular type of heater, as listed below:

- Part number (five characters consisting of four digits and a letter)

- Unit price (a typical value is $1033.67)

- Weight in pounds (a typical value is 104.5)

- Length of heating element in inches (for example, 18.8)

- Volume of test water in gallons (0-99 gallons used)

- Test data, recorded as a table consisting of six time readings followed by six temperature readings. Each time reading is a three-digit number representing whole minutes, and each temperature reading is a three-digit number representing degrees to the nearest degree. A typical card is shown in Figure 7.3.

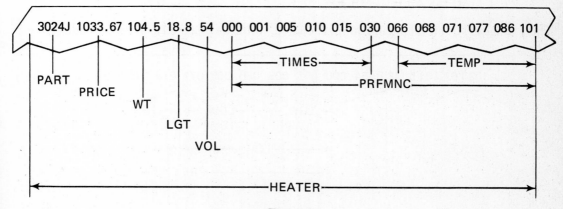

Figure 7.3

The data contained on such cards can be organized into a structure by means of the following declaration:

DECLARE 1 HEATER,

  2 PART **CHARACTER**(5), 2 PRICE **FIXED**(6,2),

  2 WT **FIXED**(4,1), 2 LGT **FIXED**(3,1), 2 VOL **FIXED**(2),

  2 PRFMNC,

    (3 TIME(6), 3 TEMP(6)) **FIXED**(3);

Having organized the data in this manner, we can refer to any element as we did before. Thus, TIME(2) refers to the second time reading on the card.

    A wide variety of alternative structural organizations can be specified, depending on the programmer's particular needs. Let us suppose that each of these industrial heaters has two operating modes (low and high) and that the first three of the six time-temperature readings are always obtained in the low operating mode. This distinction could be reflected in a declaration that reads as follows:

DECLARE 1 HEATER,

  2 PART **CHARACTER**(5), 2 PRICE **FIXED**(6,2),

 2 WT **FIXED**(4,1), 2 LGT **FIXED**(3,1), 2 VOL **FIXED**(2),

  2 PRFMNC,

    3 LOW,

      (4 TIME(3), 4 TEMP(3)) **FIXED**(3),

    3 HIGH,

      (4 TIME(3), 4 TEMP(3)) **FIXED**(3);

This change in structural organization, of course, would be reflected in a corresponding change

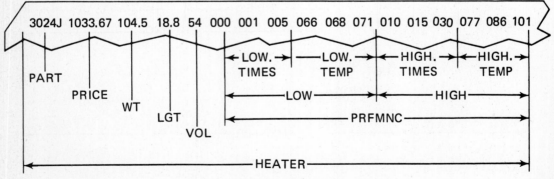

Figure 7.4

in the order of the values on the data card. Accordingly, the sample values shown before would be rearranged as seen in Figure 7.4. Under this type of organization, note that the names TIMES and TEMP each can refer to two separate and distinct arrays. It is now necessary to use a qualified name (such as LOW.TEMP) to distinguish the array of readings obtained at low operating mode from those recorded under the alternative conditions.

VII.5.2   Arrays of Structures

When a programmer finds it desirable to declare and maintain a number of identically organized structures, he can, if he wishes, consider each structure a member of an array of structures. By using this method of organization, it is possible to refer to an entire collection of structures by a single name and to distinguish one structure from another by attaching a suitable subscript to that name.

The declaration of an array of structures is developed in exactly the same way as it would be for an ordinary array: the dimensions of the array are specified within parentheses immediately following the name of the structure. Thus, the statement

DECLARE 1 A(3), 2 B, 3 C **FIXED**(2), 3 D **CHARACTER**(5),
$\qquad$ 2 E **FLOAT**(7), 2 F(2) **FIXED**(3);

will cause PL/I to allocate storage for the following variables:

- A one-dimensional array C consisting of three fixed-point decimal numbers with precision (2,0)

- A one-dimensional array D consisting of three strings containing five characters each

- A one-dimensional array E consisting of three seven-digit floating-point decimal numbers

- A two-dimensional array F consisting of three rows and two columns, with each element containing a three-digit fixed-point decimal integer

The organization of this storage can be depicted as follows:

The construction of a subscripted qualified name may assume several legitimate forms. These alternatives result from the ability to move any or all of the subscripts to any portion of the name, as long as their order is maintained. We can examine this flexibility by listing the various ways of referring to the element circled above. These are

$$A(2).F(1) \quad A(2,1).F \quad A.F(2,1) \quad F(2,1)$$

The organization of structures into arrays is not restricted to major structures. If it suits the programmer's convenience, he may declare a single major structure that contains one or more arrays of minor structures. Use of this facility can conveniently be illustrated by employing it as a shorthand method for declaring the structure used in Illustration 18. Referring to that declaration, we see that the minor structure NVNTRY contains three structures of identical composition. Consequently, we can express NVNTRY as an array in which each of these three structures is a member. The resulting declaration will read as shown in Table 7.4, and the organization of our structure can now be expressed as follows:

1. SOAP is still a single major structure.

2. NAME and DATE each are minor structures as before, containing their previous structural element.

3. NVNTRY is now replaced by an array of three structures named SIZE(1), SIZE(2), and SIZE(3).

4. BOXWT is now an array of structures, each containing two fixed-point decimal variables. Thus, the location containing the value representing the number of pounds in a giant box of a particular soap is now identifiable by the name SIZE(2).LBS, or merely LBS(2).

5. Finally, NBOX is a one-dimensional array containing three fixed-point numbers.

TABLE 7.4 Structure Declaration for
Inventory Card Using Arrays

```
DECLARE 1 SOAP,
   2 NAME,
      3 TRADE CHARACTER(15),
      3 TECH CHARACTER(8),
   2 DATE,
      (3 MONTH, 3 DAY) FIXED(2),
      3 YEAR,
         (4 DECADE, 4 UNIT) FIXED(1),
   2 SIZE(3),
      3 BOXWT,
         (4 LBS, 4 OZ) FIXED(2),
      3 NBOX FIXED(6);
```

Arrays of structures need not be unidimensional. The structure

DECLARE 1 A(2,2), 2 B, 2 C;

specifies B and C as two-dimensional arrays. PL/I offers extremely flexible combinations. The structure

DECLARE 1 A(2), 2 B(4,3);

makes A an array of two structures, and B, within A, thus has dimensions $2 \times 4 \times 3$.

Arrays of structures may be manipulated like other arrays. When they appear in an assignment, whether with the **BY NAME** option or not, all of the participating arrays must have the same number of dimensions and the same bounds. The process for evaluating such assignment statements is the same as described in Chapter VI, with the compiler operating on each set of corresponding array elements (individual structures in this case) in turn.

PROBLEMS

1. There are a number of commonly used documents whose contents can be represented conveniently as a PL/I structure. Select one or more such documents and declare an appropriate structure for each. Some suggestions follow:

    a. Driver's license.

    b. Library card.

    c. Medical care card (such as Blue Cross, Medicare).

    d. Bank credit card.

    e. Ticket to a sporting event, concert, or play.

    f. Airline or rail ticket.

    g. Stock transaction form (record of purchase or sale of shares).

    h. Gas or electric bill.

2. From the following statements

        DECLARE 1 A, 2 B, (3 C, 3 C1, 3 CL) **FIXED** (3,1),
        3 D, (4 C1, 4 C2) **FIXED** (3,1), 2 E **FIXED** (2),
        2 G, (3 G1, 3 G2) **FIXED** (3,1), 2 H **FIXED** (2); **GET LIST** (A);

and from the card shown below

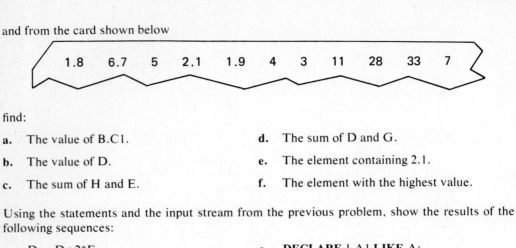

find:

a. The value of B.C1.

b. The value of D.

c. The sum of H and E.

d. The sum of D and G.

e. The element containing 2.1.

f. The element with the highest value.

3. Using the statements and the input stream from the previous problem, show the results of the following sequences:

a. D = D+2*E;

    PUT DATA(D);

b. D = D+B−3*H;

    PUT DATA(D);

c. G = H−G; H = H+2*G2;

    PUT DATA(G,H);

d. A = A−1; B = B+.5;

    D = D+G−C1;

    PUT DATA(A);

e. **DECLARE 1 A1 LIKE A**;

    A1.B = 2+A.B;

    A1.D = A.G−A1.C;

    A1.E = A.H; A1.H = 7;

    A1.G = A1.D+A.H;

    PUT DATA(A1);

f. **DECLARE 1 B1 LIKE B**;

    B1.C1 = 6; B1.C2 = H;

    B1.C = 2*(B1.C1+B1.C2−E)

    PUT DATA (B1);

4. *Organic Computing*, a monthly magazine, maintains data for each of its subscribers on a punched card. The items listed on each card are in the following order:

    subscriber's name (up to 20 characters)
    subscriber's account number (six digits)
    length of subscription (1, 2, 3, 4, or 5 years)
    subscription's last month
    subscription's last year
    initial month and year for this account

At the beginning of each month, the magazine would like to obtain a list of all accounts whose subscriptions are up for renewal two months hence. Write a procedure that provides such a service. For each expiring subscription, the program is to print a line of output containing the account number, name, length of subscription (assumed to be the same as it was), rate per year, and total amount due. Normally, the rates are $8.00, $15.00, $21.00, $26.00, and $30.00 for 1 to 5 years, respectively. However, there is an additional discount for longtime subscribers amounting to 2 percent of the subscription cost for each year in excess of five years that the account has subscribed. (No, *Organic Computing* has not been around nearly long enough for some subscribers to be getting it free.) The columns are to be headed. After the final subscriber has been processed, the program is to print a summary (on a separate page) listing the number of renewals for that month for each time period, together with the corresponding total billing for that time period. Then, after skipping two lines, a final line of output is to show the grand totals.

5. We have the statements

```
DECLARE 1 A(2,3), 2 B FIXED(3),
    2 C, (3 C1,C2) FIXED(3),
    2 D(3), (3 D1, 3 D2) FIXED(3),
        3 D3, (4 E1, 4 E2(2)) FIXED(3);
GET LIST (A);
```

and the following data stream:

> 61,111,39,17,4,2,31,70,120,66,44,51,26,33,80,73,53,95,16,104,6,
> 79,45,62,36,11,54,28,82,114,112,3,21,24,41,43,69,35,12,93,15,8,
> 102,48,27,57,84,32,106,105, 96,47,13,124,56,23,115,97,52,77,123,
> 49,5,76,55,121,98,86,83,25,127,118,19,64,38,68,103,42,29,7,22,
> 58,117,34,88,107,46,14,37,20,90,113,50,67,125,30,1,92,108,72,
> 9,100,40,59,18,91,116,63,65,10,71,118,94,75,87,85,101,60,81,78

a. How many values are accounted for by the structure declaration?

b. Rewrite the values for the structural elements to portray the organization of the structure.

c. Write all of the acceptable names that refer to the value 121.

d. Repeat part c. for the value 95.

e. What is the value of E2(1,3,2,2)?

f. What is the value of A(2,2).D(2).D2?

g. Assuming nothing has been read yet, write a statement that will read in the values 39, 66, 62, 55, 25, and 71.

6. Using the declaration and the data from Problem 5, write a program that reads in enough values to fill A and then:

a. Rearranges the elements in each of the six structures of any A so that they are in ascending order (within their respective structures).

b. Rearranges the structures so that each structure still contains its original values (in ascending order), but now structure A(1) is the one whose elements have the smallest sum, A(2)'s sum is the next smallest, and so on. Print the original structure, skip four lines and print the new structure, leaving a blank line between A(1) and A(2), A(2) and A(3), and so on.

7. The venerable firm of Frères ZaVodnik produces eleven kinds of liqueur, which it packages under customers' brand names. Nine different bottles are available for all eleven types, with the following price schedule:

prices (dollars per bottle)

size type	pint	fifth	quart
plain	4.20	7.75	9.05
opaque	5.20	8.95	11.15
decanter	7.80	10.15	12.35

The liqueur flavors are known to ZaVodnik as Apple, Apricot, Banana, Canteloupe, Cherry, Guava, Peach, Pear, Pineapple, Plum, and Rungleberry for types 1-11, respectively. Customers may supply their own flavor names, limited to 12 characters or less. If such a name is not given, ZaVodnik's is used by default.

Each order for a given flavor is submitted on a separate card which contains the customer's brand name, customer's flavor name (if one is desired), flavor type (a number from 1-11), numerical designations for bottle size and type, and the number of bottles ordered.

Write a program that produces two lines of print for each order. The first one shows the brand name and flavor name to be used; the second is to show the bottle size, bottle type, number of bottles ordered, and the total cost. These sets of output are to be separated by a blank line. After the last order is processed, the program is to print a separate page summarizing the total number of bottles and corresponding dollar amounts for each of the eleven flavors. A final line of output is to indicate the grand totals.

8. Write a program that meets the same requirements specified for the previous problem with the following exception: Output for each order is to appear as a single line of print. (Note: Since the **PUT LIST** or **PUT DATA** statements are limited to five output items per line, something must be done to express the required information in terms of five items. A fruitful approach would be to combine the bottle size and type into a single designation.)

9. Specific Motors Corporation makes six basic types of automobiles, named Meteor, Savage, Orwell, Phoenix, Oedipus, and Omnivor. Each of these types comes in several models and each model has a name.

Meteor	Savage	Orwell	Phoenix	Oedipus	Omnivor
Streak	Claw	Super	Chimera	Special	Adrena
Flash	Talon	Deluxe	Unicorn	Custom	Platina
Whoosh			Dragon	Deluxe	Delancey
				Oracle	

Each time a car is sold, a card is filled out containing the following information: type and model name, month purchased (01 through 12), region in which sold (01 through 18), purchase price (to the nearest cent), and allowance for trade-in (to the nearest cent).

Write a program that will print any or all of the following:

a. Total number of cars sold in any month, and total sales dollars.

b. Total number of cars sold in any region in any month, and total sales dollars.

c. Total number of cars of a given type sold in any month, and total sales dollars.

d. Region with most cars sold in a given month, and total sales dollars.

e. Most popular type in each region (by month or overall).

f. Most popular model in each region (by month or overall).

g. Most popular model in each month.

h. Least popular type and least popular model, for each month and overall.

i. Region giving the highest total trade-in allowance.

j. Average price paid for each type and each model.

SUMMARY OF IMPORTANT TERMS

BY NAME

An option that may appear in an assignment statement involving internal manipulation of several structures. When used, it allows a single set of operations (expressed once) to apply in turn to sequences of similarly organized subsets of structures whose overall organizations need not be identical.

Level

In the context of structure declaration, a numerical designation indicating the hierarchical position of the structural component with regard to other parts of the structure. Higher level numbers signify a lower (that is, more subordinate) hierarchical position.

LIKE

A declared attribute that allows the implicit specification of an entire structure's organization merely by giving its name. The **LIKE** attribute is used to link this name with that of an explicitly described *reference structure* (which see), whereupon PL/I automatically supplies all the necessary allocations to replicate the organization.

Major structure

An entire structure; thus, the major structure name is the only name in that structure having a level of 1 and is an implied collective reference to all of the elements in the structure.

Minor structure

A structure contained in a major structure (that is, its numerical level must be 2 or greater).

Qualified name	A reference to a structural element or minor structure in which the specific name is augmented by associated names in hierarchical order. Thus, if X is an element in minor structure Y, which in turn is contained in major structure Z, X's qualified name would be Z.Y.X.
Reference structure	An explicitly declared structure whose organization is to be replicated in a subsequent declaration by means of the **LIKE** attribute.
Structural element	The lowest component of a structure.
Structure	A collection of data items with arbitrarily different attributes linked together organizationally by means of a hierarchical relationship among them.

VIII TRANSMISSION OF DATA STREAMS

Perhaps the most striking evidence of PL/I's great flexibility in handling information is seen by the extensive choice of techniques offered for sending data to and from the processor. This versatility relieves the programmer of having to be concerned with physical input or output devices. By interacting closely with the supervisory software under which it functions, PL/I is able to handle all of the intricate bookkeeping required to keep track of input sources and output destinations. The programmer need only identify his data to the system. If the identification is adequate, the system will select the external device containing the data and locate the data on that device for input purposes, or determine which device is to be used for output and if it is a sharable device such as a disk, allocate storage on the device. We have already seen that when no identification is included with the source program, PL/I assumes that all data transmission will occur between the processor and standard input and output files, and acts accordingly.

Another aspect of PL/I's input/output flexibility gives the user virtually limitless options for specifying the form and arrangement of his input data and for defining the desired appearance of his output. He may choose to treat his data readings as a continuous *stream* of information, or as a series of definite groupings or *records*. The first mode, called *stream input/output*, operates by considering the data to flow continuously into or out of the processor with no required awareness of physical breaks, such as the end of a punched card, a reel of tape, or a printed line. The stream itself is treated as being a continuous flow of characters, interruptible only by an instruction from the programmer. In dealing with input/output, we have exploited these facilities through the **GET** or **PUT** statement. When transmitting input, we have (indirectly) drawn the program's attention to information that tells it how many characters to intercept from the input stream (hence, the word **GET**) and into what form they are to be converted before they are stored in their designated locations. Conversely, the activities unleashed by the **PUT** statement lead the program to information required to find the proper locations, access their contents, and put them in the output stream. Although stream input/output need not recognize the existence of card boundaries or print line endings, PL/I does allow the programmer to take some cognizance of these features if he so desires. This is handled by means of the **SKIP** option and other facilities, which we shall meet presently.

In contrast, the *record* input/output transmission mode considers the data to be prearranged in certain groupings termed *records*, with separations between such records usually corresponding to actual physical separation. The organization of data in the form of structures (which we explored in the previous chapter) is provided primarily as a vehicle for the internal representation of data that are stored on external media as records. Accordingly, a record-oriented input statement (**READ**) causes an entire record to be transmitted to the processor (with the programmer usually having made arrangements to store the record in a structure). Similarly, a record-oriented output statement (**WRITE**) transmits an entire record from storage to an external medium. In either direction, this transmission is always literal, involving no conversion from one form to another.

In this chapter we shall concern ourselves with the exploration of the features provided for stream input/output. These are most conveniently examined by dividing them into four groups: List-directed (**GET/PUT LIST**), data-directed (**GET/PUT DATA**), edit-directed (**GET/PUT EDIT**), and string transmission (**GET/PUT STRING**). Since we have already accumulated some experience with the first two of these, it will not be necessary to spend too much time on them. Accordingly, our treatment of these facilities will emphasize those features not yet discussed, with the other types of stream input/output receiving more detailed scrutiny.

VIII.1 LIST-DIRECTED STREAM TRANSMISSION: THE **GET/PUT LIST** STATEMENTS

Use in illustrative procedures and assigned problems has established the simplicity of list-directed input/output by now. Hence, our discussion will be limited to a brief review, accompanied by some additional features.

VIII.1.1   The **GET LIST** Statement

The general form for reading data in a list-directed mode from the standard input unit (which we are considering to be the card reader) is

GET LIST (name1, name2, etc);

where the parenthesized list contains variable names, separated by commas. These names designate the locations into which the input values are to be placed. The rules governing the use of the **GET LIST** statement are quite straightforward and may be summarized as follows:

1. Variable names in the parenthesized list may refer to single values (subscripted or unsubscripted), arrays, array cross sections, structures, or adequately defined parts of structures.

2. Input data are recorded as actual values separated by commas or one or more blanks.

3. The number of values obtained from the input stream is governed by the number of elements specified in the **GET** statement; the locations to which they are assigned correspond to the order in which the names are listed.

4. When an input stream contains two consecutive commas with zero or more blanks between them, PL/I considers this to be a *null* reading. The location that would have been filled at that point is skipped, thereby retaining its previous contents. For example, if locations A, B, and C currently contained values of 10, 12, and 14, respectively, and we have data punched on a card as represented below,

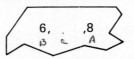

the statement **GET LIST**(B,C,A); will change the respective values in A and B to 8 and 6, while leaving the contents of C at its previous value of 14.

5. If the data stream ends before all the elements in the list are filled, an error condition will result.

6. Arrays are transmitted in row major order (see Chapter VI); elements of major or minor structures are transmitted in the order in which they are declared.

7. Complex numbers must be recorded with no blanks between the real part and the sign connecting it with the imaginary part. ($3+4I$ is valid; $3+ 4I$ and $3 +4I$ are not.)

8. Values of character strings must be enclosed by single quotation marks. Blanks or commas must still separate adjacent values anyway.

Utility of the **GET LIST** statement may be extended by additional facilities. These are discussed below.

VIII.1.1.1   List-Directed Input of Arrays

If X is an array defined by the statement

DECLARE X(24) **FLOAT** (6);

we can read the entire array with a single statement such as

GET LIST (X);

When circumstances call for part of an array to be read, the input statement can be made part of a **DO** loop (as developed in Chapter VI). Thus, if the next 12 items in the data stream are to be placed in X(8) through X(19), then we can specify that activity with the following loop:

DO I = 8 **TO** 19;

GET LIST (X(I));

END;

VIII.1.1.2   The **DO** Loop in a **GET LIST** Statement

A more compact (and generally more efficient) form of the same process allows the loop to be included as a syntactic part of the **GET** statement:

GET LIST ((X(I) **DO** I = 8 **TO** 19));

Note that the extra set of parentheses is required; their omission produces an error condition which precludes successful execution. Since the input and looping activities are combined within the construction of a single statement, PL/I obtains sufficient information that the **END** statement is not required; in fact, its inclusion is unacceptable. Such loops are processed right along with other parts of an input list, so it is possible to specify arbitrary combinations of input sequences. For example, the statement

GET LIST(Y,(X(I) **DO** I = 8 **TO** 19), Z);

will read the next 14 items from the data stream. Assuming Y and Z to be declared as single-valued variables, the first item in the data stream will be stored in Y, the next 12 in X(8) through X(19), respectively, and the fourteenth and final item read by that statement will be placed in location Z. This type of facility also comes in handy when part of an array is to be filled from the input stream but the number of elements is not known in advance. In many situations the circumstances of the particular problem make it possible to specify that number as part of the input. Thus the statement

GET LIST(N,(X(I) DO I = 1 TO N));

will bring in the next N + 1 values. The first of these, having been read and stored in variable N, now becomes available and is used by the program to determine the number of subsequent input items to be transmitted. Because of the specifications in the **DO** loop, these N values will be placed in X(1),X(2), ..., X(N).

Several loops may be included in a single **GET** statement to read different parts of a given array or parts of separate arrays. Accordingly, if X and Y have both been declared as arrays, the statement

GET LIST((X(I) DO I = 2 TO 8), N,(Y(J) DO J = N TO N+4));

accounts for the transmission of the next 13 items from the input stream: X(2) through X(8) are filled with the first seven values; the eighth value, N, is used by the program to determine the destination of the last five input items. Hence, if N is 6 for a particular run, the next five values will be placed in Y(6) through Y(10), respectively.

Although it is very convenient to read two entire arrays with a simple statement such as

GET LIST(X,Y);

it is not always true that the data will be arranged so obligingly. In fact, it is much more common to find data for two arrays arranged in the sequence X(1), Y(1), X(2), Y(2), and so on. If the sequence is regular, its transmission can be handled by an input/output statement containing a **DO** statement. For example, if TIME and PRESSURE are each declared as 50-element arrays and each pair of elements is punched on a card as shown,

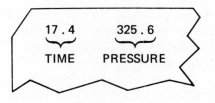

the statement

GET LIST((TIME(I),PRESSURE(I) DO I=1 TO 50));

will produce the desired operations.

VIII.1.2   The **PUT LIST** Statement

This command, written in the general form

PUT LIST (name1, name2, etc.);

will cause the program to access the locations enumerated in (name1, name2, etc.) in the order specified and place their contents in the output stream, which will eventually find its way to the standard output device (the line printer, in our case). The physical appearance of a value written by a **PUT LIST** statement reflects the form in which it was stored and is, therefore, in accordance with the attributes declared for it or assigned by default.

In order to maintain its simplicity, PL/I has not burdened the **PUT LIST** statement with extensive features for controlling the output format. Thus, the programmer has no direct means of controlling the number of items printed on a particular line. Instead, this is a fixed quantity whose value depends on the particular version of the compiler being used. (Most present compilers set this number at five or six items.) Thus, if an output list contains more than the prescribed number of items for a single line of print, the printer's carriage will automatically be shifted to the next line at the appropriate point in the list. Because of this restriction, the programmer cannot directly control the spacing between adjacent values on a line.

VIII.1.2.1   The **PAGE** Option

The programmer can cause his next line of output to be printed at the top of a new page by including the word **PAGE** somewhere in his **PUT** statement. Since PL/I will cause a new page to be started when it finds this word in an output statement, its placement is not important. The most commonly used forms are

PUT PAGE LIST (name1, name2, etc.);

or

PUT LIST (name1, name2, etc.) **PAGE**;

The data items enumerated in (name1, name2, etc.) will then be printed on the first line of the new page. The programmer can also go to the beginning of a new page without printing anything (many programmers like to include such an instruction at the beginning of their programs as a matter of habit) merely by writing **PUT PAGE**.

VIII.1.2.2   The **LINE** Option

This feature allows the programmer to specify the line number on which he wants a particular list of output values to appear. The most commonly used form for this option is

PUT LINE (w) **LIST** (name1, name2, etc.);

where (w) specifies the line number on which the output is to be printed. Most line printers are constructed to accommodate a page 14-7/8 inches wide and 11 inches long, containing 66 lines and as many as 132 characters per line. However, the number of lines that can be printed on a particular page is set at some particular value for each compiler and can be changed by the programmer if he desires. Hence, when the limiting line is reached, the printer's carriage will automatically be restored to the first line of the next page.

The line number specification (w) can be a decimal integer constant or a variable expression that will be evaluated and converted to an integer. Hence, the programmer can control the line number on which some particular output is to appear, based on prevailing conditions in his program at any particular time. This option may appear in an output statement by itself or together with the **PAGE** option. Thus, the statement

PUT PAGE LIST(7) **LIST**(A,B,C); or **PUT LIST** (A,B,C) **PAGE LINE**(7);

will cause the program to print the current values of A,B and C on the seventh line of a new page. If we wrote

PUT LINE(7);

without any additional information, the program would position the page at the seventh line. If the line number specified by the programmer is less than the current line number, a new page is started and printing continues on the first line of the new page; if the line number thus specified equals the current line, the same thing happens unless no data has yet been printed on the current line, in which case the print position is left undisturbed. Line numbers falling outside the page limits are replaced by 1.

VIII.1.2.3 The **SKIP** Option

Since **PUT** is a stream operation, each **PUT** statement normally continues where the previous one left off; a new line is started only when the current line has been completely filled. This activity can be changed and controlled by the programmer through the use of the **SKIP** option. We are already familiar with this option through its use in previous chapters. For reference purposes, its general form is

PUT SKIP(n) **LIST** (name1, name2, etc.);

where (n) represents the number of lines to be skipped before printing. As in the case of the **LINE** option, n may be constant, variable, or legitimate arithmetic expression that will be evaluated and truncated to the nearest integer. If n is specified as being 0 or less, movement of the carriage will be suppressed altogether, so the net effect is to print the next set of output values on top of those printed previously. This turns out to be a very useful procedure for producing patterns of light and dark characters for certain visual effects. (This technique is known as gray shading.) However, the restrictions imposed by list-directed output limit its usefulness so that its exploration would be more fruitful with edit-directed output. The **SKIP** option may not be combined with either the **PAGE** or **LINE** options in the same output statement.

VIII.1.2.4   Expressions in **PUT LIST** Statements

In contrast to input statements, the specification of output need not be limited to a list of variables. Instead, such lists may contain constants, variables, and expressions, freely inter-mixed in any order. Any legitimate string of characters can be included in an output line by specifying that string between single quotation marks as part of the parenthesized list in the **PUT** statement. The number of such strings specified and their positions relative to the variables in the output list are not restricted.

The members of an output data list need not be restricted to variables alone. Any legitimate expression may be specified, as long as the terms in that expression all have current values. Thus, if A and B contain numerical values and C and D contain character strings, a statement such as

PUT LIST(2*A**3 − B/4, C, D ‖ 'ES');

is perfectly legitimate. Note that the members of the list shown above are expressions and not complete assignment statements. PL/I will perform the indicated operations and place the results in reserved areas of storage allocated without the user's knowledge or intervention. At the appropriate time, these results are added to the output data stream.

VIII.2   DATA-DIRECTED TRANSMISSION: THE **GET/PUT DATA** STATEMENTS

While still retaining the simplicity inherent in list-directed statements, this mode of transmission provides the user with the additional advantage that his output will be automatically labeled when it is displayed. If this method is to be used for input, the user is obligated to supply adequate identification as part of the input stream. This is a very handy feature for programmers wishing to use the simplest means possible for producing clearly labeled output, without too much regard for format control. If one wishes to take advantage of the automatic labeling capabilities presented by data-directed output and it is inconvenient or inappropriate to fulfill the similar obligations imposed by data-directed input, the programmer has the prerogative of reading his input in list-directed mode (if it is appropriately arranged) and printing his output using the data-directed statement.

VIII.2.1   The **GET DATA** Statement

It is possible to bring data-directed input into the processor with the most basic of input statements, namely,

GET DATA;

This is sufficient to cause PL/I to read variables into the processor and store them in designated locations. The number of values brought in by such a statement is determined by the construction of the input stream itself. Each value in a data-directed stream is specified in the form

identifier = value

Consecutive specifications are separated by blanks or commas, and the last value to be read in by a given **GET DATA** statement is immediately followed by a semicolon.

When the basic **GET DATA** statement is used for numerical values, PL/I will make the necessary conversions so that each value is stored with its declared base, scale, mode, and precision. If an undeclared numerical variable is read in, it will be assigned default attributes and the value read will be stored in that form. Input character values must be enclosed in single quotation marks and all character variables must be declared.

Data-directed input statements may also take the more restrictive form

GET DATA (name1, name2, etc.);

When this form is used, it is necessary for every name in the data stream (up to the next semicolon) to appear in the input list; other wise an error condition will occur. The reverse is not true, however, since the entire list need not be fulfilled by the values in the data stream. If a set of readings is punched as shown below,

B=12 , C=25 , A=6 ;

the statement

GET DATA (A,B,C,D);

will work, but the statement

GET DATA (D,B,A);

will not. Note that the order in which the variables are listed does not have to be the same as that presented by the data stream. Note also that D's value will not change since a new value does not appear in the stream.

VIII.2.1.1   Data-Directed Input of Arrays

If X is a declared array name, the statement

GET DATA (X);

serves the dual purpose of reading in the entire array or any part of it. This is a very convenient feature for such situations where an array is already in storage and it is desired to modify it by reading in individual values. The number of values and/or their subscripts need not be known in advance. Assuming that X is a five-element one-dimensional array with attributes **FIXED** (3), the statement

GET DATA (X);

will take care of any combination of X's elements. For example, either of the following cards

```
X(2)=7 , X(4)=3 , X(1)=132 ;
```

```
X(2)=-18 , X(3)=778 , X(1)=6 , X(5)=0 ;
```

will be handled properly by the statement given before. Note, however, that it is not possible to specify individual subscripted elements in a **PUT DATA** statement; in fact, it is illegal. A single list may, of course, include any number of array and single-valued variable names in any order.

VIII.2.1.2   Data-Directed Input of Structures

Entire structures or any parts thereof can be entered using data-directed transmission in much the same way as is used for arrays, with the additional capability of specifying individual elements. PL/I allows the names in the **PUT DATA** statement to be qualified, but not to be subscripted. Internally it is willing to deal with partial qualifications; also, when qualified names are subscripted as well, PL/I allows great flexibility internally to interleave the subscripts within the qualified name (see Chapter VII). In the data stream, however, the story is quite different: all structure element names must be fully qualified, whether such qualification is needed or not; moreover, all subscripts must be brought over to the right in order for the **GET** statement to operate. If we declare an array of structures S as follows:

DECLARE 1 S(3), 2 A **FIXED**(4), 2 B, 3 C(5) **FIXED**(2), 3 D **FIXED**(2);

and we wish to read in the fourth C value in the second of the S structures (let us say its value is 12) we could say

GET DATA(S.B.C);

or

GET DATA(S.B);

If we refer to this element internally, we could say S(2).B.C(4) or S(2,4).C; but the value must appear in the stream as

S.B.C(2,4)=12;

VIII.2.2   The **PUT DATA** Statement

The basic form for data-directed output is

PUT DATA (name1,name2,etc.);

When encountering such a statement, PL/I accesses the appropriate values from storage in the order listed, attaches their identifiers to them, and places them in the output stream. The display format for each value printed is

name = value

with the number of values per line being set by the compiler as in the **PUT LIST** statement. Adjacent values are separated by one or more blanks (the number depends on the particular version of the compiler), and the last value printed by a given statement is followed by a semicolon. Character variables are printed enclosed in single quotation marks. The three format control options available for list-directed output (**PAGE,LINE,** and **SKIP**) can also be used with the **PUT DATA** statement, with the same rules and restrictions as stated previously. In contrast to the **PUT LIST** statement, the variables in a data-directed output list cannot appear in expressions.

   Entire arrays can be printed in data-directed form with a single statement. Each element will appear with its full subscript, and the order will be the same as that used for storage (row major order for multidimensional arrays). When only certain elements of an array are to be printed, their subscripts may be specified as constants, variables, or expressions. The resulting printout will show these elements whose subscript values are obtained by evaluating the expressions in the **PUT DATA** statement and truncating to the nearest integer.

   For example, if X is a nine-element, one-dimensional array and A, B, and C are single-valued variables whose current contents are 12, 4, and 7 respectively, the statement

PUT DATA(X((A+B)/C), X(A−12+B+C/2), X((B−A)/4+1.5*B);

will produce the line

X(2)=value, X(7)=value, X(8)=value;

When a single **PUT DATA** statement is used to print a complete structure, each element will appear with its fully qualified name in the order given in the original **DECLARE** statement. If we defined a structure A by the statement

DECLARE 1 A, 2 B **FIXED**(3), 2 C, (3 D, 3 E) **FIXED**(3),

2 F **FIXED**(3), 2 G, 3 H, (4 X, 4 Y) **FIXED**(3), 3 Z **FIXED**(3);

and Y had a value of 114, the statement

PUT DATA (Y);

would produce

A.G.H.Y = 114;

Subscripted elements of structures will appear with all subscripts appended to the last (right-most) identifier in the qualified name.

For certain situations that may occur during the debugging process it is helpful to obtain a printout of all the data stored by the procedure. This can be specified very conveniently simply by writing

PUT DATA;

PL/I treats this as a license to reveal all; accordingly, it prints (in data-directed form) the current values for all the variables used in the procedure. Since this uninhibited display could range from a trickle to a deluge, the programmer is cautioned to use this feature prudently.

VIII.3   EDIT-DIRECTED DATA TRANSMISSION

The third type of stream input/output differs substantially from the other two; it is designed primarily to allow the programmer maximum flexibility in describing the form and organization of his data. On the input side, he can arrange his variables in as compact a manner as he wishes, as long as the arrangement is consistent from one set of readings to the next. When generating output, the user has the opportunity to exercise complete and detailed control over the appearance and organization of his printout. While edit-directed input/output is considered a stream operation, it is generally not practical to use it without paying strict attention to card boundaries and the beginning and end of print lines. Nevertheless, it is the programmer's responsibility to use options such as **SKIP** to achieve the required positioning of the stream. An unavoidable consequence, of course, is that the statements specifying these input and output formats can become much more complex than with list-directed and data-directed forms. However, once the fundamental rules for using the edit-directed features are understood, the synthesis of very involved statements becomes relatively straightforward.

VIII.3.1   Edit-Directed Input: The **GET EDIT** Statement

Until now we have been dealing with input for which the important organizational criteria were order and form. PL/I was able to accept input and store it as required as long as the attributes were compatible with the declaration (either directly or by conversion) and as long as the readings were properly sequenced. (For data-directed input, it was seen that even the latter prerequisite was not always necessary.) Punctuation (separation between variables) received only the most casual attention in that PL/I looked for blanks or commas between readings and required a semicolon at the end of a data-directed input list. Placement of the variables on the punched card or other medium was of no concern at all.

In edit-directed input, the placement of the data is of major importance. When a number of data cards are to be read in, each containing a set of readings for the same variables, PL/I expects the reading for a given variable to be in exactly the same place and with exactly the same form on each of the cards. A completely detailed, column-by-column description of the data card format must be made available to PL/I. This latter point is perhaps the most fundamentally distinguishing feature of edit-directed input. The compiler does not deduce the data description from the input card itself. Instead, it must be given a detailed map or specification of the data.

The ability to provide such a detailed data map undeniably complicates the construction of input statements, but it also introduces a sizeable advantage. It allows the user to represent his data in the most compact way possible by obviating the need for separating consecutive readings on a card. For example, if we wished to record a variable called HOURS as a two-digit integer (XX) followed by one called RATE as a three-digit number with two digits to the right of the decimal point (Y.YY), an edit-directed specification will allow us to run this together, namely, XXY.YY. We can further reduce the number of columns by implying rather than including the decimal point (XXYYY instead of XXY.YY) and letting the format specification take care of the bookkeeping. This saving of space may not be much of an advantage when dealing with a small number of cards containing readings for a small number of variables. In many real cases, however, it can mean the difference between the use of one card per set of readings versus two, with resulting benefits in machine time reduction and in improved handling convenience. An additional benefit closely allied with those described above is the increased efficiency of data collection and preparation. Although the **GET LIST** and **GET DATA** statements are very convenient, their use is most appropriate for small amounts of input, usually prepared by the programmer. When large numbers of readings are involved (as in most data processing situations), it is more effective to record the raw data on a form from which it can be transcribed directly onto some machine-compatible input medium by clerical personnel. The design of such forms and the corresponding allocation of card columns or other input storage locations for each of the variables are greatly facilitated when done with the intention of using edit-directed input.

VIII.3.1.1   Basic Form of the **GET EDIT** Statement

The general statement for edit-directed input has the form

GET EDIT (name1, name2, etc.) (spec1, spec2, etc.);

(name1, name2, etc.) is a list of input variable names given in the order the readings appear in the input stream. (spec1, spec2, etc.) is a list of descriptions that supplies PL/I with the information required to identify the form of an item in the stream, as well as the location of its initial and final characters or digits. The number of descriptive specifications does not necessarily equal the number of data items listed in the (name1, name2, etc.) portion of the **GET EDIT** instruction. If there are too many format specifications in the statement, PL/I will use as many as required and ignore the rest. If there are too few format specifications, PL/I will use them all and then go back and go through them again as many times as necessary to fulfill the input list.

There are several types of specifications for describing data. These relate to the data as they are presented in the input stream and have nothing to do with how they are stored in the processor. This final form is still dictated by the attributes in the **DECLARE** statement. The combination of the two types of specifications provide PL/I with the information as to what type of conversion to perform, if any.

VIII.3.1.2   The **COLUMN** Specification

Since edit-directed transmission lends itself to fixed formats, we need a method of directing the processor to the proper starting column of each card (usually column 1). This is handled by the column specification, which is written as

COLUMN(n) or **COL**(n)

where n may be a constant, variable, or expresion. If c is the first column that has not yet been read, l the length of the input record (usually $l = 80$ since we shall be dealing with punched card input), and n is the numerical value accompanying the **COL** specification, then the following rules operate:

1.   If $n \leq 0$ or $n > l$, the next card is read and the transmission continues with column 1 of that new card.

2. If $1 \geqslant n \geqslant c$, then $n - c$ columns are ignored, and transmission continues with column n; (note that if $n = c$, nothing happens).

3. If $1 \leqslant n < c$, a new card is read and transmission continues with column n of that new card.

For example, to read a four-digit number from columns 1-4 of each card and store that number in X, we would write

GET EDIT(X) (**COLUMN**(1), **F**(4));

(The **F** specification is discussed in the next section). If the number were punched in columns 10-13, the input statement would become

GET EDIT(X) (**COLUMN**(10),**F**(4));

VII.3.1.3   The **F** Specification

Input data that will be in the form of fixed-point numbers may be read using the **F** specification, whose general form is

F(w,d,s)

where w is the number of columns in the input field containing the value. The number itself must be in the form of a valid PL/I fixed-point decimal constant and, of course, may have a sign and/or decimal point. If the number requires fewer than w columns to express, it may be located anywhere within the field, with blanks either before or after; however, there may not be any blanks within the number, or between the sign and the number.

If a decimal point is not punched, the d, if specified, indicates the number of digits that are to the right of an *assumed* decimal point. If d is omitted, its default value is zero; it may never be negative.

If s is present, it is a positive or negative value specifying the power of ten by which the number is to be multiplied before it is stored in the location associated with the input variable name. The default value of s is zero. Note that s is effective whether or not a decimal point is punched and that it may be positive or negative; in contrast to this, d is ignored if an actual decimal point appears, and it, (d), must always be non-negative.

If the entire-column field is blank, a value of zero is stored. Remember that unless the attributes of the input variable are **FIXED DECIMAL**, the value must undergo additional conversion before it is stored.

Let us suppose we are to read and store three variables name ACCTNO, DEPOSIT, and BALANCE. These are punched on a card as tabulated below:

Name	*Card Columns*	*Form**
ACCTNO	1-6	XXXXXX
DEPOSIT	7-12	XXXX(.)XX
BALANCE	13-19	XXXXX(.)XX

*indicates the position of the implied decimal point.

Sample data would appear in accordance with this format as follows:

column 1 ⎯⎯⎯⎯⎯┐

2431650546222461793

Our declaration and edit-directed input statement would be

DECLARE ACCTNO **FIXED**(6), DEPOSIT **FIXED**(6,2), BALANCE **FIXED**(7,2);

GET EDIT(ACCTNO, DEPOSIT, BALANCE)(**COLUMN**(1), F(6),F(6,2),F(7,2));

with the result being that ACCTNO will contain 243165, DEPOSIT will have a value of 0546.22, and the value in BALANCE will be 24617.93. If the specification for DEPOSIT had been given as F(6,2,1), it would be stored as XXXXX(.)X. When a decimal point is punched as part of the data and its position is not that indicated by the format specification, the specification implied by the data is the one used. Bear in mind that when a decimal point is actually punched as part of a value, it occupies a column and must therefore be included in the count. Thus a value punched as 72.634 requires $w = 6$. Since the decimal point is punched, the value of d is irrelevant.

VIII.3.1.4   The **E** Specification

If the programmer wishes to read input that may be recorded in floating-point scale, he must use the E specification, which has the general form

E(w,d,s)

where, as before, w is the total number of columns making up the input field. The input number may be located anywhere within the w columns, with blanks either before or after; it must be a valid PL/I fixed- or floating-point decimal constant. If the entire field is blank, a **CONVERSION** error occurs. If there is no decimal point present in the number, then d specifies the number of digits to be assumed to the right of the decimal point; otherwise, d is ignored. The s parameter specifies the number of significant digits to be displayed when the E specification is used for output; it has no effect when the specification is used for input but is permitted to appear for compatibility. For example, assuming that X, Y, and Z are suitably declared, the statement

GET EDIT$(X,Y,Z)(\text{COL}(1),E(12,5),E(10),E(8,3));$

would be adequate to read the following card:

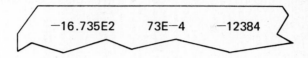

and would result in X, Y, and Z having the values $-1.6735E+3$, $7.3E-4$, and $1.2382E+1$, respectively.

VIII.3.1.5 The C Specification *Complex*

An edit-directed complex input value is specified in a **GET EDIT** statement by the letter **C** followed by two numerical specifications (any combination of **F**, **E**, and/or **P** descriptions can be used). Thus, if we had an input value punched as

0 (.)	7	2	4	E	+	0	2	+	1	6	(.)	1	3	1

the specification for it would read $C(E(8.3),F(6,3))$. If only one specification is given, PL/I will use it for both the real and imaginary components. Note that the letter **I** must not appear as part of the data.

VIII.3.1.6 The A Specification

The **A** specification states that the w character input field is to be treated like the value of a character string of length w and assigned to the variable in the **EDIT** list with any necessary conversion being performed. In most situations, of course, the variable is a character string already; but there is no rule preventing it from being a numeric variable. For example, the sequence

DECLARE A CHARACTER(5), **B CHARACTER**(7) **VARYING**,X **FLOAT**(6);

GET EDIT(A,B,X) $(\text{COL}(1),A(4),A(4),A(4));$

assigns the values 'GOOD ','BAD ', and $-6.5E+1$ to A, B, and X, respectively, if the input card is punched as

```
GOODBAD  −65
```

VIII.3.1.7   The **P** Specification   *Picture*

Picture specifications may be used for numerical or character data by following the same rules described for declarations (see Chapter V). As an example, the statement

GET EDIT(ACCTNO,DEPOSIT,BALANCE,LIMIT)

   (**COL**(1),**P'(6)9'**,**P'9999v99'**,**P'(5)9V99'**,**P'9V9E99'**);

could be used to obtain data from an input card punched as

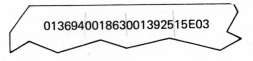

013694001863001392515E03

to produce 013694, 0018.63, 00139.25, and 1.5E+3, respectively. Character strings can also be specified with the **P** form by using the appropriate symbols. The variables ACCTNO, DEPOSIT, BALANCE, and LIMIT in the above example may have any arithmetic attributes; they need not be numeric character variables.

PL/I is very flexible about reading negative data in edit-directed mode. Two forms are commonly used for preparing negative data. The most straightforward one is merely to reserve an extra column in front of the leftmost digit for the sign when it is known that a variable may take on negative values. However, when it is desired to conserve space on a card, negative values can also be indicated by punching the minus sign along with the last (rightmost) digit of the value. For example, if a value A is to be punched as a floating-point number in the form $\cup$XXXXEXX, a value of $-.7234 \times 10^{-2}$ would appear as $\boxed{7}\ \boxed{2}\ \boxed{3}\ \boxed{4}\ \boxed{E}\ \boxed{0}\ \boxed{2}$. This technique is known as *overpunching* and is handled with the **P** specification by means of the **T**, **I**, and **R** codes. These are explained in terms of output generation later on in this chapter, but their use for describing input is identical.

VIII.3.1.8   The **X** Specification   *Skip Columns*

In addition to the **COLUMN** specification, PL/I provides the programmer with an alternate mechanism for specifying the location of an input value by allowing him to skip columns in the input stream. The specification

X(n)

will cause the next n spaces in the input stream to be skipped, regardless of the contents of these spaces. Let us suppose that a bank record is punched on a card as follows:

Name	Card Columns	Form
REC	1-4	XXXX
NAME	5-24	Character string
ADDRESS	25-49	Character string
ACCTNO	50-55	XXXXXX
DEP	56-61	XXXX$_{(.)}$XX
TAKE	62-67	XXXX$_{(.)}$XX
BAL	70-76	XXXXX$_{(.)}$XX

We can write statements to store NAME, ACCTNO, DEP, and BAL without reading the other variables as shown below:

DECLARE NAME **CHARACTER**(20), ACCTNO **FIXED**(6),
  DEP **FIXED**(6,2), BAL **FIXED**(7,2);

GET EDIT(NAME, ACCTNO,DEP, BAL)(**COL**(1),**X**(4),
  A(20),**X**(25),**F**(6),**F**(6,2),**X**(8),**F**(7,2));

Of course, we could replace each **X** with an appropriate **COLUMN** specification. The choice is purely a matter of personal taste.

VIII.3.1.9   The **SKIP** Specification

The **SKIP** specification causes the input to be repositioned to column 1 of the next card (record). This is true regardless of the location on the current record. Because of this it is not quite the same as **COLUMN**(1), which does nothing if we happen to be in column 1 to begin with. **SKIP** can have a parameter of the form

  SKIP(n)

where n may be a constant, variable, or expression that specifies the number of cards (records) to be skipped. The default for n is 1. **SKIP** may also be used as an option in the **GET** statement itself. For example, the following three statements

GET SKIP EDIT(X,Y)(**F**(8,4),**X**(6),**F**(7,3));

GET EDIT (X,Y)(**SKIP**,**F**(8,4),**X**(6),**F**(7,3));

GET EDIT(X,Y)(**F**(8,4),**X**(6),**F**(7,3)) **SKIP**;

are all equivalent. Use of **SKIP** with n greater than 1 is helpful when the relevant data values occur on every nth card. For instance, we may have patient records that are punched on three cards (per patient), and only be interested in variables that happen to be on the second card of each group of three cards. This situation can be handled easily by the following technique:

GET SKIP EDIT(variables)(format);   **GET SKIP**(2);

The first statement begins by skipping the first card of the group, reading the variables, and leaving the stream positioned somewhere on the second card. The second statement then skips the rest of the second card and all of the third card, leaving the stream at column 1 of the first card of the next group. This will work properly even if the last column read by the first statement is column 80 of the second card. This is because PL/I makes a distinction between "being on the second card just after column 80" and "being on the third card just before column 1." Since this distinction does exist, the **SKIP** specification must be used with a certain amount of care.

VIII.3.2   Iterative Specifications

Shorthand methods similar to those used in declarations may be applied to format specifications. The statement

GET EDIT(A,B,C,D)(**COL**(1),**X**(3),**F**(2),**F**(2),**F**(2),**F**(4,1));

can be rewritten as

GET EDIT(A,B,C,D)(**COL**(1),**X**(3),3 **F**(2),**F**(4,1);

Similarly, the statement

GET EDIT(A,B,C,D,E,F,G)(**COL**(1),**X**(3),**A**(4),**F**(6,1),**X**(3),**A**(4),

   F(6,1),**X**(3),**A**(4),**F**(6,1),**F**(5));

can be simplified to

GET EDIT(A,B,C,D,E,F,G)(**COL**(1),3 (**X**(3),**A**(4),**F**(6,1)),**F**(5));

If we were not concerned with G, we could simply write

GET EDIT(A,B,C,D,E,F)(**COL**(1),3 (**X**(3),**A**(4),**F**(6,1)));

If we can also assume that the stream already is positioned to column 1, we can simplify even further by writing

GET EDIT(A,B,C,D,E,F)(**X**(3),**A**(4),**F**(6,1));

since the program will repeat the format as necessary.

VIII.3.3   Blank Data

*Note
Caution*

Since a blank is a particular PL/I character with its unique internal representation, its inclusion in an input character string offers no particular problem. However, when a piece of numerical data is missing and this condition is designated by blanks (as it often is), PL/I's processing may present some difficulties. When PL/I encounters a field of blanks where it expects to see a numerical value, it automatically places zeros in the designated location. (This is true except for the **E** specification or in **P** specifications not allowing blanks.) Since zero can also be a legitimate data value and there is no way of directly distinguishing between a zero that was read in and a zero that resulted from conversion of a blank input field, the dilemma could be a serious one. This distinction can be preserved by using **GET STRING**, which is discussed later on in this chapter. Another frequently used method for handling missing data is to avoid blanks altogether and use something like −1 instead.

VIII.3.4   Operation of the **GET EDIT** Statement

Now that we have seen several illustrations of edit-directed input, we can describe a conceptual mechanism for the process. PL/I works with three "pointers": one to keep track of the location in the input stream, a second to keep track of the position in the data list, and a third to keep track of the position in the format list. Let us call these pointers S (stream), D (data), and F (format), respectively. At the beginning of the program S points to just before the character of the first card. At the beginning of each **GET** statement S points wherever it was left by any previous **GET** statement, whereas D and F are set to the beginning of the data and format list. Now the whole process can easily be described by a flowchart such as the one shown in Figure 8.1.

VIII.3.5   Edit-Directed Input of Data Aggregates, *Structures*

PL/I handles edit-directed input arrays and structures as it does in the other stream-oriented input mechanisms. If X is declared as an array, the statement

   GET EDIT(X)(spec1, spec2, etc.);

will cause the entire array to be read in and stored in the same sequence as described for other **GET** statements. The same holds true for entire structures. Single-subscripted names or qualified structural elements may be given in a **GET EDIT** list, but they must, of course, be in the same order as the values appear in the data stream.

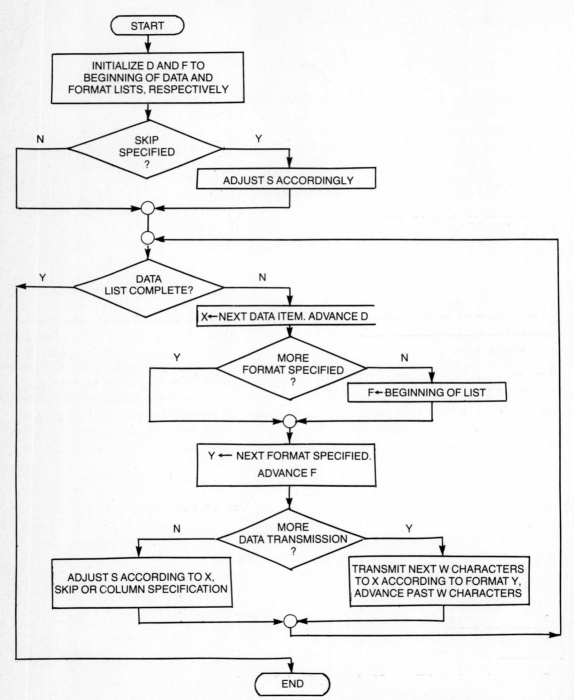

Figure 8.1

VIII.3.5.1 Edit-Directed Input of Entire Arrays

To illustrate the edit-directed input of arrays, let us suppose that we wish to read in an array X consisting of 15 fixed-point decimal values with precision (5,1). These are punched on 15 data cards so that each card contains an X value as follows:

Either of the following statements could be used:

GET EDIT(X)(**COL**(33),**F**(5,1));

or

GET EDIT(X)(**X**(32),**F**(5,1),**X**(43));

We use this latter form to illustrate further the behavior of the stream pointer; note that it behaves consistently. Since PL/I knows it is to read the next 15 values from the data stream according to the format specifications, the program will repeat the full format list 14 times. During the 15th and last time around, the program exhausts the data list without processing the X(43). Hence, execution of the **GET EDIT** statement will end with the pointer sitting at column 38 of the 15th data card. If the program is such that additional reading is going to be done, the programmer must remember that those last 43 columns have *not* been skipped. If we were to write

GET EDIT(X)(**X**(32),**F**(5,1),**X**(43);   **GET SKIP**;

he would not have to remember.

Note also that because of the contents in which they appear, PL/I has no difficulty in distinguishing the times when X refers to an array and those in which **X** is used as a format specification.

VIII.3.5.2 **GET EDIT** Statements with Built-in **DO** Loops

The inclusion of a **DO** loop in a **GET EDIT** statement is no different from its use as described for **GET/PUT LIST**.

Illustration 19

Suppose that A and B are 25-element fixed decimal arrays with precision (5,1) and (4), respectively, and C is a 25-element array of character strings with length (6). Furthermore, each input card contains corresponding elements of each array as follows:

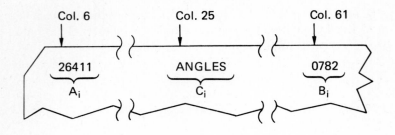

Now let us say that we have N such cards, containing the first N elements of the three arrays. These are preceded by a single card on which N is keypunched in columns 1 and 2. Assuming that everything has been properly declared, we can accommodate this situation with the following:

```
ILL19: PROCEDURE OPTIONS (MAIN);

       DECLARE A(25) FIXED(5,1), B(25) FIXED(4), C(25) CHARACTER(6), N;

/*--------------------ADDITIONAL STATEMENTS.--------------------*/

       GET EDIT (N) (F(2)) ( (A(I),C(I),B(I) DO I = 1 TO N) )
           (SKIP,X(5),F(5,1),X(14),A(6),X(30),F(4));

/*--------------------ADDITIONAL STATEMENTS.--------------------*/

       END ILL19;
```

Note that the double grouping of (data list) (format description) (data list) (format description) is valid and may be repeated as many times as the situation requires. (This is somewhat more efficient than using separate **GET** statements.) Since the input point is positioned at column 65 of the card containing the Nth set of elements, a final **GET SKIP**; could be added if we wanted to be ready for the first column of the next card.

VIII.3.6   Extension of Format Capabilities   *Data to vary.*

When a program is written to process a specific collection of variables prepared according to a particular format, the proper description of that format in a **GET EDIT** statement is sufficient for the purpose of that program. In many instances, however, a particular type of analysis or information processing procedure is useful for a variety of data collections. When this is the case, it would be highly inefficient and uneconomical to prepare and maintain special programs, each of which differs only in its description of the input data format. PL/I makes this unnecessary by allowing the data format to vary. It is also possible to use a single set of format specifications in several places throughout a program.

VIII.3.6.1 Remote Format Specification

Occasions often arise for which it is desirable to read and distinguish different groups of input variables, where each has its own set of names but all groups share a common format. Ordinarily, there would be separate **GET EDIT** statement for each set, complete with a string of format specifications. It is possible to replace the separate format specifications with references to a single description placed in some other part of the program. This is done by using the form

   GET EDIT (name1, name2, etc.) (**R**(label));

where "label" is the statement label of a **FORMAT** statement that has the following general form:

   label: **FORMAT** (spec1,spec2,etc.);

One useful application of this feature occurs in situations where diverse input statements share a common format. The following procedure illustrates this.

Illustration 20

The Cockamamie Research Company has embarked on a project in which experimental data are collected at each of three sites. During each experiment, values are obtained for L, M, and N (each of which is a three-digit integer) and X and Y (each of which is a number in the form n.nn), from which a value Z is computed as

$$Z = N \frac{x}{y} + L - M$$

Data for each experiment are to be recorded on a card in the following form:

Column(s)	Item	Format
1	site no.	1, 2, or 3
4-5	experiment no.	XX
8-10	X	X(.)XX
13-15	Y	X(.)XX
18-20	L	XXX
23-25	M	XXX
28-30	N	XXX

A program is to be written to compute and print Z for each set of inputs, along with the corresponding site number, experiment number, X, and Y. After all the individual values are printed, the program is to print a summary showing the total number of experiments for each site, along with the average Z. Finally, there is to be a line showing the total number of experiments and overall average Z.

Everything seemed fine until the data arrived. At that time it was discovered that although site 2's data were good and proper, the same, alas, could not be said for sites 1 and 3. The correct columns were used and the individual values were accurate; however, the positions of some variables were transposed. (Some people hinted darkly that they were not at all surprised.) After careful scrutiny, it was determined that the situation was as follows:

Column(s)	Item for Site 1	Item for Site 3
1	site no.	site no.
4-5	experiment no.	experiment no.
8-10	X	Y
13-15	Y	X
18-20	N	M
23-25	M	L
28-30	L	N

```
ILL20: PROCEDURE OPTIONS (MAIN);

/******************************************************/
/*   SITE AND EXP ARE THE SITE AND EXPERIMENTS NUMBERS  */
/*   NUM IS AN ARRAY OF COUNTERS FOR THE EXPERIMENTS    */
/*   ZAVG IS AN ARRAY WHERE Z AVERAGES WILL BE STORED   */
/*   NSUM IS THE TOTAL NUMBER OF EXPERIMENTS            */
/******************************************************/
          DECLARE (X,Y,Z,ZAVG(3),L,M,N,NUM(3), EXP FIXED(2),
              (SITE,NDFL) FIXED (1);

          NUM = 0;       ZAVG = 0;      NDFL = 0;
          ON ENDFILE (SYSIN) NDFL = 1;
          PUT PAGE LINE(3) LIST ('COCKAMAMIE RESEARCH REPORT');
          PUT SKIP LIST ('SITE','EXP.NO.','X','Y','Z');
          PUT SKIP;
          GET EDIT (SITE)(F(1));

          DO WHILE (NDFL = 0);
            IF SITE=1
              THEN GET EDIT (EXP,X,Y,N,M,L)(R(HOW));
              ELSE IF SITE=2
                    THEN GET EDIT (EXP,X,Y,L,M,N)(R(HOW));
                    ELSE GET EDIT (EXP,X,Y,M,L,N)(R(HOW));
   HOW:       FORMAT(X(2),F(2), 2 (X(2),F(3,2)), 3 (X(2),F(3)));
              /***THE FORMAT STATEMENT'S PLACEMENT IS IMMATERIAL***/
              GET SKIP;
              Z=N*(X/Y)*M-L;
              NUM(SITE)=NUM(SITE)+1;
              ZAVG(SITE)=ZAVG(SITE)+Z;
              PUT SKIP LIST(SITE,EXP,X,Y,Z);
          END;

          PUT PAGE LINE(3) LIST ('SUMMARY');
          PUT SKIP LIST('SITE','NO.OF EXP.','AVG.Z');
          PUT SKIP;
          DO I=1 TO 3;
            ZAVG(I)=ZAVG(I)/NUM(I);
            PUT SKIP LIST(I,NUM(I),ZAVG(I));
          END;
          NSUM=SUM(NUM);    Z=SUM(ZAVG)/NSUM;
          PUT SKIP(2) LIST ('ALL',NSUM,Z);
          STOP;

          END ILL20;
```

Now, the program must be designed to accommodate these differences.

Since the interchanged variables have identical formats, we shall be able to use three different input statements, each referring to a common format specification. Furthermore, we shall take advantage of the "continuous" nature of the input stream by using a separate **GET** statement to read the site number. Its value will then determine which of the three alternatives will be used for the rest of the input.

VIII.3.6.2   Variable Format Specifications

Although remote format specifications may be convenient for certain situations, there are many real circumstances for which they will not suffice. Consequently, PL/I includes a comprehensive facility that offers complete flexibility in handling formats. The basis is quite simple: every disignator in every type of specification (**PICTURE** excepted) can be a variable or expression as well as a constant. A statement such as

GET EDIT(VAR1,VAR2,etc.)(X(N1),F(N2,N3),X(N4),A(N5),etc.);

is quite valid as long as values for N1, N2, and so on, are available to the program at the time the **GET EDIT** is to be executed. (The easiest thing to do, of course, is to read values in as part of the input and use them to define the format for a particular run.) A very important aspect of this feature is that a value of zero for one of these designators will cause the program to ignore that specification. Thus, the specifications

(X(3),F(6,2),X(0),F(0,3),X(4),A(0),F(7,1))

and

(X(3),F(6,2),X(4),F(7,1))

are equivalent.

The same flexibility is true for repetition of formats. By writing format specifications such as

((M1)X(n1),(M2)F(N2,N3),(M3)X(N4),(M4)A(N5),etc.)

we have the opportunity to set the values of M1, M2, and so on, so that the corresponding specification is used once (for example, M1 = 1), more than once (M1 > 1), or not at all (M1 < 1). M1, M2, ... could then be read in for each run. *Note that we must enclose the repetition factors in parentheses when they are variables or expressions.*

Illustration 21

We shall write a program to read and print the values of groups of fixed-point variables. These variables are punched three to a card and may appear anywhere on the card. A particular data collection may consist of any number of such cards having a common input format. Although this format does not change for a particular collection, the format is likely to vary from one collection to the next. No variable will exceed seven digits in length or have more than five decimal places; none of the values will ever be zero. In addition to designing and writing the program, we shall show how the input specifications will look for the three different formats given below.

Case 1

Card Columns	Data Format
5-9	XXXX(.)X
10-12	XXX
16-19	XXXX

Case 2

1-6	XXX(.)XXX
7-8	X(.)X
75-79	XXXXX

Case 3

13-16	XXX(.)X
17-20	XXX(.)X
21-24	XXX(.)X

We shall declare a three-element array name VAR for the input variables. Although we are told that no variable will exceed seven digits in length or have more than five decimal places, we do not know exactly how many digits and decimal places the variable will have. In order to take care of all contingencies, we shall use a common precision of (12,5). This will take care of a number having a maximum of digits, with none of them being decimal places.

In order to accommodate any and all formats for the three variables, we shall construct a very general type of format statement. For purposes of convenience, we shall use a separate statement rather than include the specifications as part of the input statement. (Operationally, of course, it makes no difference.) Since we do not know in advance whether or not all of the variables will be punched in consecutive card columns, without intervening areas to be skipped, our general statement will include a column specification before each of the numerical specifications. Based on these considerations, our statement can look as follows:

FORMAT(COL(C1),F(W1,D1),COL(C2),F(W2,D2),COL(C3),F(W3,D3));

On inspecting this statement, it is seen that nine variable indicators are used in the specifications. Since three numbers are needed to pin down the location and extent of each input value, we shall set up three arrays (one for the C values, one for the W values, and one for the D values), instead of referring to each of these indicators by a separate name. Based on the requirements worked out in the statement above, all of them will be three-element arrays. Our general format statement can now read as follows:

FORMAT(COL(C(K)),F(W(K),D(K)));

where K will have to take on the values 1, 2, and 3 at the proper times. The specifications will be repeated three times automatically.

Having worked out the crucial arrangements for the formats, we can turn to other things. To indicate the last card in a particular collection, we shall use a fake data card with a VAR(1) value of zero. The program will be constructed to process as many different collections of cards as are submitted:

```
ILL21: PROCEDURE OPTIONS (MAIN);

/*****************************************************/
/* C, W, AND D ARE THE THREE-ELEMENT ARRAYS IN WHICH */
/* WILL BE STORED THE VARIABLE FORMAT SPECIFICATIONS: */
/* C FOR THE COLUMN SPECIFICATIONS AND W AND D FOR   */
/* THE TWO PARTS OF THE F-SPECIFICATIONS.            */
/* N KEEPS TRACK OF THE NUMBER OF INPUT GROUPS, AND  */
/* THE DATA THEMSELVES WILL BE READ INTO ARRAY VAR.  */
/*****************************************************/

        DECLARE ( (C,W,D)(3),N,NDFIL ) FIXED BINARY,
        VAR(3) FIXED (12,5);

        N,NDFIL = 0;   ON ENDFILE (SYSIN) NDFIL=1;
        GET EDIT ( (C(I),W(I),D(I) DO I=1 TO 3) )(COL(1), 9 F(2));

        DO WHILE (NDFIL = 0);
           GET SKIP;   /**RESET TO COLUMN 1 FOR NEXT CARD**/
           N = N+1;
           PUT PAGE LINE(2) LIST ('GROUP',N);
           PUT LINE (3) LIST('VAR(1)','VAR(2)','VAR(3)');
           PUT SKIP(2);
           GET EDIT ((VAR(I) DO I=1 TO 3))(R(LOOK));
LOOK:      FORMAT (COL(C(I)),F(W(I),D(I)));

    /* WE SHALL INTRODUCE ANOTHER CONDITION TESTED WITH AN "ON" */
    /* STATEMENT, I.E., THE ENDPAGE CONDITION. ENDPAGE IS RAISED */
    /* WHEN THE AUTOMATIC LINE COUNTER REACHES A PRESET VALUE DE-*/
    /* FINED FOR EACH INSTALLATION. 55 IS A TYPICAL VALUE. THE   */
    /* SYSTEM AUTOMATICALLY STARTS A NEW PAGE AND RESETS THE LINE*/
    /* COUNTER. HOWEVER, WE CAN SPECIFY ADDITIONAL ACTIONS BY THE*/
    /* STATEMENT     ON ENDPAGE ACTION;     WE SHALL USE IT IN   */
    /* THIS EXAMPLE TO PRINT THE GROUP NUMBER AND COLUMN HEADINGS*/
    /* AT THE TOP OF THE NEW PAGE BEFORE PRINTING THE NEXT SET   */
    /* OF INPUT DATA.                                            */

           DO WHILE (VAR(1) = 0);
             ON ENDPAGE
               BEGIN;
                 PUT PAGE LINE(2) LIST('GROUP',N);
                 PUT LINE(3) LIST('VAR(1)','VAR(2)','VAR(3)');
                 PUT SKIP(2);
               END;
             PUT SKIP LIST(VAR);
             GET EDIT ((VAR(I) DO I=1 TO 3))(R(LOOK));
           END;
           GET EDIT ((C(I),W(I),D(I) DO I=1 TO 3))(COL(1), 9 F(2));
        END;

        STOP;
        END ILL21;
```

The program itself is quite simple and needs no further explanation. We shall now concern ourselves with determining the required specifications for each of the three test cases given. These are easily read off from the specifications:

Case 1

$C(1)=5$	$W(1)=5$	$D(1)=1$
$C(2)=0$	$W(2)=3$	$D(2)=0$
$C(3)=16$	$W(3)=4$	$D(3)=0$

Case 2

$C(1)=1$	$W(1)=6$	$D(1)=3$
$C(2)=7$	$W(2)=2$	$D(2)=1$
$C(3)=75$	$W(3)=5$	$D(3)=0$

Case 3

$C(1)=13$	$W(1)=4$	$D(1)=1$
$C(2)=17$	$W(2)=4$	$D(2)=1$
$C(3)=21$	$W(3)=4$	$D(3)=1$

This program will work for any arrangement of three variables on one card as long as they are in the proper left-to-right order. If they are not, a more elaborate scheme must be used.

VIII.3.7   Edit-Directed Output: The **PUT EDIT** Statement

Precise control over the form and appearance of stream-oriented output is exercised by means of the **PUT EDIT** statement, whose general form is directly analogous to the **GET EDIT**:

PUT EDIT(name1, name2, etc.)(spec1, spec2, etc.);

The specifications that can be used to define the output format are the same as those described for input except that each number in these specifications now refers to a space on a printed line instead of a column on a punched card.

Aside from format considerations, the edit-directed output statement is operationally similar to the **PUT LIST** statement; the accompanying list of items to be printed need not be restricted to variable names. Headings can be included as character string constants and the variables can be invloved in any legitimate expression consistent with their form. This flexibility includes the specification of variable subscripts. Thus, if X is an array of numerical elements, A is a character string, and B, I, and Y are single-valued numerical variables, a statement such as

PUT EDIT(Y*2*X(3*B−I),B**2,A ‖ 'NESS')(spec1,spec2,spec3);

is perfectly valid.

VIII.3.7.1   Allocations of Spaces on the Print Line

When a numerical data item is printed with a **PUT EDIT** statement, its appearance is similar to that produced by other stream-oriented output statements; the decimal point is shown in its proper place rather than implied. In the other output statements, the programmer did not concern himself directly with the placement of the decimal point; this was handled internally as part of the particular output operation. With edit-directed output, however, the programmer exerts direct and detailed control over each space on the print line, since he must account for the fact that a printed decimal point occupies a space. Thus, if a value of 147.52 is contained in storage and the programmer wishes to display it that way, he must provide for six spaces with a format specification of **F(6,2)**. If a variable is expected to take on negative values from time to time, space must be allowed for the sign to be shown. When the programmer anticipates a situation in which an insufficient number of spaces may be available to take care of a particular output variable, he may set up a special PL/I diagnostic service to take note of such an occurrence and perform a programmer-defined action. This is known as the **SIZE** condition.   *SIZE*

VIII.3.7.2   Fixed-Point Output Formats

The general form for such specifications, that is,

F(w,d,s)

still operates basically as it does for input. In the output situation, an area of w spaces on a line is reserved and filled with the value contained in the corresponding location given in the data list. The decimal point is printed in the space immediately to the left of the first d digits at the right end of the number. (If no d is specified, a value of zero is assumed.) If w is longer than necessary, the value is shifted to the right end of the reserved set of spaces on the line and the unused spaces are filled with blanks. If d is larger than the available number of decimal places in the stored value, zeros are added to the right. These operations are illustrated below for the value −38.2464:

Format Specification	*Appearance*
F(8,4)	`- 3 8 . 2 4 6 4`
F(9,5)	`- 3 8 . 2 4 6 4 0`
F(8,5)	`- 8 . 2 4 6 4 0 *`
F(12,5)	`    - 3 8 . 2 4 6 4 0`
F(12,2)	`    - 3 8 . 2 4`
F(7,4)	`3 8 . 2 4 6 4`
F(8)	`- 3 8`

*This will cause the **SIZE** condition to be raised if the programmer has activated it.

The third specification, s, causes the internal value to be multiplied by 10s before arranging it in the format dictated by w and d.

The principal use of this feature is to avoid the printing or punching of the decimal point. (This is especially useful in punching data to be read back in later with the number of decimal places implied. It also finds widespread utilization for printing on preprinted forms with columnar rulings or shadings to indicate the decimal point). For example, our value −38.2464 could be transmitted with 3 decimal places, leaving the decimal point out, using the specification F(6,0,3) and would appear as $\boxed{- \mid 3 \mid 8 \mid 2 \mid 4 \mid 6}$.

VIII.3.7.3 Floating-Point Output Formats

The specification

E(w,d,s)

must be such that w reserves sufficient spaces on the print line for two signs (the extra one is for the exponent), a decimal point, an E, a two-digit exponent value, and the s digits of the number. Note that if d = 0, the decimal point is omitted.

The value s indicates the total number of numerical digits with which a particular variable is to be printed. Of the s spaces made available on the line for digits (not to be confused with w, which also includes punctuation, and so on), d of those digits will appear to the right of the decimal point and s − d will appear to the left of the decimal point. The default value of s is d + 1. We can illustrate this by the following:

Format Specification	Appearance
E(13,6)	− 3 . 8 2 4 6 4 0 E + 0 1
E(13,4)	− 3 . 8 2 4 6 E + 0 1
E(13,4,6)	− 3 8 . 2 4 6 4 E + 0 0
E(15,7)	− 3 . 8 2 4 6 4 0 0 E + 0 1
E(12,5)	− 3 . 8 2 4 6 4 E + 0 1
E(12,3)	− 3 . 8 2 4 E + 0 1
E(12,3,5)	− 3 8 . 2 4 6 E + 0 0
E(10,0,5)	− 3 8 2 4 6 E − 0 3

Once we know the value of s, we can make some general rules for minimum value of w required. When a variable's value is never expected to be negative, w can be as small as s + 5. Otherwise, it should be s + 6.

VIII.3.7.4 Other Format Specifications

The use of the C, A, and X specifications for edit-directed output introduces no special problems. Factoring and repetition of specifications can be used as in the GET EDIT statement. The ability to vary the output format by using variables or expressions for format specifications can be excercised with no reservations imposed by the compiler.

When the **PUT EDIT** statement includes a character string constant as part of its output list, an **A** specification is usually included in the format list. This does not mean that the programmer has to specify the number of characters in the string. The compiler will do the counting but requires mention of the fact that a character string is being transmitted. Consequently, if we have a variable X in storage with a current value of 117.4 and wish to produce the following line of print:

THE MAXIMUM VELOCITY IS 117.4 FEET PER SECOND

our output statement would read

PUT SKIP EDIT('THE MAXIMUM VELOCITY IS ',X,' FEET PER SECOND')(**A,F(5,1),A);**

VIII.3.7.5   Control of Line and Column Position

The **PAGE, LINE,** and **SKIP** options were described for the other types of stream-oriented output. Programmers making use of edit-directed output may avail themselves of these options and, in addition, may use the **PAGE, LINE, SKIP,** and **COLUMN** format specifications. For instance,

PUT SKIP EDIT(X,Y,Z)(**X(12),F(5,1),X(5),E(17,6),X(10),A(20));**

and

PUT EDIT(X,Y,Z)(**SKIP,COL(13),F(5,1),COL(23),E(17,6),COL(50),A(20));**

will produce identical lines of print.

As indicated before, the number of characters to be printed on a particular line is set for each version of the compiler and can be changed by the programmer through the use of the **LINESIZE** option, which will be discussed later. When a format specification includes a **COLUMN** option that specifies a value, N, smaller than the current column, PL/I will start printing the specified items at the (w) column on the next line. However, if the quantity (w) is larger than the allowable number of columns on a line, PL/I will replace (w) with 1 and start a new line. This distinction can be illustrated as follows, assuming that our limit is 120 spaces per line: Suppose we had a character string A in storage with the value CONSTITUTIONAL. The statement

PUT SKIP EDIT(A)(**COLUMN(115),A(14));**

will produce the following printout:

TUTIONAL

while the statement

PUT SKIP EDIT(A)(**COLUMN**(122),**A**(14));

will produce

CONSTITUTIONAL

VIII.3.7.6   Overprinting

There are occasions for which it is desirable to print more than one character of information in a given position on a given line. Perhaps the most common situation is one calling for certain items to be underlined. This technique, called *overprinting*, is exercised in PL/I by means of the **SKIP** option or **SKIP** specification with a modifier of zero. If essence, the general statement

PUT SKIP(0) **EDIT** (data list)(format specifications);

suppresses the printer's urge to move to the next line before printing. Thus, the output pointer still is forced to the beginning of a print line, but it is the same line on which the previous printing took place. To illustrate, we shall set up statements to print the heading LATEST SUMMARY, underlined and centered on a 120-position line. Since LATEST SUMMARY occupies 14 spaces, it will start at a position (120-14)/2 or 53 spaces from the left. Accordingly, our sequence will say

PUT SKIP EDIT('LATEST SUMMARY')(**X**(53),**A**);

PUT SKIP(0) **EDIT**((6)'_',(7)'_')(**X**(53),**A**,**X**(1),**A**);

An equivalent result could be produced with a single statement by using **SKIP** as a format item as in either of the statements

PUT SKIP EDIT('LATEST SUMMARY')(**X**(53),**A**)
                ((6)'_',(7)'._')(**SKIP**(0),**X**(53),**A**,**X**(1),**A**);

or

PUT SKIP EDIT('LATEST SUMMARY',(6)'_',(7)'_')
                (**X**(53),**A**,**SKIP**(0),**X**(53),**A**,**X**(1),**A**);

This facility may be used repeatedly to overprint as many times as is desired. By overprinting prescribed combinations of characters it is possible to produce an effect similar to halftone illustrations, known as *gray shading*. An example of gray shading with up to five layers of printing is shown in Figure 8.2.

Courtesy: R. Blocher

Figure 8.2

VIII.3.8   The P Specification , *PIC OR PICTURE*

The **PICTURE** attribute in a **DECLARE** statement describes in detail the format in which any value assigned to the variable is to be stored; if such a variable is transmitted using **PUT LIST, PUT DATA**, or **PUT EDIT** with an **A** format specification, it will appear in the *exact* form described by the picture. The **P** format specification gives the programmer the ability to specify, in the same way, the detailed format in which he desires a value to be transmitted without the need for prior assignment of that value to a **PICTURE** variable.

The **P** specification has the general form

P 'codes'

where the codes are exactly the same as those used with the **PICTURE** attribute; the only difference between the two is that the word **PICTURE** has been abbreviated to a **P** or **PIC**. Some of the picture codes have already been discussed in connection with the **DECLARE** statement; here we shall review these and introduce others.

There are three basic types of picture specifications: one type describes a character string; the second, a fixed-point numerical value that is stored in character form; the third, a floating-point value stored in character form.

VIII.3.8.1   Picture Codes For Character Strings

Pictures describing character strings may use the codes **X, A**, and **9**. At least one **X** or **A** must appear to distinguish this usage from a fixed-point number consisting solely of digits. No other picture codes are permitted. In a character picture, the **9** stands for a digit or blank. These properties are summarized in Table 8.1.

TABLE 8.1 Picture Specifications for Character Strings

E X A M P L E S

Character	Explanation	Picture	Source	Internal Form
X	indicates any character	P 'XXXXX'	'%.ABC'	'%.ABC'
		P 'XXXXX'	'12.65'	'12.65'
A	indicates A-Z or blank	P 'XXXXX'	'ABCDEF'	'ABCDEF'
		P 'AAXAA'	'AB/CD'	'AB/CD'
		P 'AAA'	'AB/CD'	error
9	indicates 0-9 or blank	P '99X99'	'12.65'	'12.65'
		P 'AAX99'	'AB-23'	'AB-23'
		P 'AAX99'	'A − 3'	'A − 3'
		P '99'	numeric character picture	

VIII.3.8.2 Picture Codes for Fixed-Point Numbers

Numeric character pictures describe the character representation of a numeric value. This representation naturally may include the digits 0-9 that go to make up the number; in addition, the sign of the number and a decimal point may appear. In writing numerical values we frequently use additional punctuation and conventions to make the number more readable. For example, commas are frequently used to set off the digits in numbers greater than 1000 (1,000); a dollar sign is usually written before a number representing an amount of money, and most people prefer $1.25 to $ 1.25; in the same way, it is more convenient to write the sign of the number directly before it. That is, −1.25 is preferable to −   1.25; finally, in entering amounts in financial ledgers, negative values are frequently indicated by showing either a minus sign or a **CR** or **DB** symbol on the right; that is, 79.37− or 79.37**CR**. Additional conventions used in writing numbers include the replacement of nonsignificant high-order zeros with blanks (1.638 instead of 0,001.638) or sometimes with asterisks (****1.638). The asterisk notation is used in writing checks to prevent the weaker members of our society from wavering.

All of these possibilities, and more, are provided in the numeric picture specification, with innumerable variations to allow for differences in individual preference or in the requirements of different jobs. The use of these codes is summarized in Table 8.2, with examples of each major type of usage.

VIII.3.8.3 Picture Codes for Floating-Point Numbers

Floating-point numbers can be conceptually divided into two fields: the value and the exponent. The boundary line between these two fields is indicated by the picture character **K** or **E**, and the exponent field must appear to the right of the value field (also known as the mantissa) and must denote an integer. Both fields may contain sign characters and insertion characters. The Optimizing and Checkout Compilers permit the sign to be at either end of the field, whereas the IBM PL/I-F compiler requires that it be at the left end. Overpunched signs may also be used, but the **CR** and **DB** symbols are not allowed. Zero suppression characters should not be used in specifying picture descriptions for floating-point numbers in that their behavior is inconsistent. The same caveat holds true for floating signs (that is, **SSS...S**) or floating asterisks (that is, ****...***). Accordingly, the picture description of floating point numbers centers around the use of **9, V, K, E**, the insertion characters, and static use of numerical sign and dollar sign indicators at the left. These rules are summarized and illustrated in Table 8.3.

TABLE 8.2 Picture Specifications for Fixed-Point Numeric Character Variables

Type	Char	Explanation	Picture	Source Data as a FIXED DECIMAL Constant	Internal Form of Numeric Character Variable
				Examples	
Digits and	V	Indicates location of radix point does not appear in string	PIC'99V99'	2.5	'0250'
	9	Indicates a digit	PIC'9Y9Y9'	1205.73	'012 5'
			PIC'ZZZ99'	124	' 124'
	Y	Indicates a non-zero digit or blank	PIC'ZZZ99'	1	' 01'
			PIC'ZZZVZZ'	1.25	' 125'
	Z	Indicates a significant digit or blank	PIC'ZZZVZZ'	0.01	' 01'
			PIC'ZZZVZZ'	0	' '
			PIC'ZZZVZZ9' illegal – if Z to right of V all Z's required		
Magnitude	*	Indicates a significant digit or *	PIC'****V**'	1.25	'***125'
			PIC'**ZVZZ' illegal – illegal to mix Z's and *'s		
			PIC'ZZ9VZZ' illegal – 9's not permitted between Z's or *'s		
Insertion Characters	B	Indicates a blank	PIC'999V.99'	1.25	'001.25'
		These characters are replaced by a blank, $, or sign unless there is a significant or unconditional digit to the left	PIC'999V,99'	1.25	'001,25'
	.	Indicates a .	PIC'99.99V99'	12.258	'00.1225'
	,	Indicates a ,	PIC'Z,ZZZV.ZZ'	1378	'1,378.00'
	/	Indicates a /	PIC'Z,ZZZV.ZZ'	0.05	' .05'
			PIC'Z,ZZZ.VZZ'	0.01	' 01'
			PIC'Z,ZZZ.VZZ'	23.95	' 23.95'
			PIC'9B9B9'	27.3	'0 2 7'
			PIC'Z9/99/99'	12474	' 1/24/74'
Signs	+	+ if ≥ 0, b if < 0	PIC'SZ9'	−2	'− 2'
	−	− if < 0, b if ≥ 0	PIC'SZ9'	2	'+ 2'
		These characters may appear either to the left or right of the digit positions. May also be used as drifting characters, below	PIC'−99'	−2	'−02'
			PIC'−99'	2	' 02'
	S	+ if ≥ 0, − if < 0	PIC'+99'	−2	' 02'
			PIC'+99'	2	'+02'
	CR	CR if < 0, bb if ≥ 0	PIC'ZZV.ZZCR'	−1.25	' 1.25 CR'
	DB	DB if < 0, bb if ≥ 0	PIC'ZZV.ZZBCR'	1.25	' 1.25 '
		These codes may only appear to the right of the digit portion of the picture	PIC'ZZV.ZZBDB'	−1.25	' 1.25 DB'
	T	12 or 11	PIC'999V.9T'	1.25	'0012E'
	I	12 or none	PIC'999V.9R'	−1.25	'0012N'
	R	none or 11	PIC'999V.9R'	1.25	'00125'

These characters are digit positions on which the indicated zones will be 'overpunched' according to the sign: 12 = +, 11 = −

Type	Spec.		Explanation	Picture	Source	Internal Value
Drifting	$	$	These characters must appear in a consecutive sequence, possibly interspersed with insertion characters. Each character is replaced by either a blank, a significant digit, or the character it stands for (which appears only once, as far to the right as possible)	PIC'$$,$$$V.$$'	365.79	' $365.79'
	S	same		PIC'$$,$$$V.$$'	1365.79	'$1,365.79'
	+	as		PIC'$$,$$$V.$$'	25.63	' $25.63'
	-	above		PIC'$$,$$$V.$$'	0.01	' $.01'
				PIC'$$,$$9V.99'	0.01	' $0.01'
				PIC'$$,$$$V.V$$'	0.01	' $01'
				PIC'$$,$$$V.$$—'	-1.25	' $1.25—'
				PIC'————9V.99'	-12.95	' —12.95'
				PIC'————9V.99'	0.25	' 0.25'
				PIC'SSSS9V.99'	0.25	' +0.25'
Scaling	F(s)		s is a decimal integer constant. The value represented by the rest of the picture is effectively multiplied by 10s	PIC'999F(3)'	16000	'016'
				PIC'V999F(—2)'	0.00125	'125'

TABLE 8.3 Picture Specifications for Floating-Point Numeric Character Variables

Type	Spec.	Explanation	Picture	Source	Internal Value
Digits and Magnitude	V	Indicates location of radix point, mantissa only	PIC'99V99K99'	10	'100000'
	9	Indicates a digit	PIC'99V99K99'	1000	'100002'
			PIC'99V99K99'	.01	'100003'
			PIC'99V99K99'	0	'000000'
Insertion	B	Indicates a blank	PIC'9,999E99'	1276	'1,27600'
	.	Indicates a period	PIC'9V.999E99'	1276	'1,27603'
	,	Indicates a comma	PIC'9.999/K99'	13690	'1,368/01'
	/	Indicates a slash	PIC'$9,999E99'	12378000	'$1,237E04'
	$	Indicates a dollar sign			
Signs	+[1]	+ if ≥ 0, blank if < 0	PIC'—9,999/K—99'	.1	'1,000—04'
	-	— if < 0, blank if ≥ 0	PIC'—9,999E—99'	—.1	'—1.000E—04'
	S	+ if ≥ 0, — if < 0	PIC'—9V.999E—99'	—.1	'—1.000E+00'
			PIC'S9V.999ES99'	1	'+1.000E+00'
	T[2]	12 or 11 overpunch	PIC'9V.99TE9T'	.1	'1.00+EOJ'
	I	12 or no overpunch	PIC'9V99TK9T'	12.75	'127EOA'
	R	11 or no overpunch	PIC'9V99TK9T'	—12.75	'127NOA'
			PIC'S9V999K9T'	—12.75	'—12750A'
Field Separators	K[3]				
	E	Indicates an E			

[1] These characters may appear to the left of all digit positions to indicate the presence of a sign. The Optimizing and Checkout compilers allow signs on the right as well.

[2] These characters designate digit positions in which the indicated zones will be 'overpunched' according to the sign: 12 = +, 11 = —.

[3] One of these characters (K or E) must be used to separate the mantissa from the exponent.

Illustration 22

The Yehyeh Record Company wishes to publish a weekly sales summary having the form shown below.

Yehyeh Record Company Sales List Week Ending 10/31/67

Name	Number	Records Sold	Revenue
Oh, Look, a Flower!	004741	3,284	$ 1,576.32
Radio Love	000812	25,977	$10,650.57

Total Records Sold = 306,744
Total Sales = $125,765.04

The operation is set up so that each time a dealer or distributor orders a shipment of a particular record, a card is punched with the following information:

Card Columns	Name	Format
1-35	Name of song under which order is placed	Character string
36-41	Record number	XXXXXX
48-53	Number of records ordered	XXXXXX
54-56	Unit price, to the nearest cent	X$_{(.)}$XX

The unit price is included because it can vary with the size of the order. Since each of these sales is listed by the name of the song under which the order was placed, it is acceptable to have two entries in the summary table for the same record number.

Write a program to produce the information required for the summary sheet and to format it properly. There is no definite limit to the number of transaction cards that may be expected for a given run, nor is there any advance knowledge as to how many different song titles will be involved or which ones they will be. The only thing known is that there are never more than 50 different song titles involved in a week's sales. The transaction cards are not submitted in any particular order. Assume that a line of print can consist of up to 120 columns and that the number of lines allowed per page is sufficient to accommodate the entire weekly summary. The first sales card is preceded by a card in which the date is punched in columns 1-6 (mmddyy).

Since we have no knowledge about which songs are sold in a particular week, one of the essential features in our program will be a loop of instructions that checks each incoming name against those already stored. If there is a match, the sales information will be added to the appropriate total; if not, the new name will be added to the array of names. When all the cards have been read and processed in this manner, the table will be formatted and printed.

The listing of song names and corresponding information about them is most conveniently built up as an array of structures, since this will facilitate the construction of the output statement. A single structure will also be provided in which to store the information as it is read in and before it is placed in its appropriate array element.

Now for the format considerations. The first heading is seen to require 17 characters (including spaces). We can center the heading on the line by starting the first character ($^{120}/_2$ minus $^{17}/_2$) or roughly column 53. The first character of the second line will be placed at column 55, and the initial character of the third line will be placed in column 50. The centering calculations for the other line in the output are obtained in similar fashion:

```
ILL22: PROCEDURE OPTIONS (MAIN);
  /*****************************************************/
  /* SALE IS THE STRUCTURE FOR AN INPUT CARD,        */
  /* SUMUP IS THE ARRAY OF STRUCTURES FOR ALL SONGS, */
  /* COUNT IS THE TOTAL NO. OF SONGS FOR THE RUN,    */
  /* #SALES IS THE TOTAL NO. OF RECORDS SOLD,        */
  /* AMOUNT IS THE DOLLAR VALUE OF #SALES.           */
  /*****************************************************/
        DECLARE 1 SALE,
                  2 NAME CHARACTER(35),     2 RECNUM CHARACTER(6),
                  2 #SOLD FIXED(6),         2 PRICE FIXED(3,2),
                1 SUMUP(50),
                  2 SONG CHARACTER(35),     2 #REC CHARACTER(6),
                  2 TOTAL FIXED(6),         2 INCOME FIXED(8,2),
                (COUNT,NDFIL,I,J) FIXED BINARY,
                #SALES FIXED(8), AMOUNT FIXED(9,2), DATE CHARACTER(6);
        TOTAL, INCOME, COUNT, #SALES, AMOUNT, NDFIL = 0;
        ON ENDFILE (SYSIN) NDFIL=1;   GET EDIT (DATE(A(6));
        GET SKIP EDIT (SALE)(A(35),A(6),X(6),F(6),F(3,2));

        DO WHILE (NDFIL = 0);
          #SALES = #SALES+#SOLD;  AMOUNT=AMOUNT+#SOLD*PRICE;
          /** WE NEED TO FIND THE MATCHING SONG. IF THERE IS  **/
          /** NO MATCH, THE NEW SONG HAS TO BE ADDED TO THE   **/
          /** ARRAY. A SPECIAL TEST AND ACTION TAKE CARE OF   **/
          /** THE FIRST INPUT CARD.                           **/
          IF COUNT = 0
            THEN DO;
                    COUNT = COUNT+1;        SONG(COUNT) = NAME;
                    #REC(COUNT) = RECNUM;   I = COUNT;
                 END;
            ELSE DO;
                 J = 0;
                 DO I = 1 TO COUNT WHILE (J = 0);
                    IF NAME = SONG(I) THEN J=1;
                 END;
                 /* IF J STILL = 0 HERE, THIS IS A NEW SONG. */
                 IF J=0 THEN DO;
                            COUNT=COUNT+1;      SONG(COUNT)=NAME;
                            #REC(COUNT)=RECNUM;   I=COUNT;
                         END;
                 END;
          TOTAL(I)=TOTAL(I)+#SOLD; INCOME(I)=INCOME(I)+#SOLD*PRICE;
          GET SKIP EDIT (SALE)(A(35),A(6),X(6),F(6),F(3,2));
        END;

        PUT PAGE LINE(3) EDIT('YEHYEH RECORD CO.')(COL(53),A)
           ('SALES LIST')(SKIP,COLUMN(55),A)
           ('WEEK ENDING ',DATE)(COL(50),A,X(3),P'99/99/99');
        PUT SKIP EDIT('NAME','NUMBER','NO.SOLD','REVENUE')
           (COLUMN(32),A,COLUMN(62),A,COLUMN(78),A,COLUMN(96),A);
        PUT SKIP EDIT((SUMUP(I) DO I=1 TO COUNT))
           (COLUMN(17),A(35),COLUMN(62),A(6),COLUMN(78),F(6),
           COLUMN(94),P'$ZZZZZZ.ZZ',SKIP);
        PUT SKIP(2) EDIT('TOTAL NO. OF RECORDS SOLD = ',#SALES)
           (COLUMN(40),A,F(8));
        PUT SKIP EDIT('TOTAL SALES = ',AMOUNT)
           (COLUMN(40),A,P'$ZZZZZZ.ZZ');
        END ILL22;
```

VIII.4   INTERNAL EDITING: THE **STRING** OPTION

PL/I provides another use of the **GET** and **PUT** statements that does not involve the flow of information between the processor and external devices. Instead, this method of transmission uses a character string stored inside the processor as a source or destination. Once a character string is established in storage, the **STRING** option allows the programmer to read from it as if it were an input stream. It is possible to place information in such a character string as if it were an output stream.

VIII.4.1   The **GET STRING** Statement

Although the **STRING** option can be used with any of the three stream-oriented types of input, its most useful application is with the edit-directed mode, since it provides the programmer with an opportunity to examine the string and use its contents to direct subsequent actions. The basic form for this type of statement is

GET STRING (stringname) **EDIT**(name1,name2,etc.)(spec1,spec2,etc);

where (stringname) is the name of the area in storage from which the information is to be transmitted. The other designations enclosed in parentheses have their previous meanings.

To illustrate how this feature can be used, we can set up an alternate method of handling data whose format is not constant. This method is general, so it can be used effectively in cases where the specification of variable formats becomes awkward or impossible. Let us suppose that we are to process a set of data consisting of an amalgamation of three separate collections of data cards obtained from different sources. Three variables (X, Y, and Z) are involved in each case, but they appear on the card in three different formats. One way to handle this, of course, is to use a simple program to rearrange two of the collections to conform to the third, or to rearrange all three to some common standard format. However, the **STRING** option presents us with another possibility. Let us assume that all three data collections have a vacant column in common (say, column 80). This fortunate condition is exploited by punching a

```
/**--ASSUME X IS FIXED(4), Y IS FIXED(5,1) AND Z IS FIXED(3).--**/
/**--FOR THIS EXAMPLE WE SHALL MAKE THESE FURTHER ASSUMPTIONS--**/
/**--IF COL. 80 HAS A 1, THAT CARD HAS X IN COLS. 5-8,      --**/
/**-~     Y IN 20-24 AND Z IN 76-78;                         --**/
/**--IF COL. 80 HAS A 2, THAT CARD HAS Y IN COLS. 2-6,      --**/
/**--     Z IN 18-20 AND X IN 42-45;                         --**/
/**--IF COL. 80 HAS A 3, THAT CARD HAS Z IN COLS. 2-4,      --**/
/**--     Y IN 16-20 AND X IN 42-45.                         --**/

        DECLARE PLACE CHARACTER(79), X FIXED(4), Y FIXED(5,1), Z FIXED(3),
                KIND FIXED(1);
        ON ENDFILE (SYSIN) STOP;
    IN: GET EDIT(PLACE,KIND)(A(79),A(1));
        IF KIND=1 THEN GET STRING(PLACE)EDIT(X,Y,Z)
                (X(4),F(4),X(11),F(5,1),X(51),F(3));
        IF KIND=2 THEN GET STRING(PLACE)EDIT(Y,Z,X)
                (X(1),F(5,1),X(11),F(3),X(4),F(4));
        IF KIND=3 THEN GET STRING(PLACE)EDIT(Z,Y,X)
                (X(1),F(3),X(11),F(5,1),X(21),F(4));
```

number in that column to designate the type of card (1,2, or 3). By reading the card into a string and examining the number, we can determine which format to use and direct the **GET EDIT** statement, through the proper format. The cards need not be in any particular order, since each card is examined individually. Our program segment is given on the preceding page.

If a **GET STRING** statement accounts for fewer characters than are present in the character string, the remaining ones are ignored. If the opposite is true, if the **GET STRING** statement requests more characters than have been allocated for the string, an error condition is raised and processing terminates.

VIII.4.2   The **PUT STRING** Statement

This statement causes the program to treat an adequately declared character string as if it were the output stream. Thus, the general statement

PUT STRING(stringname) **EDIT** (name1,name2,etc.)(spec1,spec2,etc.);

will place the sequence of variables given in (name1,name2,etc.) in the character string (stringname) in the order given and in accordance with the format instructions. As with the **GET STRING** statement, it is possible to use this option with list-directed and data-directed output as well as with the edit-directed type. However, the unique ability to place variables next to each other within a stream without intervening blanks makes the edit mode the most common one used with this option.

Specific note should be made of the **X** specification's behavior in the **PUT STRING** statement with edit-directed information. Since the destination is treated as if it were an "output stream", the **X**(w) places w blanks in that stream. This is consistent with the specification's effect in a regular **PUT EDIT** statement, and therefore the result is quite different from skipping w spaces. Accordingly, if a particular **X** specification in a **PUT STRING** statement refers to columns (positions) that already contain desired information, those values will be replaced with blanks.

PROBLEMS

1. For each of the declarations given below, show the appearance of the data card and specify the input statement required to read the data in list-directed mode. Use the following values:

    A is 17

    B is 124.25

C is 1100101₂

D is 'CYCLOPENTADECANOL'

E(1) is 11.4, E(2) is 8, E(3) is 124.67

F is 30—14;

a. DECLARE A FIXED(2), B FIXED(6,3), C BINARY FIXED(10),D CHARACTER (20), E(3) FLOAT(7), F COMPLEX FIXED(3);

b. DECLARE (A,B,C) FLOAT(6), D CHARACTER(17), E(3) FIXED(6,3), F COMPLEX(6);

c. DECLARE (A,B) BINARY FIXED(10,2),C FIXED(3),D CHARACTER(30) VARYING, E(3)FLOAT(9), F COMPLEX FIXED(5);

d. DECLARE A PICTURE '999', B PICTURE '999v999', C FIXED (8), D PICTURE '(17)A', E(3) PICTURE '999.999', F COMPLEX PICTURE '99';

2. Repeat Problem 1 for data-directed mode.

3. Given the following values:

D(1)=14, D(2)=−3.6, D(3)=7.72, D(4)=6.016,
D(5)=.71, D(6)=0, D(7)=11, D(8)=.002

and the statement

DECLARE D(8) FIXED(7,4);

show the appearance of the printout for each of the following statements:

a. PUT SKIP LIST (D);

b. PUT SKIP DATA (D);

c. I=4; PUT SKIP LIST(D(1),D(2),D(I**2−3*(I+1)));

d. J=3; PUT SKIP DATA(D,D(2*J));

e. I=4; PUT SKIP LIST(2*D,(I**3/(8)*D(1.5*I)/7));

Assume that the compiler prints five values on a line.

4. We have the following sequence of statements:

DECLARE 1 A(2),2 B,(3 C(3), 3 D)FIXED(2,1), 2 E FIXED(3), 2 F,
3 G,(4 G1, 4 G2(2)) FIXED(3,1), 3 H FIXED(1);

GET LIST (A);

and the data are punched as shown below. Show the appearance

4.1,6,.7,0,12,6.3,14,39.8,8,3,2,1.1,9,4,61,87.5,.6,3,41.7,28.6,8 of the printouts for each of the following statements (assuming the compiler prints five values per line):

a. **PUT SKIP LIST** (2*A(2));

b. **PUT SKIP DATA** (A);

c. **PUT SKIP LIST** (F);

d. **PUT SKIP DATA** (G(2(,G2(2,2));

e. **PUT SKIP DATA** (C(2,3));

f. Write a statement to print the square of the 11th value in a structure.

g. We wish to read in a new value of 7 and store it in the ninth element of the structure using data-directed mode. Write the appropriate **GET** statement and show the corresponding data card.

5. A data card is to be punched according to the specification shown below.

Card Columns	Name	Typical Value
6-8	A	12.2
9-15	B	3247J08
20-25	C	−176.24
26	D	W
31-32	E	.18
77	F	2

a. Show the data card and write a completely formatted input statement.

b. Repeat part A using **P** specifications only.

6. A data card has the following contents:

Columns	Contents
1-20	41430617341263411350
21-40	29028422365701265840
41-60	0624877931ЬЬЬЬ4382AJ
61-80	5B475125136KLIBЬЬЬ1G

List the values of the variables as a result of the following statements:

a. **GET EDIT** (A) (**COL**(1),F(8,3));

b. **GET EDIT** (A,B,C) (**COL**(1), 3 F(6,6));

c. **GET EDIT** (A,B,C) (**COL**(1), (X(14),F(4,1)));

d. **GET EDIT** (A,B,C,D) (**COL**(1),X(3),F(7,0), 2 (X(11),F(2,1),F(1)));

e. **GET EDIT** (A,B,C,D,E,F) (**COL**(1), 2 (X(3), 2 F(5,2),X(4)),F(3,1));

f. **GET EDIT**(A,B,C)(**COLUMN**(15),F(4,1),X(7),F(3),E(7));

g.   **GET EDIT(A,B,C,D)(X(2),F(2),X(1),E(5));**

h.   **GET EDIT((A(I)DO I = 1 TO 7))(F(3,1));**

i.   **GET EDIT(B,(A(I)DO I = 1 TO B))(X(3),F(1),6(X(2),F(2,1)));**

j.   **GET EDIT(A,D,E,B)(X(2),4(F(2,2),X(1));**
      GET EDIT(F,C,G)(3(X(2),F(1)));

7.   Using the same card as in Problem 6, write the variable declaration and input statements necessary to produce the following values in storage:

a.   A = 17.3, B = 341, C = .061

b.   A = 41.26, B = 617.3, C = 5B47, D = 3.0617

c.   A = 16, B = 58400, C = 73.41, D = 984.22, E = .0263

d.   A = 36KL, B(1) = 3.06, B(2) = 1.26, B(3) = 3.50, C = 24.8

e.   A = 143, B = 6KL, C = .003412, D = 512,500, E = 136

8.   A police department maintains information on traffic violations by collecting and recording data on each citation as shown below.

Card Columns	Identification	Format
1-2	Type of violation (01 to 50)	XX
3-23	Officer's name	Characters
24-29	Officer's serial number	CXXXXX*
30	Day of week (1 to 7)	X
31-32	Week of year (01 to 52)	XX
40	Conviction obtained (1 = yes, 2 = no)	X

*Serial number consists of an initial letter followed by five digits.

Write a program to produce a list giving the number of citations for each officer for each day of the week. (1 is Sunday, and so on.) A separate page should be printed for each officer as shown below:

Citation Report for Officer's Name;
Serial Number CXXXXX;
Week Number XX

Day of Week	Number of Citations
Sunday	XX
Monday	.
Tuesday	.
Wednesday	.
Thursday	.
Friday	.
Saturday	.

    Total Citations This Week = XX

Assume that all cards for a particular officer are kept together but not necessarily in any order.

9. The physics department at East Svoovik High School wishes to grade a test using a computer. The test consists of 12 questions, each of which is answerable by a three-digit number of the form $X_{()}XX$. Answers for an individual student are to be prepared on a fixed-format input card containing the student's name (last name, comma, first initial, period, the total length no more than 22 characters), followed by each of the answers in succession. Since this will be used for different tests, it is possible that any or all of the answers could be negative. Fixed column locations are to be assigned to each answer, so that omitted answers are left blank. Write a program that reads a set of correct answers and uses them to grade each student's exam. The output is to show a line of output for each student containing the student's name, number of questions answered correctly and the score, the latter based on 100 points distributed uniformly over the 12 questions. Report the score to the nearest point and provide appropriate headings for the columns and for the entire run.

10. Write the program described in Problem 9, but include the additonal provision that an answer is correct if it is within ± 10 percent of the corresponding value given on the answer card.

11. Write the program described either in Problem 9 or 10 with the following additional feature: a column of output is to be added in which each student's score is to be reported as Z, the number of standard deviations from the mean score:

$$Z_i = \frac{SCORE_i - SMEAN}{S}$$

where

SCOREi is the score for student i
SMEAN is the average score
S is the standard deviation of the scores

$$SMEAN = \frac{\displaystyle\sum_{i=1}^{N} SCORE_i}{N}$$

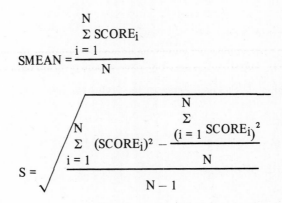

$$S = \sqrt{\frac{\displaystyle\sum_{i=1}^{N} (SCORE_i)^2 - \frac{\left(\displaystyle\sum_{i=1}^{N} SCORE_i\right)^2}{N}}{N-1}}$$

N = number of students

12. Write a program that prepares and prints a simple graphical display of X-Y data. Use a fixed display area of 50 lines $\times$ 100 spaces framed by a perimeter of dashes (horizontally) and I's (vertically). The

horizontal and vertical ranges are to be 1-100 and 1-50, respectively, with appropriate markers every ten units (See Figure 8.3). Data are to be submitted as (X,Y) coordinates, one set to a card, with X and Y values expressed as integers. The positions of these values are consistent for an entire group of cards but may vary from run to run. The program is to accept a label that is centered and printed above the display. Each point on the display is denoted by a period. After the display is shown, the program is to print the number of points read and the number of points that could not be shown (out of range).

13. Write the program described in Problem 12, but include the following: X-Y data may be submitted as mixed numbers (with precision varying from run to run), in which case the program is to round them to the nearest integer value and plot them accordingly.

14. Write the program specified for Problem 12 or 13, with the following additional feature: The display is to distinguish between single and multiple occurrences of points with a given set of coordinates. A single occurrence is to be shown as a period (same as before); two occurrences are to appear as a 2, three occurrences as a 3, and so on, with 9 representing nine or more replicates of a given (X,Y) pair.

15. Write the program specified for Problem 13 with the following change: Points to be shown on the display are produced by solving the equation

$$Y = mX + b$$

for X values of XB, XB + 1, XB + 2, ..., XE, where XB, XE, m, and b are input variables whose placement and format are fixed:

Columns	Item	Format
2-6	m	$\pm XX_{(.)}XX$
11-15	b	$\pm XX_{(.)}XX$
16-17	XB	XX
19-20	XE	XX

Precede the display with a line (centered) specifying the function:

FUNCTION IS: Y = $\pm$XX.XX * X $\pm$ XX.XX

For example, if m is −2.2 and b is 12, the line should read

FUNCTION IS: Y = −2.20* X + 12.00

16. Write the program specified for Problem 15 with the additional capability of producing displays (one to a page) for any number of input functions.

17. F. J. Yech Chemicals, Ltd., has some information on its chemicals punched so that each card contains the following data for a particular chemical

Columns	Item	Format
1-5	catalog product i.d.	characters
10-20	trade name	characters
31-40	formula	characters
51-56	melting point, °F	XXX.XX

The catalog product i.d. consists of a letter followed by four digits (such as J2127); the formula is a string of letter-number combinations in which each letter (representing an element) is followed by a one- or two-digit integer representing the number of atoms of that element present in a molecule of the chemical. For example, C2H8O2 represents a compound consisting of two atoms of carbon, eight atoms of hydrogen and two atoms of oxygen. Yech chemicals happen to contain only those elements with one-letter names (a nice thing). Write a program that prints a suitable heading (up to you) followed by a line of print for each card showing the catalog i.d., trade name, formula, melting point in degrees C (not degrees F) to the nearest .1°, and the molecular weight to the nearest hundredth. For reference purposes,

$$°C = \frac{5}{9}(°F-32)$$

Element	Atomic Weight	Element	Atomic Weight
B	10.82	N	14.01
C	12.01	O	16.00
F	19.00	P	30.98
H	1.01	S	32.07
I	126.92	U	238.07

Molecular weight $= \sum$ (no. of atoms of element i * atomic wt. of element i)

18.   Write the program described in Problem 17 with the following change: Elements represented by a single atom do not have an explicit numerical designator, thus C1H4 would appear as CH4.

19.   Churchill River Canoe Outfitters, Ltd., is a rental business handling a variety of canoeing and camping equipment. Rates for the various items are given below:

Item	Rental Price, $/Day
Canoes (with paddles)	6.00
Tents:	
2-man	2.50
3-man	3.50
4-man	4.50
5-man	5.50
Car-top carriers	0.35
Tarpaulins	0.60
Pack sacks	
small	0.50
large	0.60

Item	*Rental Price, $/Day*
Sleeping bags	
single	1.00
double	1.05
Foam mattresses	0.60
Axes	0.25
Folding shovels	0.25
Cook-and-eat kits	0.40
Raincoats	0.35
Gas stoves	
1-burner	0.50
2-burner	1.00
Life jackets	0.35
Special prepared foods	5.50 per person

For every four canoes rented, a fifth is provided free.

    The leader of each party fills out a form giving his name and home town, the size of his party, the length of their proposed trip (in days) and the quantities of equipment required for the trip. Write a program that produces the following output:

a. An invoice for each party showing the list of items required, the quantity of each item, the unit price, total price for each type of item, and the total rental cost for the party.

b. A summary showing total equipment counts and rental receipts for all parties outfitted on a given day.

Treat the price schedule as a fixed table.

20. Prepare a more flexible version of the program in the previous problem by allowing the price schedule to be variable, so that it can be read in with each day's run.

21. Prepare another alternative to the program in Problem 19 such that the schedule given in that problem is used as a standard. That is, prices on a given day may be changed for any item.

22. Varicose Sales punches the following card for each inventory item received:

Card Columns	*Item*	*Format*
1-5	i.d.	characters
6-15	item description	characters
16-17	quantity	XX
18-23	total cost	XXX.XX (the decimal point is punched)
24	code	1, 2, or 3

Write a program to produce sales tickets for the unit items. Each sales ticket is to appear as follows:

Item No.	*Description*	*Price*
A.12.34	Table lamp	40.00

Price is computed as 110 percent of cost for a code 1 unit, 115 percent for a code 2 unit, and 125 percent for a code 3 unit. Assume that these tickets will be printed on special perforated output paper, laid out so that there are two groups of tickets across the page and 20 tickets down the length of the page (a total of 40 tickets per page).

SUMMARY OF IMPORTANT TERMS

COLUMN	An option available in **PUT EDIT** statements allowing the specification of a particular column number as the starting point for the next output item. This option also may be used with the **GET EDIT** statement when reading from punched cards.
Data-directed i/o	One of the three types of stream-oriented input/output; data values in this mode of operation are accompanied by their names.
Edit-directed i/o	One of the three types of stream oriented input/output; this is the most detailed and controlled transmission mode in that each individual position in the input or output stream must be accounted for explicitly.
Editing	In the context of edit-directed output, the process of refining an output display by incorporating dollar signs, asterisks, commas, and other symbols that make the value more meaningful. Such editing often is done by means of **PICTURE** format specifications.
ENDPAGE	A condition raised automatically when PL/I's line counter reaches a preset value. The default action is to position the paper to the start of the next page. Other action may be defined in conjunction with an **ON ENDPAGE** statement.
Format specification	A series of special symbolic indicators available for use with edit-directed input/output. These provide PL/I with the information necessary for interpreting a fragment of an input stream or constructing part of an output stream. Included among these are a number of **PICTURE** specifications for extended editing (which see).
FORMAT statement	A statement containing a list of format specifications for use by an arbitrary number of **GET EDIT** or **PUT EDIT** statements elsewhere in the program.
GET statement	The general statement type for reading stream-oriented input.

GET STRING statement — A statement type that allows the programmer to treat an internally stored collection of data items (usually organized as a structure) as if it were an input stream.

LINE — An option, available for use in a **PUT** statement, that forces positioning of the printer at a designated line on the page.

List-directed i/o — One of three types of stream oriented input/output; data values are presented in sequence with intervening blanks (or commas) but without explicit identifiers.

Overprinting — A technique for producing special graphic and other visual effects by superimposing several printed characters on each other. This is implemented by specifying a **SKIP**(0) option.

PAGE — An option available for use in a **PUT** statement. Its inclusion forces positioning of the printer to the top of the next page.

PUT statement — The general type of statement used to produce stream-oriented output.

PUT STRINGS statement — A statement type that allows the programmer to construct the contents of an area in storage as if it were part of an output stream.

READ statement — The general statement type used for reading record-oriented input.

Record oriented i/o — One of two basic forms of data transmission. In this mode, data are read or written as discrete segments of data (records) of arbitrary but known length.

Remote format — A construction, used in edit-directed input/output statements, whereby the data formats are not described as a physical part of the data transmission statement. Instead, reference is made to a separate **FORMAT** statement (which see) elsewhere in the program.

SKIP — An option available for use in **PUT** statements. Its inclusion forces the printer to skip an indicated number of lines.

Stream oriented i/o — One of two basic mechanisms for data transmission. In this mode, the input or output is treated as a continuing stream of characters punctuated by special symbols or by directions contained in the associated **GET** or **PUT** statements.

Variable format — Specifications, available for use in edit-directed input/output, that allow the descriptions of data items (such as a field length, number of skipped characters, and so on, to be varied from one use to another without changing the program.

WRITE statement — The general statement type used for generating record-oriented output.

IX INTERNAL ARITHMETIC MANIPULATIONS

The use of arithmetic expressions in assignment statements, array subscripts, or as parameters of various sorts (for example, in format specifications) is certainly not new to us by this time. However, we have not explored the construction and behavior of expressions to any appreciable extent since we have employed them primarily as vehicles in developing other PL/I concepts and features. The very fact that we could treat internal data manipulations so casually points up a fundamental philosophy in PL/I's design: the intent to provide built-in actions that coincide as much as possible with those "naturally" expected by the user. Thus, to the extent that such correspondence exists, it has not really been essential to be fully aware of the compiler's underlying activities.

We are now at the point, however, where we can write more complicated expressions, whose proper use may require some knowledge of how PL/I executes internal operations. We are ready to extend our manipulating capabilities by means of a number of special features contained in the language. To permit extensive flexibility of operations, PL/I maintains and continually refers to a set of rules that govern the handling of expressions and lets PL/I determine what their components are, the order in which they are to be evaluated, and the disposition of the results. (In the interest of completeness, this chapter includes an introductory discussion of PL/I's arithmetic rules (Sections IX.1.3 and IX.1.4). This may be omitted without loss of continuity.)

IX.1   EVALUATION OF ARITHMETIC EXPRESSIONS

PL/I does arithmetic using the five basic operations of addition(+), subtraction(−), mulitplication(*), division(/), and exponentiation(**). While the use of *,/, and ** are rigid and completely straightforward, + and − each have two possible meanings. When one of these latter operators is used to connect two parts of an expression (such as A+B), it is known as an **infix operator** as are *,/ , and **.

However, a + or − operator can also be used in front of a single component of an expression, referring only to that component. In that context it is known as a *prefix operator*. The + in +B−2*A**2 is a prefix operator, as is the − in 2*A**−3. PL/I looks for and can distinguish between these usages, as will be seen.

IX.1.1   Priority of Arithmetic Operations

The strategy used by PL/I to analyze and evaluate an arithmetic expression is basically as follows: the entire expression is scanned from left to right to determine which operators are being used and in what order. Evaluation proceeds according to a priority system in which the operations implied by**, prefix +, and prefix − are performed first. Then, all multiplications and divisions are performed in order, starting with the leftmost multiplication or division in the expression. Once all of these have been done, the compiler goes back and carries out all of the indicated additions and subtractions in order, again starting with the leftmost one. The results of intermediate operations are automatically assigned to temporary locations, which are released when no longer needed. If the compiler discovers that there are two or more first-priority operations in an expression (as in the term A**−B**2), they are evaluated from right to left. Let us consider the statement

$$Y = -B**3 + 2*A*C/D**2 - 3*C/A*B;$$

According to the strategy outlined above, the evaluation would proceed conceptually (though not necessarily exactly) as follows:

1. Since the − in front of B is not connecting B with anything, it is considered a prefix operator. Because there are other high-priority operators, the activity implied by them is performed from right to left. Hence, D is squared and the result assigned to temporary storage.

2. The next first-priority operator is found and executed, resulting in a temporarily stored value of B**3.

3. The remaining first-priority operation is processed, resulting in a sign change for B**3.

4. Finding no more first-priority operations, PL/I goes back to the beginning of the expression to look for second-priority operations. The first one found is the * connecting 2 and A, forming a temporary result representing the product of these two values.

5. The next multiplication is performed, forming the product (2*A)*C, using C and the temporary value of 2*A.

6. The product formed in the previous step is divided by the value of D^2.

7. The product 3*C is formed and stored.

8. The product formed in the previous step is divided by the value of A, and that quotient is retained.

9. The result obtained in Step 8 is multiplied by the value of B.

10. The temporary results obtained in Steps 3 and 6 are added, and their sum is held for further use.

11. The value obtained in Step 9 is subtracted from the sum calculated in Step 10, and that difference, representing the desired value, is stored in location Y.

The introduction of parentheses may change the order of evaluation but not the basic strategy. The combination of terms enclosed by parentheses is treated as a separate expression that is evaluated by itself, according to the same set of procedures. The result is then stored and operated on as a single value. For instance, if the above expression were changed to read

Y − B**3 + 2*(A*C/D**2−3*C)/(A*B);

the processing sequence would be:

1. −B**3 would be evaluated and stored as before.

2. The leftmost parenthetical subexpression (A*C/D**2 − 3*C) is scanned, and the highest priority operation is carried out, resulting in the temporary storage of a value representing D^2.

3. The product A*C is obtained.

4. The quotient $A*C/D^2$ is evaluated.

5. A value for 3*C is obtained.

6. The indicated subtraction between the values obtained in Steps 4 and 5 is performed, resulting in a single value for the entire parenthetical expression.

7. The product A*B is calculated and stored.

8. Having taken care of all parentheses, the compiler begins another full scan. The first operation it finds is a multiplication between the constant 2 and the value obtained in Step 6.

9. The value obtained in Step 8 is divided by the product found in Step 7.

10. The result obtained in Step 9 is added to the value of $-B^3$ obtained in Step 1, and the final value is stored in location Y.

When parenthetical expressions contain terms enclosed in parentheses, the evaluation proceeds starting with the contents of the innermost set.

IX.1.2   Conversion in Mixed Arithmetic Expressions

Our detailed concern with the assignment of attributes to variables stands in stark contrast to the rather free-wheeling attitude with which we can combine the variables and constants to form expressions and assignment statements. The underlying support that allows us to construct and use expressions in this seemingly debonair manner consists of a rather elaborate network of conversion rules whose ultimate goal is to provide PL/I's evaluation mechanism with an expression whose terms are all of the same type. If it is an arithmetic expression, the compiler will perform all the conversions necessary to produce terms with the same base, scale and mode.

PL/I's mechanisms for providing consistency in expressions and assignment statements range all the way from very simple adjustments to elaborate conversions. The underlying intent is to free the programmer from concern with the form of the expression, so that he can concentrate on its contents. For example, when a programmer declares and initializes a variable with a statement

DECLARE A FIXED(5,2)**INITIAL**(4);

he may give no thought to the fact that the initial value he has specified does not agree with the precision attributes given in the other part of the declaration. The compiler automatically adjusts the form of the value so that although it was stipulated as 4, it is stored as 004.00, in accordance with the declaration. Similarly, the simple assignment statement

D = 3;

where D is an otherwise undeclared variable, is sufficient to activate a mechanism within the compiler that determines that there is no explicit declaration for D, assigns attributes in accordance with its name (**FLOAT DECIMAL**(6,0)), and converts the assigned value to a number having these attributes . Although it is the variable on the left side of the equals sign that determines the combination of attributes to which the expression value will ultimately be converted, there are several rules governing the evaluation of expressions prior to that point in the process when the final result is placed in the location stipulated on the left-hand side. The compiler still determines which conversions are needed for each pair of terms connected by an infix operator at that point in the evaluation process when the particular operation is to be performed. The basic rules governing these conversions are as follows:

1.   All arithmetic operations are done on numbers. Hence, if the particular operation being performed is B+C, and one or both of these variables was declared with the **PICTURE** or **CHARACTER** attribute, the compiler will make the necessary conver-

sion to numerical form before the addition is carried out. Thus, if B were declared with the attribute **PICTURE** '999V99' and it contained the digits 42761, PL/I will first change the contents in B to represent the value 427.61 before going on with the addition. Similarly, if C were declared with the **CHARACTER** attribute and had the value ' −23.5 ', this value would also be converted before the operation is performed. Because of the way PL/I must handle this conversion there is a good chance that the fractional portion, .5 in this case, would be lost in the conversion process.

2. If the two operands have different bases, the decimal operand will be converted to binary before the operation proceeds.

3. If the scales differ, the fixed point operand will be converted to floating-point. The only exception to this rule occurs when the operation is exponentiation (**) and the exponent is a fixed-point integer while the base is a floating-point number. In such a situation the exponent is left unchanged.

4. If the modes of the two operands differ, the real one is converted to complex mode (a real component having the original value of the operand, together with an imaginary component of zero). As in rule 3, when the second operand of an exponentiation is a fixed-point integer, it is not converted.

5. A set of additional rules is followed when performing exponentiation. In describing these rules, we shall make use of the general expression A**B.

   a. When A is not equal to 0 and B is 0, the result is always 1.
   b. When A is 0 and B exceeds 0, the result is always 0.
   c. When A is 0 and B is 0 or less, no operation is performed and PL/I indicates the existence of an error.
   d. A number less than 0 cannot be raised to anything but a fixed-point integer exponent. If these conditions are not met, PL/I will indicate an error.

6. When an array subscript is denoted by an expression, the final result of that expression is converted to fixed-point binary and truncated toward 0 to obtain the final integer value.

IX.1.3   Precision of Converted Results

The rules discussed above enable us to follow the progress of PL/I's automatic conversions of base, scale, and mode, but they do not say anything about the specific appearance or exact value of the results. Since there is no direct correspondence between a value with a particular combination of base and scale and its "equivalent" representation in some other base/scale combination, one cannot speak of a general rule that determines the "natural" precision resulting from a particular base/scale conversion. For example, it would be necessary to define a systematic relationship between the number of digits in a decimal integer and the number of binary digits required to represent the same magnitude. Such a correspondence would be extremely awkward and difficult to construct for fractions. Many values that can be represented in exact form as decimal fractions produce unending equivalents when converted to binary form. (For example, 0.2 is equivalent to 0.001100110...). Consequently, the desire to provide such conversions forces the implementation of a set of rules, which, though recognized as having certain shortcomings, will produce satisfactory results for the overwhelming majority of instances. Neither the origin of these rules nor a detailed examination of their behavior is appropriate here. Discussion will be limited to a presentation of their form, and references to additional material will be included at the end of the chapter. The subject of data conversion is discussed more fully in Appendix C.

To facilitate the examination of these precision rules, we shall use the following notation in describing the various types of numbers:

(w,d) is the precision of a fixed-point number

(p) is the precision of a floating-point number

The *ceiling* of a number, denoted by CEIL(n), is the smallest integer not less than that number. For example, CEIL(2.47) = 3.

MIN(exp1,exp2) is the smaller of the two numbers obtained by evaluating expressions exp1 and exp2.

ABS(n) is equivalent to |n|, the absolute value of n.

SIGN(n) is $+1$ if $n > 0$, -1 if $n < 0$, an 0 if $n = 0$. Later on we shall find that these names also represent specific built-in functions in PL/I.

IX.1.3.1   Precision Rules for Converting Binary Numbers

The rules for producing various types of numerical values whose original base in binary are summarized in Table 9.1. Note that these rules are followed consistently, as long as the precision of the result does not exceed maximum limits set by the implementation. Specifically, for the IBM 360/370, a number converted to fixed binary will not be longer than 31 digits, regardless of what the precision formula specifies; similarly, a number converted to floating-point binary cannot be longer than 53 digits (109 for the Optimizing and Checkout Compilers.) under any circumstances. For decimal values the maximum precisions are 15 and 16 for fixed and float, respectively (33 for the Optimizing and Checkout Compilers.).

It should be noted that the whole idea of floating-point decimal representation is strictly an item of convenience for the programmer and end user. There is no corresponding internal representation as far as the machine is concerned. When a variable is declared with the **FLOAT DECIMAL** attributes or is assigned those attributes by default, it eventually ends up in storage as a floating-point *binary* number and is used that way for all subsequent operations. (The same is true, of course, for constants written explicitly in exponential notation). It is only when the variable is to be displayed that a final conversion is made so that it will appear in the more convenient decimal representation.

Consequently, when we consider this fact together with the substantial possibilities that slight errors can be produced by the conversion process, we can begin to understand the

TABLE 9.1 Precision Rules for Conversion of Binary Numbers

Nature of Conversion	Precision of Result	Precision of Example Starting Value	Precision of Result
BINARY FIXED(w,d) to **BINARY FLOAT**(p)	$p = w$	(8,3)	(8)
BINARY FIXED(w,d) to **DECIMAL FLOAT**(p)	$p = \mathbf{CEIL}(w/3.32)$	(8,3) (9,2)	(3) (3)
BINARY FIXED(w,d)$_1$ to **DECIMAL FIXED**(w,d)$_2$, $d_1 > 0$	$w_2 = 1 + \mathbf{CEIL}(w_1/3.32)$ $d_2 = \mathbf{CEIL}(d_1/3.32)$	(8,3) (9,2)	(4,1) (4,1)
BINARY FIXED(w,d)$_1$ to **DECIMAL FIXED**(w,d)$_2$, $d_1 < 0$	$w_2 = 1 + \mathbf{CEIL}(w_1/3.32)$ $d_2 = \mathbf{CEIL(ABS}(d_1)/3.32)$ $\mathbf{*SIGN}(d_1)$	(8,-3)	(4,-1)
BINARY FLOAT(p)$_1$ to **DECIMAL FLOAT**(p)$_2$	$p_2 = \mathbf{CEIL}(p_1/3.32)$	(7) (9)	(3) (3)

reasons behind PL/I's apparent inability to reproduce perfectly simple numbers. (For example, see what happens as a result of the sequence A = .53; **PUT DATA(A);**).

IX.1.3.2 Precision Rules for Converting Decimal Numbers

When decimal numbers are converted to binary, the precision is handled as summarized in Table 9.2. Here again, the rules are followed consistently as long as maximum limits for precision are not exceeded. Thus, if the result is a fixed binary number, it will not have more than 31 digits, and a floating-point binary result will not be longer than 53 (or 109) digits.

When converting in this direction, the possibilities and types of errors appear more dramatic. Just to illustrate the possibilities, we shall examine a rather simple situation: suppose we have variables A and N defined by the statement

DECLARE A FIXED DECIMAL(10,5)**INITIAL**(31492.75),**N INITIAL**(732);

TABLE 9.2 Precision Rules for Conversion of Decimal Numbers

Nature of Conversion Process	Precision of Result	Precision of Example Starting Value	Precision of Result
DECIMAL FLOAT (p_1) to BINARY FLOAT (p_2)	$p_2 = \text{CEIL} (p_1 *3.32)$	(8) (15)	(27) (50)
DECIMAL FIXED (w,d) to BINARY FLOAT (p)	$p = \text{CEIL} (w*3.32)$	(8) (15)	(27) (50)
DECIMAL FIXED (w,d) to DECIMAL FLOAT (p)	$p = w$	(8)	(8)
DECIMAL FIXED $(w,d)_1$ to BINARY FIXED $(w,d)_2$ $d_1 > 0$	$w_2 = 1 + \text{CEIL} (w_1 *3.32)$ $d_2 = \text{CEIL} (d_1 *3.32)$	(8,5) (16,5) (10,5)	(28,7) (31,17) (31,17)
DECIMAL FIXED $(w,d)_1$ to BINARY FIXED (w,d) $d_1 < 0$	$w_2 = \text{MIN} (\text{CEIL} (w_1 *3.32) + 1, 31)$ $d_2 = \text{CEIL} (\text{ABS} (d_1) *3.32) * \text{SIGN} (d_1)$	(8,−5) (16,−12) (12,−8)	(28,−17) (31,−40) (31,−27)

and we used A in a subsequent expression, such as $A - N$, whose other terms forced its conversion to binary (in accordance with IX.1.2) prior to performing arithmetic on it. Since the number's initial value was specified with less precision than indicated in the declaration, PL/I dutifully provides the additional zeros, and the value ends up in storage as 31492.75000. Therefore, $w_1 = 10$ and $d_1 = 5$, and the precision rules force the compiler into a situation where obedience would produce a length (35) exceeding the maximum provided for fixed binary numbers. Accordingly, the binary conversion is stored as an intermediate value having w_2 of 31 (the maximum) and a d_2 of 17, in accordance with the stated rule. Consequently, there are 14 binary digits available for the integer portion of the converted number. However, when we convert 31492.75000, we obtain an integer portion (111101100000100) that requires 15 binary digits for its complete representation. Thus, the leftmost digit is dropped, and the converted result now becomes 15108.75. Under proper operating conditions, this precipitates a **SIZE** error, so that it is not necessary for the error to go undetected. However, it is better practice to arrange arithmetic computations so that such possibilities are anticipated and circumvented. (In this case, for example, the arithmetic expression could be preceded by a statement in which N is converted to decimal and stored in another variable, with that variable being used in place of N for the subtraction. Alternatively, we can force N to be converted to decimal without the need for an additional variable by means of the **DECIMAL** function.

IX.1.4   Precision Rules for Arithmetic Operations

When two operands in an expression are made compatible by conversion prior to the performance of some type of arithmetic operation, the implication is that steps have been taken such that the operands now share the same base, scale, and mode. Furthermore, when an individual operand was converted, it was done in accordance with the precision rules described in the preceeding section. However, this does not mean that the precisions of the two otherwise compatible operands are necessarily alike. Consequently, additional rules must be defined to govern the performance of arithmetic operations on values with differing precision. Such rules are necessarily more involved since their characteristics depend on the type of operation being performed. A detailed scrutiny of these rules is inappropriate here, but we cannot ignore them. Consequently, we shall acquaint ourselves with their behavior, and refer to sources of additional information.

IX.1.4.1 Addition and Subtraction

If we examine the two operands to be added or subtracted at a point in the process immediately after they have been converted in accordance with the rules described in the previous sections, then the precision of the resulting sum or difference is dictated by a rather simple rule:

The precision of a sum or difference represents the maximum precision of its contributing operands. Thus, if in the statement $Y = A + B + C$; A is **FIXED**(5,2) and B is **FIXED**(4,3), the temporary result $A + B$ will be stored as **FIXED**(7,3). That is, intermediate storage will be required for a number having a three-digit fractional portion (as is the case with B) and a four-digit integer portion (as is required for A with a possible carry).

A more detailed summary of these precision rules is given in Appendix C.

IX.1.4.2 Multiplication

The rules governing the precision of an intermediate product also can be stated rather simply if we restrict ourselves to those situations in which the two factors have similar attributes:

1. When both operands are fixed-point numbers having the same base, the resulting fixed-point product has an integer portion one digit longer than the sum of the operands' integer lengths; the length of the fractional portion is the sum of the two fractional lengths.

2. When both factors are floating-point numbers to the same (apparent) base, the precision of the product is merely the larger of the two precisions.

Appendix C summarizes the multiplication rules more thoroughly.

IX.1.4.3 Precision Rules for Division

When both divisor and dividend enter the operation with the same attributes, precision rules can be stated as follows:

1. If both operands are floating-point numbers to a common base, the precision of the quotient is the greater of the two precisions.

2. If both operands are fixed-point numbers, the precision of the result is tied to the maximum number of digits available for a given base (15 for decimal, 31 for binary). If

m represents that maximum number and $(w,d)_1$, $(w,d)_2$ and $(w,d)_r$ are the respective precisions of the dividend, divisor and result, then

$$w_r = m \quad \text{and} \quad d_r = m - ((w_1 - d_1) + d_2)$$

A more extensive summary is given in Appendix C.

The precision values used in following these rules are those specified (declared or implied) for the participating values. This becomes especially important when either or both operands are constants without associated names. In the absence of a declared or implied precision, PL/I obtains the precision directly from the appearance of the constant. Thus, 13.5 and 13.500 can have different effects on the precision of a result. For example if we say

DECLARE (A,B **INITIAL**(8,6)) **FIXED**(3,2);

the result obtained from the operation Á13.5 will have a precision of (15,13), whereas the operation B/13.500 will produce a result with precision (15,11).

IX.1.4.4   Precision of Exponentiation

The most common situation, in which a floating-point decimal value is raised to a power represented by a fixed-point decimal exponent, produces a result with the same precision as the base or first operand. (Appendix C contains more details.)

IX.1.4.5   Precision of Final Results

After an entire expression is evaluated, an additional, final conversion may be required to make the attributes of the result conform with those declared for its destination. Most of the rules governing this process are the same as those described before. There is, however, one area that requires special consideration. When the variable designated to receive the final result is declared as **FIXED**, it is the programmer's responsibility to make sure that the variable has been given sufficient precision to accommodate the entire value of the result. If an insufficient number of digits have been assigned, PL/I will truncate on both sides of the decimal point, and a **SIZE** error will occur if a nonzero digit is dropped on the left. Thus, if the expression on the right-hand side of the statement

Y = 3*X**2 – 12.2/X** –4;

produces a result of 15690.474 and Y has been declared with a precision of (6,2), the resulting contents of Y will be 5690.47. (We shall have further dealings with the **SIZE** error condition later on.)

IX.2   BUILT-IN FUNCTIONS FOR ARITHMETIC OPERATIONS

In earlier chapters we have had occasion to perform certain operations (such as rounding a value or summing an array) in which our view of the particular operation is considerably simpler than its actual implementation inside the processor. This disparity is bridged by handling the internal sequence of events as a distinct procedure (a *built-in function*) that is part of a predefined library. Each such procedure has a permanently assigned name so that it can be referenced by the programmer at any point in his sequence of statements and used as if it were a single operation.

As part of this reference, the programmer includes the names or values of a prescribed number of items that identify the data on which the indicated operation is to be performed and provides the compiler with additional information that regulates the use of the function. The number and type of such items (called *arguments*) supplied with a reference to a given function, depend on which function is being used and how the programmer wishes to use it.

A function is referenced by using its name in an expression having the general form

function name(arg1, arg2, etc.)

where "function name" is a unique identifier recognized by PL/I and (arg1, arg2, etc.) comprises the list of arguments on which the function will operate. Depending on the particular function, these arguments may be constants, variables, or expressions. Expressions containing function references can be used in assignment statements as they are, or they may serve as terms in larger expressions. Thus, it is quite consistent for an expression involving a built-in function to serve as an argument for another function reference.

The library of mathematical and computational functions provided as an intrinsic part of PL/I serves as further illustration of the language's concern with versatility and automatic adjustment. In addition to performing the actual computational operations implied by their names, these built-in functions are supported by auxiliary procedures that allow the user to neglect such considerations as consistency of base, scale, mode, and precision. All necessary conversions are made automatically, in accordance with the general rules described in the previous section for the basic operators.

IX.2.1   Functions for Use with Single-Valued Variables

The built-in functions described below operate on single-valued numeric arguments and produce single-valued numerical results.

IX.2.1.1   The **ABS** Function

This function operates on a single argument, which can be any legitimate arithmetic expression. If the argument is real, the result is the positive value of that argument, with the base, scale, and precision unchanged. Thus, negative values are, in effect, multiplied by -1 and positive ones remain numerically unchanged. For example, the statement

Y = **ABS**(X**2 − 14.5*X/3);

will cause the expression to be evaluated, changed to a positive value (if not already so), converted to match the attributes assigned to Y, and stored in that location. If the argument is complex, the result consists of the positive magnitude of the argument.

IX.2.1.2   The **SIGN** Function

This function takes a single argument (any numeric variable or legitimate arithmetic expression) and evaluates it. If the result is greater than 0, PL/I generates a binary number with default precision (usually (15,0)), having a value of 1. If the value of the argument is 0, the binary value of 0 is generated; if it is less than 0, a value of −1 is generated. Thus, if X has value of 2, the contents of N in the statement

N = **SIGN**(X**2 − 5);

will be −1**B**. The argument cannot be complex.

IX.2.1.3   The **PRECISION** Function

If it is desired to change the precision of an argument (a variable or the result of an expression) without changing its base, scale, or mode, an expression of the general form

PRECISION(arg1,w,d)

can be written. Arg1 can be any numeric variable or legitimate arithmetic expression. If arg1's scale is **FIXED**, the result will have precision (w,d). When these two arguments are included, they must be decimal integer constants. When they are omitted, PL/I assigns default precision. If arg1 is a floating-point quantity, d may not be specified.

IX.2.1.4   Base-Changing Functions

Binary arguments may be changed to decimal by means of the **DECIMAL** function as follows:

DECIMAL(arg1,w,d)

where arg1, w, and d have their previous meanings. As is the case in the **PRECISION** function, w and d may be omitted if default precision is desired; if arg1 is a floating-point quantity, d must be omitted.

The **BINARY** function goes in the other direction, converting decimal values to binary base, leaving the scale and mode unchanged. The form for the expression is

BINARY(arg1,w,d)

with the rules being the same as for the **DECIMAL** function.

IX.2.1.5 Scale-Changing Functions

The **FIXED** and **FLOAT** functions will perform scale changes without affecting the base and mode of the argument involved. The general form of the expressions involving these functions are:

FIXED(arg1,w,d)

and

FLOAT(arg1,w)

where arg1, w, and d have their previous meanings. The rules governing the inclusion or omission of w and d are the same as for the base-changing functions.

IX.2.1.6 Functions for Manipulating Complex Numbers

Several functions are available for converting from real to complex mode, and vice versa, and handling other operations involving complex numbers.

The **COMPLEX** function takes two arguments and is used in an expression of the general form

COMPLEX(arg1, arg2)

where arg1 and arg2 are variables or expressions representing real numerical values. The result of this operation is a complex number having arg1 and arg2 as its real and imaginary components, respectively. Since both components must have the same base, scale, and precision, appropriate conversions are made where necessary. The rules followed for such conversions are the same as described for evaluation of expressions in Section IX.1: mixed bases result in conversion to binary; mixed scales result in conversion to **FLOAT**; and different precisions produce a result having the greater precision of the two components.

The **REAL** function converts in the other direction and therefore requires a single argument that represents a complex quantity. The general form for an expression involving this function is

REAL(arg1)

and the result of the operation is a real number whose value is obtained from the real component of the argument. Base, scale, and precision are unchanged.

The **IMAG** function is similar to the **REAL** function, except that the resulting value is obtained from the imaginary portion of the single complex argument. If C is a complex quantity having the value $3 + 4I$, the statement

Y = **IMAG**(C);

will place a value of 4 in location Y.

These three functions also may be used on the left-hand side of the equals sign as pseudovariables. For instance, if RE and IM are real variables and COM is complex,

   COMPLEX(RE,IM) = COM;

has the same effect as

   RE = **REAL**(COM); IM = **IMAG**(COM);

Similarly,

   REAL(COM) = RE; **IMAG**(COM) = IM;

produce the same result as the single statement

   COM = RE + IM * 1**I**;

The **CONJG** function operates on a single complex argument, producing its conjugate value. Thus, if C1 is 2 − 7**I**, the statement

   C2 = **CONJG**(C1);

will place a value of 2 + 7**I** in location C2 (assuming, of course, the C2 has been appropriately declared).

IX.2.1.7   Basic Arithmetic Functions

A number of functions are provided to perform elementary arithmetic operations. Although at first glance these may seem redundant with respect to the operations signified by +, *, and /, they are designed to provide the programmer with additional controls if he finds them necessary.

The **ADD** function is used as an expression of the form

   ADD(arg1, arg2, w,d)

where arg1 and arg2 are numerical variables or legitimate arithmetic expressions, and w and d are decimal integer constants. As a result of this operation, arg1 and arg2 are added together. The result, if **FIXED**, is expressed with precision (w,d); if the result is **FLOAT**, d may not be specified as one of the arguments. If the base and/or scale of arg1 and arg2 are different, conversion will take place according to the rules stated previously. For example, if we wrote

   DECLARE(X,Y)**FIXED**(3,1),Z **FIXED**(4,1);

   Z = **ADD**(X,Y,5,2);

and X and Y's values were 67.8 and 49.3, respectively, the **ADD** function would generate the value 117.10, change the precision to match Z's, and place the result (117.1) in Z.

The **MULTIPLY** function works in a similar fashion to produce a product whose precision is determined by the third and fourth arguments in the expression (for **FIXED** results), or by the third argument alone if the result is in floating-point scale. Thus, if X and Y were declared as fixed-point decimal variables with precisions of (3,1) and (4,2), respectively, and if X = 124 and Y = 26.33, the expression

  MULTIPLY(X,Y,5,2)

would produce a value of 326.49, whereas the expression X*Y would produce 00326.492. This result would then be converted (if necessary) to match the attributes of the destination variable.

The **DIVIDE** function also uses three or four arguments, depending on the scale of the result, producing a value equivalent to the quotient of the first two arguments. If A is 7 and B is 3 and we wrote

  Y = **DIVIDE**(A,B,6,5);

the function would generate a value of 2.33333. Assuming Y to be declared as **FLOAT**(6), the quotient would be appropriately converted, and the value 2.333333E+00 would be placed in Y.

IX.2.1.8   The Modulus Function

One of the most powerful functions provided by PL/I is used in an expression of the general form

  MOD(arg1, arg2) $\dfrac{ARG1}{ARG2}$

The operation instigated by the **MOD** function proceeds as follows: the value obtained from arg1 is divided by arg2 to obtain an integer quotient. The remainder becomes the value of the function. This remainder, r, always satisfies the condition $0 \le r < $ **ABS**(arg2). Suppose X has a current value of 13 and we write the statement

  Y = **MOD**(X,5);

PL/I will divide the contents of X by 5, obtaining an integer quotient (2) and a remainder (3). It is this value of 3 that is placed in location Y. This function can be applied to values that are not integers. For instance,

  Y = **MOD**(13.7,2.3);

produces the value 2.2 = 13.7 − 5 * 2.3 since the integer quotient of 13.7/2.3 is 5.

Illustration 23

The convenience of the **MOD** function can be shown by writing a procedure to read a series of 30 fixed decimal numbers and produce two results: the sum of all the absolute input values divisible by 17 and the sum of the absolute values of the remaining numbers. Input values are punched 15 to a card in the form ±XXX.X in columns 1-5, 6-10, ..., 71-75. For each series of values processed, the program is to print the input values, ten to a line, followed by a line containing the two sums. Successive sets of output are to be separated by two blank lines.

For convenience we shall set up an array A for the 30 values and SUM17 and NO17 for the two sums. The coding follows:

```
ILL23: PROCEDURE OPTIONS (MAIN);
/**********************************************************/
/* THIS PROGRAM READS ARRAYS OF 30 NUMBERS AND, FOR      */
/* EACH ARRAY, COMPUTES THE SUM OF ALL ELEMENTS THAT     */
/* ARE EVENLY DIVISIBLE BY 17 (SUM17) AND THE SUM OF     */
/* THOSE THAT ARE NOT (NO17).                            */
/**********************************************************/
        DECLARE A(30) FIXED (4,1),
                (SUM17,NO17) FIXED (6,1),
                (NDFILE INITIAL(0),I) FIXED BINARY;

        ON ENDFILE(SYSIN) NDFILE=1;
        PUT PAGE;   GET EDIT (A) (2 (COLUMN(1), 15 F(5,1)));

        DO WHILE (NDFILE=0);
          SUM17,NO17 = 0;
          DO I=1 TO 30;
            IF MOD (A(I),17)=0
              THEN SUM17=SUM17+ABS(A(I));
              ELSE NO17=NO17+ABS(A(I));
          END;
          PUT SKIP(2) EDIT (A)( 3 (SKIP,X(10), 10 (F(6,1),X(5)));
          PUT EDIT ('SUM OF ABS 17 DIVISIBLES = ',SUM17,
                    'SUM OF ABS NON-17 DIVISIBLES = ',NO17)
                   (SKIP,X(10),A,F(8,1),X(5),A,F(8,1));
          GET EDIT (A)(2 (COLUMN(1), 15 F(5,1)));
        END;

        STOP;
        END ILL23;
```

IX.2.1.9 Numerical Adjustment Functions

Four functions are available for roundoff or truncation:

The FLOOR function operates on a single argument, producing the largest integer that does not exceed the argument's value. If X has a value of 12.7 and we write

$Y = FLOOR(X);$

the value of 12 would be stored in Y. On the other hand, if $X = -12.7$, the value -13 would be stored in Y. A complex argument may not be used with this function.

The **CEIL** function operates in contrast to the **FLOOR** function in that it examines a single argument to produce the smallest integer not exceeded by that argument. If X has a value of 4, the statement

$Y = CEIL(3*X/5+2*X);$

will store a value of 11 in Y. An example of a negative argument would be

$Y = CEIL(-6,3);$

which would store -6 in Y. As with the **FLOOR** function, a complex argument may not be used.

The **TRUNC** function includes aspects of the previous two, operating on a single argument arg1 as follows: if arg1 is less than zero, the function produces a value equivalent to **CEIL** (arg1); for all other values, the result is equivalent to **FLOOR**(arg1). Thus, for a value of 23.7, **TRUNC** will return 23, [**FLOOR**(23.7)] while for an arg1 value of −23.7, it will return **CEIL**(−23.7) or −23.

As we know from earlier work, roundoff is provided by the **ROUND** function. For purposes of continuity, we shall recall that two arguments are given with the function in an expression of the form

ROUND(arg1,w)

where w is a decimal integer constant indicating the digit on which the roundoff is to occur, counted from the decimal point. For this to be effective, arg1 must be in fixed-point scale. Since the decimal point in floating-point scale "floats," it does not serve as a very good landmark for rounding. As a consequence, PL/I's action when a floating-point value is rounded is to increase the last internal binary digit to 1. This has no effect unless the last bit was a zero to begin with. Thus, the **ROUND** function is not of much use on floating-point data.

IX.2.1.10   Selection Functions

The highest or lowest value can be selected from a list of arguments and made available to the programmer as follows:

The **MAX** function will find the largest value in a list of arguments (no limit on the length of the list). If A is 12, B is 12.4, and C is −3, the statement

Y = A**2+**MAX**(A,B,C);

will place a value of 156.4 in location Y. The compiler will make the necessary conversions if the bases, scales, and precisions of the arguments differ, but complex arguments may not be given.

The **MIN** function works similarly, yielding the lowest value in a list. Note that these functions return the highest and lowest values, respectively, but they do not provide any information as to which variable it is that contains this value.

IX.2.1.11   Common Algebraic Functions

Each of the following functions operates on a single numerical argument (a constant, variable, or expression) by evaluating the argument, converting it to floating-point scale, and performing the calculations implied by the function.

The **SQRT** function evaluates its argument and makes available the positive square root of the argument. Should the value of the argument turn out to be less than zero, an error condition will result. It is a good idea for the programmer to include a test for a negative value immediately preceding those places where he is obtaining a square root, so that he can preempt the error condition and provide his own action in such contingencies.

The **EXP** function, used in an expression of form

EXP(arg1)

produces a value of e_{arg1}.

The **LOG** function produces the natural logarithm of the single argument.

The **LOG**10 function gives the value of the argument's logarithm to the base 10. Similarly, the expression

LOG2(arg1)

produces the logarithm of arg1 to the base 2. All of the logarithm functions (c, d, and e above) will produce an error condition if the value of the argument turns out ot be zero or less. As in the case of the square-root function, the programmer would be well advised to test his variables and provide his own actions to avert the interruption.

All of these functions except **LOG**2 and **LOG**10 may also be used with complex arguments. The students should note that it is usually preferable to write **SORT**(A) rather than A**.5. The first form is not only more accurate but also faster. This is one of only five known counter examples to Murphy's Law. (Foozleman, G.B., Kapuchnikoff, H.Y. and Toot, B., "There are Counter Examples to Murphy's Law," Journal of *Gaelic Legal Mathematics*, vol. 22, no. 6, pp. 259-262 (1933).)

IX.2.1.12   Trigonometric Functions

PL/I calculates and returns to the programmer a wide variety of trigonometric functions. As with the other built-in calculation procedures, the compiler is very flexible with respect to the attributes of the arguments submitted.

SIN(arg1) will return the sine of the angle represented by the numerical value of arg1. PL/I assumes that this value is in radians.

When the name **SIND** is specified instead, the value of arg1 is assumed to be an angle expressed in degrees.

The function **COS** works exactly the same way, delivering the cosine of arg1, the latter being treated as an angle in radians.

COSD does the same thing, treating the argument as an angle expressed in degrees.

TAN(arg1) gives the tangent of arg1, treating the latter as an angle in radians.

TAND(arg1) returns the tangent of arg1 by assuming that the latter is an angle expressed in degrees.

Trigonometric functions can be applied either to real or complex numbers. Using these basic facilities as building blocks, other trigonometric functions of either real or complex arguments may be obtained by means of identities found in any text on the subject.

IX.2.1.13 Hyperbolic Functions

The following hyperbolic functions are available:

SINH(arg1) returns the hyperbolic sine.

COSH(arg1) returns the hyperbolic cosine.

TANH(arg1) returns the hyperbolic tangent of the argument.

The hyperbolic funtions are also applicable to both real and complex arguments.

IX.2.1.14 Inverse Functions

Frequently the tangent of an angle is known or can easily be computed, and it is desired to find the angle itself. For such purposes, PL/I includes the **ATAN** function. Accordingly, the expression **ATAN**(arg1) will return an angle in radians whose tangent is equal to arg1. When the argument is a complex value, the function is still valid, although the result no longer represents an angle in the usual sense.

An error condition will result if the argument happens to be $0 + i$. The **ATAN** function also will accept two real arguments; this is to take care of situations where there would be a danger of dividing by zero. When this does occur, the results are as follows:

arg1	arg2	Value of **ATAN**(arg1,arg2)
anything	>0	$\tan^{-1}(\text{arg1}/\text{arg2})$
>0	0	$\pi/2$
<0	0	$-\pi/2$
≥ 0	<0	$\pi + \tan^{-1}(\text{arg1}/\text{arg2})$
<0	<0	$-\pi + \tan^{-1}(\text{arg1}/\text{arg2})$
0	0	error

The **ATAND** function operates as **ATAN** except that it returns a value in degrees. The two-argument form may be used for this function with the following results:

ATAND(arg1,arg2) = $(180/\pi)$***ATAN**(arg1,arg2);

ATAND will not accept complex arguments.

The Optimizing and Checkout Compilers also include inverse sine and cosine functions, their respective names being **ASIN** and **ACOS**.

The **ATANH** function will return a value whose hyperbolic tangent is equal to the argument. An error condition will result if **ABS**(arg1) ≥ 1. Here also the argument may be complex.

IX.2.1.15 Error Functions

This complicated but very useful function is accessed by the name **ERF** and requires a single argument. The result returned by the function is as follows:

$$\text{ERF(argl)} = \frac{2}{\sqrt{\pi}} \int_0^{\text{argl}} e^{-t^2} dt$$

A value representing $1 - $ **ERF**(argl) is obtained by using the function **ERFC**(argl). Complex numbers may not be given as arguments for either function.

IX.2.2   Built-in Functions for Data Aggregates

The functions described in the preceding section will accept arrays as arguments wherever those arguments need not be decimal integer constants. For example, if we said

DECLARE(X(12), Y(12))**FIXED**(5,2); **GET LIST**(X); Y = 5.5***SQRT**(X);

PL/I will read in the 12 values for X, compute the square root for each element, multiply it by 5.5 and store the result in the corresponding element of Y. Similarly, the statements

DECLARE A(20)**FIXED**(4),B(20)**FIXED**(7,3);

GET LIST(A);

B = **SQRT**(**LOG**(A)/(**COS**(2*A)));

will cause the program to read in the 20 values of array A and perform the indicated operations on each one in succession, placing the result in the corresponding element of B. As implied by the above statement, built-in functions may be combined to any desired extent. The use of such functions with data aggregates is limited to arrays. They may not be used in this way with structures or arrays of structures.

IX.2.2.1   The Summation Function

In addition to the capabilities described above, PL/I provides several built-in functions that are specifically intended for use with arrays. One such function is used to form an expression having the general form

SUM(argl)

where argl is the name of an array or any legitimate array expression. Each element of argl is converted to floating-point and added to the contents of a temporary location in storage. Thus, if X is an array consisting of ten elements and we wrote

Y = **SUM**(2*X**3) + 14;

each of the ten elements in array X will be converted to floating-point (if not already expressed that way), cubed, that value will be doubled, and the result added to a temporary location containing a running total. When all of the elements have been added in this fashion, 14 is added to that total and the result is stored in location Y. [Note that this is different from **SUM**(2*X**3 + 14.)]

IX.2.2.2   The Product Function

The function referred to by the name **PROD** works exactly as the **SUM** function except that instead of adding each element of a temporary location, PL/I multiplies the contents of that temporary location by each element. Thus, if array X consists of five elements, **PROD**(X) will generate the value X(1)*X(2)*X(3)*X(4)*X(5).

IX.2.2.3   The Polynomial Function

This particular set of operations finds frequent use in numerical analysis and related mathematical work. The function is used in an expression of the general form

POLY(arg1,arg2)

where each of the arguments can be a single value or a vector (a one-dimensional array, a single row or column from a two-dimensional array, and so on). If V1 is the first vector with subscript numbers going from L1 to H1, and V2 is the second vector with subscript going from L2 to H2, then

$$\text{POLY}(V1,V2) = V1(L1) + \sum_{i=1}^{H1-L1} \left[V1(L1+i) * \prod_{j=0}^{i-1} V2(L2+j) \right]$$

If $(H2-L2) < (H1-L1-1)$ then the second vector would run out of elements before the complete summation is fulfilled. In that case, the last element V2(H2) is used over and over. For example, if X is a six-element vector going from X(1) to X(6) such that

$$X_1 = 1, X_2 = 2, X_3 = 3, X_4 = 4, X_5 = 5, \text{ and } X_6 = 6$$

and Y is a three-element vector such that

$$Y_1 = 7, Y_2 = 8, \text{ and } Y_3 = 9$$

then L1 = 1, H1 = 6, L2 = 1, H2 = 3, and

POLY(X,Y) = 1 + 2*7+ 3*7*8+ 4*7*8*9 + 5*7*8*9*9 + 6*7*8*9*9*9 = 269823.

If the first array consists of a single value (H1=L1), the processing degenerates and the final result returned by the function is equal to V1(L1).

The function gets its name from the fact that if the first argument (V1) is a vector and the second argument (V2) is a single value (a scalar), the computed value will represent the sum of the terms in the polynomial

$$V1(L1) + V1(L1+1)*V2 + V1(L1+2)*V2**2 + V1(L1+3)*V2**3$$

and so on.

It should be pointed out that the **MAX** and **MIN** functions will not operate with arrays. That is, if X is an array and Y is a single-valued variable, we cannot say Y = **MAX**(X); with the expectation that Y will contain a value representing the largest element in X. Instead, this must be done by programming.

Several additional functions are available for obtaining descriptive information about arrays; however, their utility will not be apparent until we have explored some additional storage allocation concepts. These will be introduced in a subsequent chapter.

IX.3   SOME COMPUTATIONAL DIFFICULTIES

In examining the rules for conversion and precision we have seen that there are occasions where seemingly reasonable computations can produce "unreasonable" results. A great many of these are due to PL/I's approach, which seeks to provide a set of operating rules that the user can ignore for most circumstances. Yet, along with this objective, there is an often conflicting effort to implement a fairly uncomplicated set of rules that will not add excessively to the compiler's overhead. Thus, for example, the rules for selecting the precision of converted results or of quotients could be improved at the expense of greater complexity.

Consequently, we shall look at the more commonly occurring instances of these shortcomings and use the language's versatility to get around them.

Perhaps the most annoying difficulty deals with fixed-point division and the rules governing the precision of the results.

To illustrate, let us use the very simple formula for converting degrees Centigrade to degrees Fahrenheit:

$$F = \frac{9}{5}C + 32$$

Suppose C is given to the nearest degree and has been declared as **FIXED**(2). Then, it might seem reasonable to construct a statement that reflects the familiar appearance of the formula; that is,

    F = (9/5)*C + 32;

Now we shall determine what happens for a C value of 30:

1.   The division 9/5 is performed. Because of their appearances, both values have precisions of (1,0), giving a resulting precision of (15,15−1) or (15,14).

2. The newly developed quotient, 1⸱80000000000000, is multiplied by C's value. Since the two precisions are (15,14) and (2,0), the rules compel PL/I to use a precision of (18,14) for the product. The maximum number of digits for expressing a fixed-point number is 15, so we end up with 4⸱00000000000000 instead of 5⸱400000000000000, and a **FIXEDOVERFLOW** condition. (Note that this differs from the **SIZE** condition in that it is precipitated by the production of an oversized result in an arithmetic operation; **SIZE** occurs when there is an attempt to assign a value to a variable too small to hold it or when a converted result is too large for the target.)

Rearrangement of the operations will help in this situation. If we use the form

C*9/5 + 32

the multiplication will precede the division, giving a product with precision (4,0) (that is, $2+1+1,0+0$). Then, when that product is divided by 5, the quotient's precision is $(15,15-4)$ or (15,11). Now, when PL/I attempts the final edition, the precision of the sum would be $(1+4+11,11)$ or (16,11), which becomes (15,11) because 15 is the maximum available. Since the final value, 86, will fit within this precision, no error occurs. However, there would still be trouble if the value to be added were large. The problem lies in the excessive number of fractional digits that PL/I sets up for a division. One way out would be to set up a temporary variable (say, R) whose declared precision is adequate for the situation. Thus, with a precision like (3,1) we could say

R = 9/5; F = R*C+32;

An alternative (and perhaps more appealing) approach would be to wrest control from PL/I and define the required precision ourselves:

F = **DIVIDE**(9,5,3,1)*C + 32;

Of course, in this example, there is an even more obvious solution, namely

F = 1,8 * C + 32;

Since the values involved in this division are both constants, the division should be done away with entirely. In general, however, the quantities will be variables, so one of the methods described above will have to be used to solve this problem.

It is good practice for the programmer to exercise this type of control over the division process so that these idiosyncracies of the precision rules are avoided. The additional alternative of forcing the use of floating-point form is not necessary here: we can obtain the precision we require without it; furthermore, since all the terms in the expression are fixed-point values, the time required for conversion to floating point would slow things down without any benefits unless other extensive computations involved the same variable.

Another situation requiring similar attention is one in which decimal-to-binary conversion involves numbers with fractional components. Since there are certain fractions that can be represented exactly in decimal whose binary equivalents have infinite length, it is possible to convert a decimal number to binary, reconvert to decimal, and end up with a different value. Consequently, when there is a situation calling for an expression containing both decimal and binary values, the programmer must anticipate the possibility of lost digits due to conversion and avert it by controlling the process. A simple example will clarify this: suppose we have the statement

Y = 2*A*N + 3.8*I;

where Y and A are decimal variables and N and I are binary. The presence of N and I will force conversion of 2*A and 3.8 to binary, even though the final result will be in decimal, thereby requiring a reconversion, with possible losses in precision. To avoid that, we can force the arithmetic to be performed in decimal by saying

Y = 2*A*DECIMAL(N,w_1,d_1)+3.8*DECIMAL(I,w_2,d_2);

where the w's and d's are selected to suit the situation. This way, the decimal fractions will be preserved.

PROBLEMS

1. The following values are given:

$$X = 6 \quad A = 4 \quad B = 3 \quad C = 12 \quad D = 2$$

Y is declared as **FIXED**(6,2). Evaluate each of the following expressions and indicate the final value placed in Y:

a. Y = $-A**3+B**-2-A*-B/4*A*C-3*C$;

b. Y = $A**-3+(B**(-2-A)*-B)/(4*A*C-3*C)$;

c. Y = $A*B/2*A-2*A*B/3*(ÁC)$;

d. Y = $A*B/(2*A-2*A*B)/3*(ÁC)$;

e. Y = $C*X/A*B**2*C$;

f. Y = $C*X/A*B**(2*C)$;

g. Y = $C*X/ÁB/C*X$;

2. Write a program that reads in two integers N1 and N2. Starting with the smaller of these, the

program is to print a line of output showing that number, its square and its square root, the latter being shown to the nearest thousandth. A similar line of output is to be produced for each successive integer up to and including the larger of the two input values. After the limiting value is reached, the program is to skip a line and print a value indicating the number of lines in the table just printed.

The program is to print this output on a separate page for each set of input values processed. If either or both of the input values are negative, the program is to skip that set and print an appropriate message. Another, equally appropriate message is to be printed if the two input values are equal, regardless of their sign.

3. Input data consisting of three-digit decimal integers are punched on cards in columns 1-3, 5-7, 9-11, and so on. Write a program that reads these values and prints them ten to a line. After all the values have been read and printed, the program is to print the following information: the total number of values processed, number of values that are evenly divisible by 3, and the number of even values.

4. Using the same type of input as described in the previous problem, write a program that counts the number of values in which the middle digit is numerically equivalent to the sum of the outer two. For example, the numbers 264 and 880 are such values; 212 and 074 are not. All of the input values are to be printed 10 to a line as in the previous problem. However, if a value meets the criterion for inclusion in the count, its appearance in the printout is to be underscored.

5. Write a program that reads in a set of list-directed numbers and determines which of these numbers have square roots which, when truncated to the nearest integer, are prime numbers (evenly divisible only by one or by themselves). When such a number is found, print the number and its square root before and after truncation.

6. Using the same type of input described in the previous problems, write a program that treats each group of 20 values separately and defines a range for that group so that it is bounded by those multiples of ten that are closest to the group extremes. For each group, print all of the values on two lines followed by a third line showing the range. Skip a line between groups.

7. A popularly held (though unproven) claim is that every positive even number can be expressed as a sum of two prime numbers. (For instance, 28 = 23 + 5). Write a program that reads in successive integers punched one to a card, right-justified in columns 1-4. For each integer read, the program is to print a line consisting of the input value followed by two prime numbers whose sum equals that value. If a particular input value is not a positive even number, the program is to print a line showing that value followed by the message "THIS VALUE IS INELIGIBLE". After the last value has been processed, the program is to skip two lines and print the total number of input values, the number of eligible values and the number of ineligible values.

8. A highway authority has to define the path of a road through an expanse of mountainous terrain. Each mountain presents a problem as to whether to tunnel through or go around it. Figure 9.1 summarizes the problem for a portion of the distance. In this figure, A and B define the points under

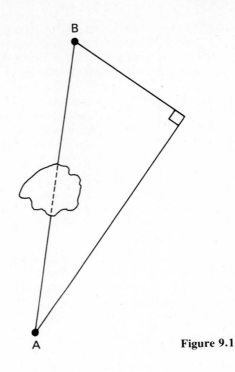

Figure 9.1

consideration. If the direct route is used, a tunnel must be built at a cost C. If the mountain is to be circumvented, the road must detour from point A at an angle ALPHA and then make a right angle and continue to point B. In any event, there is a construction cost RATE associated with each mile of roadway (exclusive of tunnel costs) that may change for each section. Data for this project are punched so that each card contains the following information for a given section:

Card Columns	Identification	Format
1-3	Section number	XXX
4	Number of mountains in section	X(1 or 0)
5-10	Tunneling cost, dollars	XXXXXX(.)
11-14	Number of miles from point A to B	XX(.)XX
15-20	Construction cost, dollars per mile	XXXXXX(.)
21-22	Value of angle ALPHA, degrees	XX(.)
23-24	Value of fractional portion of ALPHA, minutes	XX(.)

Write a program that decides whether to tunnel or detour for each section read in. The printout should contain the following information: section number and total distance for each section, for direct as well as detour route; cost for each section using the alternative approaches; minimum cost for total road project and corresponding highway length; and total cost with no detours and corresponding highway length.

9. A metallurgical firm places the following test data on cards:

Card Columns	Identification	Format
1-4	Alloy number	XXXX
7-8	Length of sample, feet	X(.)X
9-10	Width of sample, feet	X(.)X
15-20	Applied load, pounds	XXXXX(.)X

The applied load represents that load sufficient to buckle the sample. A number of such samples are prepared for each alloy, and 20 alloys are compared in a given run. Write a program that prints the average buckling stesss (expressed in pounds per square inch) for each alloy and prints the following at the bottom of the output page:

ALLOY NO. xxxx EXHIBITS THE HIGHEST AVERAGE
BUCKLING STRESS OF xxxxx.x PSI

10. A computing facility punches a card for each job it processes. The information shown on that card is as follows:

Card Columns	Identification	Format
1-4	Job number	XXXX(.)
5-6	Time in hours	XX(.)
7-8	Fractional hour, minutes	XX(.)
9-11	Fractional minute, seconds	XX(.)X
12-13	Time out, hours	XX(.)
14-15	Time out, minutes	XX(.)
16-18	Time out, seconds	XX(.)X
19	Cost rate	Character*
20	Job type	Character‡
21-40	Customer's name	Character
41-60	Customer's city	Character
61-62	Month	XX
63-64	Year (last two digits)	XX

*Cost rate is punched as F (free), I ($300/hr), or E($600/hr).
‡Job type is punched as B (business, S (scientific), P (political), or D (debugging).

Write a program that prints a line for each job showing the job number, elapsed time (in hours, minutes, and seconds), job type, customer's name, and cost for the job. After the final job, the program is to skip two lines and print the total number of jobs processed, average duration per job, total cost and average cost per job.

11. Using the data in Problem 10, write a program that will print the following information for each customer on a separate page:

                              Customer's Name
                              Customer's City
                    USAGE REPORT FOR month year

JOB TYPE	NO. OF JOBS	AVERAGE JOB LGTH.	TOTAL TIME	AVERAGE COSTS	TOTAL COST
C					
S					
P					
D					

TOTAL NO. OF JOBS   =
OVERALL AVG. JOB LENGTH   =
TOTAL TIME   =
TOTAL COSTS   =

Assume that all cards for a given customer are together but in no order.

12. Write a program that will produce the printout in Problem 11 for each city. (Expect no more than 20 cities.) Assume the same card arrangement as for Problem 11.

13. Archaeologists working with a number of ancient sites have determined that these sites, though all from the third Paleolithic period and all generally related to the Mousterian prototype, actually divide into four somewhat distinct categories. This contention was developed after intensive examination of artifacts found at the various sites and the associated criteria that define the site types are based on the appearance of the artifacts:

Mousterian site of Acheulian Tradition (standard)
No. of hand axes/total no. of tools: >20%
No. of denticulates/total no. of tools: >10%
No. of scrapers/total no. of tools: >20%
Backed Knives: present
Projectile points: present
Borers   present
Gravers   present
Typical Mousterian Site
No. of hand axes/total no. of tools: >5%
Keena Mousterian Site
Scalar retouch on scrapers/total scrapers   >50%
No hand axes
No backed knives
No. of side scrapers/total no. of tools: >25%
Denticulate Mousterian Site
No. of hand axes/total no. of tools: <20%
No. of scrapers/total no. of tools: <10%
No. of denticulates/total no. of tools: >50%

The findings at each site are reported on a separate punched card using the following format:

Cols.	Item	Format
1-3	Site identification	characters
4-6	No. of hand axes	XXX
7-9	No. of Levalloisian side scrapers	XXX
10-12	No. of Levalloisian end scrapers	XXX
13-15	No. of non-Levalloisian side scrapers	XXX
16-18	No. of non-Levalloisian end scrapers	XXX
19-21	No. of scrapers with scalar retouch	XXX
22-24	No. of backed knives	XXX
25-27	No. of projectile points	XXX
28-30	No. of denticulates	XXX
31-33	No. of borers	XXX
34-36	No. of gravers	XXX

(Note that "scrapers with scalar retouch" describes an attribute of some of the scrapers and, therefore, is not a separate type of tool.)

Any site that does not fulfill any of these criteria suffers the fate of being labeled an "atypical site."

a.   Identify the site category for each submitted site card by calculating the percentage of tool types and comparing it to the category standards.

b.   Determine whether each site is of Levalloisian facies by establishing whether the percentage of scrapers produced by this technique exceeds 20 percent.

c.   When a site is found to be "atypical", print the percentages for each tool type at that site.

d.   Print a summary showing the percentage of sites in each category, and the percentage of sites of Levalloisian facies.

Use the following data cards for your run:

```
W34032000000029017005003011019010023
B 1709304102700000001702301200073072
M09000038025009000046000008015003020
J 25007002001003000000001002005003004
D 57009002004000001002000013063019006
A 40009000003000000000000002001000011
M79006000000048035000026008028007010
T 120020130210000000050180320003005000
H 28000004000038031058000005012023014
Q 65008003001005004000003002004002004
```

14.   Even by today's frenzied standards among international conglomerates, Acquisitive Enterprises is considered to be unusually aggressive, adding and shedding companies in rapid order. To help systematize these transactions, certain data are accumulated for each subsidiary and used to compute several financial measurements which (presumably) aid management in subsequent decision-making:

Item	Format	Coded Name
Company code	characters	CODE
Cash	XXXXXX.XX	A1
Accounts receivable	XXXXXX.XX	A2
Notes receivable	XXXXXX.XX	A3
Inventory	XXXXXXX.XX	A4
Fixed assets	XXXXXXX.XX	A5
Accounts payable	XXXXXX.XX	L1
Salaries payable	XXXXXX.XX	L2
Notes payable	XXXXXX.XX	L3
Capital stock	XXXXXXX.XX	L4
Retained earnings	XXXXXX.XX	L5

the financial measurements derived from these readings are as follows:

a. Current ratio $= (A1+A2+A3+A4)/(L1+L2)$
b. Asset test ratio $= (A1+A2+A3)/(L1+L2)$
c. Debt ratio $= (L1+L2+L3)/A1+A2+A3+A4+A5)$
d. Equity ratio $= (L4+L5)/(A1+A2+A3+A4+A5)$

Raw data for these computations are to be entered on cards for the various subsidiaries. Accordingly, devise an input card format and, using that format, write a program that will produce a financial ratio analysis (appropriately labeled) for each subsidary.

15. The Smith Company has a file of data cards punched as follows:

Card Columns	Item	Format
1	Warehouse number	X
2-3	Item number	XX
4-7	Quantity	XXXX
8-11	Unit cost	XX(.)XX

Write a program that reads an unknown number of such cards and produces the following summaries:

a. A summary for each item showing the total quantity available and the corresponding total cost.

b. A summary for each warehouse showing the total number of items available (regardless of type) and the corresponding total cost.

16. The PB Company is setting up a new filing system. There will be 2000 files in all, numbered 0001 to 2000. For a number of reasons it is desired to obtain a computer-produced set of appropriately numbered file labels. Each label is to contain the file number followed by a dash and a check digit, the latter being derived from the digits in the file number and based on a cycle of eight. Write a program that produces such labels and prints them, 15 to a line and 40 lines to a page. To help define

the pattern for the check digit, the first fifteen file labels are shown below (though not on one line):

0001-0   0002-1   0003-2   0004-3   0005-4
0006-5   0007-6   0008-7   0009-0   0010-1
0011-2   0012-3   0013-4   0014-5   0015-6

SUMMARY OF IMPORTANT TERMS

Argument	A constant, variable, or expression used by a built-in function (or any other function) in its prescribed processing.
Ceiling	The ceiling of a value is the smallest integer equal to or larger than that value.
FIXEDOVERFLOW condition	The condition raised when a fixed-point number is produced that exceeds the largest expressible fixed-point value.
Floor	The floor of a value is the largest integer equal to or less than that value.
Infix operator	An operator whose proper use requires its placement between two operands. (For example, the * in A*B represents an infix operator.)
Prefix operator	An operator whose proper use requires its placement directly ahead of a single operand. (For example, the − in −A is a prefix operator.)
SIZE condition	The condition raised if a fixed-point value exceeds the storage space assigned to it by declaration or default. (This mechanism must be explicitly activated by the programmer).

SUPPLEMENTARY READING

Conway, R., and others, *User's Guide to PL/C*. Ithaca: Cornell University Press, 1971.

Marasa, J.D., and Matula, D. W., "A Simulated Study of Correlated Error Propagation in Various Finite-Precision Arithmetics," *IEEE Transactions on Computers*, vol. C-22, no. 6, June 1973, pp. 587-597.

Matula, D.W., "A Formalization of Floating-Point Numeric Base Conversion," *IEEE Transactions on Computers*, vol. C-19, no. 8, Aug. 1970, pp. 681-692.

Matula, D.W., "Significant Digits: Numerical Analysis or Numerology," *Information Processing 71*. Amsterdam: North-Holland, 1972.

PL/I Language Reference Manual, IBM Document No. GC28-8201. White Plains, N.Y.: IBM Corporation, pp. 44-48, 270-278.

X MANIPULATION OF CHARACTER STRINGS

Our previous use of character string operations (Chapter V), though limited, established the idea that PL/I treats the manipulation of such data as an endeavor paralleling arithmetic computation. Accordingly, there is in PL/I an identifiable group of facilities and techniques associated with character strings. This chapter will deal with their properties, use, and interaction with the spectrum of computational operations.

X.1 DEVELOPMENT OF CHARACTER STRING EXPRESSIONS

Unlike arithmetic computations, there is no set of well-established notation for basic character string operations. Thus, PL/I's approach is to supplement the elemental process of concatenation with a collection of special built-in functions that serve as building blocks for a potentially limitless variety of more intricate activities.

X.1.1   Concatenation of Strings

As seen in previous chapters, we can build character strings by concatenating smaller strings, which may be either constants or variables. For example, the sequence

DECLARE (A,B) **CHARACTER** (3), W **CHARACTER** (14);

A = 'CON'; B = 'ATE';

W = A II 'C' II B II 'N' II B;

will fill string W with the 14 characters   CONCATENATEⱠⱠⱠ

X.1.1.1   Expansion of Strings

This basic operation can be used in a somewhat different context when applied to character strings declared with the **VARYING** attribute. Recall that the (apparent) length of such a string changes with its contents (limited only by the maximum length associated with the declaration). Accordingly, it is possible to build such a string by "grafting" another string onto it, thereby obtaining a new length. For instance, the result of the action of the sequence

DECLARE B **CHARACTER**(15) **VARYING**, C **CHARACTER**(4);

D = ''; C = 'TAPE';

B = C; B = B II 'S';

would be as follows: string B is initialized to the null string (that is, nothing at all) and the four characters TAPE are placed in C. Then, by assigning C's contents to B, the apparent length of the latter is increased from zero characters to four characters, with the contents as indicated. Finally, string B is made to grow again by concatenating it with the constant 'S'. Consequently, its final contents consist of the characters TAPES and the final length is 5.

X.1.1.2   The **LENGTH** Function

PL/I provides a very useful accessory for dealing with variable-length character strings. By writing an expression of the form

LENGTH(arg1)

the programmer can obtain a fixed binary integer of default precision specifying the current length of the character string named in arg1. For example, if the variable-length character string B currently contains the characters PLURAL and we wrote

Y = 14 + **LENGTH**(B);

a value of 20 would be placed in location Y. Of course, **LENGTH** also will work with fixed-length strings.

Illustration 24

As an example of this buildup process we shall develop a procedure to handle input cards punched in accordance with the following format:

Column(s)	Item	Format
1-4	X	XXXX
8	Y	characters

The program is to examine each card (there may be as many as 40 in a run) and, if the rightmost digit of X is odd, the program is to build a string S by augmenting it with the value of Y obtained from that card. Every time S grows in this manner, the program is to print a line of output showing the sequence number of the card (for example, 21 if it is the 21st card read), X, Y, S, and the current length of S. If it turns out that there was a particular run in which none of the X values was odd, the program is to print a special message saying "NO ELIGIBLE NUMBERS FOUND THIS RUN".

We shall handle this situation by setting up a varying string S with a maximum length of 40. By initializing S to the null string, we can construct a loop in which input cards are systematically read and tested. When an eligible card is found, we can concatenate the corresponding Y value onto the string built thus far. This automatically provides us with a test for a completely futile run: since the defined length of a null string is zero, the persistence of that value at the end of the run will tell us that the string has not grown. The appropriate statements are shown below and sample output is given in Figure 10.1.

```
ILL24: PROCEDURE OPTIONS (MAIN);
        DECLARE S CHARACTER(40) VARYING INITIAL (''),
                Y CHARACTER(1),
                (X,NDFILE,SEQ) FIXED BINARY;

        NDFILE,SEQ = 0;
        ON ENDFILE (SYSIN) NDFILE=1;
        PUT PAGE LINE(3) EDIT ('CARD NO.','X','Y','S','LENGTH OF S')
            (COL(11),A,COL(22),A,COL(30),A,COL(55),A,COL(78),A);
        PUT SKIP;   GET EDIT(X,Y)(F(4),X(3),A(1));   GET SKIP;

/**********************************************************************/
/*   NOW THE SYSTEM IS INITIALIZED AND "PRIMED" WITH THE FIRST    */
/*   SET OF INPUT. NOTE THAT S IS SET AT A LENGTH OF ZERO.        */
/**********************************************************************/

        DO WHILE (NDFILE=0);
          SEQ = SEQ+1;
          IF MOD (X,2) = 1
            THEN DO;
                S = S || Y;
                PUT SKIP EDIT(SEQ,X,Y,S,LENGTH(S))
                    (COL(14),F(2),COL(21),F(4),COL(30),A,COL(35),A,
                        COL(83),F(2));
                END;
          GET EDIT (X,Y) (F(4),X(3),A(1));   GET SKIP;
        END;

        IF LENGTH(S) = 0
          THEN PUT SKIP(2) EDIT ('NO ELIGIBLE NUMBERS THIS RUN')
                            (X(10),A);
        END ILL24;
```

```
CARD NO.    X         Y                         S                    LENGTH OF S
    1       2317      G       G                                           1
    2        533      R       GR                                          2
    5        515      O       GRO                                         3
    7       7575      O       GROO                                        4
    9       2123      B       GROOB                                       5
   11        667      L       GROOBL                                      6
   12        655      N       GROOBLN                                     7
   13       3333      I       GROOBLNI                                    8
```

Figure 10.1

X.1.1.3   The **REPEAT** Function

As its name implies, this function provides a convenient facility for replicating a character string or character string expression. The basic usage is in an expression of the form

REPEAT(arg1, n)

where arg1 is a character string constant, variable or expression, and n is a decimal integer constant that specifies the number of times the character string is to be concatenated with itself. Thus, if C represents a character string, the expressions C || C || C || C and **RE-PEAT**(C,3) are equivalent. Note that if n ≤ 0 the argument is returned unchanged.

X.1.2   Extraction and Decomposition of Character Strings

The ability to build and expand character strings through concatenation is complemented by powerful facilities for obtaining and manipulating arbitrarily defined parts of strings. The keystone of this capability is provided by the extremely flexible **SUBSTR** built-in function.

X.1.2.1   Basic Properties of the Substring Function

This function allows the programmer to identify and work with any contiguous set of characters drawn from some larger string (and referred to as a *substring*). The form calls for two or optionally three arguments. In the general expression

SUBSTR(arg1,arg2,arg3)

arg1 is a character string or an expression that will be converted to a string, and the other two arguments can be any legitimate arithmetic expressions. This function evaluates the second and third arguments (if a third is included) and converts the results to integers. Using these as guides, PL/I reproduces that portion of the string specified by arg1, starting with the position indicated by arg1, starting with the position indicated by arg2 and continuing for that number of characters specified by arg3. Thus, if A and B are character strings of a particular length, the statement

B = **SUBSTR**(A,3,4);

will extract four characters from string A (specifically the third, fourth, fifth, and sixth characters) and place them in string B. Note that the positioning of the substring in the destination variable is fixed. The first character in the substring is placed in the leftmost position of the string specified on the left-hand side of the equals sign. If the specified length of the substring (arg3) is greater than the number of characters available in arg1, starting from the position specified in arg2, the **STRINGRANGE** condition will be raised if it is enabled. If this particular error detection mechanism is not in force at the time such a situation arises, the action PL/I will take would vary with the compiler. For example, PL/I-F will go ahead and operate on whatever data happen to be where the nonexistent part of the string would be if it did exist; on the other hand, the Checkout compiler will print an error message anyway, even though **STRINGRANGE** is not enabled. If the destination variable is declared with insufficient length, PL/I will stuff it with as much of the substring as it can. Omission of the third argument causes the compiler to assume that the substring is to go out to the end of arg1. These operations are summarized in Table 10.1.

TABLE 10.1 Summary of Operations with the
SUBSTR Function

A = 'POPOCATEPTL'   B = **SUBSTR**(A,m,n)

Length of B	M	N	Contents of B
10	1	10	POPOCATEPT
10	2	10	OPOCATEPTL
10	7	10	error result undefined
5	6	5	ATEPT
9	4	not given	OCATEPTLƀ
3	5	5	CAT

Once a substring has been identified, it may be used like any other character. For example, the sequence

DECLARE E **CHARACTER**(6), F **CHARACTER**(2), G **CHARACTER**(8);

G = 'THANKFUL'; F = 'BL';

E = F ‖ **SUBSTR**(G,3,3) ‖ 'S';

will place the six characters BLANKS in the string E.

X.1.2.2   Substrings as Pseudovariables

A major shortcoming of the replacement operation is that the destination character variable is replaced in its entirety by the string specified on the right-hand side of the equals sign. This is true even when that new string is not long enough to fill the destination variable, in which case

PL/I obligingly pads the remaining positions with blanks. The **SUBSTR** function provides a powerful extension to this capability by allowing the programmer to replace arbitrarily defined parts of strings. This is implemented by a special feature called a *pseudovariable*, whereby the programmer is allowed to use the term **SUBSTR**(arg1,arg2,arg3) on the left side of the equals sign in an assignment statement as if it were a variable name. The general form for such an assignment is

    SUBSTR(arg1, arg2, arg3) = expression;

As an example, suppose we have a ten-character string A, which currently contains 'CON-FECTION'. The statement

    SUBSTR(A,4,2) = 'CO';

would change A to 'CONCOCTION'.

Pseudovariables can also be used as members of a data list in a **GET** statement, so that an input character string can be read and used to replace part of a character string already in storage. Other built-in functions can also be used as pseudovariables, including **COMPLEX**, **REAL** and **IMAG**, as we have already seen.

X.1.2.3   The **STRING** Pseudovariable

A special pseudovariable is available for placing a character expression into a character string array or structure. If C is a one-dimensional array with elements of length n and exp is a legitimate character string expression, the statement

    STRING(C) = exp;

will place the first (leftmost) n characters of exp in C(1), the next n characters in C(2), and so on until C is filled or until exp runs out of characters, in which case the remainder of C is padded with blanks. For example, the sequence

    DECLARE A(3) **CHARACTER**(4), B **CHARACTER**(6),
                 C **CHARACTER**(2), D **CHARACTER**(12);

    B = 'BRAIDS'; C = 'AT';

    D=**SUBSTR**(B,2,4)||**SUBSTR**(B,1,2)||C||**SUBSTR**(B,3);

    STRING(A) = D;

will store RAID, BRAT, and AIDS in A(1), and A(2), and A(3), respectively. If an array used with the **STRING** pseudovariable has more than one dimension, then the elements are filled in row major order. If the array has the **VARYING** attribute, each element is filled to its maximum length.

STRING is also a built-in function. When used as a function it concatenates all the elements of its argument (in their natural order) to form one giant string.

Illustration 25

Input cards (an unknown number) are available with a ten-letter string punched in columns 11-20 of each card. For each card processed, the procedure is to print a line of output containing the original string followed by the string with the letters in reverse order and with each **E** replaced by *. After the last line is printed, the program is to skip two lines and print the total number of strings processed for that run.

The algorithm is straightforward enough: after the input string is read, a **DO** loop will be used to place each character in a new string in reverse order. Once placed, that character can be examined to determine whether or not a substitution is required. The resulting procedure is shown below, and sample output is reproduced in Figure 10.2.

```
WORD1               WORD2
GOOGLEFEER          R**F*LGOOG
EDWARDIANS          SNAIDRAWD*
FEDWAYSEWR          RW*SYAWD*F

     NO. OF WORDS PROCESSED =    3
```

Figure 10.2

```
ILL25: PROCEDURE OPTIONS (MAIN);
       DECLARE (WORD1,WORD2) CHARACTER(10),
       ((NWT,NDFILE) INITIAL(0), I,J) FIXED BINARY;

       ON ENDFILE (SYSIN) NDFILE=1;
       PUT PAGE LINE(3)EDIT('WORD1','WORD2')
                (COL(10),A,COL(30),A,SKIP);
       GET EDIT (WORD1)(X(10),A(10));    GET SKIP;

       DO WHILE (NDFILE=0);
         NWT = NWT+1;
         DO I=1 TO 10;
           J = 11-I;
           SUBSTR(WORD2,J,1) = SUBSTR(WORD1,I,1);
           IF SUBSTR(WORD2,J,1)='E'
             THEN SUBSTR(WORD2,J,1)='*';
         END;
         PUT SKIP EDIT(WORD1,WORD2)
                  (X(9),A(10),X(11),A(10));
         GET EDIT (WORD1)(X(10),A(10));    GET SKIP;
       END;

/**********************************************************************/
/* TO ILLUSTRATE THE USE OF EXPRESSIONS WITH SUBSTR, WE SHALL RE-*/
/* PEAT THE PROCESSING WITHOUT USING J. INSTEAD, WE SHALL EXPRESS*/
/* THE REVERSE ORDER OF THE ITH POSITION IN TERMS OF I.        */
/**********************************************************************/

       DO I=1 TO 10;
         IF SUBSTR(WORD1,I,1) = 'E'
           THEN SUBSTR(WORD2,11-I,1) = '*';
           ELSE SUBSTR(WORD2,11-I,1) = SUBSTR(WORD1,I,1);
         END;
       PUT SKIP EDIT(WORD1,WORD2)
                (X(9),A(10),X(11),A(10));
       GET EDIT (WORD1)(X(10),A(10));    GET SKIP;
       END;

       PUT SKIP(2) EDIT('NO. OF WORDS PROCESSED = ',NWT)(X(10),A,F(3));
       END ILL25;
```

X.1.2.4   Automatic Replacement: The **TRANSLATE** Function

When a situation requires extensive character-for-character replacement, the process can be automated by means of the **TRANSLATE** function. An expression involving this function has the general form

TRANSLATE(arg1,arg2,arg3)

where arg1 identifies the string in which replacement is to occur, arg2 indicates the string containing the replacement symbols and arg3 refers to the string of characters to be replaced. That is, each occurrence in arg1 of a character in arg3 is replaced by the character in the corresponding position of arg2. For example, if arg2 and arg3 contain 123 and ABC, respectively, then all A's in arg1 will be replaced by ones, all B's by twos, and all C's by threes.

Illustration 26

We shall restate the problem in Illustration 25 by imposing the following complication: Each input string is to be printed with the characters in forward (original) and reverse order, as before. In addition, all E's, D's, W's and A's in the input strings are to be replaced by *'s, T's, X's, and U's, respectively, in the processed strings.

The reversing process will still be handled by a loop, with subsequent replacement being specified by a single assignment statement. The listing is given below and sample output is shown in Figure 10.3.

```
WORD1                WORD2
GOOGLE FEER          GOOGL*F**R
EDWARDIANS           *TXURTIUNS
FEDWAY SE WR         F*TXUYS*XR

     NO. OF WORDS PROCESSED =    3
```

Figure 10.3

```
ILL26: PROCEDURE OPTIONS (MAIN);
         DECLARE (WORD1,WORD2) CHARACTER(10),
              (S1,S2) CHARACTER(4),
              ((NWT,NDFILE) INITIAL(0), I,J) FIXED BINARY;

         S1 = 'EDWA';   S2 = '*TXU';
         ON ENDFILE (SYSIN) NDFILE=1;
         PUT PAGE LINE(3) EDIT ('WORD1','WORD2')
                   (COL(10),A,COL(30),A,SKIP);
         GET EDIT (WORD1)(X(10),A(10));   GET SKIP;

         DO WHILE (NDFILE=0);
           NWT=NWT+1;
           DO I=1 TO 10;
             J=11-I;
             SUBSTR(WORD2,J,1) = SUBSTR(WORD1,I,1);
           END;
           WORD2 = TRANSLATE(WORD1,S2,S1);
           PUT SKIP EDIT (WORD1,WORD2)(X(9),A(10),X(11),A(10));
           GET EDIT (WORD1)(X(10),A(10));   GET SKIP;
         END;

         PUT SKIP(2) EDIT ('NO. OF WORDS PROCESSED = ')
                   (X(10),A,F(3));
         END ILL26;
```

X.2   EXAMINATION OF CHARACTER STRINGS

PL/I's facilities for building and dissecting character strings are supported by basic, but powerful, functions for searching strings and constructing versatile tests of their contents.

X.2.1   The **INDEX** Function

This procedure provides a very valuable comparison tool; it allows the programmer to test for similarity between portions of strings by actually performing some searching operations. The basic expression performed is

INDEX(arg1,arg2)

where arg1 and arg2 are names of character strings. This function operates by trying to find a portion of arg1 which coincides with arg2. If such a situation is found (that is, if the characters in arg2 represent a particular substring of arg1), the function will return a binary integer of default precision giving the position of the character in arg1 where the substring begins. If no such correspondence can be found, the function returns a value of zero. For example, if variable A contains the string 'BALEFUL' and variable B contains 'ALE', the statement

L = **INDEX**(A,B);

will place a value of 2 in location L.

One of the most flexible uses of the **INDEX** function is implemented by combining it with the **SUBSTR** function to provide a complete search of a string. Note that the **INDEX** function, when applied by itself, is content after finding the first (leftmost) occurrence of a specified string in another string. Thus, if we were to look for the string AN in the name of the famous Eastern scholar Rangananthanantharan with the statement

M = INDEX('RANGANANTHANANTHARAN','AN');

a value of 2 would be placed in M and that would be that.

Illustration 27

We shall exemplify a more general method for searching a string by writing a procedure that reads a two-character string S1 in columns 1-2 of the first input card and searches succeeding input for all occurrences of S1. Each input string (S2) will appear in columns 1-20 of a card. For each card, the program is to print a line showing S1 followed by the number of occurrences of S2, followed in turn by a list of the positions at which those occurrences were found. Thus, the output for the venerated scholar's name would say

RANGANANTHANANTHARAN   6   2 5 7 11 13 19

Output columns are to be appropriately headed and an initial line is to show the value of S2:

```
ILL27: PROCEDURE OPTIONS (MAIN);

/** SINCE A 2-CHARACTER STRING CANNOT OCCUR MORE THAN 19 TIMES IN **/
/** A 20-CHARACTER STRING, A 19-ELEMENT ARRAY (NUM) WILL HANDLE   **/
/** THE OCCURRENCES' POSITIONS. BY INITIALIZING TO ZERO AND FIL-  **/
/** LING NUM AS OCCURRENCES ARE FOUND, WE CAN KEEP TRACK OF THE   **/
/** NUMBER OF OCCURRENCES (N) AND PRINT ONLY THAT MANY.           **/

        DECLARE S1 CHARACTER(2),  S2 CHARACTER(20),
                (N,NUM,N1,J,NDFILE) FIXED BINARY;

        NDFILE=0;  ON ENDFILE(SYSIN) NDFILE=1;
        GET EDIT(S1)(A(2));   GET SKIP EDIT(S2)(A(20));
        PUT PAGE LINE EDIT('S1 = ',S1)(X(5),A,A(2))('S1','N',
            'OCCURRENCES')(SKIP,X(15),A(2),X(17),A,X(15),A,SKIP);

/*FIRST, WE SHALL CHECK FOR ANY OCCURRENCES AT ALL. IF NOT, WE CAN*/
/*AVOID THE COMPLETE SEARCH. WHEN THE INDEX FUNCTION IS USED SUC- */
/*CESSFULLY ON A SUBSTRING, THE RESULTING VALUE OF THE POSITION OF*/
/*THE MATCH IS RELATIVE TO THE BEGINNING OF THE SUBSTRING, NOT    */
/*THE PARENT STRING. THUS, WHEN AN OCCURRENCE IS FOUND, ITS APPA- */
/*RENT POSITION HAS TO BE ADJUSTED TO GET ITS ACTUAL POSITION RE- */
/*LATIVE TO THE ORIGIN OF THE ENTIRE STRING. J, THEN, WILL BE USED*/
/*TO INDICATE THE START OF THE PART OF THE STRING STILL TO BE     */
/*SEARCHED, AND M1 WILL INDICATE THE POSITION OF THE MATCH.       */

        DO WHILE (NDFILE=0);
          N,NUM = 0;
          M1 = INDEX(S2,S1);
          IF M1 = 0
            THEN PUT SKIP EDIT(S2,'0','NO OCCURRENCES')
                          (X(5),A(20),X(9),A,X(15),A);
            ELSE DO;
                 N=1;   NUM(1)=M1;   /* INITIALIZATION */
                 DO WHILE (NUM(N) < 19);
                   J = NUM(N)+1;
                   M1=INDEX(SUBSTR(S2,J),S1);
                   IF M1 > 0
                     THEN DO;        /* THERE IS A MATCH */
                           N = N+1;
                           NUM(N) = M1+NUM(N-1);
                          END;
                 END;
               END;
          PUT SKIP EDIT(S2,N,(NUM(I) DO I=1 TO N))
                   (X(5),A(20),X(9),F(2),X(13),(N)(X(1),F(2)));
          GET SKIP EDIT(S2)(A(20));
        END;

        END ILL27;
```

X.2.2   The VERIFY Function

A different type of search may be specified by means of the **VERIFY** function, whose form requires two arguments:

VERIFY (arg1,arg2)

where arg1 indicates the string to be searched and arg2 represents the reference string against which the search is to be conducted. Starting at the left end, each character in arg1 is scrutinized to determine whether it matches one of the characters in arg2. If a match is found, the search continues with the next character in arg1 being compared against each character in arg2. If all of arg1's characters are present somewhere in arg2, **VERIFY** produces a zero; otherwise it stops at the first mismatch and develops a fixed binary integer (with default precision) that indicates the position of the non-conformist. For example, if A, B, and C are character strings containing CANNA, TRIFLES, and NACHITE, respectively, the statements

N = **VERIFY**(A,C); and M = **VERIFY**(B,C);

will give N a value of 0, and M will have a value of 2.

Note that the search stops at the first mismatch. Accordingly, a complete search of arg1 must be implemented with a loop, as was done with the **INDEX** function.

X.3 RELATIONS WITH OTHER DATA FORMS

As part of the language's tremendous flexibility, it is possible, under specific conditions, to include character strings in legitimate arithmetic expressions. More generally, facilities are provided for controlled conversion between character strings and numbers.

X.3.1 Character Strings in Arithmetic Expression

If a string contains a valid arithmetic constant or a complex expression consisting of a real constant plus or minus an imaginary constant, it is possible to assign that string to a numerical variable. For example, if we define variables V and W with the statements

DECLARE V **CHARACTER**(6) **INITIAL**(' −12.75'),

      W **FIXED**(6,3);

and we specify the simple assignment W = V; the six characters −12.75 will be converted to numeric form and (in this case) extended with zeros to match the precision of the destination. Thus, the value −012(.)750 will be stored in W. This type of automatic conversion will produce the expected result for fixed- or floating-point destinations as long as their precisions are adequate to accept the result and as long as the character string contains nothing but digits, a sign, and a period.

As soon as a character string appears in an arithmetic expression, a different conversion mechanism comes into play. In such situations Pl/I converts the string to an item with the same attributes that would be required if a variable with the attributes **FIXED DECIMAL**(15,0) appeared in place of the string. The expression is evaluated in accordance with the regular arithmetic conversion rules (as described in Chapter 9). This can result in the truncation of decimal places, which could have unfortunate results. For example, the sequence

DECLARE V **CHARACTER**(6) **INITIAL** ($'-12.75'$),

W **FIXED**(6,3);

W = V + 27.6;

would produce a converted value of V equivalent to -000000000000012, to which addition of 27.6 yields a value stored in W as 015(.)600. Thus, if we know (or suspect) that V will have significant digits to the right of the period, it would be better to separate the activities:

W =V; W = W+27.6;

When a string is being combined with a floating-point variable in this way, decimal places will never be lost.

X.3.2   Arithmetic in Character String Expressions

When an assignment statement is specified in which the final destination is a character string, it is obvious that the result of the indicated expression must itself be a character string before it is stored in the destination variable.

As long as the expression itself consists of character strings being processed by character string operations, everything is straightforward. However, it is possible for such expressions to include arithmetic terms and operations along with character manipulations, in which case separate conversion rules apply.

X.3.2.1   Conversion of Numbers to Character Strings

PL/I's mechanisms are designed for specific conversion from decimal numbers to character strings. Accordingly, the presence of a binary number or variable in a character string expression activates the regular binary-to-decimal conversion facilities (Chapter IX) in advance of the final transformation to character string form.

The rules governing decimal-to-character conversion are summarized in Table 10.2. To illustrate the operation of these conversions, let us assume that variables A, B, and C are defined as follows:

DECLARE A **FIXED**(4,2), B **FIXED**(3), C **CHARACTER**(5);

C = 'VALUE'; A=6.02; B=230;

TABLE 10.2 Number-to-Character Conversion Rules

Attributes of Number	Length of Converted String	Remarks about Converted Form
FIXED DECIMAL(w,0)	w + 3	No decimal point, leading zeros replaced with blanks, value right-adjusted
FIXED DECIMAL(w,d) w>=d, d>0, value has integer portion	w + 3	Decimal point appears; no + sign; if value < 0, − sign precedes first significant digit
FIXED DECIMAL(w,d) w>=d, d>=0, value is a fraction	w + 3	Decimal point preceded by single zero; no + sign; if value < 0, − sign precedes leading zero.
FIXED DECIMAL(w,d) d>w or d<0	w + 3 + n(n = number of digits to express scale factor)	No decimal point; significant digits followed by F ± n (the value of n = −d)
FLOAT DECIMAL(w) value > = 0	w + 6	bw.w...wE±nn
FLOAT DECIMAL(w) value < 0	w + 6	−w.w...wE±nn

Then the expression 'THE' ‖ (A*B) ‖ C will be developed as follows:

1. The product A*B is computed following the previously defined arithmetic rules, yielding a fixed decimal number with precision (4+3+1,2+0). Thus, the temporary value is 001384(.)60.

2. The 1384.60 is converted to a character string of length 11 (that is, 8 + 3) with the numerical digits right-justified. Accordingly, the string is stored as ƀƀƀƀƀ1384.60 just prior to concatenation.

3. Final concatenation produces the twenty characters THEƀƀƀƀƀ1384.60VAL-UE . Thus, if some other variable D were to be declared as **CHARACTER**(20), the statement

    D = 'THE ' ‖ (A*B) ‖ C;

would place the resulting string snugly in D. Note, however, that if D had been declared with a greater length, say, **CHARACTER**(23), the assignment would place the computed result in the twenty *leftmost* positions of D, filling the rest with blanks.

For example, if we say

DECLARE W FLOAT(6) **INITIAL**(72641), Y **CHARACTER**(14);

  Y = W+4;

the sum W + 4 would be developed as a floating-point value with precision (6), and that value would be converted to a character string with length 12 (that is 6 + 6), represented as b̷7.26450E+04 . Subsequent placement in Y would be *left-justified*, thereby giving Y a value of b̷7.26450E+04b̷b̷ . Additional examples are shown in Table 10.3.

TABLE 10.3 Examples of Number-to-Character Conversion*

Attributes of A	Value of A	String value of A	Value of lgth	String placed in B
FIXED(4)	184	b̷b̷b̷b̷184	8	b̷b̷b̷b̷184b̷
			6	b̷b̷b̷b̷18
	−184	b̷b̷b̷−184	7	b̷b̷b̷−184
			5	b̷b̷b̷−1
FIXED(5,2)	72.8	b̷b̷b̷72.80	5	b̷b̷b̷72
			8	b̷b̷b̷72.80
	−72.84	b̷b̷−72.84	8	b̷b̷−72.84
	−.29	b̷b̷b̷−0.29	7	b̷b̷b̷−0.2
			9	b̷b̷b̷−0.29b̷
FIXED(5,5)	.12764	b̷0.12764	9	b̷0.12760b̷
FIXED(5,6)	.012764	b̷12764F−6	8	b̷12764F−
		w n	10	b̷12764F−6b̷
FIXED(5,−3)	−71852000	−71852F+3	8	−71852F+3
		w n		
FLOAT(5)	329.67	b̷3.2967E+02	12	b̷3.2967E+02b̷
			9	b̷3.2967E+0
	−.07414	−7.4140E−02	11	−7.4140E−02
			8	−7.4140E−

*A is a numerical variable, B is **CHARACTER** (lgth), statement is B = A;

X.3.2.2 The **CHAR** Function

The **CHAR** function allows the programmer to specify the length to which a converted length is truncated or padded on the right. When used in the form

CHAR(arg1,n)

arg1 specifies the expression to be converted and n is a decimal integer constant giving the desired length of the converted string. For example, if we have the sequence

DECLARE A **FIXED**(4,2) B **FIXED**(3), D **CHARACTER**(13);

A = 6.02; B = 230; D = **CHAR**(A*B,13);

the value of A*B, generated as 001384ₒₒ60 (see previous section), is converted to the 13-character string ␢␢␢␢␢␢1384.60 and stored as such in D. By omitting the second argument (n) we permit PL/I to use its own rules to determine the length of the result. Thus, if we rewrote the final assignment statement to read

D = **CHAR**(A*B);

the string ␢␢␢␢1384.60␢␢ would be placed in D. Hence, the final result is the same. If control over the conversion process is really desired, it is preferable to use a numeric character variable.

PROBLEMS

1. The following variables have been declared:

Name	Attributes	Value
A	**CHARACTER**(12)	
B	**CHARACTER**(6)	BLOWER
C	**CHARACTER**(4)	MAUL
D	**CHARACTER**(12)**VARYING**	
X	**FIXED**(2)	24
Y	**FLOAT**(5)	
W	**FIXED**(1)	6
Z	**FIXED**(4,2)	

Show the value in the appropriate destination variable or variables resulting from each of the following statements or sequences of statements:

a.   A = C || **SUBSTR**(B,5) || 'S';

b.   A = **SUBSTR**(C,1,1) || **SUBSTR**(B,3) || ' # ' || W;

c.   A = **SUBSTR**(B,6,1) || **SUBSTR**(B,3,3) || 'S' || **SUBSTR**(C,1,2) || X:
     Y = X/6***LENGTH**(D);

   d.   D = **SUBSTR**(B,4,2) ‖ ' ' ‖ **SUBSTR**(C,1,2) ‖ 'Y' ‖ **SUBSTR**(A,2);

             SUBSTR(D,3,3) = **SUBSTR**(D,3,3);

             Z = W + **LENGTH**(D)***INDEX**(B,**SUBSTR**(B,4,2));

   e.   A = **SUBSTR**(B,1,2) ‖ **REPEAT**(**SUBSTR**(B,3,1),1) ‖ **SUBSTR**(C,1,1) ‖

             SUBSTR(B,5);

             Y = X/(2***INDEX**(**SUBSTR**(A,3),**SUBSTR**(B,5)));

2. Sentences of text are keypunched on cards in columns 1-76, with sequential card numbers in 77-80 (for example, 0001, 0002, and so on). When a word ends in column 76, column 1 of the next card is blank. A word broken in column 76 continues right in column 1 of the next card (no hyphen). Thus, the text is presented as if each 76-column segment of a card is part of a continuous string of columns. A sentence can end only with a period and is separated from the next sentence by a single blank.

    Write a program that reads a group of such cards and prints each sentence on a separate line. A final line is to show the number of sentences printed.

3. Using the same text as in the previous problem, write a program that prints each sentence on a line, along with the number of words in that sentence. After the last sentence, the program is to print the number of sentences, the number of words and the average word length.

4. Using the same text as in the previous problem, print the text, one sentence to each line. Then skip two lines and print the number of words having two letters, three letters, and so on. Note, however, that they are to be printed by decreasing frequency. That is, the most popular length first, the least popular length last.

5. Using the same text as in the previous problem, print the text, one sentence on each line. Then, skip two lines and print each letter along with the number of occurrences for that letter. These are to be printed with the most frequently used letter appearing first, and so on.

6. Text is punched on cards starting in column 1 and going as far as column 76. If a word cannot be finished by column 76, the remaining columns are left blank and the word is started in column 1 of the next card. Moreover, there may be any number of blanks between words or at the beginning of a sentence.

    Write a program that prints the text, one sentence to a line, with only one blank between words or after a sentence.

7. Words up to 20 letters long are punched, one to a card, starting in column 1. In columns 31-32 of each card is a two-digit integer that specifies a replacement code for the letters in that word. For example, if a particular card has 04 in those columns, then each letter in the word is to be replaced by the letter four positions removed in alphabetical order (for example, all A's replaced by E's, B's by F's, W's by A's, X's by B's, and so on).

    Write a program that prints a line for each card processed showing the word as received, its length, the value of the two-digit integer, and the newly produced string.

8. Strings of nonblank characters are punched in columns 1-80. Write a program that prints each card on a line followed by a second line that shows that same string with the vowels removed and the remaining consonants squeezed together. On that same line print the length of the compressed string. Separate pairs of lines by a blank line.

9. An input list consists of 100 common words used in rhymes. Write a program that will classify these words into rhyming categories. A rhyming category is defined here as a group of words with the same ending. In order for two words to belong to the same category, at least the final three letters must match. Assume that plurals, present participles, and so on are not used. The printout should show each group separately in some appropriate format.

10. An input list consists of 100 words that may or may not be 100 different words (some may be different forms of the same word). Write a program that finds such words and reduces them to standard forms using the following rule: two words belong to the same root if the total number of dissimilar letters at the ends of the two words is less than six. Thus, the two words

F A R M I N G

F A R M E R

are classified as coming from the same root (farm) because the total number of dissimilar letters is five. Similarly, the words

T R A V A I I L

T R A V E L E R

are considered different since there is a total of seven letters from the point at which the two words ceased being identical. (This is by no means an inviolable rule. For example, the words "farming" and "farmland" would be wrongly classified.) The program should print each root form, the number of words assigned to that form, and the total number of forms identified.

11. The city of Bowdlersville wishes to implement a censoring program that checks all newspaper copy before it goes to press. A device exists that allows this copy to be produced as punched cards. The censoring program is to replace all four-letter words with ****. To simplify matters, the device is designed so that no word is split between two cards and the last card is followed by a card containing all (80) asterisks. Do these folks a favor and write such a program.

SUMMARY OF IMPORTANT TERMS

Left-justified	Placement of a data item in storage such that the beginning of that item occupies the leftmost position of its assigned location. PL/I automatically left-justifies character strings.

Right-justified

Placement of a data item in an assigned location such that the right extremity of that item coincides with the rightmost position of the assigned location. As expected, PL/I automatically right-justifies numerical values.

STRINGRANGE condition

An error detection mechanism that, when activated by the programmer, automatically issues a message when there is a reference to a string that extends beyond its bounds.

Substring

An arbitrary number of contiguous characters contained within a string. The **SUBSTR** function allows the convenient description of a substring in terms of its length and starting position within the containing string.

SUPPLEMENTARY READING

PL/I Language Reference Manual, IBM Document No. GC28-8201. White Plains, N.Y.: IBM Corporation, pp. 270-278.

XI BIT STRINGS

Although the combination '1001101' is a perfectly legitimate character string and can be stored as a value of an appropriately declared variable, it is often desirable to make use of a string that can contain nothing but ones and zeros, without actually treating it as a binary number. To provide for such situations, PL/I included facilities for a type of constant or variable known as a *bit string*. These strings have all the properties of character strings; they can be read in, shifted around, concatenated, printed out, and compared in the same way. In addition, however, there are a number of operations specifically intended for bit strings. These are designed to treat each bit in the string not as a numerical one or zero but rather as a binary switch that can exist only in one of two states (one or zero). For convenience, these states are referred to as "on" or "off," respectively. The method of storing a bit string is different and considerably more compact than that used for character strings. It is possible to store a bit string of length 8 in the same amount of storage required for a single character, even when that character is a one or zero.

XI.1   REPRESENTATION OF BIT STRING DATA

Since a bit string is still treated as a sequence of symbols, it must be surrounded by single quotation marks as is a character string. However, some means must be provided to distinguish a bit string from a character string consisting of ones and zeros. This is done by including a **B** immediately after the closing quotation mark. Hence, the constant '10110011' is treated as a character string while '10110011'**B** is treated as a bit string and stored in memory accordingly. (It requires only one-eighth the amount of memory used by '10110011'.)

Bit string variables must be named in an explicit declare statement having the general form

DECLARE name **BIT**(n);

where "name" is any legitimate variable name and (n) is a decimal integer constant specifying the length (number of bits) to be assigned to the variable. As with character strings, the **VARYING** attribute may be specified if desired. Omission of a specification of (n) will result in a default length assignment of one.

The shortened form shown previously for character strings can also be used for bit strings, so that the statements

A = (7)'101'**B**;

and

A = '101101101101101101101'**B**;

are identical. In addition, declarations of bit strings may be factored in the usual way.

Bit string variables may be organized into arrays and structures according to the same rules and limitations discussed for the other types of variables. All of the attributes assignable to character string aggregates apply to bit strings as well.

XI.2   INPUT/OUTPUT OF BIT STRING DATA

Since bit strings constitute a specific, but perfectly legitimate, type of data, they can be transmitted to and from the processor by means of the same mechanisms available for numerical and character string variables. We shall confine our discussion in this chapter to an exploration of stream-oriented input/output.

XI.2.1   List-Directed and Data-Directed Transmission

In order to be read by a **GET LIST** statement, bit strings must be identified as such by actually punching the **B** right along with the string itself. Once this is done and the particular variable has been declared as a bit string having sufficient length, input can occur in the usual fashion.

An ordinary **PUT LIST** statement will take the current value of a properly declared bit string from storage and print it in full form, including the quotation marks and the **B**. A bit string constant, as a character string constant, can be specified as part of an output statement. The statement

PUT LIST('1011001'**B**);

for example, will produce a printout of '1011001'**B**.

A command to print a binary variable automatically causes its value to be converted to decimal form before it is printed. If the programmer should wish to see such output directly in binary form (as a sequence of ones and zeros), he can do so by first converting the value to a bit string and printing it in that form. This is illustrated by the statements

DECLARE A **FIXED BINARY** (6), B **BIT** (6);

A = 100101B; B = A; **PUT LIST**(A,B);

The line of output resulting from the **PUT LIST** statement would appear as

37'100101'**B**

PL/I will accept data of other types, converting them to bit strings. If we wrote

DECLARE (A,C)**BIT**(8), B **BIT**(6), D **BIT**(10)**VARYING**;

GET LIST (A,B,C,D);

and our data card appeared as

'10011001'**B** 110010B '100101' 26

PL/I would covert all of the values to bit strings and store them as such. Specifically, the first value would be stored in A as is (without the quotation marks and the **B**), and the second value would be converted to a string representing '110010'**B** and stored in B, the third, a character string, would be converted by changing character ones to bit ones and character zeros to bit zeros, and zeros would be added to the right to fill C's length, thus placing the string '1001010000'**B** in that location. (Were it the other way around, C would be filled to capacity starting with the leftmost input digit, and the rest would be lost.) The fourth value would first be converted from **FIXED DECIMAL**(2) to **FIXED BINARY**(7), giving the value 0011011B, which would then be converted to a bit string of length 7 and assigned to D.

If one of the input values had been expressed as a number with fractional places, it still would have been converted, but somewhat less directly. Before conversion to a bit string, the number is converted to a binary integer with the fractional portion being lost. Whenever a number of any kind is converted to a bit string the sign is also lost. Table 11.1 summarizes the rules for conversion of numerical values to bit strings. N in this table is the maximum allowable number of (binary) digits in a PL/I binary value. (This can vary with the conversion of the compiler but is usually 31.)

TABLE 11.1 Rule for PL/I's Conversion from Numbers to Bit String

Base	Scale	Precision	Precision of Resulting Binary Number (Length of Final Bit String)
Binary	Fixed	(w,d)	$MIN(N,MAX(w-d,0))$
Binary	Float	(w)	$MIN(N,w)$
Decimal	Fixed	(w,d)	$MIN(N,MAX(CEIL((w-d)*3.32),0))$
Decimal	Float	(w)	$MIN(N,CEIL(w*3.32))$

We shall examine this conversion more closely by working out two examples (using $N = 31$). Suppose that A were declared as **BIT**(10), and an input value punched as 11.25 were to be stored in A. Hence, P, the length of the intermediate binary number, would be obtained as

$$P = MIN(31,MAX(CEIL((4-2)*3.32),0))$$

$$= MIN(31,MAX(CEIL(6.64),0))$$

$$= MIN(31,MAX(7,0))$$

$$= 7$$

The 11.25 would be converted to a seven-digit binary integer, or 0001011**B**. Since A was assigned ten positions, the extra ones (to the right) will be filled with zeros, so that the resulting bit string will be '000101100'**B**.

Now let us look at an input value of 1011.01000**B**, which is to be read into A, declared as before. This time, w is 9 and d is 5. According to our rule for conversion from fixed binary numbers, we drop the fractional portion and produce a bit string whose length, P, is

$$P = MIN (31,MAX(9-5,0))$$

$$= MIN(31,MAX(4,0))$$

$$= MIN(31,4)$$

$$= 4.$$

The remaining positions in A will be filled with zeros, producing the final value '1011000000'**B**.

Data-directed input/output of bit strings follows all the rules that apply for other data forms. Conversions from arithmetic and character string forms will take place as long as the constraints discussed for list-directed bit string input are followed. Output will appear with quotation marks and the **B**.

XI.2.2   Edit-Directed Transmission

When bit strings are read in under edit-directed input, the values should be recorded as ones and zeros without the surrounding quotation marks and without the trailing **B**. The format specification for handling data is written as

B(W)

where (w) is a constant, variable, or expression that, when reduced to an integer, determines the number of columns to be read in or printed. A repetition factor may precede the **B** [for example, 3**B**(6)] as with any other format specification. When (w) for a particular variable in an output format exceeds the number of places assigned in the declaration, the compiler causes the bit string to be printed as stored, adding blanks to the right to fill the field. For instance, if **D** were a bit string with current contents of '101110'**B** and we wrote

PUT EDIT(D)(**COLUMN**(20),**B**(10));

our output would appear as

col. 20

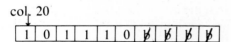

When (w) in a **PUT EDIT** statement is smaller than the number of bits used to store the bit string value named in the data list, the first (leftmost) w characters will be written and the rest will be truncated.

XI.3   INTERNAL MANIPULATIONS

The operators = and ‖ are used with bit strings exactly as with character strings. If an expression involves both bit string and character string values, the latter is considered to be the "higher" type, so that all necessary conversions are made to character strings before the expression is evaluated.

Bit strings may also appear in numerical expressions. When this happens, PL/I treats each bit string as if it represented a fixed binary integer and makes the appropriate conversion. For example, if X is 3, Y is 2.4, and A is '1001'**B**, the statement

Z = 2*X − Y + (A‖'110'**B**);

will be evaluated as

$Z = 6 - 2.4 + 1001110_2$

$= 6 - 2.4 + 78$

$= 81.6$

XI.3.1   Logical Operations

In many instances it is fruitful to think of each bit as a switch. One way of looking at such a switch is to consider it to be in one of two positions, either "on" or "off." This implies that we are not treating the digit as a number but as an indicator of a state or a condition. It would not be inconsistent to designate these alternative states by any pair of terms. Instead of referring to the existence of a one or a zero as "on" or "off" we could just as plausibly call these states "a" or "b," "present" or "absent," "yes" or "no," or "true" or "false,". The usage of "true" and "false" is especially interesting in that it leads us directly to the idea of using a binary digit to represent the status of an event. By the same token, we can use multidigit bit strings as a symbolic summary of the status of a sequence of events. When this is supported by a set of operators that allow us to manipulate these bit strings, we are presented with a powerful logical network for representing conditions or events, combining them into sequences analyzing these combinations and regulating subsequent activity according to their outcomes. We shall examine these capabilities as applied to a bit string containing a single digit, with the implication that the same operations apply to longer strings.

The diagram in Figure 11.1 depicts the setup for the classic Kolchikoff Triangular Rat Situation. (Kolchikoff, I., Grischchick, S. and Upf, A., "Rat Situations," *Iranian Journal of Clinical Psychology*, vol.31, 1924, pp 171-188.) In it the rat, standing at point P1, is faced with the task of eventually obtaining the cheese located at point P3. This immediately defines the basic event in this system for us, namely, the success or failure of the rat to get at

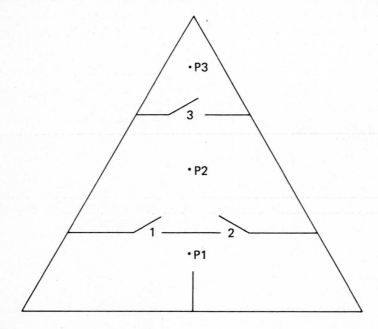

Figure 11.1

the cheese. Since the event can be clearly stated, we can easily represent it by a symbol, and we shall do that by letting Y represent the event "the rat obtains the cheese." Since this event can only have one of two possible outcomes (success or failure), we can represent Y by a single- character bit string whose value will be 1 when Y is true (the rat gets the cheese) and 0 when it is false (the rat does not). From the diagram it is clear that the value of Y (success or failure) depends on the position of the three doors 1, 2, and 3. Each of these doors can exist in one of only two possible states (open or closed) as far as our problem is concerned. We can assign symbols to each of these events:

Let A represent the event "Door 1 is open."

Let B represent the event "Door 2 is open."

Let C represent the event "Door 3 is open."

As before A, B, and C can each be represented by single-digit bit string variables containing a 1 when the event is true and a 0 when it is false. We can now go about the process of building up a logical expression reflecting the dependency of the value of Y on the conditions of A, B, and C.

First of all, our rat must get to point P2 before we can talk seriously about a final assault on the cheese. We can define that intermediate event by letting X represent the event "He arrives at point P2." To make X true (to allow the rat's arrival at point P2), it is necessary for door 1 or door 2 to be open. Note that X will also be true if both doors are open, but it is not a necessary condition. This relationship can be expressed in PL/I as

   OR

$X = A|B;$

The operator connecting A and B is known as the **OR** operator, and the statement is read "X equals A or B." Sometimes this condition is referred to by the expression "A and B are **OR**'d together." The **OR** operator provides a very compact way of saying "When either A or B or both are true, the event X will be true; otherwise X will be false." A very handy way of analyzing a logical statement is to construct a *truth table*. This type of structure (shown below left, for the statement $X = A|B;$) is developed by considering all possible combinations of conditions for the events represented on the right-hand side of the equals sign (A and B in our case) and determining the outcome of the remaining event (X) for each combination listed. The same truth table in terms of bit string values is shown below right. Although this may appear to be unnecessary for the simple situation $X = A|B;$ the construction and use of a truth table becomes very helpful for more complicated situations.

Condition of A	Condition of B	Condition of X	Value of A	Value of B	Value of X
True	True	True	1	1	1
True	False	True	1	0	1
False	True	True	0	1	1
False	False	False	0	0	0

Now that we have examined all of the conditions under which our rat will or will not achieve point P2, we can extend our analysis to an examination of the conditions that must prevail for penetration to point P3. These can be stated verbally as follows: "To get at the cheese, the rat must attain point P2 and door 3 must be open." This can be written in PL/I as

Y = X&C;

X and C in these statements are connected by a link known as the **AND** operator (that is, variables X and C are **AND**ed together). (A surprisingly small amount of jargon has managed to entrench itself among designers and users of computer languages. Computerniks are fundamentally literate people, because they must often be facile in many tongues; they refrain almost naturally from violent transgressions against good taste in English usage. To those who cringe with us at the sight of such things as **OR**ing and **AND**ing, we offer the consoling thought that it could have been worse.) [(2nd ed.) It is worse.] Use of the **AND** operator carries the implication that the event on the left-hand side of the = sign (Y in our case) can only be true when both variables connected by the **AND** operator (X and C in our case) are true; under all other conditions Y will be false. We can represent this statement by the following truth table on the left repeated on the right in terms of bit string values.

Condition of X	Condition of C	Condition of Y	Value of X	Value of C	Value of Y
True	True	True	1	1	1
True	False	False	1	0	0
False	True	False	0	1	0
False	False	False	0	0	0

We can now produce a symbolic description for the complete Kolchikoff Triangular Rat Situation by replacing X with its equivalent expression, so that the outcome of Y is expressed in terms of the outcomes of the three events A, B, and C. Symbolically stated,

Y = (A|B) & C;

The complete truth table for this expression is shown above. Note that the parentheses are needed because & has higher priority than |. If we were to write

Y = A|B&C;

the result would be quite different for some combinations of values. This difference is completely analogous to the difference between (A + B)*C and A + B*C. To see this difference more clearly, consider the statements

Y = (A|B)&C;   and   Y = A|(B&C);

These two statements obviously represent two different logical situations, as can be seen by comparing the following table on the left, representing the KTRS, with the table on the right, summarizing the second of the two statements.

A	B	A|B	C	Y		B	C	B&C	A	Y
1	1	1	1	1		1	1	1	1	1
1	0	1	1	1		1	0	0	1	1
0	1	1	1	1		0	1	0	1	1
0	0	0	1	0		0	0	0	1	1
1	1	1	0	0		1	1	1	0	1
1	0	1	0	0		1	0	0	0	0
0	1	1	0	0		0	1	0	0	0
0	0	0	0	0		0	0	0	0	0

A third logical operator, known as the **NOT** operator, is available for use with bit strings. If we write the statements

$$D = \neg \; E;$$

the conditions implied by the operator are that whenever E is true, D is false, and vice versa. **NOT** may be combined with either of the other two logical operators to form legitimate logical expressions. As an illustration, the following is a truth table for the statement

$$F = D \& \neg E;$$

The two logical operators **AND** and **OR** cannot appear consecutively without an intervening bit string constant or variable. In other words, $\neg$ is a *prefix* operator while | and & are *infix* operators.

E	¬E	D	F
1	0	1	0
1	0	0	0
0	1	1	1
0	1	0	0

Having developed the basic usage for the three logical operators, we can now extend their application to longer bit strings. Logical operations with these longer strings proceed in exactly the same way as with single bits. The indicated operation is performed sequentially on the first bit of each string, then the second, and so on, until each pair has thus been processed. Table 11.2 shows the results of several logical operations on three particular bit strings of equal length. If two bit strings combined by a logical operator are of unequal length, and the bit string to contain the result contains sufficient positions

TABLE 11.2 Logical Operations on
            Multicharacter Bit
            Strings*

Statement	Contents of D
D = A&B;	'100001'B
D = AIBIC;	'111111'B
D = A&B&C;	'000001'B
D = A&B&¬C;	'100000'B
D = (A& ¬B)IC;	'011111'B
D = A&¬(BIC);	'000010'B

* A = '100011'B
  B = '101001'B
  C = '011101'B;
  D is declared as **BIT**(6).

to accommodate the longer of the strings, the operation will be performed after adding zeros to the right of the shorter string to fill it out. Hence, the statements

DECLARE (A,B) **BIT** (4), C**BIT**(2);

A = '1101'B;

C = '10'B;

B = A & C;

will produce a value of '1000'B in location B.

XI.3.2   Expressions Involving Bit Strings of Length One

The bit string of length 1 has an additional special use in PL/I. Certain types of expressions can be written to generate such a bit string whose value will reflect the conditions prevailing in that expression. It is possible to write an expression such as

Y = A > B;

Assume that A and B were numeric variables and Y is a bit string of length 1. The value '1'B will be stored if A is greater than B; otherwise, a '0'B will be placed in Y. If Y is not declared it will be **FLOAT DECIMAL**(6) and the bit string will be converted.

The expression that will generate this type of bit string may contain any of the eight relational operators. Each time a statement such as this is encountered, the value of the bit string will change depending on the truth or falsity of the relational expression. We have been exploiting these operations until now without being aware that they actually generate bit strings. If a relational expression involving the = operator is assigned to a variable we get a statement of the form

Y = A = B;

which must be interpreted carefully to avoid confusion: the equals sign on the left is the replacement or assignment operator; the one on the right is a relational operator.

Since an expression in which two terms are linked by a relational operator produces a bit string, we can link this expression with another bit string or another such expression by means of an appropriate logical operator to create an even more extensive expression. For example, if X, Y, and Z are bit strings obtained from the respective statements

X = A > (B+2);   Y = A < (B**2−17);

(assuming A and B had previously received some values), the statements

Z = X & Y;   and   Z = (A > (B + 2)) & (A < (B**2−17));

would both assign to Z a bit string whose value will reflect the truth or falsity of the relationship between numerical variables A and B. (Incidentally, the second of the two expressions given above can be rewritten without any of the parentheses without effect.) Table 11.3 illustrates the results of several such constructions.

TABLE 11.3 Examples of Expressions
            Generating Single-Bit Strings*

Expression	Value of B
B = X = 5	'0'B
B = X<Y|X<Z;	'0'B
B = X>Y&X>2*Z;	'1'B
B = X = 12&¬(X>Y + Z);	'1'B
B = X = 2*Z|Y¬<2*Z;	'0'B

*X = 12;
Y = 8;
Z = 5;

Illustration 28

We have the following program segment:

DECLARE (A,B) **FIXED**(6,2), **Y BIT**(1);

GET LIST (A,B);

Y = (2*A<3*B)&¬(A**2>12*B);

PUT LIST (Y);

END;

The problem is to find the value printed by the **PUT LIST** statement when values of 3 and 9 are read in for A and B, respectively.

We shall evaluate each of the expressions in parentheses and then perform the indicated logical operation on them. When A = 3 and B = 9, 2*A(6 in this case) is indeed less than 3*B (27 in this case), so that the comparison indicated in the first expression is true, and we can represent that condition by establishing a bit string (in concept) whose value is one. In the second expression, A**2 (9 in this case) is not greater than 12*B (108 in this case), so the current condition of that comparison is false. We shall represent that condition by a mental bit string with a value of zero. Remaining now is the task of evaluting the resulting expression '1'**B** & ¬'0'**B**. Performing the **NOT** first changes the expression to '1'**B** & '1'**B**. The resulting value placed in Y, and hence, printed by the **PUT LIST**, is '1'**B**.

XI.3.3   General Expressions Involving Logical and Comparative Operators

We saw that the evaluation of arithmetic expressions proceeds in terms of a priority system in which the following sequence is observed:

1.   Prefix +, prefix −, **
2.   *, /
3.   Infix +, infix −

We can now work with an expanded set of operators, for which a similar order of precedence must be established. When an expression involves string, logical, and comparison operators as well as arithmetic ones, PL/I proceeds according to the following general priority schedule:

1.   ¬, prefix +, prefix −, **
2.   *, /
3.   infix +, infix −
4. ||
5.   > =, >, ¬ >, ¬ =, <, ¬<, < =, =
6.   &
7. |

Parentheses still exert the same effect; they alter the priorities in the overall expression. As an example, let us examine the statement

$$Y = ((A*B**2>12*A\&3*A< = 15)||(B\neg>7)) + 3;$$

for $A = 4$ and $B = 5$:

1. The square of B is calculated and stored.
2. AB^2 is calculated.
3. $12*A$ is calculated.
4. $3*A$ is calculated.
5. AB^2 is compared to 12A and value $'1'B$ is generated, since $4(25)^2$ is greater than 12(4).
6. $3*A$ is compared to 15, and a $'1'B$ is generated, since 3(4) is less than 15.
7. The two bit strings produced in Steps 4 and 5 are **AND**ed together, producing a single $'1'B$.
8. B is compared to 7 and, since the indicated relation is true, a $'1'B$ is produced.
9. The two values of $'1'B$ are concatenated, resulting in $'11'B$.
10. $'11'B$ is changed to 11_2 and added to 3, producing a value of 6.
11. The final conversion is made, if necessary, to match Y's attributes and the 6 is placed in Y.

XI.3.4   Bit Strings and the **IF** Statement

The ability to manipulate logical expressions in this fashion gives us some additional insight as to the mechanism behind the operation of the **IF** statement. Based on the properties of PL/I regarding bit strings, we can now restate the operations of the **IF** statement in more detail. The expression to be tested in an **IF** statement may be any expression that defines a bit string or can be converted to a bit string. If the string contains a 1 in any position, the program takes appropriate action by executing the statement following the word **THEN**. To illustrate, we can dissect the statement

IF $A\neg <B$ **THEN** C = D;

into the equivalent statements

$Y = A\neg <B;$ **IF** Y **THEN** C=D;

Of course, in a simple case like this, PL/I does not actually need to construct the bit string and test it since it can foresee the outcome of the test once the comparison has been made.

XI.3.5 Built-in Functions for Bit Strings

Several of PL/I's built-in functions for character string manipulations apply to bit strings as well. Specifically, the **REPEAT, STRING, SUBSTR, LENGTH, INDEX, TRANSLATE,** and **VERIFY** functions will operate with bit strings replacing the character string arguments. In addition, there are functions aimed at exploiting the on-off properties of bit strings to provide the programmer with virtually limitless capabilities for true-false decision structures.

XI.3.5.1 The **BOOL** Function

The **BOOL** function is a very useful operation whereby it is possible for the programmer to set up and use as complicated a true-false decision network as he finds necessary, with a relatively minor amount of inconvenience and toil.

The basic form for this function is

BOOL(arg1, arg2, arg3)

where arg1 and arg2 are two-bit strings to be combined and arg3 is a four-bit string which specifies the set of rules to be used. The operation works as follows: each position in arg1 is considered along with the corresponding position in arg2. Since only 1's or 0's are involved, there are only four possible situations that can exist. These correspond to the four positions of arg3, as shown below.

Contents of Position in arg1	Contents of Position in arg2	Value of Result Bit
0	0	Position 1 in arg3
0	1	Position 2 in arg3
1	0	Position 3 in arg3
1	1	Position 4 in arg3

For example, if Position 1 of arg3 contains a 1, the program will generate a 1 each time any pair of corresponding positions in arg1 and arg2 contain 0's. Similarly, if Position 3 in arg3 contains a 1 as well, the program will also generate a 1 wherever a position in arg1 contains a 1 and the same position in arg2 contains a 0. This process continues for each position over the entire length of the strings. If arg1 and arg2 have different lengths, PL/I will pad the shorter one with 0's (to the right) until the lengths match. Thus, by making a bit string available in an assignment statement such as

Z = **BOOL**(X,Y,W);

the programmer will end up with Z containing a series of 1's and 0's reflecting the outcome of the sequential application of the rule defined by W to the corresponding positions in X and Y.

The student should observe that the use of **BOOL** with the third argument equal to '0111' or

'0001' corresponds to the operation | and &, respectively. Similarly, '1100' corresponds to
¬applied to arg1 (ignoring arg2 entirely).

Illustration 29

The Mate-Arama Matching Service is interested in bringing suitable soul mates together for
high purposes by storing people's characteristics (physical information, likes, dislikes, opin-
ions, and so on) and using these data to find optimally matched couples. The "client profile" is
compiled by having the individual answer a series of 18 "yes or no" questions, with each "yes"
being recorded as a 1 and each "no" as a 0. For purposes of this illustration, a file of 331 female
client profiles is stored in memory, and each male client's profile is read individually and
compared to the entire file. The matching rules are as follows:

1. If boy and girl both answer "yes" to the same question, score a 1.
2. If boy and girl both answer "no" to a given question, score a 1.
3. If they disagree on a question, score a 0.
4. A boy and a girl are "matched" if their "compatability profile" contains at least
    twelve 1's.

The data for each profile are punched on a card with the profile in columns 1-18 and the
indentification number in columns 77-80.

Write a program to list the possible soul mates, using a separate page for each male client.
Show the results of the matching procedures for a boy with the profile

0	1	1	0	0	0	1	1	0	1	0	1	1	0	1	1	0	0

and a girl with the profile

1	1	0	0	1	0	0	1	1	0	1	0	1	0	0	0	1	0

We shall start by organizing the data into a very simple structure form. Female profiles will
be stored as an array of structures consisting of the profile itself, which we shall treat as an
18-position bit string, and the i.d. number. The male data will be similarly organized, but we
shall not need an array.

Our decision rules can be used to construct a four-position bit string as follows:

1. Since we want two "noes" (by boy and girl) to be scored as a 1, the first position of
    arg3 in our **BOOL** function setup must be 1.
2. Positions 2 and 3 in our arg3 will be 0's, in accordance with rule 3 above.
3. By the same token, position 4 will be a 1, since it reflects the presence of two 1's.

We shall store the results of the comparisons on a place called COMPAT. Using the self-
explanatory qualified names BOY.PROFILE and GIRL.PROFILE, our comparison statement would read

COMPAT = **BOOL**(BOY.PROFILE, GIRL.PROFILE, '1001'**B**);

Now we can incorporate this into our program as follows:

```
ILL29: PROCEDURE OPTIONS (MAIN);
       DECLARE 1 BOY,
                 2 PROFILE BIT(18),
                 2 IDENT FIXED BINARY,
               1 GIRL(331),
                 2 PROFILE BIT(18),
                 2 IDENT FIXED BINARY,
               COMPAT BIT(18),
               (COUNT, SCORE, NDFILE, J) FIXED BINARY;

       NDFILE = 0;   ON ENDFILE (SYSIN) NDFILE=1;
       GET EDIT (GIRL) (R(SHAPE));
SHAPE: FORMAT(B(18),X(58),F(4));
       GET EDIT (BOY) (R(SHAPE));

/** IN OUR PROCESSING LOOP, EACH BOY WILL BE COMPARED TO EACH **/
/** OF THE 331 GIRLS' PROFILES IN TURN. THE COMPATABILITY WILL**/
/** DEVELOPED AS AN 18-BIT STRING USING THE BOOL FUNCTION. THE**/
/** SCORE WILL BE COMPUTED BY GOING THROUGH THAT STRING.     **/

       DO WHILE (NDFILE = 0);
         PUT PAGE LINE(3) EDIT ('REPORT FOR BOY NO.  ',BOY.IDENT)
            (X(20),A,F(4),SKIP);      COUNT=0;
         DO I=1 TO 331;
           COMPAT = BOOL(BOY.PROFILE, GIRL.PROFILE(I), '1001'B);
           SCORE = 0;
           DO J=1 TO 18;
             SCORE = SCORE + SUBSTR(COMPAT,J,1);
           END;
           IF SCORE >= 12
             THEN PUT SKIP EDIT('NO. ',GIRL(I).IDENT,
                  'MATCHES WITH A SCORE OF ',SCORE)
                  (X(10),A,F(4),A,F(2));
           COUNT = COUNT+1;
         END;
         IF COUNT = 0
           THEN PUT SKIP(2) EDIT ('SORRY, WE HAVE NO ONE FOR YOU')
                          (X(10),A);
           ELSE PUT SKIP(2) EDIT ('TOTAL NO. OF MATCHES = ',COUNT)
                          (X(10),A,F(3));
       END;

       END ILL29;
```

Based on our decision rule ('1001'**B**), we can compare the two profiles and determine the resulting compatibility profile. This is shown as follows:

Value of BOY.PROFILE	0	1	1	0	0	0	1	1	0	1	0	1	1	0	1	1	0	0
Value of GIRL.PROFILE	1	1	0	0	1	0	0	1	1	0	1	0	1	0	0	0	1	0
Position number for decision rule	2	4	3	1	2	1	3	4	2	3	2	3	4	1	3	3	2	1
Value in COMPAT	0	1	0	1	0	1	0	1	0	0	0	0	1	1	0	0	0	1

Adding the 1's together in COMPAT, we find a total value of 7, which, sad to say, is not sufficient for a match. There are better uses for computers.

XI.3.5.2   The **UNSPEC** Function

Each character is uniquely distinguished from all others by having a particular internal representation assigned to it. As seen in Appendix B, these representations can be expressed in terms of bit strings (eight bits being required to represent each single character). When a value is placed in a particular location, it is stored as the concatenation of these bit strings, the composition of which depends on the type of data being stored as well as its value. PL/I provides the program with the ability to obtain this internal representation by means of the **UNSPEC** function. By writing an expression of a general form,

UNSPEC(arg1)

UNSPEC will return a bit string showing the internal coding for arg1. The argument may be any legitimate single valued expression. Thus, assuming that variable Z is declared with the attributes **BIT**(8), the statement

Z = **UNSPEC**('W');

$$E\ 6$$

will place the string '11100110' in location Z, reflecting the internal representation of the character W. This is especially helpful in tracing error sources in a program, since it can be used to obtain a visual display of a location's contents which, with an ordinary **PUT** statement, would appear to be blank or zero. **UNSPEC** may also appear as a pseudovariable.

XI.3.5.3   The **HIGH** and **LOW** Functions

Although these are actually character string functions, they are closely tied in with the internal representation of digits, symbols, and characters. Since each type of character sets up a unique code in memory which can be expressed as an eight-position bit string, that string can also be treated as a binary number with a magnitude unique for the particular character. For example, the internal code for the letter T is '11100011', or binary value of 227, while the slash (/) is coded internally as '01100001'; or 97. In this sense, T is "higher" than / (Appendix B shows the entire list). Each type of processor is designed to accept a particular set of characters; one will be "highest" and one will have the "lowest" value.

If the PL/I programmer wishes to place the processor's highest character in a particular location, he can use the **HIGH** function in a statement of the form

A = **HIGH**(n);

when (n) is a decimal integer constant indicating how many times the highest character is to be repeated in location A (which presumably was declared as a character string of length n). Similarly, the statement

B = **LOW**(n);

would place n duplicates of the processor's "lowest" characters in location B.

These functions are needed for two reasons:

1. The highest and lowest characters '11111111'**B** and '00000000'**B** are usually unassigned, so the programmer has no convenient way to represent them.

2. Even if the above were not the case, the character corresponding to '11111111'**B** might be different on different processors; thus, the use of **HIGH** would make the program "machine-independent."

XI.3.5.4   The **ANY** and **ALL** Functions

Two built-in functions are provided specifically for use with arrays of bit strings. The **ALL** function operates on a single argument (the name of a bit string array) in the following manner. When used in a statement such as

Y = **ALL**(X);

where Y is a bit string variable of the same length as an element in array X, corresponding positions in all of the elements are examined. If all of them contain a 1, a 1 is placed in that position of Y. Otherwise, a 0 is placed there. Thus, if X is an array of three bit strings, each eight positions long, and Y is a single bit string of the same length, the statements

X(1) = '10110111'**B**;

X(2) = '00100001'**B**;

X(3) = '10011001'**B**;

  Y = **ALL**(X);

will place the value '00000001'**B** in location Y. In other words, all of the elements of X are **AND**ed together and the result placed in Y.

XI.3.5.5   The **BIT** Function

This is exactly analogous to the **CHAR** function; it will convert character strings or numbers containing 1's and 0's to bit strings. The form

BIT(arg1)

converts the entire argument and places it as directed by the programmer. The alternative argument form

BIT(arg1,n)

allows the programmer to limit the number of digits or characters that are converted.

PROBLEMS

1. Assuming that X, Y, Z, and A are each bit strings of length 1, construct truth tables for the following statements:

    a. A = ¬ X & Y;

    b. A = (X & ¬ Y)|Z;

    c. A = (X & Y) & (Z| ¬ Y);

    d. A = X|(Y & Z) & (¬ Z|'1'**B**);

    e. A = X¬ (Y/Z) & Y & (Y|X);

2. C is declared as **BIT**(5) and

    X = '10101'**B**

    Y = '01110'**B**

    Z = '10001'**B**

    W = '110'**B**

    Find the contents of C for

    a. C = X|Y;

    b. C = X|(Y|¬ Z);

    c. C = X|(Y&Z);

    d. C = X&W&¬ Z;

    e. C = (X&¬ Y) & (¬ Z|¬ W);

    f. C = W|(Y&X&¬ Z);

3.　If　$X = 12$
　　　$Y = 7$
　　　$Z = 4$
　　　$W = 3$

determine the contents of A for the following statements:

a.　$A = 2*X = 2*W*Z;$

b.　$A = X*Y|Z*W \neg > W+3;$

c.　$A = \textbf{SQRT}(X*W)|Z < (Y+Z)|W;$

d.　$A = (Z**W|X \neg < Y|Z) \ \& \ (Y*Z \neg = W*X-6);$

e.　$A = (Z**W|X \neg < Y|(Z+W))|\neg(Y*Z \neg = W*X-6);$

f.　$A = Z**2 + W*Y + (Z+W = Y);$

g.　$A = W*X|(Y+2) - (2*Y>W**2);$

4.　If　$X = $　'11010'**B** and
　　　$Y = $　'01101'**B** and
　　　Z is declared as **BIT**(5)

find the contents of Z for the following statements:

a.　$Z = \textbf{BOOL}(X,Y,'1111'\textbf{B});$

b.　$Z = \textbf{BOOL}(Y,X,'0110'\textbf{B});$

c.　$Z = \textbf{BOOL}(X,Y,'0010'\textbf{B});$

d.　$Z = \textbf{BOOL}(X,Y,'0101'\textbf{B});$

e.　$Z = \textbf{BOOL}(X,Y,'1010'\textbf{B});$

5.　An examination consists of 50 multiple-choice questions. Only one of the four choices for each question is the correct one. The examinations are graded by a machine which punches the answer to each question (1,2,3, or 4) in a separate column of a punched card, so that each paper generates a card with data in columns 1-50. If more than one choice is marked, a 5 is punched in the corresponding column and the answer is scored as incorrect. If no choice is given, a 6 is punched, and the answer is, of course, marked as being "wrong." Columns 51-70 contain the examinee's name and 75-80 contain the student's number. A minimum score of 36 is required to pass.

　　　Write a program that prints the names of all individuals who passed. Assume that the first data card contains the correct answers in columns 1-50.

6.　A specialized library wishes to institute a procedure for automatically providing key personnel with new documents of specific interest to them. Their classification scheme contains 32 subject headings. Each document, upon acquisition, is classified by assigning a 1 to each subject considered pertinent, with zeros being assigned to the remainder of the subjects. The results are recorded in columns 1-32 of a punched card, along with the document identification number, which is punched in columns 75-80. Similarly, each key person has examined the list of subject categories and selected a particular combination which reflects his interests. Each of these combinations is punched in columns 1-32 of a separate card, along with the person's name (columns 50-75) and department number (columns 77-80). The library has such cards for 237 users.

The system is to examine the week's new document cards and determine which document abstracts are to be sent to which user according to the following rules: if a particular subject is not marked for either the document or the user, score a 1 for that subject; if a particular subject is marked for both document and user, score 1 for that subject; score zero for all other contingencies. The minimum score required for a document abstract to be sent to a user is not fixed for the system. It is set for each user and appears in columns 45-46 of his card.

Write a program that prints the following page for each of the users:

User's Name		Department Number
	Minimum Score =	XX
Document Number		Score
XXXXX		XX
XXXXX		XX
etc.		etc.

7. After some additional experience, the library has decided that the decision rules described in the previous problem are not particularly realistic. For example, if Jones is interested in Transcendental Meditation and Botany, and document 236129 deals with Astrophysics, the score comes out 29. To improve the selectivity, the following rules are proposed: (a) if a subject is marked for both the document and the user, score 5; (b) if a subject is marked for the document but not for the user, score −1. Modify the program to incorporate this new executive thinking.

8. Suggest another method that would give each user of the library even greater control of the selection criteria to be used in identifying documents for him.

SUMMARY OF IMPORTANT TERMS

Bit	The attribute associated with bit strings. This attribute always must be explicitly declared.
Bit string	A sequence of independently manipulable 1's and 0's having a specified length and declared with the **BIT** attribute.
KTRS	The Kolchikoff Triangular Rat Situation.
Logical constant	'1'**B**(true) or '0'**B**(false).
Logical expression	A combination of terms whose resulting value can either be true or false.

Logical operator   The prefix operator ¬ and the infix operators & and |
                          available in PL/I for combining logical constants, vari-
                          ables, and expressions to construct more extensive log-
                          ical expressions.

Logical variable   A bit string of length 1 (or a one-bit substring of a larger
                          string). The value of a logical variable can be either $'1'\mathbf{B}$
                          or $'0'\mathbf{B}$.

Relational operator   One of eight types of comparisons ($=$, ¬ $=$, $<$, $<=$, $>$,
                          $>=$, ¬ $<$, ¬ $>$) available in PL/I for combining two
                          arithmetic expressions to form a logical expression.

Truth table   A summary showing the resulting values of a logical
                          expression for all possible combinations of values that
                          can be taken on by each term in that expression.

SUPPLEMENTARY READING

Korfhage, R.R., *Logic and Algorithms*. New York: Wiley, 1966. See, especially, Chapters 1 and 2.

XII CONTROL OF SEQUENCE IN A PROCEDURE

Using the **IF** statement, the **DO-WHILE** construct, and other controlled loops, we have been able to exercise sufficient control over the operating sequence in a procedure to construct and incorporate some fairly involved decision mechanisms. However, we have been making use of only a portion of the many facets of Pl/I's control facilities. Although this has not limited us too severely in terms of the type of procedures attempted thus far, it will constitute an impediment in subsequent explorations of the language. Before attempting to build more complex decision mechanisms we shall review the basic ones and build on them, so that we can acquaint ourselves with a wide range of PL/I's decision and control facilities.

In dealing with decisions and cyclic activities thus far, we have pointedly avoided the use of a very basic vehicle for redirecting the sequence of operations in a PL/I procedure. This vehicle is the **GO TO** statement. As the discussion in the next section shows, the **GO TO** statement is very explicit and straightforward. However, it is its very simplicity that has caused it to be overused to a point where the flow of events can be very cumbersome and difficult to follow, even in a relatively simple procedure. Consequently, such overuse has been identified with programs that are poorly designed and ultimately, difficult to develop and maintain. As is true with any such generalization, there will be an inevitable temptation to extrapolate, and some will not resist. Accordingly, the spectrum of practitioners includes a substantial number who equate badly structured (or unstructured) programs with the presence of **GO TO** statements, and (it is just a small step after that) good structure with the absence of **GO TO** statements.

A more helpful criterion, in our view, is clarity and legibility. There may be occasions where the judicious use of a **GO TO** statement represents a simple way to express a particular process, in which case its use is preferable to an alternative which is made awkward and convoluted specifically in order to avoid such usage. Consequently, we shall describe the statement and its properties, after which its usage will be considered in the larger (and more useful) context of overall procedural clarity.

XII.1   THE **GO TO** STATEMENT

The basic form for this statement (known as the *unconditional* **GO TO** statement) is

$$\text{GO TO label;}$$

The word "label" represents an identifier attached to a particular statement by the programmer. Thus far, the procedure statement that begins a program and the **FORMAT** statement that describes a format referred to by one or more **GET EDIT** or **PUT EDIT** statements have represented the only occasions where labels were needed. Almost any type of PL/I statement can be labeled. (The **DECLARE** statement cannot be labeled, and the **IF** and **GO TO** statements should not be labeled). In addition, it is possible to have a label without any statement at all. For instance, the construction

$$\text{OVER: ;}$$

is legitimate. This is known as a *null statement*. An additional capability (which we mention for completeness) allows the attachment of more than one label to a single PL/I statement. Thus, for example, the following statement

$$\text{WHERE: DEST: X=2*X;}$$

can be referred to by either of the two labels attached to it.

It is possible to enhance the flexibility of the **GO TO** statement by providing a choice of destinations. PL/I provides one way of doing this by recognizing variable labels. These are treated as another data type, in the same general category as numbers, character strings, or bit strings. The pertinent forms and properties are discussed in the following sections.

XII.1.1   Statement Label Variables

To increase the opportunities for control of sequences in a PL/I procedure, provisions are included for a special type of variable whose values represent statement labels. Such variables are defined by declaration, using the **LABEL** attribute:

DECLARE name **LABEL**;

The name of a statement label variable may be any legitimate variable name. The values assigned to such a variable must appear as statement labels on some statement in the program. Such values should not be confused with character strings, even though they seem to have that form. The most obvious use for this type of designation is to create the possibility for a **GO TO** statement to have a variable destination. Instead of directing a program to a particular statement identified by a specific label, the program can be constructed to direct its attention to the statement whose label is currently stored in the statement label variable. To illustrate, let us consider the following sequence:

DECLARE (A,B) **FIXED**, PLACE **LABEL**;

GET LIST (A,B);

IF A<B **THEN** PLACE = HERE1;

  ELSE IF A = B **THEN** PLACE = HERE2;

             ELSE PLACE = HERE3;

GO TO PLACE;

     .
     .
     .

HERE1: statement;

     .
     .
     .

HERE2: statement;

     .
     .
     .

HERE3: statement;

As a result of this processing, the newly read values in A and B are compared to each other. The outcome of that comparison places a particular statement label constant in label variable PLACE. Accordingly, the ensuing **GO TO** statement acts as a pivot to one of three possible destinations. Of course, the particular action illustrated here could have been handled just as easily by placing the appropriate **GO TO** statements in place of the assignments to PLACE and eliminating PLACE entirely. Label variables provide another alternative, which is sometimes more convenient.

One of the most common errors regarding statement label variables is the attempt to use them like other variables. (We already have indicated that they are not character strings and cannot be used interchangeably with them.) There is no direct way to use such variables for input or output except with the Checkout Compiler; attempts to do so will produce an error condition.

XII.1.2   Declaration of Label Variables for Efficient Processing

It is possible to restrict the use of label variables to a particular set of names by writing a declaration such as

DECLARE name **LABEL** (label2, label3,label4,etc.);

where "name" is still any legitimate variable name. The parenthesized list represents a set of actual labels assigned to statements elsewhere in the program. This type of declaration limits the choice of names to be placed in the statement label variable to those specified in the list. As such, it frequently permits the compiler to handle the variable more efficiently, especially if all values to be assigned to the variable are within the block in which the variable is declared. Furthermore, each name given in this list must appear as an actual label in a statement. If it does not, a message to that effect will be generated.

XII.1.3   Arrays of Label Variables

Label variables may be declared as arrays having single or multiple dimensions. This adds to the overall versatility of such variables because it is possible to use such array elements in two distinct ways: First, each element serves as an ordinary label variable in that a statement label constant may be assigned to it. Second, it is also permissible to use the actual subscripted element name as a statement label constant. Thus, if we write the statement

DECLARE WHERE(3) **LABEL**;

PL/I will set up an array named WHERE, each of whose three elements (WHERE(1), WHERE(2) and WHERE(3)) may itself appear as a statement label constant.

A simple example will illustrate how this could work: Suppose that our procedure requires the input of sets of values for variables N, X, Y, Z, A, and B. Furthermore, the processing of these variables may take one of three paths, depending on N. Using the previous declaration for array WHERE, we can construct the following sequence:

GET LIST (N,X,Y,Z,A,B);

GO TO WHERE(N);

.

.

.

WHERE(1): statements;

.

.

.

WHERE(2): statements;

.

.

.

WHERE(3): statements;

.

.

.

Now, every time a new set of values is read in, the destination of the **GO TO** statement will be determined by the most recent value in N. Of course, in order for the mechanism to work, N's value always must be either 1, 2, or 3. In a more complete development of such a procedure, additional steps would be introduced to detect and handle situations in which N's value turns out to be out of range.

XII.2   THE CASE CONSTRUCT

From the very start, we have been building decision mechanisms with the **IF-THEN-ELSE** construct. This fundamental two-way selection vehicle has been seen to carry over directly into PL/I programming statements. Because of its fundamental nature, it can be used as a building block to construct more elaborate and complex decision networks. One such extension that suggests itself immediately is the type of situation in which there are more than two choices from which the mechanism must select.

While such structures can be implemented readily from combinations of the basic **IF-THEN-ELSE**, an additional construct often is used as a more convenient alternative. This is known as the *case construct*, the name reflects the implied decision activity: "Select case *i* from among the *n* available choices and perform the activity associated with case *i*". The flowchart representations in Figure 12.1 emphasize the fact that the entire process of making the choice and performing the corresponding activity is perceived as a single (structural) activity. This is underscored further by the following observations about the structure:

1.   The activities available as choices can be completely arbitrary. For instance, one of the activities may be long and complex while another may consist of nothing at all

(i.e., a *null activity*). Moreover, two or more of the choices may prompt the same activity. In any event, each choice is linked with its corresponding (conceptual) activity. Once that activity is concluded (regardless of what it might entail) processing reunites at the common thread. Thus, as is true with any other well-designed program construct, there is one entry and one exit.

2. The basic integrity of the construct is unaffected by any changes in the details. Thus, modification or replacement of an activity, or changes in the number of choices, leave the structure unperturbed.

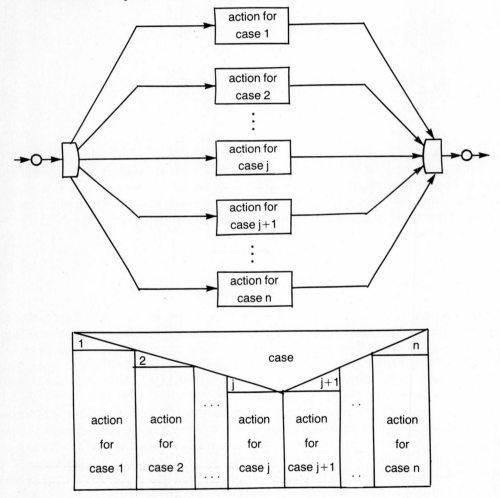

Figure 12.1

One way to implement the case construct in PL/I is to construct each of the alternative activities with a label attached to its first statement. The conceptual relationship among these activities is established by making these labels members (elements) of the same label array. The selection process determines which of these activities to pursue by defining an integer value that is used as the label array's subscript. Each activity ends with an unconditional **GO TO** statement that reunites the individual flows at a common junction symbolizing the conclusion of the case construct. Since this common junction has no activity associated with it (it is merely a conceptual point in the flow of events), a labeled null statement serves that purpose. For example, if the array of labels is named WHICH and J indicates the particular activity chosen, the general construct can be represented as shown in Figure 12.2.

```
          DECLARE  WHICH (10) LABEL, ....., J FIXED BINARY, ..... ;
                   .........
                   ........
          /** A VALUE IS ASSIGNED TO J BASED ON THE PARTICULAR CASE **/
                   .........
                   ........
          GO TO WHICH (J);

                          /** ACTION FOR CASE 1 **/
          WHICH(1):            .....
                               .....
                               .....
                          GO TO XCASE;

                          /** ACTION FOR CASE 2 **/
          WHICH(2):            .....
                               .....
                          GO TO XCASE;

                               ..
                               ..
                               ..
                          /** ACTION FOR CASE 10 **/
          WHICH(10):           .....
                               .....

                          /** CONCLUSION OF CASE CONSTRUCT **/
          XCASE: ;
```

Figure 12.2

Illustration 30

A utility company recognizes six types of users and provides a rate structure for each of them based on the amount of usage (in kilowatt hours) according to the following schedule:

Type of User	Discount	Rate Schedule
1 (single-unit residential)	5% if use < 750	14.50 + $0.04 per kwhr for usage > 500 kwhr up to 1000 kwhr + $0.06 per kwhr for usage above 1000 kwhr.
2 (multiple-unit residential)	5% if use < 850	$14.50 + $0.04 per kwhr for usage > 500 kwhr up to 1000 kwhr + $0.055 per kwhr for usage above 1000 kwhr.
3 (single-unit commercial)	5% if use < 1650	$17.00 + $0.045 per kwhr for usage > 1000 kwhr up to 1500 kwhr + $0.065 per kwhr for usage over 1500 kwhr and up to 2000 kwhr + $0.080 per kwhr for usage over 2000 kwhr.

4	(multi-unit commercial)	5% if use < 1750	$17.00 + $0.045 per kwhr for usage > 1000 kwhr up to 1500 kwhr + $0.065 per kwhr for usage over 1500 kwhr and up to 2000 kwhr + $0.078 per kwhr for usage over 2000 kwhr.
5	(industrial)	5% if use < 1900	$24.00 + $0.043 per kwhr for usage > 1500 kwhr up to 2000 kwhr + $0.060 per kwhr for usage over 2000 kwhr and up to 3000 kwhr + $0.075 per kwhr for usage over 3000 kwhr.
6	(special industrial)	none	$42.50 + $0.082 per kwhr for usage over 2000 kwhr.

Data for each customer is recorded on a card containing an integer customer number in columns 1-6, a single digit usage code (1,2,3,4,5, or 6) in column 8, and the usage, to the nearest tenth of a kilowatt hour, in columns 11-15. For each user, the program is to print a line of output containing an echo of the input along with the gross billing amount, discount, and net billing amount.

The heart of the program is a case construct in which the proper rates are selected and used to determine the billing amounts. Note that the code for usage type serves as the subscript for the appropriate computation.

XII.3   EXPANDED USES OF THE **IF** STATEMENT

The **IF** statement already has played a very significant role in the work we have done thus far. However, we should recognize that the form in which we have employed it represents but the beginning of its capabilities. When used in this basic form, the **IF** statement allows the programmer to execute one of two arbitrarily complicated alternatives depending on the outcome of some comparison or the state of a particular set of conditions. Building on this foundation, it is possible to expand the complexity of the decision criteria to the point where entire networks of comparisons can be constructed to motivate correspondingly intricate webs of actions. Yet, by applying relatively simple expansions to the **IF...THEN...ELSE** syntax, such decision rules and consequences can be defined in a straightforward manner.

Illustration 30A

The expanded **IF** statement, especially the **ELSE IF** clause, provides a convenient alternative to label arrays for implementing the case construct. Many practitioners prefer this approach because its syntax is more "natural". We shall illustrate its use by rewriting the case construct from the previous example program. Note that the array of label variables no longer is needed. It is also relevant to point out that the programmer may be able to take advantage of this construction if he or she knows enough about the application to anticipate the relative likelihood of the appearance of a particular type. Such knowledge can be used to influence the

```
ILL30: PROCEDURE OPTIONS (MAIN);
/************************************************************/
/* USE:        ELECTRICAL USAGE, XXXX.X KWHRS           */
/* USERNO:     6-DIGIT USER I.D.                        */
/* TYPE:       USER TYPE (1,2,3,4,5, OR 6)              */
/* CASE:       A 6-ELEMENT LABEL ARRAY; EACH LABEL      */
/*             IS ATTACHED TO THE FIRST STATEMENT OF    */
/*             THE CORRESPONDING RATE COMPUTATION.      */
/* A USERNO VALUE OF 0 ENDS THE RUN.                    */
/************************************************************/
        DECLARE USERNO CHARACTER(6),
                (USE,GROSS,NET,DISC,TMP,TMP1,TMP2) FLOAT DECIMAL(6),
                CASE(6) LABEL,
                (TYPE,NDFILE) FIXED BINARY;

        NDFILE = 0;    ON ENDFILE(SYSIN) NDFILE=1;
        PUT PAGE LINE(3) EDIT ('ELECTRIC BILLING REPORT')(X(48),A);
        PUT SKIP EDIT('USER NO.','TYPE','KWHRS','GROSS AMT','DISCOUNT',
                'NET AMT')(COL(10),A,COL(25),A,COL(40),A,COL(55),A,
                        COL(70),A,COL(85),A,SKIP(2));
        GET EDIT(USERNO,TYPE,USE)(A(6),X(1),F(1),X(2),F(5,1)); GET SKIP;

        DO WHILE (NDFILE=0);
          DISC = 0;
          GO TO CASE(TYPE);
CASE(1): GROSS = 14.5;
        TMP = USE-500;    TMP1 = USE-1000;
        IF TMP > 0
          THEN DO;
                IF TMP1 > 0 THEN GROSS=GROSS+20+0.06*TMP1;
                        ELSE GROSS=GROSS+0.04*TMP;
               END;
        IF USE < 750 THEN DISC = 0.05*GROSS;
        GO TO ENDCASE;
CASE(2): GROSS = 14.5;
        TMP = USE-500;    TMP1 = USE-1000;
        IF TMP > 0
          THEN DO;
                IF TMP1 > 0 THEN GROSS=GROSS+20+0.055*TMP1;
                        ELSE GROSS=GROSS+0.04*TMP;
               END;
        IF USE < 850 THEN DISC=0.05*GROSS;
        GO TO ENDCASE;
CASE(3): GROSS = 17;
        TMP = USE-1000;    TMP1 = USE-1500;    TMP2 = USE-2000;
        IF TMP > 0
          THEN DO;
                IF TMP2 > 0 THEN GROSS=GROSS+22.5+32.5+0.08*TMP2;
                        ELSE DO;
                                IF TMP1 > 0
                                   THEN GROSS=GROSS+22.5+0.065*TMP1;
                                   ELSE GROSS=GROSS+0.045*TMP;
                             END;
               END;
        IF USE < 1650 THEN DISC=0.05*GROSS;
        GO TO ENDCASE;
CASE(4): GROSS = 17;
        TMP = USE-1000;    TMP1 = USE-1500;    TMP2 = USE-2000;
        IF TMP > 0
          THEN DO;
                IF TMP2 > 0 THEN GROSS=GROSS+22.5+32.5+0.078*TMP2;
                        ELSE DO;
                                IF TMP1 > 0
                                   THEN GROSS=GROSS+22.5+.065*TMP1;
                                   ELSE GROSS=GROSS+0.045*TMP;
                             END;
               END;
        IF USE < 1750 THEN DISC=0.05*GROSS;
        GO TO ENDCASE;
```

```
CASE(5): GROSS = 24;
         TMP = USE-1500;    TMP1 = USE-2000;    TMP2 = USE-3000;
         IF TMP > 0
            THEN DO;
                     IF TMP2 > 0 THEN GROSS=GROSS+21.5+60+.075*TMP2;
                               ELSE DO;
                                       IF TMP1 > 0
                                          THEN GROSS=GROSS+21.5+.06*TMP1;
                                          ELSE GROSS=GROSS+.043*TMP;
                                    END;
                  END;
         IF USE < 1900 THEN DISC=0.05*GROSS;
         GO TO ENDCASE;
CASE(6): GROSS = 42.5;
         TMP = USE-2000;
         IF TMP > 0 THEN GROSS=GROSS+0.082*TMP;
ENDCASE: ;
         NET = ROUND(GROSS-DISC,2);
         PUT SKIP EDIT(USERNO,TYPE,USE,ROUND(GROSS,2),ROUND(DISC,2),NET)
            (COL(10),A(6),COL(27),F(1),COL(40),F(6,1),COL(55),P'$9999.99',
            COL(72),P'$999.99',COL(85),P'$9999.99');
         GET EDIT(USERNO,TYPE,USE)(A(6),X(1),F(1),X(2),F(5,1)); GET SKIP;
      END;

      END ILL30;
```

order in which the tests are specified. If such information is not available, it is reasonable to assume that the various types will appear with equal likelihood, so that the order of the tests is immaterial. The listing for the revised program is shown below. Note that with only six different cases, we already are beginning to compromise the program layout and are pressing against the right-hand margin. When this type of situation occurs, the programmer is encouraged to experiment with other indentations, blank lines, conspicuous borders (implanted as comments) and other layout and formatting aids that will overcome this restriction and still provide the visual clarity that allows the case construct to stand out and be identified easily. (In this regard, the layout of the case construct implementation exemplified in Illustration 30 has some slight advantage in that it is insensitive to the number of cases in a particular construct).

XII.3.1   The **THEN IF** Clause

As a first step toward an expansion of our comparison and decision-making capabilities, we can use another **IF** statement immediately after the **THEN**. This provides the opportunity to undertake additional comparisons if an initial one turns out to be true. Consider the sequence

IF X>4 **THEN IF** X<Y **THEN PUT LIST**('X IS WITHIN RANGE');

ELSE PUT LIST('X STILL TOO LARGE');

ELSE PUT LIST('X STILL TOO SMALL');

NEXT: next statement;

The **THEN...ELSE** combinations are treated very similarly to sets of parentheses; they are

```
ILL30A: PROCEDURE OPTIONS (MAIN);
        DECLARE USERNO CHARACTER(6),
                (USE,GROSS,NET,DISC,TMP,TMP1,TMP2) FLOAT DECIMAL(6),
                (TYPE,NDFILE) FIXED BINARY;

        NDFILE = 0;    ON ENDFILE(SYSIN) NDFILE=1;
        PUT PAGE LINE(3) EDIT ('ELECTRIC BILLING REPORT')(X(48),A);
        PUT SKIP EDIT('USER NO.','TYPE','KWHRS','GROSS AMT','DISCOUNT',
                'NET AMT')(COL(10),A,COL(25),A,COL(40),A,COL(55),A,
                        COL(70),A,COL(85),A,SKIP(2));
        GET EDIT(USERNO,TYPE,USE)(R(INPTFM));    GET SKIP;
INPTFM: FORMAT(A(6),X(1),F(1),X(2),F(5,1));

        DO WHILE (NDFILE=0);
         DISC = 0;
         IF TYPE = 1
         THEN DO;
                GROSS = 14.5;  TMP = USE-500;   TMP1 = USE-1000;
                IF TMP > 0
                THEN IF TMP1 > 0 THEN GROSS=GROSS+20+.06*TMP1;
                                 ELSE GROSS=GROSS+0.04*TMP;
                IF USE < 750 THEN DISC = 0.05*GROSS;
              END;
         ELSE IF TYPE = 2
              THEN DO;
                     GROSS = 14.5;  TMP = USE-500;   TMP1 = USE-1000;
                     IF TMP > 0
                     THEN IF TMP1 > 0 THEN GROSS=GROSS+20+.055*TMP1;
                                      ELSE GROSS=GROSS+0.04*TMP;
                     IF USE < 850 THEN DISC = 0.05*GROSS;
                   END;
              ELSE IF TYPE = 3
                   THEN DO;
                          GROSS = 17; TMP=USE-1000; TMP1=USE-1500;
                          TMP2=USE-2000;
                          IF TMP > 0
                          THEN IF TMP2 > 0
                               THEN GROSS=GROSS+55+.08*TMP2;
                               ELSE IF TMP1 > 0
                                    THEN GROSS=GROSS+22.5+.065*TMP1;
                                    ELSE GROSS=GROSS+.045*TMP;
                          IF USE < 1650 THEN DISC=.05*GROSS;
                        END;
                   ELSE IF TYPE = 4
                        THEN DO;
                               GROSS = 17;  TMP=USE-1000;
                               TMP1=USE-1500; TMP2=USE-2000;
                               IF TMP > 0
                               THEN IF TMP2 > 0
                                    THEN GROSS=GROSS+55+.078*TMP2;
                                    ELSE IF TMP1 > 0
                                         THEN GROSS=GROSS+22.5+.065*TMP1;
                                         ELSE GROSS=GROSS+.045*TMP;
                               IF USE < 1750 THEN DISC=.05*GROSS;
                             END;
                        ELSE IF TYPE = 5
                             THEN DO;
                                    GROSS=24; TMP=USE-1500;
                                    TMP1=USE-2000; TMP2=USE-3000;
                                    IF TMP > 0
                                    THEN IF TMP2 > 0
                                         THEN GROSS=GROSS+81.5+.075*TMP2;
                                         ELSE IF TMP1 > 0
                                              THEN GROSS=GROSS+21.5
                                              ELSE GROSS=GROSS+.043*TMP;
                                    IF USE < 1900 THEN DISC=.05*GROSS;
                                  END;
```

```
                                  ELSE IF TYPE = 6
                                       THEN DO;
                                               GROSS=42.5;
                                               IF USE-2000 > 0
                                               THEN GROSS=GROSS+0.082*(USE-2000);
                                            END;
                                       ELSE DO;
                                               PUT SKIP LIST('USER NO. ',USERNO,
                                               'HAS AN ILLEGAL TYPE NO. OF ',TYPE);
                                               GO TO NXTIN;
                                            END;
                     NET = ROUND(GROSS-DISC,2);
                     PUT SKIP EDIT(USERNO,TYPE,USE,ROUND(GROSS,2),ROUND(DISC,2),NET)
                        (COL(10),A(6),COL(27),F(1),COL(40),F(6,1),COL(55),P'$9999.99',
                         COL(72),P'$999.99',COL(85),P'$9999.99');
              NXTIN: GET EDIT (USERNO,TYPE,USE)(R(INPTFM);    GET SKIP;
                  END;

       /*   NOTE THAT THIS VERSION OF THE EXAMPLE IS MORE COMPLETE THAN ILL30 */
       /*   IN THAT IT INCLUDES AN EXPLICIT TEST FOR EACH OF THE SIX TYPES.   */
       /*   THE PREVIOUS VERSION ASSUMES THAT IF A USER'S TYPE IS NOT ONE OF  */
       /*   THE FIRST FIVE, IT IS AUTOMATICALLY THE SIXTH - A SHAKY BUSINESS. */
       /*   CONSEQUENTLY, WE OMITTED THE TEST IN THE PREVIOUS VERSION SO THAT */
       /*   IT COULD BE POINTED OUT MORE EMPHATICALLY: IT IS GOOD PRACTICE TO */
       /*   MAKE SURE THAT ALL SUCH POSSIBILITIES ARE COVERED. THIS EXAMPLE   */
       /*   ALSO ILLUSTRATES THE USE OF AN EXPLICIT GO TO STATEMENT AS A      */
       /*   SIMPLE WAY OF AVOIDING AN ACTIVITY. IN THIS INSTANCE, ONCE WE     */
       /*   FOUND THAT THE TYPE WAS IN ERROR, THERE WAS NO POINT IN PRINTING  */
       /*   THE REGULAR OUTPUT LINE. SO, WE SIMPLY BYPASSED IT AND JUMPED TO  */
       /*   THE POINT WHERE THE NEXT INPUT VALUES ARE READ. WE EMPHASIZE THAT */
       /*   THE PURPOSE WAS SIMPLIFICATION. (YOU ARE INVITED TO TAKE A LOOK AT*/
       /*   WHAT KIND OF ADDITIONAL PROGRAMMING WOULD BE NECESSARY TO AVOID   */
       /*   USING THE GO TO IN THAT SITUATION).                               */

           END ILL30A;
```

analyzed from the "innermost" pair outward. Perhaps this can be seen more clearly if we rewrite the previous sequence in the following form:

IF X>4

    THEN IF X<Y **THEN PUT LIST** ('X IS WITHIN RANGE');

                  ELSE PUT LIST ('X STILL TOO LARGE');

    ELSE PUT LIST ('X STILL TOO SMALL');

  next statement;

In situations such as this, the programmer should take full advantage of PL/I's tolerance to variations in source program formats in order to facilitate the job of keeping track of such relationships.

Based on what we have learned about bit strings (Chapter 11), a little thought should reveal that this dual comparison could have been simplified by writing

IF X>4 & X<Y **THEN PUT LIST** ('X IS WITHIN RANGE');

                  ELSE PUT LIST ('X IS OUT OF RANGE');

  next statement;

This comparison will certainly work and may be simpler to write. However, the programmer loses the opportunity to provide special action at each stage of a chain of comparisons. When such flexibility is necessary, he can make use of any number of **IF...THEN...ELSE** combinations.

Although the compiler is equipped to do some of the bookkeeping, it is really up to the programmer to make sure that the **IFS** and **ELSES** are balanced. If there is an extra **ELSE**, the compiler will usually detect it and alert the programmer. In some cases, however, it will go ahead and delete one of them, arbitrarily deciding that the last one it finds is the extra one. If the programmer supplies one **ELSE** too few, the deficiency will not be noticed during compilation. Instead, it may go undetected until such time as it is needed in a particular run. As an example, let us examine the following sequence:

```
GET LIST(A,B,C,D);

IF A = 2*B

   THEN IF C = 3*A

          THEN IF D = B THEN PUT LIST(A);

                        ELSE PUT LIST(B);

          ELSE PUT LIST(C);

              .
              .
              .
```

This sequence is perfectly valid; however, it may or may not be what the programmer intended. Suppose that this procedure were executed using input values of 10, 5, 20, and 12, for A, B, C, and D, respectively. Since A is in fact equal to twice the value of B, the expression in the first **IF** statement will be true, and C will be compared to 3*A. Since this equality is not true for this set of values, the third **IF** (and the **ELSE** that goes with it) will be skipped, and the value of C will be printed accordingly. Suppose, however, that A = 9 (with the other three remaining as they were). Now the expression in the first **IF** statement would be false, causing the program to skip the two subsequent **IF**s, together with their corresponding **ELSE**s; it would therefore print nothing. If this is what was desired, everything is fine; otherwise the programmer may need to add an additional **ELSE** clause to provide an action for every alternative.

If the programmer finds it unnecessary or undesirable to provide an alternative action for each **THEN** clause, he need not do so. However, in an involved series of comparisons, it may be of help to provide a symmetrical situation in which each **THEN** clause is balanced by a corresponding **ELSE** clause, even when the latter specifies no action. This is done by using a *null* **ELSE** (also known as an *empty* **ELSE**), consisting of the word **ELSE** followed by a semicolon. The inclusion of such a statement does not actually do anything; it allows PL/I to match the clauses in accordance with the intentions of the programmer.

To accomodate those situations in which the existence of a certain conditon (rather than its absence) calls for no action, it is possible to specify an empty **THEN**. Thus, suppose we had the following decision rule: "If Y exceeds the square root of X, do nothing; if it does not, double it." Obviously, we can turn it around and use the form

IF Y <= **SQRT**(X) **THEN** Y = 2*Y;

next statement;

or even

IF Y   > **SQRT**(X) **THEN** Y = 2*Y;

next statement;

However, if we want to preserve the decision rule as it is represented in English we can do so by saying

IF Y > X **THEN**;

          ELSE Y = 2*Y;

next statement;

XII.3.2   The **ELSE IF** Clause

The expanded **IF** statement can be combined with the word **ELSE** and used to initiate any kind of chain of decision structures, including additional **THEN** clauses, **ELSE** clauses, and so on.

Illustration 31

As an additional example we shall consider the following situation:

The Nocturnal Aircraft Company uses the following procedure to estimate the approximate weight of an airplane:
The nominal weight is established by using the equation

$$\text{Weight} = 4960 \times \text{length}^{1.1}$$

where the weight is in pounds and the length is given in feet.
    If the length is 30-50 feet, 8 percent is added to the nominal weight.
    If the length is greater than 50 feet but less than 60 feet, 9 percent is added to the nominal weight.
    For lengths 60 feet or greater, but less than 80 feet, 10.5 percent is added to the nominal weight.

```
TLL31: PROCEDURE OPTIONS (MAIN);
/*****************************************************************/
/** LTH IS THE LENGTH;            WNG IS THE WINGSPAN;      **/
/** WN IS THE NOMINAL WEIGHT;    WT IS THE TOTAL WEIGHT;   **/
/** CL AND CSP ARE THE CORRECTION FACTORS FOR LENGTH, SPAN.**/
/*****************************************************************/

        DECLARE CONFIG CHARACTER(5),
               (LTH,WNG,WN,WT,CL,CSP) FLOAT DECIMAL(6),
               NOFILE FIXED BINARY INITIAL (0);

        ON ENDFILE(SYSIN) NOFILE=1;
        PUT PAGE LINE(3) EDIT ('NOCTURNAL AVIATION WEIGHT ANALYSIS')
                        (X(43),A);
        PUT SKIP(2) EDIT ('CONFIGURATION','WEIGHT','SPAN','NOM.WT.',
           'TOTAL WT.')(X(10),A,X(6),A,X(4),A,X(6),A,X(10),A);
        PUT SKIP(2);
        GET EDIT (CONFIG,LTH,WNG)(R(INFMT));      GET SKIP;
INFMT: FORMAT (A(5),X(1),F(4),X(6),F(4,1));

        DO WHILE (NOFILE=0);
/*---WE SHALL SEPARATE THE PROCESSING INTO--*/
/*---THOSE CONFIGURATIONS WITH LTH < 30    --*/
/*---AND THE OTHERS; THE FORMER WILL BE     --*/
/*---BYPASSED AND A MESSAGE PRINTED.       --*/
/*---FIRST, THE LENGTH CORRECTION (CL)--*/

            IF LTH >= 30
            THEN DO;
                    IF LTH <= 50
                      THEN CL = 0.08;
                      ELSE IF LTH < 60
                            THEN CL = 0.09;
                            ELSE IF LTH < 80
                                  THEN CL = 0.105;
                                  ELSE CL = 0.122;

                    /**----WINGSPAN CORRECTION---**/

                    CSP = 0;
                    IF WNG < 0.6*LTH
                      THEN CSP = -0.037;
                      ELSE IF WNG > 0.7*LTH THEN CSP = 0.045;
                    WN = 4960 * LTH**1.1;
                    WT = WN * (1+CL+CSP);
                    PUT SKIP EDIT(CONFIG,LTH,WNG,WN,WT)(X(10),A(5),
                        X(15),F(5,1),X(4),F(5,1),X(6),F(11,3),X(5),F(11,3);
                END;
            ELSE PUT SKIP EDIT(CONFIG,LTH,WNG,
                'INSUFFICIENT LENGTH: NO WEIGHT COMPUTED')
                (X(10),A(5),X(15),F(5,1),X(4),F(5,1),X(6),A);
            GET EDIT (CONFIG,LTH,WNG)(R(INFMT));    GET SKIP;
        END;

        END TLL31;
```

For all lengths 80 feet and over, a standard 12.2 percent is added to the nominal weight. If the wingspan is less than 60 percent of the length, deduct 3.7 percent from the nominal weight.

If the wingspan is at least 60 percent but not more than 70 percent of the length, no weight adjustment is necessary.

All other wingspans require a 4.5 percent addition to the nominal weight calculated from the equation.

The adjustments all refer to the nominal weight and are independent of each other.

Write a program that reads in the length and wingspan for a given configuration and prints the nominal weight and estimated total weight. The data for each configuration are punched on a card as shown below:

Card Columns	Identification	Format
1-5	Configuration number	4 digits followed by a letter
7-10	Length in feet	XXX X
17-20	Wingspan, feet	XXX X

We shall implement the adjustment rules by means of a set of **IF...THEN...ELSE** combinations.

XII.4   THE **DO** STATEMENT

Although the **DO** statement has already demonstrated its usefulness and flexibility, we have employed only part of its capabilities. Generalization of these facilities will allow the convenient implementation of more extensive cyclic processes as well as more powerful decision structures.

XII.4.1   Nesting of **DO** Groups

Since the intent of the **DO** group is to provide a general vehicle for constructing a "compound" statement, one would expect PL/I to allow the inclusion of an **IF** statement as part of that synthesized activity. Such construction, of course, is quite legal. In that light, it would seem natural to specify another **DO** group as an activity precipitated by the embedded **IF** statement. This, too, is permitted. In fact, we have already used such construction earlier (Illustration 27), doing so without any fanfare precisely because it is straightforward and appears reasonable. Such *nested* **DO** groups may be developed to any depth. When this is done, PL/I must follow some rules so that it can keep track of which **END** statement goes with which **DO** statements. The guidelines followed by the compiler are exactly the same as those used for matching left and right parentheses. This is summarized diagrammatically in Figure 12.3. To help the programmer keep track of loose **END**s, the capability of the **END** statement to refer back to the label of the corresponding **PROCEDURE** or **BEGIN** statement is extended to include **DO** groups.

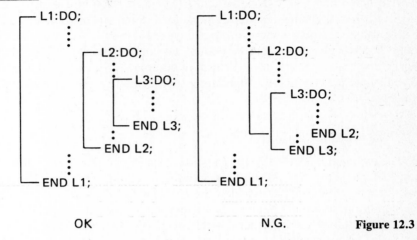

OK   N.G.   **Figure 12.3**

An **END** statement may also have a statement label just as any other statement. This gives the programmer the opportunity (when it seemed appropriate) to use that statement as the destination of a **GO TO**, so that he or she can execute only a portion of the group's statement if that is required. We saw an example of this in Illustration 30A, and the following sequence exemplifies such usage further:

```
IF A = B
  THEN SAME: DO;
                GET LIST(C);
                IF C = A THEN GO TO FINISH;
                D = A*SORT(C);
                PUT DATA(A,C,D);
    FINISH: END SAME;
  ELSE DO; B = B-1;
           A = A+1;
           B = B-1;
           PUT LIST ('A AND B ARE NOT EQUAL.');
     END;
  RESUME: next statement;
```

In group beginning with the statement label SAME, a test is made for equality of C and A. If they are equal, the program goes to the end of the group and from there directly to the statement labeled RESUME.

XII.4.2   Extensions to the **DO** Loop

On numerous occasions we have been able to set up a sequence of activities that repeat automatically, either with an index value changing systematically from some starting value to some limiting value, or with a test condition being used to monitor the repetition or curtailment of the loop. The **DO** statement that embodies the control specifications is a very powerful vehicle for defining a much broader spectrum of automatic cycles than that exploited heretofore. We shall examine the facilities that allow such flexibility and see how they enhance the cyclic process.

XII.4.2.1   The **WHILE** Clause

Thus far we have used the **DO-WHILE** construct as a structure for controlling the repetitive processing of input data. Specifically, the condition monitored by this construct has been expressed in terms of a variable (usually named NDFILE) whose value is changed by the end-of-file condition, and that change triggers an escape from the loop. This is just one very simple instance of a much more general mechanism that makes it possible to specify a wide range of criteria for loop control. The parenthesized test attached to the **DO WHILE** statement may be any expression that can be converted to a bit string. A simple example will serve to illustrate this capability: suppose we started with two values, A and B, which we wish to adjust until their product reached or just exceeded 26.91. The variable A is to be adjusted by adding 0.01 to it, and B is to be adjusted by adding 0.05 to it. Accordingly, we can express this process as follows:

```
DO WHILE(A*B > 26.91);
   A = A+0.01;
   B = B+0.05;
END;
PUT SKIP DATA (A,B);
```

next statement;

Illustration 32

To see the effectiveness of the **WHILE** clause in a more complete context we shall write a procedure to handle the following situation: X and Y are four-digit integers punched in columns 1-4 and 7-10 of a card. After that card is read and the values printed, the program is to read successive cards, each containing a two-digit integer Z in columns 15 and 16. Running totals are to be kept of odd and even values of Z. This process is to continue as long as the odd sum stays below X and the even sum stays below Y. As soon as one of those sums reaches or exceeds its respective limit, the program is to print both sums, along with the number of input values used in accumulating that sum. (Neither X nor Y will be zero.)

Once the variables have been defined, the procedure consists of four basic sections: The first of these takes care of the particular situation in which the program runs out of data before either sum reaches its respective ceiling. A second component reads the limiting values and initializes the sums and counters, and the fourth section prints the summary information. The third section is the nucleus of the procedure, and is constructed as a **DO** loop that cycles an unanticipated number of times under control of the **WHILE** clause:

```
ILL32: PROCEDURE OPTIONS (MAIN);
       DECLARE (X,Y,Z,NUMODD,NUMEVN,SUMODD,SUMEVN) FIXXED BINARY;

       ON ENDFILE (SYSIN)
         BEGIN;
           PUT SKIP(2) DATA (SUMEVN,NUMEVN);
           PUT SKIP EDIT ('NOT ENOUGH INPUT TO REACH X OR Y')(X(5),A);
           STOP;
         END;

       GET EDIT (X,Y)(F(4),X(2),F(4));       GET SKIP;
       PUT PAGE LINE(3) DATA (X,Y);
       NUMODD,NUMEVN,SUMODD,SUMEVN = 0;

 LOOP: DO WHILE (SUMODD < X & SUMEVN < Y);
         GET EDIT (Z) (COLUMN(15),F(2));
         IF MOD (Z,2) = 0
           THEN DO;
                   NUMEVN = NUMEVN+1;     SUMEVN = SUMEVN+Z;
                END;
           ELSE DO;
                   NUMODD = NUMODD+1;     SUMODD = SUMODD+Z;
                END;
       END LOOP;

       PUT SKIP(2) DATA (SUMODD,NUMODD);
       PUT SKIP DATA (SUMEVN,NUMEVN);
       END ILL32;
```

Illustration 33

To see the **WHILE** option in a somewhat different context, we shall handle the situation: values of N, X, and Y are punched in columns 5-6, 11-13, and 14-16. N is a two-digit integer and X and Y have precision (3,1). For each card read, the program prints X, Y, and N, after which it computes and prints values for J and the quantity $J(X+Y)$, where J is 1, 2, 3,...,N. After the last card has been processed, the program is to print the number of cards in the run.

The basic calculations, along with the output display, are handled in an ordinary **DO** loop, with J as the index and the number of cycles controlled by the limiting value N. This module, in turn, is embedded in another loop that regulates the acquisition of new values for X, Y, and N. This time, the variable controlling the **DO WHILE** construct is a single bit (S) which is initialized to "true" (i.e., '1'B) and changed to "false" only by the end-of-file condition. Accordingly, the test can be expressed simply as

DO WHILE(S);

The listing for this program is shown below.

XII.4.2.2 Multiple Iterative Specifications

The flexibility of the basic **DO** loop may be increased by attaching any number of iterative specifications to the initial **DO** statement. Referring to our 10-element array X, suppose that we

```
ILL33: PROCEDURE OPTIONS (MAIN);
        (N,NRUNS,J) FIXED BINARY,
        (X,Y,Z) FLOAT (6),
        S BIT (1) INITIAL ('1'B);

        NRUNS = 0;    ON ENDFILE (SYSIN) S='0'B;
        GET EDIT (N,X,Y)(R(FM));
    FM: FORMAT(COLUMN(15),F(2),X(4),2 F(3,1));

        DO WHILE (S);
          PUT PAGE LINE(3) EDIT ('X = ',X,'Y = ',Y,'N = ',N)
                (X(5),A,F(4,1),X(3),A,F(4,1),X(3),A,F(2));
          PUT SKIP(2) EDIT ('J','J*(X-Y)')(X(6),A,X(8),A,SKIP);
          NRUNS = NRUNS+1;
          DO J = 1 TO N;
            Z = J*(X-Y);
            PUT SKIP EDIT(J,Z)(X(5),F(2),X(8),F(7,1));
          END;
          GET EDIT (N,X,Y)(R(FM));
        END;

        PUT SKIP(2) DATA (NRUNS);
        END ILL33;
```

wanted to process it so that elements 2, 3, 5, 7, 8 and 9 are replaced by their square roots, while the others remain unchanged. The form for handling this is

DO I = 2 **TO** 3, 5, 7 **TO** 9;

   X(I) = **SQRT**(X(I));

END;

Note that we did not have to specify "5 to 5" to obtain the square root replacement for the single element X(5); by omitting the **TO** phrase in that instance, the compiler assumes that only one cycle is desired and acts accordingly.

XII.4.2.3   Re-use of a **DO** Loop Index

Since the starting value for the index must be specified at the beginning of a **DO** loop, it is possible to use a particular index name for more than one loop in a procedure, as long as only one loop is being processed at a particular time. Returning to our somewhat shopworn but still useful array X, suppose that we wish to replace elements 2, 3, 5, 7, 8, and 9 with their respective square roots as we did before. In addition, we would like to replace the other elements with half their values. To do this, we can set up two consecutive loops:

DO I = 2 **TO** 3, 5, 7 **TO** 9;

   X(I) = **SQRT**(X(I));

END;

DO I = 1, 4, 6, 10;

   X(I) = .5*X(I);

END;

The index name I may also be used for any legitimate purpose outside the bounds of the loop it controls.

XII.4.2.4   Changing the Repetition Increment: The **BY** Phrase

The flexibility of the **DO** loop can be extended in yet another direction by controlling the rate at which the index is changed for each cycle of the loop. The fact that we have made no such specification up to this point implies that we have made use of another PL/I default activity that adds 1 to the index for each repetition. (The use of multiple specifications has enabled us to force the program to skip certain index values, but this has no effect on the basic incrementing mechanism.) Control of that portion of the processing is exercised by use of the **BY** phrase, whose appearance in the **DO** statement follows either one of three general forms:

DO index = starting value **TO** limit **BY** increment;

DO index = starting value **BY** increment **TO** limit;

DO index = starting value **BY** increment;

As with "starting value" and "limit", the value of "increment" may be a constant or any legitimate expression that may be evaluated to a single value. Hence, we can say that a default (no **BY** phrase at all) is the same as writing

DO index = starting value **TO** limit **BY** 1;

If a **TO** phrase and/or a **BY** phrase are used, the specification stipulates that iteration is required. When **BY** is omitted, the default, as we have seen, is +1. When **TO** is omitted, the iteration is indefinite and must be terminated by some other means: either a **WHILE** clause or a **GO TO** statement that transfers control out of the loop may be used for this purpose. If both **TO** and **BY** are omitted, then the statements in the loop are executed just once, as we have already seen. Thus, if we wanted to replace the even-numbered elements of the 10-element array X with the square roots of their current values, our loop would read

```
DO I = 2 TO 10 BY 2;
   X(I) = SQRT(X(I));
END;
```

Not every increment value will cause the index to arrive exactly at the limiting value. For instance, suppose that we would like to double the value of the odd-numbered elements in array X and wrote

DO I = 1 **TO** 10 **BY** 2;

   X(I) = 2*X(I);

END;

The cycling mechanism will start at X(1), double its value, and press forward by processing X(3), X(5), X(7), and X(9) in turn. Since the conditions of the **DO** statement have not yet been satisfied (the limiting value of 10 has not been reached), the program will add the increment (2 in this case) to the index and will try to process X(11). Since this is beyond the range specified in the **DO** loop, the cycling process will cease, and the program will continue with the statement following the loop. We can make the general statement that the compiler will try to fulfill the requirements implied by the increment, going as far as it can within the bounds set by the initial and limiting values.

If multiple specifications are used in a **DO** statement, any or all of these may be augmented with **BY** phrases so that the loop

DO I = 1 **TO** 3 **BY** 2, 4 **TO** 5, 6 **BY** 3 **TO** 10;

   X(I) = 3*X(I);

END;

will triple the values in X(1), X(3), X(4), X(5), X(6), and X(9).

XII.4.2.5   Negative Increments

DO loops can be set up in which the index is decremented rather than incremented. When this is done, the increment (the value following the word **BY**) must be specified as a negative number or an expression that works out to a negative number. In this situation the limiting value must be algebraically less than the starting value or the loop will not be executed at all. This is because the test for termination is reversed when the increment is negative; thus, a loop with a negative increment is terminated when the index becomes *less* than the limiting value. Therefore, a statement such as

DO I = 10 **TO** 1 **BY** − 2;

   X(I) = − X(I);

END;

will cause the sign to be changed in elements X(10), X(8), X(6), X(4), and X(2), in that order.

Since the default increment is always 1, a negative increment can never be inferred. A programmer could not write a statement as

DO I = 7 **TO** 3;.....**END**;

and expect the loop to operate on A(7), A(6), A(5), A(4), and A(3). As written, this statement will cause the entire loop to be skipped, since the index is greater than the limiting value to begin with.

XII.4.2.6   Nonintegers as Increments in a **DO** Loop

The index variable of a **DO** loop need not be an integer value. With a noninteger index; a noninteger increment or decrement can be specified, and it will be applied as stated. This facility expands the usefulness and versatility of the **DO** loop to a considerable extent. It is particularly useful in the construction of procedures for generating tables. All the facilities of the **DO** loop also may be used in **DO** specifications in data lists.

Illustration 34

One of the most important thermodynamic properties of materials is the specific heat, which is an indicator of the amount of heat energy (usually expressed in calories or British thermal units) required to raise the temperature of some unit weight of the material (usually one gram or one pound) by one degree (Centigrade or Fahrenheit, depending on the heat and weight units). For many substances it is possible to calculate this property (C_p) for a given temperature t by using a set of characteristic constants in an equation of the form

$$C_p = A_0 + A_1 t + A_2 t^2$$

We are interested in writing a program that will produce a series of tables showing the specific heat values for various substances at specified temperatures. The data for each substance will be placed on a separate card using the following format:

Card Columns	Identification	Format
1-20	Name of substance	Characters
31-34	Value of A0	X$_{(.)}$XXX
36-40	Value of A1	$_{(.)}$XXXXX
45-50	Value of A2	$_{(.)}$XXXXXX
57-60	Starting temperature, degrees Fahrenheit	XXX$_{(.)}$X
67-70	Final temperature, degrees Fahrenheit	XXX$_{(.)}$X

Although the initial and final temperature values may change from one substance to the next, the range will always be ten degrees. The temperature increment will always be the same; specific heat values will be calculated at 0.2-degree intervals for all substances specified, so that each table will always contain 51 entries. Each table is to start on a separate page and is to be headed by the name of the substance and the equation used for it.

   The entire procedure can be constructed rather simply by using the two input temperatures as starting and limiting values in a **DO** loop placed within a single **PUT** statement which prints the entire report. This also illustrates that **GET** and **PUT** statements may be made arbitrarily complicated. The temperature itself (which we shall call TEMP) will be used as the index:

```
ILL34: PROCEDURE OPTIONS (MAIN);
       DECLARE 1 CHEM,
               2 NAME CHARACTER(20),
               (2 A0, 2 A1, 2 A2, 2 TEMP1, 2 TEMP2) FLOAT DECIMAL (6),
               TEMP FLOAT DECIMAL (6);

       ON ENDFILE (SYSIN)
         BEGIN;
               PUT SKIP (2) LIST ('END OF RUN.');
               STOP;
         END;

       DO WHILE ('1'B);
         GET EDIT (CHEM) (COL(1),A(20),X(9),F(5,3),F(6,5),X(3),F(7,6),
                          2 (X(5),F(5,1)));

         /** WE SHALL SPECIFY VIRTUALLY THE ENTIRE SET OF **/
         /** ACTIVITIES IN A SINGLE PUT STATEMENT: THE    **/
         /** FIRST PART HANDLES THE OVERALL HEADING, THE  **/
         /** NEXT PART ECHOES THE THREE COEFFICIENTS, THE **/
         /** THIRD PART SPECIFIES THE COLUMN HEADINGS, AND**/
         /** THE FINAL PORTION USES A DO LOOP TO ENUMERATE**/
         /** ALL THE TABLE VALUES. ALL OF THE FORMATTING  **/
         /** IS INCLUDED IN THE STATEMENT AS WELL. LESS   **/
         /** THAN A CENTURY AGO, STUDENTS USED TO GET     **/
         /** MASTERS AND DOCTORATE DEGREES FOR PREPARING  **/
         /** SUCH TABLES BY HAND.                         **/

         PUT EDIT ('SPECIFIC HEAT DATA FOR ',NAME,
                   'A0 = ',A0,'A1 = ',A1,'A2 = ',A2,
                   'TEMP.','CP',
                   (TEMP,A0+(A1+A2*TEMP)*TEMP
                    DO TEMP=TEMP1 TO TEMP2 BY .2))
                  (PAGE,COLUMN(45),A,A,
                   SKIP(3),COL(43), 3 (A(4),F(10,6),X(3)),
                   SKIP(2),COL(58),A(5),X(7),A(2),
                   SKIP(2), (51)(COL(57),F(7,1),F(12,4)));
       END;

       END ILL34;
```

XII.4.2.7 The Full-Blown **DO** Statement

The **WHILE** clause may be combined with the **TO** and **BY** phrases to produce the following general form:

DO index = starting value **TO** limiting value **BY** increment **WHILE**(test);

Suppose that we wanted to calculate and print successive values of Y for odd-numbered elements of array X, where

Y = 2*X(I);

We want this process to continue as long as the value of Y has not fallen below 14. The current values of X(1), X(3), X(5), X(7), and X(9) are 9, 12, 8, 6 and 10, respectively. The required **DO** loop would look as follows:

DO I = 1 **TO** 10 **BY** 2 **WHILE** (Y>=14);

    Y = 2*X(I); **PUT SKIP DATA** (X(I),Y);

END;

As a result, the program will calculate and print values of Y for X(1), X(3), and X(5). A value of Y would then be calculated for X(7) and tested against the conditions stipulated in the **WHILE** clause. Since these conditions are no longer met, execution would be terminated at this point and the program would proceed to the instruction following the conclusion of the **DO** loop. This happens even though the limiting value stipulated by the **TO** phrase has not been reached. It makes no difference that X(7) is followed by another odd-numbered element for which the specified condition is true.

The **DO** statement can be extended to its full-blown form by treating the specification from immediately past the = sign through the **WHILE** clause as a unit that can be repeated any number of times. Thus, if Z is an array declared with a sufficient number of elements, a statement such as

DO I = 1 **TO** 9 **BY** 2 **WHILE** (Y<**SQRT**(Z(I))), 10 **TO** 20 **WHILE** (Y>=.5*Z(I));

is perfectly legitimate.

XII.4.3 **DO** Loops with Multidimensional Arrays

All of the capabilities available through the **DO** statement may be used with nested **DO** loops. It is very simple to visualize the operation of such multiple cycling processes by comparing them to the hands of an ordinary clock. The two hands of the clock cycle at different rates; the minute hand must go through a complete cycle (a complete revolution around the face of the clock) before the hour hand advances one increment. Similarly, the inner loop in a nested pair completes its specified number of cycles before the next cycle of the outer one is executed.

This can be illustrated by a simple example in which we wish to double certain elements of the two-dimensional array X. By writing the following sequence of instructions

DECLARE X(3,4) **FIXED**(2);

DO I = 2 **TO** 3;

    DO J = 2 **TO** 4;

        X(I,J) = 2*X(I,J);

    END;

END;

we cause elements X(2,2), X(2,3), X(2,4), X(3,2), X(3,3), and X(3,4) to be doubled in that order. The inner loop is completely cycled (from 2 to 4) before the index for the outer loop is incremented. Separate indexes are, of course, required for each loop, and the conclusion of each loop must usually be signified by its corresponding **END** statement. This is not necessary if both loops end at the same place. The above example is a case in point, and in this instance one of the **END** statements may be omitted if the other one refers back to the label of the outer loop.

The order in which the elements are processed can be altered by changing the indexes. Thus, if we rewrote the above sequence as

    DECLARE X(3,4) **FIXED**(2);

CYCLE: **DO** J = 2 **TO** 4;

      DO I = 2 **TO** 3;

        X(I,J) = 2*X(I,J);

    END CYCLE;

the results would be the same, but the sequence in which they are obtained would be as follows: X(2,2), X(3,2), X(2,3), X(3,3), X(2,4), and X(3,4).

Illustration 35

An aircraft engine company summarizes the performance characteristics for a jet engine by producing a table in which the thrust is shown for combinations of 10 altitudes and 20 flight speeds. (A thrust value is given in the form XXXXX.X and is expressed in pounds.) After generating such a table for engine XH23W5-D, it was found that the apparatus was miscalibrated, and consequently gave erroneous figures for certain values. Recalibration indicated that the table could be corrected by making the following adjustments (assuming that rows are altitudes and columns are speeds):

```
ILL35: PROCEDURE OPTIONS (MAIN);
        DECLARE (THRUST(10,20), CORR(10,20)) FLOAT DECIMAL (6),
                (I,J) FIXED BINARY;

        /** CORRECTIONS WILL BE STORED IN THE ARRAY CORR. **/
        /** NOW WE SHALL DEVELOP AND PRINT COLUMN LABELS. **/

        PUT PAGE LINE(3) EDIT ('REVISED THRUST TABLE FOR ENGINE XH23W5-D')
                              (COLUMN(40),A);
        PUT SKIP(2) EDIT (' ')(X(17),A);      /* THIS STARTS THE LINE */
        DO I = 1 TO 20;
           PUT EDIT ('ALT(',I,')')(X(4),A(4),F(2),A);
        END;
        GET EDIT (THRUST)(F(6,1),X(74));      /* THIS READS THE ENTIRE TABLE */

        /** NOW FOR THE 200 CORRECTIONS, COMPUTED VIA SEVERAL LOOPS **/

        DO I = 1 TO 4;
           DO J = 1 TO 20;
              IF J = 1 | (J > 6 & J < 11)
                 THEN CORR(I,J) = 0.024;
                 ELSE IF J > 10
                         THEN CORR(I,J) = 0.021;
                         ELSE CORR(I,J) = 0.030;
           END;
        END;

        DO I = 5 TO 7;
           DO J = 1 TO 20;
              IF J < 7
                 THEN CORR(I,J) = -0.017;
                 ELSE CORR(I,J) = -0.015;
           END;
        END;

        CORR(8,*) = 0.013;      /* THAT TAKES CARE OF ALL OF ROW 8 */

        DO I = 9,10;
           DO J = 1 TO 20;
              IF MOD(J,I) = 0
                 THEN CORR)I,J) = -0.006;
                 ELSE IF J < 8
                         THEN CORR(I,J) = -0.008;
                         ELSE CORR(I,J) = 0;
           END;
        END;

        THRUST = ROUND(THRUST*(1+CORR),1);  /* THIS CORRECTS THE ARRAY. */

        PUT SKIP;
        DO J = 1 TO 20;
           PUT SKIP EDIT ('SPEED',J,')',(THRUST(I,J) DO I=1 TO 10)(R(FM));
        END;
FM:     FORMAT(X(5),A(6),F(2),A,X(4), 10 (X(4),F(7,1)));

        END ILL35;
```

Rows 1-4: Columns 2, 3, and 5 must be increased by 3 percent; columns 1, 7, 8, 9, and 10 must be increased by 2.4 percent; columns 11-20 must be increased by 2.1 percent.

Rows 5-7: Columns 1-6 must be lowered by 1.7 percent; columns 7-20 must be lowered by 1.5 percent.

Row 8: Columns 1-20 must all be increased by 1.3 percent.

Rows 9-10: Columns 1, 3, 5, and 7 must be lowered by .8 percent; columns 2, 4, 6, and 8-20 must be lowered by .6 percent.

The remaining values are correct as they stand. Assuming that each original value is punched in columns 1-6 on a separate card and that the cards are arranged in row major order, write a program to produce a corrected table. Format it in such a way that the ten altitudes are strung out across the width of the page and the 20 velocities turn down the length. Use ALT(1), and so on, and SPEED(1), and so on, as output labels, assuming that 132 spaces are available across the page.

We shall generate our row and column headings as character string arrays called ROW and COL, and the two-dimensional array of thrust values will be named THRUST. The decision criteria will be built into two **DO** loops. The output format will require some attention because of the way we named our rows and columns. The rows in the array will appear as columns on the page, and vice versa.

XII.4.4   Transmission of Multidimensional Arrays

The order in which multidimensional array members are read in or printed out can be controlled in a variety of ways by providing the basic input or output command with an appropriate **DO** statement for each dimension of the array being handled. Suppose that we declared a two-dimensional array as follows:

DECLARE Y(2,4)**FIXED**(3,1);

and we had eight values punched as shown below. If we were to read these in with the simple statement

GET LIST(Y);

| 14.1 | 15.3 | 16.5 | 17.7 | 21.0 | 23.1 | 25.2 | 27.3 |

the eight values would be organized as

14.1	15.3	16.5	17.7
21.0	23.1	25.2	27.3

Let us say, however, that it suited our purpose more closely to have these values stored and treated as

14.1	16.5	21.0	25.2
15.3	17.7	23.1	27.3

We can gain a clearer insight as to how to accomplish this with an input command containing two **DO** statements by assuming temporarily that such statements are not available, thus compelling us to write straightforward **DO** loops to read the values in

```
DO J = 1 TO 4;
    DO I = 1 TO 2·
        GET LIST(Y(I,J));
    END;
END;
```

Exactly the same results can be achieved by arranging two **DO** statements within a **GET LIST** instruction

GET LIST(((Y(I,J) **DO** I = 1 TO 2) **DO** J = 1 TO 4));

When the statement is written in this manner, PL/I will arrange for the instruction to be executed such that the **DO** statement closest to the array name (the leftmost **DO** statement) is cycled through completely for each single cycle of the outer (rightmost) **DO** statement.

Illustration 36

Since its establishment is 1912, the Mary Worth Sampler Company has been producing doilies embroidered with heartwarming and/or inspirational messages suitable for framing. Until the death of its founder in 1962, it was the company's unwavering policy to introduce five new samplers each year, each dealing with one of five standard subjects. Although the company is primarily in the missile business, continuing demand places it under an obligation to store and make available a complete inventory of its samplers. To fulfill this obligation, the company finds it necessary to maintain a double set of identifiers. For the convenience of the customers, each sampler is assigned a heartwarming/inspirational name consisting of ten characters, while the warehousing and manufacturing groups make use of a corresponding six-digit numerical part number. It is desired to write a program that will

a.   Print the name of each of the five samplers produced during a specified year on a separate line, together with its corresponding part number.

b.   Print the information in (a) above for any specified sequence of years.

c.   Print the name and part number on a separate line for every sampler of a specified type.

d.   Print (c) above for a specified sequence of years.

e.   Print the entire identification chart, one line, containing all five samplers for a given year.

Our strategy will be to maintain an array of structures with two corresponding elements for the name and number so that a particular sampler name and its matching part number will have identical row and column numbers. In this way, the location of a particular sampler name will immediately produce the appropriate part number. Each type of printout will be signaled by an input request containing a unique code word that will be recognized by the program and cause a particular set of instructions to be executed. To provide such indicators, it will be necessary to define three types of input cards.

```
ILL36: PROCCEDURE OPTIONS (MAIN);
       DECLARE 1 WORTH(1912:1962,5),
                 2 DOILY CHARACTER(10),
                 2 PART FIXED BINARY (31),
               REQ CHARACTER(5),
               (YEAR1,YEAR2,TOPIC,I,J) FIXED BINARY;

       ON ENDFILE (SYSIN) STOP;
       OPEN FILE (SYSPRINT) LINESIZE(132);
       GET EDIT (((WORTH(I,J) DO J=1 TO 5) DO I=1962 TO 1912 BY -1))
                 (A(10),F(6));

       DO WHILE ('1'B);
         GET LIST (REQ);
         PUT PAGE LINE(3) EDIT ('MARY WORTH SAMPLER CO.')(X(45),A);
         IF REQ = 'THEME'
           THEN  HEART: DO;
                         GET LIST (TOPIC,YEAR1,YEAR2);
                         IF TOPIC <= 5 & YEAR1 >= 1912 & YEAR2 <= 1962
                           THEN DO;
                                PUT SKIP(2) EDIT ('TYPE','TOPIC',
                                          'SAMPLERS')(X(5), 2 (A,X(10)),A);
                                PUT SKIP;
                                DO I=YEAR1 TO YEAR2;
                                  PUT SKIP EDIT (I,WORTH(I,TOPIC))
                                      (X(5),F(4),X(10),A(10),X(5),F(6));
                                END;
                                END;
                         ELSE DO;
                                IF TOPIC > 5
                                  THEN PUT SKIP EDIT
                                    ('THERE IS NO TYPE AS ',TOPIC)
                                      (X(5),A,F(1));
                                IF YEAR1 < 1912 ! YEAR2 > 1962
                                  THEN PUT SKIP EDIT
                                    (YEAR1,' AND/OR ',YEAR2,' OUT OF RANGE')
                                      (X(5), 2 (F(4),A));
                                END;
                         END HEART;

           ELSE IF REQ = 'YEARS'
                   THEN  TIMES: DO;
                                GET LIST (YEAR1,YEAR2);
                                IF YEAR1 >= 1912 & YEAR2 <= 1962
                                  THEN DO;
                                        PUT SKIP(2)EDIT('SAMPLERS FOR YEARS ',
                                        YEAR1,' TO ',YEAR2)
                                        (X(44), 2 (A,F(4)));
                                        PUT SKIP EDIT (('DOILY','PART'
                                           DO I=1 TO 5))
                                        (X(5), 5 (A(5),X(10),A(4),X(7)));
                                        PUT SKIP;
                                        DO I=YEAR1 TO YEAR2;
                                          PUT SKIP EDIT ((WORTH(I,J)
                                                DO J=1 TO 5))
                                          (X(5), 5 (A(10),X(5),F(6),X(5)));
                                          END;
                                        END;
                                ELSE PUT SKIP EDIT (REQ,' IS NOT VALID .')
                                        (X(5),A,A);
                                END TIMES;
       END;

       END ILL36;
```

Request for a display of the total inventory, the listing for a given year, and the listing for a given sequence of years can all be taken care of with a single routine. We shall define the input card for such processing as consisting of the character string 'YEARS' followed by two four-digit numbers representing the first and last year in the sequence to be shown. If these two numbers are equal, the program will recognize the fact that only one year is to be displayed. If the two numbers are 1912 and 1962, this will signify a request for the total printout.

We shall stipulate that the use of the character string 'THEME' will indicate an input request for all sampler names and part numbers dealing with one of the five basic subjects. Recognition of this character string will cause the program to look for a 1, 2, 3, 4, or 5 as an appropriate identifier. Following the identifier, there will be two 4-digit numbers indicating the first and last year in the sequence to be shown. This will work as outlined for the year-by-year display, so that the user has the option of specifying any length of time ranging from a single year to the entire reign of Mary Worth.

To provide flexibility, the program should be designed to handle any number of requests submitted in any order.

Based on these considerations, we can now assign names to our variables:

DOILY will be used for the array containing sampler names.
PART will be the array name for the part numbers.
REQ will be the name of the variable containing the request indicator.
YEAR1 will be the variable containing the initial year requested.
YEAR2 will be the variable containing the final year requested.
TOPIC will contain the type number specified on a THEME card.

The beginning of each request will be headed by an appropriate label.

We shall take advantage of the ability to shift subscript ranges by assigning row subscripts numerically equal to the corresponding years.

To illustrate the flexibility of the input mechanism, we shall impose the following additional requirement: The names and part numbers for the five samplers for a given year are punched on a single card in columns 1-10 and 11-16, 17-26 and 27-32, and so on. Moreover, the cards are in reverse order by year, that is, the most recent year first.

PROBLEMS

1. Consider the following situation:

When X is	Y,Z and W are computed as
200.0	$Y = 1.89e^{.007X} + X^{0.65}$
	$Z = Y/6 + \log(Y)$
	$W = Y - Z$
200-299.9	$Y = 2.62e^{.008X} + X \sin(X)$
	$Z = X(Y/5.5 - .0505(600-X))$
	$W = 0$
300.0-499.9	$Y = e^{.0056X}/(1+0.04X)$
	$Z = 1.77Y - \log(Y)$
	$W = 0$
500.0-599.9	$Y = 2.02^{.011X}$
	$Z = Y$
	$W = (Y-Z)/(Y+Z)$
600	$Y = 2.12^{.010X}$
	$Z = Y$
	$W = 0$

(a) Show a flowchart (either ANSI or N-S construction) for the representation of this situation as a case construct.

(b) Write a sequence of PL/I statements to implement this processing using a label array.

(c) Write a sequence of PL/I statements to implement this processing using ELSE IF construction.

2. The Zungian Intelligence Service receives its messages in a double code: Before decoding this message, the original form has to be transformed into an intermediate form. Each message consists of a string of 160 characters punched on two cards. The rules for this initial transformation are as follows:

(a) All blanks in the original text are removed.

(b) Each T, V, or B is replaced by *

(c) Each C or D is replaced by a W unless it is followed by a vowel. (Y is not considered a vowel here). When the C or D is followed by a vowel, it is replaced by WH. If the C or D is followed by a K, it is deleted.

(d) Any two vowels in succession are replaced by an X.

a. Draw a suitable flowchart for a program designed to read and process any number of such messages. For each message, the program is to print the original message (on two lines, 80 characters per line) followed by the transformed message (80 characters per line, with the last line displaying whatever number of characters it happens to display). The last line of each transformed text is followed by a line showing the length of the output string.

b. Write a program that meets these requirements.

3. For the following sequence of statements

IF B = 2*A **THEN**
  IF C = 4*D **THEN**
    IF B = C − 4 **THEN** Z = 12;
    ELSE IF A = D+6 **THEN**
      IF C = A + 14 **THEN** Z = 22;
      ELSE Z = 11;
        ELSE Z = 21;
    ELSE Z = 31;
  ELSE Z = 41;

state the value of Z when

a. A = 10, B = 20, C = 24, D = 6

b. A = 9, B = 20, C = 24, D = 6

c. A = 10, B = 20, C = 24, D = 7

d. A = 3, B = 6, C = 4, D = 5

e. A = 2, B = 4, C = 8, D = 16

4. A series of five-digit decimal integers are punched on separate cards (columns 6-10). Write a program that counts and prints the number of values read in and the number of values ending with a 6 and evenly divisible by 4.

5. Pairs of decimal integers are punched in columns 2-5 and 21-23. Write a program that performs the following operations:

  a. Counts (and prints) the number of pairs of values in which the product is not more than ten times the ratio of the first value to the second.

  b. Calculates the sum of the products of all pairs meeting the criteria in part a.

  c. Calculates the product of the sums of all pairs in which both values are even.

  d. Counts the number of times the digit 2 appears in the data.

No two members of a pair will ever have the same value. Provide appropriate labels for all output.

6. Text material is punched continuously on cards (that is, all 80 columns are used on each card, even though a card may end in the middle of a word). Write a program that counts the number of times each of the 26 letters appears in a series of cards. Print the results in table form, along with a second table that expresses the number of appearances for each letter as a percentage of the total number of letters in the data.

7. Write a program that reads an array of 200 numbers and counts the number of values that do not contain a 7. Each value is a decimal integer punched in columns 12-15 on a separate card. Use zero as a fake value. Print these values in descending order.

8. Generate and print a five-digit table of logarithms to the base 3 for numbers ranging from 1 to 10 in increments of 0.01. Format the output so that the values are printed ten across.

9. An electrical equipment company checks the performance of its motors by recording the output (measured as XXX.X watts) at 20 standard speeds. The testing setup requires that the recorded value be adjusted according to the following schedule before the performance table is issued:

    Speeds 1-5:   Multiply reading by .97
    Speeds 6-11:   Multiply reading by .98
    Speeds 12-17: Multiply reading by .99
    Speeds 18-20: Multiply reading by .995

    Each speed is punched in columns 1 and 2 as a percentage of the maximum, and the corresponding power value is punched in columns 51-54. Each group of readings is preceded by a card containing the motor's serial number in columns 1-7 (an initial letter followed by six digits). Write a program to print a performance chart for each motor on a separate page.

10. Mr. Carlotta Frump (Loch Sheldrake, New York) has won the Rock of Ages Baking Company's Third Prize for her Rhubarb-Garlic Cotillion Pie and is entitled to select $1000 worth of clothes and accessories from the Svelte Boutique. Assuming the following prices:

Coats	$500 each
Gowns	$250 each
Dresses	$100 each
Hats	$ 50 each
Purses	$ 25 each
Gloves	$ 10 a pair

    write a program that counts the number of different wardrobe combinations Mrs. Frump can buy.

11. A secret message center receives coded signals over a wireless device. These signals are automatically recorded on punched cards as groups of seven letters separated by a blank. The last group of letters is followed by seven 9s.

    The first step in the decoding process is to replace each letter by a substitute, according to a table that changes each day and is read in ahead of the message. This table is punched in columns 1-26 on a separate card in the order in which its members are to be used (that is, the letter in column 1 replaces A, the letter in column 5 replaces E, and so on). Write a program that prints the original message as received, formatted as 12 groups across a line, and on a separate page prints the partially decoded message as six groups of 14 letters per line. Each of these latter groups consists of an interweaving of two adjacent seven-letter groups as in the following:

group1	group2	amalgamated group
BABOSMS	ENLSOIM	BEANBLOSSOMISM

12. The 100 members of a fixed-decimal array are punched on cards with precision (3,0), 25 to a card in

columns 1-3, 4-6, 7-9, 10-12, ..., 73-75. The order in which they are punched is by decreasing magnitude, so the lowest value is last.

Write a program to print that section of the array whose values lie between certain minimum and maximum limits, each of which is read in as part of the input. The values are to appear in increasing order.

13. One of the most useful techniques for reducing random disturbances in various types of data recorded at equal intervals over a time span is known as "moving averages." This method is applied by replacing a given point with the average of that point and a number of subsequent readings. (The number of points used for averaging is selected to suit each situation.) Thus, if we were to use a four-point moving average on a set of 40 points, point 1 would be replaced by the average of points 1, 2, 3, and 4, point 2 would be replaced by the average of points 2, 3, 4, and 5, and so on. When there are not enough points left to calculate moving averages, the remaining points are either discarded or left unchanged. Hence, in our example, point 37 would be replaced by the average of points 37, 38, 39, and 40, and the remaining three points would be handled as the user sees fit. It is desired to calculate eight-point moving averages on a series of points whose total number is variable, but will never exceed 220. The number of points will be specified in columns 1-3 of a card preceding the data cards. The variable to be processed in TEMP, and each value is punched in columns 25-28 of a card in the form $XXX_{()}X$. The corresponding time (TIME) appears as $XXX_{()}X$ in columns 1-4. The program is to print a table showing TIME, TEMP, and revised TEMP for each reading. For simplicity, discard the last seven points.

SUMMARY OF IMPORTANT TERMS

BY phrase	An optional part of a **DO** statement, which specifies the increment to be added to a loop's index each time that loop is cycled.
Case construct	A structured program component expressing a decision mechanism in which a particular action is selected from three or more mutually exclusive alternatives; a generalization of the **IF-THEN-ELSE** construct.
Decrement	An amount to be subtracted from an index or counter each time a cyclic process is repeated. Decrements are used in those processes where it is more convenient to start the cycles with an index (counter) set at a maximum value and systematically decreased (decremented) until some prescribed minimum value is reached.
ELSE...IF clause	A second stage of testing specified as an alternative consequence of an initial test. The second test is performed if the outcome of the initial test is "false."

Empty **ELSE** clause | See "Null **ELSE** clause."
Increment | An amount that is systematically added to an index or counter during each cycle of a repetitive process. In a PL/I **DO** loop, the increment is +1 by default, or may be explicitly defined by means of a **BY** phrase.

LABEL attribute | The attribute associated with label variables. This attribute must be explicitly declared.

Label variable | A variable (definable only by explicit declaration) which may take on values of labels associated with various statements in the same procedure (that is, statement label constants).

Nesting | An organizational structure within a program wherein program components (such as **DO** loops or **BEGIN** blocks) are completely embedded in other components of the same type.

Null **ELSE** clause | Part of an **IF** statement consisting merely of the keyword **ELSE** to provide an explicit indicator that there is to be no action if the outcome of a particular test is "false." (Note that it is syntactically possible to specify a null **THEN** clause.)

THEN...IF clause | A subsequent stage of testing specified as a consequence of a prior test and performed only if the outcome of that first test were "true."

TO phrase | An optional part of a **DO** statement, which specifies the limiting value of the loop's index.

WHILE clause | An optional part of a **DO** statement, which specifies a logical expression whose truth or falsity is tested each time the loop is repeated. Cycling is terminated as soon as the outcome of such a test is "false."

SUPPLEMENTARY READING

Ashcroft, E., and Manna, Z., "The Translation of GO TO Program to WHILE Programs," *Information Processing 71*. Amsterdam: North-Holland, 1972.

Bochman, G. V., "Multiple Exits from a Loop without the GO TO," *Communications of the Association for Computing Machinery*, vol. 16, no. 7, 1973.

Dijkstra, E. W., "Notes on Structured Programming," Technische Hogeschool, Eindhoven, Netherlands, 1969.

Hopkins, M. E., "A Case for the GO TO," *Proceedings of the ACM National Conference*, Boston, 1972.

XIII CONTROL OF PL/I PROGRAM ORGANIZATION

Although we have been rather offhand about interchanging the terms "program" and "proce-dure", they refer to two different concepts in PL/I. Since we have not as yet found it necessary to do otherwise, all our programs have consisted of single procedures beginning with a **PROCEDURE** statement and concluding with an **END** statement. It is possible, however, to construct a program as a collection of several organizational components (*blocks*). Some of these may be procedures, each of which can be independently designed and developed as a self-standing entity. Others may be dependent procedures that act somewhat differently. Still others may be certain sequences of statements that are not procedures but still have their own set of properties. In many situations, this organizational approach presents substantial advan-tages over the technique of writing a program as one long procedure. One of these benefits becomes apparent when a particular information-handling task requires a very long program, in which case it is often better to design it as a group of modules. This facilitates the development and checkout of the program, since the modules can be tested and examined separately. Administratively, it presents the opportunity (often a crucial one) to divide the programming task among several people, each of whom is charged with designing and developing a particular block under the overall cognizance of a supervisor. If the requirements for each procedure are properly specified, the subsequent job of welding them into a consistent and well-integrated program is not unduly difficult.

A second important advantage of organizing a program as a group of blocks makes itself felt when a number of specific information-handling processes are used over and over again by a particular installation for a variety of applications. When such processes are expressed as separate blocks, they can be prepared as independent procedures. Once they are developed, the appropriate sets of instructions can be incorporated bodily into any and all programs requiring them, thus obviating the effort required to write and rewrite them for each application. PL/I makes extensive use of this organizational concept in many of its aspects; perhaps the most notable is the repertoire of built-in functions. While some of these (such as **MOD, FLOOR, MAX,** and **MIN**) are just names for processing sequences for which there is no convenient operational notation, most of the others are actually constructed and stored as a library of procedures. When the compiler analyzes a set of source statements and finds that one of them refers to a particular function it consults the library of procedures, finds the one that calculates the value of the function, and adds it to the user's program, together with whatever mechanisms are required to make use of it. The procedure need appear only once, even though it may be used on several occasions in different sections of the program.

A third type of payoff makes itself felt in terms of more efficient use of storage and greatly increased flexibility in the internal manipulation of data. The programmer is given the ability to isolate specific portions of his program from any or all other portions, leading to such possibilities as the specification of values recognized by one part of the program and not by the other, or the unambiguous use of the same names with different meanings in different contexts.

XIII.1   TYPES OF BLOCKS

When the choice is made to synthesize a PL/I program from a number of component blocks, a programmer may call on a variety of such modules, each with its specific set of properties and limitations. Each type of block is surrounded by its own introductory and concluding statements serving as identifying signals to the compiler. Once such identification is established, the compiler automatically follows the approprate set of rules for handling the instructions and data within that block.

XIII.1.1   Procedures

All PL/I procedures are introduced by a **PROCEDURE** statement and concluded with an **END** statement. This general structure can be represented symbolically as label: **PROCEDURE** ····;   *PRIMARY ENTRY POINT*

statements;

.

.

.

.

label#1: **END** label; *optional*

The **PROCEDURE** statement may contain various types of specifications (including none), depending on the type of procedure it is and how it is used. The word "label" refers to any legitimate statement label constant. Each procedure must have such a label attached to its **PROCEDURE** statement, since that statement (also known as the *heading statement*) indicates the beginning of the procedure and its label, and therefore supplies the procedure's name. When the compiler encounters a **PROCEDURE** statement, its label is not classified as an ordinary statement label constant. Instead, it is assigned the **ENTRY** attribute, indicating it does not merely identify a statement but denotes the point at which a procedure is entered when it is brought into use. It is possible to provide several entry points for a procedure, as we shall see later on. For this reason, the **PROCEDURE** statement is also referred to as the *primary entry point*.

The execution of procedures in a program is not related to the sequence of their appearance in the program. One of the procedure's basic properties is that it can be used any number of times at any number of places in the program. To support this flexibility, PL/I provides the necessary logical mechanisms to keep track of the point at which the sequence was broken when particular reference to a procedure was made, so that "normal" sequential processing can resume once execution of the procedure has been concluded.

All procedures must conclude with an **END** statement, which may or may not include the procedure's name. This repeated reference is optional and is intended primarily as an aid to the programmer rather than a signal to the compiler. "label#1" indicates that the **END** statement may itself be labeled so that it can serve as the destination of a **GO TO** statement (for example, **GO TO** label#1;), should the programmer find a need for this.

Although a procedure must be named, there is no particular limit on the number of names a procedure may carry. If the programmer should find it desirable to attach more than one name, he may do so by using the general form

label:label2:**PROCEDURE**....;

As a result, PL/I will be able to identify the procedures with any of the names preceding the heading statement. Any PL/I statement may have multiple labels, but we shall restrict our usage to single labels.

XIII.1.1.1   External Procedures

The basic rule governing the placement of procedures in a program is directly analogous to the one defining the use of **DO** groups. Procedures may be stacked adjacent to each other, with each organized as an independent entity, or they may be wholly contained in other procedures. When the former is the case, when a procedure is not contained inside another one, it is known as an *external procedure*, and its name an *external name*. In addition, PL/I nomenclature assigns special meaning to the word "contained" in this context; all of the text in a procedure, with the exception of its name (or names), is considered to be *contained in* that procedure.

A specific type of external procedure crucial to every program is the *main procedure*, whose heading statement takes the form

label: **PROCEDURE OPTIONS (MAIN)**;

Every program must include one main procedure. The handling of programs with more than one main procedure is controlled by the supervisory software under which a particular PL/I implementation operates. If a program consists of only one procedure, it must be a main procedure. A program consisting of three external procedures can be represented as follows:

EPMAIN: **PROCEDURE OPTIONS (MAIN)**;

      statement;

         .
         .
         .

      END EPMAIN;

    EP2: **PROCEDURE**;

      statement;

         .
         .
         .

      END EP2;

    EP3: **PROCEDURE**;

      statement;

         .
         .
         .

      END EP3;

If the user should wish to facilitate the development of such a program by compiling and debugging the procedures separately, each one can be tested in conjunction with a fake main procedure. In essence, this creates three separate programs that can be compiled independently. Note that although the instructions above in EP2 and EP3 physically follow those in EPMAIN, references to the subservient procedures from EPMAIN will cause them to be executed before EPMAIN is finished, so that the last statement processed in the program is **END** EPMAIN;.

XIII.1.1.2   Internal Procedures

A procedure whose entire text is embedded in another block is called an *internal procedure*. The structure is similar to that of an external procedure, beginning with a labeled **PROCEDURE** statement and concluding with an **END** statement that may or may not be labeled. Internal procedures may themselves contain other procedures, according to organizational rules, that are exact parallels to those for **DO** loops. Any arrangement of procedures is organizationally correct as long as no procedure is only partially contained in another. Thus, on the following page, the arrangement on the left is acceptable, but the one on the right is not. The organization on the left represents a program consisting of two external procedures EPMAIN and EP2, the first of which is the main procedure. EPMAIN contains the internal procedure IP1, and EP2 contains the three internal procedures IP2, IP3, and IP4. The one on the right is illegal because the **END** statements for IP2 and EP2 are improperly placed.

XIII.1.2   The **BEGIN** Block

Having used the **BEGIN** block earlier (Chapter VI), we shall limit its consideration here to a review of its properties and an examination of its relation to other procedural blocks.

This basic program component has the general structure

> label: **BEGIN**;
>
> ~~~~~~/ statements;
> *optional*
>
> .
>
> .
>
> .   — *optional*
>
> label#1: **END** label;
> *optional*

The **BEGIN** block is basically different from the procedure block, as it is not referenced remotely by the program (that is, not used out of sequence). Instead, the block is placed at that point in the program where it is intended to be used, and it is executed as the program reaches it in its normal sequence. There is no specific necessity for a heading label, but one (or more) may be included if desired. The **END** statement may, but does not have to, repeat the heading label, and that statement may itself be labeled.

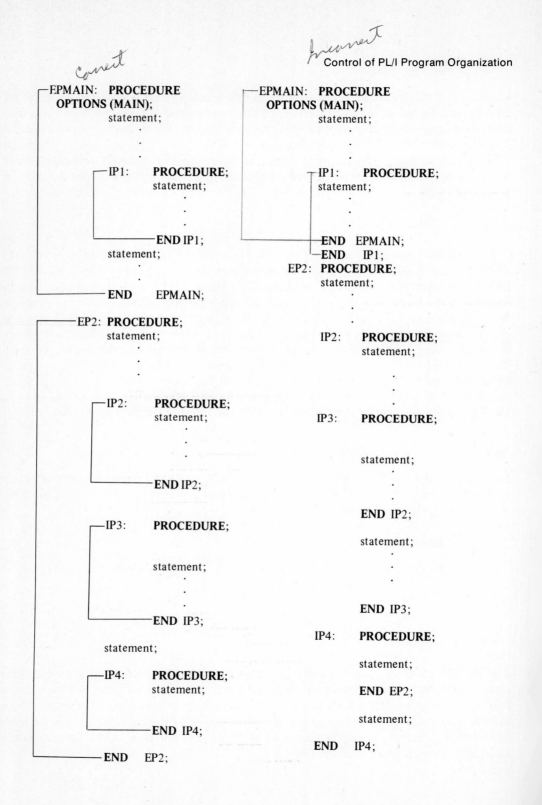

Correct

```
┌─EPMAIN:  PROCEDURE
│  OPTIONS (MAIN);
│      statement;
│          .
│          .
│          .
│      ┌─IP1:      PROCEDURE;
│      │      statement;
│      │          .
│      │          .
│      │          .
│      └──────END IP1;
│          statement;
│              .
│              .
│              .
└────── END          EPMAIN;

┌─EP2:  PROCEDURE;
│      statement;
│          .
│          .
│          .
│      ┌─IP2:      PROCEDURE;
│      │      statement;
│      │          .
│      │          .
│      │          .
│      └──────END IP2;
│
│      ┌─IP3:      PROCEDURE;
│      │
│      │      statement;
│      │          .
│      │          .
│      │          .
│      └──────END IP3;
│          statement;
│      ┌─IP4:      PROCEDURE;
│      │      statement;
│      │          .
│      │          .
│      │          .
│      └──────END IP4;
└───── END    EP2;
```

Incorrect

```
┌─EPMAIN:  PROCEDURE
│  OPTIONS (MAIN);
│      statement;
│          .
│          .
│          .
│  ┌─IP1:      PROCEDURE;
│  │  statement;
│  │      .
│  │      .
│  │      .
└──┤ END   EPMAIN;
   └─END    IP1;
    EP2:  PROCEDURE;
        statement;
            .
            .
            .
        IP2:      PROCEDURE;
            statement;

                .
                .
                .
        IP3:      PROCEDURE;

            statement;
                .
                .
                .
        END  IP2;
            statement;
                .
                .
                .
        END  IP3;
        IP4:      PROCEDURE;
            statement;
        END  EP2;

            statement;
        END    IP4;
```

Because of this difference in use, there can be no such thing as an external **BEGIN** block. The only way it can be used at all is by being fully contained in some type of procedure block (either external or internal) or in another **BEGIN** block, as long as that one is in turn included in a procedure. *pg345*

Strictly speaking, of course, there is one concept in which the usage of a **BEGIN** block may occur out of normal sequence. We have seen this in Illustration 32, where such a block is used to specify the action to be performed on encountering **ENDFILE**. Accordingly, that action preempts other processing when this condition occurs, even though the pertinent statements are elsewhere in the procedure.

XIII.1.3   Relationships between Blocks in a Program

Although each block in a program is a separate organizational entity that can name its own variables, assign and release its own storage, perform its own input-output, and so on, it must still carry some link to other procedures in the program. The nature of these relationships and the nomenclature associated with them can be explored with the aid of the following program:

```
EPMAIN:   PROCEDURE OPTIONS (MAIN);
            statement1;
            statement2;
              IP1:  PROCEDURE;
                    statement3;
                      B1:   BEGIN;
                            statement4;
                            statement5;
                            statement6;
                            END B1;
                    statement7;
                      IP2:  PROCEDURE;
                            statement8;
                            statement9;
                            END IP2;
                    statement10;
                    END IP1;
            statement11;
            END EPMAIN;
EP2:  PROCEDURE;
      statement12;
        B2: BEGIN;
            statement13;
            statement14;
            END B2;
      END EP2;
```

1. Basically, this program consists of two external procedures. The first of these EP-MAIN, contains the internal procedure IP1 which in turn, contains the **BEGIN** block B1 and the internal procedure IP2. The second external procedure, EP2, contains the **BEGIN** block B2.

2. The word "contain" is also used to describe the extent of a block. In general, *a block is said to contain all of its text with the exception of its heading name (or names).* The first external procedure above contains everything starting from "**PROCE-DURE OPTIONS(MAIN)**;" through "**END EPMAIN,**". Note that "**EPMAIN;**" is not considered to be contained in the procedure.
    Internal procedure IP1 is said to contain everything starting with the **PROCEDURE** statement through "**END IP1;**".
    Block B1 contains everything starting with "**BEGIN;**" through "**END B1;**."
    All text starting immediately after "IP2;" and ending with "**END IP2;**" is contained in procedure IP2.
    EP2 contains everything starting immediately *after* the label "EP2;" through the statement "**END EP2;**".
    The block B2 contains all information from its "**BEGIN**" through "**END B2;**."

3. The phrase "internal to" has a special meaning in PL/I, distinct from the description "internal." When a block B is included in some other block A, there is information in A outside of B's limits. If such information is not within the limits of any other block contained in A, this information is said to be *internal to block* A. For the program above, the implications are as follows:

    Statement1, statement2, the designation "IP1:", and statement11 are all internal to the procedure EPMAIN. Note that "IP1:" is included, based on the usage of the word "contained" in in the previous definition.
    Statement3, the designation "B1:," statement7, "IP2:" and statement10 are all internal to procedure IP1.
    By virtue of the definition of "internal to," **BEGIN**, statement4, statement5, and statement6, and the statement **END** B1 are internal to block B1; similarly, the statement **PROCEDURE**, statement8 and statement9, and **END** IP2 are all internal to IP2.
    The information internal to procedure EP2 consists of **PROCEDURE**, statement12, the designation "B2:" and "**END EP2;**".
    That leaves us with the information internal to block B2, which consists of "**BE-GIN;**", statement13 and statement14, and "**END B2;**".

Although this may seem an excessive burden of definitions, the importance of these organizational concepts will become apparent when we deal with the recognition of variables in blocks.

XIII.1.4   The **PROCESS** Statement   — *Used in compilation*

One of the most conspicuous advantages of building programs by combining distinct procedural modules is that such components can be developed independently. When the component procedures are brought together in source language form to compose a program, it is often appropriate to retain some of them as external procedures. (This is particularly true when the source modules come from different contexts; additional information is referenced at the end of the chapter.)

PL/I provides special support for the compilation of several external procedures into a single program. The primary vehicle for this purpose is the **PROCESS** statement, its basic form being

   * **PROCESS**;

The asterisk must appear in column 1 of a new card. The keyword **PROCESS** may appear anywhere within the area of the card in which PL/I statements are permitted (usually columns 2-72). This type of card is placed between adjacent *external* procedures in a program. Thus, if we were to compile the program whose organization is shown in the previous section, there would be a **PROCESS** card between EPMAIN and EP2 as follows:

```
Col. 1                  .
 |                      .
 |                      .
 |           statement11;
 |           END EPMAIN;
 *  PROCESS;
       EP2: PROCEDURE;
            statement12;
                        .
                        .
                        .
                        .
```

If desired, the programmer may (optionally) specify a variety of compiler options on the **PROCESS** card enclosed in parentheses between the word **PROCESS** and the semicolon. The exact format and use of these options depends on the version of the compiler being used.

XIII.2 TRANSFER OF CONTROL BETWEEN PROCEDURES

When a program is organized as a combination of several procedures, the division of labor is usually such that each procedure executes and is responsible for a particular assignment in the overall processing scheme. For example, it is often organizationally advantageous to provide a separate procedure for handling all input transactions, another for output transactions, and others for specific groups of internal manipulations. Consistent with this delegation of work, it becomes the duty of the main procedure to steer the entire sequence of operations by turning control over to the proper procedure at the proper time. Programmers in many installations routinely design main procedures consisting of little more than a series of references to other procedures whose composite effort achieves the desired information-processing objectives.

The main procedure acts as a focal point from which directions are issued regarding the disposition of the processing. Since each procedure in such a program is a separate organizational entity, the main program provides the mechanism for turning over control of the processing to each procedure as it is needed. Once the procedure's job is done, the main procedure automatically resumes control, and exectution of its instructions proceeds in normal sequence. When the subordinate procedure is in control, it may make use of other procedures to which it relinquishes control temporarily.

PL/I provides several types of statements for this general purpose. The choice depends on the type of procedure being referenced and the nature of the processing it is designed to do.

Procedures are not executed in sequence. The boundaries of a procedure are carefully protected so that even an attempted penetration by means of a **GO TO** statement will be thwarted. PL/I provides two basic processes for transferring control from one procedure to another (a process known as *invocation*). One of these, known as a *function reference*, invokes a procedure (called a *function*) by using its name in an expression in the invoking procedure in the same way that a built-in function is referenced. The second mechanism used to invoke a *subroutine*, a procedure whose construction differs slightly from that of a function, is activated by means of a separate command known as the **CALL** statement.

XIII.2.1   Function Procedures

Perhaps the most common type of job assigned to a separate procedure is the generation of a value that bears some specific relation to the value or values supplied to that procedure. This is the exact purpose of the built-in functions. The value or values supplied to the functions as a list of arguments are operated on in some prescribed manner, and the single result of these manipulations is returned to the programmer. PL/I makes it possible for the programmer to develop his own functions for use in exactly the same manner. This purpose is fulfilled by the function procedure, whose construction is depicted on the next page. "Label" once again is the compulsory heading name for the procedure, and (parm1, parm2, etc.) is a list of names used by the function procedure in performing its operations.

    label: **PROCEDURE** (parm1,parm2,etc.);

       statement1;

       statement2;

        .

        .

        .

       RETURN(expression);

  label#1: **END** label;

These names, called *parameters*, do not specify actual variable names. Instead, they are general in nature, serving to indicate the number of arguments to be supplied to the particular procedure and what type these arguments are to be. "Expression" is any legitimate PL/I expression (arithmetic or otherwise) whose evaluation produces a single (scalar) value. This value is transferred back to the invoking procedure by means of the **RETURN** statement.

To illustrate, suppose that a particular organization is engaged in a series of analyses, many of which involve the calculation of annular areas (the area between two concentric circles). Instead of including instructions to calculate such an area each time it is required, it was decided to write a function procedure to do the job once and for all. Hence, if RBIG is the radius of the larger circle and RSMALL is the radius of the smaller circle, A (the area of the resulting annulus) is calculated as

  $A = 3.14159*(RBIG**2-RSMALL**2);$

or

  $A = 3.14159*(RBIG+RSMALL)*(RBIG-RSMALL);$

(assuming RBIG and RSMALL are in the same units). The required function procedure could be written as

  ANNL: **PROCEDURE**(RBIG,RSMALL);

       RETURN (3.14159*(RBIG+RSMALL)*(RBIG-RSMALL));

       END ANNL;

By incorporating this function procedure somewhere in the program, it can be invoked once or many times, from virtually anywhere in the program.

XIII.2.1.1. Invocation of Function Procedures

Once a function procedure has been designed and added to a program, the program can use it as it would a built-in function. The procedure will be referenced, its operations performed, and its results made available to the program by means of the **RETURN** statement. PL/I treats the **RETURN** statement quite literally. After evaluating the attached expression, it drops whatever it is doing and climbs out of the procedure, returning control to the point of invocation. For all intents and purposes, the invoked procedure is terminated, even though it may contain additional statements that were not executed.

The function is invoked by using the procedure name, together with an appropriate argument list, in some legitimate statement. Let us suppose that we have a program whose main procedure reads in values D, V, a large radius R2, and a small radius R1. Using these values, it is desired to calculate a result W equal to the product and D and V multiplied by the annular area bounded by R2 and R1. The appropriate main program could appear as

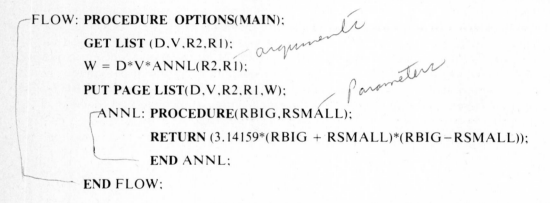

```
FLOW: PROCEDURE  OPTIONS(MAIN);
      GET LIST (D,V,R2,R1);          arguments
      W = D*V*ANNL(R2,R1);
      PUT PAGE LIST(D,V,R2,R1,W);          Parameters
      ANNL: PROCEDURE(RBIG,RSMALL);
            RETURN (3.14159*(RBIG + RSMALL)*(RBIG – RSMALL));
            END ANNL;
      END FLOW;
```

Although the use of the name ANNL in the assignment statement for W looks as if it could refer to an array with subscript (R2,R1), PL/I will permit it to act as if it were the name of a procedure. Finding that the program includes a function by the name of ANNL, PL/I can then transfer control to the first statement in ANNL.

XIII.2.1.2 Arguments Versus Parameters

Note that the names specified in the argument list of the main program's function reference are not the same as those given in the parameter list of the function's heading statement. These parameters are included for internal reference purposes and not as actual variable names. This usage is indicated by the compiler, which assigns the attribute **PARAMETER** to each of the names accompanying the **PROCEDURE** statement. When a function is referenced, each of the parameters in the **PROCEDURE** statement is paired with the argument in the same position of the invoking reference and used accordingly. This process is known as *binding*. Thus, in the previous example, R2 is used where RBIG appears, and R1 is used where there is a reference to RSMALL. As a result, the values used in determining W will be

$$W = D*V + 3.14159*(R2+R1)*(R2-R1);$$

If too many or too few arguments are given, PL/I will use the number given by the parameter list, but it will produce a warning message.

attribute

XIII.2.1.3 Attributes of Returned Values—The RETURNS Option

Contrary to what one might expect, the attributes of the value developed by a function procedure are tied (by default) to the *name* of the procedure rather than the attributes of the terms in the returned expression. The conventions are the same as those in force for variable names: Unless otherwise specified, functions named by identifiers beginning with I, J, K, L, M, or N will return **FIXED BINARY** values with default precision; the other (legitimate) starting characters force the return of a floating-point value. Thus, if a function begins with the statement

ANNL: **PROCEDURE**(RBIG,RSMALL);

its name (ANNL) will cause it to return a **FLOAT DECIMAL** value even if RBIG and RSMALL were declared as **FIXED**.

This mechanism does no particular harm in most situations where the function develops a numerical value and the invoking procedure expects one. However, when this is not the case a mismatch in attributes produces an error condition. Without an explicit way to overcome this, it would be impossible, for instance, to develop (and use) a function that returns a nonnumeric character string.

PL/I handles the necessary communication of attributes by means of the **RETURNS** feature. Applied to the function procedure, it is an option that is used when returned attributes must be defined explicitly. For example, if the opening statement of the function ANNL says

ANNL: **PROCEDURE** (RBIG,RSMALL) **RETURNS** (FIXED DECIMAL(5,2));

there is sufficient direction to motivate PL/I to convert the computed value to **FIXED**(5,2).

Once the **RETURNS** option is specified for a function, it *must* be specified in the procedure that invokes the function. In this context, **RETURNS** is an *attribute* and, as such, appears in a declaration. For example, a procedure using ANNL as specified above would include the declaration

DECLARE ANNL **ENTRY RETURNS** (FIXED(5,2));

This may be a separate **DECLARE** statement (as shown here) or part of another declaration. The **ENTRY** attribute indicates that ANNL is a procedure to be invoked. Note that the use of the **RETURNS** option in ANNL ensures the return of a value with the specified attributes. However, it does not guarantee that the invoking procedure will *expect* a value with those attributes. In fact, if **RETURNS** does not appear as a declared attribute in the invoking procedure, that procedure will be looking for a set of attributes consistent with the function's name. It has no information to the contrary and cannot receive such information. Consequently, the situation must be set up in advance as an intrinsic part of the invoking procedure—hence the required declaration.

Since the presence of the **RETURNS** attribute makes sense only in a very specific context, it is not necessary to include the **ENTRY** attribute. A PL/I default will add this automatically, so that the statement

DECLARE ANNL **RETURNS(FIXED**(5,2));

is equivalent to the one shown before.

The handling of the situation described above varies somewhat from compiler to compiler. The IBM PL/I-F compiler treats internal and external function procedures the same, and the programmer must act as outlined above in either case. On the other hand, the Optimizing and Checkout Compilers behave somewhat differently in the case of internal procedures: since the procedure is internal, the compiler takes the liberty of "looking inside" to discover the attributes of the parameters and the return value; therefore, with these compilers, not only is it unnecessary, but it is illegal to include a **DECLARE** statement for an *internal* entry point. Such a declaration is still necessary, however, for an *external* entry point.

XIII.2.1.4   Alternate Entries for Function Procedures

It is often desirable to construct a function with more than one starting point. This can be done by providing secondary entries through the use of the **ENTRY** statement, whose general form is

label:**ENTRY**;

This statement is placed in the function procedure immediately ahead of the point at which the alternative start is to occur. The compulsory label attached to the **ENTRY** statement supplies the name for this secondary entry point and has given the **ENTRY** attribute by virtue of its attachment to the **ENTRY** statement. A procedure may have any number of entry points.

Since a procedure can assume control at this secondary entry point instead of its primary one, this point must also be equipped to receive argument values. Consequently, a suitable list of parameters must be attached to the **ENTRY** statement in the same manner as for the **PROCEDURE** statement. This list need not be identical to the one attached to the primary entry point.

Illustration 37

The use of a secondary entry point can be illustrated by a simple extension of the function procedure ANNL, used in the previous example. Suppose the situation is such that the program has to read and process two sets of input values. The first of these consists of values for D, V, and two additional values, R1 and R2; the second set also contains D and V, but R1 and R2 are replaced by measurements representing diameters rather than radii. In order to handle both contingencies with a single function procedure, we shall design it so that the primary entry point (at the **PROCEDURE** statement) expects the arguments to be submitted as diameters. We shall incorporate a secondary entry point wherein the arguments can be submitted as radii. Between entry points, of course, we shall include a statement to calculate the radii from the diameters. Consequently, our program could look as follows:

```
STMT  LEVEL NEST
  1                    ILL37: PROCEDURE OPTIONS (MAIN);
  2     1                     DECLARE D FIXED(5,2),
                                (V,W) FIXED (4,2),
                                (X1,X2) FLOAT DECIMAL (6),
                                (T,N INITIAL(0)) FIXED BINARY,
                                S BIT(1) INITIAL('1'B),
                                (ANNL,ANNL1) ENTRY RETURNS (FIXED(6,2));

                           /* IF T = 1, X1 AND X2 ARE RADII; IF T = 2, */
                           /* THEY ARE DIAMETERS. IN EITHER CASE, X1   */
                           /* OR X2 MAY BE THE LARGER DIMENSION.       */

  3     1                     ON ENDFILE(SYSIN) S = '0'B;
  5     1                     PUT PAGE LINE(3) EDIT ('RUN','D','V','R1','R2',
                                'D1','D2','W')
                                (X(5),A,X(4),A,X(9),A,X(6), 4 (A,X(8),A));
  6     1                     PUT SKIP;

  7     1                     DO WHILE (S);
  8     1   1                    GET LIST (T,D,V,X1,X2);
  9     1   1                    N = N+1;
 10     1   1                    IF T = 1
 11     1   1                       THEN DO;
 12     1   2                          W = D*V*ANNL1(X1,X2);
 13     1   2                          PUT SKIP EDIT(N,D,V,X1,X2,W)
                                          (X(5),F(2),X(4),F(6,2),X(4),F(5,1),
                                          2 (X(4),F(5,2)),X(25),F(5,1));
                                       /***************************************/
                                       /* NOTE THAT X1 AND X2 ARE POSITIONED */
                                       /* UNDER THE COLUMNS HEADED R1 AND R2.*/
                                       /***************************************/
 14     1   2                          END;
 15     1   1                       ELSE DO;
 16     1   2                          W = D*V*ANNL(X1,X2);
 17     1   2                          PUT SKIP EDIT(N,D,V,2*X1,2*X2,W)
                                          (X(5),F(2),X(4),F(6,2),X(4),F(5,1),
                                          X(23), 2 (F(5,2),X(5)),F(5,1));
 18     1   2                          END;
 19     1   1                    END;

 20     1                     ┌─────────────────────────────────────────────────────┐
 21     2                     │  ANNL: PROCEDURE (X,Y) RETURNS(FIXED(6,2));          │
 23     2                     │       X = X/2;      Y = Y/2;                         │
 24     2                     │  ANNL1: ENTRY (X,Y) RETURNS(FLOAT DECIMAL(6));       │
 25     2                     │       RETURN (3.14159*(X+Y)*ABS(X-Y));               │
                              │       END ANNL;                                     │
                              └─────────────────────────────────────────────────────┘

 26     1                     PUT SKIP(3) DATA (N);
 27     1                     END ILL37;
```

The organizational relations between the procedures is indicated by the "Level" column given with the listing. While normally unobtrusive, this can be a valuable diagnostic aid in determining the activity of various statements and the availability of the variables to which they refer.

Further organizational information is provided by the "Nest" column, which shows the extent of contained **DO** groups.

In this program, the function that computes annular areas has two entry points: ANNL takes care of the arguments when they are submitted as diameters; ANNL1, the secondary entry point, avoids the halving operations that convert diameters to radii. We have introduced the ABS function to illustrate that the use of a PL/I built-in function in a procedure is perfectly legitimate. The purpose of **ABS** in this context is to make the order in which the two arguments are specified immaterial. The proper magnitude will be calculated regardless of whether X1 is less than X2 or vice versa.

XIII.2.1.5   Multiple Returns in a Function

When the situation calls for it, a decision mechanism may be included in a function such that its outcome is used to dictate the type of calculation to be performed. This is done by specifying the alternative calculations in separate **RETURN** statements and providing appropriate linkages to them.

Illustration 37A

To illustrate, we shall institute a change in the function ANNL: If the ratio of the smaller radius to the larger radius is greater than 0.7, it turns out that 8 percent of the annular area is unavailable, and the effective area has to be calculated as 92 percent of the geometric area.

```
ILL37A: PROCEDURE OPTIONS (MAIN);
        DECLARE D FIXED (5,2),
                (V,W) FIXED (4,2),
                (X1,X2) FLOAT DECIMAL (6),
                (T,N INITIAL(0)) FIXED BINARY,
                S BIT (1) INITIAL ('1'B),
                (ANNL,ANNL1) ENTRY RETURNS (FIXED(6,2));

        ON ENDFILE (SYSIN) S = '0'B;
        PUT PAGE LINE(3) EDIT ('RUN','D','V','R1','R2','D1','D2','W')
           (X(5),A,X(4),A,X(9),A,X(6), 4 (A,X(8)),A);
        PUT SKIP;

        DO WHILE (S);
          GET LIST (T,D,V,X1,X2);
          N = N+1;
          IF T = 1
            THEN DO;
                    W = ROUND(D*V*ANNL1(X1,X2),1);
                    PUT SKIP EDIT(N,D,V,X1,X2,W)
                       (X(5),F(2),X(4),F(6,2),X(4),F(5,1),
                        2 (X(4),F(5,2)),X(25),F(5,1));
                 END;
            ELSE DO;
                    W = ROUND(D*V*ANNL(X1,X2),1);
                    PUT SKIP EDIT(N,D,V,X1,X2,W)
                       (X(5),F(2),X(4),F(6,2),X(4),F(5,1),
                        X(23), 2 (F(5,2),X(5)),F(5,1));
                 END;
        END;


          ANNL: PROCEDURE (X,Y) RETURNS (FIXED(6,2));
                X = X/2;           Y = Y/2;
          ANNL1: ENTRY (X,Y) RETURNS (FLOAT DECIMAL(6));
                IF MIN(X,Y)/MAX(X,Y) <= 0.7
                   THEN RETURN (3.14159*(X+Y)*ABS(X-Y));
                   ELSE RETURN (0.92*3.14159*(X+Y)*ABS(X-Y));
                END ANNL;


        PUT SKIP(3) DATA (N);
        END ILL37A;
```

We shall retain our previous features—namely, the two entry points and the use of the **ABS** function to allow the two radii (or diameters) to be transmitted to ANNL in either size order. To handle the fact that the ratio must be obtained with the smaller radius as the numerator, we shall avoid having to find out explicitly which is which by using the **MAX** and **MIN** functions. Note that this organization was used just to illustrate the use of multiple **RETURN**s in a function. It would have been more efficient (and somewhat easier) to assign the appropriate calculation to an auxiliary variable and return that. For instance,

C = 3.14159*(X + Y)***ABS**(X − Y);

IF **MIN**(X,Y)/**MAX**(X,Y)<= .7 **THEN**;

                                  ELSE C = .92*C;

RETURN(C);

XIII.2.2   Subroutines

A function procedure returns a single value each time it is invoked. (Although most of the PL/I built-in functions can be used in array expressions, each of them really returns a scalar value.) To handle situations in which multiple values are to be returned, and a wide variety of other contingencies, PL/I provides the more versatile *subroutine procedure*. The construction of a subroutine is basically the same as that used for a function, except that the results of the subroutine's processing are not transmitted by the **RETURN** statement. As with functions, subroutines may be internal or external procedures.

XIII.2.2.1   Invocation of Subroutine Procedures

Invocation of a subroutine is effected by means of a **CALL** statement having the general form

  CALL procedure-name (arg1,arg2,etc.);

where "procedure-name" is the label (or one of the labels, if there are several) attached to any of the entry points and (arg1, arg2, etc.) have their previous meanings. The **CALL** may appear anywhere in the procedure, either by itself or as part of a conditional statement. That is, it is quite legitimate to set up a test condition (for example, an **IF** or **ON** statement) where the **CALL** is a consequent action.

XIII.2.2.2   Formal Parameters in a Subroutine

Entry statements for a subroutine contain a list of parameters that play exactly the same roles as they do in functions.

Illustration 37B

As an example let us modify the previous program by converting ANNL from a function to a subroutine. For this purpose, we shall introduce an additional parameter, A, which will be used to denote the annular area. AREA will be the name for the corresponding argument. We shall use a version of the program having both primary and secondary entry points.

```
ILL37B: PROCEDURE OPTIONS (MAIN);
        DECLARE D FIXED (5,2),
                (V,W) FIXED (4,2),
                (X1,X2,ARAN) FLOAT DECIMAL (6),
                (T,N INITIAL(0)) FIXED BINARY,
                S BIT(1) INITIAL ('1'B),
                (ANNL,ANNL1) ENTRY;

        ON ENDFILE (SYSIN) S = '0'B;
        PUT PAGE LINE(3) EDIT ('RUN','D','V','R1','R2','D1','D2','W')
            (X(5),A,X(4),A,X(9),A,X(6), 4 (A,X(8)),A);
        PUT SKIP;

        DO WHILE (S);
          GET LIST (T,D,V,X1,X);
          N = N+1;
          IF T = 1
            THEN DO;
                    CALL ANNL1(X1,X2,ARAN);
                    W = D*V*ARAN;
                    PUT SKIP EDIT (N,D,V,X1,X2,W)
                        (X(5),F(2),X(4),F(6,2),X(4),F(5,1),
                          2 (X(4),F(5,2)),X(25),F(5,1));
                 END;
            ELSE DO;
                    CALL ANNL(X1,X2,ARAN);
                    W = D*V*ARAN;
                    PUT SKIP EDIT (N,D,V,X1,X2,W)
                        (X(5),F(2),X(4),F(6,2),X(4),F(5,1),
                          X(23), 2 (F(5,2),X(5)),F(5,1));
                 END;
        END;


        ANNL: PROCEDURE (X,Y,Z);
              X = X/2;                 Y = Y/2;
        ANNL1: ENTRY (X,Y,Z);
               IF MIN(X,Y)/MAX(X,Y) <= 0.7
                 THEN Z = 3.14159*(X+Y)*ABS(X-Y));
                 ELSE Z = 0.92*3.14159*(X+Y)*ABS(X-Y));
               RETURN;
               END ANNL;


        PUT SKIP(3) DATA (N);
        END ILL37B;
```

This subroutine (ANNL) could just as easily have been written as an external procedure. The **RETURN** statement requires no parenthesized expression, as the information is transferred by modifying the parameter Z. Since the **RETURN** statement is last in the procedure, it would be omitted entirely; the **END** statement would serve as well.

XIII.2.2.3   Processing of Arrays and Structures in Subroutines

In order for PL/I to know that a particular subroutine is to process arrays or structures, sufficient information must be included in the procedure to describe the aggregate completely. Thus, if we wish to design a procedure for adjusting each of the 20 values of a one-dimensional array Z by using a reference value ZREF as a common divisor and expressing each element as a proportion of ZREF, we must identify one of the parameters as an array. This is done with a suitable declaration:

ADJUST: **PROCEDURE**(ZREF,Z);

        DECLARE (ZREF, Z(20))**FIXED**(6,3);

        Z = Z/ZREF;

        END ADJUST;

The arguments in the invoking procedure must, of course, be correspondingly declared. If the array declaration in the invoked procedure is dimensioned with asterisks rather than numbers, PL/I is signaled to expect an array, but there is no constraint on its size. Hence, if we wrote ADJUST as

ADJUST: **PROCEDURE**(ZREF,Z);

        DECLARE (ZREF, Z(*))**FIXED**(6,3);

        Z = Z/ZREF;

        END ADJUST;

the procedure would accept a one-dimensional array of any size as an argument, as long as its value were **FIXED**(6,3).

To ensure the proper processing of structures, the subroutine must include a declaration in which the anatomy of each structure named in the parameter list is clearly defined.

XIII.2.2.4   Alternate Returns from Subroutines

In contrast to the function procedure, *the subroutine does not return a value directly through the* **RETURN** *statement*; it need not return any values at all. For example, a subroutine may be called upon to arrange and print data that had been read in by another subroutine and processed internally by a third one.

Because of these contingencies, it may be useful to terminate processing in a subroutine by some mechanism besides the **RETURN** statement. One alternative is the **END** statement itself. In addition to indicating the physical endpoint of the subroutine, this statement will activate the mechanism that transfers control back to the invoking procedure.

A third possibility for return from a subroutine is the **GO TO** statement, when its destination is a statement outside of the procedure. This technique is rather restrictive, however, on the location of the destination. Consistent with the general mechanism handling the transfer of control between procedures, the **GO TO** statement can only be used in an internal procedure and must send the program to a statement in a block that contains that internal procedure.

Termination of a procedure is also possible by means of the more drastic **STOP** and **EXIT** statements, each of which terminates the entire program.

XIII.2.3   Activation of Internal Procedures

PL/I imposes a restriction on how nested internal procedures (for example, a procedure within a second procedure within a third) may be invoked. In situations such as these, direct transfer of control may occur only between two procedures immediately related to each other. This is exemplified by the external procedure symbolically structured in Table 13.1:

TABLE 13.1   A Program Organized with Nested Procedures

```
EP:   PROCEDURE OPTIONS (MAIN);
          statement1;
C1:   CALL IP1;
C2:   CALL IP2;
          statement2;
C3:   CALL IP1;
          IP1:  PROCEDURE;
                    statement3;
          C11:  CALL IP3;
          C12:  CALL IP2;
                    statement4;
                    IP3:  PROCEDURE;
                              statement5;
                              statement6;
                              END IP3;
                    statement7;
                    END IP1;
          IP2:  PROCEDURE;
                    statement8;
                    statement9;
                    statement10;
                    END IP2;
          statement11;
          END EP;
```

This program consists of a single external procedure, EP, which is also the main procedure. Internal procedures IP1, IP2, and IP3 are contained in EP; IP3 is contained in IP1. Since EP is the main procedure, it controls the activities of the other procedures in the program and therefore is said to remain active during the entire set of processing operations. We can trace the sequence of events in this program as follows:

1.   When processing begins, EP is the only active procedure in the program. This situation remains unchanged through the execution of statement1. During this time, the program does not "know" anything about procedures IP1 or IP2 except that such procedures are available to it by means of the primary entry names IP1 and IP2.

2. Immediately after statement1 is executed, the **CALL** to IP1 activates that internal procedure. (The main procedure EP remains active, of course, so that control can be transferred back to it once IP1 is finished.)

3. Activation of IP1 causes execution to start on the statements contained in that procedure; the entry names IP2 and IP3 are now available to IP1. It is only at this point that the entry name IP3 first becomes "available." Conseqently, IP3 could not have been called directly by EP, even though the former is contained in EP. By the same token, although IP1, when activated, "knows" of IP3, the procedure IP2 does not, so that in this situation IP1 is the only procedure which can issue a direct **CALL** to IP3. The exact same restrictions hold true for function references.

4. After execution of statement3, IP3 is activated, followed by execution of statement5 and statement6.

5. Upon reaching IP3's **END** statement, control is returned to IP1 at the point immediately after **CALL** to IP3.

6. This is followed by a **CALL** to procedure IP2, which is activated, and statement8, statement9, and statement10 are executed. Upon reaching the **END** statement, control passes back to IP1, and processing resumes in that procedure with statement4, followed by statement7 and the **END** statement.

7. Control now returns to the main procedure, which invokes IP2.

8. Statement8, statement9, and statement10 are executed, and the subsequent **END** statement sends control back to the main procedure at statement2. Since IP2 and IP1 are both contained in EP but neither is contained in the other, the IP2 does not "know" anything about the existence of IP3 and, therefore, could not have called that procedure. IP1, on the other hand, could have been invoked.

9. Following the execution of statement2, a second call is made to IP1, causing executtion of statement3, all the statements contained in IP3, and all the statements contained in IP2, followed by execution of statement4, statement7, and return of control to the main procedure at statement11.

10. Following the execution of statement11, the end of the main program is encountered and processing is concluded.

To summarize, the availability of entry names to procedures allows EP to invoke IP1 and/or IP2 (but not IP3); IP1 may invoke IP3 as well as IP2; IP2 can invoke IP1 (but not IP3); and IP3 can invoke nothing at all. If it were found necessary to transfer control out of one of these procedures before reaching its **END** statement, the **GO TO** statement could be used as follows: a **GO TO** in procedure IP1 or IP2 could transfer control to any of the statements internal to EP (statement1, statement2, statement11, or any of the three **CALLS**). A **GO TO** in procedure IP3 can have as its destination any of the statements internal to IP1 as well as those internal to EP.

Stated as a general rule, the **GO TO** statement, when used to transfer control out of an internal procedure, may have as its destination any statement (with the exception of entry points) in any containing procedure. It cannot be used to go the other direction (from an outer procedure to one contained in it). Similarly, a **GO TO** cannot be used to transfer control between two separate procedures (such as IP1 and IP2 in our example). This is summarized (for the example in Table 13.1) in Tables 13.2 and 13.3.

Note that although IP2 may be called by IP1, it may not transfer to a point within either of these procedures via a **GO TO**. Thus, if IP2 were to be invoked from IP1, say, any such transfer would be to a point in EP and would therefore terminate not only IP2, but IP1 as well.

TABLE 13.2 Allowable Invocations
among Procedures*

Procedure	May **CALL**	May Be **CALL**ed by
EP	IP1,IP2	none
IP1	IP3,IP2	EP,IP2
IP2	IP1	EP,IP1,
IP3	none	IP1

* Referred to Program Organization in Table 13.1.

TABLE 13.3 Allowable Use of **GO TO** Statement to
Transfer Out of a Procedure*

Procedure Containing a **GO TO** Statement	Allowable Statements in Destination Procedure			
	EP	IP1	IP2	IP3
EP	all legal destinations	none	none	none
IP1	statement1, statement2, statement11, C1,C2,C3	all legal destinations	none	none
IP2	statement1, statement2, statement11, C1,C2,C3	none	all legal destinations	none
IP3	statement1, statement2, statement11, C1,C2,C3	statement3, statement4, C11,C12	none	all legal destinations

*Referred to Program Organization in Table 13.1

Although we have dwelt for some time on the effect of transferring out of a procedure (or block) with a **GO TO**, we should point out that in general this is a very questionable practice. Such a technique is not only very expensive in terms of the computer time it consumes, but also makes the flow of control within the program difficult to follow. As a consequence, it should be used only when all other ways of achieving the same objective are even more "unnatural" and awkward.

XIII.3   TRANSFER OF INFORMATION BETWEEN PROCEDURES

As part of the process of transferring control from one procedure to another, suitable mechanisms must be set up and activated to ensure the proper transfer of information as well. In order for such a mechanism to be established, the programmer must supply certain descriptive information to both procedures involved in the exchange of control. Both the parameter and argument lists must be accompanied by specifications that provide a complete definition of the arguments being transferred to the invoked procedure, as well as the attributes of the values expected by it. As with other operations, PL/I will attempt to make certain assumptions regarding the attributes of these arguments and parameters when they are not explicitly specified. In many instances, however, the default mechanism cannot compensate for deficiency in specifications, and error conditions will result.

XIII.3.1   Transfer of Numerical Information

Thus far we have discussed and written programs in which procedures were invoked and returns were effected without the inclusion of descriptive information regarding the attributes or arguments or parameters. As a result, we have implicitly relied on PL/I's default mechanisms to assign the attributes and handle any necessary conversions. For example, in Illustration 37B, the compiler will treat arguments X1, X2, and ARAN as floating-point decimal numbers of default precision in accordance with its rules for variable names. Similarly, the names assigned to ANNL's parameter list define the acceptable attributes of the values to be transferred to that procedure when it is invoked. Hence, ANNL expects three floating-point decimal numbers of default precision. If the attributes of the arguments do not match these implied requirements, PL/I will not attempt to make the necessary conversions unless the programmer supplies additional descriptive information. This can be done, of course, either by providing suitable declarations in both procedures or by performing the necessary conversions in the invoking procedure prior to the function reference or **CALL** statement. The most frequent source of this problem lies in providing fixed decimal constants as arguments when **FIXED BINARY** or **FLOAT DECIMAL** values are expected by the subroutine or function.

Illustration 38

The first of these approaches is more straightforward and can be illustrated by modifying the program in Illustration 37B so that the processing is performed on fixed-point decimal values:

```
ILL38: PROCEDURE OPTIONS (MAIN);
       DECLARE (D,V,W,ARAN,X1,X2) FIXED (6,2),
       (T,N INITIAL(0)) FIXXED BINARY,
       S BIT (1) INITIAL('1'B),
       (ANNL,ANNL1) ENTRY;

       ON ENDFILE (SYSIN) S = '0'B;
       PUT PAGE LINE(3) EDIT ('RUN','D','V','R1','R2','D1','D2','W')
          (X(5),A,X(4),A,X(9),A,X(6), 4 (A,X(8)), A);
       PUT SKIP;

       DO WHILE (S);
          GET LIST (T,D,V,X1,X2);
          N = N+1;
          IF T = 1
             THEN DO;
                   CALL ANNL1(X1,X2,ARAN);
                   W = D*V*ARAN;
                   PUT SKIP EDIT(N,D,V,X1,X2,W)
                      (X(5),F(2),X(4),F(7,2),X(3),F(7,2),
                       2 (X(2),F(7,2)),X(25),F(7,2));
                END;
             ELSE DO;
                   CALL ANNL(X1,X2,ARAN);
                   W = D*V*ARAN;
                   PUT SKIP EDIT(N,D,V,X1,X2,W)
                      (X(5),F(2),X(4),F(7,2),X(3),F(7,2),
                       X(21), 2 (F(7,2),X(3)), F(7,2));
                END;
       END;

          ANNL: PROCEDURE (X,Y,Z);
                DECLARE (X,Y,Z) FIXED (6,2);
                X = X/2;          Y = Y/2;
          ANNL1: ENTRY (X,Y,Z);
                IF MIN(X,Y)/MAX(X,Y) <= 0.7
                   THEN Z = 3.14159*(X+Y)*ABS(X-Y));
                   ELSE Z = 0.92*3.14159*(X+Y)*ABS(X-Y));
                RETURN;
                END ANNL;

       PUT SKIP (3) DATA (N);
       END ILL38;
```

XIII.3.2 Arithmetic Expressions as Arguments

When a member of a parameter list is specified as a numerical value with certain attributes, it is not necessary for the corresponding argument to be a single variable. Instead, it may be any legitimate arithmetic expression that, when evaluated, will produce a single value whose attributes match those specified for the parameter. If the terms in such an expression possess attributes not consistent with those given for the parameter, conversion will *not* take place automatically. The expression will be evaluated in accordance with PL/I's internal conversion rules, with the attributes of the result being assigned accordingly. If additional conversion is to take place, the invoking procedure must be notified by means of an appropriate declaration listing the attributes of each argument as expected by the invoked procedure. Thus, if an internal procedure IP begins with the statement

IP: **PROCEDURE**(X,Y,Z);

   DECLARE (X,Y) **FIXED**(6,2), Z **FIXED**(10,4);

and an invoking procedure EP is to reference IP with the statement

CALL IP(3*A,B*C,C);

where A and B are declared as **FIXED**(4,1) and C is **FLOAT**, EP must somewhere contain a statement saying

DECLARE IP **ENTRY(FIXED**(6,2), **FIXED**(6,2), **FIXED**(10,4));

so that EP will know what the final values of the three arguments must look like. This will allow EP to calculate 3*A and B*C, convert the results to **FIXED**(6,2), and to convert C's value to **FIXED**(10,4), so that the attributes of the argument list match those of X, Y, and Z.

XIII.3.3   The **GENERIC** Attribute

In certain instances it may be necessary to design several procedures, each of which performs the same type of processing. The nature of the operational sequence may be such that a separate procedure is required for each type of argument. This is actually the case with many of PL/I's built-in functions. Although the user may be unaware of it, PL/I may invoke one procedure if the arguments are **FIXED**, a second if they are **FLOAT**, a third if they are **COMPLEX**, and so on. (For example, all of the trigonometric functions work this way.) The mechanism that makes this possible is the **GENERIC** attribute, which allows a number of functions to be identified by a common name referring to an entire family of functions, each of which has its unique name and a unique list of parameters. When the user invokes such a family of functions, he references them by using the generic name, treating it as if it were an ordinary entry point, and supplying it with an appropriate list of arguments. The program will examine this list and, depending on its composition, will select the appropriate member of the function family and transfer control to that specific procedure.

The general form for constructing such families of functions is to treat each one as a separate procedure, supplied with its own entry name and its own set of parameters. To make use of such a family in an invoking procedure, a declaration of the following type is made:

DECLARE family **GENERIC** (entry1(att1,att2,),entry2(att1,att2),etc.);

where "family" refers to the generic name to be used when one of the functions is invoked. Each of the functions to be included in this generic family must be identified by its unique entry name represented in the general statement by (entry1,entry2,etc.). To each entry name must be attached a list of expected attributes for each argument to be transferred to that entry point represented by (att1,att2,etc.). Thus, if we write

DECLARE FIXIT **GENERIC**(HOLD(**FIXED**(5,2),**FLOAT**(6)),

   TRY(**FLOAT**(4), **FIXED BINARY**(15)), WORK(**FLOAT**(5),**FLOAT**(5)));

we shall have informed the invoking procedure that three functions are available under the generic name FIXIT. The first of these, using HOLD as its entry point, will operate on two decimal arguments having the respective attributes **FIXED**(5,2) and **FLOAT**(6). The second, named TRY, expects its two arguments transferred as a four-digit floating-point decimal number and a 15-digit binary integer. The third member of this family, known as WORK, expects both its arguments to be five-digit floating-point decimal numbers. A typical invocation of this generic function is made by a statement such as

   Y = FIXIT(A,B);

The program will examine the attributes of the two arguments stipulated in the function reference statement and invoke the procedure whose list of parameter attributes match those of the arguments. Note that the generic name itself has no other attributes except **GENERIC**. In order for this mechanism to serve its purpose, the attribute list attached to each entry name in the family must be unique.

XIII.3.4   Nonnumeric Arguments

When a procedure is designed to process nonnumeric values, an explicit declaration must always be included in the procedure, since there is no way for PL/I to identify the type of variable from its name alone.

XIII.3.4.1   Character and Bit String Arguments

As long as suitable declarations are present in both the invoking and invoked procedures, character and bit values may be transferred between procedures with no basic restrictions. To extend the versatility of functions and subroutines designed to operate on such values, the **VARYING** attribute may be included in the declaration of the parameters so that the procedure is not tied to arguments of a given length.

Illustration 39

Write a program that reads pairs of five-character strings, transforms each string according to certain rules, concatenates the results, and prints each newly formed string, as well as the two original strings from which it was produced.

The transformations proceed as follows. If corresponding positions in a given pair of strings contain the same character, that character is replaced with a $ sign in both strings. Otherwise, if either of the characters in corresponding positions is a W, both characters are replaced with a #. There are no other reasons for changes.

Write the program so that the transformation is handled by a separate internal procedure. The two members of each character string pair are punched in columns 1-5 and 11-15 on a card.

We shall use CHAR1 and CHAR2 for the character string names, and CHANGE will be used for the internal procedure's entry name. Based on these considerations, our program will look as follows:

```
ILL39: PROCEDURE OPTIONS (MAIN);
        DECLARE (CHAR1,CHAR2,C1,C2) CHARACTER (5),
                LONG CHARACTER (10),
                S BIT(1) INITIAL ('1'B);

        ON ENDFILE (SYSIN) S='0'B;
        PUT PAGE LINE(3) EDIT ('CHANGES')(X(57),A);
        PUT SKIP(2);

        DO WHILE (S);
          GET EDIT (CHAR1,CHAR2)(A(5),X(5),A(5));
          GET SKIP;
          C1 = CHAR1;        C2 = CHAR2;
          CALL CHANGE (C1,C2);
          LONG = C1 !! C2;
          PUT SKIP EDIT (CHAR1,CHAR2,LONG)(X(19),A(5),X(15),A(5),X(15),A(10));
        END;


            CHANGE: PROCEDURE(C1,C2);
                    DECLARE (C1,C2) CHARACTER (5),
                            I FIXED BINARY;
                    DO I = 1 TO 5;
                      IF SUBSTR(C1,I,1) = SUBSTR(C2,I,1)
                        THEN SUBSTR(C1,I,1),SUBSTR(C2,I,1) = '$';
                        ELSE IF SUBSTR(C1,I,1) = 'W'   !
                                SUBSTR(C2,I,1) = 'W'
                             THEN SUBSTR(C1,I,1),SUBSTR(C2,I,1) = '#';
                    END;
                    RETURN;
                    END CHANGE;


        END ILL39;
```

XIII.3.4.2   Use of Statement Labels as Arguments

It is possible to include statement label names among the values transferred to a procedure when it is invoked. The usual preparations must be made by ensuring that the invoking procedure recognizes the argument as a label and the invoked procedure expects to receive a label. The former requirement is taken care of by an explicit declaration or a contextual one, the latter being set up by attaching that label to a statement. (Remember that the **LABEL** and **ENTRY** attributes are separate and distinct, so that such a label cannot be attached to a **PROCEDURE** or **ENTRY** statement.) The second requirement is fulfilled by assigning the **LABEL** attribute to the appropriate parameter in the invoked procedure. One way in which the label argument may be used is demonstrated on the following page.

Since L2 and L3 are contextually defined as labels by being attached to statement4 and statement7, respectively, they can be used as arguments to IP1 without any further explicit declarations in EP1.HANDLE has been declared as a label variable in IP1, so the procedure will expect the name of the third argument to refer to a label. With these features having been established, we can trace the execution of EP1.

1.   EP1 is started, and execution continues sequentially through statement2. (We are assuming that values were placed in A and B by some means during this portion of the program.)

2.   IP1 is invoked by the **CALL** statement, causing a transfer of the two numerical values A and B and the statement label constant L2.

3.   The **IF** statement in IP1 is evaluated. Should it turn out to be true, the **GO TO** statement will transfer control out of IP1 before it is completed, and processing will resume in EP1 at the statement labeled L2 (statement4). As a result, statement3 will also be bypassed. On the other hand, if the conditions turn out to be false, the **GO TO** will not be executed, IP1 will be concluded in normal fashion, and control will

return to EP1 at a point immediately following the **CALL**. Consequently, statement3 will be executed, followed by statement4 and statement5 in normal sequence.

4. Processing continues in EP1 until the second **CALL** to IP1 is made. The third argument is still a label, but this time it is L3.

5. The condition specified by the **IF** statement is evaluated again. If found to be true, the **GO TO** statement transfers control out of IP1 to statement7, thus bypassing statement6 and the **GO TO** that follows it. If false, the procedure is terminated in the usual way, and control returns to EP1 at statement6. Consequently, the **GO TO** is executed, bypassing statement7.

6. In either case, control eventually ends up at statement8, which is executed, and the program concludes.

```
EP1:    PROCEDURE OPTIONS (MAIN);
        DECLARE (A,B) FIXED (6,2);
             .
             .
             .

        statement1;
             .
             .
             .

L1:     statement2;
        CALL IP1 (A,B,L2);
        statement3;
            IP1:    PROCEDURE (X,Y,HANDLE);
                    DECLARE (X,Y) FIXED (6,2), HANDLE LABEL;
                    IF X > 2*LOG (Y) THEN GO TO HANDLE;
                    X = X + LOG (Y);
                    END IP1;
L2:     statement4;
        statement5;
        CALL IP1 (A,B,L3);
        statement6;
    GO TO L4;
    L3:     statement7;
    L4:     statement8;
        END EP1;
```

XIII.3.4.3   Use of Entry Points as Arguments

If a procedure performs some calculations involving other procedures, it is not necessary to specify the actual contributing procedure names as part of the permanent sequence of instructions. Instead, the programmer can include these procedure names as members of an argument list, thus giving him the ability to change the procedure to be used during a given invocation. This turns out to be extremely useful when it is desired to design a procedure that makes available a selection of built-in functions, the choice of which need not be made until the procedure is invoked.

Illustration 40

As an example, let us suppose we have a situation in which a program reads in values for X and Y and operates on them according to the following rules:

If X/Y is less than 0.25, a value Z is to be calculated as the square root of the sum of X and Y.

If the ratio X/Y is greater than .25 but less than .65, Z is to be calculated as the natural logarithm of the sum of X and Y.

For all other values of X/Y, Z is to be calculated as the logarithm to the base 2 of the sum of X and Y.

One way of doing this is shown below:

```
ILL40: PROCEDURE OPTIONS (MAIN);
       DECLARE MODIFY ENTRY (FIXED(6,3),FIXED(6,3),FIXED(6,3),ENTRY),
               S BIT (1) INITIAL ('1'B),
               (N25,N65,N66) FIXED BINARY;

       ON ENDFILE (SYSIN) S = '0'B;
       N25, N65, N66 = 0;
       PUT PAGE LINE(3) EDIT ('W-Z WORKUP PROGRAM ANALYSIS')

       DO WHILE (S);
         GET LIST (X,Y);
         W = X/Y;
         IF W < 0.25
           THEN DO;
                   N25 = N25+1;
                   CALL MODIFY (X,Y,Z,SQRT);
                END;
           ELSE IF W < 0.65
                   THEN DO;
                           N65 = N65+1;
                           CALL MODIFY(X,Y,Z,LOG);
                        END;
                   ELSE DO;
                           N66 = N66+1;
                           CALL MODIFY(X,Y,Z,LOG2);
                        END;
         PUT SKIP DATA (X,Y,W,Z);
       END;
```

The use of entry names in this manner is certainly not restricted to those assigned to PL/I's built-in functions. Any legitimately declared entry name can be used in this way, as long as a corresponding entry point exists.

Note that when an entry name is given in an argument list, together with a set of arguments for that entry name, it is the *value* produced by that function (not its name) that is transferred to the procedure being invoked. For example, if we rewrote the **IF...ELSE** complex in the previous example to read

IF W < 0.25 **THEN CALL** MODIFY(**SQRT**(X),Y,Z,**SQRT**);

ELSE IF W < 0.65 **THEN CALL** MODIFY(**LOG**(X),Y,Z,**LOG**);

   ELSE CALL MODIFY(**LOG2**(X),Y,Z,**LOG2**);

and conditions were such that the first **CALL** was executed, the three values transferred to the procedure MODIFY would represent the square root of X, the value of Y, the location of Z, and the entry name **SQRT**.

XIII.3.4.4   Dummy Arguments

The transmission of entry points and expressions points out a distinction that the programmer should understand. As a rule, PL/I passes arguments from invoking procedures to invoked procedures *by reference*. That is, if a variable is specified as an argument, the location of that variable is passed to the invoked procedure. (This is in contrast to some languages in which arguments are transmitted *by value*, wherein only the current value and not the location is made known.) This becomes a problem when the argument is not a variable. For example, the expression X+FUNC(7.4) implies an invocation of FUNC with an argument of 7.4. To guard against the destruction of the constant 7.4 if FUNC would happen to modify its argument, Pl/I sets up a *dummy argument* whose location is passed to FUNC. The same is true for an expression. When an expression is specified as an argument, the expression is evaluated, a dummy argument is set up to contain the value, and it is that location (unknown and unavailable to the programmer) that is sent to the invoked procedure. Thus, the transmission is ultimately by reference or location, even though the effect is sometimes equivalent to transmission by value.

The programmer can force (effective) transmission by value for arguments ordinarily transmitted by reference. This is done merely by enclosing the argument in parentheses. For example, if PR is a procedure requiring three arguments, the statement

   CALL PR(A,B,X);

transmits A, B, and X by reference, whereas

   CALL PR(A,(B),X);

transmits A and X by reference as before. However, B is evaluated, and that value is placed in a dummy argument whose location is transmitted to PR.

To see the importance of this distinction, consider the following example:

.
.
.

DECLARE (X,Y,Z) **FLOAT INITIAL**(10);

.
.
.

CALL SUBR(X,Y,(Z));

PUT LIST (X,Y,Z);

.
.
.

    SUBR: **PROCEDURE** (U,V,W);

        DECLARE (U,V,W) **FLOAT**;

        X = 5; Z = 7; **PUT LIST** (U,V,W);

        V = 4; W = 2;

        END;

.
.
.

The first **PUT** statement to be executed (that is, the one in SUBR) prints the three values 5 10 10. The modification of X is reflected in the parameter, U, since the CALL was by reference, whereas the modification of Z is not reflected in the parameter, W, since the **CALL** was (effectively) by value. The second **PUT** statement prints the three values 5 4 7. Modification of V shows up in Y, whereas that of W does not have an effect on Z.

  This example also points up the inadvisability of routinely modifying parameters and variables declared outside the procedure. A situation can easily develop in which the procedure has two (or more) ways of referring to the same location without being aware of it. Accordingly, a change made to either U or X in this example is also a change to the other. Unless this situation is intentional (and if so, then why have two names?) it probably will lead to anomalies that are both unexpected and difficult to diagnose.

XIII.4   RECOGNITION OF NAMES IN A PROGRAM

One of the unique aspects of the PL/I compiler is that the basic design of its logical mechanisms is motivated by a deep concern with the type of machine-language instructions generated from source commands. Whereas most previous compilers were constructed to apply fairly rigid translation techniques to the conversion of high-level language statements to more basic machine instructions, a PL/I compiler makes an extensive and determined effort to be efficient about such conversion. This characteristic manifests itself in terms of a complex of analytical routines that examine the source statements and, wherever possible, employ those conversion algorithms that will produce the shortest sequence of machine instructions, or the sequence that, when executed, will consume the shortest amount of computer time, or some reasonable compromise between these two requirements. This has no direct effect on the PL/I programmer, since the "correctness" of his program is not substantially influenced. There is, however, a more subtle though nonetheless definite effect, which can become very important when dealing with programs that are very large or that will be used frequently. In such situations, experimentation with alternate PL/I algorithms can quickly identify one of them as being the most advantageous (with respect to running time and/or consumed storage).

One basic mechanism resulting from this concern with program optimization is PL/I's handling of storage areas. The compiler not only determines the amount and location of storage required to accommodate a particular piece of data, but also decides when that storage is to be made available. In direct contrast to many previous languages, PL/I is not compelled to maintain a particular area of storage under a given name for the entire duration of a program. Instead, mechanisms are included that, in conjunction with appropriate hardware features, analyze the storage requirements for the entire program and schedule the allocation of storage as it is needed. When the need disappears, the storage is released to a general pool for further use by some other portion of the program. Should the program require a reallocation of storage for a given name, such an assignment will be made at the proper time, although the storage thus reserved probably will not be the same area used previously. This capability, known as *dynamic allocation*, can operate automatically at the discretion to the compiler, or it can be controlled by the programmer. The various techniques available for exerting such control will be discussed in a later chapter. In this section, we shall concern ourselves with the compiler's activities in this regard, because they are tied in very intimately with the use of procedures and **BEGIN** blocks.

XIII.4.1   The **STATIC** and **AUTOMATIC** Attributes

Since the complete description of a variable in PL/I requires the specification of a large number of attributes, it is common practice to declare some of the attributes explicitly, allowing PL/I's default mechanisms to supply the remainder. (For example, we have often taken advantage of this facility by declaring a particular variable as being **FIXED**(4,1), knowing that the compiler will automatically assign the attributes **REAL** and **DECIMAL**.) As part of this default activity, PL/I takes the opportunity to optimize its use of memory by assigning the **AUTOMATIC** attribute as well. By doing this, PL/I provides itself with the facility to assign adequate temporary storage for this variable to be released when it is no longer needed. A crucial aspect of this capability lies in the fact that this variable is not necessarily recognized (or *known*) throughout the entire program. The extent of the program over which this variable is known (called the *scope* of a declaration) is very carefully defined by a set of internal rules.

XIII.4.1.1   Scope of Variables

When a particular name is defined as having certain attributes (either by explicit declaration or by default) and that definition takes place in an external procedure, the scope of that declaration extends over the entire procedure, including all procedures contained in it. As an example, let us consider the following situation:

```
EXT: PROCEDURE OPTIONS(MAIN);
       DECLARE(A,B,C)FIXED(6,3);
       GET LIST(A,B);
       CALL INT;
       PUT PAGE DATA(A,B,C);
          INT:PROCEDURE;
             C = 2*COS(A + B);
          END INT;
       END EXT;
```

Since the subroutine INT is contained in procedure EXT, the declaration of A, B, and C in the latter procedure makes those variables known to INT. Hence, the reference to A in that procedure was sufficient for that program to locate the variable and use it as a numerical value with the attributes specified in the declaration. INT could be constructed without a parameter list and called without an argument list. Had we constructed this program as two external procedures,

```
EXT: PROCEDURE OPTIONS(MAIN);
       DECLARE(A,B,C)FIXED(6,3);
       GET LIST(A,B);
       CALL EXT2;
       PUT PAGE DATA(A,B,C);
       END EXT;
  * PROCESS;
EXT2: PROCEDURE;
          C = 2*COS(A + B);
        END EXT2;
```

EXT2 would have no idea what A, B, and C were in the program EXT. Since A, B, and C are used but not declared, the compiler will assign default attributes. When EXT2 is called, A and B will be uninitialized variables since they are completely independent of the A and B in EXT. Declaring A, B, and C in EXT2 will not change things.

If the programmer wishes to override the **AUTOMATIC** attribute set by default, he may do so by specifying the attribute **STATIC**. A typical declaration of this type would be

DECLARE B **FIXED**(5,1)**STATIC**;

or

DECLARE B **STATIC FIXED**(5,1);

When a variable is declared with this attribute, PL/I will allocate storage for that variable on a permanent basis for the duration of the entire program. This does *not* mean that there is any extension in the area over which the variable is known. The rules governing the scope of the declaration are still the same. If a name is declared in an internal procedure, that variable is known throughout that procedure and is given the **AUTOMATIC** attribute by default. As soon as control is returned from that procedure, the storage for that variable is released.

XIII.4.1.2   Scope of Entry Names

A name used to designate the entry point for an external procedure is recognized as such by every other external procedure in the program. This is consistent with the relations between external procedures, since any external procedure can call any other one. The scope of an internal entry name is also consistent with the rules for invoking procedures. Because an internal procedure can be directly activated only by the procedure in which it is contained, its entry name is known only to the containing procedure.

XIII.4.1.3   Alteration of Scope

In a sense, the scope of a variable as set by the compiler can be viewed as a default activity because it represents an automatic action, and preventive mechanisms exist for avoiding this action. The scope of a variable declared in an external procedure can be reduced by using the same name in a declaration in an internal procedure. By doing this, the programmer can reserve separate storage just as if he were using an entirely different name. This duplicate declaration can, but need not, include the same attributes used in the external procedure. If we have a program constructed as follows:

```
EXT: PROCEDURE OPTIONS(MAIN);
      DECLARE(A,B,C)FIXED(3);
      statement1;
      statement2;
      CALL INT;
      statement3;
        INT: PROCEDURE;
              DECLARE(A,B,C)FLOAT(8);
              GET DATA(A,B,C);
              statement4;
              PUT DATA(A,B,C);
              END INT:
      statement5;
      PUT SKIP DATA(A,B,C);
      END EXT:
```

the variables A, B, and C declared in INT are known only to that procedure and refer to a set of locations completely different from those assigned to the same names in EXT. By the same token, the **PUT** instruction following statement5 will always print the values of A, B, and C from EXT. This would be true even if the attributes assigned in both declarations were identical. (Internally, of course, PL/I uses its own naming system, so there can be no confusion.)

XIII.4.1.4 The **BUILT-IN** Attribute

The ability to use the same name in the same program for different purposes can be extended to include those names PL/I recognizes as built-in functions. For example, the programmer may use a name such as **COS** in a declaration, assigning to it any legitimate combination of attributes, as he would with any other name. This nullifies the use of the built-in function by that name throughout the scope of the declaration. If the programmer should wish to declare a built-in function name as a variable name in an external procedure but would like to retain its identity as a built-in function in a contained procedure, he may do this by using the **BUILT-IN** attribute as shown in the following program consisting of one external procedure containing two internal ones:

```
EXT: PROCEDURE OPTIONS (MAIN);
        DECLARE (A,B,SQRT,C) FIXED (8,4);
        GET LIST (A,B,SQRT);
        CALL INT1;
        CALL INT2;
        PUT PAGE DATA (A,B,SQRT,C);
            INT1:   PROCEDURE;
                        C = A + B + 2*SQRT;
                        END INT1;
            INT2:   PROCEDURE;
                        DECLARE SQRT BUILTIN;
                        C = C + 0.7*SQRT (C);
                        END INT2;
        END EXT;
```

SQRT is declared in EXT as a fixed-point decimal value with precision (8,4). Ordinarily, the scope of this declaration would extend over the entire program. However, by including the **BUILT-IN** declaration in the internal procedure INT2, the scope is modified so that SQRT is treated as a built-in function in procedure INT2 and as a single-valued, fixed-decimal variable throughout the rest of the program.

The **BUILT-IN** attribute may be declared for an entry name. When this is done, that name may have no other attributes. A second restriction in the use of this attribute is that it cannot be declared for any member of a parameter list.

XIII.4.2   Extensions of Scope: The **EXTERNAL** and **INTERNAL** Attributes

When it is necessary for a particular variable to be known in a program beyond the boundaries of the external procedure in which it is declared, this extension of scope can be achieved by means of the **EXTERNAL** attribute. In order for a particular variable to be known in several external procedures, each of those procedures must contain an identical declaration for that variable, including the explicit specification **EXTERNAL**. All the other attributes must be included, since each of these declarations refers to the same locations. A program organized to make use of this attribute is shown symbolically in Table 13.4 and the scopes of the various names are summarized in Table 13.5.

Examination of this program indicates that the following allocations are made: There are three separate locations reserved by the name A. The first of these is allocated by the declaration in statement L1 as a fixed-point decimal number of the **EXTERNAL** attribute. As such, it is also given the **STATIC** attribute by default, so that it is always available to any procedure in which it is known. The second location name A contains a seven-digit floating-point decimal number known only to procedure INT2. The third is a floating-point decimal number with the **INTERNAL** attribute allocated only while procedure INT3 is active and released upon termination of the procedure. The A declared in the statement L7 is the same A declared in L1.

Similarly, there are three different B's. The first is declared in statement L1, and the second is declared in statement L5 and is known only to procedure INT1. Even though it is also a fixed-point decimal number with the same precision as the B declared in L1, the fact that it is explicitly declared in an internal procedure results in a separate allocation and release upon termination of that procedure. The declaration in statement L8 reserves a third location under the name B.

This program assigns five different locations using the name C, since there is no point at which the **EXTERNAL** attribute is assigned to that name. Hence, there is a fixed-point decimal C declared in L1 which is different from the fixed-point decimal C declared in L5. Still a third value, having nothing to do with the other two, is declared in L6 and is known only to procedure INT2. The fourth value, a four-digit floating-point number, is declared in statement 17, and is known only to all of the statements internal to procedure EXT2. This is because a fifth and separate value of C is declared in L8 for use in procedure INT3, thus limiting the scope of the fourth value.

TABLE 13.4 A Program Organization to Illustrate
EXTERNAL and **INTERNAL** Attributes

```
EXT1:  PROCEDURE OPTIONS (MAIN);
  L1:    DECLARE     ((A,B) EXTERNAL, C) FIXED (6,3);
         statement1;
  L2:    CALL INT1;
  L3:    CALL EXT2;
  L4:    CALL INT2;
         statement2;
           INT1:   PROCEDURE;
             L5:   DECLARE (B,C) FIXED (6,3);
                   statement3;
                   END INT1;
           INT2:   PROCEDURE;
             L6:   DECLARE C FIXED (6,3),A FLOAT (7);
                   statement4;
                   END INT2;
         statement5;
         END EXT1;
  *PROCESS;
  EXT2:  PROCEDURE;
  L7:    DECLARE (A,B) FIXED (6,3) EXTERNAL, C FLOAT (4);
         statement6;
         CALL INT3;
         statement7;
           INT3:   PROCEDURE;
             L8:   DECLARE (A,B,C) FLOAT (4);
                   statement8;
                   END INT3;
         statement9;
         END EXT2;
```

TABLE 13.5 Scope of Variables in Program Organization of Table 13.4

Statement Label	Name	Attributes	Scope
EXT1	EXT1	**ENTRY,EXTERNAL**	Entire program
L1	A	**FIXED,EXTERNAL**	All of EXT1 except for INT2, all of EXT2 except for INT3
	B	**FIXED,EXTERNAL**	All of EXT1 except for INT1, all of EXT2 except for INT3
L1	C	**FIXED,INTERNAL**	EXT1 except for INT1 and INT2
INT1	INT1	**ENTRY,INTERNAL**	All of EXT1
L5	B,C	**FIXED,INTERNAL**	All of INT1
L6	C	**FIXED,INTERNAL**	All of INT2
L6	A	**FLOAT,INTERNAL**	All of INT2
EXT2	EXT2	**ENTRY,EXTERNAL**	Entire program
L7	A,B,	**FIXED,EXTERNAL**	Same A and B as declared in L1
L7	C	**FLOAT,INTERNAL**	All of EXT2 except for INT3
INT3	INT3	**ENTRY,INTERNAL**	All of EXT2
L8	A,B,C	**FLOAT,INTERNAL**	All of INT3

XIII.4.3   The **BEGIN** Block

Our use of the **BEGIN** block thus far has been in the context of a convenience that provides flexibility in defining and manipulating data aggregates whose size need not be set in advance.

```
  EXT: PROCEDURE OPTIONS(MAIN);

       DECLARE(A,B,C)FIXED(3);

       statement1;

       statement2;

         BEGIN;

         DECLARE(B,C)FIXED(4);

         statement3;

         statement4;

         END;

       statement5;

       END EXT;
```

Now we shall take another look at this organizational component, this time within the wider perspective of names and their scope.

The basic characteristic distinguishing the **BEGIN** block from a **DO** group is that the **BEGIN** statement can signal a change in scope. In this respect, the block acts in the same manner as an internal procedure. Names known in the containing procedure are also known in the **BEGIN** block. However, if the same name appears in a separate declaration in such a block, a separate storage location is allocated for it, and the **INTERNAL** attribute is assigned automatically. (If such a declaration appeared in a **DO** group, PL/I would treat it as a redundant declaration and signal an error, since that name already appeared somewhere else in the procedure.) Thus, in the program shown on the preceding page there are two sets of locations assigned under the names B and C. The set with precision (4) is released just before statement5 is reached. On the other hand, A is known throughout the entire program.

XIII.5   RECURSIVE PROCEDURES

In our discussion of procedures thus far, the underlying assumption has been that once a procedure is invoked it will run its course to some point of completion and return to the procedure that invoked it. This process implies that the invoked procedure, by virtue of its completion, is no longer active and can be invoked again (that is, reactivated) later.

Within this very general framework, certain instances could arise where it may be necessary to invoke a procedure and then invoke it again before its prior execution has been completed. In fact, it is not very unusual for such circumstances to occur in which the invoked procedure actually invokes itself. A frequently cited example of such self-invocation occurs in the computation of factorials. By definition, the factorial of a positive integer N can be stated as

$$N! = N(N - 1)(N - 2)(N - 3)...(1)$$

A PL/I function to handle these computations could be constructed as follows:

```
F: PROCEDURE (A) RETURNS FIXED BINARY(31);

   DECLARE A FIXED (2), B FIXED BINARY(31) INITIAL(1);

IF A<2 THEN B = 1;

     ELSE DO I=2 TO A;

           B=B*I;

           END;

RETURN(B);

END F;
```

An alternate formulation can produce the same result:

$$N! = N(N - 1)!$$

A direct "translation" into a procedure, that is,

  F= **PROCEDURE**(A) **RETURNS FIXED BINARY**(31);

      DECLARE A **FIXED**(2), B **FIXED BINARY**(31) **INITIAL**(1);

        IF A<2 **THEN RETURN**(1);

           ELSE RETURN(A*F(A−1));

  END F;

would not compile properly because we are asking the procedure F to invoke itself while it is still active. The attendant difficulties are fairly easy to perceive: Suppose that procedure F is invoked initially and given an argument containing the value 5. In going through the computation for 5!, it finds that it needs the value 4! before it can complete the process. Accordingly, it invokes itself to obtain 4!. To obtain that value, it finds that it needs 3!, and so on. Consequently, before it can deliver the final function value to the procedure that specified the original invocation, it needs several such function values, each for a different argument value, but all available "simultaneously."

This type of procedure is called a *recursive* procedure, and the process of self-invocation is called *recursion*. PL/I includes facilities for identifying and handling such procedures. The basic vehicle is the **RECURSIVE** option, whose general form is

  label: **PROCEDURE RECURSIVE**;   or

  label: **PROCEDURE** (parameter list) **RECURSIVE**;

This attribute specification informs the compiler that the intended use of this procedure will include self-invocation while the procedure is still active. Accordingly, PL/I will set up an internal mechanism for saving the arguments, internal automatic variables, and return linkage before performing a new invocation. It will also set up the machinery to restore these values when the program works its way out of the recursion.

Illustration 41

We shall write a program that reads successive values of X and, for each one read, prints a line containing X, X!, and a value Y computed as $1 + \sqrt{X!}$. X! will be calculated by invoking a recursive function:

```
ILL41: PROCEDURE OPTIONS (MAIN);
        DECLARE Y FIXED(8,2),
                (X,Z) FIXED BINARY (31),
                S BIT(1) INITIAL ('1'B),
                FC ENTRY RETURNS (FIXED BINARY(31));

        ON ENDFILE (SYSIN) S = '0'B;
        PUT PAGE LINE(3) LIST ('X', 'Z','Y');
        PUT SKIP;

        DO WHILE (S);
          GET LIST (X);
          Z = FC(X);
          Y = ROUND(1+SQRT(Z),2);
          PUT SKIP LIST(X,Z,Y);
        END;

            FC: PROCEDURE (A) RECURSIVE RETURNS (FIXED BINARY (31));
                DECLARE A FIXED BINARY(31);
                IF A < 2
                  THEN RETURN (1);
                  ELSE RETURN (A*FC(A-1));
                END FC;


        END ILL41;
```

Special note should be made of the allocation of **AUTOMATIC** variables used in procedures with the **RECURSIVE** attribute. Each time a recursive procedure calls itself, new storage is allocated for all **AUTOMATIC** variables known in that procedure, and the newest values are recognized. If a recursive procedure contains an internal procedure in which these variables are known, the values in the internal procedure will not be the same as those in the containing procedure. Of course, if a particular variable is to be maintained throughout all invocations, it can be declared with the **STATIC** attributes in the usual manner.

PROBLEMS

1. Trace the sequence of execution for the following program:

    EXT1: **PROCEDURE OPTIONS(MAIN)**;

          statement1;

          CALL EXT2;

          CALL INT3;

          statement2;

            INT1: **PROCEDURE**;

               statement3;

               CALL INT2;

               statement4;

    (program continued next page)

```
        INT2: PROCEDURE;
                statement5;
                statement6;
                statement7;
                END INT2;
            CALL INT2;
            statement8;
            END INT1;
        statement9;
        CALL INT1;
            INT3: PROCEDURE;
                statement10;
                statement11;
                END INT3;
        statement12;
        CALL EXT2;
        END EXT1;
    EXT2: PROCEDURE;
                statement13;
                statement14;
                statement15;
                END EXT2;
```

2. A program consists of the following procedures:

    EXTERNAL__1
      INTERNAL__1__1
        INTERNAL__1__1__1
      INTERNAL__1__2
    EXTERNAL__2

    Consider three variables with the following attributes (unless stated otherwise):

    X is **FIXED DECIMAL**(6,3)

    Y is **FLOAT DECIMAL**(4)

    Z is **BINARY FIXED**(10,3)

    Write the appropriate **DECLARE** statements to produce the following situations:

    a. X, Y, and Z are to be accessible to all procedures.

    b. X, Y, and Z are accessible only to EXTERNAL__1 and INTERNAL__1__2.

    c. X, Y, and Z are accessible only to EXTERNAL__1 and INTERNAL__1__1__1.

d. X is to be accessible to all procedures, while Y and Z are accessible to EXTERNAL__2, INTERNAL__1__1__1__1, and INTERNAL__1__2.

e. X, Y, and Z are to be treated as **FIXED DECIMAL** in INTERNAL__1__1__1 and with the previously defined attributes everywhere else.

3. Write a function procedure to operate on four arguments. The value to be returned by this function is calculated as the square root of the product of the largest arguments subtracted from the square root of the sum of the squared values of the other two arguments. Name the function CHANGE and assume that each of the four arguments is a fixed-decimal number with precision (5,2).

4. Modify the function procedure in Problem 3 so that the four arguments can be either all **FIXED DECIMAL**, all **FLOAT DECIMAL**, or two **FIXED** and two **FLOAT**. The fixed-point arguments may contain as many as seven digits, of which 0-7 may be to the right of the decimal point. Floating-point arguments may be as long as eight digits.

5. Using the CHANGE function from Problem 3, write a program that reads in data from punched cards where each contains the following variables:

Variable Name	Card Columns	Format
A	1-5	XX(.)XX
B	11-15	XXX(.)XX
C	41-45	XXX(.)XX
D	61-65	X(.)XX

For each card read, the program is to print a line containing the values of A, B, C, D, and CHANGE(A, B, C, D).

6. Rewrite the program in Problem 5 to accomodate the following situation. The first set of values of A, B, C, and D are read in and processed as before. After that, the values on each subsequent card must be adjusted by multiplying A, B, C, and D by the value of CHANGE(A, B, C, D) which was calculated using the values on the previous card.

7. A network of data consists of six arrays named C, D, E, F, G, and H. Each array contains ten rows and 12 columns, and a set of elements (one from each array) is recorded on a punched card as shown below:

Element Name	Card Columns	Format
C	3-4	X(.)X
D	8-10	XX(.)X
E	11-12	XX(.)
F	20-24	XXX(.)XX
G	30	X(.)
H	35-37	XX(.)X

The four arguments to the function CHANGE are named X, Y, Z, and W, and are calculated as follows:

$X = C + 2*E$

$Y = D + E*F*G$

$Z = D - X$

$W = F + G - H$

Assume that the cards are arranged in row major order. For each set of elements, print a line containing the values of C, D, E, F, G, H, and CHANGE(X, Y, Z, W).

8. Using the input format from Problem 7, write a program to read in the six arrays C, D, E, F, G, and H and calculate the four arguments to CHANGE as follows:

   a. If $C(I,J) > D(I,J)$, then $X(I,J) = C(I,J) + LOG2(D(I,J))$.

       Otherwise, $X(I,J) = C(I,J) + LOG(D(I,J))$.

   b. If $E(I,J) = F(I,J)$, then $Y(I,J) = 2*E(I,J)$. Otherwise, $Y(I,J) = E(I,J)*F(I,J)$.

   c. If $G(I,J) > 2*H(I,J)$, then $Z(I,J) = G(I,J)**2 + H(I,J)**2$.

       Otherwise, $Z(I,J) = G(I,J)^{1.5} + H(I,J)^{1.5}$.

   d. $W(I,J) = X(I,J) + Y(I,J) - 2*Z(I,J)$.

9. Rewrite the program in Problem 8 so that a separate procedure is used to prepare W, X, Y, and Z for the CHANGE function. The main program is to do nothing but read data and print the results.

10. The Maple Leaf Rag Company, Ltd. is Canada's leading producer of fine papers. Recently it decided to computerize payroll processing for its hourly employees. Since much of this processing is currently handled on punched card equipment, certain formats are already defined. Specifically, a card is prepared at the end of each week for each employee in accordance with the following layout:

Card Col.	Item	
1-20	Employee name	Characters
21-25	Employee number	XXXXX
26-27	No. of dependents	XX
28-30	Hourly rate	X(.)XX
32-34	No. of reg. hrs. worked	XX(.)X
35-37	No. of overtime hrs.	XX(.)X
38-44	Total earnings thus far this year	XXXXX(.)XX

The Form label appears at the left, with Card / Col. and Item as column headings.

These input cards are preceded by a single card that gives the date of the last day of the week for which these cards are prepared. The following rules exist for determining gross pay:

a. Overtime is paid at the rate of 1.5 times regular time for each hour in excess of 40.

b. Fractional hours (both regular time and overtime) are prorated.

c. No more than 20 hours of overtime can be paid to an employee during a week.

The following deductions are applied:

a. Unemployment insurance: 0.9% of gross pay over $30, but not exceeding a maximum deduction of $1.35.

b. Deductions for income tax and group health plans are tied to number of dependents as follows:

Dependents	Income Tax	Group Health
0 (self)	22% of gross pay	$2.50 per week
1	20% of gross pay	$3.60 per week
2	18% of gross pay	$5.10 per week
3	16% of gross pay	$6.00 per week
4	13% of gross pay	$6.50 per week
5 or more	10% of gross pay	$6.90 per week

c. Canada Pension Plan deducts 1.8% of gross pay above $600 per year and not exceeding $5400.

Write the payroll program for Maple Leaf so that it produces a wage summary consisting of a line of print for each employee. This line contains employee name, number, hourly rate, regular hours worked, overtime hours worked, gross pay, unemployment insurance deduction, income tax deduction, Canada Pension Plan contribution, hospital insurance premium, total amount deducted, and net pay. After individual employee figures are printed, the program is to print a separate page showing summary figures for gross pay, each type of deduction, and net pay. Include appropriate page and column headings.

SUMMARY OF IMPORTANT TERMS

Argument	An item of information on which a function or subroutine procedure operates (see Summary of Important Terms at the end of Chapter 9).
AUTOMATIC	An attribute (assigned implicitly or by explicit declaration) that permits the storage for its associated variable to be retained only while processing occurs within that particular block; once control leaves that block, the storage is released automatically.
BEGIN block	A procedural component consisting of an arbitrary sequence of statements starting with a **BEGIN** statement and concluding with an **END** statement. Such blocks are executed in normal processing sequence and storage for variables declared within these blocks is allocated dynamically when such processing occurs.
Binding	The process whereby arguments are paired with parameters during the invocation of a procedure.
Block	A recognizable structural component of a program (such as, procedure, **DO** group, and so forth).
CALL	The statement type used to invoke a subroutine procedure.

Contained	In the context of PL/I program organization, this characterizes the status of a block completely embedded (except for its heading name) inside another (*containing*) block.
Dummy argument	An area of storage, set up automatically to provide a reference for an argument value that is newly generated and, therefore, has no prior associated location.
Dynamic allocation	A process whereby the provision of storage for a specified purpose is delayed until the time that storage actually is needed (as is done for declared variables in a **BEGIN** block).
ENTRY	The attributes associated with an entry point of a procedure.
Entry point	A designated point in a procedure (not necessarily the beginning) to which control is to be transferred as the result of an invocation.
EXTERNAL	An attribute associated with a particular variable (either implicitly or by explicit declaration) whereby that variable is recognized outside the bounds of its block.
External procedure	A procedure whose placement in a program is such that it is contained in no other procedure.
Function procedure	A procedure that returns a single value and is invoked by referring to its entry point in an expression.
GENERIC	An attribute that sets up a mechanism for establishing a family of function procedures, each of which is designed to perform similar processing on items with different combinations of attributes.
Heading name	The statement label constant attached to the first (**PROCEDURE**) statement of a procedure.
Heading statement	The initial (**PROCEDURE**) statement of a procedure.
INTERNAL	An attribute associated with declared items whose scope is limited to the internal procedure in which they are declared.
Internal procedure	A procedure that is contained in (internal to) some other procedure.
Invocation	The process whereby control is transferred from one procedure (the *invoking* procedure) to another (the *invoked*) procedure. Implied in the process is an eventual resumption of control by the invoking procedure. (See "Return.")
Main procedure	In a given program, the procedure that assumes initial control when that program starts execution.
Parameter	An identifier (attached to a heading statement of a procedure) whose associated attributes are used to establish the requirements for corresponding arguments to be passed to the procedure when it is invoked.
Procedure	The smallest complete structural component of a program. Its general structure is **PROCEDURE;....END;**
Procedure name	See "Heading name."
Procedure statement	The initial statement of any procedure. The *primary entry point*.
PROCESS	A structural statement used to indicate the explicit inclusion of an additional external procedure in a program.

Program   In PL/I's context, an arbitrary number of procedures, one of which is a main procedure.

Recursion   A process whereby a procedure is invoked while it is still active—that is, it has not yet completed the work stemming from a prior invocation (for example, a procedure invoking itself).

RECURSIVE   The attributes associated (explicitly) with a procedure if its intended invocation will involve recursion.

Return   A process whereby control is transferred from an invoked procedure back to the invoking procedure, with the latter resuming its activities just after the point of invocation. The underlying mechanism, in PL/I, is established via the **RETURN** statement.

RETURNS option   The vehicle used for explicit definition of the attributes of a value to be returned by a procedure. (Omission of this option forces the use of default attributes derived from the procedure's heading name.)

Scope   The extent (in terms of procedural boundaries) over which a particular programmer-assigned name is recognized by the program and associated with a given set of attributes and a particular storage location.

STATIC   The attribute (assigned by explicit declaration) that forces the compiler to retain the storage associated with a particular variable for the entire extent of the program.

Subroutine   A procedure whose construction allows the return of an arbitrary number of results for each invocation. A subroutine is invoked by means of a **CALL** statement.

Transmission by reference   Delivery of an argument to an invoked procedure by informing the procedure of the argument's location rather than producing its value directly.

Transmission by value   Delivery of an argument to an invoked procedure by providing its current value at the time of invocation without any reference to its location in storage.

SUPPLEMENTARY READING

Maurer, W. D., *Programming: An Introduction to Computer Languages.* San Francisco: Holden-Day, 1968, pp. 147-154.

PL/I Language Reference Manual, IBM Document No. GC28-8201. White Plains, N.Y.: IBM Corporation, pp. 73-88, 158-170.

XIV DATA RECORDS, DATA SETS AND FILES

For many information-handling applications, it is unduly restrictive to treat the data as a collection of individual readings, observations, or identifiers. Requirements may demand that additional consideration be given to the organization of observations into groups and further agglomeration of these groups into an overall entity, endowed with its own attributes. We have already taken the first of these steps by treating certain types of data aggregates as arrays or structures and making use of PL/I's capabilities for handling such collections. Thus far, however, our interest in organizing data has been motivated primarily by a concern for immediate processing conveniences, such as facilitating its internal manipulation and increasing control over input/output. The most important, and usually the only, final product thus far has been the informative, clearly labeled printout.

Two important aspects of data handling force an extension of this scope and emphasize the desirability of more comprehensive data organization. The first of these is the fact that the fulfillment of a project or completion of a series of analyses often requires that the pertinent data be processed by several programs, each making its own organizational demands. For example, a set of specifications describing the dimensional, structural and material details of an architectural study may be processed in turn by programs designed to estimate the total weight, stress distribution, and approximate cost. During this sequence of analyses, it may be necessary for the stress analysis procedure to use the original data, augmented by some of the results generated by the weight-estimation program. Similarly, the cost analysis procedure may require additional input supplied by the stress analysis routines.

A second and perhaps more common factor is seen in many types of processing functions requiring a periodic repetition of certain operations on a basic set of data, the results of which include some type of specific output data, a status report, and the generation of a new set of data whose contents reflect current changes. A very common example of this type of processing is seen in payroll handling. Generally, this type of procedure uses as its data base a collection of information concerning wage/salary rates, standard deductions, and identification variables for a group of employees. Each pay period, this network is matched against input containing such information as hours worked, additional deductions, and sick leave taken, resulting in the three basic types of output mentioned previously. The specific product is often a set of actual paychecks and lists of deductions, the summary report contains cumulative data of interest to fiscal personnel (for example, year-to-date earnings and deductions, and total sick leave used), and the third output product is a new set of payroll data in which new employees have been incorporated, terminations deleted, and revised pay rates, deductions, and so on have replaced obsolete ones.

Both types of applications are operationally similar; they process some collection of data whose contents undergo relatively small changes and whose structure undergoes virtually none. The external storage of the data becomes important because output generated by one run may very well constitute part of the input for a subsequent one, independent of whether the latter involves a different program or a repetition of the same one. When this is the case, it becomes much more effective to treat the entire collection as an entity (known as a *data set*) with properties of its own, transcending those of its components. (Traditionally, such collections of data were referred to as *files*. However, the rapid increase in the variety of available input/output devices coupled with the development of versatile software systems has made the fixed association between a collection of data and a particular external storage medium unnecessarily restrictive. Accordingly, we shall refer to the more flexible idea of a data set throughout this discussion.) The command structure required for creating such data sets and manipulating them in their entirety is quite separate from dealing with each item in the data set. We might think of the instructions we have mastered thus far for manipulating numbers and characters to apply to the *contents* of a data set once these contents (or part of them) have been brought into their assigned locations in storage.

A crucial consideration in constructing data sets relates to their storage and maintenance. If a data set is to be used as a basis for repeated processing, it becomes inappropriate to think of it as a collection of information on punched cards, which, when revised, will result in a new set of cards. Instead, the storage and processing of data sets must be oriented to peripheral media with higher operating speeds, such as magnetic tape, magnetic disk, or other continuous storage devices. The discrepancy between data transmission and internal processing speeds with such equipment is much less pronounced than with punched cards or perforated tape, so that the use of magnetic storage media presents immediate operational advantages. The relative compactness of data stored in this form provides additional benefits. (Direct communicating devices such as keyboards cannot, of course, be considered for data collections of any size.)

As part of its facilities, PL/I includes a number of procedures designed specifically for the organization of data sets. This is handled by instructions that allow the programmer to create data sets from raw data and assign particular attributes that control their structure and method of storage. Basic to these operations is the treatment of a data set as a unified collection of records, where each record consists of a set of related data items. (All of the payroll information for one employee will constitute a record in a payroll data set.) There is usually a relation between the record and the physical medium on which it was *originally* recorded. (For example, each record may represent the contents of one or some other fixed number of punched cards.) Once a suitable PL/I program has organized these records and transferrred the information onto its final external storage medium, the data set has a recognizable beginning and end, and each record in it, consisting of so many digits and/or characters, is augmented by indicators signaling its beginning and end.

XIV.1   ORGANIZATION OF DATA SETS

The transformation of a group of related data items into a cohesive data set is not an automatic process. Its implementation requires a sequence of instructions including sufficient information to define the contents of the data set (in terms of the composition of a record), the type of device on which it is to be stored, a description of the storage method, and an indication of the eventual use of the data set. Each of these specifications is transmitted to the program in terms of a set of attributes either stated explicitly by the programmer or supplied by PL/I's default routines.

The vehicle used in PL/I to gain access to a data set is called a *file*. In contrast to a data set, which is an actual collection of data represented on some physical medium such as cards, disk, or tape, a file has no real existence. Rather, it is an abstraction that PL/I uses as a focus for specifying the processing requirements that must be marshalled in order to access the actual data. This seemingly unnecessary indirectness actually facilitates the process of writing programs that can be used with diverse data sets. The improvement occurs because it is no longer necessary to provide detailed specifications of which data set to use (along with its specific properties) as an intrinsic part of the program. Instead, the delivery of such information now can be postponed until the program is actually executed.

XIV.1.1   Internal Construction of Records

The transition between a seemingly disjointed collection of data elements and a unified data record is bridged very smoothly in PL/I by means of the structure. We have seen (Chapter VII) that we can conveniently coalesce arbitrary combinations of numbers, character strings, and bit strings into a single organizational entity with its own name. Yet the ability to read, write, and move an entire structure does not limit our accessibility to any individual element within it. It is this versatility that makes the structure an obvious vehicle for building and manipulating data records. Thus, the components of a record are brought together in a structure and transmitted as such to an output destination. Conversely, when a record is brought into the processor as a member of a data set it is usually read into a structure, from whence its elements are available for processing.

For example, suppose a data set name STDNT consists of student records. Each record contains the following information for an individual: last name, first name, middle initial (30 characters); month of entry (2 digits); year of entry (2 digits); month, day and year of birth (2 digits each); social security number (9 digits); and, finally a code for representing the student's home state (2 letters). When stored on an external medium, the collection of records comprise the data set. To handle this information in the processor, the usual practice is to define a structure whose composition is designed to provide an exact match for one of the records:

DECLARE 1 STD__REC,

        2 ST__NAME **CHARACTER**(30),

        2 ENT__DATE,

           3 ENT__MO **FIXED**(2),

           3 ENT__YR **FIXED**(2),

        2 BTH__DATE,

           3 BTH__MO **FIXED**(2),

           3 BTH__DAY **FIXED**(2),

           3 BTH__YR **FIXED**(2),

        2 SOC__SEC **CHARACTER**(9),

        2 HM__STATE **CHARACTER**(2);

Now, when the record is first created, the individual components (whatever their source) are assembled into STD__REC. Completion of that process means that another record is available for addition to the data set. At some other time, a desire to examine one of these records would prompt its transmittal to STD__REC, from whence any or all components may be obtained. This relationship is shown diagrammatically in Figure 14.1.

XIV.1.2   Basic Declaration of Files

We have seen that the basic vehicle for accessing a data set is a file. Files in PL/I are designated

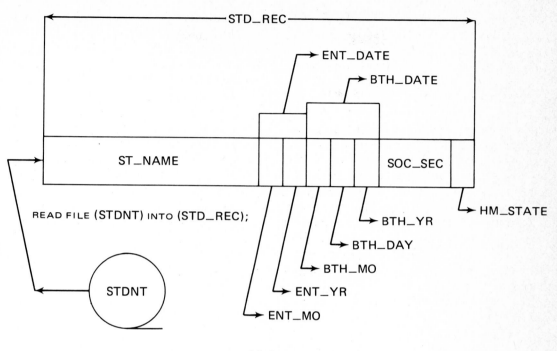

READ FILE (STDNT) INTO (STD_REC);

(a) Input

Figure 14.1a

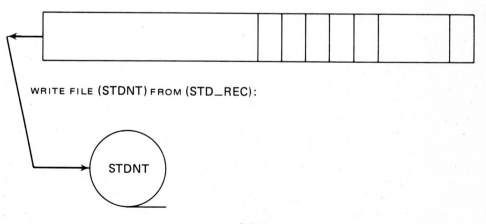

WRITE FILE (STDNT) FROM (STD_REC):

(b) Output

Figure 14.1b

by ordinary identifiers, which are given the **FILE** attribute. This identifier can be assigned in PL/I as any other name, and its composition is governed by the same rules that apply to names of numbers, character strings, labels, procedures and so on. Hence, one way of informing the compiler that a particular name is to refer to a file of data is to say

   DECLARE filename **FILE** attributes;

The word **FILE** informs PL/I that "filename" is to have the **FILE** attribute. We shall find later on that it is usually unnecessary to specify this, because we will most likely be explicitly assigning other attributes from which the compiler will deduce that the name is to be used for a file, and it will assign this attribute automatically. The form used for specifying such attributes is the same used for any other **DECLARE** statement. Any number of files may be declared in a single statement, along with any other variables.

   Once the compiler recognizes (by explicit indication or by default) that a particular name is to be associated with a file, it seeks more specific information regarding the organization of that file, its intended usage and the circumstances governing its physical transmission to or from the processor. The association between a file and an actual data set to be processed is established when the program is executed via the supervisory software. The details vary from one system to another. Further discussion on this topic is contained in Section XIV.4 at the end of this chapter.

XIV.1.3   Direction of Transmission

In order for PL/I to set up effective communications between the processor and the peripheral component, it must construct a catalog showing the intended usage for each file processed in a program. A portion of this information is provided by specifying whether the file associated with a particular name is to be used for input, output, or both.

XIV.1.3.1   The **INPUT** Attribute

   If a file is to serve as a data source, it is given the **INPUT** attribute in a declaration of the form

   DECLARE filename **INPUT**;

Since specifications of the **INPUT** attribute is meaningless for names other than those referring to files, it is not necessary to include the **FILE** attribute as part of the declaration. Specification of the **INPUT** attribute sets up the mechanism allowing that file to participate in input operations but not in output. Any attempt to use that file as the destination for output will result in an error.

XIV.1.3.2   The **OUTPUT** Attribute

   Conversely, a file name **DECLARE**d with the **OUTPUT** attribute specifies an intention to create a new data set composed of information transmitted to it by means of output instructions. By using the **PUT LIST**, **PUT DATA**, or **PUT EDIT** statement without explicit file names, for example, we were employing PL/I's default activities to create a data set on the line printer. As expected, the declaration of an output file takes the general form

DECLARE filename **OUTPUT**;

XIV.1.3.3   The **UPDATE** Attribute

In many instances, it is inappropriate to restrict the function of a data set to that of a data source or a receptacle for output. As in our payroll example, the intention may be to use the data set as a source to produce a report. During this process, the data set itself may be modified to reflect current changes so that it can serve as an updated source for the generation of a subsequent report. Since these operations involve the transmission of information to and from the data set, it would appear that the associated file must possess both the **INPUT** and **OUTPUT** attributes. This contradiction is handled by the **UPDATE** attribute, so the declaration

DECLARE WORKFILE **FILE UPDATE**;

or just

DECLARE WORKFILE **UPDATE**;

will inform the compiler that the name WORKFILE will refer to a file that will be used for such an updating operation.

XIV.1.3.4   The **PRINT** Attribute

When the information contained in a data set is eventually to be displayed on the line printer, a number of special conveniences can be utilized in organizing the data set by specifying the **PRINT** attribute. Since this attribute is in basic contradiction to the **INPUT** attribute, a declaration such as

DECLARE CHARTS **OUTPUT PRINT**;

is redundant. The statement

DECLARE CHARTS **PRINT**;

will automatically imply the **OUTPUT** attribute.

XIV.1.4   Data Transmission Attributes

In order for proper transmission to occur from a data set to the processor, or vice versa, the program must be able to determine whether such transmission is to occur in stream- or record-oriented mode. This information is supplied through the use of the keyword **STREAM** or **RECORD** in a declaration. Thus, if the programmer intended to use record-oriented transmission to generate a data set using a file called REPORT, his declaration would read

DECLARE REPORT **OUTPUT RECORD**;

When neither **STREAM** nor **RECORD** is specified, PL/I will assign the **STREAM** attributed by default. This brings us to the realization that, in performing our input/output operations, we have been dealing with data sets all along. Moreover, all the files have been assigned the **STREAM** attribute in the absence of an explicit declaration. Accordingly, the standard input file is treated as if we had said

DECLARE SYSIN **FILE STREAM INPUT**;

and our use of the standard output file presupposes the (automatically supplied) specification

DECLARE SYSPRINT **FILE STREAM PRINT OUTPUT**;

TABLE 14.1 Descriptive Attributes for Declared Files

Type of Transmission	Direction of Transmission	Ultimate Device	Applicable Input/Output Statements
STREAM	**INPUT**		**GET**
			PUT (SKIP)
	OUTPUT	**PRINT**	**PUT (SKIP, PAGE, LINE)**
RECORD	**INPUT**		**READ**
	OUTPUT		**WRITE**
	UPDATE		**READ/REWRITE/ DELETE/WRITE***

* **DIRECT UPDATE** files only.

Stream transmission (regardless of direction) enables us to treat the data set as a collection of individual data items without regard for how these items may be arranged as records. In contrast to this, record transmission handles entire records rather than individual values.

Once the transmission mode is determined, certain restrictions follow automatically. Input and output involving **STREAM** files can only proceed through the use of **GET** and **PUT** statements, respectively. Similarly, the **READ** and **WRITE** statements must be used with **RECORD** files. A file with the **UPDATE** attribute can not be handled in **STREAM** mode. Consequently, specification of the **UPDATE** attribute will automatically bring the **RECORD** attribute with it. (The converse of course, is not true). Also, PL/I cannot handle a record-oriented **PRINT** file, thus making the joint appearance of these two attributes improper. As a result, it is not necessary to specify the stream attribute when declaring a particular file as a **PRINT** file. These basic descriptive attributes are summarized in Table 14.1.

Although some of the ensuing discussion will apply also to **STREAM** transmission we shall be dealing predominantly with **RECORD** transmission, since many of the supporting facilities are designed and implemented primarily to enhance the processes for handling records.

XIV.2 ACCESS METHODS FOR DATA RECORDS

The software system under which PL/I operates contains a variety of procedures for conducting input/output operations. These techniques represent organizational variants of two basic methods for transmitting information to or from external media. A record may be an integral part of an ordered sequence, or it may be reached independently as dictated by the value of some criterion. The applicability of one or the other of these *access methods* depends on the physical characteristics of the storage device and the intended use of the data set.

Peripheral units for transmitting information from punched cards to a processor, for example, are designed to operate with a group of cards, one at a time, in the order in which they are stacked. The same holds true when a card-punching mechanism is used as an output device. Similarly, the records stored on a roll of punched tape or a reel of magnetic tape are available to the processor in a particular order. When such a data set is being generated as a series of output records, the order in which those records are written dictates their relative positions on the tape. This is known as *sequential access*. When a device such as a magnetic disk or drum is being used as a file storage medium, the order in which the individual records are written or read need no longer be fixed. Such devices are known as *random-access* or *direct-access* devices, because the ease with which a particular record may be made available to the processor or written in a particular place on the storage medium has little or nothing to do with the position from which that record is to be read or written. In physical terms, records stored on a reel of magnetic tape, for example, must each be examined in sequence until the desired one is found. In contrast, a desired record stored on a disk can be referenced directly, regardless of its proximity to the one used in the previous operation.

XIV.2.1 The **SEQUENTIAL** Attribute

When the records of a data set are to be read from or written onto an external medium in a predetermined order, the associated file is said to be a *sequential file*. This characterization is indicated by declaring the file with the **SEQUENTIAL** attribute. For example, the statement

DECLARE INFILE **FILE RECORD INPUT SEQUENTIAL;**

defines a file named INFILE whose records will be read in the order in which they physically appear on their external storage device. Similarly, the statement

DECLARE OUTGO **FILE RECORD OUTPUT SEQUENTIAL**;

defines a file named OUTGO, in which records will be stored in the same order in which they are written.

XIV.2.1.1   The **BACKWARDS** Attribute

Many computing systems are equipped with magnetic tape units designed to read information from a reel of tape while the tape is travelling past the reading mechanism in either direction. This feature can be used in many situations to save time. For example, suppose the first part of a procedure writes a series of records onto a tape and it is necessary to read those records back into the machine for further processing at some later point in the procedure. If the procedure is one in which the handling of each record does not depend on information from the other records (and such independence is the case for many types of procedures), then the ability to read records in reverse order (that is, the last one written is the first one read) avoids the time-consuming process of repositioning (*rewinding*) the tape to its beginning.

The intent to read in reverse order is applicable (obviously) only to **INPUT SEQUENTIAL** files and must be indicated explicitly. Accordingly, the statement

DECLARE TURVY **FILE RECORD INPUT SEQUENTIAL BACKWARDS**;

defines TURVY as such a file.

XIV.2.1.2   The **KEYED** Attribute

A record usually includes one or more variables that serve to distinguish each record from others in the file. (Such items as part number, employee number, name, and date are commonly used for this purpose.) This type of variable is known as a *key*. If the file is **SEQUENTIAL**, the key is not crucial in locating a particular record. However, it may be of use in a particular program as a criterion for various types of decisions to be made during the processing. Consequently, PL/I makes it possible to specify the existence of such a key by means of the **KEYED** attribute. This is added to the file's **DECLARE** statement in the same way as the other attributes.

The actual key is not assigned by specifying the **KEYED** attribute. It merely indicates that each record has previously been given a key (in the case of **INPUT** or **UPDATE** files) or that a key will be attached to each record when it is generated (in the case of an **OUTPUT** file). Although one of the variables within the record may be used as the key, it is possible to create a separate variable for that purpose. In either case, the key is assigned as a character string. If the **KEYED** attribute is assigned, certain additional input/output options become available, as we shall see in subsequent sections.

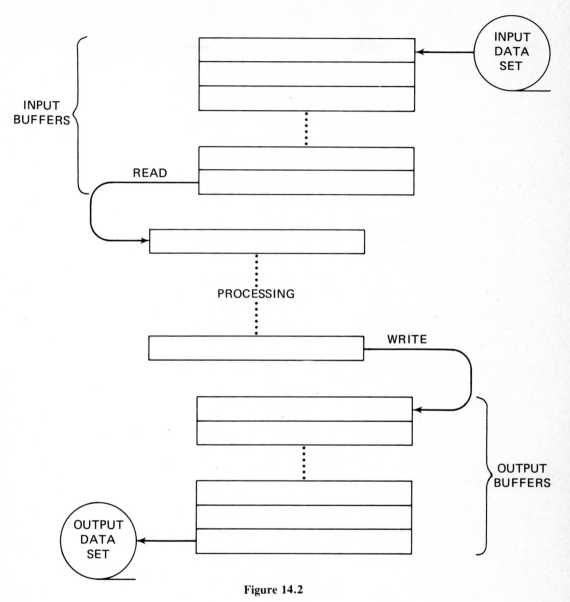

Figure 14.2

XIV.2.1.3   Buffered Input/Output Operations

Even with the fastest devices, the time required for input/output operations greatly exceeds that consumed for internal operations. Consequently, despite the fact that a processor may be performing long, complex sequences of computations on input values, it often completes its work long before the input device can deliver the next set of values. Alternatively, the processor may not be able to accept a new group of input values because it cannot dispatch the results it just computed until the much slower output device finishes with the previous set. This could easily result in a situation where the processor spends most of its available time waiting, thereby losing any benefits inherent in its operating speed. Since the processor has no moving parts and most input/output devices do, this basic speed discrepancy will persist.

However, it can be alleviated to a substantial extent by a number of organizational techniques. One of these is based on *overlapped processing*, a situation in which a computing system is equipped with hardware and software that allow data transmission and internal processing to occur simultaneously. Then, by making it possible to transmit the data to and from a separate storage area while processing continues unhindered, the benefits of high processing speeds may be largely maintained. This separate storage area is called a *buffer*, and is usually a part of central storage set aside for this purpose. Occasionally it may be in a physically independent storage device. With such capabilities, it is possible to arrange programs so that the data in a record are being processed while the next record is being read in and the previous one is being printed or written on some other output device. Instead of reading input from its stored source into the portion of memory where it is to be processed, the input is first brought into a buffer and then "read" from there. When data processing results are ready to be sent to an output device, they are diverted to an output buffer, from which the actual transmission occurs. This process is shown diagrammatically in Figure 14.2.

In a way, we have set up and used a buffer by employing the **GET/PUT STRING** feature (Chapter VIII). However, the process was manual and rather limited in scope. PL/I makes such buffering available automatically for **SEQUENTIAL RECORD** files by means of the **BUFFERED** attribute.

When an output instruction is given, the record being referred to is not transmitted to the external storage device. Instead, the record referred to in the previous output instruction is being transmitted from one output buffer to the external storage device (such as magnetic tape), and the one referred to by the current instructions is sent from the processing area to another output buffer. This type of situation in which the program stays one record ahead of itself is known as *double buffering*. The use of a higher degree of buffering is not uncommon and can be arranged in a variety of ways (such as **BUFFER** (n), mentioned later). However, as far as the PL/I programmer is concerned, such arrangements are usually made by means outside the scope of the language. Hence, when the programmer specifies the **BUFFERED** attribute, he is accepting the default level of buffering. This happens to be double buffering.

The **BUFFERED** attribute is automatically assigned by PL/I to all files having both the **SEQUENTIAL** and **RECORD** attributes. (It cannot be assigned to any other type of file.) Consequently, it need not be included in the **DECLARE** statement. Should a programmer choose to avoid this type of data transmission for a particular **SEQUENTIAL** file, he must explicitly indicate this by using a declaration such as

DECLARE filename **SEQUENTIAL RECORD UNBUFFERED**;

Although the temporary storage area for a buffered file is reserved automatically by PL/I, there are techniques available to the programmer for determining the location of this buffer area and performing operations on its contents. These will be discussed when we deal with record-oriented input/output.

XIV.2.2 The **DIRECT** Attribute

When the expectation is that the records in a file are going to be written or read in a sequence that does not necessarily bear any relation to the physical order in which those records will be stored on an external device, that file is declared with the **DIRECT** attribute. For example, a declaration such as

DECLARE FINDINGS **OUTPUT DIRECT**;

indicates that the file named FINDINGS is to be created from a series of output records stored on a direct access device. (The mechanism used to identify the actual physical device on which a file is to be created or from which a file is to be read will be discussed later. It should be noted at this point that a file declared with the **DIRECT** attribute must be assigned to a device that can be operated with the direct access method.) When neither **DIRECT** or **SEQUENTIAL** is explicitly specified, the compiler assumes the file to be **SEQUENTIAL**. As is probably apparent by now, these attributes only have meaning with respect to **RECORD** files. Sources of information on the types, construction and operational characteristics of direct access devices are given at the end of the chapter.

 DIRECT files permit access to the records in a sequence that is both variable and unpredictable. For this reason, each record in a **DIRECT** file must have a key, and the **KEYED** attribute is automatically assigned. Thus, the declarations

DECLARE REFERENCE **DIRECT KEYED**;

and

DECLARE REFERENCE **DIRECT**;

are operationally identical.

XIV.2.3 File Declaration Defaults

In discussing the various attributes that may be assigned to files as part of the declaration process, we have seen that a number of these (like **INPUT** and **OUTPUT**) are mutually exclusive. In addition, there are certain attributes that were seen to imply or exclude others. These combinations are supported by a relatively extensive network of defaults, which could be confusing until some familiarity is acquired. Accordingly, the appropriate rules are summarized in Table 14.2.

TABLE 14.2 Declared File Attributes and Defaults

Type of Attribute	Choices	Default Attribute
Direction of transmission	**INPUT, OUTPUT UPDATE, PRINT**	**INPUT**
Type of transmission	**STREAM, RECORD**	**STREAM**
Access method	**SEQUENTIAL, DIRECT**	**SEQUENTIAL**
Buffering	**BUFFERED, UNBUFFERED**	**BUFFERED** (when applicable)
Ultimate device	**PRINT***	
	KEYED‡	
	BACKWARDS	

*__STREAM OUTPUT__ only.
‡__RECORD__ only.

It is seen that some attributes may be explicitly stated or implied by default, whereas others must be specifically assigned. Their absence will not cause any assumptions to be made by the compiler. These latter attributes are called *additive attributes*, as opposed to *alternative attributes*, in which the compiler will make a choice when no explicit assignment is given. The scope of all files is assumed to be **EXTERNAL**, unless otherwise specified.

Because of the mechanisms supporting the file-handling routines, the assignment of certain attributes is restricted to specific types of files. As a result, some attributes are automatically assigned when others are present. These groupings are shown in Table 14.3.

TABLE 14.3 Implied File Attributes

If Declaration Specifies	PL/I Will Also Assign
UPDATE	**RECORD**
SEQUENTIAL	**RECORD**
DIRECT	**RECORD, KEYED**
PRINT	**OUTPUT, STREAM**
BACKWARDS	**RECORD, INPUT, SEQUENTIAL**
KEYED	**RECORD**
BUFFERED or **UNBUFFERED**	**RECORD, SEQUENTIAL**

XIV.3   THE **ENVIRONMENT** SPECIFICATIONS

The attributes discussed thus far combined to establish an association between a file and the processing to be applied to a collection of records or data set. Note, however, that the data set itself still lacks description. There is no information concerning how the records are organized to form that collection. Without such specifications PL/I cannot even begin to construct the mechanisms required to regulate the transmission processes. Of course, the irrepressible compiler will attempt to come to the the rescue with a bundle of defaults (as it has done repeatedly with SYSIN and SYSPRINT). However, there are several useful alternatives, and we shall acquaint ourselves with them now.

Information relating to the organization of records in a data set is given to PL/I through the **ENVIRONMENT** specification that appears in a declaration as follows:

DECLARE filename attr1 attr2 etc. **ENVIRONMENT**(spec1 spec2 etc.);

The options that may be specified in the environment lists do not constitute a fixed feature of the language. Instead, they can be established for each version of the compiler, depending on the requirements of the supervisory software under which it operates. We shall examine those that find most common use, with references to others given at the end of the chapter.

XIV.3.1   Files and Data Sets

To understand these specifications and work with them effectively, it is necessary to reiterate the important distinction between a file and a data set: we should think of the file as a disembodied collection of records; that is, *we should think of the term as referring to the information itself* and not to any particular device or medium on which that information happens to be represented. It may be on a reel of magnetic tape on one occasion, it may occupy part of a disk on another, or (preserve us!) it may find itself on paper tape on yet another occasion.

When a file is stored on some medium, that combination of the data and its residence is referred to as a *data set*. This distinction allows us to deal conveniently with the fact that the same file (with the same set of declared attributes) may be organized in different ways and placed on different media to produce different data sets. The conditions that govern these organizational relations between a file and a data set are described (in part) via **ENVIRON-MENT.**

XIV.3.2   Records and Blocks

When a record is stored on some magnetic device, it is automatically separated from its neighbors by a physical space (called an *interrecord gap*) that could be larger than that occupied by the record itself. A typical example will illustrate:

Suppose that we wish to create a record consisting of the contents of an entire punched card (80 characters) and our intent is to store that record on magnetic tape. Typical devices accommodate 1600 characters per inch of tape length and leave a constant gap of 0.6 inch between records, regardless of their length. Thus, a series of 80 character records will be represented on tape as a corresponding series of 0.05-inch lengths of information (80/1600) separated by 0.6-inch lengths of nothing (Figure 14.3a). In addition to the obvious waste of space this condition can slow down input/output operations, since it takes at least 12 times as long for the gap to pass the read/write mechanism as it does for the data to pass.

This situation is usually relieved by storing the data set so that several of these *logical records* are strung together and treated as one *physical record* or **block,** thereby eliminating the gaps between them. This process is known as *blocking,* and the number of logical records in a block is known as the *blocking factor.* Referring again to our example, if we allow our 80-character logical record to be treated as a physical record, we are tying up 0.65 inch of tape of which 0.05 inch actually contains data. However, if we use a blocking factor, say, of 20, our physical record now would consist of 20 logical records occupying 1.0 inch. Thus, our usage would be more respectable 1.0 inch of data for every 1.6 inches of tape (62.5 percent) compared with a paltry 0.05/0.65 or 7.7 percent for *unblocked* storage (Figure 14.3b).

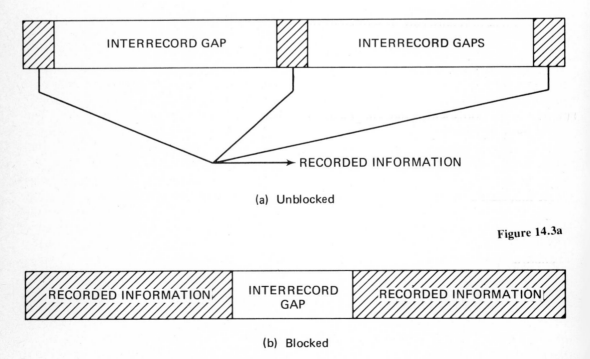

(a) Unblocked

Figure 14.3a

(b) Blocked

Figure 14.3b

Note that this gain is not achieved without some cost. In this case, the cost stems from the fact that the buffers for reading or writing the blocks must be 20 times as large, thus adding substantially to the program's storage requirements.

Since the machinery is designed to transmit a physical record (that is, the information between two interrecord gaps) each time an input/output operation is actually performed, an intervening mechanism must maintain the distinction between physical and logical records. Specifically, when the program prepares a logical record for output, that record must be combined with the proper number of other records to form the physical record. Conversely, after a physical record is brought in, something must segregate the logical records and deliver them to the program one at a time. (These processes are known respectively, as *blocking* and *deblocking*.)

All of this can be done automatically by the supervisory software, without the programmer's direct knowledge of the process or how it is implemented. However, it is up to the programmer to supply the information with which the blocking/deblocking mechanisms will operate. In PL/I this can be handled through options in the **ENVIRONMENT** specification.

XIV.3.2.1 Fixed-Length Records

The simplest type of data set organization is one in which every record has the same length. Such *fixed-length* records are described as follows:

DECLARE filename attributes **ENVIRONMENT(F**(blocksize,recordsize));

where "blocksize" refers to the number of *characters* (not records) in the block and "recordsize" indicates the number of characters in each logical record. Going back again to our 80-character records with a blocking factor of 20, we can describe an output file NEW—FL with these properties by saying

DECLARE NEW—FL **FILE OUTPUT ENVIRONMENT(F**(1600,80));

(Note that **RECORD** and **SEQUENTIAL** are assigned by default.)

XIV.3.2.2 Variable-Length Records

There are numerous occasions in which it is necessary to build data sets whose records may contain different amounts of information. For example, a record in a medical history file may consist of coded identification and diagnostic data for an individual, followed by an arbitrary amount of narrative material. Restriction to a fixed record length would require one of two concessions, neither of which may be acceptable: the amount of text would be limited to so many characters, incurring the risk of losing important information; alternatively, the size of the record would be determined by the maximum amount of text, thereby producing a situation where considerable space is tied up for blanks.

To accommodate such requirements, PL/I supports data sets that may have blocks of varying size, where the number of logical records in each block may vary and the size of the records may vary as well. In order to deal with what appears as a haphazard state of affairs, the software must handle each blocking/deblocking episode on its own terms. Consequently each record, as part of its contents, must supply information about its length. The same holds true with regard to the block length.

Length information about a record is carried in four extra bytes added to that record. Similarly, the length of the block is extended by four bytes to contain the specifications for that block. Accordingly, the programmer must account for those extra bytes when specifying length information for a data set with variable-length records (the software will provide the bytes themselves and fill them appropriately) and he must account for them when reading such a file (the software will "know" which bytes they are and how to interpret their contents).

The basic **ENVIRONMENT** option for variable-length files appears as follows:

....**ENVIRONMENT**(V(blmax,recmax));

In this construction "blmax" is the maximum block size to be encountered in the file and "recmax" is the maximum record size to be encountered. In both cases, the specifications must include these extra four-byte fields. Thus, blmax $>=$ recmax$+4$ must be satisfied or an error will result.

To illustrate, suppose we have a file OURS (already built and on tape) in which each record may contain no more than 3000 characters of data, and many records may contain less. Furthermore, for a variety of reasons, the file was developed with one record per block (that is, the records are stored on tape in unblocked form). To read this file successfully, its declaration must show a maximum record length of 3004 (3000 plus the four record description bytes) and a maximum block length of 3008 (3004 plus the four block description bytes). Thus, we would say

1 record/block

DECLARE OURS **FILE INPUT RECORD ENVIRONMENT**(V(3008,3004));

To write such a file with blocking, our declaration could say something like

DECLARE OUT **FILE OUTPUT RECORD ENVIRONMENT** (V(5000),3004));

In this case, several records would be combined to form blocks, provided that no block attains a length greater than 5000, including the control bytes.

XIV.3.2.3   Spanned Records

While extremely flexible, the variable-length capability requires the end of a block to coincide with the end of a record. Consequently, if a file includes a relatively small proportion of very long records, it would be necessary to set a very high maximum block size. To alleviate this type of contingency, it is possible to organize a data set with *spanned records*, such that a particular record may be segmented across more than one block. The specification **VS** is used to denote this, with the extra four-byte fields still being required as before. *A block in a **VS** data set cannot contain more than one record or one segement of a record.*

To see how this would work, let us declare a file SHORTY as follows:

DECLARE SHORTY **FILE OUTPUT ENVIRONMENT**(VS(200,300));

This says that any record in SHORTY may contain as many as 296 bytes of data (remember the four bytes for bookkeeping) and any block may contain as many as 192 bytes of data. Suppose that there is a 140 byte record that we wish to make part of the data set. Accordingly, the software will add the extra four bytes, making the record length 144. Throwing in the four block description bytes gives us a single block of length 148. Now, along comes a 220-byte record. Since it exceeds the specified maximum block size, the software will segment it: The first block (length 200) will contain 192 bytes of data, leaving 28 bytes for the next block.

TABLE 14.4 Block Allocations for
VS and VBS Data Sets*

Record Length(s)	Type	No. of Blocks	Block Length(s)
140	**VS, VBS**	1	148 (full record)
rec.1=80 rec.2=80	**VS**	2	1:88 (rec.1) 2:88 (rec.2)
	VBS	1	172(two full records)
320	**VS, VBS**	2	1:200(192 data bytes) 2:136(128 data bytes)
rec.1=320 rec.2=50	**VS**	3	1:200(192 bytes of rec.1) 2:136 (rest of rec.1) 3:58 (rec.2)
	VBS	2	1:200(192 bytes of rec.1) 2:190(128+4 for rec.1, 50+4 for rec.2, +4)
rec.1=320 rec.2=30 rec.3=24	**VS**	4	1:200(192 bytes of rec.1) 2:136(rest of rec.1) 3:38(rec.2) 4:32(rec.3)
	VBS	2	1:200(192 bytes of rec.1) 2:198(128+4 for rec.1, 30+4 for rec.2, 24+4 for rec.3, +4)

*VS file is declared (**VS** (200, 300)), **VBS** file is declared (**VBS** (200, 300)).

Accordingly, a second block of length 36 (28 + 4 + 4) will be written, containing a 32-byte record (28 + 4).

Another type of spanned record may be used, specified by **VBS**. With this type, an attempt is made to fill each block as much as possible, regardless of the number of records and/or segments that end up in a block. Thus, each block tends to be sized near the allowable maximum for that data set. Some comparisons are shown in Table 14.4.

XIV.3.2.4   Undefined Length Records

When the record organization is unanticipated, such files still can be processed by specifying

   ...ENVIRONMENT(U(blmax))

where "blmax" has its previous meaning. Since there is no information about the record size, the programmer is completely responsible for all blocking/deblocking operations.

XIV.3.3   Specifications of Buffers

The number of buffers can also be specified as part of most **ENVIRONMENT** option lists. This is done with the **BUFFERS** option, as in the general statement

   DECLARE filename att1,att2,etc. **ENVIRONMENT(BUFFERS**(n));

where n is a decimal integer constant. (Most compilers allow n to go as high as 256.) When the **BUFFERS** option does not appear, a value of 2 is usually assigned by default.

   Thus,

   DECLARE OUTF **FILE OUTPUT SEQUENTIAL ENVIRONMENT(F**(1000,100)**BUFFER-S**(5));

describes an output file OUTF, each of whose records is 100 bytes long. These are to be written onto some device with a block size of 100. A set of five buffers (each 100 bytes long) is to be made available to help in the blocking of physical output records.

XIV.3.4   Data Set Organization

Having stipulated an access method (**SEQUENTIAL** or **DIRECT**), we must provide more specific information regarding the arrangement of the records in the particular data set associated with a given file. When the data set is being created (that is, when the file's records are being transmitted to the data set for ultimate storage), this information guides the system in the physical placement of those records. Later on, when the records of a data set are to be accessed for internal processing, the organizational information is used to define and regulate internal search procedures that will identify a desired record and make it available to the processor.

Although there are three basic types of organization (**CONSECUTIVE, INDEXED, and REGIONAL**), the accompanying range of options that may be specified for the creation, search, retrieval, and modification of such data sets constitute the subject of an extensive study in themselves. This is complicated further by the fact that the behavior and use of such data set organizations are influenced substantially by additional specifications and options that are supplied to the software system from sources outside of the PL/I program or the compiler that analyzes it. Consequently, we shall not examine these organizational features in full detail. Rather, we shall strive to develop an understanding of the behavioral properties so that the student can become familiar with the organizational types and how they work. With this as a basis, subsequent consultation and use of the detailed specifications will be straightforward. Appropriate references to those details are given at the end of the chapter.

XIV.3.4.1   The **CONSECUTIVE** Attribute

This is the simplest type of data set organization in that the records are placed on the data set in a particular physical order with the expectation that this sequence will be maintained. The underlying idea is that such a data set will be associated with a file declared as having the **SEQUENTIAL** attribute but without the **KEYED** attribute.

When a **CONSECUTIVE** data set is being created, the file records are written onto the storage medium in the same physical sequence in which they are transmitted. Thus, even though a **CONSECUTIVE** data set may be stored on a direct-access device, it is being used as a sequential device in that the first physical record is the first one written by the program that created the data set, and so on.

When records are retrieved from a **CONSECUTIVE** data set, they are accessed in the same physical order in which they were written (or in exact reverse order if the associated file is declared with the **BACKWARDS** attribute). It is impossible to rearrange the records, and one cannot disrupt the sequence by inserting new records or removing unwanted ones. In operational terms, when we read a record from a **CONSECUTIVE** data set there is no immediate implication that we are reading a particular record. The input statement merely amounts to a specification to "read the next record." Because of this restriction, any changes to a **CONSECUTIVE** data set other than simple updating must be handled by creating a new data set that incorporates those changes. The basic capabilities are summarized in Table 14.5.

XIV.3.4.2   The **INDEXED** Attribute

There are countless occasions in which it is desired to maintain a file's records in some inherently meaningful sequence while still retaining the prerogative of retrieving individual records in random order. One very convenient way to do this is to use the **INDEXED** organization. As its name implies, a data set so organized is equipped (by the software) with an

Table 14.5   Basic Properties of Data Set Organizations

Type of Organization

Property	CONSECUTIVE	INDEXED	REGIONAL (1)	REGIONAL (2)	REGIONAL (3)
Sequence of record storage	as submitted	by ascending recorded key	by region no.	by region no.	by region no.
Allowable type of physical device	sequential or direct access	direct access	direct access	direct access	direct access
Allowable record formats	F,V,U blocked or unblocked	F,V,U blocked or unblocked	F unblocked	F unblocked	F,V,U unblocked
Record identifiers	none	recorded key	region no.	region no., recorded key	region no., recorded key
Allowable access methods for file creation	SEQUENTIAL	SEQUENTIAL	SEQUENTIAL, DIRECT	SEQUENTIAL, DIRECT	SEQUENTIAL, DIRECT
Allowable access methods for record retrieval	SEQUENTIAL	SEQUENTIAL, DIRECT	SEQUENTIAL, DIRECT	SEQUENTIAL, DIRECT	SEQUENTIAL, DIRECT
Direction of transmission for record processing	INPUT, OUTPUT UPDATE*	INPUT, OUTPUT,† UPDATE	INPUT, OUTPUT,‡ UPDATE	INPUT, OUTPUT,‡ UPDATE	INPUT, OUTPUT,‡ UPDATE
Use of standard dummy records	no provisions	(1),(3),(4)	(2),(3)	(2),(3),(4)	(2),(3),(4),(5)

* Only if data set is on a direct access device.
† Only for SEQUENTIAL files.
‡ Only for file/data set creation.

Notes:
(1) can be inserted by program during file/data set creation
(2) inserted automatically during file/data set creation
(3) automatically replace deleted records
(4) automatically ignored by READ statements
(5) special conditions for V and U record formats.

index so that it is searched in two stages: Before actually examining the records themselves, the program consults the data set's index, which directs the procedure to a considerably limited portion of the data set. The subsequent search operates over that restricted portion, the idea being that the desired record, if it exists at all, is to be found in that section. The net effect, from the programmer's viewpoint, is that he can read an **INDEXED** file as if it were **CONSECUTIVE**, without intolerable loss in efficiency. Yet, when a certain record is to be retrieved he can get it directly by saying, in essence, "find this particular record, wherever it happens to be on the data set, and bring it in."

The mechanism for identifying each record is implemented through a *key* that is associated with the record when the data set is created. This key is a character string that usually has some intrinsic relation to its associated record. For example, suppose we want to create a file called WRHS, each of whose records is to contain inventory data about a particular type of part in a warehouse: part number, number of units on hand, vendor code, unit price and location code. In this situation the part number would serve as a suitable key, since it allows each record to be distinguished from the others. With that in mind, let us examine the following sequence of statements:

```
        .
        .
        .
DECLARE WRHS FILE OUTPUT SEQUENTIAL
        ENVIRONMENT(F(23,23)INDEXED),
    1 NVNTRY,
        2 PART_ND PICTURE '99999',
        2 ONHAND PICTURE '99999'
        2 VENDOR_CODE PICTURE '9999',
        2 PRICE PICTURE '999V99',
        2 LOC_CODE CHARACTER(4);


        .
        .
        .
WRITE FILE(WRHS)FROM(NVNTRY)KEYFROM(PART_NO);


        .
        .
        .
```

NVNTRY is the structure in which an individual record is built, and WRHS is the name of the file that will be used in creating the **INDEXED** data set. The **WRITE** statement requests the transmission of a record (corresponding to the contents of NVNTRY) to the data set associated with the file. When that record is written, the system makes a note to the effect that the value in PART_NO is to be used as the key. A key specified in a transmission statement (as above) is known as a *source key*. The information from the source key is associated with the record and stored with it on the data set. In that context it is termed a *recorded key*. (In this case the source key and recorded key are identical; that may not always be true.) A recorded key may be *embedded*, in which case the actual value inside the record serves as the key; alternatively, it may be *separate*, whereby another copy of the value is made by the system and placed immediately ahead of (and attached to) the record on the data set. (Specifications as to which type of recorded key it is, as well as how long it is, are indicated to the system outside the PL/I program.)

The recorded key (separate or embedded) is the major criterion for record sequencing in an **INDEXED** data set. Thus, when such a data set is created, it must be done in conjunction with a **SEQUENTIAL** file, and the records must be written in order by ascending key value. Going back to our example, the record for part no. 7104 would have to be written before the one for part no. 20026 in keeping with this rule. (If these records were submitted in reverse order, the **KEY** condition would be raised.) If the part "number" included letters, the rule for ascending order still would hold. Thus, a part number of 35A72 would be "less than" a part number of 35C16 in accordance with the collating sequence (see Appendix C). The index, built by the system as part of the file creation process, then is available for use in accessing records in an order that is arbitrarily different from the stored sequence. In fact, records in an **INDEXED** data set may be accessed by a **DIRECT** or **SEQUENTIAL** file. With the former, records may be read, deleted, replaced, or changed in any order.

A very common situation is one in which we want to read sequentially but do not wish to start at the beginning of the data set as would be necessary with **CONSECUTIVE** organization. Accordingly, the following sequence for our file WRHS

```
DECLARE WRHS FILE INPUT DIRECT
        ENVIRONMENT (F(23,23)INDEXED),
        1 NVNTRY,
          2 ...............,
          S BIT(1) INITIAL ('1'B);
      ......
      ......
READ FILE (WRHS) INTO NVNTRY KEY ('02377');

DO WHILE (S);
      ........
      ........
     Processing
      ........
    READ FILE (WRHS) INTO (NVNTRY);
      ........
     Processing
      ........
END;
```

would allow the program to start the input with the record for part no. 2377 (regardless of the record's physical location). After that it would just keep bringing in the next record in physical sequence (that is, the one with the next higher recorded key) each time through the loop.

A special facility offers the programmer the opportunity to delete records from an **INDEXED** data set or insert records into one. Basically, this is done through the use of a *dummy record*, which is like any other record in the data set since it is no different in length or format. However, it contains a special signal to indicate that it is a dummy record and its contents are to be disregarded. This is indicated by filling the first byte (8 bits) of the record with the bit string '11111111'**B**. Generally, the data set is created without dummy records; however, the programmer can specify the inclusion of such dummy records where and when he wishes. Subsequently, when the data set is accessed, these may either be bypassed or filled with "legitimate" contents, thereby achieving the same effect as a physical insertion of a new record. Conversely, the deletion process involves the writing of the dummy indicator in the first byte of the record to be deleted. New records may be inserted even if there does not already exist a dummy record with the same key. However, as the number of such insertions increases, the access to the data set becomes less and less efficient.

These basic features are summarized in Table 14.5.

XIV.3.4.3   The **REGIONAL** Attribute

The PL/I programmer may exploit the flexibility of the direct-access device to any desired extent (limited almost exclusively by the physical operating characteristics of the device) through the **REGIONAL** data set. A wide range of possibilities exist. At the most primitive level, such data sets appear and act like arrays, with rather strict sequential limitations; when the full blown facilities are specified, the programmer may exercise detailed control over the physical positioning of individual records and over the implementation of the associated search and retrieval mechanisms.

The spectrum of capabilities is embodied in three forms of **REGIONAL** organizations.

REGIONAL(1) is the most basic level of **REGIONAL** organization in that we expect our file to be relatively simple: no duplicate keys and straightforward sequencing of records. Although such a data set must be on a direct-access device, its records must be fixed length unblocked and cannot be associated with recorded keys. Instead, each record is supplied with an implied key in the form of a unique numerical *region number* (starting with 0) that indicates that record's relative physical position in the data set. External storage for the data set is reserved outside of the program, and the extent of this storage, together with the specified record length, will determine the number of records that could be accommodated. This capacity, in turn, will define the highest region number. In any event, there is an upper limit of 16777215. Thus, if we were creating a **REGIONAL**(1) data set using a file named WRHS and the next record is to be written from location NVNTRY, the statement

WRITE FILE (WRHS) FROM (NVNTRY) KEYFROM('2729');

would identify this record as belonging in region 2729 (that is, the 2730th record in the data set).

A **REGIONAL**(1) data set has a record for every region number, even if the creating program does not supply it. For example, let us examine a procedural segment in which a loop reads a succession of cards containing values for a structure NVNTRY and a value RGNO to be used as a region number. Each of these groups is used to create a record in a file WRHS to be written on a **REGIONAL**(1) data set:

```
DECLARE WRHS FILE OUTPUT SEQUENTIAL
            ENVIRONMENT (F(23,23) REGIONAL(1)),
        RGNO FIXED (5),
        1 NVNTRY,
          2 ...........,
          ...........,
        S BIT(1) INITIAL ('1'B);

ON ENDIFLE (SYSIN) S = '0'B;
      .......
      .......
GET EDIT(RGNO,NVNTRY)(R(FORM));

DO WHILE (S);
    .......
    .......
    WRITE FILE (WRHS) FROM (NVNTRY) KEYFROM (RGNO);
    GET EDIT(RGNO,NVNTRY)(R(FORM));
END;
```

Now let us suppose that the procedure just placed a record in region 7 of the data set and the next three cards to be processed contain RGNO value of 8, 21, and 22, respectively. The first of these cards is read and the eighth record is duly written. Then, when the next card is read and the program goes to write the corresponding output record, it finds there is a gap between its region number and the previous one. Consequently, it creates dummy records for regions 9, 10, 11, ..., 20, after which it writes the specified record as the 21st one. Then, it goes ahead and routinely processes the next card, using its contents to produce the 22nd record. If the card with RGNO of 21 were followed by one with RGNO of say, 17, the **KEY** condition would be raised.

A **REGIONAL**(1) data set also may be created in conjunction with a **DIRECT OUTPUT** file. In that case, the records need not be submitted in order by ascending region number. What happens is that the entire data set is filled automatically with dummy records, after which the appropriate ones are written over with actual data in the order received.

REGIONAL(1) data sets may be accessed sequentially or directly. In either case, records may be changed or deleted. (The latter process operates by replacing a record with a dummy record). There is no mechanism for distinguishing between dummy records and those with "legitimate" contents; accordingly, the programmer must provide this. These properties are summarized in Table 14.5. *pg 432*

In a **REGIONAL**(2) data set the level of organization is set up to support more complicated search and retrieval procedures. Consequently, the underlying mechanisms are more elaborate (and more time consuming) than those provided to support **REGIONAL**(1). This means that the use of **REGIONAL**(2) to organize data sets for predominantly straightforward retrieval (for example, each record is uniquely identified and unambiguously located) is usually less efficient than **REGIONAL**(1) and may even be less effective than **INDEXED** or **CONSECUTIVE**.

Basically, a record in a **REGIONAL**(2) data set is associated with a recorded key. As with **REGIONAL**(1) data sets, there is also a region number that determines the physical placement of a record. However, this need not be part of the recorded key. There may be several records with the same region number, so that knowledge of the region number serves to define the general area in which a desired record is to be found. Once that is established, the search continues based on the comparison key. Information for the recorded key and the region number comes from a *source key* that is supplied for each record when the data set is created. The rightmost eight characters of the source key are taken to be the region number (they must be 0-9 or blanks) and the n leftmost characters form the comparison key. (The value of n for the data set is specified outside of the PL/I program.) For example, if we are creating a **REGIONAL**(2) data set using the file WRHS and the comparison key length is 6, the statement

WRITE FILE (WRHS) **FROM** (NVNTRY) **KEYFROM** ('007212ᵬᵬᵬᵬᵬᵬ417');

would cause a record to be written in region (00000)417 (leading blanks are treated as zeros) with an attached recorded key of 007112. Note that the proper number of characters are taken from the left and right ends, and the excess characters are discarded automatically. If the comparison key is sufficiently long, it is possible for the region number to be included as part of the recorded key. The rule is still the same in that the rightmost eight characters specify the region number, even though they may be part of the comparison key as well.

When a **REGIONAL**(2) data set is created in conjunction with a **SEQUENTIAL OUTPUT** file, the process is quite similar to **REGIONAL**(1) in that records must be presented one to a region, in ascending order by region number. "Missing" regions are filled with dummy records. This time, however, the dummy record is denoted differently: The first byte of its recorded key (not the data) is filled with '11111111'**B**. When created in conjunction with a **DIRECT** file, duplicate region numbers are accepted. In either case the records must be fixed length unblocked.

Sequential access of a **REGIONAL**(2) data set appears to operate like a **CONSECUTIVE** data set: The next available record is read, regardless of the value in its recorded key. Under direct access, a source key must be provided by the **READ** statement so that the system can get to the correct region and search for the specified comparison key. Unlike **REGIONAL**(1) data sets, dummy records in **REGIONAL**(2) data sets are automatically ignored regardless of access method. Table 14.5 summarizes these properties.

Although it is desirable to use a type of key that has some intrinsic meaning, it is not always best to do so. For example, suppose that we wish to store our file WRHS for direct access such that the part number is used as the key. Let us say there are 2800 different part numbers, each of which is expressed as five-digit number. That means there are 100,000 possible part numbers (00000-99999) and the **REGIONAL**(2) data set will be created with 100,000 records in it—97,200 of them dummies. To avoid this inefficiency, the usual practice is to specify the actual part number as a comparison key and develop a region number as a value computed simply and directly from the part number. One way to do this is to decide how many records (real and dummy) our data set will hold, and compute a region number on that basis. If CAP is the capacity of the data set and PART_NO is a given part number, then RGNO, the region number, when calculated as **MOD**(PART_NO,CAP), would give us a region number between 0 and CAP−1. This cuts down on the number of empty records but runs a risk of producing the same region number from different part numbers. For instance, if we decide to accommodate our 2800 records in a data set with a capacity of 3000, part numbers of 32760 and 44760 will both produce the same region number (2760). **REGIONAL**(2) would allow us to store both records, with subsequent retrieval being based on comparison keys. Note that we can avoid this complication by using an **INDEXED** organization in which the actual part number is the key and there are no vacant records. However, this may not be as desirable if the data set is going to be used for numerous and frequent direct accesses in no particular order or if it is subject to frequent changes (additions and deletions). The point is that there is considerable overlap in the capabilities of these various organizations, so the choice of one in preference to another is usually dictated by how the particular data set is going to be used.

REGIONAL(3) is the most comprehensive type of organization in that it gives the PL/I programmer more direct control over the placement of records in a data set. Such placement can be regulated to exploit the physical characteristics of the particular type of direct-access device on which that data set is to reside. Although unblocked records are still required, they may be of any format (**F**, **U**, or **V**). Consequently, if the programmer must work with variable-length records and expects to access them frequently and in unanticipated order, there are strong reasons to create (and use) his data set as **REGIONAL**(3). Furthermore, by knowing the physical characteristics of the particular device that will house the data set, the programmer can specify options (both within and outside PL/I) that will enhance the search and retrieval processes. Outside of these considerations, the basic operating characteristics do not differ substantially from those of **REGIONAL**(2) organizations. A summary is included in Table 14.5.

Additional types of attributes are stipulated as part of the **ENVIRONMENT** specification. However, they are rather specialized and their use requires additional background beyond the scope of his book. Consequently, we shall refer to appropriate sources for this information.

XIV.4   RELATIONSHIPS BETWEEN FILES AND EXTERNAL STORAGE DEVICES

In our discussion of file attributes, we have developed means for providing PL/I with a fairly extensive description of how a data set is organized (or how PL/I is to organize it) and what techniques should be made available to use it for input/output and internal manipulations. Still lacking, however, is a means for informing PL/I that a particular input file is coming from a data set on a particular storage device or that a particular output file is to be generated as a data set on a given storage device.

The establishment of the association between a particular device and a data file is not a direct process. We have already discussed the fact that the file is linked (outside the program) with a particular data set. That data set, in turn, is associated with the physical device on which it resides. This relationship, too, is defined outside of the program. The supervisory software, and not the program, is the primary agent in setting up these links. Although bypassing PL/I appears to deprive it of some control capabilities, this arrangement actually enhances the flexibility of the language and the versatility of programs written in it. By way of explanation, we must examine some of the basic features of the supervisory software and their connection with the PL/I compiler.

The types of computing systems for which PL/I is available represent substantial departures from their predecessors. Perhaps the most dramatic aspect of their growth has been the increase in the number and type of peripheral devices that can be attached to these computers. In addition to the tape drive and magnetic disk unit, each of which is available in several varieties, equipment manufactureres now provide a formidable array of other external input, output, and storage devices, with the means of incorporating them into the overall constellation. It is possible to create hundreds of different configurations, each of which is to be controlled by a network of supervisory software usually referred to as the *operating system*. It would be highly impractical to anticipate all of the possible configurations in designing the software. Instead, the approach is to construct the software system as a series of modules so that each installation can synthesize the most appropriate system to suit its particular complement of peripheral components. Contained in the resulting system is a reference table listing each individual device attached to the computing system, together with a unique name assigned to that device by the installation and description of the processor-device linkage.

When a program is written in PL/I (or, for that matter, in any other language available under an operating system organized in this manner), and that program uses or generates data sets, the association between each file name and the particular data-handling device to which it is assigned is specified as part of the set of system instructions which precede the program. Among other information, these specifications can include most of the descriptions specified as **ENVIRONMENT** options. The ability to make such specifications outside of the individual program brings with it a substantial enhancement in program flexibility. Linkages between the file name and the associated data set are much less permanent than they would otherwise be. For example, if a program uses a sequential input file named SOURCE, it is not necessary to specify the device from which SOURCE is to be read until that program is to be run. It is a very easy matter to change the specification from run to run, because such changes do not involve the program. Since these specifications can include the complete physical description of the data set to be used for a particular run (number of characters in each record, blocking information, buffering arrangement, and so on), SOURCE could be on a reel of tape for one run, a disk for another run, a magnetic drum for a third run, and so on. By the same token, a particular program can be used in many facilities whose configurations differ with respect to the number and type of peripheral units attached to the central processor. Again, it is the specifications to the system that require modification, rather than the program. Thus, it is generally a good idea to avoid using the **ENVIRONMENT** option for this type of specification and keep as many of the specifications as possible outside the program, where they are easily changed. The expected precautions have to be exercised when making these specifications in order to avoid inconsistencies between them and the attributes assigned in the program. For example, if a file name is declared in the program and given the **DIRECT** attribute, the user must make sure that the device associated with that file in the instructions to the system is a direct-access device. The forms for these specifications will not be discussed here, as they are not part of the language and may vary from one installation to another. Not all **ENVIRON-MENT** options may be so treated. For instance, **REGIONAL**(1), **REGIONAL**(2), and **REG-IONAL**(3) must always be specified within the **ENVIRONMENT** attribute.

XIV.5   ACTIVATION OF FILES

Before a file can actually be used in a program, preparations must be made to establish lines of communication among the file, processor, program, and supervisory software. The declaration of the file name accompanied by a list of attributes serves only to facilitate this preparation, which must be completed by instructing the system to activate the file and make it ready for use. If the file is a sequential input file, for example, the physical activity triggered by this preparation may include positioning of a tape unit so that the reading mechanism is set to transmit the contents of the first record of the reel. A file that is available in this manner is said to be *open*.

Although the PL/I programmer can choose one of several ways to open a file, the most straightforward method is by using an OPEN statement, whose general form is

OPEN FILE (filename) att1 att2 etc, **FILE**(filename) att1 att2 etc, ...;

where "att1 att2 etc." is a list of file attributes and "filename" is self-explanatory. In addition to triggering the activities required to prepare one or more files for immediate use, the **OPEN** statement gives the programmer the opportunity to assign additional attributes. The list of attributes that may be specified in an **OPEN** statement include all of those assignable in a **DECLARE** statement (except for **EXTERNAL**, **INTERNAL** or **ENVIRONMENT**).

Once a program has carried out all its intended operations on a file, that file need no longer remain active. Although the conclusion of the program will obviously deactivate (close) all the files used in that program, PL/I provides a specific **CLOSE** statement as a vehicle for carrying out special additional operations during the deactivation procedure. For example, many programs operating on magnetic tape files read the contents of those files more than once during a run. When this is necessary, the **CLOSE** statement is used after the first pass through the file to rewind the tape and reposition it so that its first record is available. Once this is done, all that is required for the next pass is to reactive the file with another **OPEN** statement.

XIV.5.1   The **TITLE** Option

If the programmer wishes, he can include an indirect specification of the data set to be associated with a particular file name by using the **TITLE** option. Its appearance in an **OPEN** statement is generally in the form

OPEN FILE (filename) **TITLE** (character string);

where the name specified by the **TITLE** option cannot exceed eight characters in length. The contents of the character string following the keyword **TITLE** refer to a name being used by the supervisory system to identify a particular data set. To establish the proper transfer of information between the program and the operating system, that name also appears in an instruction to the system linking that name with a particular external storage device. If we were to say

OPEN FILE (CHARTS) **INPUT SEQUENTIAL TITLE** ('UTILITY');

an instruction to the system would be included along with the program in which the name UTILITY is linked to a particular data set known to the computing system. After the program is compiled and resubmitted as a sequence of machine-oriented instructions for running purposes, the system instructions can be changed to suit the particular situation. On one occasion, UTILITY may refer to a data set that resides on tape; another time the instruction may be changed to link UTILITY with a data set on disk. In any event, the program remains unchanged and need not be recompiled.

If the **TITLE** option is not specified for a particular file name, PL/I will assume that the file name itself is to serve this purpose. The **TITLE** option has no meaning in a **CLOSE** statement.

Illustration 42

One way to use the TITLE option can be seen by examining the following situation: There are six inventory files for six different warehouses. The six **INDEXED** data sets on which these are housed have the names WD1, WD2, WD3, WD4, WD5, and WD6, respectively. Each data set is organized identically, with ten 23-byte logical records to a physical record. We wish to process input values that update the number of parts on hand for particular part numbers on one of the six data sets. The first card of a group contains the date in columns 11-16 and the warehouse number (1-6) in column 20. This is followed by an undetermined number of cards, each containing a part number of (columns 1-5) and a signed number (columns 10-15) indicating the net change in the number of units on hand. The last card of a group has a part number of zero. The program is to select the proper data set for each group, find and update the appropriate records and print them.

As in the previous declarations, we shall use the file name WRHS and the structure NVNTRY, with PART_NO serving as the key:

```
ILL42: PROCEDURE OPTIONS (MAIN);
       DECLARE WRHS FILE DIRECT UPDATE ENVIRONMENT(F(230,23) INDEXED),
               1 NVNTRY,
                 2 PART_NO PICTURE '99999',
                 2 ONHAND PICTURE '99999',
                 2 VENDRCD PICTURE '9999',
                 2 PRICE PICTURE '999V9',
                 2 LOGCD CHARACTER(4),
               1 DATE,
                 (2 MTH, 2 DAY, 2 YR) FIXED(2),
               RDPART PICTURE '9999',
               CHANGE FIXED(5),
               HNO PICTURE '9',
               (S,SKEY,SPART) BIT(1) INITIAL ('1'B);
       /***********************************************************************/
       /* S CONTROLS THE MAJOR PROCESSING LOOP, WHICH CUTS OFF WHEN   */
       /* THERE ARE NO MORE INPUT CARDS.                             */
       /* SKEY IS TRIGGERED BY THE ON KEY CONDITION, SO THAT A SPE-  */
       /* CIAL MESSAGE IS PRINTED WHEN A KEY SEARCH IS UNSUCCESSFUL. */
       /* ONCE THE MESSAGE IS PRINTED, SKEY IS RESET.                */
       /* SPART TRIGGERS THE END OF FILE FOR EACH DATA SET. WHEN     */
       /* AN INPUT PART NO. OF ZERO IS READ, SPART IS CHANGED, SO    */
       /* THAT THE PROGRAM CAN DETECT THIS AND SET UP FOR THE NEXT   */
       /* FILE. ONCE THAT IS DONE, SPART IS RESET.                   */
       /***********************************************************************/

       ON ENDFILE (SYSIN) S = '0'B;
       GET EDIT (DATE,HNO)(R(FDATE));
FDATE: FORMAT(COL(1),X(10), 3 F(2),X(3),A(1));

       DO WHILE (S);
          PUT PAGE LINE(3) EDIT ('INVENTORY UPDATE'(X(58),A)
             ('WAREHOUSE NO. ',HNO,MTH,'/',DAY,'/',YR)
             (SKIP,X(53),A(14),A,X(3),F(2), 2 (A,F(2)))
             ('PART NO. ','CHANGE','ON HAND')
             (SKIP,X(10),A(8),XB12),A(6),X(14),A(7));
          PUT SKIP;
          OPEN FILE (WRHS) TITLE ('WD' !! HNO);
          SPART = '1'B;
          GET EDIT (RDPART,CHANGE)(COL(1),A(5),X(4),F(6));
          IF RDPART = 0 THEN SPART = '0'B;
          ON KEY SKEY = '0'B;
          READ FILE (WRHS) INTO (NVNTRY) KEY (RDPART);
          DO WHILE (SPART);
             IF SKEY
                THEN DO;
                     ONHAND = ONHAND+CHANGE;
                     REWRITE FILE (WRHS) FROM (NVNTRY) KEY (RDPART);
                     PUT SKIP EDIT(RDPART,CHANGE,ONHAND)
                        (X(7),A(5),X(18),F(6),X(14),F(5));
                     END;
                ELSE DO;
                     PUT SKIP EDIT (RDPART,' IS AN INVALID PART NO.')
                        (A(5),A);
                     SKEY = '1'B;
                     END;
             GET EDIT (RDPART,CHANGE)(COL(1),A(5),X(4),F(6));
             IF RDPART = 0 THEN SPART = '0'B;
          END;
          SPART = '1'B;
          GET EDIT (DATE,HNO)(R(FDATE));
       END;

       CLOSE FILE (WRHS);
       PUT SKIP(3) LIST ('END OF RUN');
       END ILL42;
```

XIV.5.2   File Variables

The Optimizing and Checkout Compilers provide an additional feature that facilitates the redefinition of relationships between files and data sets. In fact, such associations can be set up and changed with as little complexity (on the part of the programmer) as is required to assign values to ordinary numerical variables. This flexibility is offered by means of *file variables*.

A file variable is defined in a **DECLARE** statement having the form

DECLARE filevar **FILE VARIABLE**;

The attribute **VARIABLE** indicates the filevar does not itself refer to a particular file; instead, it takes on values that are names of files. In this context, then, such assigned names can be considered as being *file constants*. To illustrate, the statement

    DECLARE WHO **FILE VARIABLE**,

             F1 **FILE**.......,

             F2 **FILE**.......,

             F3 **FILE**.......;

establishes WHO as a file variable and F1, F2, and F3 as file constants. (Associations between F1, F2, F3 and their respective data sets still are set up outside the program.) Then, the sequence

    WHO = F1;   **READ FILE** (WHO) **INTO** (place);

results in the reading of a record from the data set associated with F1 (assuming, of course, that F1's attributes allow input). Subsequent reassignment (for example, WHO=F2;) changes the implied reference in the **READ** statement without necessitating a corresponding explicit alteration in the statement itself. Accordingly, if that statement is executed subsequent to the new assignment (and prior to any further changes to WHO's value), the record will be read from F2. In this regard, file variables behave somewhat like label variables. This analogy persists in that file constants can be assigned to file variables but they cannot be read or written.

    File variables also may be set up as arrays, in which case the **VARIABLE** attribute can be implied. Thus, the statement

    DECLARE BEVY(6) **FILE**;

sets up an array of six file variable elements, each of which can be assigned a file constant value independently.

XIV.5.3   Additional Options for **PRINT** Files

When opening a file with the **PRINT** attribute, the implication is that the contents eventually will be printed regardless of the device on which the data currently are stored. Accordingly, it is possible to assign additional features that control the overall format of the file when it is printed.

XIV.5.3.1   The **PAGESIZE** Option

    Assuming that a file has been declared with the **PRINT** attribute, it is possible to specify the number of lines to be printed per page of output for that file in a statement such as

OPEN FILE (filename) **PAGESIZE** (expression);

where (expression) is any legitimate PL/I expression that can be converted into an integer value. This value is then used to determine the number of lines to be printed before the carriage is returned to the top of a new page. This number has nothing to do with the physical size of a page in the printer. The limiting value of a **PAGESIZE** for most compilers is about 32,768, and the default value is 60.

XIV.5.3.2   The **LINESIZE** Option

The programmer can specify the number of spaces to be used for each line of a **STREAM OUTPUT** file by using a statement such as

OPEN FILE (filename) **LINESIZE** (expression);

(expression) is evaluated and used in the same way as for the **PAGESIZE** option. The maximum number of spaces (characters) that may be specified for a "line" in most compilers is 32,760, and the default value is 120.

XIV.5.4   Additional Remarks Concerning the **OPEN** and **CLOSE** Statement

If the programmer wishes, he may combine the functions of the **OPEN** and **DECLARE** statements by listing all the attributes in the **OPEN** statement. There is no specific order in which these attributes and options have to be listed. It is possible (and highly advisable) to activate more than one file in a single **OPEN** statement. The advisability of doing this stems from the fact that each **OPEN** command requires PL/I to call a series of special procedures to perform the necessary activation. By writing

OPEN FILE (WORK1) **INPUT, FILE** (WORK2) **OUTPUT,**

    FILE (WORK3) **INPUT;**

instead of

OPEN FILE (WORK1) **INPUT;**

OPEN FILE (WORK2) **OUTPUT;**

OPEN FILE (WORK3) **INPUT;**

the compiler would have to make only one time-consuming call to the activating procedures instead of three.

PROBLEMS

1. The East Floogle National Bank has information pertaining to its depositors on punched cards as
    follows:

Columns	Item	Format
1-7	account no.	F(7)
11-30	last name, first name, initial	characters
34	type of account	1,2,3,4 or 5
35-40	date of last transaction	mnddyy
45-50	amount of transaction	F(6,2)
51	type of transaction	D or W
58-60	current balance	F(7,2) plus a sign

    The bank is adding magnetic tape units to its computer system and these data will form a
    record-oriented file. In preparation for the great event, write a sequence of statements to develop a
    structure that would eventually represent a record.

2. East Floogle's management wants its eventual system design set up so that there is a separate file
    for each type of account. Develop a sequence of statements that build each type of record from the
    appropriate input card.

SUMMARY OF IMPORTANT TERMS

Access method	One of two basic techniques for transmitting records to or from data sets. *Sequential access* restricts the availability of records to a fixed order, whereas the transmission of a record to or from a particular position in a *direct-access* data set is independent of the position of the record transmitted previously.
BACKWARDS	A special attribute for an input file whose associated data set records are to be accessed sequentially, but in reverse order to that in which they were written.
Blocked records	Organization of a data set such that each physical record contains more than one logical record.
Blocking	The process of concatenating several strings of data (each representing a logical record) to form a single string that ultimately will become a physical record.
Blocking factor	The number of logical records in a particular physical record.

Buffer	A storage area to or from which input/output is to be transmitted, distinct from the area in which the data are to be processed. The use of buffers facilitates exploitation of overlapped processing (which see).
CLOSE	The statement type for explicit deactivation of files.
CONSECUTIVE	The attribute assigned to a data set whose organization is intended exclusively for sequential access.
Data set	An organized collection of records residing on a specific external storage medium.
Deblocking	The process of extracting and making available single logical records from a blocked physical record.
DIRECT	See "Access method."
Direction of transmission	A set of attributes indicating that records from a data set associated with a particular file are to be transmitted to the processor (**INPUT**), from the processor (**OUTPUT** or **PRINT**), or both (**UPDATE**).
ENVIRONMENT	An option that may be attached to a file declaration to designate organizational attributes of the data set associated with a given file.
File	A disembodied (conceptual) collection of records not intrinsically associated with any physical storage device or medium. In PL/I's context, a vehicle for accessing a data set.
INDEXED	An organizational method for a data set whereby its records may be accessed directly or sequentially.
INPUT	See "Direction of transmission."
Interrecord gap	A space on magnetic recording media provided automatically by the device's mechanism to separate adjacent physical records.
Key	A character string of arbitrary length and composition used to provide a unique identifier for a record in a file. (Such files are assigned the **KEYED** attribute.)
Logical record	A collection of conceptually related data items forming the elemental structural component of a file. For example, a record in a payroll file would consist of all the information about an individual employee.
OPEN	The statement type used for explicit activation of a file, thereby making its associated data set available for processing.
OUTPUT	See "Direction of transmission."
Overlapped processing	Simultaneous performance of internal processing and input/output operations, supported by appropriate hardware facilities.
Physical record	That amount of information stored on a magnetic medium between interrecord gaps.
PRINT	See "Direction of transmission."
Record	See "Logical record" and "Physical record."
RECORD	See "Transmission mode."
Record length	The number of bytes in a (logical or physical) record.

REGIONAL	An organization method for data sets allowing either the direct or sequential access of its records.
SEQUENTIAL	See "Access method."
Spanned record	A logical record occupying more than one physical record.
STREAM	See "Transmission mode."
Transmission mode	One of two basic methods for moving information in or out of the processor. **STREAM** mode (**GET/PUT** statements) implies transmission of individual data items while **RECORD** transmission (**READ/WRITE/REWRITE/DELETE/LOCATE** statements) implies input/output of entire records.
Unblocked records	Organization of a data set such that each physical record contains only one logical record.
UPDATE	See "Direction of transmission."

SUPPLEMENTARY READING

Job Control Language, IBM Document No. C28-6539. White Plains. N.Y.: IBM Corporation.

PL/I Language Reference Manual, IBM Document No. GC28-8201. White Plains, N.Y.: IBM Corporation, pp. 112-116, 125-148.

PL/I Programmer's Guide, IBM Document No. GC28-6594. White Plains, N.Y.: IBM Corporation, pp. 21-25, 99-150.

Price, W.T., *Introduction to Data Processing*. San Francisco: Rinehart Press, 1972, pp. 203-250.

Steinhart, R.F., and Pollack, S.V., *Programming the IBM System/360*. New York: Holt, Rinehart and Winston, 1970, pp. 550-562.

XV MANIPULATION OF FILES AND DATA SETS

In handling input/output so far, we have been willing to rely on a series of PL/I defaults and operating system conventions to establish the connection between our input and output data sets (a deck of cards and a printed listing, respectively) and the PL/I files used to process these data sets (SYSIN and SYSPRINT respectively). (In some operating systems these names are different; for example, in the MTS operating system, the names SCARDS and SPRINT are used, and the PL/I compiler has been modified accordingly.) This practice enabled us to omit all mention of the files (except in the case of an **ON ENDFILE**(SYSIN) statement) since the PL/I default files for stream input and output are SYSIN and SYSPRINT. Similarly, the standard procedures for running PL/I programs in most installations see to it that the input data cards are identified to the system as SYSIN, while an appropriate printer is identified as the device to receive the data set associated with SYSPRINT.

Utilization of the expanded input/output capabilities requires two important additions to the scope of transmission instructions. First, the available commands must be generalized to allow input/output to involve a variety of files. Second, a separate repertoire of record-oriented transmission instructions must be included.

Generalization of input/output commands is achieved by qualifying the basic stream-oriented statement to the following manner:

GET   **LIST**
              FILE (filename)   (name1, name2, etc.);
PUT   **DATA**

In this generalized statement, (filename) represents the name assigned to a particular file in a **DECLARE** and/or **OPEN** statement, and (name1, name2, etc.) refers to a list of data items, as in any other stream-oriented statement. If edit-directed transmission is involved, the additional list of format specifications must, of course, be included:

GET
              FILE(filename) **EDIT** (name1, name2, etc.)(spec1, spec2, etc.);
PUT

Since the file name given in such a statement relates back to an identical name somewhere in the program or in the instructions to the system that accompanied the program, that name can be traced by association to a particular data set on some peripheral device and the appropriate communication links can be established.

If an input or output statement uses the name of a file not activated by a previous **OPEN** statement, PL/I performs what is termed an *implicit opening*. It detemines what the name of the file is from the context of the statement (it can not be anything but the parenthesized name following the keyword **FILE** or the default file SYSIN or SYSPRINT) and assigns certain default attributes to that file, depending on the type of statement in which the name appears. For example, if a particular file name appears in a **GET** statement, that file must have the attributes **INPUT** and **STREAM**. A file name appearing in the **PUT** statement must necessarily refer to a file with the **OUTPUT** and **STREAM** attributes. Although the generation and use of stream-oriented files is possible (we have been implicitly using them all along), their use is generally limited to **PRINT** files and initial input files (such as decks of punched cards) from which other files will be generated. Perhaps the one common exception is the employment of a magnetic device (such as a disk) as a temporary receptacle for a **PRINT** file, with the purpose of transmitting those data to the line printer at some other, more opportune time. When this is the case, the information is automatically divided into records, each of which represents the data that will eventually appear on a single line of print. Each of these records (known as a *line image*), together with certain signals that control the action of the printer, is stored on the external device in proper sequence.

A special service facility available for **STREAM INPUT** files is the copy option used in a statement such as

GET FILE (filename) **COPY EDIT** (....)(....);

When PL/I encounters such a statement, it will copy each item read as a result of the data list in that statement, without modification, on the standard output unit.

In the majority of instances, it is more appropriate to generate and use files with the **RECORD** attribute, which brings us to the second direction in which we must expand our input/output commands, in order to include record-oriented transmission instructions.

In our development of file declaration, we have already acquired a nodding acquaintance with the basic idea of the **READ** and **WRITE** statements—that is, the transmission of entire records, with subsequent dissection (of input) or prior syntheses (of output) being handled as distinct processes. As we explore record transmission more extensively, it will become evident that the tremendous array of organizational capabilities are tapped by a surprisingly small variety of statements and options. This apparent mismatch is easily reconciled by reemphasizing a point discussed in the preceding chapter. Though nourished by definitions and specifications from the program (such as the **ENVIRONMENT** attributes), much of the organizational work takes place beyond its bounds. With all this groundwork already in place, it is possible to design a syntax in which the same **READ** statement will transmit a record from, say, an **INDEXED** data set just as routinely as from a **REGIONAL** data set without the need for extensive restructuring of the statement.

XV.1 THE **READ** STATEMENT

For the purpose of continuity, we shall restate the basic form for record input transmission:

READ FILE (filename) **INTO** (place);

This constitutes a basic instruction to transmit the contents of the next record to a location in storage designated by the name (place). Note that no list of data items is included in such a statement. Instead, the statement assumes that the record is organized in some predetermined manner and that the storage designated by (place) has been allocated in sufficient quantity to accept the record as it is transmitted. In direct contrast to stream-oriented input, no conversion occurs as part of **READ** activities. The information in each data set record is stored exactly as it appears on the device. Variables must be unsubscripted and cannot be minor structures (that is, only level 1 is acceptable). Once an input record has been brought in, it need no longer be handled as a unit. If the assigned storage has been declared to correspond exactly to the composition of the record, each component can be treated separately.

When an **UNBUFFERED** file is read, each record is transmitted directly from external storage to its assigned location inside the machine. This bypasses the automatic, but nonetheless time-consuming, operation of moving the record from a buffer to the input area named in the **INTO** option.

Illustration 43

The Long Sleep Drug Company has a transaction file named TRANS in which each record consists of information pertaining to an individual shipment of a particular drug. When the file was created, each record was generated as a series of character strings consisting of the following components

Variable Name	Typical Value	Form
DRUG_NAME	**PLUTOCAINEßß**	12 characters
DRUG_CODE	**P39JD**	5 characters
GMS_SOLD	514.72	XXX$_{(.)}$XX
UNIT_PRICE	1.19	X$_{(.)}$XX

The records are arranged on tape so that transaction records for a given drug are together. It is desired to produce a printout summarizing the transactions for each drug. Column headings are to be consistent with the variable names given above, and the entire 132-column width of the page is to be available. To simplify matters, we shall assume that the file is sequential, the records are unblocked, and the associated data set is unlabeled. There are no more than 500 transactions for a given drug.

To handle this problem, we shall assign storage for two structures: One of these, called PLACE, will contain an input record. The other, called NEW_PLACE, will be used to construct a set of output values which will ultimately appear as a line of print. NEW_PLACE will use five characters for DRUG_NAME and five characters for DRUG_CODE, as before. GMS_SOLD and SALES each will be FIXED(7,2) and AVG_PRICE will be FIXED(4,3). We shall limit each page to 50 lines of print (excluding headings) and use separate procedures to print the headings and the output. A separate variable name CODCHK will be used to store the code of the drug that is being processed currently, so we know when it changes.

On this basis, our program is as follows:

```
ILL43:   PROCEDURE OPTIONS (MAIN);
         DECLARE   TRANS FILE INPUT RECORD SEQUENTIAL ENVIRONMENT(F(22)),
                   1 PLACE,
                     2 DRUG_NAME CHARACTER(12),
                     2 DRUG_CODE CHARACTER(5),
                     (2 GMS_SOLD, 2 UNIT_PRICE) FLOAT DECIMAL(6),
                   1 NEW_PLACE,
                     2 DRUG_NAME CHARACTER(12),
                     2 DRUG_CODE CHARACTER(5),
                     (2 GMS_SOLD, 2 AVG_PRICE, 2 SALES) FLOAT DECIMAL(6),
                     2 NTRANS FIXED BINARY,
                   CODCHK CHARACTER(5) INITIAL ('00000'),
                   LINES FIXED BINARY,
                   S BIT(1) INITIAL ('1'B);

         ON ENDFILE (TRANS) S = '0'B;
         OPEN FILE(TRANS),FILE(SYSPRINT) LINESIZE(132) PAGESIZE(60);
         CALL PGHD;
         READ FILE (TRANS) INTO (PLACE);

         DO WHILE (S);

             /** CODCHK HAS THE CODE OF THE MOST RECENTLY READ DRUG **/
             /** RECORD, OR ZEROES IF WE ARE JUST STARTING. THUS, IT**/
             /** IS COMPARED WITH THE CODE JUST READ TO DETERMINE   **/
             /** WHETHER TO UPDATE, OR TO SUMMARIZE AND CHANGE DRUGS**/

             IF PLACE.DRUG_CODE ¬= CODCHK
                THEN IF CODCHK ¬= '00000'
                        THEN DO;
                             IF LINE = 50 THEN CALL PGHD;
                                CALL SHOW;    CALL NEW;
                        END;
                     ELSE CALL NEW;
                ELSE ;

             /** NOW, WE HAVE SUMMARIZED THE FIGURES FOR THE PREVIOUS**/
             /** DRUG AND RESET THE SYSTEM FOR A NEW ONE, OR WE HAVE **/
             /** DONE NOTHING (IF THE CURRENT RECORD STILL IS PART OF**/
             /** THE DATA FOR THE SAME DRUG FROM THE PREVIOUS RECORD)**/
```

```
              NEW_PLACE.GMS_SOLD=NEW_PLACE.GMS_SOLD+PLACE.GMS_SOLD;
              SALES = SALES+PLACE.GMS_SOLD*UNIT_PRICE;
              NTRANS = NTRANS+1;
         END;

         /**--END-OF-FILE PROCESSING (PRINT THE LAST SUMMARY)--**/
         CALL SHOW;

         DO WHILE (NDFILE = 1);
           IF NTYPE = 1
              THEN DO;
                     FLCON = 4.4-2.2E-4*PYLD;
                     GLNS = MILES/FLCON;
                     NDEL1 = NDEL1+1;
                     PYLD1 = PYLD1+PYLD;
                     MILES1 = MILES1+MILES;
                     GLNS1 = GLNS1+GLNS;
                  END;
           IF NTYPE = 2
              THEN DO;
                     FLCON = 4.14-1.89E-6*PYLD**1.2;
                     GLNS = MILES/FLCON;
                     NDEL2 = NDEL2+1;
                     PYLD2 = PYLD2+PYLD;
                     MILES2 = MILES2+MILES;
                     GLNS2 = GLNS2+GLNS;
                  END;
           IF NTYPE = 3
              THEN DO;
                     FLCON = 3.96-(2.07E-4*PYLD+6.1E-7*PYLD**1.4);
                     GLNS = MILES/FLCON;
                     NDEL3 = NDEL3+1;
                     PYLD3 = PYLD3+PYLD;
                     MILES3 = MILES3+MILES;
                     GLNS3 = GLNS3+GLNS;
                  END;
           PUT SKIP DATA (NTYPE,MILES,PYLD,FLCON,GLNS);
           GET DATA (NTYPE,MILES,PYLD);
         END;
/***********************************************************/
/** PGHD: PRINTS NEW HEADINGS, RESETS THE LINE COUNTER */
/***********************************************************/
PGHD: PROCEDURE;
         PUT PAGE LINE(3) EDIT ('LONG SLEEP DRUG CO.'(X(56),A)
              ('TRANSACTION SUMMARY')(SKIP,X(56),A)
              ('DRUG NAME','DRUG CODE','GMS SOLD','AVG PRICE',
               'SALES','# TRANS')(SKIP(2),X(5), 2 (A(9),X(6)),
              (A(8),X(7),A(9),X(6),A(5),X(10),A(7));
         PUT SKIP;        LINES = 0;
         RETURN;
         END PGHD;

/***********************************************************/
/** SHOW: SUMMARIZES AND PRINTS DATA FOR A GIVEN DRUG */
/***********************************************************/
SHOW: PROCEDURE;
         AVG_PRICE = ROUND(SALES/NEW_PLACE.GMS_SOLD,3);
         PUT SKIP EDIT (NEW_PLACE)(X(5),A(12),X(3),A(5),
             (X(10),F(9,2),X(6),F(6,3),X(9),F(9,2),X(6),F(3));
         LINES = LINES+1;
         RETURN;
         END SHOW;

/***********************************************************/
/** NEW: RESETS COUNTERS, NAME AND CODE FOR A NEW DRUG */
/***********************************************************/
NEW: PROCEDURE;
         NTRANS, NEW_PLACE.GMS_SOLD, NEW_PLACE.SALES = 0;
         NEW_PLACE.DRUG_NAME = PLACE.DRUG_NAME;
         CODCHK, NEW_PLACE.DRUG_CODE = PLACE.DRUG_CODE;
         RETURN;
         END NEW;


     END ILL43;
```

Note that in specifying the **ENVIRONMENT** attribute, it was necessary to work out the total number of bytes occupied by PLACE. This comes out 22 rather than 25 because **FIXED DECIMAL** numbers occupy **CEIL**$((p+1)/2)$ bytes.

XV.1.1   The **KEYTO** Option

If a file is declared (or opened) with both the **SEQUENTIAL** and **KEYED** attributes, it is possible to isolate the key and manipulate it as an ordinary character string variable. When a key is included with each record of an input file and the programmer wishes to obtain that key, he may do so as part of the **READ** operation by means of the **KEYTO** option, whose general form is

    READ FILE (filename) **INTO** (place) **KEYTO** (stringvar);

where (filename) and (place) have their previous meanings, and (stringvar) refers to a character string variable that has been declared with sufficient length to accommodate the key. As a result of this operation, the next record from the sequential file (filename) will be reproduced in the location designated by (place), and the key for the record will be placed in (stringvar). Once the key has been placed in this manner, it can be treated as any other character string variable. Note that the **KEYED** attribute may only be applied to files associated with **INDEXED** and **REGIONAL** data sets.

XV.1.2   The **KEY** Option

When reading records from an **INDEXED** data set using a **SEQUENTIAL** file, it is possible to direct the system to a particular record via its key. This is done by means of the **KEY** option;

    READ FILE (filename) **INTO** (place) **KEY** (value);

In this case, (value) is any legitimate PL/I expression. When this statement is processed, the expression is evaluated and converted to a character string. The next record to be referenced and reproduced in the location designated (place) will be the record whose key is identical to that character string. If no such key can be found attached to any of the records in the file, the **KEY** condition is raised. This operation is possible because of the index associated with an **INDEXED** data set, which enables any record to be found quickly. This type of action is *not* possible with **REGIONAL** data sets. Once the particular record has been found, subsequent **READ** statements without the **KEY** option will cause consecutive records to be *read in* in normal sequence.

    While reading with a **DIRECT** file, the **KEY** option must be used in this way for each **READ** operation for both **INDEXED** and **REGIONAL** data sets. Thus, it is possible to read every record of the data set using a **DIRECT** file only if we have a way to generate every key that actually corresponds to a record. (If we try to read the record corresponding to a key that does not exist, the **KEY** condition will be raised. However, this generally is not a very efficient way to test whether the record is present.) For **REGIONAL**(1) data sets, generating all keys is easy. For the other types, it depends on what we know about the keys. We see, then, that the basic difference between **SEQUENTIAL** and **DIRECT** access to a data set is that with **SEQUENTIAL** access it is easy to process all records, but this can be done only in a fixed *sequence* (with a slight concession in the case of **INDEXED** organization), whereas with **DIRECT** access it is easy to go *directly* to any record whose key we happen to know, but more awkward to process each and every record systematically. As is the case with **KEYTO**, the **KEY** option is restricted to **INDEX** or **REGIONAL** data set organizations.

Illustration 44

Let us write another program for the Long Sleep Drug Company. This time we shall assume an input file that is constructed somewhat differently. Each record is still organized as it was before, with the exception that a modified DRUG__CODE is now being used as a key (the assumption being that it was attached to the record by some other program that created the file). To distinguish among records containing transactions for a given drug, the key is constructed by concatenating DRUG__CODE with a three-digit numerical character string. Thus, if the drug code happens to be AKB2W, the first transaction record for that drug will have the key AKB2W001, the next one AKB2W002, and so on. Otherwise, all of the assumptions still hold.

The program requested in this case is somewhat narrower in scope: It is supposed to read a single card with a drug code punched in columns 1-5 and produce a printout containing summary information for that one drug, as shown below:

    LONG SLEEP DRUG COMPANY

    SUMMARY FOR DRUG P39JD

    NUMBER OF TRANSACTIONS: 143

    NUMBER OF GRAMS SOLD: 2716.75

    AVERAGE PRICE PER GRAM: $1.145

    TOTAL SALES: $3110.68

We shall declare only one structure (called PLACE) to accommodate each record from TRANS. Our file will have the **SEQUENTIAL** and **INDEXED** attributes, thereby enabling us to access the first record with the desired key directly (that is, the first record for the drug with the specified code). Once that one has been read, we can proceed to read and process the remaining transactions sequentially, until there is a mismatch between the key on the record (that is, its first five characters) and the code read in from the card.

```
ILL44: PROCEDURE OPTIONS (MAIN);
       /* TRANS IS AN INDEXED FILE IN WHICH THE 5-CHARACTER DRUG CODE */
       /* IS CONCATENATED WITH A SEQUENCE NUMBER TO FORM A UNIQUE KEY */
       /* FOR EACH RECORD. ACCORDINGLY, THE CODE MATCH (AFTER A DRUG'S*/
       /* FIRST RECORD) WILL BE ON THE KEY'S FIRST FIVE CHARACTERS.  */
       DECLARE TRANS INPUT SEQUENTIAL KEYED ENVIRONMENT(F(220,22) INDEXED),
               1 PLACE,
                 2 DRUG_NAME CHARACTER(12),
                 2 DRUG_CODE CHARACTER(5),
                 (2 GMS_SOLD, 2 UNITPRICE) FLOAT DECIMAL(6),
               KEYCODE CHARACTER(8),   CODE CHARACTER(5),
               ( (GRAMS,SALES) INITIAL(0), AVG) FLOAT DECIMAL(6),
               NTRANS FIXED BINARY INITIAL (0),
               (SKEY,SSY) BIT(1) INITIAL ('1'B);

       ON ENDFILE (SYSIN) SSY = '0'B;
       PUT PAGE LINE(3) EDIT ('LONG SLEEP DRUG CO.')(X(56),A,SKIP);
       OPEN FILE(TRANS), FILE (SYSPRINT) LINESIZE (120);
       GET EDIT (CODE)(A(5));    GET SKIP;

       /*******************************************************************/
       /* THIS LOOP CYCLES ONCE FOR EACH INPUT CARD. THE TRANS FILE*/
       /* IS INITIALIZED BY TAKING THE CODE FROM THE CARD AND ATTA-*/
       /* CHING '001' TO IT, SO IT MATCHES THE FIRST KEY OF THE    */
       /* FIRST RECORD FOR THAT DRUG. THAT LETS US PROCESS AN INNER*/
       /* LOOP THAT CYCLES UNTIL THE DRUG CODE CHANGES.           */
       /*******************************************************************/

       DO WHILE (SSY);
         KEYCODE = CODE || '001';
         ON KEY SKEY = '0'B;
         READ FILE (TRANS) INTO (PLACE) KEY (KEYCODE);
         DO WHILE (SKEY);
           DO WHILE (SUBSTR(KEYCODE,1,5) = CODE);
             NTRANS = NTRANS+1;
             GRAMS = GRAMS+GMS_SOLD;
             SALES = SALES+GMS_SOLD*UNIT_PRICE;
             READ FILE (TRANS) INTO (PLACE) KEY (KEYCODE);
           END;
           AVG = ROUND(SALES/GRAMS,3);
           PUT SKIP EDIT ('SUMMARY FOR DRUG ',CODE)(X(55),A,A(5))
               ('NO. OF TRANSACTIONS: ',NTRANS)(SKIP(3),X(10),A,F(3))
               ('NO. OF GRAMS SOLD: ',GRAMS)(SKIP,X(10),A,F(9,2))
               ('AVG. PRICE/GRAM: ',AVG)(SKIP,X(10),A,P'$$.99')
               ('TOTAL SALES: ',SALES)(SKIP,X(10),A,P'$$$$$$.99');
         END;
         IF SKEY = '0'B
           THEN DO;
                 PUT SKIP(2) EDIT ('NO RECORDS FOR DRUG WITH CODE ',CODE)
                             (X(10),A,A(5),SKIP);
                 SKEY = '1'B;
                END;
         GET EDIT(CODE)(A(5);    GET SKIP;
       END;

       END ILL44;
```

XV.1.3 The **IGNORE** Option

When using a sequential input file, the programmer is able to skip over a specified number of records at any point in the file by using the **IGNORE** option as follows:

READ FILE(filename) **IGNORE** (n);

where (n) is a legitimate PL/I expression that can be evaluated to an integer. That integer specifies the number of records to be skipped. Note that no actual transmission takes place. If the input file FOUNT is positioned at its first record and we have a statement

READ FILE(FOUNT) **IGNORE** (18);

the first 18 records in the file will be skipped over. At the end of this activity, the file will be ready to transmit the contents of the nineteenth record, but that transmission will not occur without an additional statement such as

READ FILE(FOUNT) **INTO** (place);

The **IGNORE** option can be used at any point in a sequential file. Suppose, for example, we are processing an input file called FOUNT in which the key of each record is continually being checked against the five-character string '33244'. As soon as a match is found, we would like to ignore the next 12 records and then continue processing as before. Assuming each record is read into a place in storage called STORE and key is read into a place called CHKEY, our program segment would appear as

BRING: READ FILE (FOUNT) **INTO** (STORE) **KEYTO** (CHKEY);

    IF CHKEY = '33244' **THENREAD FILE** (FOUNT) **IGNORE** (12);

                ELSE..........;

    GO TO BRING;

A single record can be skipped by writing a **READ** without using the **INTO** phrase. Thus, the statements

READ FILE(FOUNT);

and

READ FILE(FOUNT)**IGNORE**(1):

are equivalent. A summary of the **KEY, KEYTO** and **IGNORE** options and their allowable usage for input is given in Table 15.1.

TABLE 15.1 Use of **KEY, KEYTO,** and **IGNORE** Options, in **READ** Statements for **INPUT** Files
Option

	KEYTO		KEY		IGNORE
Access Method	SEQUENTIAL		SEQUENTIAL	DIRECT	SEQUENTIAL
Data set organization	INDEXED	REGIONAL	INDEXED	INDEXED REGIONAL	CONSECUTIVE INDEXED REGIONAL
Buffering	BUFFERED	BUFFERED UNBUFFERED	BUFFERED	not applicable	BUFFERED UNBUFFERED*

*Except **INDEXED**.

XV.1.4   Buffered Files

All the examples we have dealt with have used **BUFFERED** files by default. Greater under-standing will be achieved, however, if the buffering process is studied in more detail. Although many forms of the **READ** statement apply to both **UNBUFFERED** and **BUFFERED** files, the underlying processes differ considerably. As implied earlier (Figure 14.1), the use of input buffering allows us to take advantage of the computer's ability to perform input/output operations and computations simultaneously (*overalpped processing*). For example, suppose that we have a file TRANS defined by the statement

> **DECLARE** TRANS **FILE INPUT SEQUENTIAL**
>
> **BUFFERED ENVORONMENT (F(22,22)INDEXED)**;

and there is a structure named NVNTRY that is to serve as a destination for one of TRANS's records. Since TRANS is **BUFFERED** but the number of buffers is not specified, PL/I assigns two buffers by default. These are unnamed and inaccessible as far as the programmer is concerned. Nevertheless, they are there and they provide a way station for these records as they come in. Thus, when there is a statement like

> **READ FILE (TRANS) INTO (NVNTRY)**;

the program does not generally respond by reading a record from the associated data set and placing it in NVNTRY. No, indeed. Chances are that the desired record is already in one of the buffers (say, BUF1, just to give it a name). Accordingly, that record is moved from BUF1 to NVNTRY while the *next* record is being brought into the other buffer (let us call it BUF2 to be imaginative) at the same time. As soon as the move is completed, the input device is instructed to bring the second record following into BUF1 so it will be there when needed. Then when another **READ** is executed, BUF2's record is moved to NVNTRY and the reading of a new record into BUF2 is initiated. As would be expected, this read/move pairing would shuttle back and forth between the two buffers, with PL/I having set up the mechanism that automatically keeps track of the alternation. Thus, the program has a record to work on (in NVNTRY) while another one is being read. Sometimes, two buffers are inadequate and a large number must be assigned. A typical case in point would be one in which the amount of time required to process a record is sufficiently small so that the much slower input mechanism cannot deliver the next record when the processor is ready for it (that is, the buffers are emptied faster than they can be filled). For such a situation, it would be advisable to use more buffers and, perhaps, reorganize the data set with a higher blocking factor. You might remark, "How can this help? After all, if the input device is too slow to keep up, it is too slow no matter how many buffers there are." The answer is that the large number of buffers allows the device to get ahead while the computer works on some other job; that way there is lots of work waiting when it turns its attention to this job. In any event, this method of processing is termed *move mode* input.

XV.1.4.1   Locate Mode Input

In certain circumstances, a situation may develop in which the internal movement of data from buffer to designated storage is undesirable. For instance, the time for data movement may be excessive or there may be insufficient storage available for both areas. When this happens, it would be helpful to be able to do the internal processing right in the buffer. This would allow us to retain the advantages of buffering without going through the additional data movement. But if we are working with several nameless buffers whose duties are rotated automatically, we face the problem of even getting at the buffers, much less keeping track of the rotation.

Capabilities for handling such difficulties are provided by means of a special technique for establishing and maintaining contact between the program and the buffer areas. The basic vehicle, known as *locate mode* input, operates on the idea that each time a record is to be read, no movement will occur. Instead, the *location of the record within the appropriate buffer* will be made available to the program so that it has a way of getting at the contents. At the same time, some other buffer may be filled with a block of logical records from the input device. Then, when its turn comes in the rotation, each logical record in *that* buffer will be made available, in turn, by letting the program know where it is.

XV.1.4.2   Pointers and Pointer Variables

pg. 329

Thus far we have been dealing primarily with variables whose contents represent data values that we use for computation, comparison, and so on. One exception has been the label variable (Chapter XII), where, in a restricted sense, the contents were seen to represent addresses corresponding to labeled statements elsewhere in the procedure.

Along those same basic lines, but in a much more general sense, PL/I has a type of variable whose specific purpose is to locate some other variable. This is called a *pointer* (seems reasonable), and such variables are said to have the **POINTER** attribute. This concept is especially helpful (in fact, it is specifically intended to be so) in situations where the variable of interest is elusive, bounding hither and yon through storage. Of course, such is the case before us, with the variable being first in one buffer, then in the next, a dizzying prospect. With a pointer to give unerring chase, we can answer the question "which buffer?" by saying "the one the pointer is indicating."

XV.1.4.3   Based Variables and Pointers

The association between a pointer and its quarry is established in PL/I by means of a *based variable*. This facility has many uses in other contexts, which we shall explore later. At present we shall examine the way in which it functions with regard to locate mode input.

If we want to set up a pointer for keeping track of our input buffers, we use a based variable to describe the composition of the record. To illustrate, let us look at a record description for a file TRANS and indicate some small, but crucial, additions:

NO STORAGE TO BE ALLOCATED

POINTER

DECLARE 1 NVNTRY **BASED** (NOSE),

    2 PART__NO **PICTURE** '99999',

    2 ONHAND **PICTURE** '9999',

    2 VENDOR__CODE **PICTURE** '9999',

    2 UNIT__PRICE **PICTURE** '999V99',

    2 LOC__CODE **CHARACTER** (4);

The attribute **BASED** indicates that NVNTRY specifies a structure for which *no storage is to be allocated.* It merely provides descriptive information. NOSE, specified in the indicated context, tells PL/I that the pointer associated with NVNTRY has the name NOSE. Therefore, any location that is indicated by NOSE will be treated as having the components (and their names and attributes) described by NVNTRY. In other words, NVNTRY now serves as a template to be overlaid on any location referred to by NOSE.

XV.1.4.4   The **SET** Option

We can put the based variable and its associated pointer to work in a **READ** statement and study the effect. This is done by using the form

    READ FILE (filename) **SET** (pointer);

Now that we have some idea of the underlying mechanism, the absence of the **INTO** phrase in this type of **READ** statement is easily explained: There is no predetermined destination to be designated by the **INTO**. (Remember that NVNTRY in our example is not associated with any actual storage). Instead, the location of the next record in the buffer is ascertained and the pointer is set to the location of the record so that its contents are accessible to the program for processing. Referring to the **BASED** structure NVNTRY described before, the statement

    READ FILE (TRANS) **SET** (NOSE);

brings the next records from TRANS into a buffer and the address of that record is stored in NOSE. Since NOSE is associated with the structure NVNTRY, references to NVNTRY or any of its components (such as ONHAND or LOC__CODE) are recognized and handled routinely. The **SET** option may be combined with either the **KEYTO** or **KEY** option.

XV.1.4.5   Handling Variable Format Record Files

Although record-oriented input does not permit the freedom of format available with stream-oriented transmission, it is possible to introduce a certain amount of flexibility by making arrangements to read records with different formats from the same file. This is done by incorporating a variable in each record of the file which identifies the format of that record. The program reading that file contains a description of a based variable for each of the formats used in the file. By assigning the same pointer variable to each of these based variables, the format indicator can be tested and its value used to impose the proper set of attributes on the buffer.

Let us suppose that a file named INFO contains three types of records:

First Format

Variable Name	Format
FORM_ID	1
A	XX(.)XX
B	(.)XX
C	5 characters

Second Format

FORM_ID	2
D	7 characters
E	XX(.)
F	XX(.)
B	(.)XX

Third Format

FORM_ID	3
D	7 characters
G	4 characters
A	XX(.)XX

To make sure that each type of record is recognized and handled properly, we shall describe it as a based variable and use TYPE to determine which of these descriptions should be imposed on the input buffer. The resulting sequence of instructions would appear as follows:

```
DECLARE INFO FILE INPUT BUFFERED,
    1 HOME1 BASED(TYPE), 2 FORM_ID FIXED(1),
        2 A FIXED(4,2), 2 B FIXED(2,2), 2 C CHARACTER(6),
    1 HOME2 BASED(TYPE), 2 FORM_ID FIXED(1),
        2 D CHARACTER(5), (2 E, 2 F) FIXED (2),
        2 B FIXED(2,2),
    1 HOME3 BASED(TYPE), 2 FORM_ID FIXED(1),
        2 D CHARACTER(7), 2 G CHARACTER(1),
        2 A FIXED(4,2);
```

.
.
. *(continued next page)*

```
            .
            .
            .
     READ FILE (INFO) SET(TYPE);
     IF FORM_ID = 1 THEN USE1:  DO;
                                        .
                                        .
                                        .
                               statements for HOME1
                                        .
                                        .
                                        .
                               END USE1;
       ELSE  IF FORM_ID = 2 THEN USE 2:  DO;
                                              .
                                              .
                                              .
                                     statements for HOME2
                                              .
                                              .
                                              .
                                     END USE2;
         ELSE  IF FORM_ID = 3 THEN USE 3:  DO;
                                                .
                                                .
                                                .
                                       statements for HOME3
                                                .
                                                .
                                                .
                                       END USE3;
                               ELSE CALL HM_ERROR;
            .
            .
            .
```

XV.2   THE **WRITE** STATEMENT

The basic record-oriented output statement has the general form

WRITE FILE (filename) **FROM** (place);

Here again, no data list is specified. Instead, it is presumed that the programmer has made the necessary arrangements to create the entire record and store it in the location designated by (place). The **WRITE** statement will then transmit the entire contents of that variable to the data set implied by (filename), instigating all the necessary activity to produce a record in conformance to the attributes specified or implied for that file.

XV.2.1 The **KEYFROM** Option

A key must be added to an output record by using the **KEYFROM** option in a **WRITE** statement if the data set is **INDEXED** or **REGIONAL**. The form, then, is

WRITE FILE (filename) **FROM** (place) **KEYFROM** (stringvar);

The general names in parentheses have their previous meanings. As a result of this statement, the contents of (place) will be used as the next record to be reproduced on the file designated by (filename). The contents of (stringvar) will be used, without alteration, as the key for that output record and also for the region number.

The relationship between **KEYTO** and **KEYFROM** can be illustrated by the following simple example: Suppose we had a program that created an indexed data set using an output file called TABLES. If the program were arranged to gather the information for a single record in a place called CONTENTS, and the key for that record were formed as a five-character variable named CODE, the statements required to create the key for a particular output record and write the record might appear as

CODE = 'K237G';

WRITE FILE (TABLES) **FROM** (CONTENTS) **KEYFROM** (CODE);

At some subsequent time, this newly created data set could be used as input in conjunction with a sequential input file (also called TABLES) in another program that stores the individual record in a place called WORKAREA and places the key in a location called SYMBOL. In order for this to work properly, WORKAREA must be declared with the same length as CONTENTS, and SYMBOL must have the same length as CODE in the previous program. Assuming these conditions to be met and that we are at a point in our subsequent program where we are about to read the same record as we wrote before, the statement

READ FILE (TABLES) **INTO** (WORKAREA) **KEYTO** (SYMBOL);

will place that record in WORKAREA, and the contents of SYMBOL will be K237G.

Illustration 45

The basic use of the **WRITE** statement can be exemplified by writing a procedure to develop the file named TRANS with records as described in Illustration 44. To do this, let us say that each transaction comes in on a separate card with the following format:

Columns	Item	Form
1-12	DRUG_NAME	12 characters
16-20	DRUG_CODE	5 characters
21-25	GMS_SOLD	XXX(.)XX
28-30	UNIT_PRICE	X(.)XX

The cards are arranged so that all transactions for a given drug are together. To provide a unique key for each record while still retaining a common code for the transactions pertaining to a given drug, the key will be eight characters long, constructed from the five-character drug code and a string of three numerical characters. The program also illustrates the use of the **DEFINED** attribute to accomplish this without recourse to concatenation. TRANS will be declared as **INDEXED** and **SEQUENTIAL**. For illustrative purposes, we shall declare SYSIN as a **RECORD** file, and treat each card as a logical record. The program follows:

```
ILL45: PROCEDURE OPTIONS (MAIN);
        DECLARE TRANS FILE OUTPUT SEQUENTIAL ENVIRONMENT(F(250,25)INDEXED),
                SYSIN FILE RECORD INPUT ENVIRONMENT(F(80)),
                1 PLACE,
                  2 DRUG_NAME CHARACTER (12), 2 DRUG_CODE CHARACTER(5),
                  2 GMS_SOLD PICTURE '999V99', 2 UNIT_PRICE PICTURE '9V99',
                KEYBUILD CHARACTER (8) INITIAL ('*****     '),
                CODE CHARACTER (5) DEFINED KEYBUILD,
                SUPPL PICTURE '999' DEFINED KEYBUILD POSITION (6),
                1 CARD BASED (FINGER),
                  2 DRUG_NAME CHARACTER (12), 2 NOT1 CHARACTER (3),
                  2 DRUG_CODE CHARACTER (5), 2 GMS_SOLD PICTURE '999V99',
                  2 NOT2 CHARACTER (2), 2 UNIT_PRICE PICTURE '9V99',
                  2 NOT3 CHARACTER (50);
        /** NOT1,NOT2 AND NOT3 WILL NOT HOLD DATA; THEY ARE DEFINED **/
        /** TO 'HOLD' THE UNUSED CARD COLUMNS.                     **/
        ON ENDFILE (SYSIN) BEGIN; PUT PAGE LINE(3) LIST ('END OF RUN'); END;
        OPEN FILE (SYSIN), FILE (TRANS);

        DO WHILE ('1'B);
          READ FILE (SYSIN) SET (FINGER);
          IF CODE ¬= CARD.DRUG_CODE
            THEN DO;
                    SUPPL = 0;    CODE = CARD.DRUG_CODE;
                    PLACE.DRUG_NAME = CARD.DRUG_NAME;
                    PLACE.DRUG_CODE = CARD.DRUG_CODE;
                 END;
          PLACE.GMS_SOLD = CARD.GMS_SOLD;
          PLACE.UNIT_PRICE = CARD.UNIT_PRICE;
          SUPPL = SUPPL+1;      KEYBUILD = CODE || SUPPL;
          WRITE FILE (TRANS) FROM (PLACE) KEYFROM (KEYBUILD);
        END;

        END ILL45;
```

XV.2.2   The **LOCATE** Statment

Although the **READ** statement serves both move and locate modes of input, the **WRITE** statement handles only move mode output. A separate statement, **LOCATE**, is used specifically to allocate space for a record in an output buffer and indicate its location in an associated pointer. Its general form is

LOCATE name **FILE** (filename) **SET** (pointer);

This statement does not cause any immediate data transmission; buffer space for the record described by the based variable named after the keyword **LOCATE** is allocated and the address of the space is placed in (pointer). Since the variable name in (pointer) indicates the location of this buffer, the programmer can now move data to that buffer as necessary (by assigning to name) to form a record. Although that record will ultimately be added to the data sets, that final step is not instigated by the execution of the same statements that allocate the buffer. Transmission occurs with the next execution of the **LOCATE** statement or the execution of another **LOCATE** or **WRITE** statement that refers to that file. Upon encountering that statement, the program writes the record from the output buffer and proceeds to prepare for the next one. When the file is closed, the contents of the final buffer are transmitted to the data set storage device as part of the closing procedure. The **LOCATE** statement may also be used in conjunction with the **KEYFROM** option.

Illustration 45A

The use of locate mode output can be exemplified by modifying Illustration 45 so that PLACE is a based variable with an associated pointer (which we shall call **NOSE**):

```
ILL45A: PROCEDURE OPTIONS (MAIN);
        DECLARE TRANS FILE OUTPUT SEQUENTIAL ENVIRONMENT (F(250,25)) INDEXED,
                SYSIN FILE RECORD INPUT ENVIRONMENT (F(80)),
                1 PLACE BASED (NOSE),
                  2 DRUG_NAME CHARACTER (12), 2 DRUG_CODE CHARACTER (5),
                  2 GMS_SOLD PICTURE '999V99', 2 UNIT_PRICE PICTURE '9V99',
                KEYBUILD CHARACTER (8), CODE CHARACTER (5) DEFINED KEYBUILD,
                SUPPL PICTURE '999' DEFINED KEYBUILD POSITION (6),
                1 CARD BASED (FINGER),
                  2 DRUG_NAME CHARACTER (12), 2 NOT1 CHARACTER (3),
                  2 DRUG_CODE CHARACTER (5), 2 GMS_SOLD PICTURE '999V99',
                  2 NOT2 CHARACTER (2), 2 UNIT_PRICE PICTURE '9V99',
                  2 NOT3 CHARACTER (50);

        ON ENDFILE (SYSIN) BEGIN; PUT PAGE LINE(3) LIST ('END OF RUN'); END;
        CODE = '*****';  OPEN FILE (TRANS), FILE (SYSIN);

        DO WHILE ('1'B);
          READ FILE (SYSIN) SET (FINGER);
          IF CODE ¬= CARD.DRUG_CODE
            THEN DO;
                    SUPPL = 0;   CODE = CARD.DRUG_CODE;
                 END;
          SUPPL = SUPPL+1;
          LOCATE PLACE FILE (TRANS) KEYFROM (KEYBUILD);
          PLACE.DRUG_NAME=CARD.DRUG_NAME;   PLACE.DRUG_CODE=CARD.DRUG_CODE;
          PLACE.GMS_SOLD=CARD.GMS_SOLD;   PLACE.UNIT_PRICE=CARD.UNIT_PRICE;
        END;

        END ILL45A;
```

If both input and output records are constructed identically, there is usually no need to use locate mode in both directions of transmission. By setting up a common buffer with a **READ...SET** statement and then writing from it with an ordinary **WRITE...FROM** statement, the data can be processed with only one movement. Any modification can take place between the **READ** and the **WRITE**.

If the output file is **UNBUFFERED** in addition, there will be no movement of data from input to output buffer; the record is processed where it is and is then written directly. This is the main application for unbuffered files, since it completely eliminates nonproductive data movement.

When records are blocked, their movement in locate mode may cause difficulty in some PL/I implementations. There is a possibility that boundary requirements relative to the machine's storage organization could cause misalignment of adjacent records in a block. More detailed information is cited at the end of the chapter.

XV.2.3   Punched-Card Output

It is sometimes useful to produce output on punched cards. In many smaller systems, for example, input cards containing individual items of information often are processed by a program to produce punched cards with summary information. These serve as input to another program for subsequent processing. While this type of fragmentation may not be necessary for many PL/I installations, there are numerous occasions for which it is convenient to produce such punched output as a standard vehicle for data to be disseminated to users of an arbitrary mixture of computing system types.

This is done conveniently in PL/I by using a sequential file named **SYSPUNCH**, whose ultimate relation to the output card punch device is defined as a standard part of the system. Records are written onto **SYSPUNCH** in the usual way.

Illustration 46

We shall write a program that reads cards and punches new ones with the information in reverse order (input column 1 in output column 80, etc.); also, just for fun, we shall list both forms on the printer:

```
ILL46: PROCEDURE OPTIONS (MAIN);
       DECLARE SYSIN FILE RECORD INPUT ENVIRONMENT (F(80)),
               SYSPUNCH FILE RECORD OUTPUT,
               FIRST CHARACTER (80) BASED (POINT),
               SECOND CHARACTER (80) BASED (OPT),
               I FIXED BINARY;

       ON ENDFILE (SYSIN)  BEGIN; PUT SKIP(3) LIST ('END OF RUN'); STOP; END;

       DO WHILE ('1'B);
         READ FILE (SYSIN) SET (POINT);
         LOCATE SECOND FILE (SYSPUNCH);
         DO I = 1 TO 80;
           SUBSTR (SECOND,81-I,1) = SUBSTR (FIRST,I,1);
         END;
         PUT SKIP EDIT (FIRST,SECOND)(2 (SKIP,X(5),A(80)));
       END;

       END ILL46;
```

XV.3 UPDATE FILE HANDLING

When a file is declared with the **UPDATE** attribute, the intent is to use that file both for input and output. That is, the basic processing sequence consists of reading in a file record, operating on it, and rewriting it onto the same data set from which it came. The name **UPDATE** is particularly appropriate, since the type of processing in which such files are involved usually consists of modifying the records so that their contents reflect a current state of affairs. A file of loan records maintained by a bank represents a typical example. Each record in this type of file may contain such information as the loan number, name and address of borrower, balance due, and the amount of principal and interest comprising that balance due, and the amount of principal and interest comprising that balance. Periodically the records in the file are matched against a set of input cards, each of which contains data about a payment made against a particular loan. The cards are arranged in the same order (perhaps by loan number) as the records on the file. When the loan payment data for a particular borrower are read in, they are matched against his file record. After his payment is deducted to obtain the new balance due, and so on, the updated record is written in the same position on the file, erasing what was previously there, and the procedure continues until the changes have been recorded for all the loan payments.

To implement such processing, the programmer may employ all the forms of the **READ** statement available for **INPUT** files. The restrictions, governing the usage of the various options (the **INTO, KEYTO, SET, IGNORE**, and **KEY**) are dictated by whether or not the file is **SEQUENTIAL** or **DIRECT, BUFFERED** or **UNBUFFERED,** and are the same for **UPDATE** and **INPUT** files. For output purposes, however, the repertoire of instructions does not always correspond to those available for **OUTPUT** files, since the transmission of the record to an **UPDATE** file often results in the replacement of an existing record rather than the addition of a new record to the file. Consequently, the **WRITE** statement is available only for **UPDATE** files with the **DIRECT** attribute and must take the form

    WRITE FILE (filename) **FROM** (place) **KEYFROM** (stringvar);

XV.3.1 The **REWRITE** Statement

The **REWRITE** statement is specifically intended for the replacement of existing records on **UPDATE** files. Its basic form is

    REWRITE FILE (filename);

Without any additional specifications, this statement will cause the record that had last been read from the file designated by (filename) to be written in the position from which it had been read. Since no key information is specified, nor does the string include any explicit indication as to where the record is stored, this form can only be used with **BUFFERED SEQUENTIAL UPDATE** files. In other situations, the **FROM** (place) option must be added to the statement.

(Of coure, it can be included here, too.) In either case, the programmer must make sure that no input/output statement involving the same file intervenes between the **READ** statement that brought in the particular record and the **REWRITE** statement replacing that record. (This rule does not apply to **DIRECT UPDATE** files.) When the **UPDATE** file is also **DIRECT** (and therefore **KEYED**), any **REWRITE** referring to that file must include the **KEY**(value) phrase in addition to the **FROM** (place) designation:

    REWRITE FILE (filename) **FROM** (place) **KEY** (value);

XV.3.2   Deletion and Addition of Records

Since the records in a **DIRECT** file can be processed in any order, it is possible to change the number of records in a **DIRECT UPDATE** file by erasing those records found no longer useful. The PL/I programmer can exploit this facility through the **DELETE** statement, whose general form is

    DELETE FILE (filename) **KEY** (value);

As a result of this statement, the program will locate the record identified by the specified key and delete it from the file. Note that "deletion" in this context is not analogous to a physical

TABLE 15.2 Use Characteristics of **UPDATE** Files

Statement	Allowable Access Method	Allowable Data Set Organization
READ FILE(name)**INTO**(place);	**SEQUENTIAL**	**CONSECUTIVE, INDEXED, REGIONAL**
READ FILE(name)**IGNORE**(expr.);		
READ FILE(name)**SET**(pointer);	**SEQUENTIAL BUFFERED**	
READ FILE(name)**INTO** or SET **KEY**(expr);	**SEQUENTIAL BUFFERED**	**INDEXED**
READ FILE(name)**INTO**(place) **KEY**(expr.);	**DIRECT**	**INDEXED, REGIONAL**
REWRITE FILE(name);	**SEQUENTIAL**	**CONSECUTIVE, INDEXED, REGIONAL**
REWRITE FILE(name)**FROM**(place);		
REWRITE FILE(name)**FROM**(place) **KEY**(expr.);	**DIRECT**	**INDEXED, REGIONAL**
WRITE FILE(name)**FROM**(place) **KEYFROM**(expr.);	**DIRECT**	**INDEXED, REGIONAL**
DELETE FILE(name);	**SEQUENTIAL**	**INDEXED**
DELETE FILE(name)**KEY**(expr.);	**DIRECT**	**INDEXED, REGIONAL**

removal of the record and closing of the gap. Recall (from Chapter XIV) that certain types of files can be equipped with dummy records recognizable as such. Correspondingly, the deletion process replaces the unwanted record with a dummy record, thereby preserving the relationship among the records, their locations on the associated data sets, and any supporting structure (such as an index) built for them. If a file named in a **DELETE** statement has not been activated earlier in the procedure, it will be opened implicitly as part of the processing.

By including appropriate specifications (outside of the PL/I program), it is possible to add new records to the end of certain types of **UPDATE** files. Table 15.2 indicates the eligible types, along with other summary information. More information about these specifications external to PL/I is to be found in the references indicated at the end of the chapter.

```
ILL47: PROCEDURE OPTIONS (MAIN);
        DECLARE DEP FILE SEQUENTIAL UPDATE KEYED ENVIRONMENT
                    (F(480,48) INDEXED),
                SYSIN FILE RECORD INPUT,
                1 LOAN_REC,
                  2 ACCT PICTURE '999999', 2 NAME PICTURE '(30)X',
                  2 AMT PICTURE '9999V99', 2 LOAN_CODE PICTURE '(6)X',
                1 PAY_REC BASED (NOSE),
                  2 NUM PICTURE '(6)9', 2 U1 PICTURE 'XXXX',
                  2 PAYMT PICTURE '9999V99', 2 U2 PICTURE '(64)X';

        ON ENDFILE (SYSIN)  BEGIN; PUT SKIP(3) LIST ('END OF RUN.'); STOP; END;
        OPEN FILE (SYSPRINT) LINESIZE (132), FILE (SYSIN), FILE (DEP);
        PUT PAGE LINE(4) EDIT ('EAST FLEEGLE BANK')(X(58),A)
            ('LOAN DEPARTMENT')(SKIP,X(59),A);    PUT SKIP;

        /** THE TWO READ STATEMENTS READ A CARD AND OBTAIN THE DEP RECORD **/
        /** WITH A MATCHING KEY PREPARATORY TO A LOAN/PAYMENT COMPARISON. **/
        DO WHILE ('1'B);
          READ FILE (SYSIN) SET (NOSE);
          READ FILE (DEP) INTO (LOAN_REC) KEY (NUM);
          IF PAYMT = AMT
            THEN DO;
                    PUT SKIP EDIT ('ACCT. NO.: ',ACCT)(X(5),A,A(6))
                        ('FINAL PAYMENT:  ',AMT)(SKIP,X(5),F(7,2),SKIP);
                    DELETE FILE (DEP);
                END;
            ELSE DO;
                    AMT = AMT - PAYMT;
                    REWRITE FILE (DEP);
                END;
        END;

        END ILL47;
```

Illustration 47

The East Fleegle Bank acts as an agent for the goverment's interest-free loan program to deserving agencies. For this purpose, the bank uses a **SEQUENTIAL** file named DEP to access loan records for its borrowers. Each record has the following information:

Item	Form
ACCT	XXXXXX
NAME	30 characters
AMT	XXXX⌄XX
LOAN__CODE	6 characters

The records (with ACCT as the key) are arranged in order by increasing ACCT number on an **INDEXED** data set.

Input cards containing account number (columns 1-6) and payment amount (columns 11-16) are submitted for use in updating the data set. The cards are in the same relative order as the records. We have written a program that reduces the amount due by the current payment. If the payment equals the amount, relevent output is printed and the record is deleted. (Of course, if no payment is made, the record is unchanged).

XV.4 USE OF FILE NAMES AS ARGUMENTS

PL/I permits the use of file names as parameters and arguments, so the programmer can transmit them from one procedure to another as he would any other type of information. The name used in the parameter list must be declared as a file name in the invoked procedure, since there is no contextual information from which PL/I can deduce this. In general, the specified attributes of the file name in the parameter list should match those of the argument file. If this is not the case, the programmer must make sure that the implied attributes match. For example, he cannot use a **BUFFERED** file name as an argument for a procedure in which the file name in the parameter list is declared as **DIRECT**. Since **BUFFERED** implies that the file is **SEQUENTIAL**, the resulting mismatch would constitute an error.

PROBLEMS

1. Modify the program in Illustration 45A so that it includes facilities for accumulating and printing the following information:

   a. The number of input cards read:

   b. The number of different drug types processed;

   c. The drug code with the largest number of records, along with that number.

2. Modify the program in Illustration 47 so that the following processing is added.

   a. Print the number of accounts processed this run;

   b. Print the number of loans closed out during this run;

   c. Print the total amount of the payments processed during this run;

   d. Print the total amount paid toward loans that are still open.

3.   Write a program to create a sequential file from a series of cards where each record represents the contents of an entire card.

4.   Write a program similar to the one in the Problem 1 except that each record in the new file is to consist of the contents of three cards. As in the previous case, the formats may vary from run to run. However, the card number (1, 2, or 3) will always be punched in column 80. The program should include a mechanism for informing the user when his cards are out of order.

5.   Modify the program in Problem 1 so that it keeps track of the number of cards read in and creates a key for each record consisting of the current value of this counter, preceded by the contents of columns 77-79 of the card. The maximum number of cards comprising a set of cards is 5000.

6.   A hospital makes up a summary card at discharge of each patient according to the following outline:

Card Columns	Item	Format
1-20	Patient's last name	
21-25	Identification number	XXXXX
26-30	Hospitalization number (all zeros if patient does not belong to hospitalization plan)	First letter of last name followed by a 4-digit integer
31-36	Date of admission	Month, day, year
37-42	Date of discharge	Month, day, year
43-46	Discharge diagnosis	A letter followed by a 3-digit integer
47-48	Patient's age	XX
49	Patient's sex	M or F
50-51	Room cost base (dollars per day)	XX(.)
52-58	Total bill	XXXXX(.)XX
59-63	Cost for special medical services	XXX(.)XX
64-68	Cost for special nomedical services	XXX(.)XX

Construct a sequential file for such cards, assuming that all items are filled in for all patients and that the cards are arranged by increasing order of identification number.

7.   Using a file from Problem 4, write a program to update the file, adding newly discharged patients and removing those who have paid in full. When an input card is punched for a patient making a payment, the amount is placed in columns 69-75 (format XXXXX(.)XX), the date and payment in columns 37-42 and 52-58 respectively, and the name, identification number, and hospital number in the columns shown in Problem 4.

8.   Modify the program in Problem 5 to include the following information:

A list of all members discharged during the month.
A summary page indicating

Number of patients on input file
Number of patients who settled their accounts this month
Number of patients who made a partial payment
Total number of patients who made a payment
Total number of newly discharged patients
Number of patients on output file

9.   Using the updated file from Problem 5, write a program that processes the patient file. Compute and print the average length of hospital stay for all patients with a particular diagnosis.

10.   Using the updated summary files from Problem 5 and the payment cards from Problem 5, write a program that produces a list of delinquent accounts (those patients for whom no payment has been recorded in 3 months).

11.   Add a routine to the program in Problem 8 that will count and print the number of delinquent accounts for each day of the week, that is, the number of delinquent accounts discharged on Monday, and so on. (*Hint*: One way is to read in a card on which a particular date is associated with a day of the week and use that as a basis to assign a day-of-week designation to each patient's record.)

SUMMARY OF IMPORTANT TERMS

Based variable	A variable explicitly declared with the **BASED** attribute, indicating that the location of that variable is subject to arbitrary change; the current value of that location is stored in an associated pointer (which see).
DELETE	A statement type used to (effectively) remove a record from a **DIRECT UPDATE** file without subsequent replacement.
Dummy record	Space in a data set sized for one of its records but devoid of meaningful contents and skipped automatically when that data set is processed; for example, the result of a **DELETE** statement.
IGNORE	An option, specifiable as part of a **READ** statement for **SEQUENTIAL** files, that forces the program to skip over a specified number of records before reading occurs.
KEY	A clause (incorporated in a **READ** statement) whose associated character string value is used to identify the particular record desired from an **INDEXED** data set.
KEYFROM	A clause (inserted in a **WRITE** statement) whose associated character string specifies the value or source of the key to accompany a record to be written.
KEYTO	The option used to obtain the key from a **KEYED** file during a **READ** statement.
LOCATE	The statement type used to write records in locate mode.
Locate mode	An arrangement whereby records can be processed in the same storage area (buffer) into which they had been read, without further internal movement of the data.

Move mode	A processing arrangement whereby records are read into a particular storage area (buffer) set aside for that purpose. Subsequent processing requires an intervening internal movement of the data.
Pointer	An item of information that specifies the location (address) or some other item.
POINTER	The attribute declared for a variable whose value will represent the current location of an associated (based) variable.
READ	The statement type used for record-oriented input.
REWRITE	The statement type used to write (change) records in an **UPDATE** file.
SET	The option used to locate a newly allocated buffer by storing its address in (that is, *setting*) an associated pointer.
WRITE	The statement type used to produce record-oriented output. (For a specific exception, see **REWRITE**.)

SUPPLEMENTARY READING

PL/I Language Reference Manual, IBM Document No. GC28-8201. White Plains, N.Y.: IBM Corporation, pp. 117-123, 411.

PL/I Programmer's Guide, IBM Document No. GC28-6594. White Plains, N.Y.: pp. 123-141.

XVI CONTROL OF EXECUTION

By now a statement such as

ON ENDFILE (SYSIN) **GO TO** ENDUP;

is quite familiar. We perceive it as a constantly recurring test to determine whether there are any more cards to be read. While the supply lasts, processing continues in normal fashion; the first unsuccessful attempt to read a card forces the program to take the action indicated by the **ON** statement. The important distinction between this behavior from that of an ordinary **IF** statement lies in the fact that the **ON** test is not localized.

Rather, it is in effect over a section of the procedure whose extent is controllable by the programmer. (Thus far we have allowed the **ENDFILE** test to apply over the entire procedure.) Its effectiveness does not depend on the number of input statements within its jurisdiction, nor on their placement within that scope.

In this chapter we shall explore this capability more extensively; besides studying the other types of conditions that may be dynamically tested this way, we shall examine the mechanisms for controlling the scope of these tests. In order to exploit this large set of controls to its fullest extent, the programmer not only must have accumulated considerable experience but must be acquainted with the functioning of operating systems, particularly the one at his facility. Because of this merging of layers of software, it will be difficult to give detailed examples, since they would take us far afield. However, the examples included will enable the student to understand the structure of the execution control mechanisms so that he can acquire the fundamentals of their manipulation.

We may begin by recalling that a variety of statements, combinations, terms, and expressions have been referred to as illegal or inconsistent. When this situation occurred, it was often accompanied by the remark that the illegal usage raised some particular condition.

When PL/I recognizes an anomalous condition during execution, termination is not immediate or automatic; it is the result of a decision process in which the inconsistency is examined and subsequent action is dictated by the type of error encountered. The fact that a decision-making procedure exists indicates that the step immediately following the recognition of an illegal situation constitutes the suspension of a "normal" processing activity. Based on the operation of the decision mechanism, such activities may or may not be resumed. This type of suspension, generally termed an *interrupt*, may stem from a variety of causes. Many times the programmer may wish to cause such a suspension intentionally so that he can activate his own decision structure.

To allow the programmer to control execution in this manner, PL/I provides a spectrum of commands and built-in functions for detecting the presence of a variety of conditions that would cause suspension of processing. By using these facilities, the programmer can, if he wishes, provide his own consequent action in place of that taken by default. Some of these tests are valuable for detecting errors in a program (for example, an attempt to divide by 0) and are usually included by the programmer as temporary aids while a particular program is under development. Once its checkout is complete, the test instructions can be removed and the final version is recompiled. Other tests are valuable as permanent components and are incorporated into the program's decision networks. These differ from the error detection tests in that the conditions they are designed to recognize do not constitute illegalities. For example, we have been using the **ENDFILE** condition to cause an interrupt after the last record in a file has been read. As long as the records are still available from that file, processing continues. As soon as the last record is read (as signaled by a special indicator provided as part of the file generating process), normal sequential processing is suspended, and the program takes whatever action is indicated by the **ENDFILE ON** unit.

Yet another type of execution control that can be exercised by the programmer allows him to alter the relationship between internal activities in the processor and those concerned with its peripheral components. For example, it is possible to suspend the execution of internal statements and delay such processing until a particular data transmission activity is completed.

XVI.1   SERVICE OPERATIONS

When a particular program is loaded into the central processor and its statements are executed, the supervisory system under which it operates supplements this processing by maintaining a variety of records for its own bookkeeping purposes. Since some of this information can be of use to the programmer, the software system makes it available to him through features in PL/I and other high-level languages under its jurisdiction. Although the availability of certain items represents a convenience to the programmer, saving him the job of maintaining them himself, other items cannot be duplicated by alternate means within the structure of the language.

XVI.1.1   General Aids

Two built-in service functions are included to provide the user with conveniences for labeling and documentation.

XVI.1.1.1   The **TIME** Function

Fearful that users would accuse PL/I of not giving them the time of day, its designers have included a function that does just that. The name **TIME**, unless specifically declared otherwise, is recognized by the compiler as a built-in function that obtains the current time of day from the operating system and returns it to the programmer. Each processor contains a very accurate digital clock in which timed pulses are counted. The current value in that counter is translated into a nine-character string in which the first two characters represent the hour, the next two represent the minutes, the next two represent the second, and the final three specify milliseconds, usually to the nearest $16^2/_3$ milliseconds. Thus, if it happens to be 19 minutes, 51 seconds, and 358 milliseconds after 4 in the afternoon, the statement

PUT EDIT(TIME)(COLUMN(40),A(9));

will produce a printout showing the string 161951358.

XVI.1.1.2   The **DATE** Function

The programmer can use **DATE** in much the same way as the **TIME** function. Today's date is returned as a six-character string in which the first pair represents the year, the next two characters indicate the month, and the final two show the date. Thus, a program run on Mozart's birthday anniversary in 1986 would show the date 860127.

XVI.1.2   Communications with the Operator

Although the design of modern software systems minimizes human intervention during the course of a run, occasions arise necessitating the interruption of processing to allow an operator action. A common interruption of this type occurs when the operator must change a reel of tape. PL/I allows the programmer to build such interruptions into his procedures and to include for the operator instructions that are displayed when such an interruption occurs. (Most processing systems include a typewriter or other keyboard device for such purposes.)

XVI.1.2.1   The DISPLAY Instruction

The programmer can transmit a message to the operator by writing the statement

DISPLAY (expression);

(expression) consists of any legitimate PL/I expression whose evaluation will produce a single result. PL/I evaluates the expression, converts the result to a character string, and prints the string on the console output device. The length of the message may vary within a maximum limit set for the particular version of PL/I. In most cases, that maximum is 72 characters.

XVI.1.2.2   The REPLY Option

The **DISPLAY** statement can be extended by adding the **REPLY** option:

DISPLAY (expression) **REPLY** (stringvar);

When this option is added, processing does not resume until the operator submits a message to the program by means of the console keyboard. (The **DISPLAY** statement alone will not cause such a suspension.) When the message is received, it is treated as a character string and stored in the location designated by (stringvar). The maximum allowable length is usually the same as that imposed on the displayed message.

XVI.1.3   Input/Output Services

Several of the "housekeeping" services performed by the operating system and available through PL/I keep track of data transmission activities. The resulting statistics can often preclude the necessity for assigning counters in the program.

XVI.1.3.1   The COUNT Function

When a stream-oriented file is involved in a transmission operation (a **GET** or **PUT** statement), the programmer may obtain information revealing the number of data items transmitted in the most recently executed input/output statement by using the **COUNT** function. Generated as a fixed-point binary integer of default precision, this quantity is available by writing a statement such as

E = **COUNT** (filename);

where E is an appropriately declared numerical variable.

XVI.1.3.2   The LINENO Function

When transmitting the contents of a **PRINT** file to the line printer, the system counts the lines being printed on each page so that the programmer can always determine the number of the line currently being printed. This is done by invoking the **LINENO** function in a statement such as

   C = **LINENO** (filename);

where C is a numerical variable. As with **COUNT**, the value is generated as a fixed-point binary integer of default precision and is subject to PL/I's standard conversion rules.

Illustration 48

To examine the operation of some of these service functions we shall write a little procedure as follows: we shall read a card containing an integer N, indicating the number of subsequent **GET DATA** statements to be processed. The subsequent cards may have groups of one to four numerical values in data-directed form. To provide a separation between the reading and processing of successive groups, the program is to reset the four variables (A, B, C, and D) to zero after each is processed. For each group read, the following decision rules will be used:

1. If four values are present, the program is to print each of them.
2. If three values are present, the program is to compute and print the sums of all combinations of three variables (using 0 for the absent one).
3. If two input values are given, the program is to compute and print the sums of all pairs. (Thus, one of these sums will be 0).
4. If only one input value is present the program is to print a single sum for all four variables (three of which will be 0).

In addition, the output produced for each group is to include the number of values read and the number of values printed. Furthermore, the program is to show the date and the time at start (just before N is read) and the time after the last result has been printed.

The program is constructed in straightforward fashion. Operation with the sample data shown below produces the results seen in Figure 16.1:

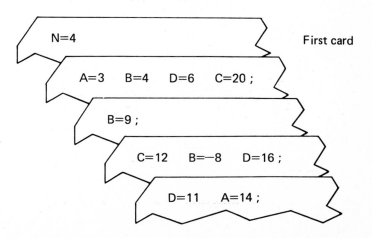

```
ILL48: PROCEDURE OPTIONS (MAIN)$
       DECLARE (A,B,C,D,F1,F2,F3,F4,F5,F6,D1,D2,N,I) FIXED BINARY (31),
               CLOCK CHARACTER (9)$

       CLOCK = TIME$                       /* RECALL SECTION XVI.1.1.1 */
       PUT PAGE LINE(3) EDIT ('DATE: ',DATE)(X(10),A,A(6)) /*SEC XVI.1.1.2*/
           ('TIME AT START: ',CLOCK)(SKIP,X(10),A,A(9))$
       GET DATA (N)$              PUT SKIP DATA (N)$

       DO I = 1 TO N$
         A,B,C,D = 0$     GET DATA (A,B,C,D)$     D1 = COUNT (SYSIN)$
         IF D1 = 4
           THEN PUT SKIP EDIT (A,B,C,D)(4 (X(5),F(4)))$
           ELSE IF D1 = 3
                   THEN DO$
                        F1 = A+B+C$  F2 = A+B+D$  F3 = A+C+D$  F4 = B+C+D$
                        PUT SKIP EDIT (F1,F2,F3,F4)( 4 (X(5),F(4)))$
                   END$
                ELSE IF D1 = 2
                   THEN DO$
                        F1 = A+B$  F2 = A+C$  F3 = A+D$
                        F4 = B+C$  F5 = B+D$  F6 = C+D$
                        PUT SKIP EDIT (F1,F2,F3,F4,F5,F6)
                            (6 X(5),F(4)))$
                   END$
                ELSE DO$
                        F1 = A+B+C+D$  PUT SKIP EDIT(F1)(X(5),F(4))$
                END$
         D2 = COUNT(SYSPRINT)$   PUT SKIP DATA (D1,D2)$      PUT SKIP$
       END$

       CLOCK = TIME$
       PUT SKIP EDIT ('TIME AT FINISH: ',CLOCK)(X(10),A,A(9))$
       END ILL48$
```

```
                DATE: 740322
                TIME AT START: 170227660
    N=           4                    FLNAME='':
                 3          4          20          6
    D1=          4                    D2=          4:

                 9
    D1=          1                    D2=          1:

                 4          8          20
    D1=          3                    D2=          3:

                14         14          25          0          11         11
    D1=          2                    D2=          6:

                TIME AT FINISH: 170241850
```

Figure 16.1

XVI.2   THE HANDLING OF INTERRUPTIONS

In contrast to the endless variety of numerical and logical conditions the programmer can check by means of the **IF** statement, there are a number of specific types of events whose occurrence triggers a series of signals and indicators that the computer hardware itself is designed to recognize. Processing is usually terminated when such a signal is received. However, because the software is constructed to interact intimately with the logical circuitry, it can intercede and prevent complete termination, replacing that action with an interruption. Under such circumstances, normal processing activities are suspended rather than terminated, thus presenting the opportunity for a decision to be made regarding the disposition of the particular processing job. The nature of the decision depends upon the type of situation encountered and is built into the software. In general, the decision may call for a resumption of normal processing or curtailment of activity on that job and initiation of the next job. If the job is to be terminated, the system generates a message that informs the user that a particular type of interruption has occurred. This type of response is known as a *standard system action* and is analogous to a PL/I default activity.

To expand the usefulness and versatility of such suspensions, PL/I permits the programmer to anticipate such interruptions and provide his own responses in preference to the system's. These responses may be in force for the entire program or for a designated portion of it. It is possible to suppress one or more interruption mechanisms completely, a process known as *disabling*. This condition can also be made temporary, so that if the programmer wishes to reenable a particular interrupt mechanism he may do so.

We can generalize from our experience with **ON ENDFILE**, recognizing that the **ON** statement provides a basic vehicle for detecting interruption and defining "nonstandard" responses:

ON condition action;

where "condition" is usually a specific keyword recognized by the system and associated with a particular type of interruption, and "action" is a response specified by the programmer in the form of an unlabeled executable statement or an unlabeled **BEGIN** block. (In the former, the response consists of execution of the single statement; in the latter, the entire block is executed when the specified interruption occurs.) There are certain statements that may not be designated as reactions to interruption. These include the **DECLARE, DO, END, FORMAT, PROCEDURE,** and **RETURN** statements. If a **BEGIN** block is specified as the response, that block may not contain a **RETURN** statement. When the response statement is a **CALL** or a **GO TO**, control is transferred in the usual manner when the specified interruption occurs. In addition to a series of specific types of interrupt conditions recognized by the system and designated in PL/I by unique keywords, the programmer can define his own conditions which he can then precipitate at will by means of the **SIGNAL** statement.

The **ON** statement sets up a mechanism to monitor the stated condition. If that condition should occur after the **ON** statement is executed and before it is nullified (either by another **ON** statement for the same condition, by return from the procedure in which the **ON** statement appears, or by execution of a **REVERT** statement for the condition), then processing will be interrupted and the indicated action will be performed.

It is useful to contrast the actions of the **IF** and **ON** statements:

- The **IF** statement says, "If this test is satisfied *now* then do this action *now*."

- The **ON** statement says, "Do not do anything now; but, if this condition should come up at some future time, stop whatever is being done and perform this action. When the action is complete, then take up where you left off if you can."

XVI.2.1   Computational Conditions

Among the interruptions that can be intercepted and controlled by the programmer are a series of conditions precipitated by numerical operations. This type of interruption usually occurs where the program encounters an inconsistent calculation or a violation of one of PL/I's restrictions.

XVI.2.1.1   The **CONVERSION** Condition

When a variable is declared with a specific set of attributes (either explicitly or by default), PL/I will attempt to convert any value assigned to that variable so that its attributes will match those required by the programmer. When such conversion from **CHARACTER** to some other type is impossible, an interruption will occur, and the system will terminate processing, informing the user that a conversion error has been encountered. Such situations occur, for example, when the program attempts to convert from character string to bit string using a character string containing something other than 1's or 0's. Similarly, a command to read a string that includes a letter into a location declared with numerical attributes will cause a conversion error. If the programmer wishes to substitute some response besides termination, he may do so with a statement of the form

ON CONVERSION action;

Should the programmer want processing to resume after the interuption, he must specify a type of response that will successfully change the situation that caused the interruption. If this is not done, the program, after executing the statement (or statements) specified by "action," will attempt the conversion again. Consequently, there is a very real possiblity that the specification of an improper type of action will cause the program to go into an endless loop in which conversion is attempted, followed by an interruption, followed in turn by another unsuccessful conversion attempt.

To help the programmer find the type of response likely to succeed in overcoming the illegal conversion condition, PL/I provides a number of functions that offer information regarding the possible reason for the interruption. Access to such information may allow the programmer to rectify the condition so that execution can proceed.

XVI.2.1.2   The **ONCHAR** Function

Since character conversion in PL/I is performed on one character at a time, the inability to handle a single character is sufficient to precipitate an interruption. If this is the case, the **ONCHAR** built-in function identifies the offensive character. Thus, if B is declared as a single-character string, the statement

B = **ONCHAR**;

will place the particular character causing the conversion error in location B. **ONCHAR** can also be used as a pseudovariable, thus providing a very convenient and effective means for changing the character that caused the conversion error so that processing could be resumed. For example, the statement

ON CONVERSION ONCHAR = '0';

would replace the offending character with a 0 and continue where it left off. If the particular variable being processed contains additional characters to be converted, each illegal character will produce an interruption, resulting in the substitution of a 0 until processing on that field is complete. Note that not every **CONVERSION** error can be attributed to a single character. For instance, Z = 'ᵬᵬᵬ-' will cause an error if Z is numeric; the error here is the *lack* of any digit after the *legal* character '-'.

XVI.2.1.3   The **ONSOURCE** Function

This function is a more general variant of the **ONCHAR** function. With this function, the programmer can reference the entire field that caused the interruption. Hence, the statement

ON CONVERSION ONSOURCE = '99999';

will replace the value of the guilty variable with a series of 9's. If the expression to the right of the = sign produces a character string shorter than the one involved in the interruption, it is used to replace the leftmost characters in that string, with the remainder being filled with blanks.

These functions find common usage in situations where a particular field is to be tested for errors. Suppose that a program reads and processes a series of data cards in which each card contains an identification variable X in columns 1-5, and two readings Y and Z punched in columns 11-15 and 21-25, respectively, each with the implied format $XXX_{\cup}XX$. Let us assume that these variables are declared as follows:

DECLARE (Y,Z) **FIXED**(5,2),X **PICTURE** 'A999A';

As a result of this declaration, a value of X composed of any combination of characters besides a letter, three digits, and another letter, in that order, will raise the **CONVERSION** condition. By using the **ON** statement followed by some type of error routine, we can intercept each card with an improperly recorded value of X, print an appropriate error message, ignore that card, and read the next one:

ON CONVERSION BEGIN;

    PUT SKIP LIST (ONSOURCE,'IS AN ILLEGAL VALUE');

        GO TO BRING;

  END;

     ·

     ·

     ·

BRING: GET EDIT (X,Y,Z)(P'A999A',2 (X(5),F(5,2)));

     ·

     ·

     ·

Note that the **ON** statement, accompanied by the **BEGIN** block that specifies the programmer's response to the interruption, precedes the input statement, thus activating the response in time for it to be of use. As long as the value of X contains the proper combination of characters, the **BEGIN** block is ignored and processing continues normally. (Presumably, the statements operate on the data in some manner and send control back to the input statement BRING.) When the **CONVERSION** condition occurs, the error message is printed, including the illegal value of X, after which the processing of that card is bypassed and control is returned to BRING.

XVI.2.1.4   The **SIZE** Condition

During our exploration of numerical data attributes, we saw that each particular version of PL/I imposes its limitations on the magnitude of numbers, the maximum number of digits that can be used, and so on. Violation of one of these restrictions raises one of several conditions that can be intercepted by the programmer. We have already mentioned a very useful one, the **SIZE** condition, in discussing the arithmetic conversion rules (Chapter IX). We shall review it here and add a little more detail.

If the number of digits in a value assigned to a particular variable exceeds the number allocated for it, PL/I tries to accommodate the value by truncating digits to the left and right of the radix point as required, so as to maintain proper alignment of the radix point. If a nonzero digit is truncated on the left, PL/I can detect such an attempt on request, and will raise the **SIZE** condition as a result. This violation may occur as the result of an assignment statement, because an excessively long value has been read in or when a decimal value being converted to binary exceeds the maximum permissible binary value. In any event, the **SIZE** condition will occur if the number of digits in the value is greater than that assigned by the **DECLARE** statement or if the limit set up by the compiler is exceeded.

The **SIZE** condition is supported by software and requires extra instructions in the program. If the system is left to its own devices, the occurence of a **SIZE** condition will not be detected since it is not normally enabled. To supply his own action, the programmer must enable **SIZE** and specify an **ON SIZE** statement with a suitable action. To enable **SIZE**, the condition must be mentioned in a *prefix* on the **PROCEDURE** or **BEGIN** statement of the appropriate block. By way of illustration, such a statement might appear as follows:

(SIZE) : PROGRAM: PROCEDURE OPTIONS (MAIN);

The Optimizing and Checkout Compilers have a similar condition, **STRINGSIZE**, which is raised, if enabled, when a string assignment causes truncation. Also, these compilers do not require the enabling prefix to be on a **PROCEDURE** or **BEGIN** statement.

XVI.2.1.5   The **FIXEDOVERFLOW** Condition

The generation of a value with an excessive number of digits may also occur as the result of a series of calculations. When this happens, an interruption results, which is detected by the hardware and is separate and distinct from the **SIZE** condition and can be intercepted independently.

When a particular calculation involves fixed-point quantities and the result exceeds the maximum allowable number of digits, the **FIXEDOVERFLOW** condition is raised. Unless preempted by the programmer, the system will print a message and raise the **ERROR** condition. The use of the keyword **FIXEDOVERFLOW** in an **ON** statement in the usual manner allows the programmer to subsitute a different response:

ON FIXEDOVERFLOW action;

FIXEDOVERFLOW is very long keyword. For those wishing to write shorter keywords, most PL/I implementations accept **FOFL** as an alternative. Other legal abbreviations are listed in Appendix E.

XVI.2.1.6   The **OVERFLOW** Condition   *Floating Point*

When floating-point numbers are involved, a similar violation produces the **OVERFLOW** condition. The type of processing used with floating-point numbers does not influence the total number of digits in the result, and the violation manifests itself as an excessively high exponent value. The standard system action again is to issue a message and raise the **ERROR** condition. The **ON OVERFLOW** statement gives the programmer the opportunity to intercept the **OVERFLOW** condition and define his own action.

XVI.2.1.7   The **UNDERFLOW** Condition   *floating point*

In many situations (such as those in which a very small floating-point number is divided by a very large one), it is possible to generate a floating-point result in which the exponent is smaller than the minimum value allowed by the compiler. The interruption thus caused is known as the **UNDERFLOW** condition, and the appropriate statement for interception has the standard form:

ON UNDERFLOW action;

The standard action is to substitute a result of zero and ignore the condition.

XVI.2.1.8   The **ZERODIVIDE** Condition

In a statement such as

Y = X/(W − Z);

it sometimes happens that the values of W and Z are sufficiently close to each other that the attempt to divide produces a quotient too large to be represented in the maximum number of digits allowed. Occurrence of this situation raises the **ZERODIVIDE** condition. Since it is inappropriate to use the result of such an operation, the system takes the more sensible way out and prints a pertinent message immediately before raising the **ERROR** condition. The keyword **ZERODIVIDE** may be used in an **ON** statement in the usual manner.

XVI.2.1.9   The **SUBSCRIPTRANGE** Condition

When the subscript of an array element is specified by means of a variable or expression, there is a possibility in concept and often in actuality that the resulting integer is outside of the range declared for the array. The interruption thus caused is known as the **SUBSCRIPT-RANGE** condition. Like the **SIZE** condition, this situation will not be detected unless the condition is enabled. Once enabled, the standard action is to print a message and raise the **ERROR** condition. Using an **ON** statement, the programmer may specify his own action as usual. Note that no distinction is made between a subscript value that is too large and one that falls below the minimum level. If an array is multidimensional, each subscript value is tested individually, so that the **SUBSCRIPTRANGE** condition can occur for each one in succession.

XVI.2.1.10   The **STRINGRANGE** Condition

If it is enabled, the **STRINGRANGE** condition is raised whenever a reference to the **SUBSTR** built-in function results in a violation of the rules governing its operation. Such violations can be defined by recalling the general form for invoking this function:

SUBSTR (string,arg2,arg3)

where "string" is the name of the character string variable from which the substring is to be extracted, arg2 is a value indicating the character number at which the substring is to start, and arg3 specifies the number of consecutive characters to be used. In terms of this reference, the **STRINGRANGE** condition will occur if:

1. The value of arg2 exceeds the length of "string."*
2. The value of arg2 is less than or equal to zero.
3. The value in arg3 exceeds the number of available characters starting from the point defined by arg2.
   *If arg3 = 0, arg2 may lie outside the string without causing an error.

Unless otherwise specified by the programmer, the appearance of this condition will not cause execution to be curtailed. Instead, the **SUBSTR** function will be executed with revised arguments that essentially specify the part of the original substring that overlaps the existing string.

XVI.2.2   Input/Output Interrupt Conditions

Many systems are designed to suspend processing when encountering one of several conditions during data transmission operations. These may be an organizational difference between a data file and its specifications in the program or an actual physical (hardware) difficulty during a transmission operation.

XVI.2.2.1   The **NAME** Condition

PL/I's rules governing the use of the **GET DATA** statement allow the list of items in the statement to include variable names for which values do not appear in the input stream. The reverse situation causes an interruption known as the **NAME** condition. The appropriate test statement takes the form

   ON NAME (filename) action;

After the programmer's specified action is carried out, the program will resume execution by reading in (or attempting to read in) the data item in the input stream immediately following the one that caused the **NAME** condition.

If the programmer wants to know the contents of the data item that caused the **NAME** condition, he may reference the value by using the **DATAFIELD** function. When there is no **ON** statement, or on return from the **ON** unit, the program continues with the next name, ignoring the erroneous **ON**. Note that if an illegal name occurs in a **GET STRING** (...)**DATA**(...); statement, the **ERROR** condition is raised instead.

XVI.2.2.2   The **UNDEFINEDFILE** Condition

Since the attributes that can be assigned to a data file by an **OPEN** statement include those assignable in a **DECLARE**, the situation may arise wherein the attributes added to the file by the **OPEN** statement are in conflict with those specified or implied by declaration. When this happens, the **UNDEFINEDFILE** condition is raised and may be detected by a statement of the form

    ON UNDEFINEDFILE (filename) action;

If such a test is not included, the standard system action consists of writing an error message and raising the **ERROR** condition. This condition is also raised if the corresponding data set has not properly been made known to the operating system.

XVI.2.2.3   The **TRANSMIT** Condition

As part of the circuitry that directs transmission of information to and from peripheral devices, computing systems include control mechanisms that check to determine whether the input or output signals are of the proper type and strength. Occasionally, the quality of such signals may deteriorate because of physical imperfections on the storage medium. One common cause of such difficulties stems from uneven or worn-out magnetic coating on a portion of a tape reel, caused by faulty manufacture or excessive wear. As a result, it is quite likely that a signal will be misinterpreted, causing erroneous data to be read into the processor or written on the tape. When the system detects such a situation, it raises the **TRANSMIT** condition. The standard action is to print an error message and raise the **ERROR** condition. The **ON** statement must include the filename, namely,

    ON TRANSMIT (filename) action;

On return from the **ON** unit, processing continues as though the erroneous record were correct.

XVI.2.2.4   The **RECORD** Condition

This condition is raised when there is a disagreement between the size of a record and that of a variable to which that record is assigned and from which it is to be filled. If such a discrepancy is encountered, the standard action is to print a message and raise the **ERROR** condition. If an **ON** statement is specified, then on return the following action is taken: If the record is too large to be contained in the variable reserved for it, the excess data are lost. If the reverse is true, the results are that on input the entire record is read into the variable and the excess portion of the variable retains its previous contents, and on output only those data that can be accommodated by the record will be transmitted from the variable.

The **ON RECORD** statement may be used to test for the **RECORD** condition, regardless of whether it is caused by a **READ, REWRITE**, or **WRITE** statement. (Note that its contextual usage prevents confusion with the keyword **RECORD** when used as a file attribute.)

XVI.2.2.5   The **KEY** Condition

A number of different discrepancies may arise when handling keyed records (see Chapter

12). Any of the following raise the **KEY** condition: a **READ** statement in which the specified **KEY** value cannot be matched by any of the records in the referenced file; an improper specification of a character string representing the key; specification of a **KEY** value in a **WRITE** or **LOCATE** statement where a record already exists with the key; (Except for a **REGIONAL**(1) file opened for **UPDATE**.) and a **REWRITE** or **DELETE** statement referring to a nonexistent key.

To preempt the standard action (the printing of an error message and raising the **ERROR** condition), the **ON KEY** (filename) statement is used in conjunction with some desired response. Once this specified action is carried out, the program resumes normal processing at the statement following the one that raised the **KEY** condition. As in all other file handling conditions, the name of the file must be specified in the **ON** statement, so that its appearance takes the form

ON KEY (filename) action;

The offending key value may be referenced by means of the **ONKEY** built-in function (note the absence of blanks between the two words) with a statement such as

OFFENDER = **ONKEY**;

XVI.2.2.6 The **ENDPAGE** Condition

As we saw in the **LINENO** function, the program automatically keeps track of the number of lines written on a given page. It compares that number to the limit specified by the **PAGESIZE** designation. When that limit is exceeded, the **ENDPAGE** condition is raised. If no programmer action is specified, the system will merely start a new page, reset the line counter, and resume processing. Although this does not appear to be particularly damaging, the programmer may often want to substitute his own action, such as going to a new page and printing a set of page headings before processing is resumed.

When the programmer uses a statement such as

ON ENDPAGE (filename) action;

the system takes the following action at the point that an attempt is made to increase the line counter to a value greater than **PAGESIZE**: the **ON** unit is entered with the current line being one greater than **PAGESIZE**. The programmer may carry out whatever action he wishes, including the execution of **PUT** statements on the same file. These will not interfere with the **PUT** statement that was interrupted. Such **PUT** statements may transmit any amount of information on the current page and, if desired, may also start a new page, transmitting any amount of information on the new page as well.

Resumption of processing following the specified action will cause the next item in the data list of the **PUT** statement that raised the condition to be transmitted to the current line (which may well have been changed as a result of the **ON** unit action). This is true even if the indicated action did not include the use of the **PAGE** option. Once this has happened, the testing of the line counter is disabled; the program will continue to produce lines of output, the value in the line counter will continue to increase, but the **ENDPAGE** conditon will not be raised again.

These facilities are very useful and provide great flexibility. For example, the **ENDPAGE** condition can be used as a natural criterion for invoking a procedure to print a new set of headings, increment a page counter, and so on.

XVI.2.3   Interruptions as Debugging Aids

In addition to these specific types of interruption, PL/I allows the programmer to refer to certain system indicators that provide more information about a particular incident causing suspension of processing. The opportunity exists for further investigation by means of additional tests, with the possibility of reconstructing an entire sequence of processing.

XVI.2.3.1   The **SNAP** Option

When the programmer is testing for the occurrence of a particular type of interruption by means of an **ON** statement, he may request more detail about the processing preceding that interruption. This is done by including the **SNAP** option:

ON condition **SNAP** action;

Before the indicated action is taken, the system will trace the sequence of execution prior to the interruption by identifying the statement that caused the interruption and referring to the entry point of the procedure containing that statement. If the statement is part of a procedure invoked by another one, the **SNAP** routines will also list the entry point of the invoking procedure. If that procedure was called, in turn, by another one, its entry name will also be given. This type of trace may not always be complete, because it can show only those procedures having remained active during the invoking sequence. The format of these trace displays varies with the particular type of compiler.

Illustration 49

We shall examine the results of some of these options by equipping a program with several tests and using it with input designed to force the occurrence of the associated condition. Since our emphasis here is on the tests and their effects, the processing itself will be very simple. We shall read sets of eight values into an array X declared as **FIXED**(2). Each set is accompanied by N and Z, each integers. Then, for each set, the program is to compute the first N elements of an array Y (also declared as **FIXED**(2)) such that

$$Y_i = \frac{X_i Z}{X_i - Z}$$

The program prints X, followed by N, Z, and the N values of Y.

Our implementation of the program will include tests for **FIXEDOVERFLOW, SUBSCRIP-TRANGE**, and **ZERODIVIDE**. Figure 16.2 shows several sets of input, together with the corresponding results.

```
                (SIZE,SUBSCRIPTRANGE):
     ILL49: PROCEDURE OPTIONS (MAIN);
            DECLARE (X(8),Z,N,NRUN INITIAL(1),I) FIXED BINARY (31),
                    Y(8) FLOAT DECIMAL (6),    S BIT(1) INITIAL ('1'B);
            PUT PAGE LINE(5) EDIT ('ARRAY COMPUTATIONS')(X(51),A); PUT SKIP(2);

            ON ENDFILE (SYSIN)
              BEGIN;
                    NRUN=NRUN-1; PUT SKIP(2)EDIT('NO. OF RUNS: ',NRUN)(X(5),A,F(2));
                    STOP;
              END;

            DO WHILE ('1'B);
               GET LIST (X,Z,N);
               PUT SKIP(2) EDIT ('RUN ',NRUN)(X(5),A,F(2));
               PUT SKIP(0) EDIT ('_____')(X(5),A);
               PUT SKIP EDIT ('X = ',X)(X(5),A, 8 (X(5),F(2)))
                             ('N= ',N,'Z= ',Z)(SKIP, 2 (X(5),A,F(2)));

               ON SIZE
                 BEGIN;
                     PUT SKIP EDIT ('---SIZE ERROR IN RUN ',NRUN,'---')
                         (X(10),A,F(2),A);              S = '0'B;
                 END;
               ON FIXEDOVERFLOW
                 BEGIN;
                     PUT SKIP EDIT ('---FIXED OVERFLOW IN RUN ',NRUN,'---')
                         (X(10),A,F(2),A);              S = '0'B;
                 END;
               ON SUBSCRIPTRANGE
                 BEGIN;
                     PUT SKIP EDIT ('---N IS TOO LARGE IN RUN ',NRUN,'---')
                         (X(10),A,F(2),A);              S = '0'B;          '
                 END;
               ON ZERODIVIDE
                 BEGIN;
                     PUT SKIP EDIT ('---X(I)=Z FOR I OF ',I,'IN RUN ',NRUN,'---')
                         (X(10),A,F(1),A,F(2),A);       S = '0'B;
                 END;

               DO WHILE (S);
                 DO I = 1 TO N;
                    Y(I) = ROUND(X(I)*Z/X(I)-Z),2);
                 END;
                 PUT SKIP EDIT ('Y = ',(Y(I) DO I=1 TO N))(X(5),A,(N)(X(3),F(7,2)));
               END;
               NRUN = NRUN+1;
               S = '1'B;
            END;

            END ILL49;
```

XVI.2.3.2   The **ONLOC** Function

If the programmer wants to reference and use the name of the entry point of the procedure containing the statement causing a particular type of interruption, he may do so by means of the **ONLOC** function, which is used in the same way as **ONCHAR** and **ONKEY**. In certain situations, the identification of the procedure will allow the programmer to adjust the argument values so that when control returns to the statement that caused the interruption, it will now be executed without incident. A statement such as

ON ZERODIVIDE BEGIN;

.

.

.

END;

may include statements in which **ONLOC** is used to identify the procedure in control at the time the interruption occurs. Before the **BEGIN** block is concluded, the necessary adjustments will have been made and processing will resume.

```
                                      ARRAY COMPUTATIONS


  RUN__1_
  X =            12       7       16        4       15       13       11        9
  N=  8      Z=   6
  Y =         12.00       42.00       9.60     -12.00       10.00       11.14       13.20       18.00

  RUN__2_
  X =             7       4        1       11        6       14       20       -6
  N=  6      Z=   8
  Y =        -56.00       -8.00      -1.14      29.33      -24.00      18.67
              ---SIZE ERROR IN RUN   3---

  RUN__4_
  X =             5       4        3       -2        5        5       14       13
  N= 11      Z=  12
              ---N IS TOO LARGE IN RUN    4---

  RUN__5_
  X =            10       9        8        7        4       1C        7        2
  N=  8      Z=   7
              ---X(I)=Z FOR I CF 4 IN RUN    5---

  RUN__6_
  X =            14      15       12       16        8        6        6       16
  N= 17      Z=  26
              ---N IS TOO LARGE IN RUN    6---

  NO. OF RUNS:   6
```

Figure 16.2

XVI.2.3.3   The **ONCODE** Function

As we have seen, PL/I designates each type of interruption by a special keyword that can be used in an **ON** statement. Underlying these keywords is a more elaborate network of codes that dissect many types into two or more subtypes. For instance, when there is an anomaly in the organization of a data file, PL/I raises the **UNDEFINEDFILE** condition. There is no distinction made between an interruption due to the use of an undefined data set or one whose attributes supplied by the **OPEN** statement are in conflict with those supplied in the **DECLARE**, or one that is inadequately specified (for example, no information concerning block size). In the system, each of these discrepancies is recognized as a separate error and is designated as such by a unique error code available through Pl/I by means of the **ONCODE** function, whose use parallels that of **ONKEY**. The function value is given to the programmer as a binary integer corresponding to a particular entry in a table of error codes. This table is rather long, and its composition may vary with each type of operating system. (The one used in the IBM/360 operating system, for example, is given in the *PL/I Programmer Guide*, IBM Publication Number C28-6594.)

XVI.2.3.4 The **ERROR** and **FINISH** Conditions

For many of the interrupt conditions, we have seen that the standard action has been to print a particular error message and raise the **ERROR** condition. There are other circumstances where an error occurs that are difficult to classify. In these cases, also, the **ERROR** condition is raised. Once the **ERROR** condition is raised, the standard response is to print a message (if one has not already been printed) and, in turn, raise the **FINISH** condition. The **FINISH** condition is raised whenever the program is about to be terminated and its standard action consists of actually going through with the termination. By virtue of this definition, the **FINISH** condition includes normal termination, such as the **STOP** and **EXIT** statements and the **RETURN** or **END** statements in a main procedure.

The programmer may specify a statement of the form

ON FINISH action;

The action specified in such a statement may consist of any type of processing that can be used with other **ON** statements. Once this action is carried out, processing is terminated. Of course, if the action includes a **GO TO** statement, the termination can be forestalled. This must be used with caution in order to avoid an infinite loop that can only be broken by explicit operator intervention.

In the same way, the programmer may specify an **ON** statement for the **ERROR** condition:

ON ERROR action;

Normal return from the action causes **FINISH** to be raised; and again, if he so desires, the programmer can cause the program to continue by exiting from the **ON** unit by means of a **GO TO** statement.

XVI.2.3.5 The **CHECK** Condition

An effective technique that often can be of help in debugging is to trace the history of a particular variable during a processing sequence. In many instances this is done by inserting instructions to print the values of specified variables at a number of strategic points, thus providing the programmer with a running record of the values assumed by those variables. By comparing the values with those known to be correct for a given situation, it is often possible to pinpoint an error in procedural logic. Once a source of error is identified and corrected, the superfluous output statements are removed and the program is recompiled.

This process may be automated in a PL/I program by means of the **CHECK** condition. When activated, this facility provides a method for obtaining histories of value changes in minute detail. The basic mechanism consists of identifying the variables to be traced by attaching their names to a **PROCEDURE** or **BEGIN** statement. Once such identification has been established, the program automatically prints a variable (its name and value) each time its value changes.

Variables for automatic checking are named in a *check prefix* having the following form:

(**CHECK**(name1,name2,etc.)):label:**PROCEDURE** .....;

Having established that these variables are to be traced, PL/I will do so for the entire scope of the procedure unless it encounters an explicit statement to the contrary. (We shall deal with such statements a little later in the chapter.) Types of variables that may be specified in a check prefix include statement label constants, entry names, and variable names, including those of arrays and structures (or qualified names therein). The following types of identifiers are *not* permitted: names with attached subscripts; based variables (those with locations indicated by a pointer); names used as parameters in a procedure; and defined variables.

Illustration 50

To see how this automatic facility operates, we shall write a simple procedure that reads a succession of integer values for N. For each value, the procedure computes two numbers, S and T, using the following relations:

$$s = \sum_{i=1}^{N} (1 + \sqrt{i}); \quad t = N^2 / s$$

```
ILL50: PROCEDURE OPTIONS (MAIN);
       DECLARE (NRUN INITIAL(0), N,K) FIXED BINARY (31),
               (T,S INITIAL(0)) FLOAT DECIMAL;

       ON ENDFILE (SYSIN) GO TO ST;
       PUT PAGE LINE(3) LIST ('VALUE OF N','VALUE OF T');

       DO WHILE ('1'B);
         GET LIST (N);
         IF N = 0 THEN GO TO ST;
         NRUN = NRUN+1;
         DO K = 1 TO N;
           S = S+1+SQRT(K);
         END;
         T = N*N/S;
         PUT SKIP LIST (N,T);
       END;

ST:    PUT SKIP(2) DATA (NRUN);
       END ILL50;

           VALUE OF N              VALUE OF T
               3                   1.25939E+00
               4                   9.25255E-01
               5                   8.15000E-01
               6                   7.57789E-01
               7                   7.20756E-01
               8                   6.93466E-01
               9                   6.71664E-01
```

Figure 16.3

Upon completion of the calculation, the procedure is to print N and the corresponding value of T.

Such a procedure, together with the output for a number of input values, are given in Figure 16.3. Inspection of the output indicates that the program execution was complete and a full set of results were obtained. However, their values arouse some suspicion: we note that, although T is a rather simple function of N, there does not appear to be the kind of systematic change in T that one might expect. To probe a little further, we shall incorporate a check prefix

```
              (CHECK(K,S)):
ILL50A: PROCEDURE OPTIONS (MAIN):
        DECLARE (NRUN INITIAL(0), N, K) FIXED BINARY(31),
               (T, S INITIAL(0)) FLOAT DECIMAL:
        PUT PAGE LINE(3) LIST ('VALUE OF N','VALUE OF T'):
        ON ENDFILE (SYSIN) GO TO ST:

        DO WHILE ('1'B):
          GET LIST (N):
          IF N = 0 THEN GO TO ST:
          NRUN = NRUN+1:
          DO K = 1 TO N:
            S = S+1+SQRT(K):
          END:
          T = N*N/S:
          PUT SKIP LIST (N,T):
        END:

ST:     PUT SKIP(2) DATA (NRUN):
        END ILL50A:


        S= 0.00000E+00;



        VALUE OF N                    VALUE OF T

        K =         1;

        S= 2.00000E+00;

        K =         2;

        S= 4.41421E+00;

        K =         3;

        S= 7.14626E+00;

        K =         4;

                    3                 1.25939E+00

        K =         1;

        S= 9.14626E+00;

        K =         2;

        S= 1.15604E+01;

        K =         3;

        S= 1.42925E+C1;

        K =         4;

        S= 1.72925E+C1;

        K =         5;
```

Figure 16.4   4   9.25255E-C1

for S and for K, the index variable in the summation loop. This will produce printed values of these variables for each cycle through the loop (N such displays) before the computed value of T is printed. The revised procedure and corresponding output for part of the run are given in Figure 16.4. We see that intermediate values of S for the first value of N are ascending nicely and N and T are printed forthwith. Then, however, when K reappears as 1 (indicating that the looping process is about to start for a new value of N), we find that there is no printed value of S preceding it. In fact, as the loop keeps cycling, S just keeps getting larger and larger. Terrible. It is clear now that S is not being reinitialized for each new N (confirmed, of course, by a quick glance at the listing). Consequently, the appropriate correction can be made and the check prefix removed (Figure 16.5). It would be misleading to proceed tacitly from this point, leaving the impression that the **CHECK** condition will point quickly to all such errors and allow their swift and sure correction. However, it is a very powerful debugging facility, and accumulated experience in its usage can pay off handsomely in substantial savings of time and aggravation.

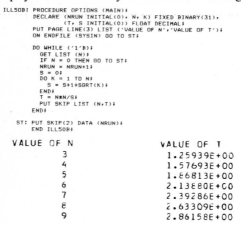

```
ILL50B: PROCEDURE OPTIONS (MAIN);
        DECLARE (NRUN INITIAL(0), N, K) FIXED BINARY(31),
                (T, S INITIAL(0)) FLOAT DECIMAL;
        PUT PAGE LINE(3) LIST ('VALUE OF N','VALUE OF T');
        ON ENDFILE (SYSIN) GO TO ST;

        DO WHILE ('1'B);
          GET LIST (N);
          IF N = 0 THEN GO TO ST;
          NRUN = NRUN+1;
          S = 0;
          DO K = 1 TO N;
            S = S+1+SQRT(K);
          END;
          T = N*N/S;
          PUT SKIP LIST (N,T);
        END;

    ST: PUT SKIP(2) DATA (NRUN);
        END ILL50B;
```

VALUE OF N	VALUE OF T
3	1.25939E+00
4	1.57693E+00
5	1.86813E+00
6	2.13880E+00
7	2.39286E+00
8	2.63309E+00
9	2.86158E+00

Figure 16.5

Additional flexibility may be obtained with the form

ON CHECK (name1,name2,etc.) action;

where (name1,name2,etc.) represents a list of identifiers that the programmer wishes to be checked during processing. Now, instead of printing the name and its current value each time that particular variable is involved in an activity, the action taken in such situations may be as simple or extensive as the programmer wishes. The following are circumstances under which the **ON CHECK** interruption occurs:

When the name is a statement label constant, processing will be interrupted immediately before the referenced statement is about to be executed. No interruption will occur if the particular label refers to a nonexecutable statement, such as **DECLARE** or **FORMAT**.

If the name refers to a procedure's entry point, interruption occurs just as the entry is about to be invoked. In cases where that entry is referred to by more than one name, the **CHECK** condition will be raised only when the program makes reference to the same name given in the **ON** list.

When the name in the **ON CHECK** list refers to a single-valued variable, the **CHECK** condition will be raised each time when: (a) the variable appears to the left of the = sign in an assignment statement; (b) the value of the variable is changed by a pseudovariable appearing on the lefthand side of an assignment statement; (c) the variable appears as one of the control variables in a **DO** statement (the index, initial value, limiting value, increment, or in a **WHILE** option); (d) the variable appears in an input list of a **GET LIST** or **GET EDIT** statement; (e) the variable appears in a **GET DATA** statement and a current value for the variable already exists; (f) the variable appears in a **PUT STRING** statement; (g) the variable is used as a member of an argument list when invoking a procedure that ends with a **RETURN** statement; (h) the variable appears in the **SET** option of a **READ** or **LOCATE** statement; (i) the variable is named by a **REPLY** portion of a **DISPLAY** statement.

An interruption will *not* occur if the value of the variable is set by the **INITIAL** option, or if the variable is used as a base upon which another variable is defined and the value of the defined variable changes.

If the variable refers to an entire array, the above circumstances will raise the **CHECK** condition when any element of that array is involved.

When the variable refers to a structure, it refers by implication to any element in that structure.

If the variable named in an **ON CHECK** list is an element of a structure, processing will be interrupted when any element in the structure containing the named element is involved in one of the situations above.

Each member of the **ON CHECK** list is handled independently; the names do not have to appear in any particular combination for an interruption to occur. If a particular statement contains several members of an **ON CHECK** list, an interruption will occur for each of them, in the order in which they appear in the statement (not in the list).

If a member of a **CHECK** list appears in a **DO** loop, the condition will be raised for each iteration of that loop.

The standard action taken by the system when the **CHECK** condition is raised consists of writing the new value of the variable (or the name of the statement or entry label) on the standard output file, after which processing is resumed. This provides a chronological trace of the processing sequence. Since the program has no way of anticipating which names are to be involved in the **CHECK** condition, this type of interruption does not exist by default, as do the other interruptions discussed before. If the programmer desires such an interruption to occur, he must explicitly provide for it, whether or not he specifies his own action or prefers the system's. If the latter is the case, he must indicate this by a statement such as

ON CHECK (name1, name2, etc.) **SYSTEM**;

This informs the program that he would like to implement the **CHECK** facility for the identifiers given in the list and that he is content with the standard response. In subsequent discussions we shall see that the **SYSTEM** option can be used to change the reaction to a particular type of interruption from that specified by the programmer to the one taken by the software.

XVI.2.4   Do-It-Yourself Interruptions

PL/I provides an additional mechanism that is very useful in certain applications such as real time, teleprocessing, and list processing, and also for program checkout. This technique can be considered to consist of two facets: the first allows the programmer to define his own interrupt conditions and test for them as he would any condition recognized by the system; the second allows him to precipitate the condition and also, if he desires, any of those defined by the system as well.

XVI.2.4.1   The **ON CONDITION** Statement

When a programmer wishes to test for a condition he has defined himself, he uses the **ON CONDITION** statement in the following form:

ON CONDITION (name) action;

The identifier in parentheses refers to a condition name specified by the user, and "action" has the same meaning as in any other previously described **ON** statement. Since the condition is not one of those usually recognized either by PL/I or the underlying operating system, the standard action is simply to print a message and otherwise ignore the condition.

The homemade interrupt condition is precipitated by the **SIGNAL** statement

SIGNAL CONDITION(name);

where (name) has the same meaning as in the **ON CONDITION** statement. The setup and use of a programmer-defined condition can be illustrated by the following: Suppose the programmer wishes to interrupt processing when certain subtraction operations produce results less than zero (a condition he decides to call DEFICIT). This interruption is brought about by the statement

SIGNAL CONDITION(DEFICIT);

By using the **ON CONDITION** statement to test for this interruption and supply the necessary response, it is possible to write a sequence of statements such as

ON CONDITION (DEFICIT) **PUT SKIP LIST**('A DEFICIT.');

.

.

.

IF BALANCE < TAKEOUT **THEN SIGNAL CONDITION**(DEFICIT);

.

.

.

IF CREDIT < CHARGE **THEN SIGNAL CONDITION**(DEFICIT);

Thus, the DEFICIT condition can be raised for a variety of reasons. Each time this interruption occurs, the indicated message will be printed, and processing will resume at the point following the statement causing the interruption.

XVI.2.4.2   Simulation of Standard Interruptions

The **SIGNAL** statement may also be used to induce any specified interruption whenever desired. For example, the statement

SIGNAL ENDFILE (filename);

will suspend processing in exactly the same manner as the detection of the last item on a data file. If a programmer-defined action is specified in an appropriate **ON** statement, it is executed, and control is returned to the statement immediately following the **SIGNAL**. If no such statement is included, the standard system action is taken. This can be used to advantage to test **ON** units for conditions that are not too likely to come up. It is also especially useful to precipitate an **ENDPAGE** condition to produce page headings on the first page of output.

XVI.2.5   Enabling and Disabling Interrupt Conditions

Once a particular action has been defined for a given type of interruption, that action is by no means irrevocable. PL/I provides a number of facilities for defining a new response to an interruption, returning to the standard system action or eliminating the interruption altogether.

As part of the system's preparation for the execution of a program's statements, arrangements are made to activate the **OVERFLOW, UNDERFLOW, FIXEDOVERFLOW, ZERODIVIDE**, and **CONVERSION** conditions automatically. When a situation exists such that an interruption could be precipitated, that interruption occurs, and the supervisory software takes the standard action. If the programmer wants the condition to remain enabled but desires to substitute his own action, he uses an appropriate **ON** statement, as discussed previously. Thus, when that statement appears in the program, its stipulation is in force for all subsequent statements in the program until the appearance of another **ON** statement which countermands it. (This is explored in more detail in Section XVI.2.6.)

The **CHECK, SIZE, SUBSCRIPTRANGE,** and **STRINGRANGE** conditions are *not* enabled automatically at the beginning of each program. Unless the programmer specifically activates these mechanisms, the situations that would cause suspension of processing will go unnoticed since processing will continue unhindered. Subsequent results may be affected, however, depending on the nature of the circumstances. For example, a calculation that would ordinarily raise the **SIZE** condition (if it were activated) could produce a result in which some of the digits are lost due to truncation, and this error would be propagated in subsequent processing without the user's being aware that such truncation had taken place.

PL/I provides no mechanism for implicit activation of an interrupt condition (as it does for the implicit opening of a file with a **READ** statement). The appearance of an **ON SIZE** statement will not enable that condition. In order for such activation to occur, the programmer must specify the type of interruption in a *condition prefix* in the general form of

(condition): label: statement;

where "condition" is the specific keyword used by PL/I to identify the particular interrupt condition. "Statement" represents any legitimate executable statement, which may or may not be labeled. (**CHECK, SIZE, SUBSCRIPTRANGE** and **STRINGRANGE** are exceptions in that they can be attached only to **PROCEDURE** or **BEGIN** statements.) The usual practice is to attach one or more of the condition prefixes to a **PROCEDURE** statement so that the activation of the indicated condition for the duration of that procedure is clearly designated. Thus, the statement

(**SIZE**): FIND: **PROCEDURE**;

will cause the **SIZE** condition to be activated for the duration of the procedure named FIND, with the standard system action being taken whenever such an interruption occurs. Now the programmer can change the response to a **SIZE** interruption by placing an appropriate **ON** statement at that point in the program where he wants the alternative action to begin taking effect. The specification of several condition prefixes is illustrated by the statement

(**SUBSCRIPTRANGE, STRINGRANGE, SIZE**): LOOK: **PROCEDURE**;

It is also possible to use condition prefixes to deactivate interrupt conditions by placing the word **NO** directly in front of the particular conditions named (no intervening blanks). Thus, the statement

(**NOOVERFLOW,SIZE,NOZERODIVIDE**):FIND:**PROCEDURE**;

will activate the **SIZE** condition and deactivate the **OVERFLOW** and **ZERODIVIDE** conditions for the procedure FIND. The only condition names that may appear in a prefix (either as is or with the **NO** preceding them) are **CONVERSION, FIXEDOVERFLOW, OVERFLOW,**

UNDERFLOW, and **ZERODIVIDE**, which are automatically enabled at the beginning of a program, and **SIZE, CHECK, SUBSCRIPTRANGE,** and **STRINGRANGE**, which are automatically disabled at the beginning of each program.

If the **SIZE, SUBSCRIPTRANGE, STRINGRANGE,** or **CHECK** is enabled in a procedure, it may be disabled for a single statement.

XVI.2.6   Scope of an Interrupt Condition

If a particular interrupt condition is enabled at the beginning of a procedure (either explicitly or automatically), the action triggered by that interruption can be changed at various points in the procedure by using a new **ON** statement. Consequently, the scope of each type of action is directly related to the placement of the corresponding **ON** command, as illustrated by the following sequence:

LOOK: **PROCEDURE OPTIONS (MAIN)**;

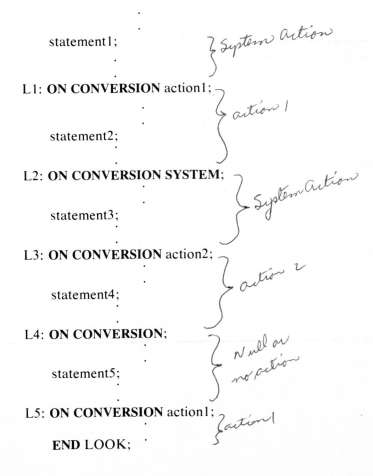

statement1;   } System Action

L1: **ON CONVERSION** action1;   } action 1

statement2;

L2: **ON CONVERSION SYSTEM**;   } System Action

statement3;

L3: **ON CONVERSION** action2;   } action 2

statement4;

L4: **ON CONVERSION**;   } Null or no action

statement5;

L5: **ON CONVERSION** action1;   } action1

END LOOK;

where "action1" and "action2" represent two different responses specified by the programmer. Since the **CONVERSION** condition is enabled automatically at the beginning of the procedure and no programmer action is specified until statement L1, the system action will be taken for any **CONVERSION** condition occurring up to that point. Beyond L1, the system response is replaced by the one specified by "action1". This reaction is in force until statement L2, at which point the programmer has specified that he wants the normal system action to be taken again. At statement L3, the system action is replaced by another programmer designed response, namely, the one specified by "action2." This will prevail until statement L4, at which point the program stipulates a *null* **ON** *statement* (an **ON** statement with no specified response). As a result, no action at all will be taken when the **CONVERSION** condition is raised. Of course, this causes the **ERROR** condition to be raised since **ONSOURCE** or **ONCHAR** has not been changed. At statement L5, the condition is again enabled, with the resulting response being "action1."

If the program consists of several procedures, any special responses specified by means of an **ON** statement apply only to the procedure in which that response was stipulated and any other procedures activated by it. If a procedure specifies a particular action and the programmer wishes a different action to be taken in a contained procedure, he must indicate this accordingly. Thus, in the sequence below,

SEE: **PROCEDURE OPTIONS (MAIN)**;
.
.
.
ON OVERFLOW action1;
.
.
statement1;
CALL INT;
statement2;

　　　　　INT: **PROCEDURE**;
　　　　　　　ON OVERFLOW SYSTEM;
　　　　　　　　.
　　　　　　　　.
　　　　　　　　.
　　　　　　statement3;
　　　　　　　　.
　　　　　　　　.
　　　　　　　　.
　　　　　　END INT;
statement4;
END SEE;

omission of the **ON OVERFLOW SYSTEM** statement in the internal procedure INT would mean that "action1" will be taken whenever the **OVERFLOW** condition is raised anywhere in the program.

The **REVERT** statement can be used as a convenient means for changing the response to a particular type of interruption in the middle of an invoked procedure. Its general form is

   REVERT condition;

where "condition" represents the name of a particular type of interruption whose action is to be changed. When used in an invoked procedure, the **REVERT** statement will nullify the most recent action specified for that interruption in that procedure and implement the one designated in the calling procedure. As an example, let us rewrite the instructions above with the inclusion of a **REVERT** statement:

SEE: **PROCEDURE OPTIONS (MAIN)**;

    .
    .
    .

    ON OVERFLOW action1;

    statement1;

    CALL INT;

    statement2;

        INT: **PROCEDURE**;

           ON OVERFLOW SYSTEM;

               .
               .
               .

} System action

           statement3;

           REVERT OVERFLOW;

           statement4;

               .
               .

} action1

           END INT;

    statement5;

    END SEE;

As a result, an **OVERFLOW** condition in the internal procedure INT will cause the standard system action to be taken if that interruption occurs anywhere in the procedure from the entry point through statement3. When the condition is raised in a statement beyond that point, the response is replaced by the one specified in the calling procedure, that is, the execution of "action1." The **REVERT** statement will work the same way in a **BEGIN** block or when the invoked procedure is an external one.

XVI.2.7   Scope of Condition Prefixes

Although they appear to repeat the function of the null **ON** statement, the specific nature of condition prefixes makes them very useful for a variety of additional situations. These expanded interruption-handling possibilities can be effectively described by stating the rules regarding their scope.

If a condition prefix is attached to a **PROCEDURE** or **BEGIN** statement, that condition is enabled (or disabled, if **NO** is attached to it) for the entire block, including all blocks internal to it. Condition prefixes may be respecified for internal blocks without affecting the situation in the calling procedure. In the following, the **SIZE** condition is enabled throughout all of EXT except for INT1:

```
(SIZE): EXT: PROCEDURE OPTIONS (MAIN);
            statement1;              } system action
                .
                .
            statement2;
        L1: ON SIZE action1;         } action'
                .
                .
            statement3;
            CALL INT1;
            statement4;
        (NOSIZE): INT1: PROCEDURE;   } nosize
                    .
                    .
                    END INT1;
            INT2: PROCEDURE;
                    .
                    .                 } action'
                    END INT2;
            statement5;
            CALL INT2;
                .
                .
            statement6;
            END EXT;
```

For all statements through statement2, a **SIZE** interruption will produce the standard system action. From statement L1 through statement3, the programmer-specified "action1" replaces that of the system. When INT1 is called, **SIZE** is suspended while that procedure is in control. After its conclusion, **SIZE** is once again enabled, with the response specified in L1, for the remainder of EXT (including INT2).

Separate specifications must be made for external procedures, even when they are called by a procedure in which the primary entry point is prefixed.

The following also is valid:

MAIN: **PROCEDURE OPTIONS(MAIN)**;

    ON SIZE BEGIN; .....**END**;

    .
    .
    .

    CALL F1;

    .
    .
    .

    CALL F2;

    .
    .
    .

(**SIZE**): F1: **PROCEDURE**;....**END**;

(**SIZE**): F2: **PROCEDURE**;....**END**;

    END;

This brings out the difference between specifying the action to take and enabling the condition.

The **CHECK** condition may be specified in a **PROCEDURE** or **BEGIN** statement, together with a list of identifiers, namely,

(**SIZE, CHECK**(A,B,C)):LOOK:**PROCEDURE**;

When this is done, the enumerated variables will be checked over the same scope described before, unless a particular variable is separately declared in an internal procedure. In that case, a separate **CHECK** prefix must be attached. Thus, the variables A and B, declared separately in the procedure INT1 of (a) below will not be included in the checking procedure, while those in (b) will.

(a)

(CHECK(A,B,C)): EXT: **PROCEDURE OPTIONS (MAIN);**
                   DECLARE (A,B,C) **FIXED**(4,1);

                                    .
                                    .

                   CALL INT1;
                          INT1: **PROCEDURE;**
                                    DECLARE (A,B) **FIXED**(4,1);
                                    .
                                    .
                                 END INT1;
                   END EXT;

(b)

(CHECK(A,B,C)): EXT: **PROCEDURE OPTIONS (MAIN);**
                   DECLARE (A,B,C) **FIXED**(4,1);

                                    .
                                    .
                                    .

                   CALL INT1;
                   (CHECK(A,B)): INT1: **PROCEDURE;**
                                       DECLARE(A,B))
                                          FIXED(4,1);

                                       .
                                       .

                                 END INT1;

                                    .
                                    .
                                    .

                   END EXT;

When a prefix is attached to an **ON** or **IF** statement, its scope does not include any statements or groups of statements attached to the basic command. Thus, if we want the overflow condition to be suppressed for the entire statement

IF X $>$ 2*Y*Z/(Y +4*Z) **THEN** W = 3*X**2;

ELSE W=1.1*X**1.5;

we have to write

(NOOVERFLOW): IF X $>$ 2*Y*Z/(Y +4*Z) **THEN (NOOVERFLOW)** :W=3*X**2;

ELSE **(NOOVERFLOW)** :W=1.1*X**1.5;

If a prefix is attached to an **IF** or **ON** statement and that statement calls a procedure, the scope of the prefix does not carry over to that procedure, as it would in the case of the **ON** statement. In a statement such as

IF C = A*B **THEN (NOOVERFLOW): CALL** INT:

the **OVERFLOW** condition will not be affected in the internal procedure INT, unless that prefix is also attached to INT's **PROCEDURE** statement.

The attachment of a particular condition prefix to any other type of statement enables or disables that condition for that statement only. (For example, the prefix attatched to a **DO** statement will hold for that statement and not for the group it initiates.) Thus, the programmer can implement or nullify a particular test for a single assignment statement without affecting any of the preceding or subsequent instructions.

PROBLEMS

1. Modify the program in Illustration 44 so that it prints the message "NONEXISTENT DRUG CODE", along with the offending code, for each input card containing a code that does not have a match in the file TRANS.

2. Modify the program in Illustration 45 (or the expanded version in problem 1 of Chapter XV) so that it detects and bypasses all input cards in which (accidentally) nonnumeric information appears in those places intended for numeric values. For each such card, the program is to print the message "BAD INPUT DATA", along with the erroneous values. At the end of the run, the program is to print the total number of cards processed, along with the number of cards which could not be processed due to erroneous data.

SUMMARY OF IMPORTANT TERMS

CHECK   A condition that may be enabled in conjunction with selected variables, thereby setting up a mechanism that automatically displays those variables when their values change.

CONDITION   The mechanism for setting up the criteria for an arbitrarily
                        defined condition that can then be raised like any other condi-
                        tion.

Condition prefix   The specification of a condition name (attached to some other
                        statement) in order to enable that condition (if it is disabled) or
                        vice versa.

Disable   The explicit deactivation of a specified condition (by means of
                        an appropriate condition prefix) so that, by definition, the
                        condition cannot be raised.

Enable   The activation of a condition so that violation of its associated
                        criteria will raise the condition and force some type of action
                        in response. (Some conditions are enabled initially; others
                        require explicit activation.)

ERROR   A general condition raised by the system after its response to
                        one of a variety of interrupt types (for example, **OVER-
                        FLOW, ZERODIVIDE**).

FINISH   A general condition raised by the system prior to its intended
                        termination of a program.

Interrupt   An intrinsic system mechanism that automatically curtails
                        "normal" processing under certain circumstances (for exam-
                        ple, reference to a nonexistent address) and instigates a pre-
                        scribed action in response. In PL/I's context, the occurrence
                        of a given type of interrupt raises a particular condition.

ON   The statement type used to associate the occurrence of a
                        given condition with an accompanying programmer-defined
                        action.

ON unit   An organizational component within a procedure, consisting
                        of an **ON** statement followed by an arbitrary sequence of
                        statements that define the action to be performed when the
                        designated condition is raised.

REVERT   The statement type that changes the action precipitated by a
                        designated condition to an alternative action specified previ-
                        ously.

SIGNAL   The statement type used to simulate the occurrence of a
                        designated condition so that its associated action can be
                        forced.

Trace   A systematic display of variable values, destinations of con-
                        trol transfers, procedure invocations, and so on, thereby de-
                        picting the progress of a program's execution.

SUPPLEMENTARY READING

Bell, C. G., and Newell, A., *Computer Structures*. New York: McGraw-Hill, 1971, pp. 82-83.
PL/I Language Reference Manual, IBM Document No. GC28-8201. White Plains, N.Y.: IBM Cor-
    poration, pp. 171-175, 308-320.
PL/I Programmer's Guide, IBM Document No. GC28-6594. White Plains, N.Y.: pp. 281-285.

XVII CONTROL OF STORAGE

Although PL/I in its full form requires a computing system with substantial storage capacity, the problems imposed by insufficient storage cannot be ignored, even on large systems. In fact, considerable effort and resources have been invested in developing hardware and software components to support "virtual storage," an organizational structure that allows the user to operate as if he had practically unlimited storage available. (Some fundamental material is cited at the end of the chapter.) Thus, it is not surprising that PL/I pays some serious attention to the conservation of storage. We have had occasion (in a limited context) to concern ourselves with such economy by making use of the **BEGIN** block to reserve storage for an array of unanticipated size (Section VI.5.2). Such *dynamic allocation* allowed us to tie up only that amount of storage required for a particular situation. This is but one aspect of a generalized facility for appropriating and releasing arbitrarily sized quantities of storage. We have made limited use of another form of storage management when we used based variables to refer to input or output buffers in conjunction with the **SET** option, as seen in Chapter XV.

These capabilities are but the top layer of a powerful language resource that gives the

pg460

programmer the means for controlling the use of storage. Instructions are provided for reserving storage as it is needed, giving it up immediately after it has served its purpose, so that it may be reassigned to some other use. Stemming from this capability is an entire repertoire of commands and techniques for list processing, an area of rapidly increasing importance in computer science and its applications.

XVII.1   BASED VARIABLES

The use of based variables (and their associated pointers) for processing input data within the buffer is one specific application of a very general facility that provides the programmer with convenient and powerful ways to manage storage. By examining the features related to based variables, we shall acquaint ourselves with techniques for applying the same name to several locations and for producing results equivalent to the internal movement of data without moving the data.

XVII.1.1   Declaration of Based Variables

Whenever storage is allocated for a based variable, the location of such storage (which is likely to differ from that used for the previous allocation) must be indicated by setting a corresponding pointer. For file-handling purposes, there was no need for further concern with pointers. In the list-processing context, however, the contents of pointer variables and the methods for manipulating them become more important and must be considered in greater detail.

A based variable is declared with the **BASED** attribute, with the addition of a pointer designation:

DECLARE name att1, att2, etc., **BASED** (pointer);*

*The Optimizing and Checkout Compilers permit this pointer designation to be omitted. In this case, all references must explicitly mention a pointer.

att1, att2, etc. represent a combination of data attributes to be included in the declaration, and (pointer) represents the name of a variable whose contents are to indicate the location of the variable specified in "name". Based on its usage in such a declaration, PL/I will automatically assign the **POINTER** attribute to the pointer name. This is recognized as a separate and distinct type of variable in PL/I, and the attribute may appear in a legitimate declaration. For example, the statement

DECLARE (A,B,C)**POINTER**;

will reserve storage under the names A, B, and C, with the implication that these variables will be used to point to the location of other variables. Note that this declaration provides no information regarding which variables will be pointed to by A, B, and C. These variables are "free agents" that have not been associated with particular based variables. We shall see that such associations can be made as the programmer sees fit. A pointer can be declared in conjunction with several based variables.

VIII.1.2   Allocation of Based Variables

When storage is dynamically allocated for a based variable, it is necessary to select a location for that variable and to place that location in an appropriate pointer. This is accomplished by the **ALLOCATE** statement, which takes the form:

ALLOCATE name **SET** (pointer);

Several variables may be allocated in a single statement, and the **SET** option is not necessary unless some pointer is to be used other than the one declared with the variables. Accordingly,

implied

DECLARE A FIXED(3) BASED(P), B FLOAT BASED(P), (ARROW,P) **POINTER**:

ALLOCATE A, B **SET** (ARROW);

is perfectly legitimate. Storage is allocated for A and a reference to it is established automatically by placing A's address in pointer variable P. Since P is associated with A in the declaration, the action can be implied. Explicit association of pointer ARROW with variable B causes the location of the newly allocated storage to be placed in ARROW rather than in P. If the **SET** option were omitted in this example, P would contain only the location of the storage allocated for B at the completion of the statement. Thus, the location of A would be lost forever.

The based variable appearing in an **ALLOCATE** statement may be an element variable, an entire array, or a major structure. If the last is the case, only the major structure name is given. An element of the structure may not be used.

XVII.1.2.1   Multiple Allocations of Based Variables

When successive **ALLOCATE** statements are used to appropriate storage for the same based variable, duplicate storage is actually reserved and the previous value (or values) is (are) retained. Because of the use of pointers, however, all of the previously allocated values can be made available at one time. This is possible because the pointer variable specified in the **SET** option of the **ALLOCATE** statement need not be the same one declared with the based variable. Thus, as a result of the sequence

DECLARE B FIXED(4) BASED (ARROW1), (ARROW2,ARROW3) **POINTER**:

L1: **ALLOCATE** B **SET** (ARROW2);

L2: **ALLOCATE** B **SET** (ARROW1);

L3: **ALLOCATE** B **SET** (ARROW3);

there will be three areas of storage reserved. The location of the one reserved earliest in the program (allocated by statement L1) is contained in ARROW2. Similarly, ARROW1 and ARROW3 contain the locations of the other allocations. In subsequent sections we shall see that there is actually a way of answering a question such as "which B do you mean?" by symbolically replying, "I mean the B pointed to ARROW3."

XVII.1.2.2   Allocation of Based Arrays

Arrays may be dynamically allocated in normal fashion. Thus, if we say

DECLARE X(20) **FIXED**(3) **BASED**(P1);...**ALLOCATE** X;

a 20-element array of three-digit fixed-point integers is duly allocated, with P1 pointing to it. The dimension bounds of a **BASED** array must be constants.

Three built-in functions are available to help the programmer monitor such dynamically allocated arrays:

1. The **DIM** function returns the value of a specified dimension for an array X. For example, if M = 3 and N = 5 for a particular allocation, then the statement

    BIG = **DIM**(X,2);

    will place a value of 5 in Y.

2. The **HBOUND** functions return the value of the upper bound of a given dimension. For instance, if X is defined by the statement

    DECLARE X(M1:M2,N1:N2).....;

    and the array is allocated at a subsequent point, the statement

    HIGHER = **HBOUND**(X,1);

    will place the current value of M2 in HIGHER.

3. Similarly, **LBOUND** returns the lower bound of a specified dimension. Thus, for the previous example,

    LOWER = **LBOUND**(X,2);

    would place the current value of N1 in LOWER.

Several situations can produce errors when these functions are used. The most common ones occur when the particular array is not allocated or when the dimension number given in the second argument is higher than the highest dimension of the array as currently allocated.

XVII.1.2.3 Allocating Based Structures

When a structure is declared as **BASED**, it may be allocated any number of times, as is the case with an array or single valued variable. A single statement, with reference to the major structure name, allocates the entire structure. Thus, if T is declared by the statement

DECLARE 1 T **BASED** (T1),

   (2 S1, 2 S2) **FIXED**(4),

   2 G, (3 G1, 3 G2) **CHARACTER**(6),

a statement like

ALLOCATE T;

is all that is required for a complete allocation of T. Once allocated, each component (or the entire structure) may be accessed through a reference to T.

XVII.1.2.4 The **REFER** Option

The based structure may be given additional flexibility in dynamic allocation by providing a component that contains *self-defining data*. To help understand this, recall the fact (Chapter XIV) that variable-length records are organized so that each record includes an explicit piece of information that specifies its length. That is an example of self-defining data. In the same sense, it is possible to define a based structure containing an array, such that the size of the array is not known until that structure is allocated. Furthermore, the size is obtained from outside the structure and made available to another element of the same allocation of that structure. Thus, once the structure is allocated, it carries the size of its own array.

This is implemented through the **REFER** option, using the following general form:

DECLARE 1 structure **BASED** (pointer),

   2 inside **FIXED BINARY**,

   2 array (outside **REFER** (inside));

where "structure" is the name of the based structure being declared; "array" is an array contained in that structure; "outside" is the name of an appropriately declared variable outside of the structure from which the size of the array will be obtained when the structure is allocated; and "inside" is a variable contained in "structure." Each time "structure" is allocated, the current value stored in "outside" will be duplicated in "inside," from whence it will be used to set the size of "array."

For example, suppose we had the following sequence:

> .
> .
> .

    DECLARE 1 XR **BASED** (PX),

        2 NA **FIXED BINARY**,

        2 W, 2 V **FIXED** (4),

        2 A (B **REFER**(NA)) **CHARACTER**(5),

    B **FIXED BINARY**;

> .
> .
> .

    B = 17;

> .
> .
> .

  L1: **ALLOCATE** XR SET (PX);

> .
> .
> .

When statement L1 is executed, structure XR will be allocated, its storage consisting of fixed-point binary variable NA (containing a value of 17 transmitted to it from B), a floating-point variable W, a four-digit fixed-point integer V, and a 17-element array A of five-character strings.

This option can be used only within the following restrictions:

1. It may appear only once in a structure.
2. It can be used only to specify the upper bound of the leading dimension of an array or the length of a string. Thus the declaration

    DECLARE 1 XR **BASED** (PX),

      2 NA **FIXED BINARY**,

      2 Y (1:B **REFER**(NA), 3:10),

    B **FIXED BINARY**;

is valid: When XR is allocated, the allocated storage will include room for an array Y consisting of eight columns (numbered 3-10) and some number of rows (that value having been passed from B to the newly allocated NA). However, the declaration

DECLARE 1 XR **BASED**(PX),
    2 NA **FIXED BINARY**,
    2 Y (4, 1:B **REFER**(NA)),
  B **FIXED BINARY**;

would be illegal.

3.   This option may be used only with the final element in the structure declaration or in the minor structure containing the final element.

4.   Neither "outside" nor "inside" can be subscripted; however, "outside" may be qualified or based.

In addition to these restrictions, early versions of the IBM-F compiler required that both "outside" and "inside" be **FIXED BINARY** variables with default precision (15,0). Later versions of the F compiler have relaxed this rule to allow any precision capable of containing the values to be used, as long as both "outside" and "inside" have the same precision. The Optimizing and Checkout Compilers are still more liberal: "inside" may have any attributes (of course, conversion to and from integer must be possible); "outside" may be any expression that can be converted to an integer as long as it does not depend on any variable within the structure containing the **REFER** option; finally, rules 1-4 above have also been relaxed considerably—in particular, several uses of the **REFER** option can occur in the same structure subject to additional rules too complicated to explain here. The student is referred to the appropriate manual (see references at the end of this chapter) for details.

XVII.1.3 Pointer Qualifiers

The ability to manipulate based variables and pointers in PL/I is extended by means of a special mechanism known as a *pointer qualifier*. This feature allows the programmer to distinguish among based variables reserved during several allocations by referring to them through their respective pointers. The symbol used for this mechanism consists of a minus sign followed immediately by a "greater than" sign: $->$. Thus, if Y is a based variable and ARROW a pointer variable, the term

ARROW $->$ Y

can be read as "the value of Y pointed to by ARROW" or "ARROW pointing at Y." As a simple example, let us examine the sequence

DECLARE BASIS **FIXED**(3) **BASED** (BEAM),*

(NEON,ARGON,ZENON) POINTER;

L1: **ALLOCATE** BASIS **SET**(ARGON);

L2: **ALLOCATE** BASIS **SET**(XENON);

L3: **ALLOCATE** BASIS **SET**(BEAM);

L4: **ALLOCATE** BASIS **SET**(NEON);

Don't understood NEW −> BASIS, BASIS = 8;

ARGON −> BASIS = BASIS + 2;

XENON −> BASIS = ARGON −> BASIS + 2;

*Based variables may not have the **INITIAL** attribute except in the Optimizing and Checkout Compilers. Here it takes effect only upon execution of an **ALLOCATE** statement or a **LOCATE** statement.

Based on this sequence, a reference to ARGON −> BASIS designates the variable allocated in statement L1. Consequently, the instruction

PUT LIST (ARGON −>BASIS);

will produce a value of 10. By the same token, the statement

PUT LIST (XENON−>BASIS, BASIS);

will produce adjacent values of 12 and 8, respectively. Taking this a step further, we can write the sequence

NEON−>BASIS = 27 + 2 * BASIS;

PUT LIST (NEON−>BASIS);

which will result in a value of 43 being printed.

XVII.1.4   Basic Properties of Pointer Variables

In previous sections we have seen that PL/I recognizes a pointer as a separate type of variable with its own attributes and properties. For purposes of review and consolidation, we shall restate the explicit and contextual conditions under which the **POINTER** attribute is assigned to a variable name:

Summary: Basic Properties of Pointer Variables

1. By specific use of a **DECLARE** statement with the **POINTER** attribute.
2. By the appearance of the pointer's name in parentheses immediately following a **BASED** specification in a **DECLARE** statement.
3. By appearing in parentheses immediately following the **SET** option in an **ALLOCATE**, **READ**, or **LOCATE** statement.
4. By appearing as a pointer qualifier.

XVII.1.4.1 Declaration of Pointers

As seen before, pointers may be declared with or without other types of variables in an ordinary **DECLARE** statement. For example,

DECLARE X,Y, (P1,P2(6)) **POINTER** N(8);

defines P1 as a pointer, P2 as a one-dimensional array of six pointers, X and Y as floating-point variables and N as an array of eight fixed binary elements.

When explicitly declared as such, pointer variables may be assigned any of the storage class attributes (**STATIC/AUTOMATIC/BASED/CONTROLLED**) and/or the scope attributes (**INTERNAL/EXTERNAL**). However, such variables cannot participate in most manipulative operations. There is no conversion mechanism from pointer to any other type of variable (Except **OFFSET**.) or vice versa, and such variables may not appear in most types of expressions. The contents of two pointer variables may be tested on equality or inequality, but no other type of comparison can be made. Such variables may not be transmitted to or from the processer in stream-oriented mode but can be used as arguments when invoking procedures. Note that there are no "constants" to which pointers may be set in the same sense that some numerical variable X can be set to a value of, say 17. The information in a pointer is construed, by definition, to be an address or location, and the assignment of actual addresses is out of the programmer's reach.

XVII.1.4.2 Assignment of Values To Pointer Variables

The establishment of pointer values by means of the basic mechanism activated by the **SET** option is supplemented by three additional features that provide somewhat more extensive programmer control.

The most straightforward of these is a simple assignment statement whereby the contents of one pointer variable may be duplicated in another, thus creating two pointers that point to the same location. Thus, if we write the sequence

DECLARE B **CHARACTER**(7) **BASED**(ARROW1) (ARROW2,ARROW3) **POINTER**;

ALLOCATE B; ARROW2, ARROW3 = ARROW1;

we will produce a situation in which all three pointers indicate the location of B.

XVII.1.4.3   The **ADDR** Function

PL/I provides a built-in function for the specific purpose of creating pointer values. The address function, as it is known, uses the key word **ADDR.** When used with a single keyword in a statement such as

T = **ADDR**(B);

the *location* (not the value) of B is placed in location T, where T has been declared (explicitly or implicitly) as a pointer variable. Thus, T has been made to point to variable B.

XVII.1.4.4   The **NULL** Built-in Function

In constructing lists, we shall see that it is useful to have a special pointer value that points nowhere. PL/I provides such a value through a special built-in function named **NULL.** Its actual composition is of no direct concern to the programmer and may vary from compiler to compiler. If ARROW is a pointer variable, the simple statement

ARROW = **NULL**;

is sufficient to place that special value in location ARROW. In effect, we are saying that ARROW points to nothing. **NULL** does have a unique value that can be tested, making it perfectly legitimate to have such a statement as

IF ARROW = **NULL THEN GO TO** NOMORE;

Illustration 51

We shall exemplify the use of based variables by developing a procedure that reads and processes sets of input cards as follows: In each set, an initial card specifies NC, the number of data cards in that set; then, there are NC more cards to that set. Each data card consists of a string of nonblank characters starting in column 1 and ending somewhere or other, but never beyond column 72. The rightmost columns (however many) are all blank. For each set, the program is to print the character strings one per line in order of length, with the longest string appearing first. NC is in columns 1-2 and no two strings in any set will have the same length.

The program will be implemented by reading NC and using its value to allocate the required number of items for that input set. Each item will be allocated as a based structure (CARD) consisting of 72-character string (STR) and a numeric variable (L). Correspondingly, an array of pointers (PT) will be allocated to go with CARD. A separate procedure named **FIND** will be used to determine the string's length by starting at its right end and looking to the left until it encounters a nonblank. The resulting length will be stored in L. Once all the lengths are known, the strings will be rearranged by shifting the values in their respective pointers. The program is shown below. Note that the roundabout way of assigning pointers stems from the fact that a member of a pointer array cannot be used as a pointer qualifier; its value must be assigned to an unsubscripted pointer which, in turn, is used as a qualifier:

```
ILL51: PROCEDURE OPTIONS (MAIN);
        DECLARE (NSETS INITIAL(0), NC, I, J, K) FIXED BINARY,
                (NOSE, N1) POINTER,
                1 CARD BASED (NOSE),
                  2 STR CHARACTER (72),
                  2 L FIXED BINARY;

        ON ENDFILE (SYSIN) STOP;

        DO WHILE ('1'B);
          GET EDIT(NC) (COLUMN(1),F(2));
          BEGIN;
              DECLARE (PS,PT(NC)) POINTER;
              NSETS = NSETS+1;      PUT SKIP (2) DATA (NSETS);
              DO I = 1 TO NC;
                ALLOCATE CARD;    PT(I) = NOSE;    PS = PT(I);
                GET EDIT (STR)(COLUMN(1),A(72));
                PUT SKIP EDIT (STR)(X(5),A(72));
                DO J = 72 TO 1 BY -1 WHILE (SUBSTR(STR,J,1) = ' ');
                  L = J-1;         /*---L WILL BE LENGTH OF NON-BLANK STRING--*/
                END;
              END;
              DO I= 1 TO NC-1;       /*--SORT THE STRINGS IN ORDER OF--*/
                NOSE = PT(I);        /*--INCREASING LENGTH BY          --*/
                DO K = I+1 TO NC;    /*--REARRANGING THE POINTERS.     --*/
                  N1 = PT(K);
                  IF N1 -> L > L
                     THEN DO;
                             PT(K) = NOSE;     NOSE = N1;
                          END;
                END;
                PT(I) = NOSE;
              END;
              PUT SKIP;
              DO I=1 TO NC;
                NOSE = PT(I);
                PUT SKIP EDIT (STR,L)(X(5),A,COLUMN(80),F(2));
              END;
          END;
        END;

        END ILL51;
```

XVII.1.4.5   Use of Based Variables to Describe Other Variables

A fundamental property of a based variable is that a reference to it does not cause a direct access to the contents of a particular location. Instead, that reference causes the program to consult the associated pointer, from which the location to be reference is determined.

Since a pointer value can be set independently, even when that pointer is associated with a based variable, it is possible to use a single based variable to refer to one of several other variables that need not be based. The following example illustrates this:

```
DECLARE (A STATIC, B, C INITIAL(18),
     ROCK BASED (ARROW))FIXED(4);
     A = 12; B = 20;


ALLOCATE ROCK; ROCK = 6;


L1: PUT SKIP LIST(ROCK); ARROW = ADDR(A);
                6


L2: PUT SKIP LIST(ROCK); ARROW = ADDR(C);
              12


L3: PUT SKIP LIST(ROCK); ARROW = ADDR(B);
                18


L4: PUT SKIP LIST(ROCK);
                20
```

Since the pointer ARROW is initially associated with the based variable ROCK, allocation of that variable automatically sets ARROW at its address. Consequently, the statement labeled L1 will print a value of 6. Following that, however, the contents of the pointer are changed so that it now points to the location of variable A. Since it is still associated with the based variable ROCK, a reference to that variable will still cause the program to check ARROW, which, in turn, indicates the location of A. A statement to print the contents of the based variable (statement L2) is, in essence, an instruction to print the contents of the variable currently pointed to by ROCK's pointer, A. By the same token, statements L3 and L4 will print the current values of C and B, respectively, because the contents of ARROW have been altered prior to each output statement. Thus, the resulting printout will show

6

12

18

20

XVII.1.5   The **AREA** Attribute

A limited amount of control may be exercised over the placement of variables in storage with respect to one another by reserving a unified section of storage and assigning the desired variables to that section. Such a region of storage is known as an *area* and is designated by a declaration of the form

DECLARE name **AREA**;

where "name" is a legitimate PL/I identifier subject to the usual rules. As a result of such a declaration, PL/I will assign a section of storage to that name and keep track of the amount consumed by subsequent assignments. The size of the area thus reserved is a default activity that can vary for each version of the compiler. (A typical default is 1000 bytes.)

The programmer may override the default by specifying a length (in bytes) as part of the declaration:

DECLARE name **AREA**(size);

where "size" may be a constant or an expression. The limit on "size" also varies with the type of compiler. The IBM PL/I-F compiler accepts areas up to 32768 bytes, whereas the IBM PL/I Optimizing Compiler allows a whopping 16,777,216.

A group of areas can be organized into an array, and an area can be declared as part of a structure. Such a variable may not be assigned any other attributes except for **STATIC/AUTOMATIC, BASED/CONTROLLED**, and/or **EXTERNAL/INTERNAL**.

XVII.1.5.1   Allocation of Areas

If an area is based, its declaration does not make storage available for it; an explicit **ALLOCATE** statement is required. Thus, if we say

DECLARE A1 **AREA BASED** (P1), A2 **AREA**(2000) **BASED**(P2), (Q1,Q2) **POINTER**;

> .
> .
> .

ALLOCATE A2, A1, A2 **SET** (Q2);

a 2000-byte section of storage will be allocated for A2 and its address stored in P2, and a 1000-byte area will be allocated for A1 (by default) and P1 set to its address. Then, a second 2000-byte area is allocated for A2, with its address placed in Q2. Consequently, the first allocation of A2 can be accessed by a reference to P2 $->$ A2, and the second allocation is reached by Q2 $->$ A2.

XVII.1.5.2   Allocation of Storage in Areas

Once an area is allocated, variables may be allocated in that area by using the form

ALLOCATE name **IN** (area) **SET** (pointer);

or

ALLOCATE name **SET** (pointer) **IN** (area);

Any number of allocations may be made in a given area (as long as there is room). Moreover, it is possible to make several allocations of the same variable in a given area. For example,

DECLARE A1 **AREA** (2000) **BASED** (P1),

   B1 **FIXED**(2) **BASED** (Q1),

   B2 **BASED** (Q2), R1 **POINTER**;

   .
   .
   .

ALLOCATE A1;

ALLOCATE B1 **IN** (A1) **SET** (Q1);

ALLOCATE B2 **IN** (A1);

ALLOCATE B1 **IN** (A1) **SET** (R1);

   .
   .
   .

will result in area A1 having three identifiable occupants: B2, Q1−>B1 and R1−>B1.

XVII.1.5.3   The **AREA** Condition

As part of the activity supporting areas and allocations within them, the program will update its information concerning the amount of available storage in that area. If a particular allocation requires more storage than is available in the designated area, processing is suspended. This interrupt is known as the **AREA** condition and can be tested for with an appropriate **ON** statement. The standard system action is to print a message and raise the **ERROR** condition.

XVII.1.5.4   Offset Variables

When working with a based variable in a based area (The Optimizing and Checkout Compilers allow offsets to refer to nonbased areas as well.) it is often useful to know the location of that variable with respect to the beginning of the area. Since the pointer associated with an area locates the beginning of the area, it cannot be used for other components. Instead, PL/I provides the *offset variable*, which must be explicitly declared along with the area. The basic form is

DECLARE name1 **OFFSET**(name2);

where name1 is the name of the offset variable and name2 is the name of the area for which it is to be used. This declaration is more commonly included as part of the area declaration:

DECLARE name2 **AREA BASED**(pointer), name1 **OFFSET**(name2);

Although an **OFFSET** variable is very much like a pointer in that its contents locate a particular item of information, it cannot be handled in quite the same way. Specifically, the only way such a variable can receive a value is by means of an assignment statement (it cannot be used with the **SET** option). (The Optimizing and Checkout Compilers allow offsets in the **SET** option of an **ALLOCATE** statement.) For example, let us look at the sequence

DECLARE ROOM **AREA** (100) **BASED**(P1),

    PUSH **OFFSET** (ROOM), V1 **BASED**(Q1), V2 **BASED**(Q2),VAR **BASED**(R);

ALLOCATE ROOM; **ALLOCATE** V1 **IN** (ROOM); **ALLOCATE** V2 **IN** (ROOM);

ALLOCATE VAR **IN** (ROOM);

PUSH = R;

These statements will produce the following results:

1. 100 bytes of storage are reserved under the name ROOM, with P1 locating the beginning of that area.
2. V1, a **FLOAT DECIMAL** variable with default precision, is allocated in ROOM; its address is placed in Q1.
3. A second **FLOAT DECIMAL** variable, V2, is allocated within the boundaries of ROOM, with its address stored in Q2.
4. VAR (also having the attributes **FLOAT DECIMAL**) is allocated in ROOM, its pointer being R.
5. The final assignment converts R (which gives the actual location of VAR) to a *relative address* that indicates the location of VAR in terms of its distance from the beginning of ROOM. Thus, if ROOM starts at location 4580 and the storage allocated for VAR begins with location 4588, P1 will contain 4580, R will contain 4588, and PUSH will contain 8.

These relationships are shown in Figure 17.1.

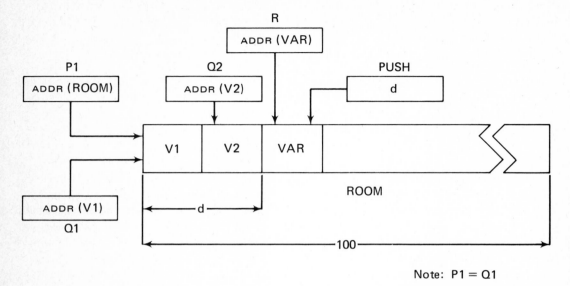

Figure 17.1

The offset variable differs from the pointer in another respect: If the contents of a based area undergo some manipulation (such as input or output), its pointers have to be reset to provide proper location indicators. Since an offset variable points to a relative location, such adjustment is not necessary.

Values for offset variables may be assigned only from pointers or other offset variables. Offset values may be compared with other such values (as in an **IF** statement), but the usable relational operators are restricted to = and ¬=. Offsets cannot be used as qualifiers. (Except in the Optimizing and Checkout Compilers. For the Optimizing and Checkout Compilers **NULLO** does not exist and **NULL** is used instead. A **NULL** offset converts to a null pointer, and vice versa.)

XVII.1.5.5   The **NULLO** Built-in Function

Even though an offset variable can be assigned a value from a pointer variable, proper conversion will not take place if the pointer value happens to be **NULL**. To place a null value in an offset variable the special function **NULLO** must be used:

off = **NULLO**;

It is usually good practice to avert this situation by preceding each offset variable assignment statement with a test for the null value. For example, if POINT is a pointer variable and OFF an offset variable we would write

IF POINT = **NULL THEN** OFF = **NULLO;**

ELSE OFF = POINT;

XVII.1.5.6 Other Properties of Areas

Contents of areas may be assigned to other areas, with the result that items allocated in the source area will be duplicated in the destination area in the same relative positions. This can be very useful in situations where successive allocations within a given area have exceeded their capacity. The action specified by the programmer in conjunction with an **ON AREA** statement can move the information to another area (by changing the address in the associated pointer).

Areas can serve as sources or destinations for file records. Thus, it is possible to read or write an entire group of based variables by referring to the area in which they are allocated. However, in doing so, the programmer must be aware of the area's length. Specifically, when an area of a certain *size* is allocated, that specifies (or implies) the number of bytes available for allocated items. The actual amount of storage allocated (the *length* of the area) includes an additional 16 bytes used by the system to keep track of the number of bytes allocated within the area at any given time. (This is called the *extent* of the area.) Thus, when an area is written from or read into as part of a file, the record length must include those 16 bytes.

Areas may be specified as parameters and arguments in procedures. Similarly, the items returned by a procedure may include an area.

XVII.1.6 Freeing Based Variables

The ability to provide a specified amount of storage exactly when it is needed is complemented by equally convenient means to dispose of it. This is handled by the **FREE** statement, whose basic form is

FREE based_variable;

As a result, the indicated storage is no longer available to the program in that context. It is returned to a collection of "uncommitted" storage that is potentially available for subsequent allocation. For example, suppose that we have the following sequence:

DECLARE 1 A **BASED**(P),

   2 A1 **FIXED** (3),

   2 A2 **CHARACTER** (4);

     .
     .
     .

ALLOCATE A; **GET LIST**(A);

     .
     .
     .

FREE A;

The effect is sufficiently straightforward in that A is available and may be used like any other variable until it is freed.

Several based variables may be freed with a single **FREE** statement. Thus, if variables X, B, and W were allocated earlier, the statement

FREE X,B,W;

will free them all.

XVII1.6.1   Freeing Amidst Multiple Allocations

Since a based variable can be allocated several times, it is consistent for the **FREE** statement to be used several times to get rid of as many of the allocations as is desired. As with any reference to a based variable, it is possible to pinpoint the particular allocation to be freed by using a pointer qualifier. To illustrate, let us consider the statements

DECLARE V **BASED** (P1),

   (P2,P3,P4) **POINTER**;

     .
     .
     .

ALLOCATE V;

     .
     .
     . *(continued next page)*

.
.
.

ALLOCATE V SET (P3);

FREE V;

ALLOCATE V SET (P2);

FREE P3 – >V, P2 – >V;

.
.
.

The first allocation of V sets P1 by implication (since it is the pointer associated with V in its declaration). Correspondingly, the first **FREE** statement releases P1 – >V in the absence of a pointer qualifier. Subsequent allocations and releases are self-explanatory. Note, however, that the programmer must make sure that only allocated variables are freed. Releasing an unallocated variable produces unpredictable results, the only sure thing being that they will be erroneous.

XVII.1.6.2   Freeing Parts of Areas

Based variables allocated in areas may be released with the following form of the **FREE** statement:

FREE variable **IN** (area);

or

FREE pointer – >variable **IN** (area);

Several releases can be specified in a single **FREE** statement. For instance,

FREE A **IN** (AREA1), P1 – >A1 **IN** (AREA2);

P2 – >A **IN** (AREA1);

releases three allocated variables: An allocation of A1 in AREA2 and two allocations of A, both in AREA1.

XVII.1.6.3   The **EMPTY** Built-in Function

An entire area may be cleared of allocated items simply by stating

area = **EMPTY**;

The result is equivalent to that obtained by freeing each of the area's allocated variables individually. Accordingly, an **EMPTY** area is available for new allocations. By the same token, a newly allocated area automatically is set to **EMPTY**. Since an area can be assigned to another area, the use of an **EMPTY** source area in such an assignment empties the destination area. Thus, in the sequence

DECLARE A **AREA** (500) **BASED** (P1),

     B **AREA** (500) **BASED** (Q1),

      (P2,Q2) **POINTER**,

C **FIXED** (2) **BASED** (R1), D **FIXED** (2) **BASED** (S1);

ALLOCATE A; **ALLOCATE** B;

ALLOCATE C **IN** (A) **INITIAL** (40);

ALLOCATE C **IN** (A) **INITIAL** (35) **SET** (P2);

ALLOCATE D **IN** (B) **INITIAL** (10) **SET** (Q2);

ALLOCATE D **IN** (A) **INITIAL** (80);

    .

    .

    .

B = **EMPTY**; A = B;

the last two assignments empty all the areas. The result is equivalent to what would have been obtained by saying

FREE C **IN**(A), P2 –>C **IN**(A), D **IN**(A), Q2 –>D **IN** (B);

XVII.2 LIST PROCESSING

Although its general definition is relatively vague in that it does not imply a particular structure or formalism, the term "list" as used in this context implies a type of data organization that is set apart from other collections by a rather specific set of properties. Originally, the techniques surrounding the construction and manipulation of such data lists were used in a relatively small number of fairly specialized computer applications. Because of this relatively limited interest, the designers of most popular high-level languages paid little or no attention to list-processing requirements. Instead, those concerned with lists and their uses developed special languages for that purpose. More recently, however, the usefulness of this versatile tool has been more widely recognized, and it is being applied in a variety of areas ranging from information retrieval to urban planning. PL/I has been designed to include a number of features that allow the programmer to perform list-processing operations with relative convenience.

Although a comprehensive discussion of list processing techniques is outside the intent of this book, it is important to state some of the underlying principles to provide perspective. (Additional reference material is indicated at the end of the chapter.) Situations often arise where a number of related data items are not stored in contiguous locations, as they would be in an array. This can occur when the processor's storage is allocated so that a sufficient amount is available to contain the entire collection, but the locations are scattered throughout storage rather than being adjacent to each other. Consequently, some means other than the physical location of an individual member must be used to establish its placement with respect to the other values in the collection. The basic technique for this purpose involves the attachment of an additional piece of data to each member of the list. This value acts as a pointer, indicating the internal address of the next member. By equipping each member with such a pointer, we can effectively link together an entire collection regardless of the proximity of its members. An organization of this type is referred to as a *chained list* or simply a *list*. This concept is central to list processing and many pertinent techniques stem from it. A simple type of list organization is shown in Figure 17.2a. Examination of this diagram will help establish some of the basic definitions and properties.

The first member of the list is called the *head* and as such is associated with a separate pointer that provides users with initial access to the list. Having thus found its beginning, it is possible to work one's way through the list by following the succession of pointers. The last member of such a list, usually called the *tail*, has a pointer containing a special value to indicate that there are no subsequent members. In effect, this pointer points "nowhere," and many systems acknowledge this concept by referring to that special value as the *null value*. Sometimes, however, it is useful for the tail's pointer to point to the location of the first member of the list, thus completing a circular route. When this is done, the list is known as a *ring* (Figure 17.2b). A more complicated type of list involves the attachment of two pointers to each value, one indicating the address of the next member of the list and the other pointing to the location of the preceding member. This is known as a *bidirectional list*, as opposed to the *unidirectional list* described previously. The organizational properties of these data organizations are compared in Figure 17.2.

The obvious penalty incurred in constructing such lists is the inefficient use of storage, since a list may require twice or even three times as much storage as an array composed of the same number of data items. On many occasions, however, this penalty is a small price to pay for the increased flexibility such lists offer. For many applications, certain types of operations can be performed more efficiently with lists than with any other type of data organization. For example, a member of a list may be deleted without leaving a gap. It is a relatively simple matter to "open up" a list to insert a new member without requiring a change in the location of any other members.

The features incorporated in PL/I to support list-processing activities are not advanced. Commands for list-processing operations are not immediately available to the programmer in the sense that they are for algebraic and trigonometric manipulations. Instead, the programmer is provided with a set of fundamental tools for assigning and releasing storage and changing pointers that can be used to synthesize the desired routines.

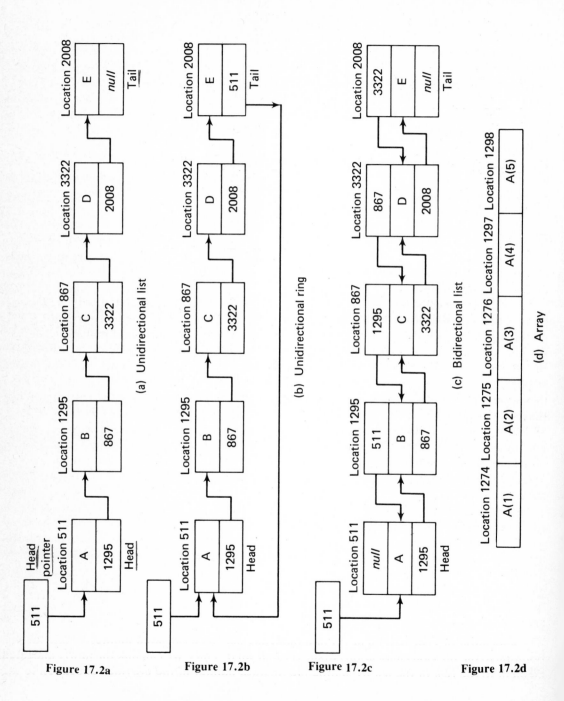

(a) Unidirectional list

Figure 17.2a

(b) Unidirectional ring

Figure 17.2b

(c) Bidirectional list

Figure 17.2c

(d) Array

Figure 17.2d

XVII.2.1   Organization of Lists

A convenient way to construct list elements in PL/I is to treat each element (data item(s) and pointer(s)) as a structure. For example, if we want to build a unidirectional list in which each element E consists of a floating-point number V and forward pointer FWD, such an element can be defined by the statement

DECLARE 1 E **BASED** (W),

   2 V,

   2 FWD **POINTER**;

Then when E is allocated, W automatically is set to point to it, and FWD is available for assignment as a pointer to the next member of the list. The versatility of the PL/I structure can be used to organize list elements containing any number of data items and any number of pointers for a multitude of purposes.

   When a new E is allocated, its associated pointer is set to the new address. Consequently, it is up to the programmer to make sure that the new addition is properly connected to the other members. An effective technique for doing this is to set an additional pointer to the newly allocated member so that its address still will be available to the programmer after the next allocation. This allows the programmer to construct statements that will set the forward pointer of a list element to the address of the subsequent allocation, thereby adding the latest link to the chain. To illustrate, let us define a pointer T and show its use in two consecutive allocations of the structure E. We shall assume that at least one such element has already been allocated, so we can operate on the basis that T indicates the address of the most recent allocation. Bearing that in mind, we can write the following:

A1: **ALLOCATE** E;

   T–>FWD = W;

   T = W;

   .

   .

   .

A2: **ALLOCATE** E;

The allocation of E in statement A1 automatically sets its associated pointer W and finds T pointing to the previous allocation (whatever that was). Thus, we can link the newly allocated element to the rest of the list by setting the forward pointer of the previous allocation to the address of the current one (such as W), using T as a pointer qualifier. Having served its purpose, T now can be updated to point to the current allocation, and this is done by setting it equal to W. Then the next allocation (specified in statement A2) resets W to the new address and finds T pointing to the previous one. Of course, the two allocations are shown above in separate statements for illustrative purposes; in a properly constructed program this would be handled by means of an appropriately controlled loop.

When such a list is completed, it will be possible to find each member by means of the forward pointer of its predecessor. The beginning of the list would be accessible through a separate head pointer, and the end of the list would be discernible since the forward pointer of the final element would be set uniquely to **NULL**. Note, however, that under these circumstances it is impossible to find any given member of that list directly; any search must start at the head of the list and work its way through the chain. If this is not satisfactory in a particular situation, the programmer can provide permanent independent access to key members of the list as part of the construction process.

Illustration 52

Each of a series of input cards contains a value V in columns 1-5 (with format F(5,2)) and a character string C in columns 11-18. Each of these pairs is to form an element of a unidirectional list of no more than 20 elements. V is to appear as a floating-point number. When all of the pairs have been read and added to the list, the program is to print a value NP, the number of elements in the list.

We shall use the techniques discussed before to build this list. Accordingly, each element will be built as a structure containing V, C, and forward pointer FWD. A pointer HD will be used to indicate the head of a list, and T will be used as a temporary pointer to assist in the linkage process:

```
ILL52: PROCEDURE OPTIONS (MAIN);
        DECLARE 1 E BASED (W),
                2 V FLOAT DECIMAL,
                2 C CHARACTER (8),
                2 P POINTER,
                (HD, T) POINTER,
                (NP, I) FIXED BINARY INITIAL (0),
                V1 FLOAT DECIMAL,
                C1 CHARACTER (8);

        ON ENDFILE (SYSIN) BEGIN; PUT SKIP(2) DATA (NP); STOP; END;
        PUT PAGE LINE (3) EDIT ('LIST BUILDER')(X(54),A);
        PUT SKIP EDIT ('ELEMENT','V','C')(X(3),A,X(4),A,X(11),A); PUT SKIP;
        HD = NULL;

        DO WHILE ('1'B);
          GET EDIT (V1,C1)(COLUMN(1),F(5,2),X(5),A(8));
          NP = NP+1;              CALL BUILD;
          PUT SKIP EDIT (NP,V,C)(X(5),F(2),X(5),F(7,2),X(5),A(8));
        END;

        BUILD: PROCEDURE;
                ALLOCATE E;     V=V1;       C=C1;
                W -> P = NULL;
                IF NP > 1
                  THEN T -> P = W;
                  ELSE HD = W;
                T = W;
                RETURN;
                END BUILD;

        END ILL52;
```

XVII.2.2   Manipulation of Lists

Once a list is created it can be subjected to a variety of operations. We shall examine some of the pertinent PL/I-based techniques to establish foundations for the construction of more complex list processing procedures.

XVII.2.2.1   Chaining through a List

Given the name of its head pointer, the very nature of a list allows us to work our way through its successive members quite easily. To illustrate, let us assume that the list built in Illustration 52 is in storage with HD pointing to its head. If we wanted to print the items in the list (V and C in each element), one pair to a line, we could do it with a simple loop after initializing W so that it points to the first element:

```
             .
             .
             .
             .

W = HD;
DO WHILE (W ⌐ = NULL);
PUT SKIP EDIT (V,C) (X(5),F(7,2),X(5),A(8));
END;
             .
             .
             .
             .
             .
```

XVII.2.2.2   Searching a List

The technique for chaining through a list provides a convenient basis for implementing an inquiry procedure. As an example, we shall show a procedural segment that reads in successive values of a number X and search the list referred to in the previous example. When we find an element whose numerical variable V is within ±5 percent of X, the procedure is to print X, V, the corresponding C, and the sequence number of the element. If the search is unsuccessful, the procedure is to print X and the message "SEARCH IS UNSUCCESSFUL":

```
IN: GET LIST(X); W=HD;
    DO N=1 BY 1 WHILE (W ¬ = NULL);
    IF ABS(X/−1)<.05 THEN DO;
                    PUT SKIP EDIT(X,V,C,N)
                    (2 (X(5),F(7,2)),X(5),A(8),X(3),F(3));
                    GO TO IN;
                    END;
                ELSE W=P;
    END;
    PUT SKIP EDIT(X,'SEARCH IS UNSUCCESSFUL')
        (X(5),F(7,2),X(5),A);
    GO TO IN;
```

XVII.2.2.3 Insertion in a List

The advantages of a list become somewhat more apparent when considering the type of situation in which it is desired to add an element at some arbitrary position in a collection of similar elements. When the collection is an array, it is necessary to "make room" by shifting all subsequent elements (that is, those with higher subscripts) further back. Thus, if X is an array currently occupied from $V(1)$ through $V(N)$ and we wish to insert a new item G in some location $V(J)$, we could do this by a loop such as

```
INSRT: DO K = N TO J BY −1;
        V(K+1)=V(K);
        END INSRT;
        V(J)=G;
```

This insertion is depicted in Figure 17.3a.

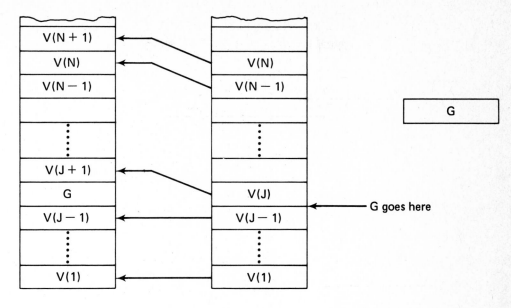

Figure 17.3a   (a)

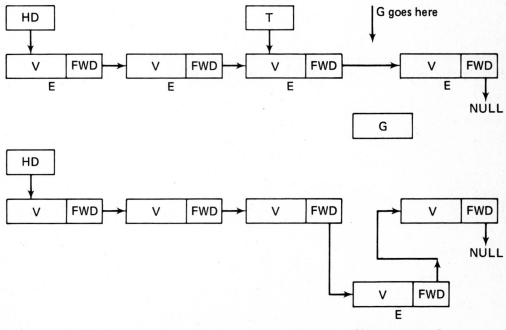

Figure 17.3b   (b)   New home for G

Though simple and straightforward, this sequence could be relatively time-consuming. With the elements organized as a list, the operation is more direct. Allocate a new element and set it in place by adjusting the pointers. Let us consider the same situation in this context: We have a list in which each element E consists of a value V and a forward pointer FWD. An item G is to be placed in a new element whose position has been determined by a prior search. Just as an array search would tell us that we want G to be placed in A(J), the list search would result in a pointer (let us say T) having been set to the element preceding the new one. Assuming that E is declared as a based structure with associated pointer W, the insertion would go as follows:

.
.
.

ALLOCATE E **SET** (W);

W−>FWD = T−>FWD;

T−>FWD = W;

W−>V = G;

.
.
.

This process is depicted schematically in Figure 17.3b. (G is shown separately for purposes of clarity; depending on G's origin, we might very well allocate the new element at the time G appears.)

XVII.2.2.4   Deletion from a List

The technique for this process is, so to speak, the "mirror image" of that for insertion. Accordingly, the elimination of A(J) from an array of M entries and "closure" of the array is handled by

BYE: **DO** K = J **TO** M − 1;

A(K) = A(K+1);

END BYE;

With a list organization (assuming elements named E as before, with T pointing to the element preceding the unwanted one), the deletion process could be implemented as follows:

.
.
.

```
W = T->FWD;
T->FWD = W->FWD;
FREE W->E;
```

.
.
.

Pointer W is set to the address of the element to be deleted. This allows us to get at the next element (through W->FWD) and link it to the preceding one (T->E), thus bypassing the undesirable W->E.

XVII.2.3   Lists and Areas

By using areas and offset pointers within them, it is possible to construct lists and store them as such on external media. That is, we can preserve the value-pointer relations, thereby avoiding the necessity of reconstructing the list each time the data are to be read in.

To circumvent the fact that pointer values will change from one usage to the next, each list element can be allocated and constructed within an area. Accordingly, the pointers linking consecutive elements would be expressed as offset values referenced to the beginning of the area. Once an area is filled it can be written as a record, just like any other record. (Note that a variable declared with the **POINTER** or **OFFSET** attribute can be transmitted as part of a record but not as part of a stream.) Subsequent input of that record into an appropriately declared structure makes that list available for processing. Since offsets cannot be used as qualifiers, each one can easily be assigned to a pointer as it is needed.

To illustrate, suppose that we wanted to create a record RC whose contents represent five elements of a unidirectional list. Each element E consists of a floating-point value V, an eight-character string C, and variable HERE, which locates the next element in the list. Consequently, each element will require 16 bytes in the area: 4 for V, 8 for C, and 4 for HERE. (A summary of storage requirements is given in Table 17.1.) Thus, the area will be 80 bytes long. (The actual length will be 96, as explained in Section XVII.1.5.7. This would have to be indicated when specifying the record length in the file declaration.) With these defined properties, let us consider the following sequence:

.
.
.

```
    DECLARE RC AREA (80) BASED (NOSE),
        1 E BASED (W),
            2 V, 2 C CHARACTER(8),
            2 HERE OFFSET(RC),
        P POINTER;
```

.
.
.

```
    ALLOCATE RC;
```

.
.
.

```
    DO I = 1 TO 5;
S1: ALLOCATE E IN(RC);
    GET EDIT (V,C) (format);
    IF I > 1 THEN P -> HERE = W;
S2: P = W;
    END;
    HERE = NULLO;
```

.
.
.

```
    WRITE FILE (OUT) FROM (RC);
```

.
.
.

After area RC is allocated, we fill it with five of the E's by means of a loop. The allocation of E sets W, and the input is duly read. P is set to W so that the next time around W points to the most recent allocation of E and, until statement S2 is executed, P points to the one before that. Thus, each offset HERE is set to the relative position of the *next* element. When all five elements have been built and linked, the offset in the fifth element is set to **NULLO** (outside the loop) and the record is written.

TABLE 17.1 Storage Requirements for PL/I Variables

	Attributes		Storage, bytes
FLOAT	**BINARY**(p)	P < 22	4
		21 < p < 54	8
		53 < p < 110	16*
	DECIMAL(p)	P < 7	4
		6 < p < 17	8
		16 < p < 34	16*
FIXED	**BINARY**(p,d)	p < 16	2
		p > 15	4
	DECIMAL(p,d)		**CEIL**((p + 1)/2)
CHARACTER(n)			n
PICTURE 'c...c' (except **V**, **K**, scale factor)			one byte/picture character
BIT(n)			**CEIL**(n/8)
LABEL			8
POINTER			4
OFFSET			4
AREA(n)			n + 16

* Optimizing and Checkout Compilers only.

XVII.3   CONTROLLED STORAGE

PL/I provides a second major type of dynamic storage allocation under direct control of the programmer. It is known as *controlled storage*, and is set up by specifying the **CONTROLLED** attribute. That is, the statement

DECLARE F **FIXED**(9,2) **CONTROLLED;**

lays the groundwork for subsequent dynamic allocation(s) of a variable F with the indicated attributes. As is the case with based variables, the declaration does not allocate storage; it merely specifies preparatory information. The allocation itself is triggered by an **ALLOCATE** statement, and subsequent release is effected by a **FREE** statement. Moreover, it is possible to have several allocations of a controlled variable, each one potentially available until its eventual explicit release.

XVII.3.1   Special Properties of Controlled Variables

Although the ideas of multiple allocations and releases for controlled variables parallel those associated with based variables, there are important differences between the two types that make each one uniquely suited to a particular kind of usage. We shall discuss two basic areas that apply specifically to controlled variables and give them their special characteristics. One of these stems from the fact that, although each allocation of a controlled variable leaves its predecessors intact, only the latest allocation is immediately available. The other property stems from the perseverance of controlled variables across procedural boundaries. (Based variables are also preserved across such boundaries.)

XVII.3.1.1   The "Pushdown" and "Pop-up" Concept

When the programmer specifies successive allocations for a based variable, each allocation is independently accessible as long as the programmer has provided and set corresponding pointers that ensure unambiguous distinction. With controlled variables there are no pointers. If a particular controlled variable is named in an **ALLOCATE** statement and assigned a value, and then that same variable is named in a subsequent **ALLOCATE** statement and assigned another value without an intervening **FREE** statement, PL/I assigns duplicate storage, maintaining both values in what is known as a "pushdown stack." The name is derived from the spring-loaded plate dispensers used in many restaurants and is applied to this situation because only the most recently allocated value of the variables is directly available to the programmer. Suppose that we wrote the sequence

DECLARE A **FIXED**(5,2) **CONTROLLED**, B **FIXED**(5,3);

ALLOCATE A **INITIAL**(12);

.

.

.

ALLOCATE A;

A = 14;

B = 2 * A − 4;

PUT DATA(A);

The printed output would read

B = 24.000;

Although the most recently generated value of A was used, the previous value is still maintained, and can be made available by preceding any reference to it with a **FREE** statement.

When this is done, the most recently generated value is peeled away (eliminated) from the pushdown stack, and the next most recent one is "popped up," thus preserving the analogy to a plate dispenser. Hence, if we were to follow the sequence in the above example with the additional statements

FREE A;

B = 3 * A − 4;

PUT DATA(B);

the resulting printout would read

B = 32.000;

There is no practical limit on the number of items allowed in any particular pushdown stack (the number of successive allocations for a given variable). It is up to the programmer, however, to make sure that he knows which member of the list is available to him at any particular time.

XVII.3.1.2   The **ALLOCATION** Function

The programmer can determine the status of a controlled variable at a given time by means of the **ALLOCATION** built-in function. If storage is currently allocated for a particular variable named in the argument for the function, PL/I will generate a '1'**B**; otherwise it will generate '0'**B**. (With the Optimizing and Checkout Compilers, the **ALLOCATION** function returns a **FIXED BINARY** (15) value indicating the number of generations that currently exist.) This function may not appear as a pseudovariable but can be used in an assignment statement as any other built-in function; for example,

Y = **ALLOCATION**(X);

The argument (X in the above statement) must have the **CONTROLLED** attribute.

XVII.3.1.3   Controlled Variables As Parameters

Unlike based variables, controlled variables may be specified as parameters. These are termed *controlled parameters* to distinguish them from all other types (that is, *simple parameters*). When a parameter is specified with the **CONTROLLED** attribute, the corresponding argument must be controlled but need not be allocated. It is then possible to allocate storage under that name with the result being the creation of an allocation under the corresponding arguments' name. When the parameter is simple, the argument may be controlled but must be allocated, and only the current allocation is passed. To illustrate, consider the following sequence:

.
.
.

DECLARE A (20) **FIXED**(3) **CONTROLLED,**N **FIXED BINARY;**

.
.
.

GET LIST(N);
CALL INT(A,N);

.
.
.

PUT LIST(A);
 ALLOCATE A; **GET LIST**(A);

.
.
.

F1: **FREE** A;

.
.
.

F2: **FREE** A;

INT: **PROCEDURE** (X,NUM);
DECLARE X(NUM)**FIXED**(3)**CONTROLLED,**NUM **FIXED BINARY;**

.
.
.

ALLOCATE X; X = 27;

.
.
.

RETURN;
END INT;

.
.
.

Array A is declared as **CONTROLLED** and N is an ordinary fixed-point binary integer with default precision. (Since the number of elements is specified as 20, each simple (unqualified) **ALLOCATE** statement automatically sets up a 20-element array for A.) Let us suppose that the **GET LIST** statement reads a value of 6 for N. Then, the subsequent **CALL** to INT passes the names A and N to parameters X and NUM. Since X is a controlled parameter whose size (number of elements) depends on NUM, the subsequent **ALLOCATE** statement sets up storage for a six-element allocation of array A. Accordingly, the ensuing assignment statement will fill the newly allocated A with 27's (six of them).

Upon return to the invoking procedure, this allocation is still in existence and the output statement will print the six 27's even though they were allocated and assigned in an already concluded procedure. The subsequent allocation sets up a second array A, this time with 20 elements as declared, pushing down the previous allocation. Consequently, statement F1 frees this latest allocation, popping the six-element A (with the 27's) back to the top of stack, from whence it is vaporized by statement F2.

XVII.3.2   Asterisk Notation for Controlled Variables

When dimension sizes are specified for a controlled array, those values are available for successive allocations and may be implied by using asterisks in place of dimension values. If this is done, PL/I will assign the values used in the most recent allocation. For example, if we wrote the sequence

DECLARE X(10,10) **FIXED**(3) **CONTROLLED**;

ALLOCATE X(4,5);

ALLOCATE X(*,*);

(assuming no intervening **FREE** statement), the first allocation would reserve storage for a 4 × 5 array called X, and the second allocation would reserve memory for an array of identical size. It should be understood, however, that these are two separate and distinct allocations preserved in a push-down stack. A subsequent **FREE** statement would release only that array allocated most recently, popping up the first one. Had we not used asterisks and written the second allocation as

ALLOCATE X;

the program would revert to the dimensions orginally specified in the declaration, thus reserving space for a 10 × 10 array. This feature may also be used for implicit specification of bit string and character string lengths in an **ALLOCATE** statement.

The rules for asterisk notation apply for parameters. Thus, if we have the following sequence

.
.
.

   DECLARE A(10)**FIXED**(3)**CONTROLLED**;

S1: **ALLOCATE** A(8);

.
.

  CALL INT(A);

.
.

    INT: **PROCEDURE**(X);

      DECLARE X(*)**FIXED**(3)**CONTROLLED**;

.
.

   S11: **ALLOCATE** X;

.
.

   S12: **ALLOCATE** X(7);

.
.

    RETURN;

    END INT;

S2: **ALLOCATE** A;

.
.
.

we produce four allocations of array A: The first (statement S1) sets up an eight-element array. The second (statement S11) creates another eight-element array, since the asterisk in the declaration obliges X's (and therefore A's) size to be taken from the most recent allocation. The third allocation (S12) explicitly specifies seven elements; and the fourth, by virtue of its occurrence outside the procedure INT, generates storage for ten elements. Thus, our stack can be considered as follows:

Allocated	S2	A(1)	A(2)	A(3)	A(4)	A(5)	A(6)	A(7)	A(8)	A(9)	A(10)	Top
by:	S12	A(1)	A(2)	A(3)	A(4)	A(5)	A(6)	A(7)				
	S11	A(1)	A(2)	A(3)	A(4)	A(5)	A(6)	A(7)	A(8)			
	S1	A(1)	A(2)	A(3)	A(4)	A(5)	A(6)	A(7)	A(8)		Bottom	

PROBLEMS

1. Use the following input cards

First card

```
    4   6   5   24.3   −12.5   76   35.8   96.6   −14   −11   4   4   2   5

    6   13.9   −7   8   44.7   −26   35.8   57   56   3.3   14   24   4   31

5   15   97.8   −61.1   32.2   −17   22   74.8   7   9
```

and assuming the declaration

DECLARE (W,X,Y,Z)INITIAL(1);

show what the values of W,X,Y and Z would be as a result of each of the following sequences:

a. **DECLARE A BASED (P1), B FIXED(4,2) BASED (P2);**
   ALLOCATE A,B; GET LIST(A,B);
   X,Y=B;Z=A;

b. **DECLARE A BASED(P1), B FIXED(4,2) BASED (P2),**
   (Q1,Q2,Q3) POINTER
   ALLOCATE A,B;
   ALLOCATE A SET(Q1), B SET(Q2), A SET(Q3);
   GET LIST(A,P2−>B,Q2−>B,Q3−>A);
   X =B; Y =P1−>A; W=B+P2−>B;

c. DECLARE A BASED(P1), B BASED(P2), C BASED(P3), (S,Q(3)) POINTER;
ALLOCATE A,B,C; GET LIST(C,B,A);
ALLOCATE C SET(S); Q(1)=S; GET LIST(S->C);
ALLOCATE B SET(S); Q(2)=S; GET LIST(S->B);
ALLOCATE A SET(S); Q(3)=S; GET LIST(S->A,A);
S=Q(1); W=C+S->C;
S=Q(2); X=2*B-3*S->B;
S=Q(3); Y=A+S->A+2*P1->A;
Z=W+X+Y-P3->C;

d. DECLARE A BASED(P1), B BASED(P2), C BASED(P3), (S, Q(3)) POINTER;
ALLOCATE A,B,C; GET LIST(C,A,B);
DO I=1 TO 3;
ALLOCATE A SET(S);
Q(I)=S; GET LIST(S->A);
X=X+S->A;
END;
Y=X+A; Z=Y+B;

e. DECLARE A(6) BASED(P1),(P2,P3)POINTER;
ALLOCATE A, A SET(P2);
GET LIST(P2->A,A);
X=0.5*SUM(P2->A);
DO I=1 TO 4;
Y=Y+A(I)+P1->A(I+1);
END;

f. DECLARE A(6) BASED(P1), (P2,P3)POINTER, M,N;
ALLOCATE A SET(P2), A SET(P3),A;
GET LIST(A,P3->A,M,N);
DO I=1 TO M;
P2->A(I)=P1->A(I)+P3->A(I);
X=X+P2->A(I);
END;
Y=MIN(M,N)*X;

   g.   **DECLARE** 1 T **BASED**(R),

           2 M, (2 A, 2 B)**FIXED**(4,1),

           2 C(E **REFER**(M))**FIXED**(3,1),

       N, E **FIXED BINARY**, (R1, S(10)**POINTER**);

       GET LIST(N);

         DO I = 1 **TO** N;

         GET LIST(E); **ALLOCATE** T;

         S(I) = R; **GET LIST**(A,B,C);

         IF I<3 **THEN** X=X+**SUM**(C);

             ELSE Y=Y+**SUM**(C);

         IF I>1 **THEN DO**;

            R = P(I−1);

            W = W + R −> B; Z=Z + R −> C;

              END;

        END;

2. Using the input data described in Illustration 51, write a program that prints each character string on a line, followed (in columns 80-81 of that line) by a number indicating the number of times the letter E appears in that string. Instead of printing the string in order by length, they are to be shown so that the string with the most E's appears first, and so on.

3. Generalize the program in Problem 2 by preceding each set of cards with a single card containing the number of cards in the set (as before) and the character to be counted for that set. Then, when the output is printed, each set of resequenced character strings is to be preceded by a line showing the number of cards in that set and the character that was counted.

4. Data cards are available as described in Illustration 51. Each set of such cards is preceded by a single card showing NC, the number of cards in the set; CH, the character to be counted in that particular set; and OP, a coded option indicating how the output is to be printed. If OP is punched as a 1, the cards are to be printed in order by decreasing string length; if OP is a 2, that set is to be printed in decreasing order by frequency of the designated character; if OP is a 3, the cards are to be printed both ways, with decreasing string length first and blank line separating the two sections. In any case, each line of output is to show the character string followed by the number of appearances of the designated character in that string.

5. A number of input cards are available, each containing 23-digit integers punched in columns 1-3, 5-7, 9-11, and so on. Write a program that divides these data into ten groups: 0-99, 100-199, 200-299, and so on. A punched output card is to be prepared for each of these groups showing the number of values in that group (columns 1-2) followed by each of the values in descending order. Assume that the number of values in each group can be accomodated on a single card. However, it is not necessarily true that each group will be represented in a given set of input. Print a corresponding line of output for each card punched.

6. Write a more generalized version of the program in Problem 5 by allowing any number of values in each of the ten groups. Set up your output cards so that it is possible to identify the cards for a given group and the individual cards within each group. As before, represent your punched output in printed form as well.

7. Rewrite the procedure shown in Illustration 52 such that there is no specific limit on the number of list elements to be formed.

8. Write a procedure that reads data cards as described in Illustration 52 and uses their contents to form a bidirectional list in which each element contains a forward pointer FWD and a backward pointer BWD.

9. Using the input described in Illustration 52, write a program that reads a series of such cards and organizes the data into a list whose elements are sequenced in alphabetical order of character string C. Print the list in that order.

10. Using the data from Illustration 52, write a program that reads the cards and organizes the data into a list such that each element is equipped with two forward pointers FWD1 and FWD2. For any given element, FWD1 is to point to the element in the list with the next larger value of V; FWD2 is to point to the element in the list whose value of V is next in alphabetical sequence. Once this organizational part has been completed, the program is to print the elements twice: first, with the V values in ascending numerical order, followed by a blank line and followed in turn by another copy of the list with the C values in alphabetical order. Each line of output is to contain C followed by the corresponding V.

11. Using the input data described in Illustration 52, write a program that reads the cards, organizes them into a unidirectional list sequenced in the order in which the elements were originally read. However, each element in that list is to consist of four items: V and C as read, a value SEQ indicating the sequence number of that element (for example, contents of the first card will go into an element whose SEQ value will be 1, and so on), and a value AV representing the average of all the V values thus far. (Thus, AV in the first element will be a duplicate of V, AV in the second element will be the average of the first two V's, and so on.) Print the list in reverse order, one element per line, containing SEQ, C, V, and AV in that order.

12. Using the input described in Illustration 52, write a program that produces a unidirectional list in which the elements are sequenced by ascending order of V. In this particular problem the last set of input values for the list is followed by a card in which C has a unique value consisting entirely of asterisks. Having built the list, the program is to read successive pairs of integers B1 and B2. For each such pair it is to print the elements of the list whose V values fall outside of the range specified by B1 and B2. Each element is to appear on a separate line containing V, C and that element's sequence number. Output for each set of B1 and B2 values is to consist of those values followed by the elements below that range. After an intervening blank line, the program is to print all of the elements above that range. Successive output sets are to be separated by two blank lines.

13. Write a program that reads the basic input data as described in Problem 12 (with the asterisks as a special signal). This time, however, a list is constructed such that the elements are sequenced with the C values in alphabetical order. Then, the program is to read additional data cards with each card containing a character string CH in columns 1-8. For each CH read, the program is to produce a new list element that will be inserted in proper alphabetical order. The value C, of course, will be a direct duplicate of the corresponding CH, and the value of V to be placed in the newly created element will represent the average of all the V's preceding that element. If the newly created element happens to belong ahead of all the others, use a value of 0 for its V. (Do not forget to reset the head pointer if this should be the case.)

SUMMARY OF IMPORTANT TERMS

ALLOCATE	The statement type used to provide storage (dynamically) for a particular based or controlled variable.
Area	A designated amount of contiguous storage, identified by its own name and declared with the **AREA** attribute. Though treated like ordinary storage, areas provide an additional organizational facility in that the location of a variable within an area can be expressed as a displacement (or *offset*) relative to the beginning of that area.
AREA condition	A condition that is raised when an attempt is made to allocate more storage in a given area than is available at the time.
Based variable	A variable (declared with the **BASED** attribute) whose association with a particular storage address is arbitrarily changeable and not necessarily unique. Accordingly, such associations are maintained in *pointers* under the programmer's control.
Bidirectional list	A list organized such that each element includes a pointer to the previous element as well as one to the next element in the list.
Controlled variable	A variable (declared with the **CONTROLLED** attribute) whose handling is such that multiple allocations are placed in a *pushdown stack* (which see) from which only one member (representing the most recent allocation) is available to the programmer.
Controlled parameter	Assignment of the **CONTROLLED** attribute to a parameter, thereby making it possible to specify an unallocated argument when that particular procedure is invoked. This is in contrast to a *simple parameter* (which see).
EMPTY built-in function	A built-in function that clears an entire area, making all of its storage available for subsequent allocation.
FREE	The statement type used to destroy a particular allocation of a designated based or controlled variable.
Head	In the context of list processing, the first (leading) element of a list.

List	An internally stored collection of data whose relative locations are arbitrary. Connection among individual components is maintained by placing each one in a *list element* which also includes one or more pointers to adjacent members of that list.
NULL built-in function	A built-in function used to set a pointer to an "address" representing a terminus or "nowhere."
NULLO built-in function	A built-in function for offset variables equivalent to the **NULL** function.
Offset variable	A pointerlike variable used to indicate the location of a based variable relative to the beginning of the area in which that variable is assigned.
Pointer qualifier	A pointer containing the address of a particular allocation, thereby distinguishing it from other (still current) allocations of the same variable.
Pop-up operation	A process whereby the most recently added member of a stack is freed, thereby raising the next most recent allocation to the top of the stack.
Pushdown operation	The process of adding a new allocation to a stack such that it occupies the top of the stack. Accordingly that will be the one freed when the stack is popped up.
Pushdown stack	An arbitrary collection of allocated items organized such that the items are ordinarily available one at a time and in a fixed order. In PL/I, multiple allocations of a **CONTROLLED** variable are placed in such a stack, with the most recent allocation occupying the top.
REFER option	A vehicle that makes it possible to allocate a based structure containing an array whose size is not known until the allocation occurs. This is done by providing a reference to a variable (outside of the structure) in which information about the array size is to be found.
Ring	A list organized such that there is no physical terminus; that is, the element "following" the last element (tail) is the head of the list.
Self-defining data	A collection of information that includes an item describing some aspect of that information. (For example, a dynamically allocated array may be associated with a self-defining data item that gives its size by means of the **REFER** option.)
Simple parameter	A parameter that, in contrast to a *controlled parameter*, must be paired with an allocated argument.
Tail	In the context of list processing, the final element of a list.
Unidirectional list	A list organized such that each element is associated (by means of a single pointer) with only one other element (usually the next one in that list).

SUPPLEMENTARY READING

Berztiss, A.T., *Data Structures–Theory and Practice*. New York: Academic Press, 1971, pp. 289-325.

Introduction to the List Processing Facilities of PL/I, IBM Document No. F20-0015. White Plains, N.Y.: IBM Corporation.

PL/I Language Reference Manual, IBM Document No. GC28-8201. White Plains, N.Y.: IBM Cororation, pp. 167-168, 178-191.

Stone, H.S., *Introduction to Computer Organization and Data Structures*. New York: McGraw-Hill, 1972, pp. 125-126, 202-213.

XVIII CONTROL OF COMPILATION

For most high-level languages, the compilation process may be described in general terms as a procedure whereby the statements in a source program are examined, analyzed, and replaced by functionally equivalent sequences of instructions in another language either directly comprehendible by the processing system or a major step closer to that form. (This sequence is schematically depicted in Figure 18.1.) Such is not always the case with PL/I. At the programmer's option, it is possible to interject an additional component (Figure 18.2). (Such communications, called compiler options, are also available for a variety of other functions such as controlling the extent and format of the program listing, selecting the input character set, and identifying the error recovery and optimization strategies to be employed. The method of selecting the compiler options varies from one compiler to the next, as does the set of such options available.) During this new stage, known as the *processor stage*, the incoming (original) source program is inspected and, if special instructions are found, the program may be modified while still a source program. The analytical agent designed to do

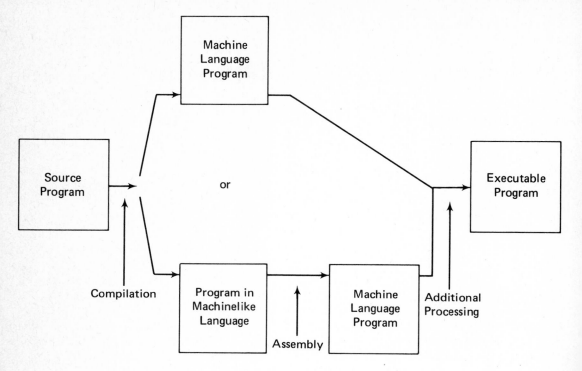

Figure 18.1

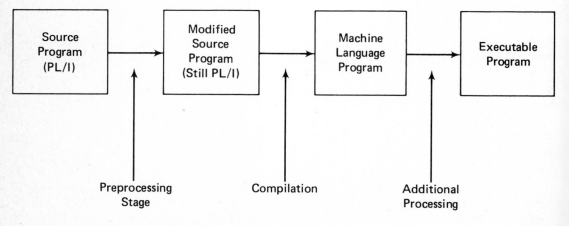

Figure 18.2

this is the PL/I *preprocessor* and its services are requested by communications to the supervisory system outside the program itself. In response to such a request, the program undergoes a separate analysis before being turned over to the regular compiler.

As a result, the PL/I statements actually compiled may not be identical in sequence or in content to those submitted by the programmer. This method of compilation offers the programmer additional controls, as he has the prerogative to augment his source program with special instructions that directly determine the nature and extent of the changes effected during the preprocessor stage.

Such instructions, termed *compile-time instructions*, are PL/I-like in form and may be interspersed freely throughout the source program. They are not part of that program, however, since they are examined, analyzed, and actually executed by the portion of the software that operates during the preprocessor stage. Although their effects are incorporated into the final version of the source program, the actual compile-time statements are no longer present.

In addition to several commands provided specifically for such purposes, the programmer may write a variety of compile-time instructions by using ordinary PL/I statements with a special signal (a preceding percent sign). A variety of purposes may be fulfilled by using such statements, including (a) prevention of compilation of certain portions of a program based on numerical, logical, or other tests; (b) substitution of variable names; (c) substitution of variable values; and (d) incorporation of additional material, including actual source statements, from external storage sources other than that being used to submit the program. In addition, the compile-time facility allows the inclusion of entire procedures which, after execution, are also eliminated from the final source program presented to the compiler.

XVIII.1   COMPILE-TIME STATEMENTS

The general form for a compile-time statement is

% statement;

Any number of blanks, including none, may be inserted between the percent sign and the statement. Such statements may be labeled in accordance with standard labeling rules. Where such a label is appended, the percent sign is placed ahead of the label, so that the form now becomes

% label: statement;

Since compile-time statements do not appear as such in the final source program submitted to the compiler, a compile-time statement label should not be used as the destination of a **GO TO** in the source program. We shall see later that there is a compile-time **GO TO** for which such a label is a legitimate though temporary destination.

It is not true that placing a percent sign ahead of any legitimate PL/I statement will automatically convert it to a compile-time instruction. The repertoire of compile-time instructions consists only of a restricted version of the assignment statement and simplified versions of the % **DECLARE**, % **GO TO**, and % **DO**. The % **ACTIVATE**, % **DEACTIVATE**, % **INCLUDE**, and the null statements are also provided in support of the compile-time facilities. Similarly, the types of compile-time variables are restricted to decimal integers of default precision and varying character strings.

XVIII.1.1   Activation and Reactivation of Compile-Time Variables

In order to grasp the function and operation of compile-time variables, it should be understood that a PL/I source program is submitted to and treated by the compiler as a long string of characters interspersed with appropriate punctuation. If such a program is altered before it reaches the compiler, we may think of such a modification as a systematic addition, deletion, or replacement of certain items in this character string. One of the primary purposes of a compile-time instruction is to direct such replacements.

When an identifier in a program is also declared as a compile-time variable, the preprocessor is alerted to the fact that the particular variable is a candidate for replacement. The scanning mechanism in the preprocessor stage examines the source program string and substitutes the current value of the compile-time variable each time it encounters the identifier in a nonpreprocessor statement. Again, let us stress that *this is a direct replacement of characters in a character string*. As a very simple example, let us suppose that a program has been written in which a particular variable that appears very frequently throughout the program has been given the name C. It is not until after the program is written and prepared as a series of punched cards (Murphy's Law being what it is) that the programmer discovers that, throughout the second half of the program, all of the C's should actually have been Z's. Faced with the prospect of having to repunch numerous cards to make the necessary substitutions, the day is saved by declaring C as a compile-time variable and defining the appropriate replacement in a compile-time statement:

% **DECLARE** C **CHARACTER**; % C = 'Z';

If the sequence is placed in the original source program at a point just before the first C that must be changed, the compiler will receive a new source program in which each reference to C in that part of the program has been replaced by a reference to Z, and the compile-time statements that triggered replacement will be obliterated. Thus, if the above sequence were to be embedded in a sequence such as

% **DECLARE** C **CHARACTER**;   % C = 'Z';

C = 2*A**2;   D = 17/C;

PUT LIST('ADJUSTMENT = ',C);   etc.

the modified sequence, as submitted to the compiler, would read

$Z = 2*A**2$; $D = 17/Z$;

PUT LIST('ADJUSTMENT = ',Z);   etc.

XVIII.1.1.1   The % **DEACTIVATE** Statement

The programmer may not always want to subject every reference to a given variable in his program to replacement operations stipulated in a compile-time statement, as in the previously described example. Such activity may be curtailed by a **DEACTIVATE** statement having the form

% **DEACTIVATE** name1, name2, etc.;

When such a statement is placed at an appropriate point in the source program, the scanning mechanism will curtail replacement operations for those references appearing after it. Note that the process of deactivation does not destroy the source program variable or change its value; all it does is prevent any further attempts to replace that identifier in nonpreprocessor statements. Such curtailment persists until the end of the program or until the next % **ACTIVATE** statement involving that variable is encountered.

XVIII.1.1.2   The % **ACTIVATE** Statement

When a source program variable can be replaced in the above manner, that variable is said to be *activated*. In our example, we activated the variable C implicitly by declaring it as a compile-time variable. If a % **DEACTIVATE** statement is used to deactivate a variable, that variable can be reactivated by means of the % **ACTIVATE** statement. Its general form is

% **ACTIVATE** name1, name2, etc.;

The % **ACTIVATE** statement may or may not be labeled. (Recall that the percent sign must appear ahead of the label if one is used.) One or several names may be activated in a single statement.

XVIII.1.2   Sequential Replacement and Rescanning

The replacement process instigated by compile-time statements need not be limited to a simple substitution. Virtually any degree of complexity may be introduced due to the mechanism underlying the scanning operation that takes place during the preprocessor stage. When a particular variable is activated, each reference to it is replaced by the current value of the variable at the time of replacement. Once that replacement has been made, however, it is not yet introduced as a final change to the string of source characters. Instead, the replacement value is scanned and compared with all active compile-time variables to determine whether any additional replacements are called for. This process is repeated until no further replacements can be made, at which point the character string, containing all the indicated modifications, is incorporated into the final version of the source program. When a replacement value is introduced, the string of characters comprising that value is inserted without change by the IBM Optimizing Compiler. The IBM PL/I-F compiler inserts a blank at either end of the replacement value.

As an example, let us examine the results of the following sequence:

% **DECLARE** (X,Z) **CHARACTER**, T **FIXED**;

% X = Z + T;   % Z = '(W+1)';

% T = 5;   Y = X + 4/Z;

As a result of the declaration, three compile-time variables are activated. W was not declared in this manner because it is used to effect a change but is not being changed itself. (Presumably, the name W is known in the program, so a newly generated statement involving W would not constitute an anomaly.)

Even though X is obviously being used in the source program as a numerical variable, the compile-time statement treats it as a character because it is interested only in replacing X with some other character or characters. Hence, as a result of the first compile-time assignment statement, the source program statement

Y = X + 4/Z;

will be modified to read

Y = Z + T + 4/Z;

The replacement for Z stipulated in the second compile-time assignment statement includes a set of parentheses, because Z appears in the denominator of the source program statement. Based on the specifications given here, rescanning of the modified source program statement will produce

Y = (W+1) + T + 4/(W+1);

The final compile-time assignment statement calls for the replacement of T with the value 5. This time the replacement is shown as a numerical substitution. However, since we are still dealing with a string of source characters, the value of T will be converted to a character string before insertion as a replacement value. Rescanning indicates that an additional replacement is called for, resulting in the new statement

Y = (W+1) +5 +4/(W+1);

A final scan would then show that no further replacements are indicated. The statement as given above will be inserted into the final source program, and the compile-time statement will be deleted.

Because of the extra blanks inserted by the preprocessor in the IBM PL/I-F implementation of the language, the replacements will appear as follows:

```
Y = X+4/Z;
Y = Z+T +4/Z;                          (first replacement)
Y =  (W+1) +T  +4/ (W+1) ;             (second replacement)
Y =  (W+1) +         5  +4/ (W+1) ; (final replacement)
```

To illustrate the effect of activating and deactivating variables in the middle of a procedure, let us enlarge and modify the above example so that the sequence reads

> % **DECLARE** (X,Z) **CHARACTER** T **FIXED**;
>
> % X = 'Z + T'; % Z = '(W+1)'; % T ='5';
>
> % **DEACTIVATE** Z;
>
> L1: Y = X + 4/Z;
>
> % **ACTIVATE** Z; % **DEACTIVATE** X;
>
> L2: S = 2*X − 6/Z − T;

Since the variable Z is deactivated before the scanning routine reaches the first source program statement, Z will not be replaced in that statement, even though compile-time instructions exist for it. The scanning and rescanning operations will produce the conceptual sequence

```
Y = X+4/Z;   Y = Z+T +4/Z;   Y= Z+      5 +4/Z;
```

Before we reach the second source program instruction, Z has been reactivated, so that the replacement indicated by the corresponding compile-time assignment statement will be carried out. However, since X has been deactivated, it will be left alone. Thus, the scanning and replacing sequence would be

```
S = 2*X −6/ (W+1)−T;
S = 2*X −6/ (W+1) −      5;
```

The final source program segment would thus be

```
Y = Z+      5 +4/Z;   S = 2*X − 6/ (W + 1) −      5;
```

XVIII.1.3   Compile-Time Declarations

As the student may have surmised from previous examples, the declaration of compile-time variables follows the same form used for source program variables. However, **CHARACTER, FIXED, ENTRY**, and **RETURNS** are the only attributes that may be specified in a compile-time declaration. When **CHARACTER** is specified, no length may be given. Instead, the PL/I preprocessor assumes a varying length with no upper limit. When **FIXED** is specified, the programmer cannot designate a precision. Instead, PL/I assigns a precision of (5,0). If a label is attached to such a statement, the percent sign must precede the label as in any other compile-time statement. Such a label would merely serve as an aid to the programmer, since it is ignored by PL/I.

Because there is much less bookkeeping with the preprocessor stage than there is with compilaton, the declaration of a compile-time variable must be processed prior to the processing of any other reference to it; otherwise, an error is incurred. Once a compile-time variable has been declared, it may be deactivated and reactivated any number of times. Its scope, however, covers the entire program.

XVIII.1.4   The Compile-Time Assignment Statement

Although compile-time assignment statements take the same form as their source program counterparts, they are subject to several basic restrictions:

- All of the variables participating in such an assignment statement must be compile-time variables.

- The only numerical values that will be operated on are decimal integer constants of precision (5,0). Each intermediate result of an arithmetic computation will be set to have precision (5,0). Thus, the result of 11/5 is 2 and not 2.20000...0. Similarly, the operation 8/12 in a compile-time expression will produce 0. There is no restriction on the appearance of character and digit string constants.

- The exponentiation operator (**) cannot be used.

- Compile-time character string variables may not contain character strings that are themselves compile-time statements. Thus, for example, the second statement in the following sequence

    % **DECLARE A CHARACTER**;   % A = '% **DECLARE B FIXED**;';

    is illegal.

XVIII.1.5   Compile-Time Decision Statements

The activity triggered by a sequence of compile-time statements need not be completely straightforward. By using compile-time versions of the **GO TO**, **IF**, **DO**, and the null statement, it is possible to change sequences and construct compile-time decision mechanisms.

XVIII.1.5.1   The % **GO TO** Statement

Although the routines used in the processor stage are prepared to scan each instruction in the submitted program, the programmer can bypass certain portions of his program by using the compile-time **GO TO** statement. This may be exemplified as follows:

> **PROCEDURE OPTIONS(MAIN)**;
>
> % statement1;
>
> % statement2;
>
> statement3;
>
> .
>
> .
>
> .
>
> .
>
> statement4;
>
> % **GO TO** C1;
>
> statement5;
>
> .
>
> .
>
> .
>
> .
>
> statement6;
>
> % C1: statement7;
>
> % statement8;
>
> statement9;
>
> .
>
> .
>
> .
>
> .
>
> statement10;
>
> **END**;

As a result of this sequence, the replacements stipulated in statements 1 and 2 will be applied to all of the source program through statement 4. At that point, the scanning routines will bypass all of the source program from statement 5 through statement 6. Scrutiny of the instructions will resume at statement 7, the destination of the compile-time **GO TO** statement, and will continue through the end of the program. The destination for such a transfer must always be a compile-time instruction. Thus, statements...statement6 are effectively removed. Of course, it would be easier to omit them in the first place; however, the real power of this facility comes from the ability to apply it selectively under control of the % **IF** statement.

XVIII.1.5.2   The Compile-Time Null Statement

Since the rules require that a compile-time **GO TO** statement must always transfer control to another compile-time statement, a mechanism must be provided for those cases in which the programmer does not wish to specify additional compile-time instructions at that point. The technique for handling such situations is to use a *null* compile-time statement, that is, an instruction that does nothing at all. By merely writing

   % label:;

a destination is provided without designating any further compile-time activity. Thus, if we did not wish to specify any additional compile-time activity beyond statement2 in the previous example (if we wanted to eliminate statements 7 and 8), we could write

   % statement2;

   % **GO TO** C1;

   statement5;

   statement6;

   % C1: ;

   statement9;

   etc.

Under these circumstances, the scanning routine will bypass the same part of the source program as before and resume with statement9, but no additional compile-time instructions will have been added. The null statement can also be used to create empty % **ELSE**s or % **THEN**s.

XVIII.1.5.3   The % **IF** Statement

The structure of the compile-time **IF** statement follows that used for source programs, with the usual inclusion of the percent sign immediately ahead of the label or ahead of the keyword **IF** when no label is used. A percent sign must also appear ahead of the keyword **THEN** and ahead of the keyword **ELSE** if an **ELSE** clause is included. Thus, the full form for this statement is

   % label: **IF** expression % **THEN** action1 % **ELSE** action2;

where "expression" is any legitimate compile-time expression, subject to the limitations described under the compile-time assignment statement. This expression is evaluated and converted to a bit string. If any member of that string is a 1, the operation stipulated by the compile-time statement (or statements) in "action1" is carried out. Otherwise, the % **THEN** clause is skipped, and the % **ELSE** clause, which must also be composed of one or more compile-time statements, is executed. action1 and action2 must also be compile-time statements and, as such, will have their own percent signs. Thus, a complete % **IF** statement could look as follows:

% **IF** A < 10 % **THEN** % A = A + 1;

   % **ELSE** % **GO TO** DONE;

XVIII.1.5.4 The % **DO** Group

The compile-time **DO** statement is a simplified form of the one in regular source programs. When such a statement is being used to initiate a compile-time **DO** loop, the variables specified in the % **DO** statement itself (that is, the index, starting value, limit, and increment) must be compile-time variables or expressions. The **WHILE** clause may not be used. It is not necessary to restrict the statements in a **DO** group to compile-time statements. The % **END** statement terminates the loop. When a source program statement is present in such a loop, that statement is not executed. Instead, it is examined for possible replacement resulting from the other statements.

This facility can be used to force a more efficient compilation in certain instances where repetition is required but execution time savings may be more important than conservation of storage. For example, the source program loop

DO I = 1 **TO** 12; X(I) = X(I)*I; **END**;

would cause the compiler to set up a sequence of instructions in which a special counter keeps track of the index I. Each time I is incremented and another value of X is processed, the special counter is tested to determine whether the cycle is to be repeated or not. This continous process of incrementation and testing is often more time-consuming than the processing represented by a straightforward sequence of statements, one for each member of the array X. By using a compile-time **DO** loop around the source statement

X(I) = X(I)*I;

it is possible to create such an incrementation and testing process on a temporary basis, resulting in the desired instruction sequence. We can examine how this happens by considering the following loop:

% **DECLARE** I **FIXED**;

% **DO** I = 1 **TO** 12;

X(I) = X(I)*I;

% **END**;

% **DEACTIVATE** I;

further source statements;

The compile-time **DO** loop will cause an incrementation and testing process to be set up during the preprocessor stage, so each time the source statement is scanned, I will have a different value. Thus, the first time through the compile-time loop, the source statement will read

X(1) = X(1)*1;

Since the compile-time variable I was declared as a fixed-point number and not as a character, a scan of the source statements will indicate that there is nothing more to be changed, and that statement will be inserted in the source character string. The compile-time loop will then increment I, producing

X(2) = X(2)*2;

Again, the scanning mechanism will not find anything to replace, and this statement will be inserted into the source character string. This process will continue until the loop is terminated, resulting in the insertion of 12 individual assignment statements. At that point, I will have a value of 13 (one more than the specified limit). The % **END** statement is followed by an instruction that deactivates I, so that it can cause no further replacement.

XVIII.1.6   **SUBSTR** as a Compile-Time Built-in Function

None of PL/I's built-in functions is available for use in compile-time statements with the exception of **SUBSTR**. When a reference to that function appears in a compile-time statement, the function is invoked in a normal manner as part of that statement's execution. If the programmer wishes to execute the **SUBSTR** function during the preprocessor stage even though that function appears in a source program statement, he may do so by including the statement

% **ACTIVATE SUBSTR**;

at some point prior to where the function is used.

XVIII.1.7 The % **INCLUDE** Statement

One of the most versatile compile-time features allows the incorporation of text from external files into the final version of a source program. Texts to be incorporated in this fashion generally consist of standardized declarations that are to be incorporated identically in all programs associated with a large project, a large table of constants, standard procedures, or sequences of statements that need to be included internally rather than as external procedures. The mechanism for introducing such external information is triggered by the % **INCLUDE** statement, whose general form is

% label:**INCLUDE** name;

or

% **INCLUDE** name;

where "name" refers to an identifier by which the external data are known to the system (that is, a file name or a data set name). When the software encounters an **INCLUDE** statement, the named material is found and scanned as if it were part of the initial source program. Appropriate replacements are made, and the scan continues as before. As an example, suppose that a data set named REF contained the following declaration:

DECLARE 1 SUMMARY,

    2 PART__NO **FIXED**(5,0);

    2 PART__NAME **CHARACTER**(8),

    2 TOTAL__ITEMS,

      3 PACKED **FIXED**(4),

      3 LOOSE **FIXED**(4);

and we wanted to incorporate this declaration into our source program except that instead of referring to the major structure as SUMMARY we wanted to call it STATUS. Our compile-time statements would appear as

% **DECLARE** SUMMARY **CHARACTER**;

% SUMMARY = 'STATUS';

% **INCLUDE** REF;

The **INCLUDE** statement will bring the information in from REF and duplicate the declaration. However, since SUMMARY, the name appearing in the declaration, is also declared as a compile-time variable, it will be replaced by STATUS, so that the final declaration to be inserted in the source program will read

DECLARE 1 STATUS,

  2 PART__NO **FIXED**(5,0),

  2 PART__NAME **CHARACTER**(8),

  2 TOTAL__ITEMS,

    3 PACKED **FIXED**(4),

    3 LOOSE **FIXED**(4);

Illustration 53

To examine the basic operation of the preprocessor, we shall present it with a simple procedure in which we wish to expand a **DO** loop and replace some variable names with more elaborate ones: X is to be replaced by VELOCITY, Y by VELOCITY__SUM, B by MAX__VELOCITY, and AV by AVG__VELOCITY. Note that we have exploited the preprocessor's concatenating ability by specifying the newly replaced X whenever we want the string VELOCITY. The original listing is shown below, followed by the revision produced during preprocessing:

```
        ILL53: PROCEDURE OPTIONS (MAIN);

COMPILE-TIME MACRO PROCESSOR
MACRO SOURCE2 LISTING

   1      ILL53: PROCEDURE OPTIONS (MAIN);
   2          % DECLARE (X,Y,B,AV) CHARACTER, I FIXED;
   3          % X='VELOCITY';    % Y=X||'_SUM';    % B='MAX_'||X;    % AV='AVG_'||X;
   4          DECLARE (X(12),B) FIXED(2), (Y,Z) FIXED(5),,AV,NRUN;
   5
   6          ON ENDFILE(SYSIN) GO TO ENDUP;    NRUN=0;
   7      IN: GET LIST(X);    NRUN=NRUN+1;    Y=0;    B=0;
   8          % DO I=1 TO 12;
   9          Y=Y+X(I);    IF X(I) > B THEN B=X(I);
  10          % END;    % DEACTIVATE I;
  11          Z=Y-B;    AV=ROUND(Y/12,2);
  12          PUT SKIP EDIT(X,Y,Z,B,AV)
  13              (X(5), 10 (F(2),X(3)), 2 (F(5),X(3)),F(2),X(5),F(6,2));
  14          GO TO IN;
  15
  16      ENDUP: PUT SKIP(2) DATA (NRUN);
  17          END ILL53;

NO ERROR OR WARNING CONDITION HAS BEEN DETECTED FOR THIS MACRO PASS.
```

```
          ILL53: PROCEDURE OPTIONS (MAIN);

               MACRO PHASE OUTPUT

               GENERATED SOURCE STATEMENTS.


ILL53: PROCEDURE OPTIONS (MAIN);                                          1
       DECLARE ( VELOCITY (12), MAX_VELOCITY ) FIXED(2), ( VELOCITY_SUM   4 1
,Z) FIXED(5),, AVG_VELOCITY ,NRUN;                                        4 1
                                                                         5
       ON ENDFILE(SYSIN) GO TO ENDUP;     NRUN=0;                         6
   IN: GET LIST( VELOCITY );     NRUN=NRUN+1;     VELOCITY_SUM =0;        7 1
MAX_VELOCITY =0;                                                          7 1
          VELOCITY_SUM = VELOCITY_SUM + VELOCITY (          1 );    IF    9 1
VELOCITY (          1 ) >  MAX_VELOCITY  THEN  MAX_VELOCITY = VELOCITY (  9 1
   1 );                                                                   9 1
          VELOCITY_SUM = VELOCITY_SUM + VELOCITY (          2 );    IF    9 1
VELOCITY (          2 ) >  MAX_VELOCITY  THEN  MAX_VELOCITY = VELOCITY (  9 1
   2 );                                                                   9 1
          VELOCITY_SUM = VELOCITY_SUM + VELOCITY (          3 );    IF    9 1
VELOCITY (          3 ) >  MAX_VELOCITY  THEN  MAX_VELOCITY = VELOCITY (  9 1
   3 );                                                                   9 1
          VELOCITY_SUM = VELOCITY_SUM + VELOCITY (          4 );    IF    9 1
VELOCITY (          4 ) >  MAX_VELOCITY  THEN  MAX_VELOCITY = VELOCITY (  9 1
   4 );                                                                   9 1
          VELOCITY_SUM = VELOCITY_SUM + VELOCITY (          5 );    IF    9 1
VELOCITY (          5 ) >  MAX_VELOCITY  THEN  MAX_VELOCITY = VELOCITY (  9 1
   5 );                                                                   9 1
          VELOCITY_SUM = VELOCITY_SUM + VELOCITY (          6 );    IF    9 1
VELOCITY (          6 ) >  MAX_VELOCITY  THEN  MAX_VELOCITY = VELOCITY (  9 1
   6 );                                                                   9 1
          VELOCITY_SUM = VELOCITY_SUM + VELOCITY (          7 );    IF    9 1
VELOCITY (          7 ) >  MAX_VELOCITY  THEN  MAX_VELOCITY = VELOCITY (  9 1
   7 );                                                                   9 1
          VELOCITY_SUM = VELOCITY_SUM + VELOCITY (          8 );    IF    9 1
VELOCITY (          8 ) >  MAX_VELOCITY  THEN  MAX_VELOCITY = VELOCITY (  9 1
   8 );                                                                   9 1
          VELOCITY_SUM = VELOCITY_SUM + VELOCITY (          9 );    IF    9 1
VELOCITY (          9 ) >  MAX_VELOCITY  THEN  MAX_VELOCITY = VELOCITY (  9 1
   9 );                                                                   9 1
          VELOCITY_SUM = VELOCITY_SUM + VELOCITY (         10 );    IF    9 1
VELOCITY (         10 ) >  MAX_VELOCITY  THEN  MAX_VELOCITY = VELOCITY (  9 1
  10 );                                                                   9 1
          VELOCITY_SUM = VELOCITY_SUM + VELOCITY (         11 );    IF    9 1
VELOCITY (         11 ) >  MAX_VELOCITY  THEN  MAX_VELOCITY = VELOCITY (  9 1
  11 );                                                                   9 1
          VELOCITY_SUM = VELOCITY_SUM + VELOCITY (         12 );    IF    9 1
VELOCITY (         12 ) >  MAX_VELOCITY  THEN  MAX_VELOCITY = VELOCITY (  9 1
  12 );                                                                   9 1
          Z= VELOCITY_SUM - MAX_VELOCITY ;     AVG_VELOCITY =ROUND(      11 1
VELOCITY_SUM /12,2);                                                     11 1
          PUT SKIP EDIT( VELOCITY , VELOCITY_SUM ,Z, MAX_VELOCITY ,      12 1
AVG_VELOCITY )                                                          12 1
               ( VELOCITY (5), 10 (F(2), VELCCITY (3)), 2 (F(5),        13 1
VELOCITY (3)),F(2), VELOCITY (5),F(6,2));                               13 1
          GO TO IN;                                                      14
                                                                        15
ENDUP: PUT SKIP(2) DATA (NRUN);                                          16
       END ILL53;                                                        17
```

Observe that the preprocessor output is not particularly readable. Also, note the need to deactivate X in order to prevent it from being replaced in the **X** format item. This illustrates the fact that language keywords should not, in general, be used as compile-time variables.

XVIII.2   COMPILE-TIME PROCEDURES

An entire procedure can be written for execution during the processor stage to produce some type of change in the source program. As with an individual compile-time statement, the procedure itself does not appear in the final source language text. Because of their nature, certain procedures cannot utilize most of the facilities available under ordinary circumstances. They must all be internal function procedures, invoked by a function reference and not by a **CALL**. Since the value returned by such a procedure is subject to the same restrictions governing compile-time variables, that value may not have any other attributes besides **CHARACTER** or **FIXED**.

As would be expected, a compile-time procedure must start with a statement having the form

% label: **PROCEDURE** (param1, param2, etc.) **RETURNS** attribute);

where "label" is the primary entry name and (param1, param2, etc.) represents the list of parameters. The **END** label; statement which terminates the procedure, must also have a preceding percent sign. Note, however, that the other statements inside a compile-time procedure must *not* be written with any percent signs, even though they are *all* compile-time statements. That is, a procedure cannot contain statements to insert text as, for example, the compile-time **DO** loop illustrated previously. The type of statements that may be included are still no more extensive than those allowed for compile-time use. These include **DECLARE**, the assignment statement, the null statement, the **IF**, **DO** group, and the **GO TO** statement, as long as its destination is not outside of the compile-time procedure. At least one **RETURN** statement is required, its usage being the same as for any function procedure, with no preceding percent sign used. When a declaration is made in a compile-time procedure, its scope encompasses only that procedure.

The attribute of the returned value must also be specified in the compile-time **PROCEDURE** statement, with the attribute being either **CHARACTER** or **FIXED** at the end.

When the scanning mechanism comes across a compile-time procedure, it is handled as a regular procedure in the source program. The scanner bypasses it and resumes its scan immediately after the **END** statement. When a reference to that procedure is found, the scanning mechanism executes that procedure, using the arguments given in the invoking statement, replacing the reference with the return value in the same manner that an activated identifier is replaced. Before any such reference is made, it is necessary to activate the compile-time procedure by means of a compile-time **ENTRY** declaration. The form is

% **DECLARE** name **ENTRY RETURNS** (attribute);

where "name" refers to the label of the compile-time procedure statement. If the procedure requires arguments to be supplied to it, the attributes of the corresponding parameters must be specified as part of the **ENTRY** declaration. (Remember that **CHARACTER** and **FIXED** are the only allowable attributes.) Thus, if we had a compile-time procedure CHANGE, requiring two arguments whose respective attributes are **FIXED** and **CHARACTER**, the declaration would read

% **DECLARE** CHANGE **ENTRY (FIXED, CHARACTER) RETURNS** (attribute);

The scanning mechanism will then look for the same number of arguments in the source program's function reference to the procedure. If the attributes do not match those specified by the declaration, the necessary conversion will be performed. The inclusion of these attributes in the declaration is not optional. If such specifications are not given, it is assumed that the procedure requires no arguments. When a source program statement invokes a compile-time procedure, it is possible that the arguments to be transferred to that procedure may themselves be subject to replacement. Transfer to the procedure is not made until the arguments are scanned and all possible replacements are performed. If the function reference were in a source statement, the return value is converted (if necessary) to character and scanned for replacement before being included in the generated program.

If the reference is in a compile-time statement, then the arguments must be compile-time variables or constants that are passed just like arguments for regular procedures.

The **ENTRY** declaration must also include a **RETURNS** option specifying the attribute of the value generated by the compile-time procedure. Thus, if the procedure named CHANGE, used in the previous sample statement, returned a character string, the full declaration would read

% **DECLARE** CHANGE **ENTRY (FIXED, CHARACTER)**

   RETURNS (CHARACTER);

The expression in the compile-time **RETURN** statement is converted to the attribute specified in the **RETURNS** attribute of the % **PROCEDURE** statement and this *must* be the same as that declared in the **ENTRY** declaration.

As an example, let us analyze the following sequences:

% **DECLARE** B **CHARACTER**, RAISE **ENTRY (CHARACTER, CHARACTER, FIXED) RETURNS (CHARACTER);**

   DECLARE (B,C,D,E)FIXED;

   % B = 'D';

   % RAISE: **PROCEDURE** (PAR1, PAR2, PAR3) **RETURNS (CHARACTER);**

   DECLARE (PAR1, PAR2,) **CHARACTER**, PAR3 **FIXED**;

   RETURN (PAR1 || ' +('||PAR2||')**'||PAR3);

   % **END** RAISE;

   B = 4 + RAISE (D,E,2);

The character string returned by the compile-time procedure RAISE consists of the three arguments concatenated together, with the first two being separated by a plus sign and the second and third by a double asterisk. The parentheses are included to assure that the exponentiation applies to the entire second argument. Since the three arguments supplied to the procedure are B, E, and 2, respectively, the source program assignment statement

    B = 4 + RAISE(D,E,2);

would be modified initially to read

    D = 4 + D + E**2;

However, the variable B is itself subject to replacement because it has been activated by the compile-time declaration, so the final source statement would read

    C = 4 + D + E**2;

The following statements illustrate the use of this procedure in different circumstances:

    E = 73 * (RAISE (B−4,C+B*D,3));

results in

    E = 73 * (D −4 + (C + D*D) **3;

whereas

    %B = RAISE (B, E+C,2);

changes the value of the compile-time variable to

    'B + (E+ C) ** 2';

and, finally,

    X = RAISE(C,D,E);

is illegal because E cannot be converted to **FIXED**.

PROBLEMS

1. Introduce appropriate compile-time variables in Illustration 51 so that a new PL/I program is produced with the following name changes:

Old Name	New Name
CARD	INPUT_DATA
PS	CURRENT_POINT
PT	POINT_ARRAY
L	STRING_LGTH

2. Modify Illustration 9 so that the compiler is given a program in which the additions and subtractions in the formulas are reversed (that is, all additions become subtractions and vice versa).

SUMMARY OF IMPORTANT TERMS

% **INCLUDE**	The statement type that provides the vehicle for incorporating sequences of text from external sources into a PL/I source program.
Activation	In the context of compile-time operations, the process of making a designated identifier available for scrutiny by the PL/I preprocessor.
Compile-time statement	A statement specifying some type of action by the PL/I preprocessor with the purpose of effecting possible alterations in the source program prior to its submittal to the PL/I compiler.
Deactivation	The process of removing a designated identifier from the scope of scrutiny by the PL/I preprocessor. This allows such scrutiny to be limited to desired parts of a source program.
Preprocessor	A procedural system designed to operate on a PL/I source program with the purpose of altering its contents by selective replacement of characters in accordance with criteria specified by the programmer.
Rescanning	A preprocessing facility that allows the implementation of arbitrarily complex character replacement procedures by repeated examination (and associated processing) of a PL/I source program segment.

SUPPLEMENTARY READING

PL/I(F) Language Reference Manual, IBM Document No. GC28-8201. White Plains, N.Y.: IBM
Corporation, pp. 205-212.

PL/I(F) Programmer's Guide, IBM Document No. GC28-6594. White Plains, N.Y.: IBM Corporation,
pp. 41-60.

XIX ASYNCHRONOUS PROCESSING

One of the most versatile features of the hardware-software complexes for which PL/I is designed is the ability of the system to perform more than one operation at the same time. For some systems, this simultaneity is restricted to the execution of data transmission instructions while the processor is handling a sequence of internal commands. Other, more elaborate configurations may include replicate control circuits, so that there are really several processes sharing common storage, with each set of control circuits overseeing its own group of internal instructions. In order to make effective use of this capability, whatever its extent may be, the programmer must be able to identify those sections of the program whose execution may proceed in parallel and specify the degree of synchronization required to insure correct execution. Control must often shift back and forth between two procedures, because the decision as to whether to continue executing the instructions in one procedure may depend on the degree of completion of the other, so there is a necessity for constant interaction between several procedures. Consequently, the programmer must be able to construct and use mechanisms that will mediate among different processing sequences, interrupt one in favor of another, recognize the completion of each one, and assume or relinquish control based on a specified set of circumstances whose occurrence is unpredictable. This type of processing is termed *parallel processing*. It is contrasted with sequential processing by the fact that under parallel processing several processing sequences (usually procedures) are allowed to begin and progress at the same time. This does not necessarily mean that several instructions are being executed at the same time, although that very well may be true. More generally, it allows individual instructions or groups of instructions from different procedures to be interspersed among each other (out of the sequence in which they were originally written) to take advantage of the system's timing characteristics or other similar features. A set of actions performed in parallel may be either *asynchronous* or *synchronous*. A set of actions is asynchronous to the extent that the time order in which they progress is irrelevant and unpredictable; actions are synchronous to the extent that there is a rigid order in which the various events leading to their successful completion must take place.

XIX.1   THE TASK CONCEPT

Although such control of execution has been provided for a variety of systems, its incorporation in PL/I represents the first instance of its availability through a major high-level language. The mechanism for its implementation hinges on the ability to provide a particular series of processing operations into a number of *tasks*. The supervisory system under which PL/I operates treats each processing assignment as a task. Thus, even though we have not stated it explicitly, the processing of each program we have written has been handled as a single task. It should be understood that the term refers to the actual execution of a particular sequence of instructions and not to the instructions themselves. Since we have not specified otherwise, each task thus far has involved the execution of a single program. When proper specifications are included, it is possible to define the task as part of a program, an entire program, or a series involving several programs. The consideration of an information-handling procedure as one or more tasks is not merely an organizational convenience. Each task is an actual operational entity, which can be given a name and may have indicators attached to it showing its importance relative to other tasks. When this type of operation is in effect, the system is said to be a *multitasking* environment.

XIX.1.1   The **TASK** Option and **TASK** Attribute

Neither PL/I nor the supervisory system under which a particular implementation is operating has any implicit mechanism for determining ahead of time that a particular program is going to use multitasking. Accordingly, such intent must be specified explicitly. The basic vehicle for presenting this information is the **TASK** option which is added to the main **PROCEDURE** statement as follows:

name: **PROCEDURE OPTIONS (MAIN,TASK)**;

The **TASK** option does not cause any tasks to be created; it merely states that the tasking facilities are to be used in the program. A task is created by a special use of the **CALL** statement. When a task is created, it may be given a name by associating it with a variable which has been declared as a task name. The form is as follows:

    DECLARE name **TASK**;

where "name" is an identifier subject to the same rules that apply to all variable names. This causes the compiler to allocate storage in which it maintains a number of items relating to the status of the associated task. A task name can be a member of an array or structure. The scope of the task name may be declared to be **EXTERNAL(INTERNAL** is assumed), and the storage class may be designated as **STATIC (AUTOMATIC** is assumed). The main procedure is always treated as a task by the system even if the multitasking facilities are not being used; its execution is known as the *major task*.

It is important to establish the fact that the declaration of a variable name with the **TASK** attribute does not associate that name with a particular task. Rather, it defines the use of that name so that it can be associated with a particular task *at the time the task is created*. In addition, it gives the programmer a way of setting a *priority* (that is, an indicator of relative urgency) for that name. Then, when that name is linked with a task, the accompanying priority is known and used by the system to help regulate its processing.

XIX.1.2   Creation and Termination of a Task

Since a task involves the execution of a sequence of instructions, it is conceptually a dynamic entity. It does not exist until it occurs, and ceases to exist upon completion or termination. The process of initiating a task is referred to as *attaching a task*, and its expiration (regardless of the circumstances) is called *task termination*.

XIX.1.2.1   Task Creation

A task is created by a **CALL** statement with one or more of the tasking options, issued from a task already in process. (Remember that the execution of the main procedure is always a task.) The basic form for the invocation is

    CALL procedure (arg1, arg2, etc.) **TASK** (name);

where "procedure" is the entry name of the procedure being invoked asynchronously and "name" is the name of the task created by the **CALL**. [Note that the **CALL** statement in this form is only valid if the **TASK** variable name has previously been assigned a **PRIORITY** value (See XIX.4.1).] This name may correspond to one previously used in a

DECLARE statement. If it has not been declared, PL/I will deduce that it refers to a task from its context. The **CALL** statement used in this way differs from an ordinary **CALL** statement in that the calling procedure is not suspended until the called procedure completes its execution; rather, it continues immediately with the next statement. Once the call is made and both tasks are proceeding asynchronously, the execution of the calling procedure is known as the *attaching task* and the execution of the invoked procedure is referred to as the *attached task*.

Note that the **CALL** may include arguments as in an ordinary (synchronous) invocation. Moreover, the task name, being like any other variable, may be subscripted or qualified. A task thus created is known as a *subtask*.

Care must be exercised if the attaching task is going to continue to refer to the arguments, especially if either task will change them. Since the two tasks are being processed asynchronously, unpredictable results are likely.

XIX.1.2.2   Termination of Tasks

A task is considered to be completed when it has executed any of the following types of statements: an **EXIT** statement; a **STOP** statement (the execution of a **STOP** statement in any task will terminate all tasks); a **RETURN** statement; or an **END** statement. Until a task is terminated (by whatever means) it is said to be active. Of course, several tasks may be active at any given time.

XIX.2   EVENTS AND EVENT VARIABLES

In order for parallel tasks to proceed properly, it may not be possible to allow totally asynchronous execution; the programmer may have to keep some track of the processing in each task. This may be necessary in cases where proper execution of certain statements in task A require values produced by a portion of task B, so task A must be informed that the particular portion of task B is completed. Such synchronization is achieved by means of *event variables*, signaling the completion of a task or part of a task.

The **CALL** statement may be amended to support the potential dependency of one task on the completion of another by specifying the **EVENT** option as follows:

CALL procedure (arguments) **TASK** (name) **EVENT** (name1);

where "name1" is an event variable that will automatically be set to a specific value when the designated task is completed. Then, some other task can test this event variable and base its action on the current value.

Note that this type of **CALL** will cause the priority of the attached task to be undefined unless "name" has been assigned a priority value at some earlier point, or the **PRIORITY** option is used.

XIX.2.1   Declaration of Events

Event variables are assigned names, as with any other variable, by means of the **DECLARE** statement, having the general form

DECLARE name **EVENT**;

The same additional attributes may be assigned to event variables as to task names. Once such a name has been declared, it can be associated with a given task and will signal the completion of the task or of a particular point in the task.

Each event variable is associated (by the compiler) with an area in storage used to accomodate information about the event. Two of these items are available to the programmer. The *completion value* is a single bit that is $'0'$**B** as long as the event is incomplete. As soon as the event is completed, the completion value is set to $'1'$**B**. Also available is a *status value* with the attributes **FIXED BINARY** (15) that indicates the circumstances under which the associated task is completed. An event variable may be defined contextually (without explicit declaration) by using it in a **CALL** statement that creates a task. A **CALL** statement with the **EVENT** option always creates a task even if the **TASK** option is omitted. For example, the statement

CALL RTN (A,B) **EVENT** (E1);

creates a task that has no name available to the programmer. This task involves the execution of procedure RTN using the arguments A and B. Associated with the task will be the event variable E1. When the **CALL** is executed, E1's completion value will be set to $'0'$**B** and its status value will be initialized to zero. Upon completion of the task, E1's completion value will change to $'1'$**B** and a new status value will be produced in accordance with the completion circumstances. The only consequence of creating an unnamed task is that the programmer loses the ability to change its priority dynamically.

XIX.2.2   Setting of Event Values

The programmer may exercise control over event variables in that he can test and/or set the completion value. This is done through the **COMPLETION** built-in function with the designated event variable as its argument. When **COMPLETION** is used as a built-in function, the resulting expression may be used like any other bit string of length 1.

The **COMPLETION** function also may appear as a pseudovariable on the left-hand side of an assignment statement.

To illustrate, suppose that we had a procedure in which we were reading records from a file named SOURCE and storing them in an array named HERE. Once we have stored 100 such records, we want to designate this as the completion of an event. Naming our event variable HAPPEN, and assuming that HERE and SOURCE have been appropriately declared, our sequence would be as follows:

Subtask	*Attaching Task*
READIT: **PROCEDURE** (HAPPEN); **DECLARE** HAPPEN **EVENT**; **DO** I = 1 **TO** 100;	**DECLARE**(END,TEST)**EVENT**; **CALL** READIT(TEST)**EVENT** (END);
READ FILE(SOURCE)**INTO**(HERE)I));	
END;	**IF COMPLETION**(TEST) **THEN**...;
COMPLETION(HAPPEN) = '1'**B**;	

Any attaching task can then determine whether or not 100 records have been read by testing the event variable passed to the parameter HAPPEN; continued execution or delay of the attaching task can be dictated by that value. **COMPLETION** can be used as any other PL/I function. For example, if HAPPEN is an event variable and C is declared as a bit string of length 1, the statement

   C = **COMPLETION**(HAPPEN);

will return a value of '0'**B** in location C if the event indicated by HAPPEN is not completed, and '1'**B** if it is.

XIX.3 SYNCHRONIZATION OF TASKS

Although it is very convenient for tasks to be processed asynchronously, the program usually reaches a point at which it is necessary for a set of asynchronous tasks to be completed before processing can continue properly. To make sure this point is reached correctly, the programmer must be able to check the progress of an attached task and delay the continued execution of the attaching one, if necessary, based on the status of a particular event variable.

XIX.3.1 The **WAIT** Statement

PL/I allows the programmer to effect such *sychronization* by means of the **WAIT** statement, whose basic form is

   WAIT (event1,event2,etc.);

where the parenthesized list refers to one or more event variables. When this statement is included in an attaching task, the program will process that task asynchronously with the one attached until the **WAIT** statement is reached. At that point, the program will test the values of the event variables listed in the statement. If each value is $'1'$**B**, processing will continue; if not, the task in which the **WAIT** statement appears will be suspended until all the event variable values are $'1'$**B**. Suppose we have the sequence shown below:

```
PROCESS: PROCEDURE OPTIONS(MAIN,TASK);

         DECLARE DO__IT TASK, (BEACON,LIGHT) EVENT;

         statement1;
              .
              .
         statement2;

         CALL ASYNC TASK(DO__IT) EVENT (BEACON);
              .
              .
         statement3;
              .
              .
         statement4;
              .
              .
         WAIT (LIGHT);

         statement5;

              ASYNC:PROCEDURE;
                   .
                   .
         statement6;

         statement7;
              .
              .
         COMPLETION(LIGHT)='1'B;
              .
              .
         statement8;
              .
              .
              END ASYNC;

         statement9;

         WAIT (BEACON);

         statement10;

         END PROCESS;
```

In this example, the main procedure PROCESS is the attaching task. Execution of the main procedure continues synchronously through statement2, at which point the task DO_IT, consisting of the procedure ASYNC, is attached. Execution of the two tasks now proceeds asynchronously until the **WAIT** (LIGHT) statement is reached in the attaching task. That task will not continue until statement7 in ASYNC is executed, following which, completion is immediately signaled. At that point, asynchronous processing can once again continue through statement9 in the main procedure. Immediately after that instruction is executed, the event variable BEACON is tested to determine whether the attached task has been completed. If it has not, processing of the statements in PROCESS is suspended until the end of ASYNC, at which point the program is again synchronized and processing can conclude with statement10 and the main procedure's **END** statement (see Figure 19.1).

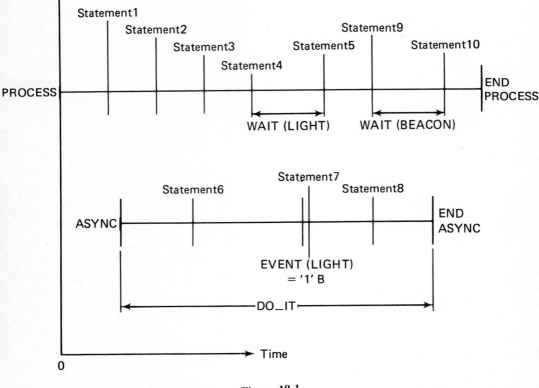

Figure 19.1

The **WAIT** statement may also take the form

WAIT(event1,event2,etc.)(expression);

where (expression) is any legitimate PL/I expression that can be evaluated to a single numerical value. This value is truncated to an integer and is used to determine the number of events that must be completed before processing is resumed. Thus, the statement

WAIT(EX1,EX2,EX3,EX4,EX5,EX6)(3);

will suspend processing until a minimum of any three event variables in the list have values of $'1'\mathbf{B}$. If the expression value exceeds the number of events in the list, the value is set equal to that number. The entire statement is nullified if the expression value is zero or less.

XIX.3.2 The **DELAY** Statement

Processing can be suspended at any point in the procedure for a desired length of time by using the **DELAY** statement. An instruction of the form

DELAY (expression);

will cause the expression to be evaluated to an integer, and processing will be suspended for that many milliseconds.

XIX.4 PRIORITY IN ASYNCHRONOUS PROCESSING

Additional control can be obtained over asynchronous processing by assigning a level of importance to various tasks. Such control can be very important in complex procedures designed to receive data from various input sources at unanticipated times. When this happens, it may be necessary to suspend the execution of one procedure in preference to another; for example, transmission of data from a remote terminal across telephone lines may halt input transmission from some other device. Such contingencies may be handled in PL/I programs by assigning relative priorities to various tasks, thus enabling the program to determine whether a particular task should be interrupted for some other one.

XIX.4.1 Setting Priorities of Tasks

The mechanism for establishing the relative "importance" of a particular task is the **PRIORITY** pseudovariable, which takes the form of

PRIORITY(task) = expression;

where (task) is the name of the task for which priority is being established, and "expression" is any legitimate arithmetic expression that can be evaluated to a decimal integer. The number obtained by evaluating this expression determines the relative priority of the task named in the pseudovariable with respect to the task in which the assignment statement is used. Thus, a statement of this form is not used in the task whose priority is being established. If the programmer wishes to set the priority of the task in that same task, no task name is given, and the assignment statement takes the more basic form

PRIORITY = expression;

The value established by the **PRIORITY** pseudovariable is used by the system within the context of established overall priorities; that is, the final priority resulting from an explicit assignment could differ from the one specified by the programmer. There is a priority associated with a particular job relative to other jobs submitted to the processing system. This priority is set outside of the program itself and is not influenced by the number of tasks associated with that job. For example, IBM's Operating System allows priority levels of 0-14, with 0 being the least "urgent." This priority level (designated by the user/operator or assigned automatically by the system) is used by the system to compute a corresponding "internal priority" for the main task. IBM's system does this by the formula

$$pi = 16 * pj + 10$$

where p_i is the "internal priority" and p_j is the priority assigned to the job. The value of p_i represents the maximum priority for any task associated with that job, including the major task. (Thus, p_i cannot exceed 234.) Then the priority p_t of any attached task will be expressed as a value relative to p_i. For example, suppose that a job is submitted with priority 5 and the major task creates a subtask, specifying **PRIORITY**(-4). Since $p_j = 5$, p_i will be 90 and the resulting priority for this subtask would be $90-4$, or 86. If a priority specification were to raise a subtask's priority above p_i, it would automatically be reset to p_i (hence the earlier reference to automatic adjustment); a computed p_t of less than zero forces an adjustment to zero.

XIX.4.2   The **PRIORITY** Function

The programmer can determine the priority of a particular task relative to some other task by means of the **PRIORITY** built-in function used in a statement of the type

X = **PRIORITY**(task);

As a result, the program will determine the priority value of the task named in the single argument and return that value to location X. Again, this is a relative value, given with respect to the task in which the function is invoked.

XIX.4.3   Use of Priorities During Task Creation

As an alternative to using the **PRIORITY** pseudovariable for assigning priorities to tasks, such values may be established right at the time the task is created, in the **CALL** statement. To do this, the statement now takes the form

CALL procedure **TASK** (name) **PRIORITY** (expression);

where (name) is the name of the attached task. The terms in (expression) will be evaluated and converted, if necessary, to a decimal integer, establishing the priority of the attached task relative to the attaching one. The **EVENT** option may be included as before.

Now that we have outlined the setting of priorities, it can be seen that the designation of a specific task name is really not essential unless the programmer wishes to assign or evaluate the priority of that task while it is active by means of the **PRIORITY** pseudovariable or function. Barring such usage, the programmer can include commands such as

CALL procedure **PRIORITY** (expression);

or

CALL procedure **EVENT** (name) **PRIORITY** (expression);

without committing any logical or procedural errors. Under these circumstances, the compiler will automatically recognize that a task is being created and will assign some type of identifier to that task without further concern by the programmer. If both **TASK** and **PRIORITY** are omitted, the system assigns a default priority equal to priority of the attaching task. If **TASK** is specified and **PRIORITY** is not, then the task variable must have previously been assigned a priority or it will be undefined.

XIX.5   HANDLING OF FILES IN ASYNCHRONOUS PROCESSING

When a task includes the handling of a particular **DIRECT UPDATE** file, it is possible to protect records in that file in such a way that no other task in the same job can read, delete, or rewrite a particular record while the given task is handling it. When such protection is required, it is established through the use of **EXCLUSIVE** attribute in the **DECLARE** or **OPEN** statement. This attribute must be explicitly included; it is not assumed.

XIX.5.1   Locking and Unlocking of Records

The actual protection process takes place while a record from an exclusive file is being read.

Once the **READ** statement is executed, the record thus transmitted is said to be *locked*. It cannot be processed by any other task until it is "unlocked" by the task that caused it to be locked. If the programmer specifically wants that record to be accessible to another task, he must say so by using the **NOLOCK** option as follows:

READ FILE(filename) **INTO** (place) **KEY** (expression) **NOLOCK**;

Once a record is locked, it can only be unlocked by the task that locks it. This may occur by means of any of the following: a **REWRITE** statement specifying the same key; a **DELETE** statement specifying the same key; a **CLOSE** statement that closes that file; completion of the task in which the record was locked; or the **UNLOCK** statement having the general form

UNLOCK FILE(filename) **KEY** (expression);

The contents of (expression) are evaluated and converted to a character string used to identify the particular record to be unlocked in the file designated by (filename). The file referred to in such an expression must have the **DIRECT, UPDATE**, and **EXCLUSIVE** attributes; otherwise, an error condition may be raised.

XIX.5.2   Use of the **EVENT** Option in File Manipulations

When a computing system is equipped with the facility to carry on input/output operation while the central processor is executing internal instructions, PL/I allows the programmer to specify such simultaneous operations by adding the **EVENT** option to **READ, WRITE, REWRITE**, and **DELETE** statements. This may be done for any type of **RECORD** file except one with the **SEQUENTIAL** and **BUFFERED** attributes. The option takes the general form

EVENT (name);

When this option is included, the event variable named in it will be set to '0'**B** until the input/output operation is completed, at which point its value will be switched to '1'**B**. Thus, if we were executing an attached task in which records were being read from a **DIRECT INDEXED** file name ROSTER, and we said

READ FILE(ROSTER) **KEY**('JK' D) **EVENT**(BULB) **INTO**(AREA);

the current value in location D would be concatenated with the string 'JK' and the result would be used to identify the record to be read. Once the input was complete, the value designated by the name BULB would be changed from '0'**B** to '1'**B**. Thus, the attaching task could use BULB in a **WAIT** statement, as explained previously. Note that it would not work to test BULB in an **IF** statement since an input/output event is not complete until the **WAIT** statement is issued. This is because it may be necessary to raise **ON** conditions at that time.

SUMMARY OF IMPORTANT TERMS

Asynchronous processing	An operating situation in which the timing relationships among concurrent processes have no effect on the proper outcome of those processes.
Attached task	The task activated by a **CALL** statement from another task.
Attaching task	The task containing the **CALL** statement that activates (attaches) another task.
Attachment	In the context of multitasking, the process of initiating a task.
Event variable	A type of variable (designated by the **EVENT** option) used to indicate the completion of a task or part of a task.
Locking	The process of assigning a designated record in a file to a particular task, thereby making it unavailable to any other task.
Multitasking	An operating environment in which several tasks may be in progress at any one time.
Parallel processing	An operating environment in which it is possible to have several (related or unrelated) processing sequences in arbitrary stages of completion. Many parallel processing systems include hardware that allows these processes to operate simultaneously.
Priority	In the context of multitasking, an indicator of the importance of a task relative to maximum and minimum numerical values defined for a particular system. This is set for a given task by the **PRIORITY** built-in function.
Synchronization	In the context of asynchronous processing, the technique of ensuring the completion of a task or part of a task (often by instituting an intentional delay) so that time-dependent events in separate tasks will occur in proper sequence.
Synchronous processing	A processing situation in which the proper outcome of concurrent tasks depends on rigid maintenance of specific time relationships among them.
Task	A conceptual unit of processing consisting of the execution of a procedure. Whereas the execution of a main procedure is a task by implication, the designation of other procedures as tasks must be handled explicitly by means of the declared **TASK** attribute.
Termination	In the context of multitasking, the expiration of a task.
Unlocking	The process of making a previously locked record available to other tasks.
WAIT	The statement type used to institute a controlled delay in a task. Regulation of its extent is governed by the completion status of designated event variables.

SUPPLEMENTARY READING

Ligomenides, P. A., *Information Processing Machines*. New York: Holt, Rinehart and Winston, 1965, pp. 10, 278-280.

Maurer, W.D., *Programming: An Introduction to Computer Languages and Techniques*. San Francisco: Holden-Day, 1968, p. 95.

PL/I Language Reference Manual, IBM Document No. GC28-8201. White Plains, N.Y.: IBM Corporation, pp. 194-203.

PL/I Programmer's Guide, IBM Document No. GC28-6594. White Plains, N.Y.: IBM Corporation, pp. 161-172.

APPENDIX A:
FLOWCHARTING

The task of developing a program can be facilitated by preparing a diagram that depicts the desired sequence of operations from which the actual source instructions are written. Such a diagram, called a *flowchart*, represents an exact representation of a program's logic and serves as a guide for subsequent implementation. When adequately constructed, the flowchart enables the programmer to examine the logic and so verify that the depicted flow of events actually will achieve the desired end. At the same time, the description of this procedure provides the information necessary for direct coding in a high-level programming language (PL/I in our case).

It is important to bear in mind that the individual designing the flowchart and the individual actually converting its flow of logic to a computer program often are not the same person. Flowcharts, therefore, describe a procedure not only for systems designers and analysts but also for others who might participate in the eventual implementation. Moreover, once the resulting program is operational, its flowchart serves as an effective item of documentation for users with widely varying technical skills, including those individuals unfamiliar with programming languages.

In order to standardize flowchart construction, the United States of America Standards Institute (now the American National Standards Institute) in June 1966 defined a set of symbols to be used for system and program flowcharts. These conventions have now been generally accepted and are outlined below.

Central to the flowcharting language is a series of enclosures of different shapes. The shape (not its size) defines the "meaning" of the symbol. For instance, a rectangular box may vary in size and in the extent of its contents, but it will always indicate one or more internal operations that correspond to one or more PL/I assignment statements.

Though many shapes are defined, there are six that may be considered as the basic nucleus for the preparation of most flowcharts.

1. The *slot* (Figure A.1) is used to denote the beginning or end of a program. As such it does not represent any particular operation, but serves as a point of reference. This symbol may also be used to show the initial and terminal points of individual procedures (where these procedures may be subroutines or other program segments).

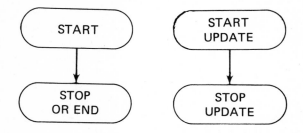

Figure A.1

2. The rectangle is used to indicate an internal operation which corresponds to one or more PL/I assignment statements. Information written in the box may describe these operations in symbolic terms or may merely state, in narrative form, which operations are carried out at that point. For example the sequence

A = 12.4 * X ** 2;
B = 3/X;
C = 4;

may be represented as

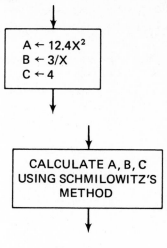

Figure A.2

3. A diamond-shaped box is used to describe some type of internal operation requiring a decision (such as that handled by an **IF** statement). Usually the decision point is stated as a yes-or-no question, so the resulting action takes on one of two alternatives. Thus, Figure A.3 shows a decision box representing a test for the last data card in a particular run.

Figure A.3

4. The trapezoid serves as a general input/output indicator, without any distinction as to the type of device involved. The usual practice is to specify the details of the data transmission (for example, type of operation, name of device) in narrative form (as shown in the example in Figure A.4).

Figure A.4

5. The rectangle with a pointed edge generally is used to indicate the start of a procedural component where a series of steps are repeated. This is illustrated for a **DO** loop in Figure A.5.

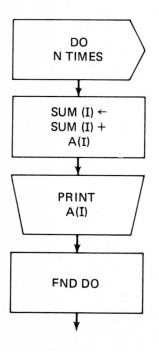

Figure A.5

6. Arrows serve to connect the various boxes in the flowchart and indicate the directions of the sequence (see Figure A.6). Loops as well as straightforward sequencing can be shown in this manner.

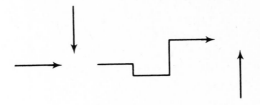

Figure A.6

The six basic symbols listed here by no means exhaust the variety used in flowcharts. Additional symbols for specifying specific parts of a flowchart in greater detail are shown in Figure A.7. Note especially the many input/output symbols whose shape suggest the type of physical medium or device being used.

In addition to portraying individual processing steps, these flowcharting symbols are used to indicate the *structure* of a program. This is done by combining certain symbols in specified ways to form well-defined unit activities or *constructs*. The integrity of each construct as an indivisible conceptual unit is underscored by the fact that it is implemented (regardless of the programming language used) with a single entry point and a single exit. In other words, a construct represents some type of processing activity that is conducted either in its entirety or not at all. Of course, there may be portions of the activity that are executed in one usage and bypassed in another, but the decisions controlling such pathways take place entirely within the construct. Accordingly the ANSI representation of a construct shows these terminal points explicitly (Figure A.8).

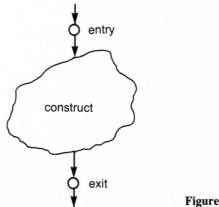

Figure A.8

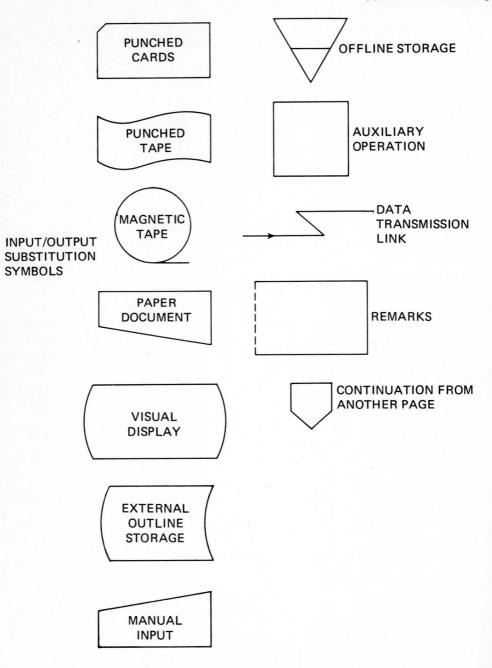

Figure A.7

the sequential construct

Processing conducted in sequence, i.e., without any branches, is depicted by the simple diagram shown in Figure A.9(a). Note that this diagram, though simpler to the one in Figure A.9(b), is structurally equivalent to it.

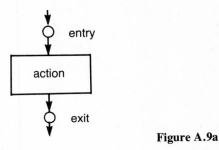

Figure A.9a

the **IF-THEN-ELSE** *construct*

This construct (Figure A.10) represents a two-way decision with an arbitrary unit action specified for each of the two alternative outcomes. The action may range from a null activity to a very complicated series of processes, with the only requirement being that it be specified as a single conceptual activity, with a single entry point and a single exit.

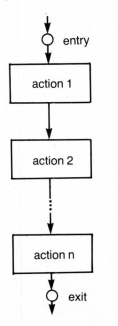

Figure A.9b

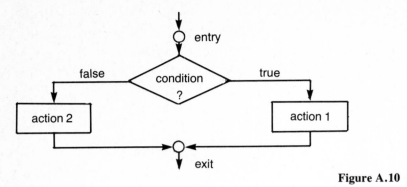

Figure A.10

the **DO-WHILE** *construct*

This is the most general construct for representing a cyclic activity. As seen in Figure A.11, the construct begins with a two-way test for the existence of some particular condition (with possible outcomes of either "true" or "false"). As long as the condition tests "true", the activity encompassed by the loop is performed. Since the test is conducted prior to each cycle (including the first one), the construct also accommodates the extreme condition whereby the condition tests "false" before the initial cycle, so that the loop is bypassed altogether.

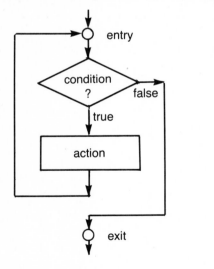

Figure A.11

the DO-UNTIL (REPEAT-UNTIL) *construct*

Unlike the **DO-WHILE** construct, this cyclic activity is characterized by the fact that it guarantees at least one performance of the specified activity. Accordingly, the activity itself precedes the test that determines whether it should be repeated or bypassed. This is reflected in the flow diagram (Figure A.12), where the single entry point is at the beginning of the activity and the single exit point follows a successful outcome of the test.

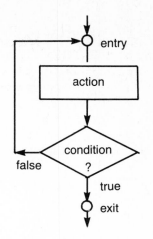

Figure A.12

the Pl/I **DO** *loop*

In this type of cyclic activity, the number of cycles, rather than a more general test condition, is of primary importance in controlling the loop. Accordingly, the **DO** loop is constructed with an explicitly defined *index* that operates within a specified range to monitor the repetitions of the loop. Since this range may be defined in a number of ways, it is awkward to categorize the **DO** loop as a **DO-WHILE** or REPEAT-UNTIL construct — its behavior may resemble either one, depending on the particular circumstances. Because of this ambivalence, a separate flowcharting representation is used to indicate the prominence of the index (Figure A.13).

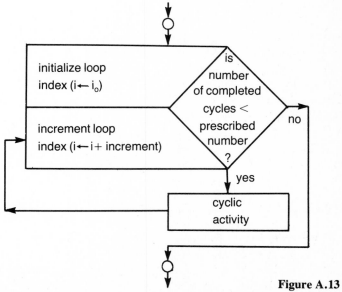

Figure A.13

the case construct

   This is a direct extension of the more basic **IF-THEN-ELSE** construct and, in fact, can be synthesized from it. Thus, its use is more a matter of convenience than a basic necessity. Specifically, it expresses a situation in which a test may have more than two mutually exclusive outcomes, with each outcome prompting its own respective action. As is true with the **IF-THEN-ELSE** construct, the entire complex (tests and activities) is treated as a single conceptual unit (Figure A.14) with a single entry point and a single exit (i.e., "perform this multi-way test to select the proper activity; then perform that activity.").

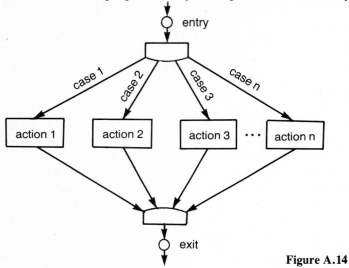

Figure A.14

   Increased appreciation and use of structured programming prompted the introduction of an alternative flowcharting system. In this type of chart, called the Nassi-Schneiderman chart (after its originators), the emphasis is on structure. This is seen in the fact that each program, routine, or other processing module is represented as an enclosed rectangle (Figure A.15) with the sequence of conceptual activities proceeding from top to bottom. Unlike the ANSI charts, there are no explicitly shown branches; instead, loops and other changes in sequence are implied by the type of activity being depicted. Since each of the N-S symbols (by definition) represents one of a specific set of construct types, it is (virtually) impossible to construct an N-S chart with components outside the realm of these specified constructs.

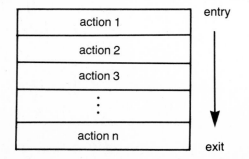

Figure A.15

the N-S sequential construct

A sequential activity is represented by a rectangle extending across the processing framework (Figure A.16). Note that the entry and exit points are not shown explicitly; their presence is implied by the upper and lower boundaries of the rectangular enclosure, and by the fact that the chart always is read from top to bottom.

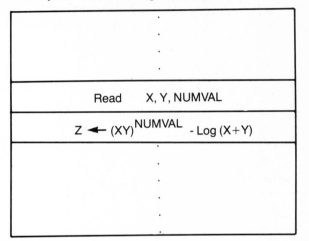

Figure A.16

the N-S **IF-THEN-ELSE** *construct*

In the N-S representation of this construct (Figure A.17), each of the alternative activities is specified under its respective motivating test outcome. The fact that the two activities are mutually exclusive is indicated by the vertical line that separates them. Conversely, the disappearance of that vertical boundary represents the reunification of the alternative pathways into a single sequential flow.

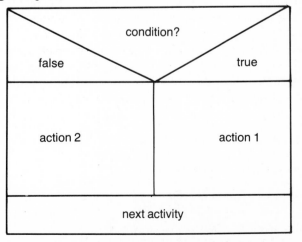

Figure A.17

the N-S **DO-WHILE** *construct*

As seen in Figure A.18, this construct is symbolized by a rectangular framework that encompasses the processing comprising the loop. "Admission" to the activities within the loop requires a positive outcome for the test at the loop's entrance. Completion of the loop (i.e., performance of the final (lowest) activity contained in the construct) implies an automatic branch back to the test at the top of the construct; failure to fulfill the conditions of the test results in a bypass of the loop to the next activity described in the chart.

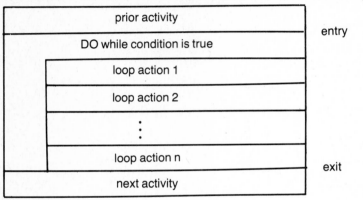

Figure A.18

Nesting of **DO-WHILE** constructs is straightforward (Figure A.19). As the diagram indicates, each cycle of the outer loop requires a complete set of cycles for the inner loop.

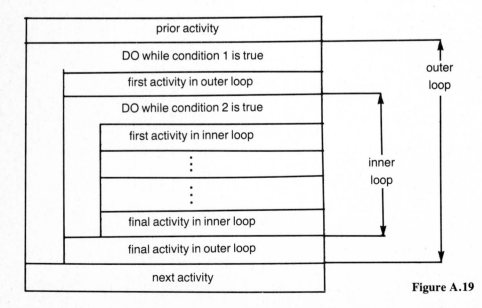

Figure A.19

the N-S **REPEAT-UNTIL** *construct*

The guaranteed first cycle of the REPEAT-UNTIL construct is reflected in the N-S representation of this construct (Figure A.20): the "admission" test follows the final activity within the loop. Thus, a successful outcome sends the process back to the beginning of the loop (i.e., the top of the construct), and an unsuccessful one causes an entry to the next activity. Nesting of REPEAT-UNTIL constructs is straightforward, following the same general form as illustrated in Figure A.19 for nested **DO-WHILE** constructs. Similarly, nesting of a **DO-WHILE** construct inside a REPEAT-UNTIL construct (or vice-versa) causes no special complications.

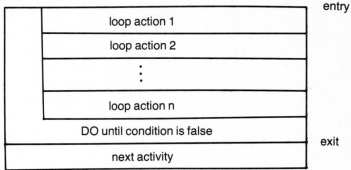

Figure A.20

the N-S **DO** *loop*

The potentially ambivalent nature of the **DO** loop is emphasized by a framework which, in essence, combines the properties of the **DO-WHILE** and REPEAT-UNTIL constructs. There is a symbolic "test" before and after the contained activity, implying that the possible conditions for loop control include those permitting zero cycles through the loop. This is seen in Figure A.21.

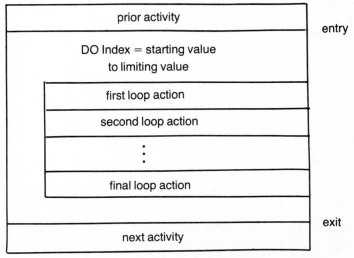

Figure A.21

the N-S case construct

This representation (Figure A.22) is a direct extension of the N-S symbol for the **IF-THEN-ELSE** construct. Each of the alternative activities is represented under its respective test outcome, separated from the others by vertical lines.

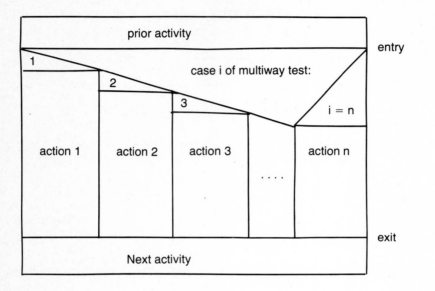

Figure A.22

APPENDIX B:
DATA CONVERSION

PL/I allows the programmer to mix variables of different types within the same expression or statement. Consequently, there are numerous situations in which the compiler must generate data conversions automatically. Used properly, this is a powerful facility, which can save the programmer much time, effort, and drudgery. Used carelessly, this facility can produce programs loaded with unnecessary conversions, which waste time and space. Moreover, this can lead to surprising and erroneous results. Such is the case in the simple example shown in Figure B.1 where careless use of mixed-mode expressions has forced the compiler to incorporate unnecessary data conversions. (Check the differences between the computed values shown in the figure and those you would have expected from exact calculations.)

To help examine the conversion mechanisms and their properties, it would be useful to categorize the various kinds of data handled by PL/I. The *type* of a variable, determined from its data attributes, refers to the nature of the data that the variable can contain and to the form in which the data are held internally. (A summary of PL/I's available types is shown in Table B.1.) Within a given type there may be finer distinctions, which we shall term *subtypes*. For example, one subtype of the arithmetic type is described by the attributes **BINARY FIXED COMPLEX** (15,3). The following rules qualify the behavior of these attributes:

```
        B1: PROCEDURE OPTIONS (MAIN);

STMT LEVEL NEST
  1                     B1: PROCEDURE OPTIONS (MAIN);
  2    1                    DECLARE X BINARY FLOAT (21), I BINARY FIXED (15);

  3    1                    PUT FILE (SYSPRINT) PAGE EDIT ('    I       X')(A);   PUT SKIP;

  5    1                    DO I=1 TO 20;
  6    1    1               X=.05*I-.01;   PUT SKIP EDIT(I,X)(F(4),F(8,3));
  8    1    1               END;

  9    1                    END B1;


    I     X

    1    0.039
    2    0.086
    3    0.133
    4    0.180
    5    0.227
    6    0.273
    7    0.320
    8    0.367
    9    0.414
   10    0.461
   11    0.508
   12    0.555
   13    0.602
   14    0.648
   15    0.695
   16    0.742
   17    0.789
   18    0.836
   19    0.883
   20    0.930
```

- Attributes shown on the same line in the table are mutually exclusive.
- A variable of a given type may have only those attributes shown within the section of the table corresponding to that tape.
- The **VARYING** attribute conflicts with the **PICTURE** attribute.
- The solid horizontal lines divide the table into regions; conversions are possible only between that which lie within the same region.

Our discussion will restrict itself to conversions between problem data types.

Whenever a conversion is necessary in PL/I, there are two values involved: The value before conversion (the *source*) and the value after conversion (the *target*). When a conversion is carried out in more than one step, each result along the way is called an *intermediate target*.

TABLE B.1 Summary of Data Types and Attributes

Type		Attributes
Problem data:		
Arithmetic	**BINARY DECIMAL** **FLOAT**(p) **FIXED**(p,q) **COMPLEX REAL**	
Numeric character	**PICTURE** 'nnn...n' **COMPLEX REAL**	nn...n = numeric picture (not using characters **A** or **X**)
Character string	**CHARACTER**(l) **PICTURE** 'cc....c' **VARYING**	ccc..c = character string picture (using only **A**, **X**, and **9**; at least one **A** or **X**)
Bit string	**BIT**(l) **VARYING**	
Locator data:		
Pointer	**POINTER**	
Offset	**OFFSET**	
Miscellaneous data:		
Area	**AREA**	
Label	**LABEL**	
Event	**EVENT**	
Task	**TASK**	
Entry*	**ENTRY**	
File*	**FILE**	

* Optimizing and Checkout Compilers only.

B.1   CONVERSION SITUATIONS

Data conversions may be necessitated by the following situations: assignment; arguments; subscripts, formats, and options; and expressions.

B.1.1   Assignment

When a value is being assigned to a variable for any reason, that value will be converted, if necessary, to the attributes of the variable to which it is being assigned. That variable may be: (a) the destination variable in an assignment statement; (b) initialized by the **INITIAL** attribute; (c) in a **LIST**, **DATA**, or **EDIT** list in a **GET** statement or in the **INTO, SET**, or **KEYTO** options of a record input/output statement; (d) in the **STRING** option of a **PUT** statement; (e) in the **SET** option or the **REFER** option of an **ALLOCATE** statement; (f) the index variable of a **DO** statement.

B.1.2   Arguments

When an argument is being passed to a procedure or function, the value of the argument is converted, if necessary, to the attributes declared by the programmer for the corresponding parameter. The converted value is stored in a temporary variable, which is then passed to the procedure or function. Similarly, the expression in a **RETURN** statement is converted to the data type specified in the **RETURNS** attribute of the **PROCEDURE** or **ENTRY** statement. An unexpected conversion of a procedure argument can lead to the loss of a result if the procedure assigns a value to the corresponding parameter because the field that receives the assigned value will be the *temporary variable* containing the converted argument rather than the actual variable that the programmer intended.

B.1.3   Subscripts, Formats, and Options

When the programmer uses a variable or expression as a subscript, in a format item, or in an input/output option (such as **PAGESIZE** or **LINESIZE**) where PL/I expects a binary integer, the variable or expression will automatically be converted if it is of some other type. Similarly, in the **KEY** , **KEYFROM**, and **TITLE** options, where a character string is expected, a variable of any other type is converted automatically to **CHARACTER**.

B.1.4   Expressions

In evaluating an expression that involves one or more operators, conversions may be necessary if the operands differ in type or are not of a type acceptable to the operator. This general situation is supported by a rather elaborate mechanism since each type of operation, while represented by a single symbol, actually refers to an entire family of operations. Thus, for example, though '+' can be treated by the programmer as representing the general process of addition, PL/I must select one of several available machine instructions, depending on the base, scale, and mode of the operands. Accordingly, if the programmer writes an expression such as $A + B$, where A is **BINARY FIXED** and B is **DECIMAL FLOAT**, PL/I must first convert one or the other (or both) of the operands to the form in which the operation will be done. In this particular example, the rules that PL/I uses require that both operands be converted to **BINARY FLOAT**.

Such rules, once defined, can be followed in a straightforward manner as long as the type to which each operand must be converted is known at the time of compilation. This is not always so. For example, it is quite legitimate to write an expression such as C + D where both C and D are declared to be **CHARACTER** (15). However, in this situation, PL/I cannot determine (at compile time) whether to provide for **REAL** or **COMPLEX** addition, nor can it tell which base or scale should be used. Moreover, the operation will not even be valid unless both operands contain numeric characters. Thus, PL/I cannot decide what is to be done until it sees the data. The rule used by PL/I is that a **CHARACTER** string used in such a situation is converted to whatever form would have been necessary for a variable having the attributes **DECIMAL FIXED** (15) appearing in place of the string. This can result in the loss of fractional digitals. For example, if we assign to C the value '1.375' and to D the value '1.925', then the result of evaluating the expressions C + D will be 2, rather than 3.300.

PL/I's conversion rules and procedures include circumstances under which conversions explicitly will *not* be performed. One important case is the situation in which PL/I expects a constant of a specific type. For example, the values in the precision attribute in a declaration must be decimal integer constants. Accordingly, it is an error to specify any other type of value. Similarly, a string repetition factor and some of the arguments of certain built-in functions (such as **ROUND, ADD, SUBTRACT, MULTIPLY, DIVIDE, PRECISION, BINARY** and **DECIMAL**) must be decimal integer constants. Another instance is the **REFER** option. Here, both variables involved must be **BINARY FIXED** of default precision (15,0). (Note that recent versions of the IBM-F compiler have relaxed this rule somewhat, and the Optimizing and Checkout Compilers have relaxed it still further.) Also, in the case of the IBM-F compiler, arguments will be converted unless the programmer has declared a parameter attribute list for the entry point.

B.2 DETERMINATION OF SOURCE AND TARGET ATTRIBUTES

In most situations, the source and target attributes of data to be converted are known either from language rules (for example, the first letter of a variable name, other defaults or from the declared attributes of the particular variables). However, such knowledge is not immediately available when conversions are required as part of the process of expression evaluation. Here the target attributes must be deduced from the source attributes of the operands in accordance with rules that vary with the types of operations to be performed.

B.2.1 Conversions in Arithmetic Operations

If the operands of an arithmetic operator are in arithmetic form (or have been prepared that way by prior conversion), no further conversion is required for operands associated with prefix operators. For the infix operators +, −, *, and / the subtype to which the operands are converted is determined by the *highest characteristic rule*: if the base, scale, or mode of the two operands differ, the attribute that prevails is **BINARY** for differing bases, **FLOAT** for differing scales and **COMPLEX** for differing modes.

Exponentiation requires different rules:

- If the first operand (the number being raised to a specified power) is **FIXED** and the exponent is an unsigned integer constant, the operation will be performed as a series of multiplications on the first operand, provided that the result will fit within the maximum allowable precision (15 for **DECIMAL** and 31 for **BINARY**). If the result exceeds the maximum precision, then the first operand is converted to **FLOAT**.

- If the first operand is (or has been converted to) **FLOAT** and the second operand is **FIXED** with no fractional digits, the result is computed without any required conversions.

- In all other cases the scale of both operands is converted to **FLOAT**, and other attributes are determined by the highest characteristic rule.

If an operand of an arithmetic operator is not in arithmetic form, conversion is always required and proceeds as follows:

- Arithmetic attributes of a numeric character variable are implied by its picture and guide the conversions in accordance with the rules stated before.

- Character strings are converted to the form to which a **FIXED DECIMAL** (15) variable would have been converted if it had appeared in place of the character string.

- Bit strings are converted to the form to which a **FIXED BINARY** (p) variable would have been converted where p = min(31, length of bit string).

When the attributes of a converted arithmetic operand have been deduced from the source attributes and the operator, it is also necessary for PL/I to deduce the appropriate precision:

- In expression evaluation, the conversion always will be in the direction of higher characteristics.

- For output conversion, the target base always is decimal.

A summary of these rules is given in Table B.2.

Since an arithmetic expression may have several operators, the result of one operation becomes an operand for a subsequent operation. Consequently, there are rules governing the precision of the results of arithmetic operations. These are summarized in Table B.3.

B.2.2   Conversion Rules for Relational Operands

A separate set of rules is required to handle comparisons:

- If both operands are bit strings, there is no conversion, the shorter bit string is extended on the right with zeros.

- If both operands are strings and at least one of them is **CHARACTER**, the bit operand (if any) first will be converted to character; then, the shorter of the two character strings will be extended on the right with blanks; finally, the comparison of the two character strings will be performed.

- In all other cases the comparison will be performed as an arithmetic comparison; accordingly, any arithmetic conversions will be performed using the rules for subtraction.

Table B.2   Target Precision

	Source Attributes	Target Attributes	Target Precision
Expression Evaluation	DECIMAL FIXED (p_1,q_1)	BINARY FIXED (p_2,q_2)	$p_2 = 1 + [3.32*p_1]$ $q_2 = [3.32*q_1]$
		DECIMAL FLOAT (p_2)	$p_2 = p_1$
		BINARY FLOAT (p_2)	$p_2 = [3.32*p_1]$
Stream Output and Arithmetic to Character	BINARY FIXED (p_1,q_1)	BINARY FLOAT (p_2)	$p_2 = p_1$
		DECIMAL FIXED (p_2,q_2)	$p_2 = 1 + [p_1/3.32]$ $g_2 = [q_1/3.32]$
	BINARY FLOAT (p_1)	DECIMAL FLOAT (p_2)	$p_2 = [p_1/3.32]$

Notes: $[n]$ = CEIL(n). When q is negative, the ceiling formulas are applied to the absolute value of q.

Table B.3   Precision of Results of Arithmetic Operations

Operation	Precision of Operands: FIXED (p_1,q_1), FIXED (p_2,q_2)	Precision of Operands: FLOAT (p_1), FLOAT (p_2)
+,−	$p = MIN (M,1 + MAX (p_1 - q_1, p_2 - q_2) + q)$ $q = MAX (q_1,q_2)$	$p = MAX (p_1,p_2)$
*	$p = MIN (M, p_1 + p_2 + 1)$ $q = q_1 + q_2$	$p = MAX (p_1,p_2)$
/	$p = M$ $q = M - ((p_1 - q_1) + q_2)$	$p = MAX (p_1,p_2)$
**	$p = (p_1 + 1) * n - 1 \quad M$ $q = q_1 * n$	$p = p_1$

Notes: M = 31 for BINARY operands; M = 15 for DECIMAL operands. Exponentiation is only applied to a FIXED first operand if the second operand is an unsigned integer constant that will permit the result to be contained within the maximum precision M.

B.2.3   Conversion for Logical Operators

Operands that are not bit strings are converted to bit strings; then, the shorter operand is extended on the right with zeros.

B.2.4   Conversion for Concatenation

If both operands are bit strings or binary arithmetic variables, any necessary conversions are performed such that both operands end up as bit strings. In all other cases the conversions are such that the resulting operands both will be character strings.

B.3   MECHANISMS OF CONVERSION

B.3.1   Arithmetic Conversions

Arithmetic conversions are best understood by considering changes of base, scale, mode, and precision more or less independently. (Since precision is intimately related to base and scale, it cannot be completely ignored when considering the base and scale conversions.)

B.3.1.1   Mode Conversions

COMPLEX to **REAL**: The imaginary part is dropped.

REAL to **COMPLEX**: An imaginary part having the value zero is added.

B.3.1.2   Precision Conversions

FLOAT (p_1) to **FLOAT** (p_2):

If p_1 and p_2 both imply the same internal representation (see Table B.4), no actual conversion takes place. If a change in internal representation is required, the fraction is truncated or extended with zeros on the right, depending on the direction of change. Note that no attempt is made to prevent nonzero digits from being developed in the extra digits that are present if the specified precision is not exactly equal to the precision corresponding to the internal form.

TABLE B.4   Internal Forms or Floating-Point Variables

Internal Form	Binary Precision	Decimal Precision
Short	≤ 21	≤ 6
Long	$21 < p \leq 53$	$6 < p \leq 16$
Extended*	$53 < p \leq 109$	$16 < p \leq 33$

* Supported by the Checkout and Optimizing Compilers only.

FIXED (p_1, q_1) to **FIXED** (p_2, q_2) :

$q_2 > q_1$: $q_2 - q_1$ zeros are added on the right.

$q_2 < q_1$: $q_1 - q_2$ digits are dropped on the right.

Let $p'_1 = p_1 + q_2 - q_1$. Then, if $p_2 > p'_1$, $p_2 - p'_1$ zeros are added on the left; if $p_2 < p'_1$, $p_1 - p_2$ digits are dropped on the left.

Note that if the number is **BINARY FIXED**, then the internal form of the number has $p = 15$ or $p = 31$ regardless of the declared value of p. Unless the **SIZE** condition is enabled, nonzero bits can find their way into the $(31 - p)$ or the $(15 - p)$ extra bits that are present but not accounted for. The **OVERFLOW** condition is raised only if the ultimate internal capacity $(p = 31)$ is exceeded during a computation. Similarly, if the number is **DECIMAL FIXED**, then the internal form always has an odd value of p, so that if the declared value of p is even, there is one extra digit present. Again, unless **SIZE** is enabled, a nonzero value can arise in this digit.

B.3.1.3 Base Conversions

DECIMAL FLOAT (p_1) to **BINARY FLOAT** (p_2) and vice versa: Since binary and decimal floating-point numbers both use the same internal format, no actual conversion takes place unless a change in internal form is required because of a difference in target precision (see Table B.4).

DECIMAL FIXED (p_1, q_1) to **BINARY FIXED** $(p_2 q_2)$ and vice versa: The conversion is carried out to the specified precision. This can lead to a different result than a base conversion followed by a precision conversion. For example: Let B have the attributes **DECIMAL FIXED** $(2,2)$ and the value .01, I have the attributes **BINARY FIXED** $(15,0)$ and a value of 1, and A be declared **BINARY FIXED** $(20,15)$. Then A=B; is a direct conversion producing a value 00000.000000101000111B. On the other hand, the statement A=I*B; involves an intermediate conversion, that is, **DECIMAL FIXED** $(2,2)$ to **BINARY FIXED** $(8,7)$ to **BINARY FIXED** $(20,15)$. This time the value is 00000.000000100000000B.

B.3.1.4 Scale Conversion

Since all-floating point numbers are really stored as binary, scale conversion can only take place on data which are in binary form. Thus, a scale conversion of decimal data implies a base conversion as well.

BINARY FIXED (p_1, q_1) to **BINARY FLOAT** (p_2): Let p'_1 be the number of significant digits in the source (that is, ignoring leading zeros). An exponent is developed from p'_1 and q_1. The internal form—short, long or extended—is determined from p_2.

BINARY FLOAT (p_1) to **BINARY FIXED** (p_2, q_2): Let p'_1 be the precision of the internal form (that is, 21, 53 or 109). The source behaves like a value with the attributes **BINARY FIXED** (p'_1, q_1), where q_1 is determined from the exponent. The precision is then adjusted, if necessary, in accordance with precision conversion rules.

DECIMAL FIXED (p_1,q_1) to **DECIMAL FLOAT** (p_2): Let p'_2 be the binary precision of the implied internal floating-point form (that is, if $p_2 \leq 6$, $p'_2 = 21$; if $6 < p_2 \leq 16$, $p'_2 = 53$; otherwise $p'_2 = 109$). A base conversion (It is necessary to compute the conversion to this accuracy in order to enable the internal binary form of the number to serve as a reasonable approximation of **DECIMAL FLOAT**.) is performed yielding a value with attributes **BINARY FIXED** (P,Q) where

P=**CEIL** (p_1*3.32)+p'_2

Q=**CEIL** (q_1*3.32)+p'_2−1

Next, a scale conversion is performed yielding a result having the attributes **BINARY FLOAT** (p'_2). Finally, a "base conversion" is performed yielding the final result with attributes **DECIMAL FLOAT** (p_2).

For example, in the sequence

DECLARE A **DECIMAL FIXED** (2,2),

B **DECIMAL FLOAT** (6),

C **DECIMAL FIXED** (12,10);

A=.01;   B=A;   C=B;

If the accuracy of the conversion were limited in a manner analogous to that used for fixed point data, C would have the value 00.0078125000. In the actual implementation, C's value would be 00.0099999979, which is somewhat more reasonable.

DECIMAL FLOAT (p_1) to **DECIMAL FIXED** (p_2,q_2): Let p'_1 be the binary equivalent of the internal form. Accordingly, an internal "conversion" to **BINARY FLOAT** (p'_1) is followed by a scale conversion yielding a result with the attributes **BINARY FIXED** (p'_1,q_1), where q_1 is computed from the exponent. Finally, a base conversion is performed to yield the final result.

B.3.2   Conversions between Numeric Character and Arithmetic

Numeric character variables are a representation of decimal numbers in character form. The picture attribute always implies either **FIXED DECIMAL** (p,q) or **FLOAT DECIMAL** (p). Both of these forms are converted to **FIXED DECIMAL** (p,q), where q is converted from the exponent in the floating-point case. Conversions to other arithmetic types are then performed as described previously. Conversion to numeric character from arithmetic forms involve an initial conversion to **FIXED DECIMAL** (p,q), where in the floating-point case q is chosen so that the p most significant digits are retained. The process is completed by subsequent conversion to the required numeric character form.

B.3.3 Conversions between Bit String and Arithmetic

A bit string is treated as a variable with the attributes **FIXED BINARY** (31,0), which is then converted as required. If the length of this string is less than 31, the string is right-justified; if it is greater than 31, only the rightmost 31 bits are used. When converting in the other direction, an arithmetic value is first converted (if necessary) to **REAL BINARY FLOAT** (p) or **REAL BINARY FIXED** (p,q), where p and q are deduced from the source precision. The absolute value of the integer part of the number is then computed and the P rightmost bits of this value form an intermediate bit string, where

$P = MIN(p,31)$ in the **FLOAT** case

$P = MIN(p-q,31)$ in the **FIXED** case

The intermediate string is then assigned to the final target according to the rules for bit string assignment.

B.3.4 Conversions between Character Strings and Arithmetic Types

A character string to be converted to arithmetic must have a value that represents either a valid PL/I numerical constant or a complex expression consisting of a real constant + or − an imaginary constant. Otherwise the **CONVERSION** condition is raised. Once the initial validity is assured, the string is converted to an arithmetic value with base, scale, mode, and precision attributes implied by the constant or expression. Conversion to target attributes proceeds from this point, as described before. Conversion of an arithmetic value to a character string starts with conversion (if necessary) to **DECIMAL**, keeping the scale and mode unchanged. The decimal value is then converted to an intermeditate character string as indicated in Table B.5. This string is then assigned to the final target by ordinary character string assignment. If the arithmetic value is complex, then the real and imaginary parts are converted to intermediate strings separately. The intermediate string for the imaginary part is one character longer than normal, and has an **I** appended to the value. Moreover, the value of the imaginary part is always signed and is left justified in the intermediate string. The two intermediate strings are concatinated to form the converted result of the complex variable. This is then assigned to the final target by normal string assignments.

B.3.5 Conversion between Numeric Character and Bit String

Conversion begins with the development of an intermediate arithmetic target having the attributes implied by the picture. Then the intermediate target is converted to the final value.

TABLE B.5 ARITHMETIC TO **CHARACTER** CONVERSIONS

Source Attributes	Length of Intermediate String	Format of Intermediate String
FIXED DECIMAL (p,q) $0 \leq q \leq p$	$P + 3$	Value is right-justified, has a decimal point if $q > 0$, and q decimal places, has leading zeros suppressed, and has a sign if negative.
FIXED DECIMAL (p,q) $q < 0$ or $q > p$	$p + k + 3$ $k = [\log_{10}(|q| + 10)]$*	$vF \pm q$, where v is the value of the digits expressed as an integer, with leading zeros suppressed and a sign if negative; q is the scale factor.
FLOAT DECIMAL (p)	$p + 6$	$p - 1$ $\pm X.XXXXXE \pm ee$

* $[n] = floor(n)$

B.3.6 Conversions between Numeric Character and Character Strings

Since the numeric character value is already in character form, this process is trivial. In going in the other direction, the character string must represent a valid PL/I numerical constant, which will be assigned to the numeric character variable according to the picture specifications. Excess fractional digits are ignored. Similarly, the sign is ignored unless one of the sign picture characters is present. If the string does not contain a valid PL/I numerical constant, the **CONVERSION** condition is raised.

B.3.7 Conversion between Character and Bit Strings

A character string is converted to a bit string by converting the character zero to the bit zero and the character 1 to the bit 1. If the source string contains any character other than zero or 1, the **CONVERSION** condition is raised. If the source string is shorter than the target, zeros are appended on the right. Excess characters are lost. A bit string is converted to a character string in accordance with the same kind of procedural rules.

B.4   COMMON PROBLEMS AND THEIR AVOIDANCE

B.4.1   Fixed-Point Overflow

Seemingly innocuous statements can produce fixed-point overflows because of the particular rules that PL/I uses in performing fixed-point arithmetic. For example, the statement

Y = 175*(1/2);

causes an overflow. (The student should review the material in the foregoing two sections to see why such a thing happens.) To avoid this problem, the programmer can take the following steps:

1. Reduce all subexpressions involving constants to a single constant. For instance, in the example above, write 87.5 instead of 175*(1/2).
2. Avoid the use of complicated expressions; assign the result of each simple intermediate expression to a variable with suitable declared precision. This usually allows the programmer to maintain control of the precision.
3. Use the **MULTIPLY** and **DIVIDE** built-in functions to control the precision of multiplications and divisions if necessary.

Note that the problem of spurious fixed-point overflows cannot occur, irrespective of an expression's complexity, if all of the fixed-point variables are integers of maximum precision and rule (1) is followed.

B.4.2   Inaccurate Results

Unexpected inaccuracy is usually due to careless use of mixed-mode expressions. (The illustration at the beginning of this Appendix is a good example of this.) This problem is best overcome by careful declaration of all variables and avoidance of mixed-mode expressions except where they are really necessary. Sometimes inaccuracy results from failure to use sufficient precision or from computations in fixed-point arithmetic when floating points would have been more satisfactory.

B.4.3   Difficulties in Converting Arithmetic Values to Character Strings

Arithmetic values are converted to character strings when they are to appear as output, assigned to **CHARACTER** variables, or used in a situation where a character string is required—for example as a **KEY**. The case of output seldom causes much of a problem because the value usually can be ascertained even if the format leaves something to be desired. However, especially in the case of a **KEY** or whenever the character value is used for further processing, the format of the **CHARACTER** rendition of the arithmetic value can be crucial to the success of the additional processing. Even though PL/I's rules for conversion are quite deterministic, they are sufficiently complicated that the programmer is leaving the format of the result essentially to chance if he uses a single assignment of an arithmetic value to a character string. The best thing to do in this situation is either to use a numeric character variable (where the format of the string can be controlled explicitly by means of the **PICTURE** attribute), or to use the **PUT STRING** statement with the **EDIT** option, where the format again can be controlled by means of appropriate format option.

APPENDIX C:
COLLATING SEQUENCES
FOR CHARACTER SETS

Table C.1 shows the character sets recognized by most computers. These are given for the two most commonly used systems for representing such characters internally. The EBCDIC system (Extended Binary Coded Decimal Interchange Code) is the one normally accepted by IBM systems and, therefore, serves as the default representation on them. ASCII (American National Standard Code for Information Interchange) is the other system in common use. Consequently, for purposes of compatibility, it is possible to notify the PL/I compiler (when implemented on an IBM configuration) that a source program and/or data are to be interpreted in accordance with the ASCII code.

The character set for each coding system is presented so that the lowest member in the collating sequence is at the upper left and the highest at the lower right. Thus, in the EBCDIC system, lowercase letters are "smaller" than uppercase letters, which, in turn, are "smaller" than numerical digits. On the other hand, numbers in the ASCII system are "lower" in the sequence than uppercase letters, which, in turn, are "lower" than lowercase letters. To illustrate the implications of these differences, the statement

IF $'A' < '2'$ **THEN** action;

will be true ($'1'B$) if the system assumes it is examining EBCDIC characters and false if it assumes it is examining ASCII characters.

Table C.1　　a. Collating Sequence for the EBCDIC Coding System

Symbol	Internal Representation	Symbol	Internal Representation	Symbol	Internal Representation	Symbol	Internal Representation
↑	00000000	-	01100000	↑	10001010	↑	11001010
≈ [1] ≈ through ≈	00111111	/	01100001	≈ [1] ≈ through ≈≈	through 10010000	≈≈ [1] ≈ through ≈	through 11001111
blank	01000000		01100010	j	10010001	<	11010000
	01000001	≈ [1] ≈ through ≈	through 01101010	k	10010010	J	11010001
≈ [1] ≈ through ≈	01001001	'	01101011	l	10010011	K	11010010
?	01001010	%	01101100	m	10010100	L	11010011
.	01001011	≈	01101101	n	10010101	M	11010100
⌐	01001100	¬	01101110	o	10010110	N	11010101
(	01001101	±	01101111	p	10010111	O	11010110
+	01001110	↑	01110000	q	10011000	P	11010111
‡	01001111	≈ [1] ≈ through ≈	through 01111000	r	10011001	Q	11011000
&	01010000			↑	10011010	R	11011001
	01010001	"	01111001	≈ [1] ≈ through ≈	through 10100001	≈ [1] ≈ through ≈	through 11011111
≈ [1] ≈ through ≈	01011001	:	01111010	s	10100010	↑	11100000
!	01011010	#	01111011	t	10100011	[1]	11100001
$	01011011	@	01111100	u	10100100	S	11100010
*	01011100	'	01111101	v	10100101	T	11100011
)	01011101	=	01111110	w	10100110	U	11100100
;	01011110	√	01111111	x	10100111	V	11100101
¢	01011111	[1]	10000000	y	10101000	W	11100110
		a	10000001	z	10101001	X	11100111
		b	10000010	↑	10101010	Y	11101000
		c	10000011	≈ [1] ≈ through ≈	through 10111111	Z	11101001
		d	10000100				11101010
		e	10000101	>	11000000	≈ [1] ≈ through ≈	through 11101111
		f	10000110	A	11000001	0	11110000
		g	10000111	B	11000010	1	11110001
		h	10001000	C	11000011	2	11110010
		i	10001001	D	11000100	3	11110011
				E	11000101	4	11110100
				F	11000110	5	11110101
				G	11000111	6	11110110
				H	11001000	7	11110111
				I	11001001	8	11111000
						9	11111001
							11111010
						≈ [1] ≈ through ≈	through 11111111

[1] Internal control or unassigned

TABLE C.1 Collating Sequence for the ASCII Coding System

Symbol	Internal Representation	Symbol	Internal Representation	Symbol	Internal Representation
[1]	00000000 through 00111111	[1]	00000000 through 10011111	[1]	00000000 through 11100000
blank	01000000	@	10100000		
!	01000001	A	10100001	a	11100001
"	01000010	B	10100010	b	11100010
#	01000011	C	10100011	c	11100011
$	01000100	D	10100100	d	11100100
%	01000101	E	10100101	e	11100101
&	01000110	F	10100110	f	11100110
'	01000111	G	10100111	g	11100111
(	01001000	H	10101000	h	11101000
)	01001001	I	10101001	i	11101001
*	01001010	J	10101010	j	11101010
+	01001011	K	10101011	k	11101011
'	01001100	L	10101100	l	11101100
−	01001101	M	10101101	m	11101101
.	01001110	N	10101110	n	11101110
/	01001111	O	10101111	o	11101111
0	01010000	P	10110000	p	11110000
1	01010001	Q	10110001	q	11110001
2	01010010	R	10110010	r	11110010
3	01010011	S	10110011	s	11110011
4	01010100	T	10110100	t	11110100
5	01010101	U	10110101	u	11110101
6	01010110	V	10110110	v	11110110
7	01010111	W	10110111	w	11110111
8	01011000	X	10111000	x	11111000
9	01011001	Y	10111001	y	11111001
:	01011010	Z	10111010	z	11111010
;	01011011	[	10111011		11111011
<	01011100	\	10111100		11111100
=	01011101	]	10111101	[1]	11111101
>	01011110	↑	10111110		11111110
?	01011111	←	10111111		11111111

[1] Unassigned or internal control

APPENDIX D:
PL/I COMPILERS

The discussions of various features throughout this book include stipulations that certain behavioral aspects depend on the particular language implementation being used. In this appendix we shall examine the more commonly available PL/I compilers with a view towards summarizing their important differences.

D.1 BACKGROUND

The language (PL/I stands for programming language/1) was first introduced by the IBM Company in 1964 in conjunction with its System/360 line of computers. Since that time an evolutionary process has taken place, affecting the language itself as well as the approaches to its compilation.

D.1.1   The IBM PL/I-F Compiler

By 1968 the language development process had begun to equilibrate, resulting in the emergence of the major compiler, embodying the entire set of language features. This compiler, known as the PL/I-F compiler, is probably the one in widest use today. Accordingly, the PL/I language described in this book is the language accepted by that compiler. Designed for use in a production environment, the F compiler generally produces efficient object programs at the expense of lengthier compilation time.

D.1.2   The PL/C Compiler

Because of the F compiler's production orientation, it is not particularly well suited for handling of student assignments. In response to that shortcoming, Cornell University developed the PL/C compiler. Its objective is to compile programs as rapidly as possible, even if they require more time for execution, and to handle several programs in quick succession (since many students in a class are likely to be working on homework problems at the same time). Thus it is ideal for student jobs, which require relatively little execution time anyway. In addition, PL/C attempts to supplement information about programmers' errors by some type of corrective action.

   To achieve these objectives, it was necessary to scale down the language somewhat, so there are a number of features supported by the F compiler but not by PL/C. In addition, some incompatibilities exist in that there are some features common to both compilers but implemented somewhat differently; also, PL/C contains some extensions for facilitating the debugging process that are not present in the F compiler. The most troublesome of these differences probably are the following:

1.   PL/C does not allow words that are names of PL/I statements to be used as the names of variables in a program. Thus, for example, **FREE** is a valid variable name in PL/I (even though it is also a keyword); however, it is illegal in PL/C since there is a **FREE** statement in the full language. (The **FREE** statement is not part of the acceptable PL/C subset, but, for purposes of PL/C's internal consistency, the keyword is unavailable for use as a variable name.)

2.   PL/C uses a different internal representation than does the F compiler for some types of data. This occasionally leads to differences in computed results.

D.1.3   PLUTO Compiler

The PLUTO compiler, developed at the University of Toronto, was designed for rapid processing of large numbers of student assignments, much like PL/C. Expectedly, PLUTO's performance in compilation and execution of programs is comparable to PL/C's. PLUTO's diagnostic messages are generally more meaningful (especially to students) than those provided by the F compiler, but, unlike PL/C, PLUTO does not attempt major corrections. This approach is an intentional one, used on the grounds that the student learns more by correcting his own errors. As in the case of PL/C, emphasis on efficient compilation and more helpful diagnostic services necessitated a compromise with regard to the number of features supported by the PLUTO compiler. The exact collection of features left out of PLUTO differs somewhat from those absent from PL/C. In the features that are implemented, PLUTO attempts to be totally faithful to PL/I rules.

D.1.4 The IBM Optimizing and Checkout Compilers

As experience with the language accumulated over a growing population of users in commercial/industrial/research environments, the implementation of increasingly ambitious projects directed additional attention to the disparity between compilation and execution costs. Sufficient importance was attached to these considerations to prompt the IBM Corporation to introduce a new pair of complementary compilers: the Checkout and Optimizing Compilers. Both of these compilers support the full language, although it is a slightly different version than that accommodated by PL/I-F. A few minor restrictions have been added where the F compiler was overly permissive; for the most part, however, the changes constitute extensions to the language.

The Checkout Compiler is designed for use during program development. Thus, its goals are similar to those motivating PL/C and PLUTO. However, the Checkout Compiler implements the full language and actually has fewer restrictions than the Optimizing Compiler. (For the most part, restrictions permit a more efficient object program to be constructed; their effect on the compilation process is secondary.) In performance, the Checkout Compiler is somewhere between PL/I-F and the student compilers. Thus, it may be a satisfactory compromise in some schools that want some of the advantages of the student compilers but do not want to deal with a language subset.

The Optimizing Compiler is designed to produce the most efficient possible object program. Ideally, it would be used for the final compilation, after the program has been completely debugged (would that there were such a thing!). The compilation speeds are somewhat better than PL/I-F's, at the same time its execution performance is significantly better on most nontrivial problems.

D.1.5 The IBM Subset Compiler

The unprecedented extent of PL/I's features requires the availability of a rather large processor for support of the full language. (The F in the PL/I-F compiler is a size code indicating that a minimum of approximately 65,000 bytes of main storage are required to support the compiler.)

Consequently, to make available the language's versatility on more modest configurations in a predominantly production environment, IBM developed and implemented the Subset Compiler. Like the F compiler, the emphasis is on efficient execution rather than compilation and diagnostic services have been conceived with the practicing programmer primarily in mind. The collection of features selected for inclusion differs only in a few respects from that supported by PLUTO.

D.1.6   PLAGO PL/I Load and Go

Developed at the Polytechnic Institute of Brooklyn, this implementation is designed for use by students working with PL/I at an introductory level. Accordingly, this version provides a very small subset of the language, embodying a relatively limited but effective grouping of statement types, attributes and built-in functions. A grouping of **ON** conditions are active in that they are always enabled. When raised, they provide the system action, with no opportunity for redefinition.

D.1.7   Other Compilers

As the population of PL/I users widens, additional compilers can be expected to appear, including those designed for use on processing systems produced by manufacturers other than IBM. (A number of such compilers are already in various stages of development and other compilers for IBM processors already exist.) An exhaustive presentation would be impractical in a single book; however, the choice of the F compiler as the major vehicle greatly facilitates transfer to another compiler once a basic fluency has been developed.

D.2   TREATMENT OF LANGUAGE DIFFERENCES

As stated previously, this text describes PL/I as supported by the F compiler. However, to make the book as useful as possible to those working with other compilers, an attempt has been made to point out some of the important language differences in the text.

For the most part, this effort has been confined to the differences between the F compiler on the one hand and the Checkout and Optimizing Compilers on the other. Where the differences constitute extensions, the additional features are clearly labeled as applying only to the Checkout and Optimizing Compilers. Incompatibilities are generally indicated in footnotes.

Although the differences between the F compiler and the various subset compilers are not that earth-shattering, their nature is such that to point them out as was done for the Checkout and Optimizing Compilers would clutter the text with innumerable footnotes. Accordingly, the various features are summarized in this appendix as a series of tables that can be used to identify at a glance those features present in (or absent from) a particular compiler. Although this material is informative to a certain extent, it should be understood that there is no substitute for specific information about the particular compiler available to the student. For one thing, the various compilers are constantly being upgraded, so it is best for the reader to check with his or her computing center for the latest implementation information.

D.2.1 Statement Types

Table D.1 lists each of the PL/I statements, together with codes indicating the level of support for that statement in the various compilers. These codes are defined as follows:

- F: The statement is supported in a manner that is substantially identical with PL/I-F.
- E: The particular compiler supports an extended version of the statement.
- P: The particular compiler provides only partial support.
- Dash: The statement is not supported by the particular compiler.
- Y: The statement type is supported by the particular compiler but not by the F compiler.
- A numerical entry, in brackets, refers to a corresponding note that appears after the table.

Notes for Table D.1

1. Initialization and specification of attributes is not permitted for allocation of **CØN-TRØLLED** variables. **IN** option may not be used since **AREA** is not supported.
2. Only simple assignment; the right-hand side may not contain operators.
3. In **BY NAME** assignment, there may be only one left-hand side.
4. No implied conversion between string and arithmetic.
5. Not permitted as **THEN** or **ELSE** except within a **DØ** group. This is to discourage an improper use of **BEGIN**.
6. **TASK, PRIØRITY**, and **EVENT** options not permitted.
7. Constants may not be used as arguments for arrays or structure parameters.
8. Structure arguments not presently supported.
9. Can cause dynamic loading.
10. SYSIN and SYSPRINT may not be closed.
11. The following are reserved words: **ALLØCATE, BEGIN, CALL, CLØSE, DE-CLARE, DCL, DØ, END, ENTRY, EXIT, FØRMAT, FREE, GET, GØ, GØTØ, IF, ON, ØPEN, PRØCEDURE, PRØC, PUT, READ, RETURN, REVERT, SIGNAL, STØP, WRITE, TØ, BY, WHILE, THEN, ELSE, NØ, CHECK, NØCHECK, FLØW, NØFLØW, SØURCE, NØSØURCE**. If built-in function names are used as variables, they should be explicitly declared.
12. The first appearance of a name declares it; thus if a name is to be *explicitly* declared, the **DECLARE** statement must precede all other uses of the name. Parameters must be declared in *the same order* in which they appear in the procedure statement.
13. The index variable may not be named WHILE.
14. If a label appears after **END** it must be the *leftmost* label prefix of the corresponding **DØ, BEGIN** or **PRØCEDURE** statement.

15. Equivalent to **STØP** statement.

16. **P** format item is not supported.

17. **C** format item not supported; W, D, and S may not be expressions but may be variables; S not supported for **F** format. For **F** or **E** format the decimal point must explicitly appear if there are fractional places.

18. Only **FILE(SYSIN)(SYSPRINT** for **PUT)** is supported; data list is required in **GET/PUT DATA**.

19. Not all PL/I-F conditions are supported.

20. All conditions normally enabled except **CHECK**; **FLØW** condition has been added.

21. Only one name permitted in **CHECK** condition; **SNAP** option not supported.

22. Additional conditions are supported.

23. Options permitted are **TITLE, PRINT, LINESIZE, PAGESIZE, INPUT, ØUTPUT, RECØRD, SEQUENTIAL, STREAM**.

24. Stream files (SYSIN/SYSPRINT) may not be opened; however, **LINESIZE** and **PAGESIZE** may be specified outside the program as options. RECORD files (SYSUT1, −2, −3, or −4) may have the attributes **SEQUENTIAL, INPUT, ØUT-PUT** or **UPDATE**. The **TITLE** option is supported.

25. The **TASK, REDUCIBLE** and **IRREDUCIBLE** options may not be used; **ØRDER** and **REØRDER** are recognized but ignored.

26. Only one external procedure is permitted; the **TASK** option is not supported. A function procedure with no parameters must have an empty argument list [for example, FUNC()] when used in a function reference.

27. Includes additional diagnostic options.

28. **RECØRD** I/Ø is limited to **SEQUENTIAL** files associated with data sets consisting of fixed length records without keys.

29. Only the **FILE, INTØ**, and **IGNØRE** options may be used, and file may only be opened for **INPUT**.

30. Files may be opened for **INPUT** or **UPDATE** and the **FILE: INTØ** and **IGNØRE** options may be used.

31. There is no implied conversion between string and arithmetic.

32. Files may be opened for **ØUTPUT**. Options permitted are **FILE** and **FRØM**.

33. Only the **F, E, B, X, A, PAGE, LINE, SKIP** and **CØLUMN** specifications are supported.

34. Structures are not supported.

35. **EDIT** not supported.

36. **CØNVERSIØN, ENDFILE, ERRØR, FINISH, FIXEDØVERFLØW, NAME, ØVERFLØW, STRINGRANG, SUBSCRIPTRANGE, UNDERFLØW,** and **ZERØDIVIDE** are the only ones supported and are automatically enabled.

TABLE D.1 Statements

		PL/I-F	PL/C	PLUTO	Checkout	Optimizing	IBM Subset	PLAGO
ALLOCATE		F	—	P[1]	F qu48s	F	—	—
Assignment	Element			F				F
	Array	F	F[4]	P[2]	F	F	F	F[34]
	Structure			P[2,3]				—
BEGIN		F	F	F[5]	F	F	F	F
CALL		F	F[6,7]	F[6,8]	F[9]	F[9]	F[6]	F[6]
CHECK		—	Y	—	Y	—	—	—
CLOSE		F	F[10]	F[10]	F	F	F	—
DECLARE		F	P[11]	P[12]	F	F	F	F
DEFAULT		—	—	—	Y	Y	—	—
DELAY		F	—	—	F	F	—	—
DELETE		F	—	—	F	F	—	—
DISPLAY		F	—	—	F	F	F	—
DO		F	F	F[13]	F	F	F	F
END		F	F[14]	F	F	F	F	F
ENTRY		F	F	F	F	F	F	—
EXIT		F	F[15]	—	F	F	—	—
FETCH		—	—	—	Y	Y	—	—
FLOW		—	Y	Y	Y	—	—	—
FORMAT		F	F[16]	P[17]	F	F	F[33]	—
FREE		F	—	F	F	F	—	—
GET		F	F	F[18]	F	F	F	F[35]
GO TO		F	F	F	F	F	F	F
HALT		—	—	—	Y	Y	—	—
IF		F	F	F	F	F	F	F
LOCATE		F	—	—	F	F	F	—
NOCHECK		—	Y	—	Y	—	—	—
NOFLOW		—	Y	Y	Y	—	—	—
Null		F	F	F	F	F	F	F
ON		F	F[19,20]	F[19,21]	F[22]	F[22]	F[19]	F[36]
OPEN		F	F[23]	F[24]	F	F	F	—
PROCEDURE		F	F[25]	F[26]	F	F	F	F
PUT		F	E[27]	F[18]	E[27]	F	F	F[35]
READ		F	F[28,29]	F[28,30]	F	F	F[28]	—
RELEASE		—	—	—	Y	Y	—	—
RETURN		F	F[31]	F	F	F	F	F
REVERT		F	F	F	F	F	F	—
REWRITE		F	—	F[28]	F	F	F	—
SIGNAL		F	F	F	F	F	F	—
STOP		F	F	F	F	F	F	F
UNLOCK		F	—	—	F	F	—	—
WAIT		F	—	—	F	F	—	—
WRITE		F	F[28,32]	F[28,32]	F	F	F[28]	—

TABLE D.2   Attributes

	PL/I-F	PL/C	PLUTO	Checkout	Optimizing	IBM Subset	PLAGO
ALIGNED	F	F	R	F	F	F	—
AREA	F	R	R	F	F	—	—
AUTOMATIC	F	F	F	F	F	F	—
BACKWARDS	F	R	R	F	F	F	—
BASED	F	R	F[1]	F[2]	F[2]	—	—
BINARY	F	F	F	F	F	F	—
BIT	F	F	F	F	F	F	—
BUFFERED	F	R	R	F	F	F	—
BUILTIN	F	F	F	F	F	F	—
CHARACTER	F	F	F	F	F	F	F
COMPLEX	F	F	R	F	F	—	—
CONDITION	—	—	—	Y	Y	—	—
CONNECTED	—	—	—	Y	Y	—	—
CONTROLLED	F	R	F	F	F	F	—
DECIMAL	F	F	F	F	F	F	F[21]
DEFINED	F	R	R	E[3]	E[3]	F	—
dimension	F	F	F[4]	F	F	F[20]	F
DIRECT	F	R	R	F	F	F	—
ENTRY	F	F	E[5]	E[5]	E[5]	F	—
ENVIRONMENT	F	R	R[6]	F[7]	F[7]	F	—
EVENT	F	R	R	F	F	—	—
EXCLUSIVE	F	R	R	F	F	—	—
EXTERNAL	F	F	R	F	F	F	—
FILE	F	P[8]	P[8]	F	F	F	—
FIXED	F	F	F	F	F	F	F
FLOAT	F	F	F	F	F	F	F
GENERIC	F	R	R	E[3]	E[3]	—	—
INITIAL	F	F[9]	F[10]	F	F	F	—
INPUT	F	F	F	F	F	F	—
INTERNAL	F	F	R	F	F	F	—

Table D.2 (continued)

	PL/I-F	PL/C	PLUTO	Checkout	Optimizing	IBM Subset	PLAGO
IRREDUCIBLE	F	R	R	F	F	—	—
KEYED	F	R	R	F	F	F	—
LABEL	F	F	F[11]	F[12]	F[12]	F	—
length	F	F[13]	F[14]	F	F	F	F
LIKE	F	R	R	F	F	—	—
OFFSET	F	R	R	F[15]	F[15]	—	—
OPTIONS	—	—	—	Y	Y	—	—
OUTPUT	F	F	F	F	F	F	—
parameter	F	F	F[16]	F	F	F	F
PICTURE	F	R	R	F	F	F	—
POINTER	F	R	F	F	F	F	—
POSITION	F	R	R	F	F	—	—
precision	F	F	F	F	F	F	F
PAINT	F	F	R	F	F	F	—
REAL	F	F	F	F	F	F	F
RECORD	F	F	F	F	F	F	—
REDUCIBLE	F	R	R	F	F	—	—
RETURNS	F	F	F	F	F	F	—
SEQUENTIAL	F	F	F	F	F	F	—
size	F	—	—	F	F	F	F
STATIC	F	F	F	F	F	F	—
STREAM	F	F	R[17]	F	F	F	—
TASK	F	R	R	F	F	—	—
TRANSIENT	F	R	R	F	F	—	—
UNALIGNED	F	F[18]	R	F	F	—	—
UNBUFFERED	F	R	R	F	F	F	—
UPDATE	F	R	F	F	F	F	—
VARIABLE	—	—	Y	Y	Y	—	—
VARYING	F	F	F	F[19]	F[19]	—	F

D.2.2   Attributes

Table D.2 lists all of the attributes recognized by PL/I. As in Table D.1, the extent of availability in each compiler is shown by a coded indicator. The same code scheme is used as before, with the addition of r, indicating that the attribute is recognized as such but is not supported. The particular compiler will either ignore the attribute or diagnose it as being unsupported. Again, bracketed numerical entries refer to notes following the table.

Notes for Table D.2

1. The **REFER** option is not supported.
2. The **REFER** option has been generalized considerably.
3. This attribute has been generalized.
4. Dimension bounds may not be expressions, but may be variables.
5. Variables may have the type **ENTRY** by using the attribute **VARIABLE**.
6. **ENVIRØNMENT (LRECL(N))** may be used as an **ØPEN** statement option.
7. Syntax is slightly different than PL/I-F.
8. Only **STREAM** and **SEQUENTIAL RECØRD** files are supported.
9. String repetition factors not permitted.
10. Iteration factors may be variables but not expressions. **CALL** option not supported. May not be used for **CØNTRØLLED** or **BASED** variables.
11. **LABEL** is used to declare a **LABEL** constant in a sequence such as

    DECLARE LAB **LABEL VARIABLE**, (HERE,THERE) **LABEL**;
    LAB = HERE;

    .
    .
    .

    HERE: -

    because HERE would otherwise become **FLØAT DECIMAL** by default. Thus, the attribute **VARIABLE** must be used to declare an ordinary **LABEL** variable. Subscripted prefixes may not be used to initialize.

Notes for Table D.2
(continued)

12. The attribute **VARIABLE** may also be added.
13. Maximum 256.
14. May be a variable, but not an expression.
15. Offsets may be used as qualifiers.
16. Structure parameters not presently supported.
17. The only two stream files supported, SYSIN and SYSPRINT cannot be explicitly declared, or øpened or cløsed.
18. Has relatively little effect since PL/C does not use the usual PL/I data mapping rules.
19. Varying length strings are stored differently than in PL/I-F.
20. Dimension must be decimal integer constants; the dimension attribute cannot be factored.
22. **DECIMAL** is the only base accepted and, therefore, always is implied.

D.2.3   Built-in Functions

Table D.3 lists all built-in functions. Because many of these functions are identical in all versions, these are simply listed in part (b) of the table. Part (a) lists those functions not present in all versions. The letter Y indicates that the function is supported.

TABLE D.3   Built-in Functions

(a) Functions Not Present in All Versions

Function	PL/I-F	PL/C	PLUTO	Checkout	Optimizing	IBM Subset	PLAGO
ACOS	—	—	—	Y	Y	—	—
ADD	Y	Y	Y	Y	Y	Y	—
ADDR	Y	—	Y	Y	Y	Y	—
ALL	Y	Y	—	Y	Y	Y	—
ALLOCATION	Y	—	Y	Y	Y	—	—
ANY	Y	Y	—	Y	Y	Y	—
ASIN	—	—	—	Y	Y	—	—
ATANH	Y	Y	Y	Y	Y	Y	—
BINARY	Y	Y	Y	Y	Y	Y	—
BIT	Y	Y	Y	Y	Y	Y	—
BOOL	Y	Y	Y	Y	Y	Y	—
COMPLETION	Y	—	—	Y	Y	—	—
COMPLEX	Y	Y	—	Y	Y	—	—
CONJG	Y	Y	—	Y	Y	—	—
COUNT	Y	Y	—	Y	Y	—	—
DATAFIELD	Y	Y	—	Y	Y	—	—
DATE	Y	Y	Y	Y	Y	Y	—
DECIMAL	Y	Y	Y	Y	Y	Y	—
DIM	Y	Y	Y	Y	Y	—	—
DIVIDE	Y	Y	Y	Y	Y	Y	—
EMPTY	Y	—	—	Y	Y	—	—
HBOUND	Y	Y	Y	Y	Y	—	—
IMAG	Y	Y	—	Y	Y	—	—
LBOUND	Y	Y	Y	Y	Y	—	—
LENGTH	Y	Y	Y	Y	Y	—	Y
LINENO	Y	Y	—	Y	Y	—	—
MULTIPLY	Y	Y	Y	Y	Y	—	—
NULL	Y	—	Y	Y	Y	Y	—
NULLO	Y	—	—	—	—	—	—

Table D.3 (continued)

Function	PL/I-F	PL/C	PLUTO	Checkout	Optimizing	IBM Subset	PLAGO
OFFSET	—	—	—	Y	Y	—	—
ONCHAR	Y	Y	Y	Y	Y	—	—
ONCODE	Y	Y	Y	Y	Y	—	—
ONCOUNT	Y	Y	—	Y	Y	—	—
ONDEST	—	Y	—	—	—	—	—
ONFILE	Y	Y	—	Y	Y	—	—
ONKEY	Y	—	—	Y	Y	—	—
ONLOC	Y	Y	—	Y	Y	—	—
ONORIG	—	Y	—	—	—	—	—
ONSOURCE	Y	Y	Y	Y	Y	Y	—
POINTER	—	—	—	Y	Y	—	—
POLY	Y	—	—	Y	Y	Y	—
PRECISION	Y	Y	Y	Y	Y	Y	—
PRIORITY	Y	—	—	Y	Y	—	—
PROD	Y	Y	—	Y	Y	Y	—
RAND	—	Y	Y	—	—	—	—
REAL	Y	Y	—	Y	Y	—	—
ROUND	Y	Y	Y	Y	Y	Y	—
STATUS	Y	—	—	Y	Y	—	—
STMTNO	—	Y	—	—	—	—	—
STRING	Y	Y	—	Y	Y	Y	—
SUM	Y	Y	—	Y	Y	Y	—
TIME	Y	Y	Y	Y	Y	Y	—
TRANSLATE	Y	Y	Y	Y	Y	Y	—
UNSPEC	Y	Y	Y	Y	Y	Y	—
VERIFY	Y	Y	Y	Y	Y	Y	—

TABLE D.3 Built-in Functions

(b) Functions Present in All Versions

ABS	FIXED	MOD
ATAN	FLOAT	REPEAT
ATAND	FLOOR	SIGN
CEIL	HIGH	SIN
CHAR	INDEX	SIND
COS	LOG	SINH
COSD	LOG2	SQRT
COSH	LOG10	SUBSTR
ERF	LOW	TAN
ERFC	MAX	TAND
EXP	MIN	TANH
		TRUNC

D.2.4 Pseudovariables

Table D.4 shows the pseudovariables supported by each of the compilers. As in Table D.3, the letter Y indicates support of that pseudovariable for a given compiler.

TABLE D.4 Pseudovariables

Pseudovariables	PL/I-F	PL/C	PLUTO	Checkout	Optimizing	IBM Subset	PLAGO
COMPLETION	Y	—	—	Y	Y	—	—
COMPLEX	Y	Y	—	Y	Y	—	—
IMAG	Y	Y	—	Y	Y	—	—
ONCHAR	Y	Y	—	Y	Y	—	—
ONSOURCE	Y	Y	—	Y	Y	—	—
PRIORITY	Y	—	—	Y	Y	—	—
REAL	Y	Y	—	Y	Y	—	—
STATUS	Y	—	—	Y	Y	—	—
STRING	Y	—	—	Y	Y	—	—
SUBSTR	Y	Y	Y	Y	Y	Y	Y
UNSPEC	Y	Y	—	Y	Y	Y	—

TABLE D.5   ON-Conditions

Conditions	PL/I-F	PL-C	PLUTO	Checkout	Optimizing	IBM Subset	PLAGO
AREA	Y	—	—	Y	Y	—	—
ATTENTION	—	—	—	Y	Y	—	—
CHECK	D	D	E	D	D	—	—
CONDITION	Y	Y	Y	Y	Y	—	—
CONVERSION	E	E	E[1]	E	E	E	Y
ENDFILE	Y	Y	Y	Y	Y	Y	Y[2]
ENDPAGE	Y	Y	Y	Y	Y	Y	—
ERROR	Y	Y	Y	Y	Y	Y	Y
FINISH	Y	Y	Y	Y	Y	—	Y
FIXEDOVERFLOW	E	E	E	E	E	E	Y
FLOW	—	E	—	—	—	—	—
KEY	Y	—	—	Y	Y	Y	—
NAME	Y	Y	Y	Y	Y	Y	Y[2]
OVERFLOW	E	E	E	E	E	E	Y
PENDING	—	—	—	Y	Y	—	—
RECORD	Y	Y	Y	Y	Y	Y	—
SIZE	D	E	E	D	D	D	—
STRINGRANGE	D	E	E	D	D	—	Y
STRINGSIZE	—	—	—	D	D	—	—
SUBSCRIPTRANGE	D	E	E	D	D	—	Y
TRANSMIT	Y	Y	Y	Y	Y	Y	—
UNDEFINEDFILE	Y	Y	Y	Y	Y	—	—
UNDERFLOW	E	E	E	E	E	E	Y
ZERODIVIDE	E	E	E	E	E	E	Y

[1] No reattempt on normal return; instead, **ERROR** is raised.
[2] Enabled for SYSIN only.

D.2.5   **ON** Conditions

Table D.5 lists the **ON** conditions supported by each compiler. The entry Y means that the particular condition is supported and is always enabled (that is, cannot be disabled); D means that the condition is normally disabled, whereas E means that the condition is normally enabled but can be disabled. As before, a dash means that the condition is not supported and cannot be recognized.

APPENDIX E:
ABBREVIATIONS FOR
PL/I KEYWORDS

A listing of PL/I keywords and their abbreviations is given in Table E.1.

Table E.1 Abbreviations for PL/1 Keywords

KEYWORD	ABBREVIATION	WHERE*	KEYWORD	ABBREVIATION	WHERE*	KEYWORD	ABBREVIATION	WHERE*
%ACTIVATE	%ACT	OF	DEFAULT	DFT	O	OVERFLOW	OFL	OFCP

Table E.1 Abbreviations for PL/1 Keywords

KEYWORD	ABBREVIATION	WHERE*	KEYWORD	ABBREVIATION	WHERE*	KEYWORD	ABBREVIATION	WHERE*
%ACTIVATE	%ACT	OF	DEFAULT	DFT	O	OVERFLOW	OFL	OFCP
ALLOCATE	ALLOC	O	DEFINED	DEF	OFC	PICTURE	PIC	OFC
ALLOCATION	ALLOCN	O	ENVIRONMENT	ENV	OFC	POINTER	PTR	OFCP
AUTOMATIC	AUTO	OFCP	EXCLUSIVE	EXCL	EXCL	POSITION	POS	OFC
BINARY	BIN	OFCP	EXTERNAL	EXT	OFCP	PRECISION	PREC	OFP
BUFFERED	BUF	OC	FIXEDOVERFLOW	FOFL	OFCP	PROCEDURE	PROC	OFCPG
CHARACTER	CHAR	OFCPG	GO TO	GOTO	OFCPG	%PROCEDURE	%PROC	OF
COLUMN	COL	OFCP	%GO TO	%GOTO	OFCPG	REDUCIBLE	RED	OF
COMPLETION	CPLN	O	INITIAL	INIT	OFCP	SEQUENTIAL	SEQL	OC
COMPLEX	CPLX	OFC	INTERNAL	INT	OFCP	STRINGRANGE	STRG	OFCP
CONDITION	COND	O	IRREDUCIBLE	IRRED	OF	STRINGSIZE	STRZ	O
CONNECTED	CONN	O	NONCONVERSION	NOCONV	OFCP	SUBSCRIPTRANGE	SUBRG	OFCP
CONTROLLED	CTL	OFCP	NOFIXEDOVERFLOW	NOFOFL	OFCP	UNALIGNED	UNAL	OC
CONVERSION	CONV	OFCP	NOOVERFLOW	NOOFL	OFCP	UNBUFFERED	UNBUF	OC
%DEACTIVATE	%DEACT	OF	NOSTRINGRANGE	NOSTRG	OFCP	UNDEFINEDFILE	UNDF	OFCP
DECIMAL	DEC	OFCP	NOSTRINGSIZE	NOSTRZ	O	UNDERFLOW	UNFL	OFCP
DECLARE	DCL	OFCPG	NOSUBSCRIPTRANGE	NOSUBRG	OFCP	VARYING	VAR	OFCP
%DECLARE	%DCL	OF	NOUNDERFLOW	NOUFL	OFCP	ZERODIVIDE	ZDIV	OFCP
			NOZERODIVIDE	NOZDIV	OFCP			

*O: Optimizing and Checkout Compilers. F: F compiler. C: PL/C. P: PLUTO. G: PLAGO.

Notes: 1. The IBM Subset compiler accpts no abbreviations (but will accept GOTO).
2. Inability of a compiler to recognize a given abbreviation does not necessarily mean that the corresponding keyword is not recognized (see Appendix B).

INDEX

CHARACTERS IN THIS TYPE DENOTE PL/1
KEYWORDS

A-specification, 219
Abbreviations for keywords, 636
ABS built-in function, 639
Access methods for records, 419, 423, 445
Accuracy and rounding, 97, 613
ACTIVATE statement, 565
Activation of files, 440
ADD built-in functions, 268
ADDR built-in function, 518
Address, definition of, 33
Algorithm
  definition of, 35
  implementation of, 38
ALL built-in function, 322
ALLOCATE statement, 511, 522, 531, 549
Allocation
  multiple, 511
  of based variables, 511, 513
  of controlled variables, 540
  of listed elements, 531
ALLOCATION built-in function, 541
Alphabetization of strings, 115
Alphanumeric characters, 130, 616
AND-ing, 312
ANSI flow-chart, 38, 587
ANY built-in function, 322
AREA attribute, 521
AREA condition, 522, 549
Areas, 549
  allocation and use of, 521, 527
  and lists, 537
Arguments, 285
  arrays as, 380
  attributes of, 387, 391, 394, 470
  binding of, with parameters, 399
  conversion of data in, 604
  dummy, 392, 408
  for built-in functions, 265
  numerical, 385
  versus parameters, 374, 408

Arithmetic expressions
  as arguments, 387
  bit strings in, 315
  built-in functions in, 264
  character strings in, 297
  data conversion in, 601
  evaluation of, 256, 316
  forms for, 9
  mixed modes in, 258, 601
  parentheses in, 10, 17, 257
Arithmetic operations
  accuracy and rounding in, 97
  built-in functions for, 264
  conversions in, 605
  expression of, 7, 8
  in character expressions, 298
  precision of, 263, 266
  priority of, 256
  with complex numbers, 95
Arrays
  and structures, 192
  bounds of, 512
  built-in functions for, 274
  controlled, 543
  crossections of, 150
  declaration of, 138, 141, 196
  defined attribute for, 161
  dimensionality of, 134
  in procedures, 380
  initialization of, 141
  input/output of, 156, 223
  ISUB specification for, 163
  of files, 443
  of labels, 330
  operations on, 144
  organization of, 134, 140, 162
  range check for, 486
  with variable sizes, 168, 512
ASCII character set, 617
Assignment statement, 32

Asterisk notation, 543
Asynchronous processing, 573, 583, 585
Attachment of tasks, 585
AUTOMATIC attribute, 394, 403, 407
Automatic programming, 3

B-specification, 309
BACKWARDS attribute, 420, 445
Base attribute, 64, 78
BASE conversion, 609
Base variable, 161
BASED attribute, 460
Based variables, 459, 472, 549
  allocation of, 511
  arrays as, 511
  as offsets in areas, 522
  as references to other data, 519
  declaration of, 510
  qualified by pointers, 515
  structures as, 513
Basic constructs, 21, 23
Basic instruction types, 4
BEGIN block, 169, 367, 400, 407
  and interrupt handling, 481, 504
BINARY attribute, 64
BINARY built-in function, 266
Binary numbers
  and bit strings, 305, 307
  appearance of, 71
  conversion of, 607
  precision of, 261
Bit, 325
BIT attribute, 306
BIT built-in function, 322
Bit strings
  and decision operations, 315
  and logical operations, 310
  and numbers, 308
  and the IF statement, 317
  and truth tables, 311
  as arguments, 388
  concatenation of, 309
  conversion of, 308, 322, 611
  declaration of, 306
  decomposition of, 321
  expressions with, 309, 314
  input/output of, 306
  variable length, 307
Blanks, rules for using, 18
Blocking, 427, 445
Blocks
  and records, 425, 428

  in programs, 363, 369, 407
BOOL built-in function, 318
BUFFERED attribute, 422, 458
Buffers, 421, 430, 446, 458, 466
BUFFERS specification, 430
Built-in functions, 103, 264
  arguments for, 265
  availability of, 630
BUILT-IN atttribute, 397
BY NAME option, 191, 201
BY phrase, 347, 351

C-specification, 219
CALL statement, 379, 389, 392, 407
Case constructs
  and the GO TO statement, 332
  basic intent of, 331
  flowchart for, 332
  implementation of, 334
CEIL built-in function, 260, 270, 453
Ceiling of a number, 285
Chained list — see list
CHAR function, 300
CHARACTER attribute, 107
Character sets, 616
Character strings, 103
  alphabetization of, 115
  and the POSITION specification, 167
  as arguments, 388
  as bit strings, 321
  as variables, 107
  components of, 290
  concatenation of, 113, 288, 293
  conversion of, 299, 612
  declaration of, 107, 118, 123, 167, 288
  duplication of, 290
  editing of numerical, 126
  in decision statements, 114
  initialization of, 108, 142
  input/output of, 110, 121, 219
  length of, 108, 110, 288
  literal, 112, 130, 235
  null, 109
  numerical, 118, 238, 297, 610
  padding of, 107
  replacement of characters in, 294
  representation of, 106, 321
  synthesis of, 293
  truncation of, 108
  variable length, 109, 288
CHECK condition, 493, 506, 507
CLOSE statement, 444, 446

Collating sequence, 616
COLUMN specification
  for input, 216
  for output, 235
Comments, form for, 32, 58
Comparisons — see relational op.
Compile-time facilities, 555, 571
  activation of variables in, 556
  deactivation of variables in, 557
  decisions in, 560
  declarations in, 560
  DO group in, 563
  generated source statements in, 567
  IF statement in, 560
  INCLUDE statement in, 565
  null statement in, 562
  procedures in, 568
  scanning and replacement in, 557
  statement forms in, 555
  SUBSTR function in, 564
  variables in, 556
Compilers, 630
  action of, 2, 32, 56
  control of, 553
  IBM subset, 621
  language differences among, 622
  optimizing/checkout, 621
  PL/C, 620
  PL/I-F, 620
  PLAGO, 622
  PLUTO, 620
  preprocessors for, 555
  services provided by, 50, 55
  statements supported by, 625
COMPLETION built-in function, 577
COMPLEX built-in function, 103, 267
Complex numbers, 103
  arithmetic with, 95
  representation of, 93
Complications in programming, 42, 50
Compound statements, 23, 49, 75, 78, 332, 334
Concatenation, 113, 130, 309
CONDITION condition, 498, 507
Condition prefix, 500, 504, 507
CONSECUTIVE attribute, 431, 446
Constants
  binary, 71
  bit string, 306
  character string, 107, 130
  decimal, 69
  fixed point, 69, 71
  floating point, 69, 72

  numerical, 8
Control
  counters for implementing, 20
  last-case indicators for, 24
  statements for defining, 18, 20
  within a program, 372, 383, 393
Constructs, 21, 23, 332, 593, 597
Control structures
  case construct, 331, 596, 600
  DO WHILE, 21, 40, 344, 594, 598
  DO UNTIL, 594, 598
  IF-THEN-ELSE, 23, 49, 334, 593, 597
CONTROLLED attribute, 539
Controlled parameters, 541, 549
Controlled variables, 539, 549
  and pushdown stacks, 540
  as parameters, 541
CONVERSION condition, 482
Conversion of data types
  difficulties in, 614
  errors in, 276
  in arguments, 604
  in arithmetic operations, 605
  in assignments, 604
  in formats, 604
  in logical expressions, 607
  in relational expressions, 606
  in subscripts, 604
  multistep, 602
  precision of, 259, 607
  rules for, 258, 299, 308, 322, 605
  source and target attributes, 607
COPY option for stream files, 450
COS built-in function, 272
COSD built-in function, 272
COSH built-in function, 273
COUNT built-in function, 478
Counters as aids to control, 20
Cross-reference guide, 53, 62
Cross section of arrays, 150, 158, 176
Cyclic processes, 20, 144, 154, 347, 563

Data
  bit string, 306
  bit-by-bit examination of, 321
  character string, 107
  fake values of, for control, 24
  fixed point form for, 42
  floating point form for, 6
  internal movement of, 11
  self-defining, 550
  stream transmission of, 204

transfer of, among procedures, 385
treatment of, in a computer, 5, 321
types and subtypes of, 603
Data sets, 412, 446
  access methods of, 419, 430
  and files, 413, 425
  organization of, 430, 432
  regional, 436
Data-directed input/output, 210
DATE built-in function, 477
Deactivation of files, 444
Deblocking, 427, 446
Debugging of programs, 50, 493, 506, 507
Decimal numbers
  conversion of, 527
  expression of, 68
  precision of, 261, 607
Decisions
  and IF-THEN-ELSE, 23, 49, 334, 593, 597
  at compile time, 560
  case construct for, 331, 596
  character strings in, 114
  compound statements in, 49, 75, 334
  counters for implementing, 20
  expanded facilities for, 331, 334
  last-case indicators for, 24
  logical expressions for, 315
  relational operators for, 22
  statements for specifying, 18, 20, 75
Declaration
  for compile-time use, 560
  implies, 85, 103
  of arrays, 138
  of bit strings, 306
  of character strings, 107, 118
  of events, 576
  of files, 414, 433
  of fixed point variables, 83
  of floating point variables, 6
  of pointers, 459, 510
  of structures, 178
  of tasks, 574
  of variables, 5
DECLARE statement, 5, 33
Decrementation in DO loops, 348
DEFAULT statement, 86, 103
Defaults
  alteration of, 85
  for files, 424
  for numerical data, 84
  general use of, 11, 33, 42, 62
DEFINED attribute, 161, 174, 464

DELETE statement, 468, 472
Diagnostic messages, 52, 55, 490
Dimensionality of arrays, 134, 174
DIRECT attribute, 423, 446, 454
DIVIDE built-in function, 269, 277
DO group, 49, 75, 342, 563
DO loops, 20, 154, 159, 344
  and arrays, 342
  and the WHILE clause, 21, 344
  control of, 20, 154, 344
  decrementation in, 348
  defaults, 347
  form for, 20, 347
  in input/output statements, 159, 206, 225
  increments for, 347
  indexes of, 20, 347
  iterative specifications for, 347
DO UNTIL construct, 594, 598
DO WHILE construct, 21, 40, 344, 594, 598
DO WHILE, use of, 21, 344, 351, 377
Dummy arguments, 392, 408
Dummy data, 33
    SEE ALSO last case indicators
Dummy records, 472
Dynamic storage allocation, 168, 176, 408, 509, 522, 526, 539

E-specification, 218
EBCDIC character set, 616
Echo check, 39, 62
Edit-directed input/output
    format specifications for, 217, 233
    of bit strings, 309
    properties of, 123
    string option for, 244
ELSE clause, 44, 103, 331, 340
ELSE IF clause, 340
EMPTY built-in function, 527, 549
Empty ELSE clause, 362
END statement, 5, 33
ENDFILE condition, 74, 78, 475
ENDPAGE condition, 253, 489
ENTRY attribute, 376, 387, 408
entry point, 408
ENTRY statement, 376
ENVIRONMENT specification, 425, 429, 446, 453, 458
Equals sign, use and meaning of, 7
ERF built-in function, 273
ERROR condition, 487, 493, 508
Error Detection, 491
Errors in precision, 276
Execution
    error detection during, 492

scope of controls during, 501
self-defined controls for, 498
trace of activities during, 490
EXIT statement, 381
EXP built-in function, 272
Exponentiation, rules for, 258, 272
Expressions
accuracy and rounding in, 97
bit string, 209, 314
character string, 288
conversions in, 258, 604
forms for construction of, 9
in PUT EDIT statements, 232
in PUT LIST statements, 210
logical, 311
parentheses in, 10, 256
relational, 315
temporary variables as aids in, 11
EXTERNAL attribute, 398, 408
External procedure, 366, 371, 408

F-specification, 217
Files, 442, 446
activation of, 440
and blocks, 429
and data sets, 413, 425
and events, 584
and external devices, 440
and records, 413
as arguments, 470
as arrays, 443
as variables, 442
attributes of, 418
buffered, 421, 458
deactivation of, 444
declaration of, 414, 433
defaults for, 424
implied attributes for, 424
in asynchronous processing, 583
input, 416
input/output of, 422, 434, 450, 456
keyed, 420, 454
locate mode input of, 459, 464
opening and closing of, 444
output, 416
print, 417
sequential, 419
special options for print, 443
title option for, 441
update, 417
updating of, 467
with variable formats, 460

FINISH condition, 493, 507
Fixed point data
defaults for, 42, 82
definition of, 62, 64
input/output of, 217
precision of, 66, 607
printing of, 233, 239
scaling of, 67
uses for, 89
FIXEDOVERFLOW conditions, 227, 285, 485
FLOAT built-in function, 267
Floating point data
as character strings, 120
conversion of, 607
defaults for, 84
definition of, 33
form for, 6
input of, 89, 218
output of, 90, 234, 239
overflow in, 69
precision of, 66, 607
underflow in, 69
uses for, 89
FLOOR built-in function, 270
Floor of a number, 285
Flowcharts
and program structure, 38
ANSI, 587
basic form for, 38, 587, 596
definition of, 33, 38, 587
N-S, 38, 597
symbols for, 38, 587
Form for arithmetic expression
Format
control of, with PUT DATA, 14, 213
control of, with PUT EDIT, 217, 233
control of, with PUT LIST, 208, 210, 212
remote, 227, 253
variable, 229, 460
Format description of data, 217, 229, 233, 240
FORMAT statement, 227, 253
FREE statement, 525, 549
Function procedures, 372, 378, 408

GENERIC attribute, 387, 408
GET DATA statement, 33
defaults for, 12
form for, 210
GET EDIT statement
COLUMN specification for, 216
for arrays, 223
form for, 216

format specifications for, 217
 SKIP option for, 221
GET FILE statement, 449
GET LIST statement, 117, 204, 336
GET STRING statement, 244
GO TO statement, 328, 333, 561
Gray shading, 237
Great character bucket, 108

HBOUND built-in function, 602
Heading name, 408
Heading statement, 408
HIGH built-in function, 321
Hyperbolic functions, 273

IF statement
 and bit strings, 317
 and IF-THEN-ELSE construct, 23, 49, 334
 at compile time, 562
 compound statements with, 75
 DO groups as alternatives in, 75, 78
 form for, 23, 33
 relational operators in, 22, 44
 versus the ON statement, 481
IGNORE option, 456, 472
 IMAG built-in function, 267
INCLUDE statement, 565
INDEX built-in function, 295
 index of a DO loop, 347
INDEXED attribute, 431, 446, 454
Infinite loop, description of, 36
Infix operators, 256, 285, 316
INITIAL attribute, 78, 84, 103, 108, 141
Initialization, 78, 84, 108, 141
INPUT attribute, 416, 446
Input/output
 data-directed, 90, 210
 edit-directed, 214
 list-directed, 93
 of arrays, 157, 159, 223
 of bit strings, 306, 309
 of character strings, 110, 121
 of structures, 187
 record oriented, 422, 434, 450, 456
 stream oriented, 36, 204, 210, 478
Instruction types, 4
INTERNAL attribute, 398, 408
Internal procedures, 367, 382, 408
Interrecord gap, 426, 446
Interrupts-
 disabling of, 499, 507
 enabling of, 499, 507

homemade, 498
 scope of, 501
 SEE ALSO ON, 480, 508
Invocation of procedures, 383, 389, 402, 408
ISUB specification for arrays, 163

Justification, 303, 304

KEY condition, 488
KEY option, 454, 468, 472
KEYED attribute, 420
KEYFROM option, 435, 462, 472
Keys for files, 420, 446
KEYTO option, 454, 472
Keyword, definition of, 36
Keywords, abbreviations for, 636

LABEL attribute, 329, 389
Labels, 19, 36
 as arguments, 389
 as variables, 354
 illustrative use of, 333
 rules for constructing, 58
 use of in case constructs, 332
Last case indicator, 24
 SEE ALSO dummy data
Layout of print formats, 233, 236
LBOUND built-in function, 512
Left-justification, 303
LENGTH built-in function, 181, 288
Levels in programs, 51
Levels, in structures, 181, 201
LIKE attribute, 186, 201
LINE option, 208
LINENO built-in function, 478
LINESIZE option, 444
Lists, 580
 and areas, 537
 bidirectional, 529, 549
 chaining through, 533
 construction of, 532
 deletions from, 536
 elements in, 531
 insertion in, 534
 null value in, 529
 organization of, 529
 searching of, 533
 start of, 529, 549
 tails of, 550
Literals, 112, 130, 235
Locate mode, 459, 464, 472

LOCATE statement, 464, 472
LOG built-in function, 222
Logical operations, 310, 315, 317, 325, 607
LOG10 built-in function, 222
LOG1 built-in function, 222
Loops, 19, 34
    counters for control of, 20
    last-case indicators for, 24
    as DO WHILE constructs, 21, 40, 344
LOW built-in function, 321

Machine language, 2
Main procedure, 5, 366, 408
Major structures, 181, 201
MAX built-in function, 271
Messages to the operator, 478
MIN built-in function, 271
Minor structures, 181, 201
Mixed mode expressions, 258, 297
MOD built-in function, 269
Mode, for numbers, 65, 267
Move mode, 472
Multiple labels on a statement, 365
MULTIPLY built-in fraction, 268
Multitasking, 585

NAME condition, 487
Naming of variables, 5, 42, 58, 62, 87
Negative DO loop increments, 348
Nesting
    of DO groups, 49, 342
    of DO loops, 343
    of IF statements, 49, 336, 340
    of IF-THEN-ELSE constructs, 49, 339
    of procedures, 377, 382
NOLOCK option, 584
Notation, explanation of, 1
N-S flowcharts, 38, 597
NULL built-in function, 518, 549
Null character strings, 109
Null statement, 560
NULLO built-in function, 524, 538
Numbers
    and bit strings, 308, 321
    and character strings, 297, 300, 610
    as arguments, 385
    as character strings, 118, 126, 238, 303
    base attribute for, 64, 609
    ceiling of, 259, 285
    complex, 93
    conversion of, 258, 300, 322, 607, 612
    defaults for, 11, 42, 84

    descriptive attributes for, 66
    errors in precision of, 276
    fixed point, 42, 62, 64
    floating point, 6, 64
    floor of, 270, 285
    formats for reading, 217
    formats for writing, 234
    input/output of, 92
    mode attribute for, 65
    operations on, 8
    overflow of, 69
    precision of, 66, 258
    representation of, 6, 8, 118, 238
    rounding of, 271
    scale attribute for, 64, 609
    scaling of, 67
    truncation of, 270
    underflow of, 69
    use in expressions, 9

Object program, 25, 34
OFFST attribute, 523
Offset variable, 522, 549
ON condition
    enabling of, 484
    support of, 633
ON statement, 74, 78, 475, 481, 508
    AREA, 522
    CHECK, 493, 506
    CONVERSION, 482
    ENDFILE, 74
    ENDPAGE, 489
    ERROR, 487, 492
    FINISH, 492
    FIXEDOVERFLOW, 485
    KEY, 488
    NAME, 487
    OVERFLOW, 485
    RECORD, 488
    SIZE, 484
    STRINGRANGE, 486
    SUBSCRIPTRANGE, 486
    TRANSMIT, 488
    UNDEFINEDFILE, 487
    UNDERFLOW, 486
    versus the IF statement, 481
    ZERODIVIDE, 492
ON unit, 469, 508
ONCHAR built-in function, 482
ONKEY built-in function, 489
ONLOC built-in function, 491
ONSOURCE built-in function, 482

OPEN statement, 440, 446
Operating system, 36
OR-ing, 312
Organization of programs, 364
OUTPUT attribute, 416, 446
Output operations
  data-directed, 12
  edit-directed, 214
  for punched cards, 466
  list-directed, 208
  monitoring of, 478
  SEE ALSO PUT statement;
  WRITE statement
Overflow, 69, 78, 277, 485, 613
OVERFLOW condition, 485
Overprinting, 236, 254

P-specification, 238
PAGE option, 36, 220
PAGESIZE option, 443
Parallel processing, 574, 585
Parameters, 373, 379, 408, 541, 550
Parentheses
  and expression evaluation, 257
  in arithmetic expressions, 10, 17
PICTURE attribute, 118, 131, 510
POINTER, 459, 472, 510
Pointers, 459, 472
  and based variables, 459, 510
  as qualifiers, 515, 549
  assignment of values to, 517
  declaration of, 510, 517
  null values for, 518
POLY built-in function, 275
Pop-up operation, 550
POSITION, specification, 167
Precision
  errors in, 276
  of arithmetic operations, 263
  of conversion processes, 259, 607
  of numbers, 66, 78
PRECISION function, 266
Prefix operators, 256, 285, 316
Preprocessing, 571
PRINT attribute, 417, 443, 446
Priority
  of arithmetic operations, 256, 316
  of tasks, 585
PRIORITY built-in function, 580
PRIORITY, pseudovariable, 580
PROCEDURE statement, 4, 36, 365, 569
Procedures

and the BUILT-IN attribute, 397
arguments for, 386
at compile time, 568
attributes of returned values, 375
compile-time statements in, 561
controlled parameters for, 541
definition of, 4, 36, 364, 408
dummy arguments for, 392
entry names as arguments for, 390
entry points for, 376, 389, 396
external, 364, 371
function, 372, 408
internal, 367, 382
invocation of, 374, 379, 383, 389, 402
main, 5, 366, 408
naming, 372
nesting of, 377, 382
recursive, 401
return from, 373, 378, 380
returns option in, 375, 413
self-invocation of, 401
subroutine, 379, 409
PROCESS statement, 371, 408
PROD built-in function, 275
Programs
  aids in development of, 50, 55, 377
  as combination of blocks, 364, 369, 409
  development of, 38
  execution of, 24
  limits of, 4, 372
  recognition of names in, 393, 399
  scope of variables in, 395, 399
  structured, 1, 19, 21, 38, 327
  termination of, 381
  transfer of control within, 372
Pseudovariables, 291, 581, 632
Punched cards, output of, 466
Pushdown stack, 540, 550
  and controlled variables, 540
  test of extent of, 541
PUT DATA statement
  defaults for, 12
  description of, 14, 34, 213
  format control with, 14
PUT EDIT statement
  and PICTURE variables, 238
  and remote formats, 227, 254
  expressions in, 232
  form for, 232
  format descriptions in, 233, 238
  overprinting with, 236
PUT LIST statement

expressions in, 210
for literal output, 112
form for, 208
with character strings, 112
PUT STRING statement, 245

Qualified names in structures, 184, 202
Qualifiers for pointers, 515

Random access
  (*SEE* DIRECT attribute;
  INDEXED attribute)
RANGE specification, 86, 104
Rat situations, 310
READ statement, 434, 451, 457
  IGNORE option in, 456
  KEY option in, 454
  KEYTO option in, 454
  SET option in, 460
REAL built-in function, 267
RECORD attribute, 418, 445
RECORD condition, 488
Record oriented input/output, 254
Records, 413
  access methods for, 419, 422
  and blocks, 425, 427
  and files, 413
  as structures, 414, 433
  buffers for, 421
  deletion of, 468
  dummy, 472
  length of, 427, 430, 446
  locking/unlocking of, 583
  logical, 446
  physical, 446
  spanned, 428, 447
  updating of, 466
  with variable formats, 470
RECURSIVE attribute, 402, 409
Recursive procedures, 401, 409
REFER option, 513, 560
Reference structure, 186, 202
REGIONAL attribute, 434, 438
Relational operators, 22, 62, 315
Remainders, function for, 326, 606
Remote format specifications, 227, 254
REPEAT built-in function, 290
REPLY option, 478
Rescanning, 571
RETURN statement, 373, 378, 381
RETURNS option, 375, 409, 569
REVERT statement, 481, 503, 508

REWRITE statement, 467, 472
Right-justification, 304
Rings, 550
ROUND built-in function, 97, 104
Rounding of numbers, 97, 271
Row major order, 140

Scale attribute, 64, 78, 609
Scaling of fixed point numbers, 67, 78
SCARDS, 449
Scope
  of interrupts, 501, 504
  of variables, 395, 398, 409
SEQUENTIAL attribute, 419, 446
SET option, 460, 465, 511
SIGN build-up function, 266
SIGNAL statement, 498, 508
SIN built-in function, 272
SIND built-in function, 272
SINH built-in function, 273
SIZE condition, 285, 484
SKIP option, 15, 36, 209, 221, 254
SNAP option, 490
Source program
  definition of, 25, 34
  format rules for, 58
  listing of, 50, 62
Spanning records, 428, 447
SPRINT, 449
SQRT built-in function, 271
Stack, (*SEE* pushdown stack)
Statements, construction of, 18, 58
STATIC attribute, 394, 403, 409
STOP statement, 97, 381
STREAM attribute, 447, 450
Stream data transmission, 36, 203, 255, 478
STRING built-in function, 293
STRING option, 244
STRING pseudovariable, 292
STRINGRANGE condition, 291, 304, 486
Structured programs
  attributes of, 20, 22, 23, 38, 40
  constructs for, 21, 23, 332, 593, 597
  principles, 38
Structures
  and arrays, 192
  as arguments, 380
  as list elements, 531
  at compile time, 565
  based, 513
  declaration of, 178, 196
  for describing records, 414, 433

input/output of, 187
levels in, 181
LIKE attribute in, 186
major, 181
minor, 181
naming elements in, 185
operations of, 198
organization of, 178, 183
qualified names in, 184
Subroutines, 379, 409
SUBSCRIPTRANGE condition, 486
Subscripts, 140, 143, 146, 162, 176, 486, 604
SUBSTR built-in function, 290
Substrings
  as pseudovariables, 291
  at compile time, 564
  definition of, 304
  extraction of, 290
SUB built-in function, 274
Synchronization of tasks, 585
Synchronous processing, 585
SYSIN, 14, 36, 449
SYSPRINT, 14, 36, 449
System specification, 104, 497, 502

TAND built-in function, 272
TANH built-in function, 273
Task attribute, 574
TASK option, 574
Tasks, 574, 585
  asynchronous, 574
  attachment of, 585
  creation of, 575, 583
  delay of, 581
  events in, 576
  priority of, 581
  synchronization of, 578
  termination of, 575
THEN clause, 92, 104
THEN IF clause, 336, 343
TIME built-in function, 477
TITLE option for files, 441
TO phrase, 360
Trace of program execution, 500, 505, 508
  SEE ALSO CHECK condition
TRANSLATE built-in function, 294
TRANSMIT condition, 488
Truth table, 311, 326

Unblocked records, 447
UNBUFFERED attribute, 422, 451, 466
UNDEFINEDFILE condition, 505

Underflow, 69, 78
UNDERFLOW condition, 486
UNLOCK statement, 585, 587
UNSPEC built-in function, 321
UPDATE attribute, 417, 447, 467

VALUE specification, 87
Variable format specifications, 229, 460
Variable length records, 427
VARIABLE specification, 441
Variables, 5, 36
  addresses of, 518
  allocation of, 511, 541
  and expressions, 9
  base, 175
  based, 459, 510
  bit string, 306
  character string, 107
  compile-time, 556
  controlled, 539, 543, 549
  declaration of, 5, 82
  defaults for, 11, 42, 84
  defined, 162
  event, 576
  external, 398
  files as, 442
  fixed point, 42
  floating point, 6
  initialization of, 84
  internal, 398
  label, 329
  logical, 310
  naming of, 5, 42, 58, 62
  numerical, 6, 84
  offset, 522
  pointer, 459, 517
  scope of, 395, 400
  storage requirements for, 539
  temporary, 11
  naming of, 87
VARYING attribute, 109, 288, 307
VERIFY built-in function, 296

WAIT statement, 578, 585
WHILE clause, 21, 344, 351
WRITE statement, 433, 462, 472
  KEYFROM option, 462

X-specifications, 220

ZERODIVIDE condition, 491